S0-AZX-565

Essentials of Criminal Justice

Third Edition

Joseph J. Senna
Northeastern University

Larry J. Siegel
University of Massachusetts, Lowell

Australia • Canada • Mexico • Singapore • Spain • United Kingdom • United States

Criminal Justice Editor: Sabra Horne
Development Editor: Terri Edwards
Assistant Editor: Ann Tsai
Marketing Manager: Jennifer Somerville
Project Manager: Debby Kramer
Print Buyer: Karen Hunt
Permissions Editor: Bob Kauser
Production Service: Cecile Joyner/The Cooper Company
Photo Credits on page 546

Text and Cover Designer: Delgado Design, Inc.
Photo Researcher: Linda Rill
Copy Editor: Betty Duncan
Illustrator: Delgado Design, Inc.
Cover Image: *One Market,* James Stagg
Indexer: Kay Banning
Compositor: Thompson Type, San Diego
Interior and Cover Printer: Transcontinental

Printed in Canada
2 3 4 5 6 7   04 03 02 01

For permission to use material from this text, contact us by
Web: http://www.thomsonrights.com
Fax: 1-800-730-2215 **Phone:** 1-800-730-2214

For more information, contact
Wadsworth/Thomson Learning
10 Davis Drive
Belmont, CA 94002-3098
USA
http://www.wadsworth.com

International Headquarters
Thomson Learning
International Division
290 Harbor Drive, 2nd Floor
Stamford, CT 06902-7477
USA

UK/Europe/Middle East/South Africa
Thomson Learning
Berkshire House
168-173 High Holborn
London WC1V 7AA
United Kingdom

Asia
Thomson Learning
60 Albert Street, #15-01
Albert Complex
Singapore 189969

Canada
Nelson Thomson Learning
1120 Birchmount Road
Toronto, Ontario M1K 5G4
Canada

Library of Congress Cataloging-in-Publication Data
Senna, Joseph J.
Essentials of criminal justice / Joseph J. Senna, Larry J. Siegel.--3rd ed.
p. cm.
Includes bibliographical references and index.
ISBN 0-534-52363-3
1. Criminal justice, Administration of--United States. 2. Police--United States.
3. Criminal procedure--United States. 4. Criminal law--United States.
5. Corrections--United States. I. Siegel, Larry J. II. Title.

HV9950 .S46 2000
364.973--dc21

00-029012

This book is printed on acid-free recycled paper.

About the Authors

JOSEPH J. SENNA was born in Brooklyn, New York. He graduated from Brooklyn College, Fordham University Graduate School of Social Service, and Suffolk University Law School. Mr. Senna has spent over fourteen years teaching law and justice courses at Northeastern University. In addition, he has served as an Assistant District Attorney, Director of Harvard Law School Prosecutorial Program, and consultant to numerous criminal justice organizations. His academic specialties include areas of Criminal Law, Constitutional Due Process, Criminal Justice and Juvenile Law.

Mr. Senna lives with his wife and sons outside of Boston. He is currently working on a criminal law textbook.

LARRY J. SIEGEL was born in the Bronx in 1947. While attending City College of New York in the 1960s he was introduced to the study of crime and justice in courses taught by sociologist Charles Winick. After graduation he attended the newly opened program in criminal justice at the State University of New York at Albany, where he earned both his MA and Ph.D. and studied with famed scholars such as Michael Hindelang, Gilbert Geis, and Donald Newman. After completing his graduate work, Dr. Siegel began his teaching career at Northeastern University, where he worked closely with colleague Joseph Senna on a number of texts and research projects. After leaving Northeastern, he held teaching positions at the University of Nebraska–Omaha and Saint Anselm College in New Hampshire. He is currently a professor at the University of Massachusetts–Lowell.

Dr. Siegel has written extensively in the area of crime and justice, including books on juvenile law, delinquency, criminology and criminal procedure. He is a court certified expert on police conduct and has testified in numerous legal cases. He resides in Bedford, New Hampshire with his wife Therese J. Libby, Esq. and their children.

Contents

chapter 2

The Nature of Crime and Victimization 38

chapter 3

Criminal Law: Substance and Procedure 76

PART II

The Police and Law Enforcement

chapter 4

chapter 6

Issues in Policing 164

chapter 7

Police and the Rule of Law 202

chapter 9

Pretrial Procedures 264

chapter 10

The Criminal Trial 294

chapter 14

Prison Life 428

PART V

Juvenile Justice

chapter 15

Juvenile Justice 466

Preface

On March 13, 2000, Scott B. Smith, 28, became the first Connecticut police officer to be convicted of manslaughter for fatally shooting a fleeing suspect.* The New Milford, Conn., officer chased Franklin Reid, wanted for failing to appear in court to face charges of harassment and violating probation. Reid tried to elude police by running along a local highway but was apprehended, placed on the ground, and then shot in the back. During the trial, several eyewitnesses testified that they thought the chase was over and that Officer Smith had his suspect pinned to the ground. Officer Smith testified that he shot Reid only after he resisted being handcuffed and made a sudden move as if to reach for a weapon.

Although the Smith case did not receive the widespread national press as some other cases involving police violence, it illustrates some of the most serious and perplexing problems facing the criminal justice system. Officer Smith is white, and Mr. Reid was black. Was this a case of "racial profiling" or was it simply a police officer doing what he considered to be his duty? All too often the justice system is forced to confront charges of race and gender discrimination. Is the system hopelessly biased or more evenhanded than critics think?

The Smith case also illustrates the role that discretion plays in shaping criminal justice. Smith was originally charged with murder but the trial judge honored the prosecution's request to allow jurors to consider lesser charges: intentional first-degree manslaughter with a firearm and/or reckless manslaughter with a firearm. Although the jury failed to convict the officer of murder, they did find that the situation clearly did not warrant deadly force and found Smith guilty of manslaughter. Smith might have gone free if the trial judge had chosen not to honor the prosecutor's request. How is discretion used in the justice system? Does it favor the wealthy and powerful or is it applied impartially? Events of the past few years remind us of the great impact crime, law, and justice have had on the American psyche. Each year the criminal justice system routinely processes millions of cases involving theft, violence, drug trafficking, and other crimes. How does this vast enterprise costing billions of dollars and involving millions of people operate? What are its most recent trends and policies? How effective are its efforts to control crime? What efforts are being made to improve its efficiency? We have written *Essentials of Criminal Justice* in an attempt to help answer these questions in a concise, forthright, and objective manner.

Because the study of criminal justice is a dynamic, ever-changing field of scientific inquiry and because the concepts and processes of justice are constantly changing and evolving, we have updated *Essentials of Criminal Justice* to reflect the most critical legal cases, research studies, and policy initiatives that have taken place during the past few years. It lays a groundwork for the study of criminal justice by analyzing and describing the agencies of justice and the procedures they use to identify and treat criminal offenders. It covers what most

* David M. Herszenhorn, "Connecticut Police Officer Convicted in Fatal Shooting," *New York Times*, March 14, 2000, A3.

experts believe are the critical issues in criminal justice and analyzes their impact on the justice system.

Our primary goals in writing this Third Edition remain as they have been for the previous two:

1. to provide students with a thorough knowledge of the criminal justice system,
2. to be as readable and interesting as possible,
3. to be objective and unbiased, and
4. to describe the most current methods of social control and analyze their strengths and weaknesses.

Every attempt has been made to make the presentation of material interesting, balanced, and objective. No single political or theoretical position dominates the text; instead, the many diverse views that are contained within criminal justice and characterize its interdisciplinary nature are presented. The text includes topical information on recent cases and events to enliven the presentation. We have tried to provide a text that is informative, comprehensive, interesting, well organized, and objective yet provocative and thought provoking.

Organization of the Text This new edition has been thoroughly revised and the chapter organization streamlined. The material that was contained in Chapter 4 "Confronting Crime" of the previous edition has been incorporated into Chapter 1 "Crime and Criminal Justice." Considering the importance and timeliness of the subject, there is a new chapter (Chapter 15) on the juvenile justice system. We hope this reorganization will make the text more appropriate for the Introduction to Criminal Justice course.

Part One gives the student a basic introduction to crime, law, and justice. The first chapter covers the agencies of justice, the formal justice process, and introduces students to the concept of the informal justice system, which involves discretion, deal making, and plea bargains. Chapter 1 discusses the major perspectives on justice and shows how they shape justice policy. Chapter 2 discusses the nature and extent of crime and victimization: How is crime measured? Where and when does it occur? Who commits crime? Who are its victims? What social factors influence the crime rate? Chapter 3 provides a discussion of the criminal law and its relationship to criminal justice. It covers the legal definition of crime, the defenses to crime, and issues in procedural law.

Part Two provides an overview of the law enforcement field. Four chapters cover the history and development of criminal justice organizations, the functions of police in modern society, issues in policing, and the police and the rule of law. There is an emphasis on community policing and community crime prevention, changes in police procedure, and other current issues.

Part Three is devoted to the adjudication process, from pretrial indictment to the sentencing of criminal offenders. Chapters focus on the organization of the court system, pretrial procedures, the criminal trial, and sentencing. Topics included here are bail, court reorganization, sentencing policy (for example, three strikes laws), and capital punishment.

Part Four focuses on the correctional system, including probation and the intermediate sanctions of house arrest, intensive supervision, and electronic monitoring. The traditional correctional system of jails, prisons, community based corrections, and parole are also discussed at length. Such issues as prison and jail overcrowding, house arrest, correctional workers, super-maximum-security prisons, and parole effectiveness are discussed.

Part Five explores the juvenile justice system. There is information on the development of juvenile justice, waiving youth to the adult court, and the death penalty for children.

Great care has been taken to organize the text to reflect the structure and process of justice. Each chapter attempts to be comprehensive, self-contained, and orderly.

What's New in This Edition Each chapter has been thoroughly updated.

- Chapter 1 "Crime and Criminal Justice" has been totally revised and now includes perspectives on justice. It also includes a discussion of the restorative justice concepts.
- Chapter 2 "The Nature of Crime and Victimization" has an updated section on international crime trends and the future of crime. It includes new sections on the factors influencing crime trends, including the association between crime and legalized abortion.
- Chapter 3 "Criminal Law: Substance and Procedure" reviews a number of new statutes on family abuse, software piracy, and gun control laws.
- Chapter 4 "Police in Society: History and Organization" has new sections on current trends in police technology, including crime mapping.
- Chapter 5 "The Police: Role and Function" reviews current community and problem-oriented policing programs. A *Policy, Programs, and Issues in Criminal Justice* box looks at "Zero Tolerance: Aggressive Policing in New York City."
- Chapter 6 "Issues in Policing" reviews the problems of policing, with sections on problem cops, how police discretion is influenced by race and gender, and police victimization.
- Chapter 7 "Police and the Rule of Law" has new sections on efforts to curtail the *Miranda* decision, as well as case material on traffic stops.
- Chapter 8 "Courts, Prosecution, and the Defense" updates the U.S. court system and public-defender programs, includes material on Gun Courts and Drug Courts, and reviews recent court reorganization efforts.
- Chapter 9 "Pretrial Procedures" updates the role of prosecutors in plea-bargaining and reviews efforts to reduce plea negotiations in serious felonies.
- Chapter 10 "The Criminal Trial" has a major section on the criminal trial in the 21st century, including the use of DNA evidence.
- Chapter 11 "Punishment and Sentencing" provides material on felony sentencing in state courts, updates the "three strike" sentences, and reviews the "truth in sentencing movement."
- Chapter 12 "Probation and Intermediate Sanctions" looks at the explosive growth of probation, the use of probation abroad, and new restorative justice techniques in alternative sanctions.
- Chapter 13 "Corrections: History, Institutions, and Populations" updates trends in correctional populations and shows how sentencing changes influences corrections. It also includes a new feature on prison security technology.
- Chapter 14 "Prison Life" focuses more attention on the problems of female inmates, including material on the Summer Program at the Bedford Hills

Correctional Center in New York. There is also a discussion of the "no-frills" movement.

- Chapter 15 "Juvenile Justice," a new chapter, reviews the changing view of juvenile justice in the new millennium, including new get-tough laws and statutes making it easier to waive juveniles to adult court.

New Features and Changes to This Edition To keep up with the changes in the criminal justice system, the third edition of *Essentials of Criminal Justice* has been thoroughly revised and renewed. In order to achieve this goal, we have:

- streamlined and thoroughly edited every chapter of the book in order to reduce redundancy, simplify language, and promote better student comprehension
- removed chapter 4 ("Confronting Crime") in order to keep the book at a manageable length
- incorporated stimulating vignettes to each chapter opener to inject a more cutting-edge feel
- added a running *Glossary* in the margins to ensure that students understand words and concepts as they are introduced
- integrated Internet exercises, linked to *InfoTrac College Edition*, into every chapter, to give students added experience using the Internet and doing web-based research

The evolution of crime control policy has been followed by updating the discussion of the criminal justice system with recent court decisions, legislative changes, and theoretical concepts that reflect the changing orientation of the field. To meet this goal, the text now contains five different kinds of boxed inserts that help students analyze material in greater depth:

1. *Policy, Programs, and Issues in Criminal Justice* helps students to think critically about current justice issues, policies, and practices. For example, in Chapter 11, a feature entitled "Let's Get Tough: Truth in Sentencing and Three-Strikes Laws" discusses the efforts to create tougher punishments for repeat offenders.
2. *Criminal Justice and the Media* shows how the criminal justice system is portrayed in films and TV shows and also how the media influences crime and justice. "The Media and Violence" in Chapter 2 helps answer the questions: Does the media influence behavior? Does broadcast violence cause aggressive behavior in viewers?
3. *Law in Review* gives the facts, decision, and significance of critical legal cases. For example, in Chapter 3, the *Law in Review* discusses *Kansas v. Hendricks* (1997) and *Chicago v. Morales* (1999).
4. *Race, Culture, and Gender* features help students better understand diversity issues and the justice system. For example, in Chapter 12 "Community Sentencing Abroad" addresses the issue of how other cultures are dealing with the crime problem in a nonpunitive fashion.
5. *Criminal Justice and Technology* reviews some of the more recent scientific advances that can aid the justice system. For example, in Chapter 4 a feature

on "Crime Mapping" shows how computer-generated crime maps give the police the power to create immediate, detailed visuals of crime patterns.

The book also contains many new graphs, figures, charts, and tables that make the presentation easier to understand and conceptualize.

Ancillary Material A number of pedagogic supplements are provided by Wadsworth to help instructors use *Essentials of Criminal Justice* in their courses and to aid students in preparing for exams. These include:

Instructor's Resource Manual Prepared by Michael Kaune of Radford University, the manual includes detailed lecture outlines, learning objectives, key terms, Internet resources, and eighty test questions per chapter.

ExamView® Computerized Testing Items Designed specifically for *Essentials of Criminal Justice*, this computerized testing software helps instructors create and customize exams in minutes. Instructors can easily edit and import their own questions and graphics, change test layout, and reorganize questions. This software also offers the ability to test and grade online. Available for both Windows and Macintosh.

Study Guide for Essentials of Criminal Justice Prepared by Roy Roberg of San Jose State University, the *Study Guide* features a variety of pedagogical aids for students such as chapter outlines and summaries, key terms, and sample test questions.

WebTutor for *Essentials of Criminal Justice* Designed exclusively for this text, *WebTutor* is a content rich, Web-based teaching and learning tool. For students, it offers real-time access to a full array of study tools, including flashcards, practice quizzes, on-line tutorials, and Web links. Instructors can use WebTutor to provide virtual office hours, post syllabi, set up threaded discussions, track student progress, and more.

Website for the *Essentials of Criminal Justice* Designed exclusively for this text, students can use this site as a launching point for research, meet other students in cyberspace to discuss criminal justice topics, and improve test scores by using the online quizzes.

The Introduction to Criminal Justice PowerPoint Presentation 2001 Created by Larry Bassi of SUNY Brockport, it features more than 700 color images that will aid instructors in visually representing to students the main concepts and ideas contained in the text.

Transparencies for Introduction to Criminal Justice To bring the graphic portions of the text to the classroom, 50 full-color transparency masters for overhead projection are provided. These transparencies help each instructor to fully discuss concepts and research findings with students.

Additional useful material includes:

InfoTrac® College Edition Students receive four months of real-time access *to Infotrac College Edition's* online database of continuously updated, full-length articles from hundreds of journals and periodicals. By doing a simple key word search, users can quickly generate a powerful list of related articles, then select relevant articles to explore and/or print out for reference or further study.

Criminal Justice Internet Investigator A brochure lists the most useful criminal justice links on the World Wide Web, including the most popular criminal justice sites, listservs, online newsletters, grants and funding information, and more.

Guide to the Internet for Criminal Justice Developed by Daniel Kurland and Christina Polsenberg, this easy reference text helps newcomers as well as experienced Web-surfers use the Internet for criminal justice research.

Blackenship/Vito/Hinze: *Your Research: Data Analysis for Criminal Justice and Criminology* An easy-to-use data analysis and graphics program with a companion workbook filled with examples of criminological research. Available for PCs only.

Harr/Hess: *Seeking Employment in Criminal Justice and Related Fields* This monograph provides students with information on finding employment, job interviewing techniques, and other criminal justice career information.

CNN Today Video Series Exclusively from Wadsworth/Thomson Learning, the *CNN Today Video Series* offers compelling videos that feature current news footage from CNN's comprehensive archives. *Criminal Justice in the News: Volume I* and *Criminal Justice in the News: Volume II* provide a collection of 3- to 5-minute clips on hot topics in criminal justice such as high-tech policing, registering sex offenders, cocaine/crack sentencing, juveniles behind bars, and much more. Available to qualified adopters, both videotapes are great lecture launchers as well as classroom discussion pieces.

The Wadsworth Criminal Justice Video Library This exciting collection of videos enriches lectures. Qualified adopters may select from a wide variety of professionally prepared videos covering various aspects of policing, corrections and other areas of the criminal justice system. The video selections include videos from *Films for Humanities*, *Court TV*, *A&E American Justice Series* videos, *National Institute of Crime File* videos, *ABC News* videos, and *MPI Home Videos*.

Careers in Criminal Justice Interactive CD-ROM This engaging self-exploration CD-ROM provides an interactive discovery of the wide range of careers in criminal justice. The self-assessment helps steer students to suitable careers based on their personal profile. Students gather information on various careers from job descriptions, salaries, employment requirements, sample tests, to actual video profiles of criminal justice professionals.

Crime Scenes CD-ROM The award-winning CD-ROM is the first developed specifically for the introductory criminal justice course. Highly visual and interactive, this program makes your students the decision makers in six intriguing scenarios that explore all aspects of the criminal justice system, such as a juvenile murder trial, a prostitution case that turns to manslaughter, and many more.

Mind of a Killer CD-ROM Based on Eric Hickey's book, *Serial Murderers and Their Victims*, this award-winning CD-ROM allows students to view confessions of and interviews with serial killers, and examine famous cases through original video documentaries and news footage. Included are 3-D profiling simulations, which are extensive mapping systems that seek to find out what motivates these killers.

Acknowledgments Many people helped make this book possible. Those who reviewed the second edition and made suggestions that I attempted to follow to the best of my ability include: Kelly J. Asmussen, Peru State College; Daniel A. Klotz, Los Angeles Valley College; William Kelly, Auburn University; Kathrine Johnson, Kentucky State University; Cecilia Tubbs, Jefferson State Community College; Ronald R. Brooks, Clinton Community College; Ellen F. VanValkenburgh, Jamestown Community College; and, Tom Fields, Cape Fear Community College.

We also thank our colleagues who reviewed the previous edition. These colleagues include Joe W. Becraft, Portland Community College; Bruce Bikle, Portland State University; Kathleen A. Cameron, Arizona State University; Janet Foster Goodwill, Yakima Valley Community College; Kathrine A. Johnson, Kentucky State University; and, Margaret Vandiver, University of Memphis.

Special thanks must also go to Kathleen Maguire and Ann Pastore, editors of the *Sourcebook of Criminal Justice;* the staff at the Institute for Social Research at the University of Michigan and the National Criminal Justice Reference Service.

Our editor Sabra Horne directed the form and content of this new edition. It has been a pleasure working with Sabra and my other colleagues at Wadsworth: developmental editor Terri Edwards, production manager Debby Kramer, production editor Cecile Joyner, photo editor Linda Rill, and marketing manager Jennifer Somerville. A lot of credit for getting this book out must go to Dan Alpert who helped us begin the project (before he was promoted to editor!) but remains as always patient, kind, and sensitive.

Larry Siegel
Joseph Senna

Essentials of Criminal Justice

chapter 1

Crime and Criminal Justice

On April 20, 1999, the nation's most deadly school shooting occurred at Columbine High School in Littleton, Colorado. Two heavily armed students—Eric Harris, age 18, and Dylan Klebold, age 17, members of a secretive student group called the "Trenchcoat Mafia"—went on a shooting spree that claimed the lives of twelve students and one teacher and wounded twenty-four others, many seriously. As police SWAT teams closed in, the two boys committed suicide in the school library, leaving authorities to puzzle over the cause of their deadly act. Later, their friends described Harris and Klebold as outsiders whose behavior may have been triggered by their perceived victimization at the hands of school athletes.

Then on July 28, 1999, Mark Barton, age 44 and a securities day trader, killed twelve people: He shot nine people at two stock trading companies in Atlanta, and earlier in the day, he bludgeoned his wife and two children with a hammer as they slept in their suburban apartment. After eluding authorities for five hours, Barton killed himself in his van as police closed in. In the aftermath of the incident, Barton's violent outburst was blamed on the pressures he felt from losing hundreds of thousands of dollars in the stock market.[1]

The wave of violence continued on August 10, 1999, when Buford Furrow, age 37, walked into a Los Angeles Jewish Community Center and shot five people including three young children. Furrow had strong ties with Aryan and neo-Nazi groups, as well as a long history of violent episodes. He had been arrested and later jailed in 1998 after he tried to check into a psychiatric hospital near Seattle and then threatened members of the hospital staff with a knife. At the time of his 1998 arrest, he told police officers that he sometimes had fantasies of going on a "shooting rampage." After his release from jail, Furrow openly espoused racist views and became active in far-right hate groups.[2] When he turned himself in to police after the LA shooting, Furrow told investigators he wanted his actions "to be a wake-up call to America to kill Jews."[3] ■

These acts are very perplexing. Although reassured by government reports that crime rates are now in a steep decline, the general public continues to be buffeted by a constant drumbeat of media stories dwelling on violence and death. Incidents like the Columbine shootings convince commentators that juvenile violence is still rampant; *Newsweek* magazine heralded the "new age of anxiety."[4] Yet, the current juvenile violent crime rate of 31 crimes per 1,000 youth in the general population represents a significant drop from a high of 52 violent crimes per 1,000 in 1993.[5]

Confusion also arises over what such violent outbursts actually signify. Do they signal the fact that many adolescents are alienated and depressed? Are disaffected youth such as Klebold and Harris liable to go on a violent rampage at the slightest provocation? Does living in our highly charged, fast-paced, technologically advanced society create overwhelming feelings of stress and anxiety? Is that what set Barton off on a killing spree? Has a hate-filled society developed that produces the violent outbursts of a racist such as Furrow?

On August 10, 1999, Buford Furrow, age 37, walked into a Los Angeles Jewish Community Center and shot five people, including three young children. Incidents such as this shooting help convince the public that we live in a violent society despite the fact that government reports indicate that crime rates are now in a steep decline.

Questions are also being raised about how such crimes can be prevented. Could the Columbine shootings have been prevented if gun ownership was abolished or severely restricted? Klebold and Harris's violence was blamed in part on their interest in media and Internet violence. Does viewing violent images on TV or in the movies have a catastrophic effect on troubled adolescents? If it does, should the government curtail or restrict the depiction of violence in the media? To some people, such measures smack of excessive governmental control, whereas to others they are necessary measures to curb violent crimes.

To provide solutions to the crime problem and to shape the direction of crime policy, we turn to the agencies of the **criminal justice** system. This loosely organized collection of agencies is charged with, among other matters, protecting the public, maintaining order, enforcing the law, identifying transgressors, bringing the guilty to justice, and treating criminal behavior. The public depends on this vast system, employing more than 2 million people and costing taxpayers more than $100 billion a year, to protect them from evildoers and to bring justice to their lives.

criminal justice
The decision-making points from the initial investigation or arrest by police to the eventual release of the offender and his or her reentry into society; the various sequential criminal justice stages through which the offender passes.

This text serves as an introduction to the study of criminal justice. This chapter introduces some basic issues, beginning with a discussion of the concept and the study of criminal justice. The major processes of the criminal justice system are then introduced so that you can develop an overview of how the system functions. Because there is no single view of the underlying goals that help shape criminal justice, the varying perspectives on what criminal justice really is or should be are set out in some detail.

IS CRIME A RECENT DEVELOPMENT?

We often hear older people say, "Crime is getting worse every day" and "I can remember when it was safe to walk the streets at night," but their memories may be colored by wishful thinking: Crime and violence have existed in the United States for more than two hundred years. In fact, the crime rate may actually have been much higher in the nineteenth and early twentieth centuries than it is today.

Crime and violence have been common since the nation was first formed.[6] Guerilla activity was frequent before, during, and after the Revolutionary War. Bands supporting the British (Tories) and the American revolutionaries engaged in savage attacks on each other, using hit-and-run tactics, burning, and looting.

The struggle over slavery during the mid-nineteenth century generated decades of conflict, crimes, and violence, including a civil war. After the war, night riders and Ku Klux Klan members were active in the South, using vigilante methods to maintain the status quo and terrorize former slaves. The violence also spilled over into bloody local feuds in the hill country of southern Appalachia. Factional hatreds, magnified by the lack of formal law enforcement and grinding poverty, gave rise to violent attacks and family feuding. Some former Union and Confederate soldiers, heading west with the dream of finding gold or starting a cattle ranch, resorted to theft and robbery.

Crime in the Old West

Some western lawmen developed reputations that have persisted for over a century. Of these, none is more famous than Wyatt Earp. In 1876 he became chief deputy marshal of Dodge City, Kansas, a lawless frontier town, and later moved on to Deadwood in the Dakota Territory. In 1879 Earp and his brothers Morgan and Virgil journeyed to Tombstone, Arizona, where he eventually was appointed deputy U.S. Marshal for the Arizona Territory. On October 27, 1880, "Curly Bill" Brocious—who along with Ike Clanton was a leader of the infamous "Cowboy" gang of local cattle thieves—killed Tombstone Marshal Fred White. Although it may have been an accident, this event is said to have started the bitter feud between the Earps and the Cowboys. The Earps, along with their gun-slinging dentist friend Doc Holliday, participated in the famous OK Corral gunfight in 1881, during which they killed several members of the Cowboys. The Cowboys were not the only gang that plied their trade in the Old West. Train robbery was popularized by the Reno brothers of Indiana and bank robbery by the James–Younger gang of Missouri.

Although the Civil War generated criminal gangs, it also produced widespread business crime. The great robber barons bribed government officials and intrigued to corner markets and obtain concessions for railroads, favorable land deals, and mining and mineral rights on government land. The administration of President Ulysses Grant was tainted by numerous corruption scandals.

Crime at the Turn of the Twentieth Century

From 1900 to 1935, the nation experienced a sustained increase in criminal activity. This period was dominated by Depression-era outlaws who later became mythic figures. Charles "Pretty Boy" Floyd was a folk hero among the sharecroppers of eastern Oklahoma, while the nation eagerly followed the exploits of its premier bank robber, John Dillinger, until he was killed in front of a Chicago movie house. The infamous "Ma" Barker and her sons Lloyd, Herman, Fred, and Arthur are credited with killing more than ten people, while Bonnie Parker and Clyde Barrow killed more than thirteen before they were slain in a shootout with federal agents.

Bonnie Parker vamps for the camera, circa 1930. She and her partner, Clyde Barrow, have been romanticized in song and film (*Bonnie and Clyde* with Warren Beatty and Faye Dunaway playing the leads). They are, however, believed to have killed 13 people, making them serial killers. Violence rates were higher in the 1930s than they are today. What does that suggest about such suspected causes of violence as violent TV shows and rock music?

While these relatively small and mobile outlaw gangs were operating in the Midwest, more organized gangs flourished in the nation's largest cities. The first criminal gangs formed before the Civil War in urban slums, such as the Five Points and Bowery neighborhoods in New York City. Though they sported colorful names, such as the Plug Uglies, the Hudson Dusters, and the Dead Rabbits, they engaged in mayhem, murder, and extortion. These gangs were the forerunners of the organized crime families that developed in New York and spread to Philadelphia, Chicago, New Orleans, and other major urban areas.

The crime problem in the United States has been evolving along with the nation itself. Crime has provided a mechanism for the frustrated to vent their anger, for business leaders to maintain their position of wealth and power, and for those outside the economic mainstream to take a shortcut to the "American dream." To protect itself from this ongoing assault, the public has supported the development of a great array of government agencies whose stated purpose is to control and prevent crime; identify, apprehend, and bring to trial those who choose to violate the law; and devise effective methods of criminal correction. These agencies make up what is commonly referred to today as the criminal justice system, and it is to their nature and development we now turn our attention.

DEVELOPING THE CRIMINAL JUSTICE SYSTEM

The debate over the proper course for effective crime control can be traced back to the publication in 1764 of Cesare Beccaria's famous treatise, *On Crime and Punishment.* Beccaria, an Italian social philosopher, made a convincing argument against the use of torture and capital punishment, common practices in the eighteenth century. He persuasively argued that only the minimum amount of punishment was needed to control crime if criminals could be convinced that their law violations were certain to be discovered and swiftly punished.[7]

In 1829 the first police agency, the London Metropolitan Police, was developed to keep the peace and identify criminal suspects; police agencies began to appear in the United States during the mid-nineteenth century. The penitentiary, or prison, was created to provide nonphysical correctional treatment for convicted offenders; these were considered "liberal" innovations that replaced corporal and/or capital punishment.

Although significant and far reaching, these changes were rather isolated developments. As criminal justice developed over the next century, these fledgling agencies of justice rarely worked together in a systematic fashion. It was not until 1919—when the Chicago Crime Commission, a professional association funded by private contributions, was created—that the work of the criminal justice system began to be recognized.[8] This organization acted as a citizen's advocate group and kept track of the activities of local justice agencies. The commission still carries out its work today.

In 1931 President Herbert Hoover appointed the National Commission of Law Observance and Enforcement, which is commonly known today as the Wickersham Commission. This national study group made a detailed analysis of the U.S. justice system and helped usher in the era of treatment and rehabilitation. The final report found that thousands of rules and regulations govern the system and made it difficult for justice personnel to keep track of the system's legal and administrative complexity.[9]

The Modern Era of Justice

The modern era of criminal justice can be traced to a series of research projects, first begun in the 1950s, under the sponsorship of the American Bar Foundation.[10] Originally designed to provide in-depth analysis of the organization, administration, and operation of criminal justice agencies, the ABF project discovered that the justice system contained many procedures that heretofore had been kept hidden from the public view. The research focus then shifted to an examination of these previously obscure processes and their interrelationship—investigation, arrest, prosecution, and plea negotiations. It became apparent that justice professionals used a great deal of personal choice in decision making, and showing how this discretion was used became a prime focus of the research effort. For the first time, the term *criminal justice system* began to be used, a view that justice agencies could be connected in an intricate yet often unobserved network of decision-making processes.

Federal Involvement in Criminal Justice In 1967 the President's Commission on Law Enforcement and Administration of Justice (the Crime Commission), which had been appointed by President Lyndon Johnson, published its final report entitled "The Challenge of Crime in a Free Society."[11] This group of practitioners, educators, and attorneys was charged with creating a comprehensive view of the criminal justice process and recommending reforms. Concomitantly, Congress passed the Safe Streets and Crime Control Act of 1968, providing for the expenditure of federal funds for state and local crime control efforts.[12] This act helped launch a massive campaign to restructure the justice system. It funded the National Institute of Law Enforcement and Criminal Justice (NILECJ), which encouraged research and development in criminal justice. Renamed the National Institute of Justice (NIJ) in 1979, it has continued its mission as a major source of funding for the implementation and evaluation of innovative experimental and demonstration projects in the criminal justice system.[13]

Law Enforcement Assistance Administration (LEAA)
Funded by the federal government's Safe Streets Act, this agency provided technical assistance and hundreds of millions of dollars in aid to local and state justice agencies between 1969 and 1982.

social control
The ability of society and its institutions to control, manage, restrain, or direct human behavior.

The Safe Streets Act provided funding for the **Law Enforcement Assistance Administration (LEAA),** which granted hundreds of millions of dollars in aid to local and state justice agencies. Throughout its fourteen-year history, the LEAA provided the majority of federal funds to states for criminal justice activities. On April 15, 1982, the program came to an end when Congress ceased funding it. Although the LEAA suffered its share of criticism, it supported many worthwhile programs, including the development of a vast number of criminal justice departments in colleges and universities and the use of technology in the criminal justice system.

The federal government continues to fund the National Institute of Justice (NIJ), the Office of Juvenile Justice and Delinquency Prevention (OJJDP), and the Bureau of Justice Statistics (BJS). These agencies carry out a more limited role in supporting criminal justice research and development and publishing extremely valuable data and research findings. (See Figure 1.1 for the criminal justice system time line.)

Figure 1.1
Criminal justice system time line

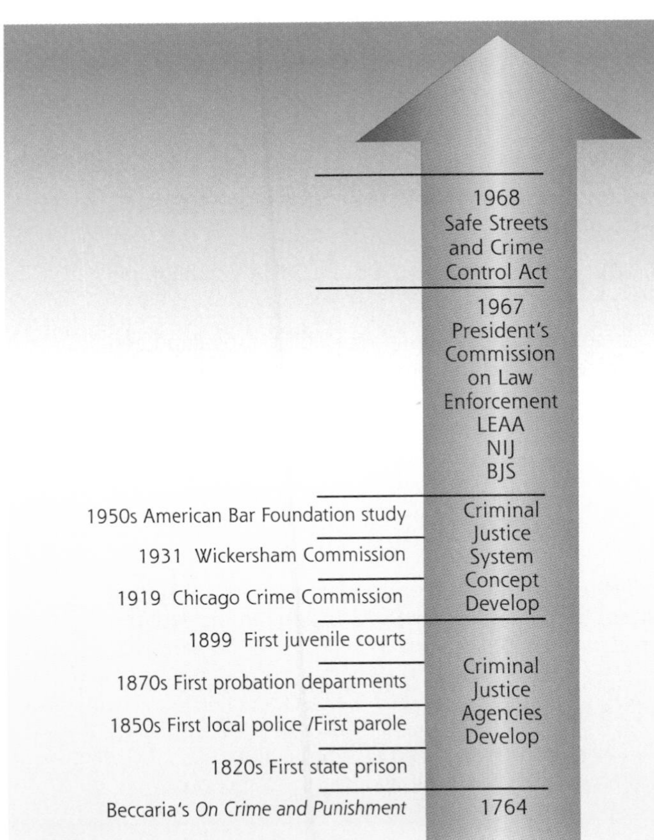

THE CRIMINAL JUSTICE SYSTEM TODAY

The criminal justice system is society's instrument of **social control:** Some behaviors are considered so dangerous that they must either be strictly controlled or outlawed outright; some people are so destructive that they must be monitored or even confined. It is the task of the agencies of justice to prevent and/or deter outlawed behavior by apprehending, adjudicating, and sanctioning lawbreakers. Society maintains other forms of informal social control, such as parental and school discipline, but these are designed to deal with moral and not legal misbehavior. Only the criminal justice system maintains the power to control crime and punish outlawed behavior through the arm of the criminal law.

The following sections set out the system, describe its major component parts, and briefly analyze its most significant processes. In the following chapters, these agencies and procedures will be discussed in more extensive detail.

Agencies of the Criminal Justice System The contemporary criminal justice system in the United States is monumental in size. It consists of over fifty-five thousand public agencies and now costs federal, state, and local governments more than $110 billion per year for civil and criminal justice, increasing more than 110 percent since 1985 (see Exhibit 1.1).

The three levels of government together spend about $400 for each resident in the United States.[14] Today the system can be divided into three main components (Figure 1.2): law enforcement agencies charged with investigating crimes and apprehending suspects; the court system where a determination is made whether a criminal suspect is guilty as charged; and the correctional system charged with both treating and rehabilitating offenders and with incapacitating them so that they may not repeat their crimes.

One reason the justice system is so expensive to run is because it employs over 2 million people, including about 900,000 in law enforcement. It consists of over 55,000 public agencies, including 17,000 police agencies, nearly 17,000 courts, over 8,000 prosecutorial agencies, about 6,000 correctional institutions, and over 3,500 probation and parole departments. There are also capital costs. State jurisdictions are now conducting a massive correctional building campaign, adding tens of thousands of prison cells. It costs about $70,000 to build a prison cell, and about $22,000 per year is needed to keep an inmate in prison; juvenile institutions cost about $30,000 per year per resident. Beyond the direct costs of funding police, court, and corrections, many more additional crime-related expenses are incurred by the federal, state, and local governments. For example, federal drug control efforts now cost an additional $17 billion per year.[15]

The system is so big because it must process, treat, and care for millions of people each year. Although the crime rate has declined substantially, about 15 million people are still being arrested each year, including more than 2.5 million for serious felony offenses.[16] In addition, about 1.5 million juveniles are handled by the juvenile courts.[17] Today state and federal courts convict a combined total of over 1 million adults on felony charges.[18]

exhibit 1.1

The Costs of Criminal Justice

- Federal, state, and local governments spent more than $112 billion per year for criminal and civil justice (1995).
- In 1995 the United States spent $48.6 billion for police protection and $39.8 billion for corrections, including jails, prisons, probation, and parole. The combined activities of courts, prosecution and legal services, and public defense accounted for $24.5 billion.
- The federal government alone spent more than $22 billion on criminal and civil justice in 1995, an increase of 253 percent since 1985. This included about $5.9 billion for grants to state and local governments. About $9 billion was spent on police protection and $4.2 billion on corrections.
- Between 1985 and 1995, expenditures for operating the justice system increased from almost $65 billion to over $112 billion, an increase of about 73 percent in constant 1995 dollars.
- The justice system employed almost 2 million people, with a total 1995 October payroll of $5.8 billion.
- More than 900,000 employees worked in police protection, 401,000 were in judicial and legal services, and 656,000 worked in corrections.

Source: Lea S. Gifford with assistance from Sue A. Lindgren, *Justice Expenditure and Employment in the United States, 1995* (Washington, D.C.: Bureau of Justice Statistics, 1999).

Police

Police departments are those public agencies created to maintain order, enforce the criminal law, provide emergency services, keep traffic on streets and highways moving freely, and create a sense of community safety. Police officers work actively with the community to prevent criminal behavior, they help divert members of special needs populations, such as juveniles, alcoholics, and drug addicts, from the criminal justice system; they participate in specialized units such as a drug prevention task force or antirape unit; they cooperate with public prosecutors to initiate investigations into organized crime and drug trafficking; they resolve neighborhood and family conflicts; and they provide emergency services, such as preserving civil order during strikes and political demonstrations.

Courts

The criminal court house is the scene of the trial process. Here the criminal responsibility of defendants accused of violating the law is determined. Ideally, the court is expected to convict and sentence those found guilty of crimes while ensuring that the innocent are freed without any consequence or burden. The court system is formally required to seek the truth, to obtain justice for the individual brought before its tribunals, and to maintain the integrity of the government's rule of law. The main actors in the court process are the judge whose responsibilities include overseeing the legality of the trial process and the prosecutor and the defense attorney who are the opponents in what is known as the adversary system. These two parties oppose each other in a hotly disputed contest— the criminal trial—in accordance with rules of law and procedure.

Corrections

In the broadest sense, correctional agencies include community supervision or probation, various types of incarceration (including jails, houses of correction, and state prisons), and parole programs for both juvenile and adult offenders. These programs range from the lowest security, such as probation in the community with minimum supervision, to the highest security, such as 24-hour lockdown in an ultra-maximum security prison. Corrections ordinarily represent the post-adjudicatory care given to offenders when a sentence is imposed by the court and the offender is placed in the hands of the correctional agency.

Figure 1.2
Components of the criminal justice system

Considering the enormous number of people processed each year, the correctional system population is at an all-time high. About 6 million people are under the control of the correctional system, including almost 2 million behind bars and another 4 million on some form of community supervision. In 1999 almost 3 percent of the nation's adult population, or about 1 in every 34 adults, were incarcerated, on probation, or on parole.[19]

THE FORMAL CRIMINAL JUSTICE PROCESS

Another way of understanding criminal justice is to view it as a process that takes an offender through a series of decision points beginning with arrest and concluding with reentry into society. During this process, key decision makers resolve whether to maintain the offender in the system or to discharge the suspect without further action. This decision making is often a matter of individual discretion, based upon a variety of factors and perceptions. Legal factors, including the seriousness of the charges, available evidence, and the suspect's prior record, are usually considered legitimate influences on decision making. Troubling is the fact that such extralegal factors as the suspect's race, gender, class, and age may influence decision outcomes. There is a significant and ongoing debate over the impact of extralegal factors in the decision to arrest, convict, and sentence suspects: Critics believe a suspect's race, class, and gender can often determine the direction a case will take, whereas supporters argue that the system is relatively fair and unbiased.[20]

In reality, few cases actually are processed through the entire formal justice system. Most are handled informally and with dispatch. The system of justice has been roundly criticized for its "backroom deals" and bargain justice. Although informality and deal making are in fact the rule, the concept of the formal justice process is important because it implies every criminal defendant charged with a serious crime is entitled to a full range of rights under law. Central to the American concept of liberty is that every individual is entitled to his day in court, to be represented by competent counsel in a fair trial before an impartial jury, with trial procedures subject to review by a higher authority. Secret and hidden kangaroo courts and summary punishment are elements of political systems that most Americans fear and despise. The fact that most criminal suspects are actually treated informally may be less important than the fact that all criminal defendants are entitled to a full range of legal rights and constitutional protections.

A comprehensive view of the formal criminal process would normally include the following:

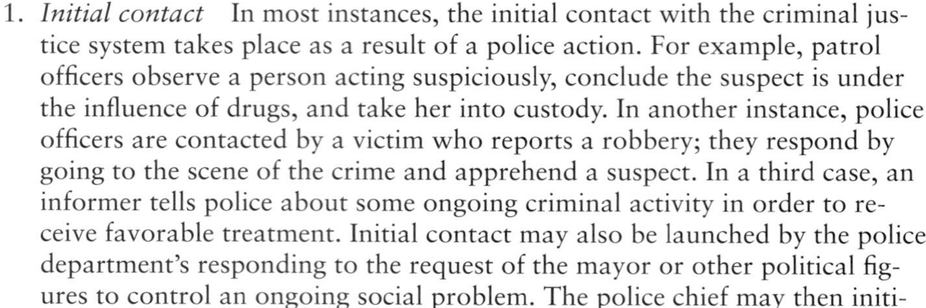

1. *Initial contact* In most instances, the initial contact with the criminal justice system takes place as a result of a police action. For example, patrol officers observe a person acting suspiciously, conclude the suspect is under the influence of drugs, and take her into custody. In another instance, police officers are contacted by a victim who reports a robbery; they respond by going to the scene of the crime and apprehend a suspect. In a third case, an informer tells police about some ongoing criminal activity in order to receive favorable treatment. Initial contact may also be launched by the police department's responding to the request of the mayor or other political figures to control an ongoing social problem. The police chief may then initiate an undercover investigation into such corrupt practices as gambling, prostitution, or drug trafficking.
2. *Investigation* The purpose of the investigatory stage of justice is to gather sufficient evidence to identify a suspect and support a legal arrest. An investigation can take but a few minutes, as in the case where a police officer sees a crime in progress and can apprehend the suspect within minutes. Or it can take many months and involve hundreds of law enforcement agents, such as the FBI's pursuit of the so-called Unabomber, which led to the eventual arrest of Ted Kaczynski. Investigations may be conducted at the local, state, or federal level and involve coordinated teams of law enforcement agents, prosecutors, and other justice officials.
3. *Arrest* An arrest is considered legal when all of the following conditions exist: (a) The police officer believes there is sufficient evidence, referred to as *probable cause,* that a crime is being or has been committed and the suspect is the person who committed it; (b) the officer deprives the individual of freedom; and (c) the suspect believes that he is now in the custody of the police and has lost his liberty. The police officer is not required to use the

A legal arrest can occur when police generate sufficient probable cause. Here suspect Scott Pennington, with coat over his head, is led away by police after shooting Deanna McDavid at East Carter High School. Police are more likely to arrest suspects who commit violent crimes than those who engage in property offenses.

word arrest or any similar term to initiate an arrest, nor does the officer have to bring the suspect to the police station. To make an arrest in a misdemeanor, the officer must have witnessed the crime personally, known as the *in-presence requirement;* a felony arrest can be made based upon the statement of a witness or victim. Arrests can also be made when a magistrate, presented with sufficient evidence by police and prosecutors, issues a warrant authorizing the arrest of the suspect.

4. *Custody* The moment after an arrest is made, the detained suspect is considered in police custody. At this juncture, the police may wish to search the suspect for weapons or contraband, interrogate her in order to gain more information, find out if the person had any accomplices, or even encourage the suspect to confess to the crime. The police may wish to enter the suspect's home, car, or office to look for further evidence. Similarly, the police may want to bring witnesses to view the suspect in a lineup or in a one-to-one confrontation. Personal information will also be taken from the suspect, including name, address, fingerprints, and photo. Because these procedures are so crucial and can have a great impact at trial, the U.S. Supreme Court has granted suspects in police custody protection from the unconstitutional abuse of police power, such as illegal searches and intimidating interrogations.
5. *Charging* If the arresting officers and/or their superiors believe that sufficient evidence exists to charge a person with a crime, the case will be turned over to the prosecutor's office. Minor crimes—that is, misdemeanors— are generally handled with a complaint being filed before the court that will try the case. For serious crimes—that is, felonies—the prosecutor must decide whether to bring the case to either a grand jury or preliminary hearing (depending on the procedures used in the jurisdiction; see item 6, next). In either event, the decision to charge the suspect with a specific criminal act involves many factors, including evidence sufficiency, crime seriousness, case pressure, and political issues, as well as personal factors such as a prosecutor's own specific interests and biases. For example, in some jurisdictions obscenity charges may be vigorously pursued, while in another they are all but ignored. After conducting a preliminary investigation of its legal merits, prosecutors may decide to take no further action in a case, referred to as a **nolle prosequi.**

nolle prosequi
The term used when a prosecutor decides to drop a case after a complaint has been formally made. Reasons for a nolle prosequi include evidence insufficiency, reluctance of witnesses to testify, police error, and office policy.

6. *Preliminary hearing/grand jury* Because a criminal suspect faces great financial and personal costs when forced to stand trial for a felony, the U.S. Constitution mandates that before a trial can take place, the government must first prove probable cause that the accused committed the crime with which he is being charged. In about half the states and the federal system, this decision is rendered by a group of citizens brought together to form a grand jury who considers the merits of the case in a closed hearing in which only the prosecutor presents evidence. If the evidence is sufficient, the grand jury will issue a bill of indictment, which specifies the specific charges on which the accused must stand trial. In the remaining states, the grand jury has been replaced with a preliminary hearing. In these jurisdictions, a charging document called an *information* is filed before a lower trial court, which then conducts an open hearing on the merits of the case. During this procedure, sometimes referred to as a *probable cause hearing,* the defendant and her attorney may appear and dispute the prosecutor's charges. The suspect will be called to stand trial if the presiding magistrate or judge accepts the prosecutor's evidence as factual and sufficient.

7. *Arraignment* Before the trial begins, the defendant will be arraigned, or brought before the court that will hear the case. Formal charges are read, the defendant informed of his constitutional rights (e.g., the right to be represented by legal counsel), an initial plea entered in the case (not guilty or guilty), a trial date set, and bail issues considered.

8. *Bail/detention* Bail is a money bond levied to ensure the return of a criminal defendant for trial, while allowing the person pretrial freedom to prepare her defense. Defendants who do not show up for trial forfeit their bail. Those people who cannot afford to put up bail or who cannot borrow sufficient funds for it will remain in state custody prior to trial. In most instances, this means an extended stay in a county jail or house of correction. Most jurisdictions allow defendants awaiting trial to be released on their own recognizance (promise to the court), without bail, if they are stable members of the community and have committed nonviolent crimes.

9. *Plea bargaining* Soon after an arraignment, if not before, defense counsel will meet with the prosecution to see if the case can be brought to a conclusion without a trial. In some instances, this can involve filing the case while the defendant participates in a community-based treatment program for substance abuse or psychiatric care. Most commonly, the defense and prosecution will discuss a possible guilty plea in exchange for reducing or dropping some of the charges or agreeing to a request for a more lenient sentence. It is generally accepted that almost 90 percent of all cases end in a plea bargain, rather than a criminal trial.

10. *Trial/adjudication* If an agreement cannot be reached or if the prosecution does not wish to arrange a negotiated settlement of the case, a criminal trial will be held before a judge or jury who will decide whether the prosecution's evidence against the defendant is sufficient beyond a reasonable doubt to prove guilt. If a jury cannot reach a decision—that is, it is deadlocked—the case is left unresolved, leaving the prosecution to decide whether it should be retried at a later date.

11. *Sentencing/disposition* If after a criminal trial the accused has been found guilty as charged, he will be returned to court for sentencing. Possible dispositions may include a fine, probation, a period of incarceration in a penal institution, or some combination of these. In cases involving first-degree murder, more than thirty-five states and the federal government now allow the death penalty.

    Sentencing is a key decision point in the criminal justice system because, in many jurisdictions, judicial discretion can result in people receiving vastly different sentences even though they have committed the same crime. Some may be released on community supervision, whereas others committing the same crime can receive long prison sentences.

12. *Appeal/postconviction remedies* After conviction, the defense can ask the trial judge to set aside the jury's verdict because she believes there has been a mistake of law. For example, in the nationally publicized Louise Woodward case, the young British nanny was convicted on the charge of second-degree murder when a Massachusetts jury found her responsible for the death of Matthew Eappen, an infant boy placed in her care. Woodward allegedly shook Matthew, causing his death. The verdict was soon set aside by the trial judge, Hiller Zobel, because he believed that the facts of the case did not substantiate the charge of second-degree murder; he instead reduced the charge to manslaughter and sentenced Woodward to time already served while she was awaiting trial.[21]

An appeal may be filed if after conviction the defendant believes that he has not received fair treatment or that his constitutional rights were violated. Appellate courts review such issues as whether evidence was used properly, a judge conducted the trial in an approved fashion, jury selection was properly done, and the attorneys in the case acted appropriately. If the court rules that the appeal has merit, it can hold that the defendant be given a new trial or, in some instances, order his outright release. For example, outright release can be ordered when the state prosecutes the case in violation of the double jeopardy clause (Fifth Amendment) or when it violates the defendant's right to a speedy trial (Sixth Amendment).

13. *Correctional treatment* After sentencing, the offender is placed within the jurisdiction of state or federal correctional authorities. She may serve a probationary term, be placed in a community correctional facility, serve a term in a county jail, or be housed in a prison. During this stage of the criminal justice process, the offender may be asked to participate in rehabilitation programs designed to help her make a successful readjustment to society.
14. *Release* Upon completion of his sentence and period of correction, the offender will be free to return to society. Most inmates do not serve the full term of their sentence but are freed via an early-release mechanism, such as parole or pardon or by earning time off for good behavior. Offenders sentenced to community supervision simply finish their term and resume their lives in the community.
15. *Postrelease* After termination of their correctional treatment, offenders may be asked to spend some time in a community correctional center, which acts as a bridge between a secure treatment facility and absolute freedom. Offenders may find that their conviction has cost them some personal privileges, such as the right to hold certain kinds of employment. These may be returned by court order once the offenders have proven their trustworthiness and willingness to adjust to society's rules.

The Criminal Justice Assembly Line

> The image that comes to mind is an assembly line conveyor belt down which moves an endless stream of cases, never stopping, carrying them to workers who stand at fixed stations and who perform on each case as it comes by the same small but essential operation that brings it one step closer to being a finished product, or to exchange the metaphor for the reality, a closed file. The criminal process is seen as a screening process in which each successive stage—pre-arrest investigation, arrest, post-arrest investigation, preparation for trial or entry of plea, conviction, disposition—involves a series of routinized operations whose success is gauged primarily by their tendency to pass the case along to a successful conclusion.[22]

This is how Herbert Packer describes the criminal justice process. According to this view, each of the preceding fifteen stages is actually a decision point through which cases flow (Figure 1.3). For example, at the investigatory stage, police must decide whether to pursue the case or terminate involvement because there is insufficient evidence to identify a suspect, the case is considered trivial, the victim decides not to press charges, and so on. At the bail stage, a decision must be made whether to set so high a bail that the defendant remains in custody, set a reasonable bail, or release the defendant on her own recognizance without requiring any bail at all. Each of these decisions can have a critical effect on the defendant, the justice system, and society. If an error is made, an

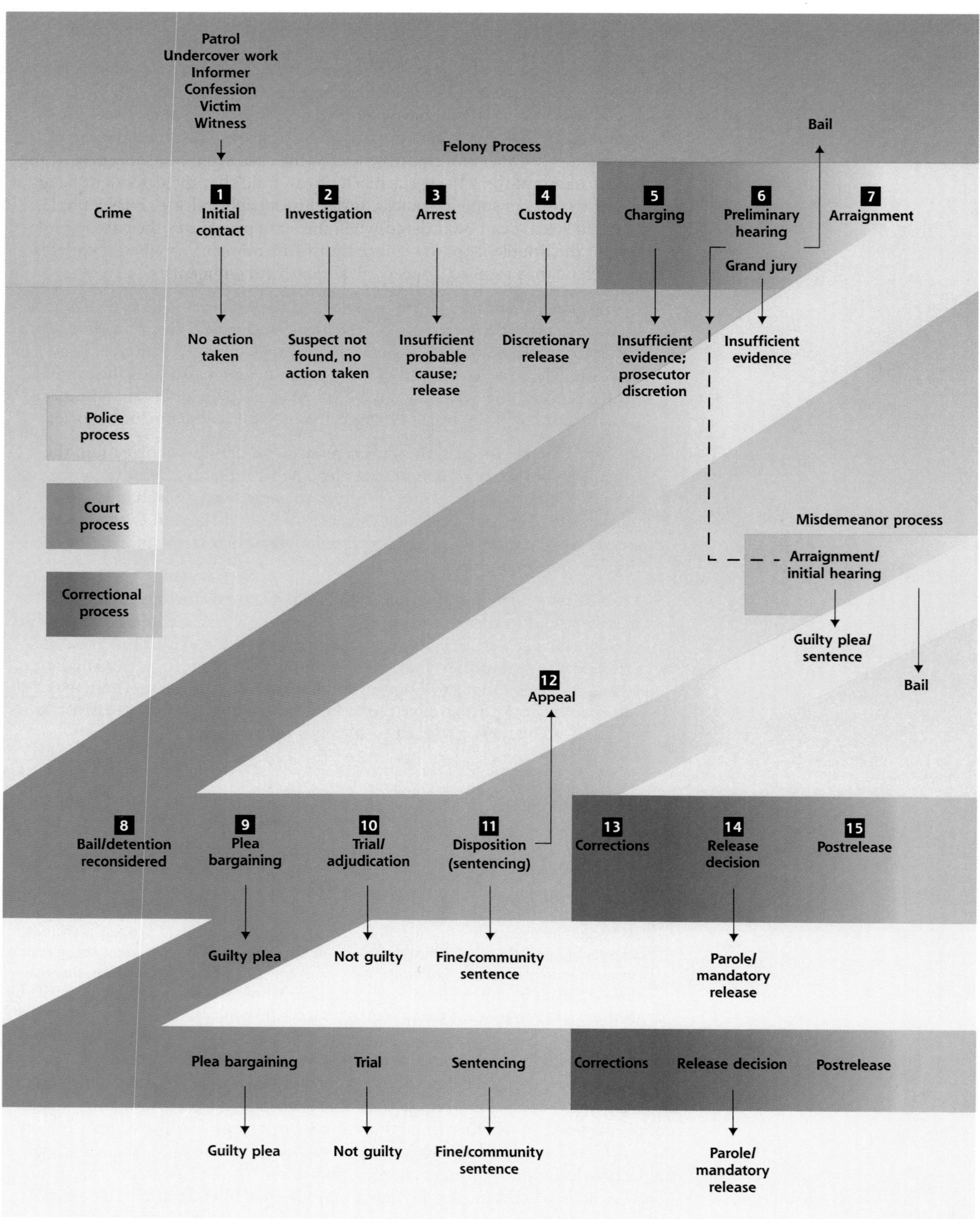

Figure 1.3
The critical stages in the justice process follow an assembly line.

innocent person may suffer or a dangerous individual may be released to continue to prey upon society.

Figure 1.4 illustrates the approximate number of offenders removed from the criminal justice system at each stage of the process. As the figure shows, most people who commit crime escape detection, and of those who do not, relatively few are bound over for trial, convicted, and eventually sentenced to prison. About 70 percent of people arrested on felony charges are eventually convicted

Figure 1.4
The criminal justice funnel

SOURCE: Patrick Langan and Richard Solari, *National Judicial Reporting Program, 1990* (Washington, D.C.: Bureau of Justice Statistics, 1993, updated 1999).

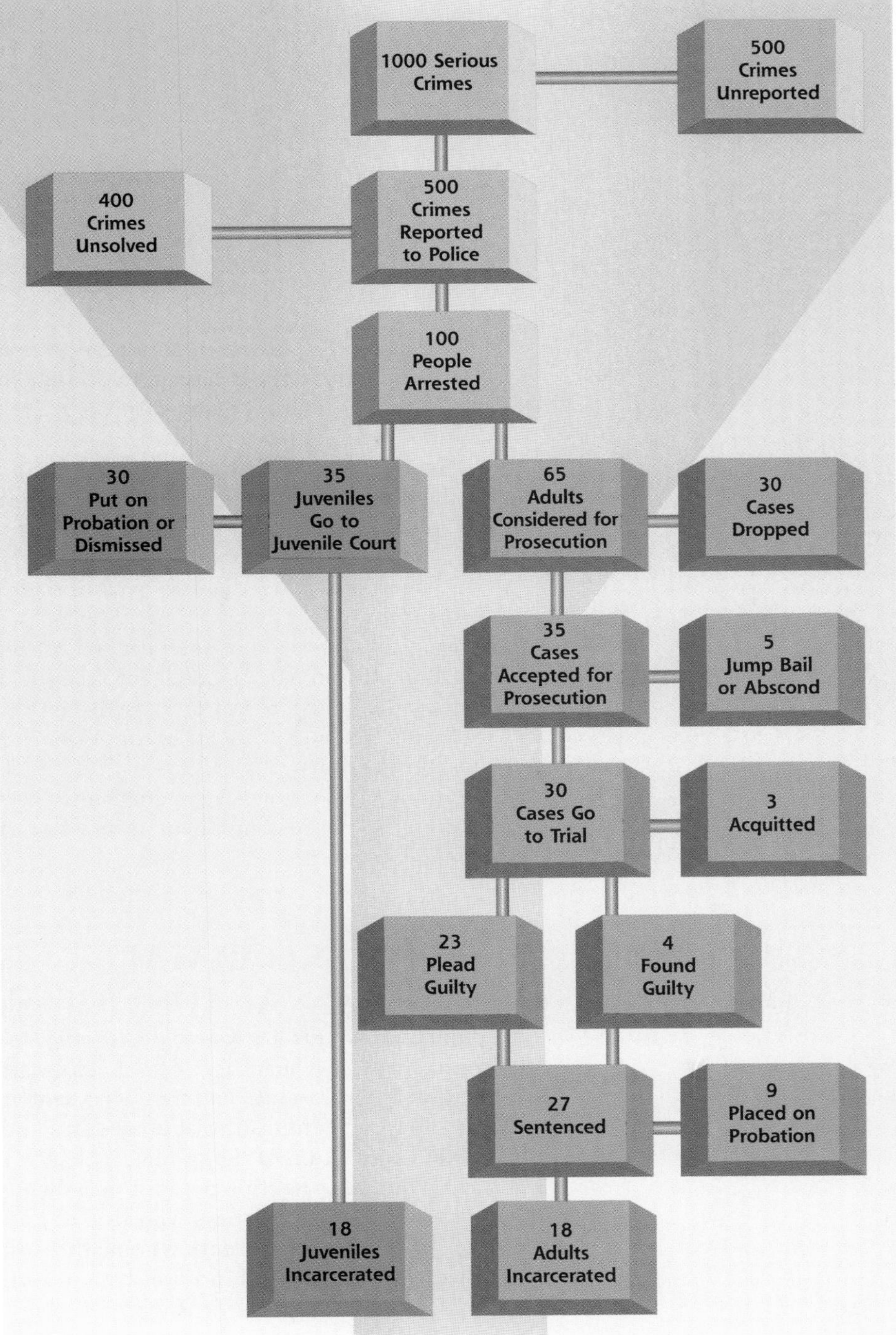

Table 1.1
The Interrelationship of the Criminal Justice System and the Criminal Justice Process

The System: Agencies of Crime Control	The Process
1. Police	1. Contact 2. Investigation 3. Arrest 4. Custody
2. Prosecution and defense	5. Complaint/charging 6. Grand jury/preliminary hearing 7. Arraignment 8. Bail/detention 9. Plea negotiations
3. Court	10. Adjudication 11. Disposition 12. Appeal/postconviction remedies
4. Corrections	13. Correction 14. Release 15. Postrelease

in criminal court; however, about 25 percent of convictees are released back into the community without having to do time in prison.[23]

In actual practice, many suspects are released before trial because of a procedural error, evidence problems, or other reasons that result in nolle prosequi. Though most cases that go to trial wind up in a conviction, others are dismissed by the presiding judge because of the defendant's failure to appear or procedural irregularities. So, the justice process can be viewed as a funnel that holds many cases at its mouth and relatively few at its end.

Theoretically, nearly every part of the process requires that individual cases be disposed of as quickly as possible. However, the criminal justice process is slower and more tedious than desired because of congestion, inadequate facilities, limited resources, inefficiency, and the nature of governmental bureaucracy. When defendants are not processed smoothly, often because of the large caseloads and inadequate facilities that exist in many urban jurisdictions, the procedure breaks down, the process within the system fails, and the ultimate goal of a fair and efficient justice system cannot be achieved. Table 1.1 shows the interrelationship of the component agencies of the criminal justice system and the criminal justice process.

THE INFORMAL CRIMINAL JUSTICE SYSTEM

The traditional model of the criminal justice system depicts the legal process as a series of decision points through which cases flow. Each stage of the system, beginning with investigation and arrest and ending after a sentence has been served, is defined by time-honored administrative procedures and controlled by the rule of law. The public's perception of the system, fueled by the media, is that it is composed of daredevil, crime-fighting police officers who never ask for overtime or sick leave, crusading district attorneys who stop at nothing to send the mob boss up the river, wily defense attorneys who neither ask clients for up-front cash nor cut office visits to play golf, no-nonsense judges who are never inept political appointees, and tough wardens who rule the yard with an iron hand. Though this "ideal" model of justice still merits concern and attention, it would be overly simplistic to assume that the system works this way for every case. Although a few cases receive a full measure of rights and procedures, many are settled in an informal pattern of cooperation between the major actors in the justice process. For example, police may be willing to make a deal with a suspect in order to gain his cooperation, and the prosecutor may bargain with the defense attorney to gain a plea of guilty as charged in return for a promise of leniency. Law enforcement agents and court officers are allowed tremendous discretion in their decision to make an arrest, bring formal charges, handle a case informally, substitute charges, and so on. Crowded courts operate in a spirit of getting the matter settled quickly and cleanly, rather than engage in long, drawn-out criminal proceedings with an uncertain outcome.

Whereas the traditional model regards the justice process as an adversary proceeding in which the prosecution and defense are combatants, the majority of criminal cases are actually cooperative ventures in which all parties get together to work out a deal; this is often referred to as the **courtroom work group.**[24] This group, made up of the prosecutor, defense attorney, judge, and other court personnel, functions to streamline the process of justice through the extensive use of plea bargaining and other alternatives. Rather than looking to provide a spirited defense or prosecution, these legal agents, who have often attended the same schools, know each other, and have worked together for many years, try to work out a case to their own professional advantage. In most criminal cases, cooperation rather than conflict between prosecution and defense appears to be the norm. It is only in a few widely publicized criminal cases involving rape or murder that the adversarial process is called into play. Consequently, upward of 80 percent of all felony cases and over 90 percent of misdemeanors are settled without trial.

courtroom work group
The phrase used to denote that all parties in the adversary process work together in a cooperative effort to settle cases with the least amount of effort and conflict.

What has developed is a system in which criminal court experiences can be viewed as a training ground for young defense attorneys looking for seasoning and practice. It provides a means for newly established lawyers to receive government compensation for cases taken to get their practice going or an arena in which established firms can place their new associates for experience before they are assigned to paying clients. Similarly, successful prosecutors can look forward to a political career or a highly paid partnership in a private firm. To further their career aspirations, prosecutors must develop and maintain a winning track record in criminal cases. No district attorney wants to become a Hamilton Burger, the fictional prosecutor who loses every case to the legendary Perry Mason. Although the courtroom work group limits the constitutional rights of defendants, it may be essential for keeping our overburdened justice system afloat. Moreover, though informal justice exists, it is not absolutely certain that it is inherently unfair to both the victim and the offender. Research evidence shows that the defendants who benefit the most from informal court procedures commit the least serious crimes, whereas the more chronic offender gains relatively little.[25]

The "Wedding Cake" Model of Justice

Samuel Walker, a justice historian and scholar, has come up with a rather dramatic way of describing this informal justice process: he compares it to a four-layer cake, as depicted in Figure 1.5.[26]

- *Level I* The first layer of Walker's model is made up of the celebrated cases involving the wealthy and famous, such as O. J. Simpson or Wall Street financier Michael Milken, or the not so powerful who victimize a famous person—

Figure 1.5
The criminal justice "wedding cake"

SOURCE: Based on Samuel Walker, *Sense and Nonsense about Crime* (Monterey, Calif.: Brooks/Cole, 1985).

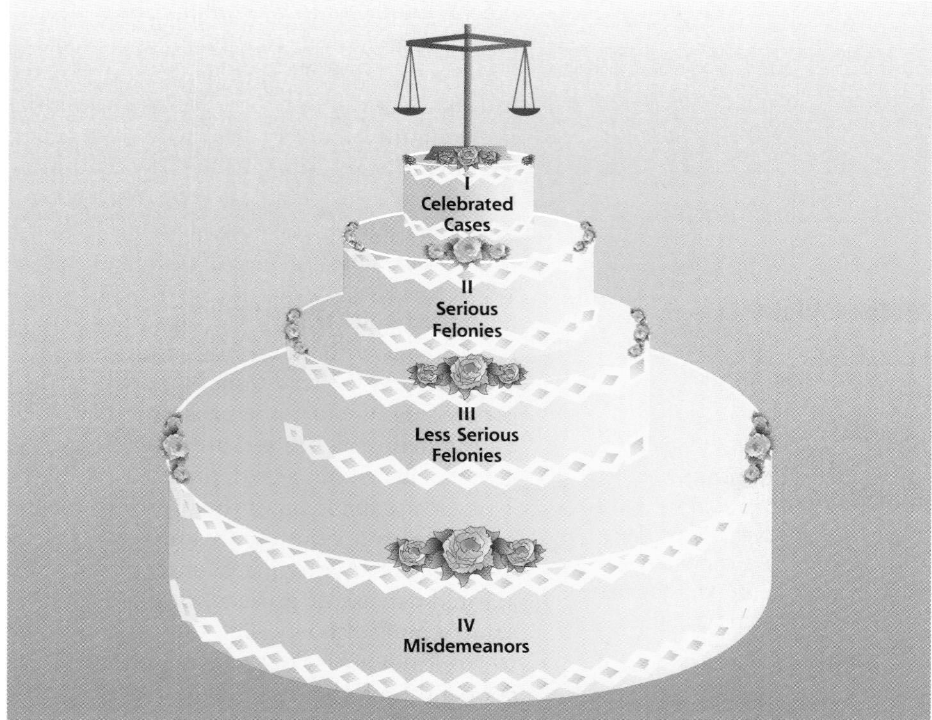

for example, John Hinckley, Jr., who shot President Ronald Reagan. Other cases fall into the first layer because they are widely reported in the media and become the subject of a TV investigation. The media usually focus on hideous or unusual cases, such as the murder of JonBenet Ramsey.

Cases in the first layer of the criminal justice wedding cake usually receive the full array of criminal justice procedures, including competent defense attorneys, expert witnesses, jury trials, and elaborate appeals. The media typically focus on Level I cases, and the movie-going public are given the impression that most criminals are sober, intelligent people and most victims are members of the upper classes, a patently false impression (see the Criminal Justice and the Media feature).

- *Level II* In the second layer are the serious felonies—rapes, robberies, and burglaries—which have become all too routine in U.S. society. They are in the second layer because they are serious crimes committed by experienced offenders. Burglaries are included if the amount stolen is quite high and the techniques used indicate the suspect is a real pro. Violent crimes, such as rape and assault, are vicious incidents against an innocent victim and may involve a weapon and extreme violence. Robberies involve large amounts of money and suspects who brandish handguns or other weapons and are considered career criminals. Police, prosecutors, and judges all agree that these are serious cases, worthy of the full attention of the justice system. Offenders in such Level II cases receive a full jury trial and, if convicted, can look forward to a prison sentence.
- *Level III* Though they can also be felonies, crimes that fall in the third layer of the wedding cake are either less serious offenses, committed by young or first-time offenders and/or involving people who knew each other or were otherwise related: An inebriated teenager committed a burglary and netted

$50; the rape victim had gone on a few dates with her assailant before he attacked her; the robbery involved members of rival gangs and no weapons; the assault was the result of a personal dispute, and there is some question of who hit who first. Agents of the criminal justice system relegate these cases to the third level because they see them as less important and deserving of attention. Level III crimes may be dealt with by an outright dismissal, a plea bargain, reduction in charges, and, most typically, a probationary sentence or intermediate sanction, such as victim restitution.

Criminal Justice and the Media

DOUBLE JEOPARDY

Agents of the criminal justice system routinely confront calculating, intelligent criminals who use guile and cunning to carry out their fiendish plots. Crime victims are wealthy, attractive, and glamorous and, if the cops can't solve the crime, they think nothing of single handedly foiling the criminals themselves. This is the theme of the popular 1999 film *Double Jeopardy.* Libby Parsons (Ashley Judd) is a wealthy Seattle socialite convicted of killing her husband. Her idyllic life is shattered when her husband, Nick (Bruce Greenwood), disappears overboard during a romantic weekend of sailing on their yacht. Though Libby (and the audience) know she is innocent of the crime, Libby is convicted of murder and sentenced to prison. She survives because of two burning desires—finding her son and solving the mystery of what happened to her husband. She tracks him down via telephone and finds that he is still alive. Prison friends tell her that she can kill him with impunity because she has already been convicted of the crime; hence, the title *Double Jeopardy.*

Libby is eventually paroled and sent to a halfway house where she is monitored by Travis Lehman (Tommy Lee Jones), a cynical and seasoned parole officer who won't tolerate any rule violations. Libby immediately escapes in order to track down her son, Matty, and Nick. Lehman goes after her in hot pursuit. After numerous ordeals and escapes, she finds Nick in New Orleans. She decides to spare his life, but he attacks her and she kills him in self-defense. In the end, Libby is united with her son who recognizes his long-lost mother.

Although an exciting adventure–action film, *Double Jeopardy* is typical of the media's romanticized vision of the criminal justice system. According to Hollywood, most cases fall in the top layer of the criminal justice wedding cake. They involve attractive victims and cunning, well-prepared criminals. The stakes are high, the law enforcement agents dedicated, street battles and shootouts common, lots of people die, and the case is always solved. Because the victims, police, and criminals are all attractive, articulate, and well-educated (after all, they are Hollywood actors), they often form a close bond and can even become romantically involved with one another. Other films of this type include *The Jagged Edge,* in which an attorney (Glenn Close) and the client she is defending on murder charges (Jeff Bridges) become romantically involved; *Basic Instinct,* in which a wealthy accused killer (Sharon Stone) and the detective investigating the case (Michael Douglas) hook up; and *The Fugitive,* in which a prison escapee (Harrison Ford), a well-known physician, and pursuing U.S. Marshal (Tommy Lee Jones) form a bond.

These films give the public a distorted view of both criminals and the criminal justice system. Some cases do involve the wealthy and glamorous, but these are actually few and far between. Most victims and criminals come from the lower end of the socioeconomic scale, living in poverty areas and not penthouses; few people are murdered on their yachts. Very few crimes involve millions of dollars; most criminals "earn" far less than minimum wage for their efforts. Rather than being intelligent and articulate, they are more likely to be drug abusing and desperate.

The most ludicrous element of *Double Jeopardy* is the way Libby's stay in the prison system is portrayed. She makes great friends, has plenty of time for reading and exercise, and comes out looking like she just spent a week at a trendy health spa. She is in such great mental and physical shape that in no time she is able to track down her missing spouse. Her hairdo and stylish clothes look great even when she is forced to jump off a ferry and then gets stuck in a coffin with a dead body. How often do you see such well-put-together criminals who have wonderful prison experiences? Probably never, unless you bought a ticket to see *Double Jeopardy!*

- *Level IV* The fourth layer of the cake is made up of the millions of misdemeanors, such as disorderly conduct, shoplifting, public drunkenness, and minor assault. These are handled by the lower criminal courts in assembly-line fashion. Few defendants insist on exercising their constitutional rights because the delay would cost them valuable time and money. Since the typical penalty is a small fine, everyone wants to get the case over with.[27]

The wedding cake model of informal justice is an intriguing alternative to the traditional criminal justice flowchart. Criminal justice officials handle individual cases quite differently, yet there is a high degree of consistency with which particular types or classes of cases are dealt in every legal jurisdiction. For example, police and prosecutors in Los Angeles and Boston will each handle the murder of a prominent citizen in similar fashion. They will also deal with the death of an unemployed street person killed in a brawl in a similar manner. Yet, in each jurisdiction, the two cases will be handled very differently. The bigwig's killer will receive a full-blown jury trial (with details on the 6:00 news); the drifter's killer will get a quick plea bargain. The model is useful because it helps us realize that all too often public opinion about criminal justice is formed on the basis of what happened in an atypical case.

PERSPECTIVES ON JUSTICE

Though it has been more than twenty-five years since the field of criminal justice began to be the subject of both serious academic study and attempts at unified policy formation, significant debate continues over the actual meaning of *criminal justice* and how the problem of crime control should be approached. After decades of effort in research and policy analysis, it is clear that criminal justice is far from a unified field. Practitioners, academics, and commentators alike have expressed irreconcilable differences concerning its goals, purpose, and direction. Some conservatives see the solution to the crime problem to be increasing the number of police, apprehending more criminals, and giving them long sentences to maximum-security prisons. In contrast, liberals call for increased spending on social services and community organization. Others worry about giving the government too much power to regulate and control behavior and to interfere with individual liberty and freedom.

This lack of consensus is particularly vexing when we consider the multitude of problems facing the justice system. The agencies of justice must attempt to eradicate such seemingly diverse social problems as substance abuse, gang violence, pornography, price fixing, and environmental contamination while respecting individual liberties and civil rights. It is also assumed that the agencies of the justice system have adequate resources and knowledge to carry out their complex tasks in an efficient and effective manner, something which so far seems to be wishful thinking. Experts are still searching for the right combination of policies and actions that will significantly reduce crime and increase public safety while maintaining individual freedom and social justice.

Considering the complexity of criminal justice, that no single view, perspective, or philosophy dominates the field is not surprising. What are the dominant views of the criminal justice system today? What is the role of the justice system, and how should it approach its tasks? The different perspectives on criminal justice are discussed next.

crime control
A model of criminal justice that emphasizes the control of dangerous offenders and the protection of society. Its advocates call for harsh punishments as a deterrent to crime, such as the death penalty

According to the crime control perspective, the focus of justice should be on the victim of crime, not the criminal. Here, friends weep over the casket of Rachel Scott, a student killed in the Columbine High School massacre. Could more effective police protection and sentences, including the death penalty, prevent such tragedies?

Crime Control Perspective More than 20 years ago political scientist James Q. Wilson made the persuasive argument that most criminals are not poor unfortunates who commit crime to survive but are greedy people who choose theft and/or drug dealing for quick and easy profits.[28] Criminals, he argued, lack inhibition against misconduct, value the excitement and thrills of breaking the law, have a low stake in conformity, and are willing to take greater chances than the average person. If they could be convinced that their actions will bring severe punishment, only the totally irrational would be willing to engage in crime. Restraining offenders and preventing their future misdeeds, he argued, is a much more practical goal of the criminal justice system than trying to eradicate the root causes of crime: poverty, poor schools, racism, and family breakup. He made this famous observation:

> Wicked people exist. Nothing avails except to set them apart from innocent people. And many people, neither wicked nor innocent, but watchful, dissembling, and calculating of their chances, ponder our reaction to wickedness as a clue to what they might profitably do.[29]

Wilson's views helped define the **crime control** perspective of criminal justice. According to this view, the proper role of the justice system is to prevent crime through the judicious use of criminal sanctions. Because the public is outraged by such crimes as the shootings at Columbine High School, it demands an efficient justice system that hands out tough sanctions to those who choose to violate the law.[30] If the justice system operated in an effective manner, potential criminals would be deterred from committing law violations, while those who did commit crime would be apprehended, tried, and punished so that they would never dare risk committing crime again. Crime rates trend upward, the argument goes, when criminals do not sufficiently fear apprehension and punishment. If the efficiency of the system could be increased and the criminal law could be toughened, crime rates would eventually decline. Recent reductions in the crime rate have been attributed to a "get tough" attitude, mandatory punishments, and expanding prison populations. Though crime control may be expensive, reducing the pains of criminal activity is well worth the price.

FOCUS ON THE VICTIM According to the crime control perspective, the focus of justice should be on the victim of crime, not the criminal, so that innocent people can be protected from the ravages of crime. This objective can be achieved through more effective police protection, tough sentences (including liberal use of the death penalty), and the construction

Victims' rights groups have become more and more vocal in trying to keep violent criminals from receiving parole. Go to www.parolewatch.org/welcome.htm **and** home.sprynet.com/~statnisle/clemency.htm **to see the tactics favored by these groups.**

of prisons designed to safely incapacitate hardened criminals. If punishment was both certain and severe, few would be tempted to break the law.

Crime control advocates do not want legal technicalities to help the guilty go free and tie the hands of justice. They lobby for the abolition of legal restrictions that control a police officer's ability to search for evidence and interrogate suspects. They are angry at judges who let obviously guilty people go free because a law enforcement officer made an unintentional procedural error.

Crime control advocates also question the criminal justice system's ability to rehabilitate offenders. Most treatment programs are ineffective because the justice system is simply not equipped to treat people who have a long history of antisocial behavior. Even when agents of the system attempt to prevent crime by working with young people, the results are unsatisfactory. For example, evaluations of the highly touted Drug Abuse Resistance Education (DARE) antidrug program indicate that it has had little impact on students.[31] From both a moral and a practical standpoint, the role of criminal justice should be the control of antisocial people. If not to the justice system, then to whom can the average citizen turn for protection from society's criminal elements?

rehabilitation perspective
A model of criminal justice that views its primary purpose as helping to care for people who cannot manage themselves. Crime is an expression of frustration and anger created by social inequality that can be controlled by giving people the means to improve their lifestyle through conventional endeavors.

Rehabilitation Perspective

If the crime control perspective views the justice system in terms of protecting the public and controlling criminal elements, then advocates of the **rehabilitation perspective** may be said to see the justice system as a means of caring for and treating people who cannot manage themselves. They view crime as an expression of frustration and anger created by social inequality. Crime can be controlled by giving people the means to improve their lifestyle through conventional endeavors.

The rehabilitation concept assumes that people are at the mercy of social, economic, and interpersonal conditions and interactions. Criminals themselves are the victims of racism, poverty, strain, blocked opportunities, alienation, family disruption, and other social problems. They live in socially disorganized neighborhoods that are incapable of providing proper education, health care, or civil services. Society must help them in order to compensate for their social problems.

You can learn about some of the constitutional questions raised by various criminal laws and procedures by going to the Web site of the American Civil Liberties Union at www.aclu.org

ALTERNATIVES TO CRIME Rehabilitation advocates believe that government programs can help reduce crime on both a macro- and microlevel. For example, on the macro-, or societal, level, research shows that as the number of legitimate opportunities to succeed declines, people are more likely to turn to criminal behaviors, such as drug dealing, in order to survive.[32] Increasing economic opportunities through job training, family counseling, educational services, and crisis intervention are more effective crime reducers than prisons and jails. As legitimate opportunities increase, violence rates decline.[33]

On a microlevel, once apprehended, criminals can benefit from well-designed treatment efforts that can reduce repeat offending. For example, counseling programs, which help offenders develop interpersonal skills, induce a prosocial change in attitudes and improve cognitive thinking patterns, both of which have been shown to significantly reduce recidivism rates.[34]

Clearly, punishing offenders and placing them in prison does not seem to deter future criminality. Society has a choice: Pay now, by funding treatment and educational programs, or pay later, when troubled youths enter costly correctional facilities over and over again. This view is certainly not lost on the public. Although the public may want to "get tough" on crime, many are willing to make exceptions, for example, by advocating leniency for younger offenders.[35]

due process
The basic constitutional principle based on the concept of the primacy of the individual and the complementary concept of limitation on governmental power; a safeguard against arbitrary and unfair state procedures in judicial or administrative proceedings. Embodied in the due process concept are the basic rights of a defendant in criminal proceedings and the requisites for a fair trial. These rights and requirements have been expanded by appellate court decisions and include (1) timely notice of a hearing or trial that informs the accused of the charges against him or her; (2) the opportunity to confront accusers and to present evidence on one's own behalf before an impartial jury or judge; (3) the presumption of innocence under which guilt must be proven by legally obtained evidence and the verdict must be supported by the evidence presented; (4) the right of an accused to be warned of constitutional rights at the earliest stage of the criminal process; (5) protection against self-incrimination; (6) assistance of counsel at every critical stage of the criminal process; and (7) the guarantee that an individual will not be tried more than once for the same offense (double jeopardy).

Due Process Perspective Advocates of the **due process** perspective argue that the greatest concern of the justice system should be providing fair and equitable treatment to those accused of crime.[36] This means providing impartial hearings, competent legal counsel, equitable treatment, and reasonable sanctions. The use of discretion within the justice system should be strictly monitored to ensure that no one suffers from racial, religious or ethnic discrimination. Though there are many views of what the true goals of justice should be, there is no question that the system must operate in a fair and unbiased manner.

Those who advocate the due process orientation are quick to point out that the justice system remains an adversary process that pits the forces of an all-powerful state against those of a solitary individual accused of a crime. If concern for justice and fairness did not exist, the defendant who lacked resources could easily be overwhelmed; miscarriages of justice are common. A report from the Institute for Law and Justice, a Virginia-based research firm, found that at least twenty-eight cases of sexual assault had been overturned because DNA evidence proved that the accused could not have committed the crimes; the inmates averaged seven years in prison before their release.[37] Evidence also shows that many innocent people have been executed for crimes they did not commit. Between 1976 and 1999, 566 people were executed. During that same period of time, 82 convicts awaiting execution were exonerated—a ratio of 1 freed for every 7 put to death.[38] Since such mistakes can happen, even the most apparently guilty offender deserves all the protection the justice system can offer.

Access to due process is rarely challenged, but a long-standing debate continues over the prerogatives and privileges of criminal suspects. How far should we go to protect individual rights? What happens when individual rights interfere with public safety? For example, if police officers discover incriminating evidence while searching a suspect but in so doing violate her constitutional right to privacy, should the information be excluded from her trial even if it means that a dangerous person goes free? Some might argue that it is better to free a guilty person than trample on the civil rights of citizens, even those who commit criminal acts. But what about the rights of actual or potential victims of crime? Should the needs of the victim take precedence over those of criminal offenders?

nonintervention
A justice philosophy that emphasizes the least intrusive treatment possible. Among its central policies are decarceration, diversion, and decriminalization. In other words, less is better.

Nonintervention Perspective Supporters of the **nonintervention** perspective believe that justice agencies should limit their involvement with criminal defendants. Regardless of whether intervention is designed to punish or treat people, the ultimate effect of any involvement is harmful. Whatever their goals or design, programs that involve people with a social control agency—such as the police, a mental health department, the correctional system, or a criminal court—will have long-term negative effects. Once involved with such an agency, criminal defendants may be watched, people might consider them dangerous and untrustworthy, and they can develop a lasting record that has negative connotations. Eventually, they may even come to believe what their official record suggests; they may view themselves as bad, evil, outcasts, troublemakers, or crazy. Noninterventionists are concerned about the effect of the stigma that criminal suspects bear when they are given negative labels such as "rapist" or "child abuser." These labels will stick with them forever; once labeled, people may find it difficult to ever be accepted back into society, even after they have completed their sentence.

decriminalization
Reducing the penalty for a criminal act but not actually legalizing it.

Fearing the harmful effects of stigma and labels, noninterventionists have tried to place limitations on the government's ability to control people's lives. They have called for the **decriminalization** (reduction of penalties) and/or legalization of nonserious **victimless crimes,** such as the possession of small amounts of marijuana, public drunkenness, and vagrancy. They demand the removal of nonviolent offenders from the nation's correctional system, a policy referred to as **deinstitutionalization.** First offenders who commit minor crimes should instead be placed in informal, community-based treatment programs, a process referred to as **pretrial diversion.**

victimless crime
An act that is in violation of society's moral code and therefore has been outlawed—for example, drug abuse, gambling, and prostitution. These acts are linked together because, although they have no external victim, they are considered harmful to the social fabric.

deinstitutionalization
The movement to remove as many offenders as possible from secure confinement and treat them in the community.

pretrial diversion
A program that provides nonpunitive community-based alternatives to more intrusive forms of punishment such as jail or prison.

widening the net
The charge that programs designed to divert offenders from the justice system actually enmesh them further in the process by substituting more intrusive treatment programs for less intrusive punishment-oriented outcomes.

Sometimes the passage of new criminal laws help stigmatize offenders beyond the scope of their actual offense, referred to as **widening the net** of justice. For example, a person who purchases pornography on the Internet is labeled a dangerous "sex offender," or someone caught for a second time with marijuana is considered a "habitual drug abuser." Noninterventionists have fought implementation of community notification–type laws that require that convicted sex offenders register with state law enforcement officials and allow officials to publicly disclose when a registrant moves into a community. Their efforts have resulted in rulings stating that these laws can be damaging to the reputation and future of offenders who have not been given an opportunity to defend themselves from the charge that they are chronic "criminal sex offenders."[39] As a group, noninterventionist initiatives have been implemented to help people avoid the stigma associated with contact with the criminal justice system.

Justice Perspective

The core of the justice perspective is that all people should receive the same treatment under the law. Any effort to distinguish between criminal offenders will create a sense of unfairness that can interfere with readjustment to society. It is frustrating when two people commit the same crime but receive different sentences or punishments. The resulting anger and a sense of unfairness will increase the likelihood of recidivism.

To remedy this situation, the criminal justice system must reduce discretion and unequal treatment. Law violators should be evaluated on the basis of their current behavior, not on what they have done in the past (they have already paid for their behavior) nor on what they may do in the future (since future behavior cannot be accurately predicted). The treatment of criminal offenders must be based solely on present behavior: Punishment must be equitably administered and based on "just desert."

The justice perspective has had considerable influence in molding the nation's sentencing policy. There has been an ongoing effort to reduce discretion and guarantee that every offender convicted of a particular crime receives equal punishment. There have been a number of initiatives designed to achieve this result, including mandatory sentences requiring that all people convicted of a crime receive the same prison sentence. *Truth-in-sentencing laws,* used in twenty-seven states, now require offenders to serve a substantial portion of their prison sentence behind bars, thus limiting their eligibility for early release on parole.[40]

Restorative Justice Perspective

restorative justice
A view of criminal justice that advocates peaceful solutions and mediation rather than coercive punishments.

According to the concept of **restorative justice,** the true purpose of the criminal justice system is to promote a peaceful and just society; the justice system should aim for peacemaking, not punishment.[41]

The restorative justice perspective draws its inspiration from religious and philosophical teachings ranging from Quakerism to Zen. Advocates of restorative justice view the efforts of the state to punish and control as crime encouraging rather than crime discouraging. The violent punishing acts of the state, they claim, are not dissimilar from the violent acts of individuals.[42] Therefore, mu-

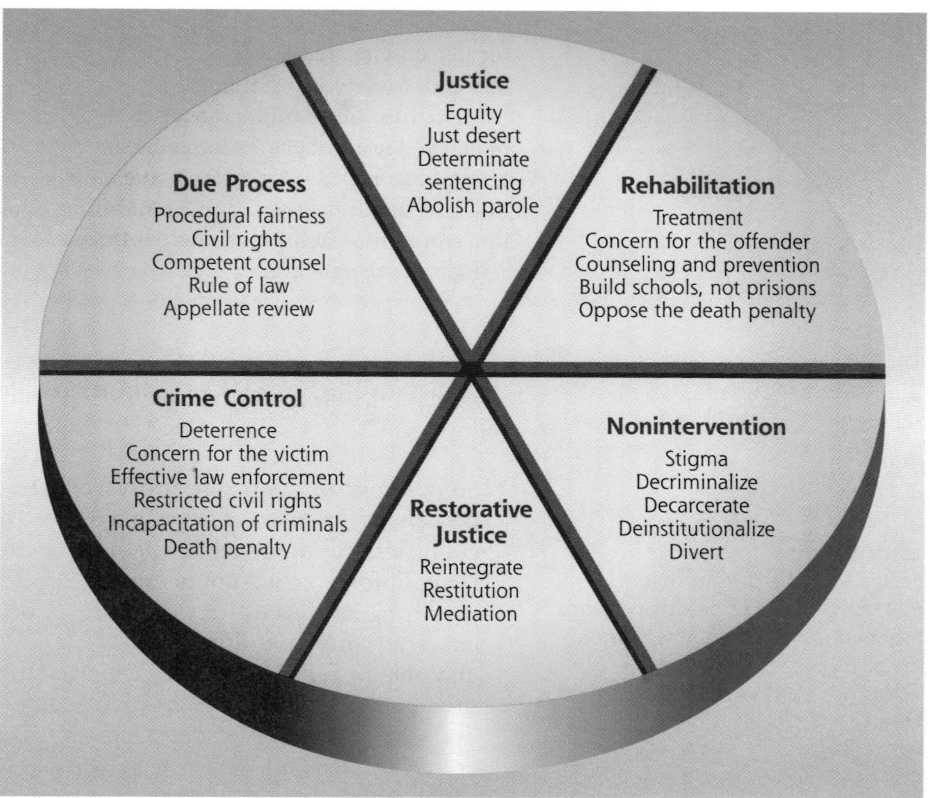

Figure 1.6
Perspectives on justice: key concerns and concepts

tual aid rather than coercive punishment is the key to a harmonious society. Without the capacity to restore damaged social relations, society's response to crime has been almost exclusively punitive.

According to restorative justice, resolution of the conflict between criminal and victim should take place in the community in which it originated and not in some far-off prison. The victim should be given a chance to voice his story, and the offender can directly communicate her need for social reintegration and treatment. The goal is to enable the offender to appreciate the damage she has caused, to make amends, and to be reintegrated back into society.

Restorative justice programs are now being geared to these principles. Police officers, as elements of community policing programs, are beginning to use mediation techniques to settle disputes rather than resort to formal arrest.[43] Mediation and conflict resolution programs are common features in many communities. Financial and community service restitution programs as an alternative to imprisonment have been in operation for more than two decades. The perspectives are summarized in Figure 1.6.

PERSPECTIVES IN ACTION: CONTROLLING THE DRUG TRADE The fact that multiple perspectives of justice exist can no where better be seen than in the "war on drugs." Reducing drug abuse is a top priority, considering its social costs. For example, the state of Florida reports that in a single year (1997) nearly forty thousand hospitalizations were linked to drug abuse, increasing the state's hospital costs by $304 million. This included more than $250 million for treating diseases and other health disorders caused by substance abuse, $46 million for detoxifying substance-addicted patients, and about $8 million for the delivery and care of newborns affected by maternal substance abuse and addiction.[44]

Because of its importance and costs, agencies of the criminal justice system have used a number of strategies to reduce drug trafficking and the use of drugs. Some have relied on a strict crime control orientation, whereas others feature nonintervention, justice, and rehabilitation strategies. The following sections illustrate how each perspective influences criminal justice efforts to control or reduce the drug trade.

Crime Control Strategies

There have been a number of efforts to control the drug trade through strict crime control efforts. These include the following:

- *Source control* A major effort has been made to cut off supplies of drugs by destroying crops and arresting members of drug cartels in drug-producing countries; this approach is known as **source control.** The federal government's Drug Enforcement Administration has been in the vanguard of encouraging exporting nations to step up efforts to destroy drug crops and prosecute dealers. Translating words into deeds is a formidable task. Drug lords are willing and able to fight back through intimidation, violence, and corruption. The drug cartels in Colombia and Mexico do not hesitate to use violence and assassination to protect their interests. Between 1994 and 1999 enforcement efforts in Peru and Bolivia have been so successful that drug crops have been significantly reduced. Rather than inhibit drug shipments, Colombia soon became the premier coca-cultivating country. When the Colombian government mounted an effective eradication campaign in the traditional growing areas, the drug cartel linked up with rebel groups in remote parts of the country for their drug supply.[45] Enforcement efforts in Colombia have promoted the emergence of Mexican drug cartels.

source control
Eradicating the drug problem through a policy of destroying crops and manufacturing plants located in source countries before the drugs can be shipped to the United States.

- *Border control* Another crime control approach to the drug problem has been to interdict drug supplies as they enter the country. Border patrols and military personnel using sophisticated hardware have been involved in massive interdiction efforts; many impressive multimillion-dollar seizures have been made. Yet U.S. borders are so vast and unprotected that meaningful interdiction is difficult. To aid law enforcement agencies, the U.S. military has become involved in stemming the flow of drugs across the border. The cost of staffing listening posts and patrolling borders is growing rapidly; today interdiction and eradication strategies costs billions of dollars, yet they do little to reduce drug supplies.
- *Police crackdowns* Local, state, and federal law enforcement agents have also been actively fighting drug dealers. One approach is to direct efforts at large-scale drug rings. However, this effort has merely served to decentralize drug dealing. Law enforcement efforts have significantly reduced the strength of traditional organized syndicates. Rather than reducing the inflow of drugs, their place has been taken by Asian, Latino, and Jamaican groups, motorcycle clubs, and local gangs. Colombian syndicates have established cocaine distribution centers on every continent, and Mexican organizations are responsible for large methamphetamine shipments to the United States. Russian, Turkish, Italian, Nigerian, Chinese, Lebanese, and Pakistani heroin-trafficking syndicates are now competing for dominance.

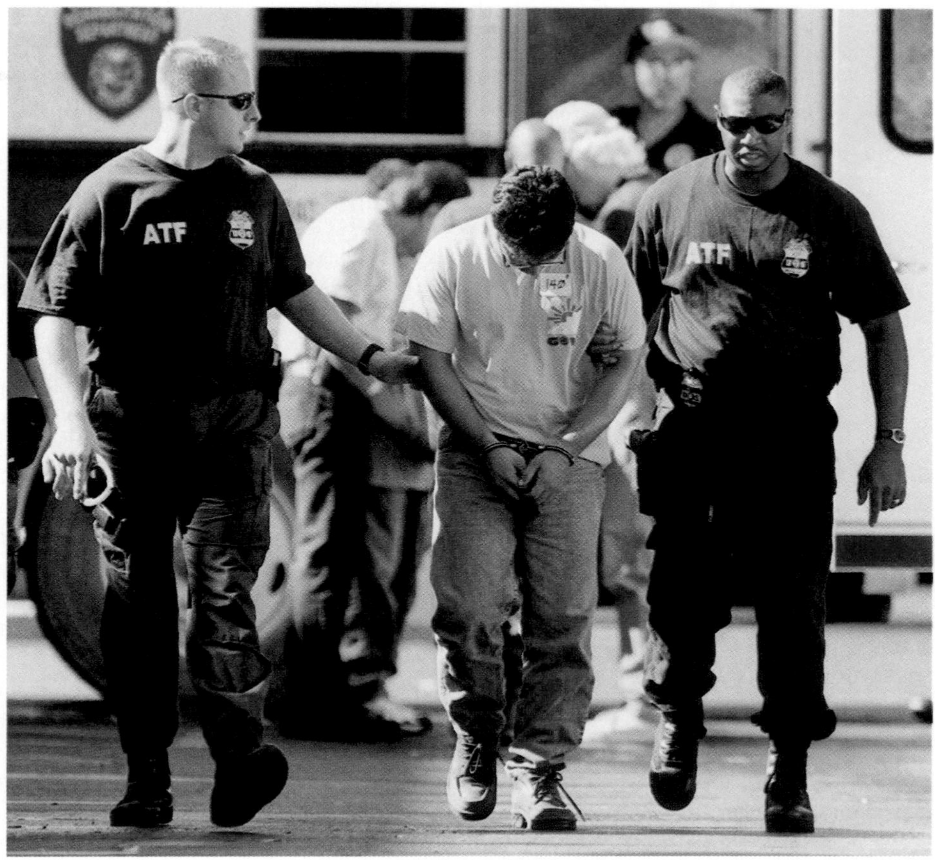

Federal agents escort an American Airlines worker arrested for smuggling in Miami. On August 25, 1999, agents arrested sixty American Airlines employees after a two year undercover effort called "Operation Ramp Rats." Although law enforcement efforts can be successful, it is still uncertain whether they can make a serious dent in the drug trade. Would legalization of drugs be a reasonable alternative to the expensive and difficult "War on Drugs"?

In terms of weight and availability, no commodity is more lucrative than illegal drugs. They cost relatively little to produce and provide large profit margins to dealers and traffickers. At an average street price of $100 per gram in the United States, a metric ton of pure cocaine is worth $100 million; cutting it and reducing purity can double or triple the value. It is difficult for law enforcement agencies to counteract the inducement of drug profits. When large-scale drug busts are made, supplies become scarce and market values increase, encouraging more people to enter the drug trade.

Aiming efforts at low-level dealers is also problematic. Some street-level enforcement efforts have been successful, but others are considered failures. Drug sweeps have clogged courts and correctional facilities with petty offenders while proving a costly drain on police resources. A displacement effect is also suspected: Stepped-up efforts to curb drug dealing in one area or city simply encourage dealers to seek out friendlier territory.

Justice Model Strategies According to the justice model, if drug violations were to be punished with criminal sentences commensurate with their harm, then the "rational" drug trafficker would look for a new line of employment. The cornerstone of this antidrug model is the adoption of mandatory minimum sentences for drug crimes, which ensure that all offenders receive similar punishments for their acts. The justice model advocates lobby for sentencing policies that will standardize punishments. The Federal Anti-Drug Abuse Act of 1988 provides minimum mandatory prison sentences for serious drug crimes, with especially punitive sentences for anyone caught distributing drugs within one thousand feet of a school playground, youth center, or other areas where minors congregate.[46] Once convicted, drug dealers are subject to very long sentences and the seizure of their homes, automobiles, boats, and other assets bought with drug-trafficking profits.

Rehabilitation Strategies Advocates of the rehabilitation model have suggested strategies aimed at reducing the desire to use drugs and increasing incentives for users to eliminate substance abuse. What strategies have been tried?

DARE
Drug Abuse Resistance Education, a school-based antidrug program initiated by the Los Angeles Police Department and now adopted around the United States.

DRUG PREVENTION One approach relies on drug prevention—convincing nonusers to not start using drugs. This effort relies heavily on educational programs that teach children to "say no" to drugs. The most well-known program is Drug Abuse Resistance Education, or **DARE**, an elementary school course designed to give students the skills for resisting peer pressure to experiment with tobacco, drugs, and alcohol. Evaluations of the program have been disappointing, indicating that it does increase knowledge about dangerous substances but has been insignificant in shaping attitudes toward drug abuse and law enforcement, increasing self-esteem, or reducing student drug use.[47]

OFFENDER TREATMENT The rehabilitation model suggests that it is possible to treat known users, get them clean of drugs and alcohol, and help them reenter conventional society.

There has been an active effort to identify drug abusers in order to get them into treatment. Drug testing of arrestees is common. Public and private institutions now regularly test employees and clients in order to determine if they are drug abusers.

Once users have been identified, a number of treatment strategies have been implemented. One approach rests on the assumption that users have low self-esteem and holds that treatment efforts must focus on building a sense of self. In this approach, users participate in outdoor activities and wilderness training in order to create self-reliance and a sense of accomplishment.[48]

More intensive efforts use group therapy approaches relying on group leaders who once were substance abusers. Group sessions try to give users the skills and support that can help them reject the social pressure to use drugs. These programs are based on the Alcoholics Anonymous approach: Users must find within themselves the strength to stay clean, and peer support from those who understand the users' experiences can help them achieve a drug-free life.

methadone
A synthetic narcotic used as a substitute for heroin in drug-control efforts.

Residential programs have been established for the more heavily involved users, and a large network of drug treatment centers has been developed. Some are detoxification units that use medical procedures to wean patients from the more addicting drugs to others, such as **methadone**, the use of which can be more easily regulated. Methadone, a drug similar to heroin, is given under controlled conditions to addicts at clinics. Methadone programs have been undermined because some users sell their methadone on the black market, while others supplement their dosages with illegally obtained heroin.

Despite their good intentions, little evidence exists that these treatment programs can efficiently end substance abuse. A stay can help stigmatize residents as "addicts," even though they never used hard drugs; while in treatment, they may be introduced to hard-core users with whom they may associate upon release. Users often do not enter these programs voluntarily and have little motivation to change.[49] Even for those who could be helped, there are simply more users who need treatment than there are beds in treatment facilities. Many programs are restricted to users whose health insurance will pay for short-term residential care; when the insurance coverage ends, the patients are often released before their treatment program is completed. Simply put, if treatment strategies are to be successful, far more programs and funding are needed. This is the topic of the following Policy, Programs and Issues in Criminal Justice feature.

Restorative Justice Strategies Restorative justice programs stress treatment and reintegration over punitive reactions to drug offenders. One example of this approach are so-called drug courts, first developed in Florida in the early 1990s. These serve as an alternative to traditional criminal justice prosecution for drug-related offenses and work to tailor nonpunitive, effective, and appropriate responses to drug offenders. Defendants eligible for the drug court program are identified as soon as possible and, if accepted into the program, are referred immediately to multiphased outpatient treatment. Treatment entails multiple weekly (often daily) contacts with the treatment provider for counseling, therapy and education and a rehabilitation program that includes vocational, educational, family, medical, and other support services.[50]

Nonintervention Strategies Despite the massive effort to control drug usage through both crime control and rehabilitation strategies, the fight has not been successful. Getting people out of the drug trade is difficult because drug trafficking involves enormous profits and dealers and users both lack meaningful economic alternatives. Controlling drugs by convincing known users to quit is equally hard; few treatment efforts have proven successful.

legalization
The removal of all criminal penalties from a previously outlawed act.

Considering these problems, some commentators, relying on a noninterventionist strategy, have called for the **legalization** of drugs. If drugs were legalized, the argument goes, distribution could be controlled by the government. Price and the distribution method could be regulated, reducing the addict's cash requirements. Crime rates would be cut because drug users would no longer need the same cash flow to support their habit. Drug-related deaths would decrease since government control would reduce the sharing of needles and thus the spread of AIDS. Legalization would also destroy the drug-importing cartels and gangs. Since drugs would be bought and sold openly, the government would reap a windfall from both taxes on the sale of drugs and on the income of drug dealers, which now is untaxed as part of the hidden economy. Drug distribution would be regulated, keeping narcotics out of the hands of adolescents. Those who favor legalization point to the Netherlands as a country that has legalized drugs and remains relatively crime free.[51]

The Internet hosts a number of organizations involved in the debate on drug policy. Drug Watch International's home page at www.DrugWatch.org **provides arguments against the legalization of drugs. The Drug Reform Coordination Network, in contrast, supports drastic changes in our drug laws. Visit its Web site at** www.drcnet.org/

DEBATING LEGALIZATION Advocates of legalization suggest that, like it or not, drug use is here to stay because using mood-altering substances is customary in almost all human societies; no matter how hard we try, people will find ways of obtaining psychoactive drugs.[52] Banning drugs serves to create networks of manufacturers and distributors, many of whom use violence as part of their standard operating procedures. Though some may charge that drug use is immoral, is it any worse than the unrestricted use of alcohol and cigarettes, both of which are addicting and unhealthy? Far more people die each year because they abuse these legal substances than the numbers who are killed in drug wars or from illegal substances (an estimated 100,000 people die each year from alcohol-related causes and another 320,000 from tobacco).[53]

Although legalization can have the short-term effect of reducing crime, critics are wary of its social consequences. Legalization may harm the well-being of the community by creating health and social damage. Individuals do not have the right to harm society even if it means curbing their freedom and personal choices—that is, the right to use drugs. If injured by their drug use, individuals would have to be cared for by the community at a very substantial cost to nondrug users.[54] Legalization would result in an increase in the nation's rate of drug usage, creating an even larger group of nonproductive, drug-dependent people, who must be cared for by the rest of society.[55] If drugs were legalized and freely available, users might significantly increase their daily intake. In countries like Iran and Thailand, where drugs are cheap and readily available, narcotic-use rates are high.

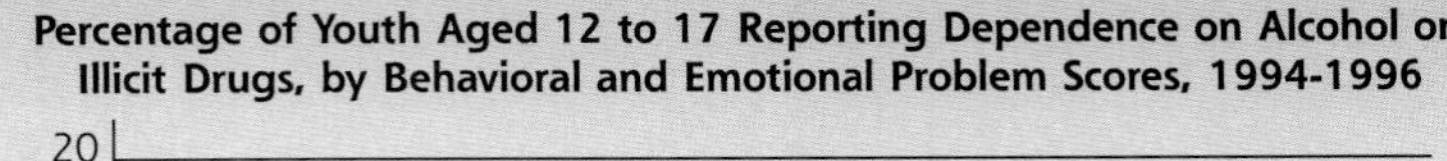

IS THERE A NEED FOR DRUG TREATMENT?

Rehabilitation strategies tactics have been thwarted because relatively few drug-dependent people are actually receiving the treatment they so desperately need. The need for treatment is evident when we consider that many people who take drugs are emotionally or psychologically troubled and would benefit from counseling and other strategies that may help them control their addictions. For example, data taken from the National Household Survey on Drug Abuse, an extensive survey sponsored by the federal government, indicates that adolescents who abuse drugs have a long history of emotional distress. As Figure A shows, those youngsters with serious behavioral problems were more than seven times more likely to report alcohol or illicit drug dependency than those with less serious problems (17.1% vs. 2.3%). In addition, youths with serious emotional problems were nearly four times more likely to report dependence (13.2% vs. 3.4%).

Unfortunately, those requiring treatment may not often receive the proper care. Although more than 4.1 million people may now be drug dependent, less than 1 million are receiving treatment. The treatment gap is most pronounced for adolescents and young adults: The number of persons ages 12–25 dependent on illicit drugs is nearly six times greater than the number receiving treatment.

Some indications show that rehabilitation can be highly successful and cost effective (Figure B). For example, the Philadelphia Target Cities Project provides publicly funded outpatient treatment services that are supplemented with referrals to social service agencies. Services provided by these agencies address an array of needs associated with state-of-the-art addiction treatment (i.e., primary health, employment, education, parenting, nutrition, and housing). The average cost per treatment episode for outpatient programs was $1,275, and the benefits gained by avoiding various "social costs" such as psychiatric care and criminal behavior were estimated at $8,408. Outpatient methadone programs treating opiate addiction yielded even greater cost benefits—$1,873 in treatment costs and $34,041 in avoided social costs.

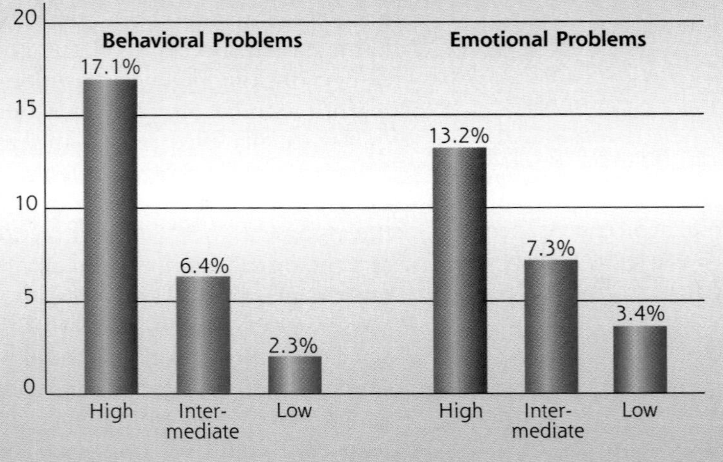

Figure A
Percentage of youth ages 12–17 reporting dependence on alcohol or illicit drugs, by behavioral and emotional problem scores, 1994–1996

Drug treatment can have benefits beyond those of reducing crime rates. An evaluation of drug treatment conducted by the Johns Hopkins University School of Medicine shows that providing treatment services to substance-abusing preg-

Others argue that the problems of alcoholism should serve as a warning of what can happen when controlled substances are made readily available. The number of drug-dependent babies could begin to match or exceed the number who are delivered with fetal alcohol syndrome.[56] Drunk-driving fatalities, which today number about twenty-five thousand per year, could be matched by deaths caused by driving under the influence of pot or crack. And though distribution would be regulated, adolescents likely would have the same opportunity to obtain potent drugs as they now have with beer and other forms of alcohol.

Perspectives in Perspective The variety of tactics being used in the war on drugs aptly illustrates the impact of the various perspectives on justice on

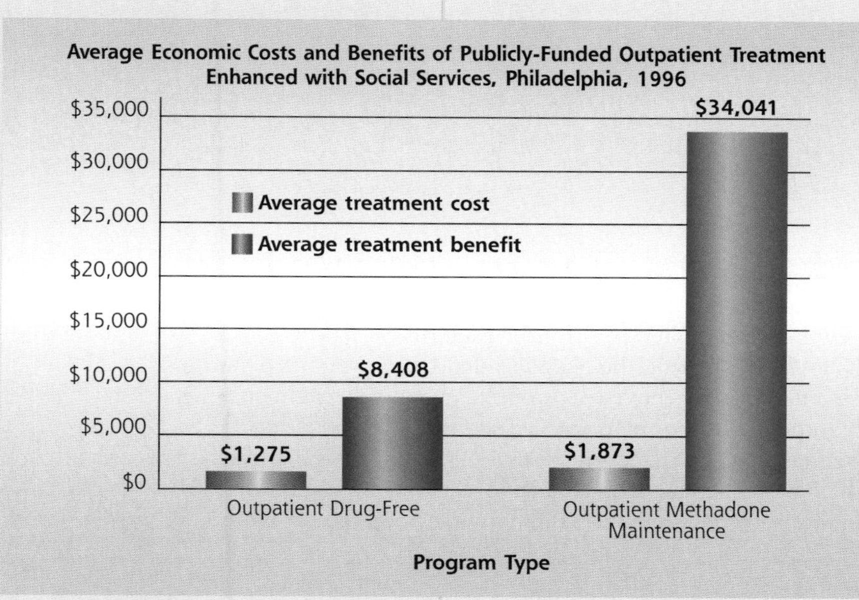

Figure B
Average economic costs and benefits of publicly funded outpatient treatment enhanced with social services, Philadelphia, 1996

SOURCE: Michael French, H. J. Jeanne Salome, Jody Sindelar, and A. Thomas McLellan, "Benefit–Cost Analysis Ancillary Social Services in Publicly Supported Addiction Treatment," 1 February 1999.

nant women can significantly reduce the costs of medical care for their infants. Neonatal intensive care unit (NICU) services were required less often by infants born to substance-abusing mothers who had received treatment than by those infants born to similar mothers who had not received treatment. Savings generated by avoiding NICU costs far exceeded the costs of providing prenatal substance abuse treatment services to the mothers. The total costs of NICU care ($12,183) for infants born to mothers who did not receive substance abuse treatment significantly surpassed the total costs ($7,539) for treatment for pregnant women ($6,639) and NICU care for their infants ($900).

Critical Thinking

These data indicate that drug treatment is not reaching many people who need it the most and that when it is received it can have a significant financial and social impact; therefore, it may be too soon to dismiss rehabilitation efforts as a strategy in the war on drugs. Do you approve of this tack? Or should the war on drugs be waged on large-scale drug importers in order to drive them out of business? If drug importation is not stopped, are we not doomed to pay for treatment efforts forever?

InfoTrac College Edition Research

Can drug treatment help improve lives and lower recidivism rates? For an answer, read

Matt Grayson, "Kicking Habits: Preparing Welfare Recipients for the Work Force," *Spectrum: The Journal of State Government* 72 (1999): 5.

Gary Field, "From the Institution to the Community: Studies Show Benefits of Continuity of Care in Reduced Recidivism, Relapse Rates," *Corrections Today* 60 (1998): 94.

SOURCES: Data provided by the Center for Substance Abuse Research, University of Maryland, College Park; Substance Abuse and Mental Health Services Administration, Office of Applied Studies, "The Relationship Between Mental Health and Substance Abuse among Adolescents," Analytic Series: A-9, 1999; Michael French, H. J. Jeanne Salome, Jody Sindelar, and A. Thomas McLellan, "Benefit–Cost Analysis of Ancillary Social Services in Publicly Supported Addiction Treatment," 1 February 1999; Dace Svikis et al., "Cost-Effectiveness of Treatment for Drug-Abusing Pregnant Women," *Drug and Alcohol Dependence* 45 (1997): 105–13.

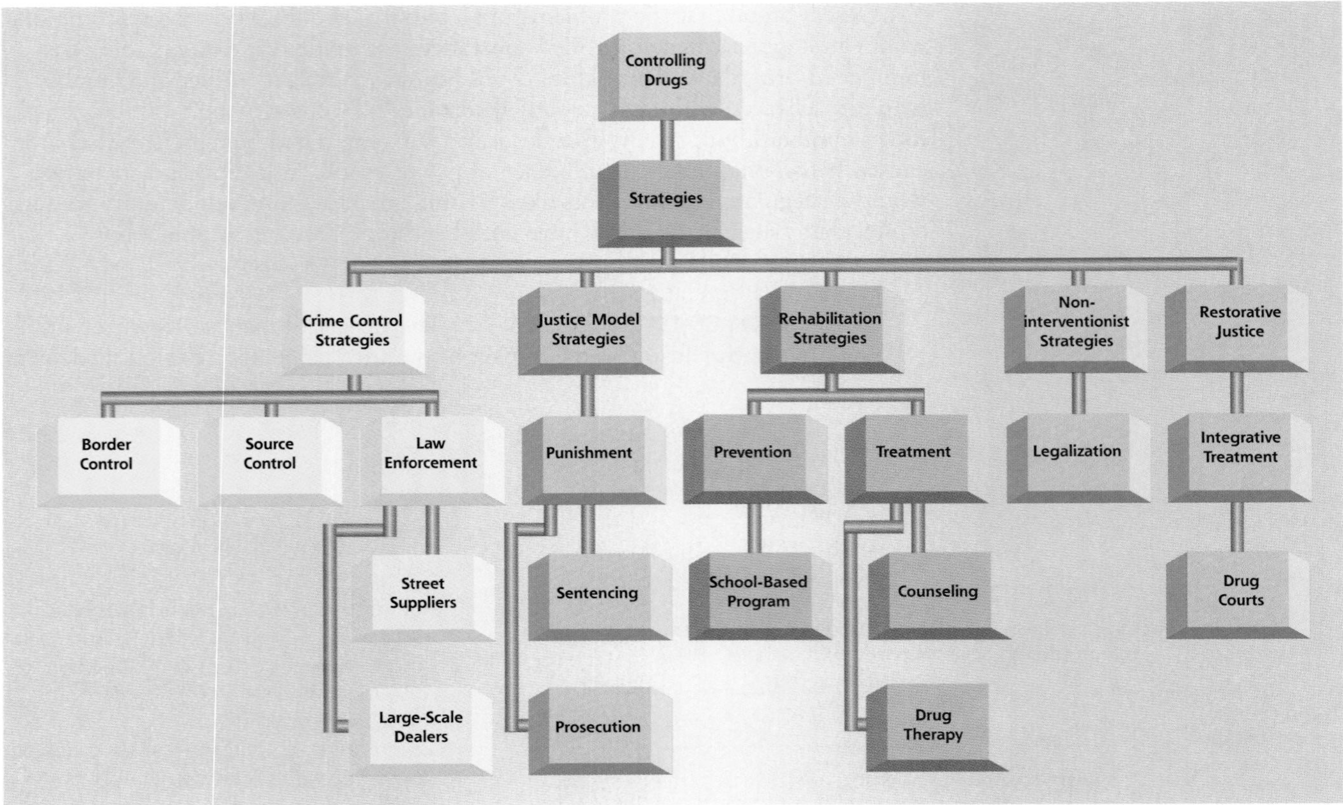

Figure 1.7
Strategies for controlling drugs

the actual operations of the criminal justice system (Figure 1.7). Advocates of each view have attempted to promote their vision of what justice is all about and how it should be. During the past decade, the crime control and justice models have dominated. Laws have been toughened and the rights of the accused curtailed, the prison population has grown, and the death penalty has been employed against convicted murderers. Because the crime rate has been dropping, these policies seem to be effective; they may be questioned if crime rates once again begin to rise. At the same time, efforts to rehabilitate offenders, to provide them with elements of due process, and to give them the least intrusive treatment have not been abandoned. Police, courts, and correctional agencies supply a wide range of treatment and rehabilitation programs to offenders in all stages of the criminal justice system. Whenever possible, those accused of crime are treated informally in nonrestrictive, community-based programs, and the effects of stigma are guarded against. Although the legal rights of offenders are being closely scrutinized by the courts, the basic constitutional rights of the accused remain inviolate. Guardians of the process have made sure that defendants are allowed the maximum protection possible under the law. For example, criminal defendants have been awarded the right to competent legal counsel at trial; merely having a lawyer to defend them is not considered sufficient legal protection. In sum, understanding the justice system today requires analyzing a variety of occupational roles, institutional processes, legal rules, and administrative doctrines. Each predominant view of criminal justice provides a vantage point for understanding and interpreting these rather complex issues. No single view is the right or correct one. Each individual must choose the perspective that best fits his own ideas and judgment—or they can all be discarded and the individual's own view substituted.

SUMMARY

The term *criminal justice* became prominent around 1967, when the President's Commission on Law Enforcement and the Administration of Justice began a nationwide study of the nation's crime problem. Since then, a field of study has emerged that uses knowledge from various disciplines in an attempt to understand what causes people to commit crimes and how to deal with the crime problem. Criminal justice, then, consists of the study of crime and of the agencies concerned with its prevention and control.

Criminal justice is both a system and a process. As a system, it ideally functions as a cooperative effort among the primary agencies—police, courts, and corrections. The process, on the other hand, consists of the actual steps the offender takes from the initial investigation through trial, sentencing, and appeal.

In many instances, the criminal justice system works informally in order to expedite the disposal of cases. Criminal acts that are very serious or notorious may receive the full complement of criminal justice processes, from arrest to trial. However, less serious cases are often settled when a bargain is reached between the prosecution and the defense.

The role of criminal justice can be interpreted in many ways. People who study the field or work within its agencies bring their own ideas and feelings to bear when they try to decide on the right course of action to take or recommend. There are a number of different perspectives on criminal justice today. The crime control perspective is oriented toward deterring criminal behavior and incapacitating serious criminal offenders. In contrast, the rehabilitation model views the justice system as a treatment agency focused on helping offenders. Counseling programs are stressed over punishment and deterrence strategies. Those who hold the due process perspective see the justice system as a legal process. Their concern is that every defendant receive the full share of legal rights granted under law.

In addition to these views, the nonintervention model is concerned about stigma and helping defendants avoid the net of justice; advocates call for the least intrusive methods possible. Those who advocate the justice model are concerned with making the system equitable. The arrest, sentencing, and correctional process should be structured so that every person is treated equally. Finally, the restorative justice model focuses on finding peaceful and humanitarian solutions to crime.

The various perspectives on justice are visible in the way the nation has sought to control substance abuse. Some programs rely on a strict crime control policy featuring the detection and arrest of drug traffickers, whereas others seek the rehabilitation of known offenders. The justice model has influenced development of sentencing policies that emphasize mandatory punishments. Another approach is to legalize drugs, thereby reducing abusers incentive to commit crimes, a policy that reflects nonintervention policies.

KEY TERMS

criminal justice
Law Enforcement Assistance Administration (LEAA)
social control
nolle prosequi
courtroom work group
crime control
rehabilitation perspective
due process
nonintervention
decriminalization
victimless crime
deinstitutionalization
pretrial diversion
widening the net
restorative justice
source control
DARE
methadone
legalization

 INFOTRAC COLLEGE EDITION EXERCISES

The issue of drug legalization has been the subject of endless debate. To get more information using *InfoTrac College Edition,* do a power search using the following terms: "drug legalization" and "decriminalization."

For a good overview of all sides of the issue, read Erich Goode, "Strange Bedfellows: Ideology, Politics, and Drug Legalization," *Society* 35, no. 1 (1998): 18.

For a more subjective view, see Charles B. Rangel, "Why Drug Legalization Should Be Opposed," *Criminal Justice Ethics* 17, no. 2 (1998): 2.

QUESTIONS

1. Which criminal behavior patterns pose the greatest threat to the public? Should the justice system devote greater resources to combating these crimes? If so, which crime patterns should be de-emphasized?
2. Describe the differences between the formal and informal justice systems. Is it fair to treat some offenders informally?
3. What are the layers of the criminal justice "wedding cake?" Give an example of a crime for each layer.
4. What are the basic elements of each model or perspective on justice? Which best represents your own point of view?
5. How would each perspective on criminal justice consider the use of the death penalty as a sanction for first-degree murder?

NOTES

1. Kevin Sack, "Gunman Slays 9 at Brokerages in Atlanta," *New York Times,* 29 July 1999, 1.
2. Martin Wolk, "Los Angeles Shooting Suspect Had Rampage Fantasies," Reuters New Service, 11 August 1999.
3. Timothy Egan, "Suspect in L.A. Shooting Was Well Known for Violent Hate," *New York Times,* 12 August 1999, 1.
4. "The New Age of Anxiety: Whether They Live in a Leafy Suburb or an Inner City, Parents Can No Longer Pretend That Their Children Are Immune from the Threat of Guns," *Newsweek,* 23 August 1999, 39.
5. Federal Interagency Forum on Child and Family Statistics, Washington, D.C., 8 July 1999, Press Release.
6. This section leans heavily on Ted Robert Gurr, "Historical Trends in Violent Crime: A Critical Review of the Evidence," in *Crime and Justice: An Annual Review of Research,* vol. 3, ed. Michael Tonry and Norval Morris (Chicago: University of Chicago Press, 1981); Richard Maxwell Brown, "Historical Patterns of American Violence," in *Violence in America: Historical and Comparative Perspectives,* ed. Hugh Davis Graham and Ted Robert Gurr (Beverly Hills, Sage, 1979).
7. Cesare Beccaria, *On Crimes and Punishments* (1764; reprint, Indianapolis: Bobbs-Merrill, 1963).
8. Samuel Walker, *Popular Justice* (New York: Oxford University Press, 1980).
9. Ibid.
10. For an insightful analysis of this effort, see Samuel Walker, "Origins of the Contemporary Criminal Justice Paradigm: The American Bar Foundation Survey, 1953–1969", *Justice Quarterly* 9 (1992): 47–76.
11. President's Commission on Law Enforcement and the Administration of Justice, *The Challenge of Crime in a Free Society* (Washington, D.C.: Government Printing Office, 1967).
12. See Public Law 90-351, *Title I—Omnibus Crime Control Safe Streets Act of 1968,* 90th Congress, 19 June 1968.
13. For a review, see Kevin Wright, "Twenty-Two Years of Federal Investment in Criminal Justice Research: The National Institute of Justice, 1968–1989," *Journal of Criminal Justice* 22 (1994): 27–40.
14. *Justice Expenditures and Employment,* 1994 data (Washington, D.C.: Bureau of Justice Statistics, 1999).
15. Office of National Drug Control Policy, *Fact Sheet: Drug Data Summary, February 1998* (updated 1999).
16. Federal Bureau of Investigation, *Crime in the United States, 1998* (Washington, D.C.: Government Printing Office, 1999), 208.
17. Jeffrey Butts, *Offenders in Juvenile Court, 1994* (Washington, D.C.: Office of Juvenile Justice and Delinquency Prevention, 1996).
18. Jodi M. Brown and Patrick A. Langan, *Felony Sentences in the United States, 1996* (Washington, D.C.: Bureau of Justice Statistics, 1999).
19. Bureau of Justice Statistics, *U.S. Correctional Population Reaches 5.9 Million Offenders,* 22 August 1999, press release.
20. For an analysis of this issue, see William Wilbanks, *The Myth of a Racist Criminal Justice System* (Monterey, Calif.: Brooks/Cole, 1987); Stephen Klein, Joan Petersilia, and Susan Turner, "Race and Imprisonment Decisions in California," *Science* 247 (1990): 812–16; Alfred Blumstein, "On the Racial Disproportionality of the United States Prison Population," *Journal of Criminal Law and Criminology* 73 (1982): 1259–81; Darnell Hawkins, "Race, Crime Type and Imprisonment," *Justice Quarterly* 3 (1986): 251–69.
21. Middlesex SS Superior Court Criminal No. 97-0433, Commonwealth Memorandum and *Order v. Louise Woodward,* 1997.
22. Herbert L. Packer, *The Limits of the Criminal Sanction* (Stanford, Calif.: Stanford University Press, 1975), 21.
23. Jacob Perez, *Tracking Offenders, 1990* (Washington, D.C.: Bureau of Justice Statistics, 1994), 2.
24. James Eisenstein and Herbert Jacob, *Felony Justice* (Boston: Little, Brown, 1977); Peter Nardulli, *The Courtroom Elite* (Cambridge, Mass.: Ballinger, 1978); Paul Wice, *Chaos in the Courthouse* (New York: Praeger, 1985); Marcia Lipetz, *Routine Justice: Processing Cases in Women's Court* (New Brunswick, N.J.: Transaction Books, 1983).
25. Douglas Smith, "The Plea Bargaining Controversy," *Journal of Criminal Law and Criminology* 77 (1986): 949–67.
26. Samuel Walker, *Sense and Nonsense about Crime* (Belmont, Calif: Wadsworth, 1985).
27. Malcolm Feeley, *The Process Is the Punishment* (New York: Russell Sage, 1979).
28. James Q. Wilson, *Thinking about Crime* (New York: Vintage Books, 1983).
29. Ibid., 128.
30. John DiIulio, *No Escape, the Future of American Corrections* (New York: Basic Books, 1991).
31. Dennis Rosenbaum and Gordon Hanson, "Assessing the Effects of School-Based Drug Education: A Six-Year Multilevel Analysis of Project D.A.R.E.," *Journal of Research in Crime and Delinquency* 35 (1998): 381–412.
32. Marilyn Chandler Ford and Francis Moore, "The Impact of Policy Shifts on Correctional Populations" (Paper presented at the American Society of Criminology meeting, Miami, November 1994).
33. Karen Parker and Patricia McCall, "Structural Conditions and Racial Homicide Patterns: A Look at the Multiple Disadvantages in Urban Areas," *Criminology* 37 (1999): 447–48.
34. Francis Cullen, John Paul Wright, and Mitchell Chamlin, "Social Support and Social Reform: A Progressive Crime Control Agenda," *Crime and Delinquency* 45 (1999): 188–207.
35. Jane Sprott, "Are Members of the Public Tough on Crime? The Dimensions of Public 'Punitiveness'," *Journal of Criminal Justice* 27 (1999): 467–74.
36. Herbert Packer, *The Limits of the Criminal Sanction* (Stanford, Calif.: Stanford University Press, 1968), 175.

37. "DNA Testing Has Exonerated 28 Prison Inmates, Study Finds," *Criminal Justice Newsletter,* 17 June 1996, 2.

38. Caitlin Lovinger, "Death Row's Living Alumni," *New York Times,* 22 August 1999, 1.

39. *Doe v. Pryor M.D. Ala,* Civ.No. 99-T-730-N, Thompson, J. 8/16/99.

40. This section is based on Paula M. Ditton and Doris James Wilson, *Truth in Sentencing in State Prisons* (Washington, D.C.: Bureau of Justice Statistics, 1999).

41. Herbert Bianchi, *Justice as Sanctuary* (Bloomington: Indiana University Press, 1994); Nils Christie, "Conflicts as Property," *British Journal of Criminology* 17 (1977): 1–15; L. Hulsman, "Critical Criminology and the Concept of Crime," *Contemporary Crises* 10 (1986): 63–80.

42. Larry Tifft, Forward to *The Mask of Love,* by Dennis Sullivan (Port Washington, N.Y.: Kennikat Press, 1980), 6.

43. Christopher Cooper, "Patrol Police Officer Conflict Resolution Processes," *Journal of Criminal Justice* 25 (1997): 87–101.

44. State of Florida Agency for Health Care Administration (AHCA), "Drug Abuse Hospitalization Costs Study," May 1999. Reported by Center for Substance Abuse Research (CESAR), College Park, Md., 23 June 1999.

45. U.S. Department of State, *1998 International Narcotics Control Strategy Report* (February 1999).

46. *Anti-Drug Abuse Act of 1988,* Public Law 100-6901 21 U.S. Ct. 1501; Subtitle A—*Death Penalty, Sec. 001, Amending the Controlled Substances Abuse Act,* 21 USC 848.

47. Dennis Rosenbaum, Robert Flewelling, Susan Bailey, Chris Ringwalt, and Deanna Wilkinson, "Cops in the Classroom: A Longitudinal Evaluation," *Journal of Research in Crime and Delinquency* 31 (1994): 3–31.

48. See, generally, Peter Greenwood and Franklin Zimring, *One More Chance* (Santa Monica, Calif.: Rand, 1985).

49. Eli Ginzberg, Howard Berliner, and Miriam Ostrow, *Young People at Risk: Is Prevention Possible?* (Boulder, Colo.: Westview Press, 1988), 99.

50. Drug Court Clearinghouse and Technical Assistance Project, *Looking at a Decade of Drug Courts* (Washington, D.C.: Government Printing Office, 1999).

51. See, generally, Ralph Weisheit, *Drugs, Crime, and the Criminal Justice System* (Cincinnati: Anderson, 1990).

52. Ethan Nadelmann, "America's Drug Problem," *Bulletin of the American Academy of Arts and Sciences* 65 (1991): 24–40.

53. Ethan Nadelmann, "Should We Legalize Drugs? History Answers Yes," *American Heritage* (February/March 1993): 41–56.

54. This and other arguments are presented in Erich Goode, *Between Politics and Reason: The Drug Legalization Debate* (New York: St. Martin's Press, 1997).

55. David Courtwright, "Should We Legalize Drugs? History Answers No," *American Heritage* (February/March 1993): 43–56.

56. James Inciardi and Duane McBride, "Legalizing Drugs: A Gormless, Naive Idea," *The Criminologist* 15 (1990): 1–4.

chapter 2

The Nature of Crime and Victimization

On October 8, 1999, two armed men entered the last car of a New York City subway train and announced a robbery. As they walked through the car, many passengers avoided eye contact or feigned sleep. Then the robbers stopped in front of sixteen-year-old Hansel Daniel Henriquez, sitting with two friends, and demanded his gold chain. Without warning one of the men fatally shot Henriquez through the right cheek. New York City police quickly identified a twenty-one-year-old suspect and charged him with the shooting; they also arrested his partner.

Hansel Daniel, the son of Honduran immigrants who live in the Bronx, was a high school sophomore. He also had two brothers and one sister. His chain though inexpensive was prized because it had been given to him by a girlfriend, and he wore it every day. Police were unsure whether Hansel was shot because he refused to hand over the chain or whether the robber's gun, a silver Davis .380-caliber, had gone off unintentionally. With tears in his eyes, Hansel's father told reporters covering the case, "I love him too much . . . I have a big space in my heart."[1] ■

Incidents such as the tragic death of Hansel Daniel Henriquez are the subject of daily newspaper stories and the 6:00 news. They help give the public the impression that violent crime is a daily feature of American life. Yet justice experts cannot rely on such media stories to either make policy decisions or evaluate program effectiveness. Administrators and policymakers must have up-to-date, accurate information about the nature and extent of crime in order to make effective choices about crime and its control. The policies and procedures of the justice system cannot exist in an informational vacuum. Unless we have accurate information about crime, we cannot be sure whether a particular policy, process, or procedure has the effect its creators envisioned. For example, a state may enact a new law requiring that anyone who uses a firearm to commit a crime serve a mandatory prison term. The new statute is aimed directly at reducing the incidence of such violent crimes as murder, armed robbery, and assault. The effectiveness of this statutory change cannot be demonstrated without hard evidence that the use of firearms actually declined after the law was instituted and that the use of knives or other weapons did not increase. Without being able to measure crime accurately, it would be impossible to either understand its cause or plan its elimination.

Another goal of criminal justice study is to develop an understanding of the nature and cause of crime and victimization. Without knowing why crime occurs or the factors that influence the crime rate, creating effective crime reduction programs would be difficult. We would never be sure whether efforts were being aimed at the proper audience or, if they were, whether these efforts were most likely to produce positive change. For example, a crime prevention program based on providing jobs for unemployed teenagers would only be effective if in fact crime is linked to unemployment. Similarly, a plan to reduce prison riots by eliminating the sugar intake of inmates is feasible only if research shows a link between diet and violence.

In addition to understanding the nature and cause of criminal behavior, it is important for criminal justice policymakers to study and understand the role of victims in the crime process. Such knowledge is essential for developing strategies to reduce the probability of predatory crime while providing information that people can use to decrease their likelihood of becoming a target of predatory criminals.

This chapter discusses some of the basic questions in the study of crime and justice: How is crime defined? How is crime measured? How much crime is there, and what are its trends and patterns? Why do people commit crime? How many people become victims of crime, and under what circumstances does victimization take place?

HOW IS CRIME DEFINED?

How can we understand the concept of crime? Actually, there are two competing models of what the term *crime* truly means. According to the **consensus view of crime,** crimes are behaviors that (1) are essentially harmful to a majority of citizens living in society and (2) have been controlled or prohibited by the existing criminal law. The **criminal law** is a set of rules that express the norms, goals, and values of a majority of society. Consequently, the criminal law has a **social control** function — restraining those who would take advantage of others' weakness for their own personal gain and thereby endanger the social framework. Although differences in behavior can be tolerated within a properly functioning social system, behaviors that are considered inherently destructive and dangerous are outlawed to maintain the social fabric and ensure the peaceful functioning of society. The consensus view is so named because it infers that the great majority of citizens agree that certain behaviors must be outlawed or controlled and that the criminal law is designed to protect citizens from harm.

consensus view of crime
The belief that the majority of citizens in a society share common ideals and work toward a common good and that crimes are acts that are outlawed because they conflict with the rules of the majority and are harmful to society.

criminal law
The body of rules that define crimes, set their punishments out, and mandate the procedures in carrying out the criminal justice process.

social control
The ability of society and its institutions to control, manage, restrain, or direct human behavior.

A second and opposing view is that the law and therefore the concept of crime is influenced by people who hold social power and use it to mold the law to reflect their way of thinking. Crime and law are not objective concepts; there is no absolute "right and wrong." Instead, crimes are subjective concepts that take on a spin reflecting the attitudes, morals, values, and needs of those in power. For example, various groups have tried to influence laws regulating the possession of handguns, the use of drugs and alcohol, and the availability of abortions and to exert social, economic, and political influence to impose their definition of right and wrong on the rest of the population.[2]

According to this **conflict view of crime,** the criminal law is a flexible instrument that may change according to the whim of powerful individuals and groups who use it to reflect their views of right and wrong. Groups able to assert their political and economic power use the law and the criminal justice system to advance their own causes and to control the behavior of those who oppose their ideas and values.[3] For example, property crimes are punished heavily in order to protect the wealth of the affluent; drug laws ensure that workers will be productive, clear headed, and sober.

conflict view of crime
The belief that the law is controlled by the rich and powerful who shape its content to ensure their continued economic domination of society. The criminal justice system is an instrument of social and economic repression.

Despite these differences, there is general agreement that the criminal law defines crime, that this definition is constantly changing and evolving, that social forces mold the definition of crimes, and that the criminal law has a social control function. Therefore, as used here, the term **crime** is defined as

> a violation of social rules of conduct, interpreted and expressed by a written criminal code, created by people holding social and political power. Its content may be influenced by prevailing public sentiments, historically developed moral beliefs, and the need to protect public safety. Individuals who violate these rules may be subject to sanctions administered by state authority, which include social stigma and loss of status, freedom, and, on occasion, their life.

crime
A violation of societal rules of behavior as interpreted and expressed by a criminal legal code created by people holding social and political power. Individuals who violate these rules are subject to sanctions by state authority, social stigma, and loss of status.

SOURCES OF CRIME DATA

Criminal justice scholars use a variety of techniques to study crime and its consequences. Some of the major sources of crime data are discussed in this section.

Survey Data

You may have read that teenage drug use has been on the rise. How can the daily substance abuse of American teenagers possibly be calculated? The answer is by having them participate in an anonymous survey asking questions about their substance abuse. A drug use survey can provide information on the percentage of students who use drugs and the type of adolescent who becomes a drug user. Conducted annually, surveys can provide information on long-term trends in alcohol and drug usage.[4]

Most survey data come from samples in which a limited number of subjects are randomly selected from a larger population. If the sample is carefully drawn, every individual in the population has an equal chance of being selected for the study. Consequently, complex statistical analysis can be used to make inferences from the small sample to the larger population. For example, a sample of ten thousand high school seniors can be selected at random and asked about the frequency of their use of alcohol and drugs. From this relatively small sample, estimates can then be made of drug use among the millions of high school seniors in the United States.

As a source of crime information, survey data consist of information obtained from interviews and questionnaires focusing on people's behaviors, attitudes, beliefs, and abilities. Criminological surveys provide a valuable source of information on particular crime problems, such as drug use, that are rarely reported to police and may therefore go undetected. Because they typically include a variety of questions, surveys provide information on the background and personal characteristics of offenders.

National Crime Victimization Survey (NCVS)
The ongoing victimization study conducted jointly by the Justice Department and the U.S. Census Bureau that surveys victims about their experiences with law violation.

Surveys are also an invaluable source of information on the nature and extent of criminal victimization. The **National Crime Victimization Survey (NCVS)**, conducted by the U.S. Department of Justice, uses a large, carefully drawn sample of citizens who are queried about their experiences with criminal activity during the past year. The NCVS enables crime experts to estimate the total number of criminal incidents that occur each year, including those that are never reported to police; it is one of the most important sources of crime data.[5]

Record Data

A significant proportion of criminal justice data comes from the compilation and evaluation of official records. The records may be acquired from a variety of sources, including schools, courts, police departments, social service centers, and correctional agencies.

official crime statistics
Compiled by the FBI in its Uniform Crime Reports, these are a tally of serious crimes reported to police agencies each year.

Uniform Crime Reports (UCR)
The FBI's yearly publication of where, when, and how much serious crime occurred in the prior year.

Records can be used for a number of purposes. Prisoners' files can be analyzed in an effort to determine what types of inmates adjust to prison and what types tend to be disciplinary problems or suicidal. Educational records are important indicators of intelligence, academic achievement, school behavior, and other information that can be related to criminal behavior patterns. However, the most important source of crime data is records compiled by police departments and annually collected and analyzed by the Federal Bureau of Investigation; these are referred to as the **official crime statistics.**

The FBI compiles the official crime data in a yearly publication referred to as the **Uniform Crime Reports (UCR)**, which is a compendium of data on where, when, and how much crime occurred during the prior year.[6]

Other Sources

Various other sources of crime information exist, besides survey and record data.

OBSERVATION The systematic observation, recording, and deciphering of behavior types within a sample or population is a common method of criminal justice data collection. Some observation studies are conducted in the field, where the researcher observes subjects in their natural environments; other observations take place in a contrived, artificial setting or a laboratory. For example, children will watch a violent TV show in a university psychology lab, and researchers will record their behavior to determine whether it undergoes a discernible change.

Still another type of observation study is called *participant observation.* In this type of research, the criminologist joins the group being studied and behaves as a member of the group. It is believed that participation enables the scientist to better understand the motives that the subjects may have for their behavior and attitudes. Participation also enables the researcher to develop a frame of reference similar to that of the subjects and to better understand how the subjects interact with the rest of the world. Participant observation studies allow the researcher to gain insights into behavior that might never be available otherwise.

INTERVIEWS Some criminal justice researchers conduct in-depth interviews with a small sample of offenders in order to gain insight into their lives. For example, a recent study by Claire Sterck-Elifson focused on the lives of middle-class female drug abusers.[7] The thirty-four interviews she conducted provide insight into a group whose behavior might not be captured in a large-scale survey. Sterck-Elifson found that these women were introduced to cocaine at first "just for fun." "I do drugs," one thirty-four-year-old lawyer told her, "because I like the feeling. I would never let drugs take over my life."[8] Unfortunately, a number later lost control of their habit and suffered both emotional and financial stress.

life history
A research method that uses the experiences of an individual as the unit of analysis, such as using the life experience of an individual gang member to understand the natural history of gang membership.

LIFE HISTORY Another technique of criminal justice data collection is the **life history.** This method uses personal accounts of individuals who have had experience in crime, deviance, and other related areas. Diaries or autobiographies can be used; sometimes an account is given to an interested second party to record "as told to."[9] Life histories provide insights into the human condition that other, less personal research methods cannot hope to duplicate.

MEASURING CRIME TRENDS

Each source of crime data collection helps criminal justice experts understand the nature and extent of criminal behavior in the United States and to measure crime trends and patterns. Usually, three separate measures are used: official record data, victim survey data, and self-report crime survey data. Each source can be used independently, but taken together they provide a detailed picture of the crime problem. The data provided by these three sources of crime data diverge in many key areas, but they have enough similarities to enable crime experts to draw some conclusions about crime in the United States. Each method is discussed in detail in the following sections.

The Federal Bureau of Investigation posts many of its statistical findings, including the Uniform Crime Report, at www.fbi.gov/ucr.htm

Official Crime Data: The Uniform Crime Reports

The Federal Bureau of Investigation's UCR is the best known and most widely cited source of aggregate criminal statistics.[10] The FBI receives and compiles records

index (Part I) crimes
The eight crimes that, because of their seriousness and frequency, the FBI reports the incidence of in the annual Uniform Crime Reports. Index crimes include murder, rape, assault, robbery, burglary, arson, larceny, and motor vehicle theft.

from over seventeen thousand police departments serving a majority of the U.S. population. Its major unit of analysis involves **index (Part I) crimes:** criminal homicide, forcible rape, robbery, aggravated assault, burglary, larceny/theft, motor vehicle theft, and arson. Exhibit 2.1 defines these crimes. The FBI tallies

exhibit 2.1

Part I Crimes	Description
Criminal homicide	(a) *Murder and nonnegligent manslaughter:* the willful (nonnegligent) killing of one human being by another. Deaths caused by negligence, attempts to kill, assaults to kill, suicides, accidental deaths, and justifiable homicides are excluded. Justifiable homicides are limited to: (1) the killing of a felon by a law enforcement officer in the line of duty; and (2) the killing of a felon by a private citizen. (b) *Manslaughter by negligence:* the killing of another person through gross negligence. Traffic fatalities are excluded. While manslaughter by negligence is a Part I crime, it is not included in the crime index.
Forcible rape	The carnal knowledge of a female forcibly and against her will. Included are rapes by force and attempts or assaults to rape. Statutory offenses (no force used—victim under age of consent) are excluded.
Robbery	The taking or attempting to take anything of value from the care, custody, or control of a person or persons by force or threat of force or violence and/or by putting the victim in fear.
Aggravated assault	An unlawful attack by one person on another for the purpose of inflicting severe or aggravated bodily injury. This type of assault is usually accompanied by the use of a weapon or by means likely to produce death or great bodily harm. Simple assaults are excluded.
Burglary	Breaking or entering. The unlawful entry of a structure to commit a felony or a theft. Attempted forcible entry is included.
Larceny/theft (except motor vehicle theft)	The unlawful taking, carrying, leading, or riding away of property from the possession or constructive possession of another. Examples are thefts of bicycles or automobile accessories, shoplifting, pocket picking, or the stealing of any property or article which is not taken by force and violence or by fraud. Attempted larcenies are included. Embezzlement, "con games," forgery, worthless checks, etc., are excluded.
Motor vehicle theft	The theft or attempted theft of a motor vehicle. A motor vehicle is self-propelled and runs on the surface and not on rails. Specifically excluded from this category are motor boats, construction equipment, airplanes, and farming equipment.
Arson	Any willful or malicious burning or attempt to burn, with or without intent to defraud, a dwelling, house, public building, motor vehicle or aircraft, personal property of another, etc.

SOURCE: Federal Bureau of Investigation, *Crime in the United States* (Washington, D.C.: Government Printing Office, 1999), 320.

nonindex (Part II) crimes
All other crimes except the eight index crimes recorded by the FBI. The FBI records all arrests made by police of Part II crimes.

and annually publishes the number of reported offenses by city, county, standard metropolitan statistical area, and geographical divisions of the United States. Besides these statistics, the UCR shows the number and characteristics (age, race, and gender) of individuals who have been arrested for these and all other crimes — **nonindex (Part II) crimes** — except traffic violations.

Data on the number of clearances involving the arrest of only juvenile offenders, data on the value of property stolen and recovered in connection with Part I offenses, and detailed information pertaining to criminal homicide are also reported. Traditionally, slightly more than 20 percent of all reported index crimes are cleared by arrest each year. Violent crimes are more likely to be solved than property crimes because police devote more resources to the more serious acts. For these types of crimes, witnesses (including the victim) are frequently available to identify offenders, and in many instances the victim and offender were previously acquainted.

The UCR uses three methods to express crime data. First, the number of crimes reported to the police and arrests made are expressed as raw figures (e.g., 18,209 murders occurred in 1998). Second, crime rates per 100,000 people are computed. That is, when the UCR indicates that the murder rate was 6.3 in 1998, it means that about 6 people in every 100,000 were murdered between January 1 and December 31 of 1998. This is the equation used:

$$\frac{\text{Number of reported crimes}}{\text{Total U.S. population}} \times 100{,}000 = \text{Rate per } 100{,}000$$

Third, the FBI computes changes in the number and rate of crime over time. For example, murder rates declined 7.4 percent between 1997 and 1998.

HOW ACCURATE IS THE UCR? Despite criminologists' continued reliance on the UCR, its accuracy has been suspect. Some criminologists claim that victims of many serious crimes do not report these incidents to police; therefore, these crimes do not become part of the UCR. The reasons for not reporting vary. Some victims do not trust the police or have confidence in their ability to solve crimes. Others do not have property insurance and therefore believe it is useless to report theft. In other cases, victims fear reprisals from an offender's friends or family. According to surveys of crime victims, less than 40 percent of all criminal incidents are reported to the police. The way police departments record and report criminal and delinquent activity also affects the validity of UCR statistics. Some departments may define crimes loosely — for example, reporting a trespass as a burglary or an assault on a woman as an attempted rape — whereas others pay strict attention to FBI guidelines. These reporting practices may help explain interjurisdictional differences in crime.[11]

Some local police departments make systematic errors in UCR reporting. Some count an arrest only after a formal booking procedure, although the UCR requires arrests to be counted if the suspect is released without a formal charge.[12] More serious allegations claim that in some cases police officials may deliberately alter reported crimes to improve their department's public image. Police administrators interested in lowering the crime rate may falsify crime reports by, for example, classifying a burglary as a nonreportable trespass.[13] Exhibit 2.2 lists other issues that have been raised about the UCR's validity.

Victim Surveys

The second source of crime data is surveys that ask crime victims about their encounters with criminals. The NCVS is conducted by the U.S. Bureau of the Census in cooperation with the Bureau of Justice Statistics

exhibit 2.2

Factors Affecting the Validity of the Uniform Crime Report

1. No federal crimes are reported.
2. Reports are voluntary and vary in accuracy and completeness.
3. Not all police departments submit reports.
4. The FBI uses estimates in its total crime projections.
5. If an offender commits multiple crimes, only the most serious is recorded. Thus, if a narcotic addict rapes, robs, and murders a victim, only the murder is recorded. Consequently, many lesser crimes go unreported.
6. Each act is listed as a single offense for some crimes but not for others. If a person robbed six people in a bar, the offense is listed as one robbery; but if he assaulted or murdered them, it is listed as six assaults or six murders.
7. Incomplete acts are grouped together with completed ones.
8. Important differences exist between the FBI's definition of certain crimes and those used in a number of states.
9. Victimless crimes such as drug sales often go undetected.
10. Many cases of child abuse and family violence are unreported.

SOURCE: Leonard Savitz, "Official Statistics," in *Contemporary Criminology,* ed. Leonard Savitz and Norman Johnston (New York: Wiley, 1982), 3–15. Updated 1999, with data from the FBI.

Warren and Minnie Singleton stand amid the rubble of their home in Brooklyn, New York. The building contractor they hired to refurbish their home absconded with their money without ever intending to finish the job, an act defined by the criminal law as fraud. If the builder's actions were not defined as a "crime," the Singletons would be left to their own devices to recoup their lost money. Now they can call upon law enforcement agencies to prosecute the culprits.

of the U.S. Department of Justice.[14] In these national surveys, samples of housing units are selected, using a complex, multistage sampling technique. Each year data are obtained from a nationally representative sample of roughly forty-five thousand households that includes more than ninety-four thousand persons. They are asked to report on the frequency, characteristics, and consequences of criminal victimization in the United States. The victims are surveyed on the number of sexual assaults, robberies, assaults, thefts, household burglaries, and motor vehicle thefts they experienced. The total sample is interviewed twice a year about victimization during the preceding six months. Households remain in the sample for about three years, and new homes rotate into the sample continually. The NCVS reports that the interview completion rate in the national sample is usually more than 90 percent in any given period. Because of the care with which the samples are drawn and the high completion rate, NCVS data are considered a relatively unbiased, valid estimate of all victimizations for the target crimes included in the survey.

The number of crimes accounted for by the NCVS (about 31 million) is considerably larger than the number of crimes reported to the FBI. For example, whereas the UCR shows that about 446,000 robberies occurred in 1998, the NCVS estimates that about 886,000 actually occurred. Victims seem to report to the police only crimes that involve considerable loss or injury. If we are to believe NCVS findings, the official UCR statistics do not provide an accurate picture of the crime problem because many crimes go unreported to the police. Exhibit 2.3 illustrates some recent patterns and trends in the victimization rate.

IS THE NCVS VALID? Like the UCR, the NCVS may also suffer from some methodological problems. As a result, its findings must be interpreted with caution. Among the potential problems are these:

- Overreporting due to victims' misinterpretation of events. For example, a lost wallet may be reported as stolen, or an open door may be viewed as a burglary attempt.
- Underreporting due to the embarrassment of reporting crime to interviewers, fear of getting in trouble, or simply forgetting an incident.
- Inability to record the personal criminal activity of those interviewed, such as drug use or gambling; murder is also not included for obvious reasons.
- Sampling errors, which produce a group of respondents who do not represent the nation as a whole.
- Inadequate question format that invalidates responses. Some groups, such as adolescents, may be particularly susceptible to error because of question format.[15]

Self-Report Surveys

The problems associated with official statistics have led many criminologists to seek alternative sources of information in assessing the true extent of crime patterns. In addition, official statistics do not say much about the personality, attitudes, and behavior of individual criminals. They also are of little value in charting the extent of substance abuse in the population because relatively few abusers are arrested. Criminologists have therefore sought additional sources to supplement and expand official data. One frequently employed alternative to official statistics is the **self-report survey.** These

self-report survey
A research approach that requires subjects to reveal their own participation in delinquent or criminal acts.

exhibit 2.3

Recent Victimization Patterns and Trends

- In 1998 U.S. residents age 12 or older experienced approximately 31.3 million crimes, of which 73% (22.9 million) were property crimes, 26% (8.1 million) were crimes of violence, and 1% were personal thefts.
- In 1998 for every 1,000 persons age 12 or older, there occurred 2 rapes or sexual assaults, 3 assaults with serious injury, and 4 robberies.
- Murders were the least frequent violent victimization—about 6 murder victims per 100,000 persons in 1998.
- Nationally, the violent crime victimization rate in urban areas was 51 per 1,000 residents.
- Between 1993 and 1998 violent crime rates fell 27%, from 50 to 37 per 1,000 persons age 12 or older. The 1998 rates are the lowest recorded since the survey's inception in 1973.
- Property crime decreased 32% from 1993 to 1998. The 1998 rate of 217 property crimes per 1,000 households is lower than both the 1997 and 1993 levels.

SOURCES: Callie Marie Rennison, *Criminal Victimization 1998 Changes 1997–1998 with Trends 1993–98* (Washington, D.C.: Bureau of Justice Statistics, 1999); James Alan Fox and Marianne Zawitz, *Homicide Trends in the United States* (Washington, D.C.: Bureau of Justice Statistics, 1999).

surveys allow participants to reveal information about their violations. Most often, self-report surveys are administered to groups of subjects through a mass distribution of questionnaires. Although the surveys might ask for the subjects' names, more commonly the responses remain anonymous. The basic assumption of self-report surveys is that anonymity and confidentiality will be ensured, which encourages people to accurately describe their illegal activities. Self-reports are viewed as a mechanism to get at the "dark figures of crime," the figures missed by official statistics. Exhibit 2.4 illustrates some typical self-report items.

Most self-report studies have focused on juvenile delinquency and youth crime, for two reasons.[16] First, the school setting makes it convenient to test thousands of subjects simultaneously because they all have the means to respond to a research questionnaire (pens, desks, and time). Second, because school attendance is universal, a school-based self-report survey represents a cross section of the community. However, self-reports are not restricted to youth crime. They are also used to examine the offense histories of prison inmates, drug users, and other segments of the population. They can be used to estimate the number of criminal offenders who have previously been unknown to the police. These respondents represent many criminals who have never figured in official crime statistics, some of whom may even be serious or **chronic offenders.**[17] In sum, self-reports provide an appreciable amount of information about offenders that cannot be found in official statistics.

chronic offender
A delinquent offender who is arrested five or more times before he or she is eighteen and who stands a good chance of becoming an adult criminal; these offenders are responsible for more than half of all serious crimes.

In general, self-reports indicate that the number of people who break the law is far greater than the number projected by official statistics. Almost everyone questioned is found to have violated some law.[18] Furthermore, self-reports dispute the notion that criminals and delinquents specialize in one type of crime or another; offenders seem to engage in a "mixed bag" of crime and deviance.[19]

Self-report surveys indicate that the most common offenses are truancy, alcohol abuse, use of a false ID, shoplifting or larceny under $50, fighting, mar-

exhibit 2.4

Self-Report Survey Questions

Please indicate how often in the past 12 months you did each act. (Check the best answer.)	Never did act	One time	2–5 times	6–9 times	10+ times
Stole something worth less than $50	____	____	____	____	____
Stole something worth more than $50	____	____	____	____	____
Used cocaine	____	____	____	____	____
Been in a fistfight	____	____	____	____	____
Carried a weapon such as a gun or knife	____	____	____	____	____
Fought someone using a weapon	____	____	____	____	____
Stole a car	____	____	____	____	____
Used force to steal	____	____	____	____	____
(For boys) Forced a girl to have sexual relations against her will	____	____	____	____	____

ijuana use, and damage to the property of others. It is not unusual for self-reports to find combined substance abuse, theft, violence, and damage rates of more than 50 percent among suburban, rural, and urban high school youths. What is surprising is the consistency of these findings in samples taken around the United States. Table 2.1 contains data from a self-report survey called *Monitoring the Future,* which researchers at the University of Michigan Institute for Social Research (ISR) conduct annually. This national survey of thousands of high school seniors, one of the most important sources of self-report data, shows a widespread yet stable pattern of youth crime since 1978.[20] As Table 2.1 shows, young people self-report a great deal of crime: About 31 percent of high school seniors now report stealing in the last twelve months, almost 20 percent said they were involved in a gang fight, about 13 percent injured someone so badly that the victim had to see a doctor, about 30 percent admitted shoplifting, and almost 25 percent engaged in breaking and entering. The facts that so many — at least 33 percent — of all U.S. high school students engaged in theft and almost 19 percent committed a serious violent act during the past year show that criminal activity is widespread and is not restricted to a few "bad apples."

ARE SELF-REPORTS VALID? Although self-report data have profoundly affected criminological inquiry, some important methodological issues have been raised about their accuracy. Critics of self-report studies frequently suggest that it is unreasonable to expect people to candidly admit illegal acts. They have nothing to gain, and the ones taking the greatest risk are the ones with official records who may be engaging in the most criminality. On the other hand, some people may exaggerate their criminal acts, forget some of them, or be confused about what is being asked. Some surveys contain an overabundance of trivial offenses, such as shoplifting small amounts of items or using false identification,

Table 2.1
Self-Reported Delinquent Activity

Self-Reported Delinquent Activity During the Past 12 Months Among High School Seniors

	Percentage Engaging in Offenses	
Crime Category	**At Least One Offense**	**Multiple Offenses**
Serious fight	9	6
Gang fight	11	8
Hurt someone badly	8	6
Used a weapon to steal	2	2
Stole less than $50	11	18
Stole more than $50	5	6
Shoplifted	11	16
Did breaking and entering	11	13
Committed arson	1	2
Damaged school property	6	7

SOURCE: *Monitoring the Future,* 1998 (Ann Arbor: University of Michigan, Institute for Social Research, 1999).

often lumped together with serious crimes to form a total crime index. Consequently, comparisons between groups can be highly misleading.

Although many criminologists believe in the reliability of self-reports, nagging questions still remain about their validity.[21] Even if 90 percent of a school population voluntarily participates in a self-report survey, researchers can never be sure whether the few who refuse to participate or are absent that day comprise a significant portion of the school's population of persistent, high-rate offenders.[22] It is also unlikely that the most serious chronic offenders in the teenage population are the most willing to cooperate with university-based criminologists administering self-report tests.[23] For example, persistent substance abusers tend to underreport the frequency of their drug use.[24]

Are the Three Sources of Crime Statistics Compatible?

Are the various sources of crime statistics compatible? Each has strengths and weaknesses. The FBI survey is carefully tallied and contains data on the number of murders and people arrested, information that the other data sources lack. However, this survey omits the many crimes that victims choose not to report to police, and it is subject to the reporting caprices of individual police departments.

The NCVS contains unreported crime and important information on the personal characteristics of victims, but the data consist of estimates made from relatively limited samples of the total U.S. population so that even narrow fluctuations in the rates of some crimes can have a major impact on findings. It also relies on personal recollections that may be inaccurate. The NCVS does not include data on important crime patterns, including murder and drug abuse.

Self-report surveys can provide information on the personal characteristics of offenders — such as their attitudes, values, beliefs, and psychological profiles — that is unavailable from any other source. Yet, at their core, self-reports rely on the honesty of criminal offenders and drug abusers, a population not generally known for accuracy and integrity.

Despite these differences, the data sources seem more compatible than was first believed. Although their tallies of crimes are certainly not in synch, the crime patterns and trends they record are often similar.[25] For example, all three sources generally agree about the personal characteristics of serious criminals (such as age and gender) and where and when crime occurs (such as urban areas, nighttime, and summer months).

CRIME TRENDS

Crime is not new to this century.[26] Studies have indicated that a gradual increase in the crime rate, especially in violent crime, occurred from 1830 to 1860. Following the Civil War, this rate increased significantly for about fifteen years. Then, from 1880 up to the time of World War I, with the possible exception of the years immediately preceding and following the war, the number of reported crimes decreased. After a period of readjustment, the crime rate steadily declined until the Depression (about 1930), when another crime wave was recorded. Crime rates increased gradually following the 1930s until the 1960s, when the growth rate became much greater. The homicide rate, which had actually declined from the 1930s to the 1960s, also began a sharp increase that continued through the 1970s.

In 1981 the number of index crimes peaked at about 13.4 million and then began a consistent decline until 1984, when police recorded 11.1 million crimes. By the following year, however, the crime rate once again began an upward trend, so that by 1991 police recorded about 14.6 million crimes. Both the number and rate of crimes have been declining ever since (Figure 2.1).

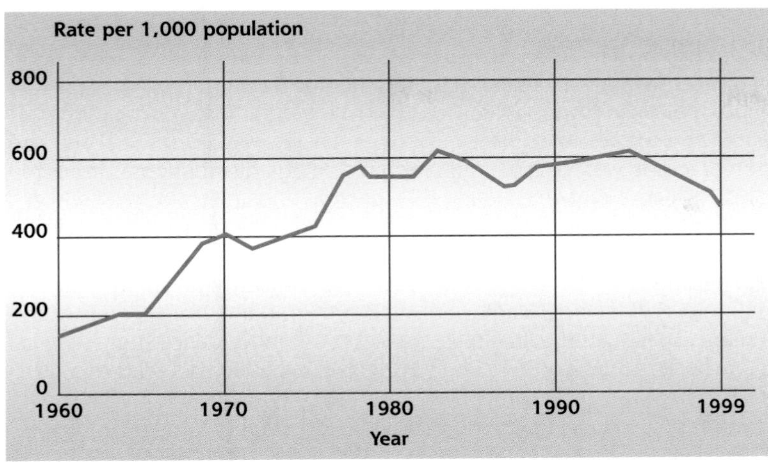

Figure 2.1
Crime rate trends, 1960–1999
SOURCE: UCR, 1996; updated 1999.

In 1998 about 12.5 million crimes were reported to the police, a decrease of about 6 percent from the preceding year. The overall crime rate declined more than 14 percent between 1994 and 1998; the number of reported crimes has declined more than 2 million from the 1991 peak. Final data from 1999 are not available, but preliminary results for the first six months of the year indicate that crime declined 10 percent during the first six months of 1999 when compared with figures reported for the same period of the previous year.[27]

What is especially encouraging is the fact that teenage criminality, a source of national concern, has been in decline during this period. Even the teen murder rate, which had remained stubbornly high, has undergone decline during the past few years.[28] The factors that help explain the upward and downward movement in crime rates are discussed in Exhibit 2.5.

Trends in Violent Crime The violent crimes reported by the FBI include murder, rape, assault, and robbery. In 1998 about 1.5 million violent crimes were reported to police, a rate of around 610 per 100,000 Americans. According to the UCR, violence in the United States has decreased during the 1990s, reversing a long trend of skyrocketing increases. The total number of violent crimes declined about 18 percent between 1994 and 1998, and the violence rate dropped nearly 21 percent. Preliminary 1999 results indicate that violent crimes dropped 8 percent in the first six months of 1999, including a 13 percent decline in murder, followed by declines in robbery of 10 percent; forcible rape, 8 percent; and aggravated assault, 7 percent.

Particularly encouraging has been the decrease in the number and rate of murders. The murder statistics are generally regarded as the most accurate aspect of the UCR. Figure 2.2 illustrates homicide rate trends since 1900. Note how the rate peaked around 1930, then fell, rose dramatically around 1960, and peaked once again in 1991, when the number of murders topped 24,000 for the first time in U.S. history. Since 1994 the murder rate has declined by 30 percent and the number of murders is down almost 28 percent. The decline in the violence rate has been both unexpected and welcome. Some major cities, such as New York, report a significant decline of over 50 percent in their murder rates through the 1990s.

Trends in Property Crime The property crimes reported in the UCR include larceny, motor vehicle theft, and arson. In 1998 about 11 million property crimes were reported, a rate of about 4,049 per 100,000 population. Property crime rates have declined in recent years, though the drop has not been as dramatic as that experienced by the violent crime rate. For example, between 1994 and 1998, property crime rates declined about 13 percent, including a 17 percent drop in burglary and 22 percent drop in the auto theft rate. Through the first six months of 1999, burglary fell 14 percent; motor vehicle theft, 12 percent; and larceny-theft, 8 percent; and overall property crimes, 10 percent. Law enforcement agencies nationwide recorded an 11 percent decline in arson.

Explaining Crime Trends

Criminal justice experts have identified a variety of social, economic, personal, and demographic factors that influence crime rate trends. Some of the most important factors are discussed here.

- **Age** Criminologists view change in the population age distribution as having the greatest influence on crime trends: As a general rule, the crime rate follows the proportion of young males in the population. With the "graying" of society in the 1980s and a decline in the birth rate, it is not surprising that the overall crime rate declined between 1990 and 1998. The number of juveniles should be increasing over the next decade, and some criminologists fear that this will signal a return to escalating crime rates. However, recent evidence suggests that population changes may have less an effect than is expected and fears of a crime wave expansion are unfounded.
- **Economy** There is a debate over the effects the economy has on crime rates. Some criminologists believe that a poor economy actually helps lower crime rates because unemployed parents are at home to supervise children and guard their possessions. Because there is less to spend. a poor economy reduces the number of valuables worth stealing. Also, it seems unlikely that law-abiding, middle-aged workers will suddenly turn to a life of crime if they are laid off during an economic downturn.

  Although a poor economy may lower crime rates in the short run, they may begin to rise during long-term periods of sustained economic weakness and unemployment. A long-term economic recession, such as the one that occurred in the late 1980s, may produce a climate of hopelessness in the nation's largest cities.
- **Racial conflict** Areas undergoing racial change, especially those experiencing an immigration of minorities into predominantly white neighborhoods, seem prone to significant increases in their crime rate. Whites in these areas may be using violence to protect what they view as their home turf. Racially motivated crimes actually diminish as neighborhoods become more integrated and power struggles diminish.
- **Abortion** John Donohue and Steven Levitt argue that the availability of abortions influences crime rates. The recent drop in the crime rate can be attributed to the availability of legalized abortion. The crime rate began to decline in 1991, approximately 18 years after abortions were legalized. Not coincidentally, the number of children being born to unwed, teenage mothers has also been in decline. It is possible that women most at risk for having children who will eventually engage in criminal activity are the ones having abortions.
- **Guns and teens** The availability of firearms may influence the crime rate, especially the proliferation of weapons in the hands of teens. There is evidence that more guns than ever before are finding their way into the hands of young people. Guns also cause escalation in the seriousness of crime. As the number of gun-toting students increases, so too will the seriousness of violent crime as, for example, a schoolyard fight turns into murder.
- **Gangs** Another factor that affects crime rates is the explosive growth in teenage gangs. Surveys indicate that there may be between 500,000 and 700,000 gang members in the United States. Boys who are members of gangs are far more likely to possess guns than nongang members; criminal activity increases when youths join gangs. The recent decline in the crime rate may be tied to changing gang values. Some streetwise kids have told researchers that they now avoid gangs because of the "younger brother syndrome"—they have watched their older siblings or parents caught in gangs or drugs and want to avoid the same fate.
- **Drug use** Some experts tie increases in the violent crime rate between 1980 and 1990 to the crack cocaine epidemic, which swept the nation's largest cities, and drug trafficking gangs, which fought over drug turf. As the crack epidemic

exhibit 2.5

The issue of guns and crime is widely debated on the Web. For the pro-gun control view, visit the Coalition to Stop Gun Control Violence at
www.gunfree.com
For the anti-gun control view, go to the National Rifle Association's site at
www.nra.org

exhibit 2.5 cont.

has subsided, so too has the violence in cities such as New York and other metropolitan areas where the crack epidemic was rampant.

- **Justice policy** Some law enforcement experts have suggested that a reduction in crime rates may be attributed to aggressive police practices that target "quality-of-life" crimes such as panhandling, graffiti, petty drug dealing, and loitering. By showing that even the smallest infractions will be dealt with seriously, aggressive police departments may be able to discourage potential criminals from committing more serious crimes.

  It is also possible that tough laws targeting drug dealing and repeat offenders with lengthy prison terms can effect crime rates. The fear of severe punishment may deter some would-be criminals, and lengthy prison sentences place a significant number of potentially high-rate offenders behind bars.
- **Crime opportunities** Crime rates may be affected by criminal opportunities. For example, the decline in the burglary rate over the past two decades may be explained in part by the abundance and subsequent decline in price of commonly stolen merchandise such as VCRs, TVs, and cameras. Criminals may perceive a drop in potential profit from crime and a corresponding increase in the opportunity to gain legitimate employment in a booming economy.

  Improvements in home, automobile, and commercial security devices may also help reduce criminal opportunity. Would-be criminals may be convinced that it is not worth taking the risk of crime. As crime rates drop, people may be less willing to spend money on security, thus increasing opportunity and theft rates.

SOURCES: John J. Donohue III and Steven D. Levitt, "Legalized Abortion and Crime" (June 24, 1999, unpublished paper, University of Chicago); Donald Green, Dara Strolovitch, and Janelle Wong, "Defended Neighborhoods, Integration, and Racially Motivated Crime," *American Journal of Sociology* 104 (1998): 372–403; Robert O'Brien, Jean Stockard, and Lynne Isaacson, "The Enduring Effects of Cohort Characteristics on Age-Specific Homicide Rates, 1960–1995," *American Journal of Sociology* 104 (1999): 1061–95; Darrell Steffensmeier and Miles Harer, "Making Sense of Recent U.S. Crime Trends, 1980 to 1996/1998: Age Composition Effects and Other Explanations," *Journal of Research in Crime and Delinquency* 36 (1999): 235–74; Bruce Johnson, Andrew Golub, and Jeffrey Fagan, "Careers in Crack, Drug Use, Drug Distribution, and Nondrug Criminality", *Crime and Delinquency* 41 (1995): 275–95; Alfred Blumstein, "Violence by Young People: Why the Deadly Nexus?" *National Institute of Justice Journal* 229 (1995): 2–9; Joseph Sheley and James Wright, *In the Line of Fire: Youth, Guns, and Violence in Urban America* (New York: Aldine de Gruyter, 1995).

Trends in Self-Reports and Victimization Self-report results appear to be more stable than the UCR. When the results of recent self-report surveys are compared with various studies conducted over a twenty-year period, a uniform pattern emerges. The use of drugs and alcohol increased markedly in the 1970s, leveled off in the 1980s, and then began to increase in the mid-1990s until 1997, when drug use began to decline. Theft, violence, and damage-related crimes seem more stable. Although a self-reported crime wave has not occurred, neither has there been any visible reduction in self-reported criminality.

Figure 2.2
Homicide rate trends, 1900–1999
SOURCE: UCR, 1996; updated 1999.

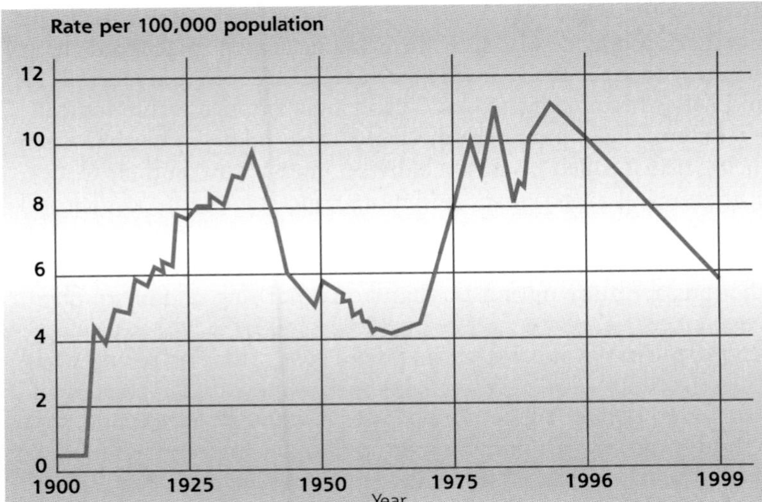

According to the most recently available NCVS data (1998), about 31 million personal crimes occur each year. Like the UCR, the NCVS also shows that crime rates have undergone a major decline in the 1990s. For example, between 1993 and 1998 violent crime rates fell 27 percent (from 50 to 37 per 1,000 persons age 12 or older). Property crime decreased 32 percent from 1993 to 1998. The 1998 rate of 217 property crimes per 1,000 households is lower than 1993 levels.

Self-report results show that the use of drugs and alcohol increased markedly in the 1970s, leveled off in the 1980s, and then began to increase in the mid-1990s until 1997, when drug use began to decline. A great deal of drug use occurs at "rave parties" held in abandoned buildings and rented warehouses.

What the Future Holds Speculating about the future of crime trends is always risky because current conditions can change rapidly. But some criminologists have tried to predict future patterns. Criminologist James Fox predicts a significant increase in teen violence if current trends persist. There are approximately 50 million school-age children in the United States, many are under age 10; this is more than we have had for decades. Though many come from stable homes, others lack stable families and adequate supervision; these are some of the children who will soon enter their prime crime years. As a result, Fox predicts a wave of youth violence that will be even worse than that of the past ten years. If current trends persist, the number of juvenile homicides should grow from fewer than four thousand today to about nine thousand in 2004.[29] Such predictions are based on population trends and other factors discussed earlier.

Fox's warnings are persuasive, but some experts dispute the fact that we are in for a big upswing in the crime rate.[30] Even if teens commit more crime in the future, their contribution may be offset by the growing senior citizen and elderly population, a group with a relatively low crime rate. Criminologists Darrell Steffensmeier and Miles Harer suggest that a growing economy, technological change, and social factors help moderate the crime rate.[31] They note that American culture is being transformed because "baby boomers" now in their forties and fifties have become less materialistic and more concerned with "kinder and gentler" cultural values.[32] These prosocial values may affect the behavior of all citizens, even crime-prone teens, moderating the potential growth of the crime rate. Their predictions are more optimistic than Fox's warning of a postmillennium crime wave.

You can find a wealth of information on cybercrimes at the CyberSpace Law Center's Web site. Go to http://cyber.findlaw.com/criminal/

Though such prognostication is reassuring, there is of course no telling what changes are in store. Technological developments such as the rapid expansion of e-commerce on the Internet have created new classes of crime. Concern about the environment in rural areas may produce a rapid upswing in environmental crimes ranging from vandalism to violence.[33] So while crime rates have trended downward, it is too early to predict that this trend will continue into the foreseeable future. In fact, as the crime rate has declined in the United States — as the following Race, Culture, and Gender feature shows — it seems to be increasing abroad.

CRIME PATTERNS

Crime experts look for stable crime rate patterns, to gain insight into the nature of crime. If crime rates are consistently higher at certain times, in certain areas, and among certain groups, this knowledge might help explain the onset or cause of crime. For example, if criminal statistics show that crime rates are consistently higher in poor neighborhoods in

Race, Culture, and Gender

INTERNATIONAL CRIME TRENDS

How do crime rates in the United States compare with those in other nations? The United States is still the "world leader" in violence, but evidence shows a disturbing upswing in violent crime abroad. For example, there has been a sharp increase in the murder rate in England, Germany, and Sweden. Racial assaults and hate crime have increased dramatically in Germany and England. Russia and the former Soviet republics have seen the rise of large-scale organized crime gangs that commonly use violence and intimidation.

Fueling the rise in European violence has been a dramatic growth in the number of illegal guns smuggled in from the former Soviet republics. Unrestrictive immigration has brought newcomers who face cultural differences, lack of job prospects, racism, and social and economic pressures, including unemployment and cutbacks in the social welfare system.

There have also been reports of increased criminal activity in Asia. For example, juvenile delinquency in the island nation of Singapore is on the rise — the number of arrests of young people more than doubled between 1991 and 1995. The delinquency increase is ironic considering that Singapore's draconian justice policies became notorious in 1993 when American teen Michael Fay was flogged after being convicted for vandalism.

Singapore is not alone among Asian nations experiencing an upsurge in crime. Authorities in Vietnam report a troubling increase in street crimes such as burglary and theft. Many crimes are drug related: There are an estimated 200,000 opium addicts in the country, and almost 50,000 acres of land are now being cultivated for growing the poppy from which heroin is produced. Although it is difficult to obtain accurate crime data from China, the world's largest nation seems to be cracking down on criminal offending. In the first few months of 1996, Chinese courts sentenced more than 100,000 street criminals, including 1,000 given death sentences and many thousands more life in prison. During a single month (June 1996), 250 people were executed. The current wave of punishments is a response to a significant increase in street crimes, including robberies and drug trafficking. Although the crime problem in China seems to be growing, research by Olivia Yu and Lening Zhang indicates that Chinese authorities may significantly undercount crime for both political and social reasons.

What factors predict high crime and violence rates around the world? A number of national characteristics are predictive of violence. These include a high level of social disorganization, economic stress (vs. support), high child-abuse rates, approval of violence by the government, political corruption, and an inefficient justice system. Children in high-violence nations were likely to be economically deprived and socially isolated, exposed to constant violence, and lacking in hope and respect for the law. Guns are common in these nations because, lacking an efficient justice system, people arm themselves or hire private security forces for protection.

Thus, although crime rates are still comparably low overseas, these trends indicate that international crime rates may yet converge.

Critical Thinking

What policies can be developed to bring the crime rate down in the United States? Is it feasible to tackle the social sources of crime by making families more cohesive, ending poverty, or reducing drug use?

Regardless of why crime rates are so high, might it not be possible to reduce them through aggressive law enforcement policies and the incapacitation of known criminals?

InfoTrac College Edition Research

To better understand the nature of crime in Eastern European nations that have transitioned from communism to democracy and the efforts now being made for its control, read

Christian Caryl, "The Very Long Arm of American Law," *U.S. News & World Report* 7 July 1997, 49.

Richard Lotspeich, "Crime in the transition economies," *Europe–Asia Studies* 47 (1995): 555.

SOURCES: Olivia Yu and Lening Zhang, "The Under-Recording of Crime in China: A Case Study," 22 (1999): 252–63; "With Women's Liberation Comes a Growing Involvement in Crime," *CJ International* 12 (1996): 19; "Crime Crackdown Continued as Statistics Increase," *CJ International* 12 (1996): 8; Sean Malinowski, "Battling an Emerging Crime Problem," *CJ International* 12 (1996): 3; "Singapore Says Delinquency Up," *Boston Globe*, 18 February 1996, 4.

large urban areas, then crime may be a function of poverty and neighborhood decline. If, in contrast, crime rates were spread evenly across the social structure, this would provide little evidence that crime has an economic basis; instead, crime might be linked to socialization, personality, intelligence, or some other trait unrelated to class position or income. In this section we examine traits and patterns that may influence the crime rate.

Gender differences in the crime rate have been explained in part by the fact that girls are socialized to be less aggressive than boys and consequently develop moral values that strongly discourage anti-social behavior. That may be changing. Here Diane Zamora sits in a Fort Worth, Texas, courtroom awaiting trial for her part in a conspiracy to kill Adrienne Jones, who had a sexual encounter with her boyfriend, David Graham. Zamora, a student at the U.S. Naval Academy, was convicted of murder in 1998.

Ecological and Seasonal Differences A distinct relationship exists between crime rates and urbanization. Areas with rural and suburban populations are more likely to have much lower crime rates than large urban areas. This finding, consistent over many years, suggests that the crime problem is linked to the social forces operating in the nation's largest cities — overcrowding, poverty, social inequality, narcotics use, and racial conflict. This pattern is illustrated by the fact that typically about 25 percent of all homicides occur in just seven cities: New York, Los Angeles, Chicago, Detroit, Houston, Philadelphia, and Washington, D.C. (although New York has had a dramatic decrease in murders since 1995).

UCR data also show that crime rates are highest in the summer months, most likely because (1) people spend so much time outdoors and are less likely to secure their homes and (2) schools are closed and young people have greater opportunity for criminal activity. Crime rates are also related to the region of the country. The West and South usually have significantly higher rates than the Midwest and New England.

Gender and Crime UCR arrest data consistently show that males have a much higher crime rate than females. The UCR arrest statistics indicate that the overall male–female arrest ratio is about 3.5 male offenders to 1 female offender; for serious violent crimes, the ratio is closer to 5 males to 1 female; murder arrests, 8.1 males to 1 female. Recent self-report data collected by the Institute for Social Research at the University of Michigan also show that males commit more serious crimes, such as robbery, assault, and burglary, than females. However, although the patterns in self-reports parallel official data, the ratios seem smaller. In other words, males self-report more criminal behavior than females, but not to the degree suggested by official data.

Traditionally, gender differences in the crime rate were explained by the biological differences between the sexes (e.g., males are stronger, hormonal differences) or by the fact that girls were socialized to be less aggressive than boys and consequently developed moral values that strongly discouraged antisocial behavior. These values help shield females from procrime influences, such as the behavior of delinquent peers, an influence to which males are decidedly more vulnerable.[34]

These views, however, are now being challenged by the rapid rise in the female crime rate. Some experts attribute this to the emergence of a "new female criminal" whose criminal activity mirrors the changing role of women in modern society.[35] As women's roles in the workplace have become more similar to men's, it is not surprising that their crime rates are converging. As a result, there has been a rise in female participation in traditionally male-oriented forms of criminality. For example, female membership in juvenile gangs appears to be on the increase. At one time a rare occurrence, recent national surveys now indicate that about 8 percent of females report gang membership (as compared with 14 percent of males). The fact that the male–female gang membership ratio is now less than 2 to 1 portends an eventual narrowing of the male–female crime rate gap.[36]

Race and Crime

Official crime data indicate that minority group members are involved in a disproportionate share of criminal activity. According to UCR reports, African Americans make up about 12 percent of the general population, yet they account for about 42 percent of Part I violent crime arrests and 27 percent of property crime arrests. They also are responsible for a disproportionate number of Part II arrests (except for alcohol-related arrests, which detain primarily white offenders). African Americans are arrested for murder, rape, and robbery at a rate higher than their relative representation in the population; an absolute majority of people arrested for murder and robbery are African Americans.

These data have proven to be controversial. Some criminologists argue that racial differences in the crime rate are caused by law enforcement practices that discriminate against African Americans.[37] In contrast, other experts view the official crime statistics as being an accurate reflection of the African-American crime rate. Their view is that racism, differential opportunity, powerlessness, and other social problems in the United States have resulted in a higher African-American crime rate as an expression of anger and frustration.[38] For example, as economic competition between the races grows, interracial homicides do likewise; economic and political rivalries lead to greater levels of interracial violence.[39]

African Americans also believe that they are unfairly targeted by a biased criminal justice system. Many young black males believe they are unfairly targeted by biased police officers. In some jurisdictions, such as Washington, D.C., almost half of young African-American men are under control of the justice system on any given day. Is it possible that this reflects racism and discrimination and a violation of their civil rights?[40] African Americans also have a significantly greater chance of being the target of violence. Nonwhites at birth are more than five times as likely to become murder victims as whites. Yet, when African Americans are the victims of crime, their plight receives less public concern and media attention than that afforded white victims.[41] These data indicate why the crime problem is of special significance for the black community.

Social Class and Crime

Researchers have used UCR data in conjunction with census data to determine whether crime is associated with poverty, unemployment, and lower-class status.[42] Official data seem to indicate that crime rates are highest in deprived, inner-city slum areas and that the level of poverty in an area can predict its crime rate.[43]

A number of explanations have been offered for the association between social class and official crime rates. One view is that the social forces in a high-risk, socially disorganized neighborhood — poverty, dilapidated housing, poor schools, broken families, drugs, and street gangs — significantly increase the likelihood that residents will engage in criminality.[44] As the social system in decayed urban areas breaks down and the rule of law becomes a distant threat, the moral vacuum of the slum acts as a magnet for criminals and deviants who help conditions grow steadily worse.[45]

Another view is that crime rates are high in deteriorated areas where the disadvantaged and the affluent live side by side. In these neighborhoods, social differences are magnified, and less affluent residents perceive a feeling of relative deprivation and social inequality that results in a higher crime rate.[46]

Age and Crime Official statistics tell us that young people are arrested at a disproportionate rate to their numbers in the population; victim surveys generate similar findings for crimes in which assailant age can be determined. Whereas youths aged 13 to 17 collectively make up about 6 percent of the total U.S. population, they account for about 25 percent of index crime arrests and 17 percent of arrests for all crimes. As a general rule, the peak age for property crime is believed to be 16 and for violence, 18 (Figure 2.3). In contrast, adults aged 45 and over, who make up 32 percent of the population, account for only 7 percent of index crime arrests. The elderly are particularly resistant to the temptations of crime; they make up more than 12 percent of the population and less than 1 percent of arrests. Elderly males aged 65 and over are predominantly arrested for alcohol-related matters (public drunkenness and drunk driving) and elderly females for larceny (shoplifting). The elderly crime rate has remained stable for the past twenty years.[47]

How can the age–crime relationship be explained? One factor is lifestyle; many young people are part of a youth culture that favors risk taking, short-run hedonism, and other behaviors that may involve them in law violation. Youths have limited financial resources and may resort to theft and drug dealing for income. The high-risk lifestyle of most youths ends as they mature and become involved in forming a family and a career.[48] Some adolescents may desist from crime when they begin to understand that the chances of winning friends, happiness, and wealth via crime are limited. A more simple explanation is biological: Young people have the energy, strength, and physical skill needed to commit crime, all of which erode with age.[49]

Figure 2.3
The relationship between age and serious crime arrests
SOURCE: UCR, 1998.

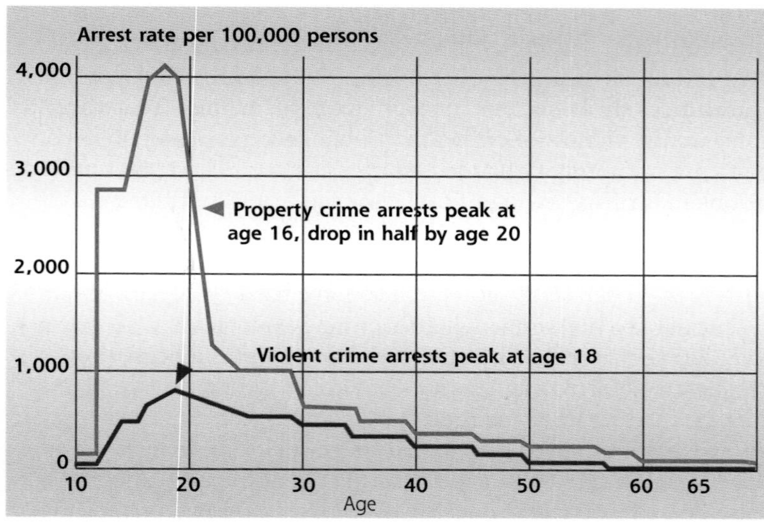

Criminologists now recognize that there are people who enter into a life of crime early in their adolescence and maintain a high rate of criminal violations throughout their life span.[50] These chronic offenders are immune to both the ravages of age and the punishments of the justice system. More important, this small group may be responsible for a significant portion of all serious criminal behavior.[51] The chronic offender is discussed in the Analyzing Criminal Justice Issues feature.

Crime Victims Whereas the UCR and self-report surveys help us determine the characteristics of criminals, the NCVS data provide a snapshot of the social and demographic characteristics of its victims. What are these characteristics?

As the level of social problems increases, so do crime rates. Increases in the number or single-parent families, in divorce and dropout rates, in nonrecreational drug use, and the number of teen pregnancies may also influence crime rates. Homeless kids and runaways may steal to survive, also contributing to rising crime rates.

GENDER Gender affects victimization risk. Men are much more likely than women to be victims of robbery and aggravated assault; they are also more likely to experience theft, but the differences are less pronounced. Although females are far more likely to be the victim of sexual assault, the NCVS estimates that 0.2 males are assaulted per 1,000 population; assuming a male population of 125 million, that means more than 20,000 males are raped or sexually assaulted each year.

When men are the victims of violent crime, the perpetrator is usually described as a stranger. Women are much more likely to be attacked by a relative than men are; about two-thirds of all attacks against women are committed by a husband or boyfriend, family member, or acquaintance. In two-thirds of sexual assaults, the victim knows the attacker.

AGE Young people face a much greater victimization risk than older persons do. Victim risk diminishes rapidly after age 25. The elderly, who are thought of as being the helpless targets of predatory criminals, are actually much safer than their grandchildren. People over age 65, who make up 14 percent of the population, account for 1 percent of violent victimizations; teens ages 12–19, who also make up 14 percent of the population, account for 32 percent of crime victims.

The association between age and victimization may be bound up in the lifestyle shared by young people. Adolescents often stay out late at night, go to public places, and hang out with other teens who have a high risk of criminal involvement. Most adolescents ages 12–19 are attacked by offenders in the same-age category, while a great majority of adults are victimized by adult criminals. Teens face a high victimization risk because they spend a great deal of time in the most dangerous building in the community: the local schoolhouse!

INCOME The poorest Americans might be expected to be the most likely victims of crime, since they live in areas that are crime prone: inner-city, urban neighborhoods. The NCVS does in fact show that the least affluent (annual incomes of

Policy, Programs, and Issues in Criminal Justice

THE CHRONIC OFFENDER

One of the most dramatic developments in the study of crime and delinquency has been the "discovery" of the chronic offender. Researchers increasingly recognize two facts: (1) Relatively few offenders commit a significant percentage of all serious community crimes, and (2) such offenders who are juveniles become chronic criminals who contribute notably to the total adult crime rate.

Chronic offenders can be distinguished from conventional criminals. The latter category contains law violators who may commit and be apprehended for a single instance of criminal behavior, usually of relatively minor seriousness — shoplifting, simple assault, petty larceny, and so on. The chronic offender is one who has serious and persistent brushes with the law, who is building a career in crime, and whose behavior may be excessively violent and destructive.

The concept of the chronic offender is most closely associated with the research efforts of Marvin Wolfgang and his associates at the University of Pennsylvania. In 1972 Wolfgang, Robert Figlio, and Thorsten Sellin published a landmark study, *Delinquency in a Birth Cohort,* that has had a profound influence on the very concept of the criminal offender. Wolfgang, Figlio, and Sellin used official records to follow the criminal careers of a cohort of 9,945 boys born in Philadelphia in 1945 until they reached age 18 in 1963. About two-thirds of the cohort (6,470) never had contact with police authorities, while the remaining 3,475 had at least one contact with the police during their minority. Of these, a relatively small group of 627 boys were arrested fives times or more. These chronic offenders were responsible for 5,305 arrests, 51.9% of the total. Even more striking was the involvement of chronic offenders in serious criminal acts. Of the entire sample, they committed 71% of the homicides, 73% of the rapes, 82% of the robberies, and 69% of the aggravated assaults. Arrest and punishment did little to deter them. In fact, punishment was inversely related to chronicity — the stricter the sanctions they received, the more likely they were to engage in repeated criminal behavior.

Since the Philadelphia survey was carried out, a number of other independent studies, including one of a larger Philadelphia cohort of children born in 1958, have also confirmed the existence of a repeat offender.

The Stability of Crime

The chronic offender research indicates that young persistent offenders grow up to become repeat adult offenders. The stability of criminal careers was detected by Paul Tracy and Kimberly Kempf-Leonard in their important follow-up study of all subjects in the second (1958) Philadelphia cohort. By age 26, those delinquents with high rates of juvenile offending, who had started their delinquent career early, who had committed a violent crime, and who continued offending throughout adolescence were the ones most likely to persist as adults. The severity of offending, not the frequency, had the greatest impact on later adult criminality.

The Cause of Chronic Offending

The existence of a chronic offender presents a dilemma for those who believe that the criminal offender can be successfully treated with some combination of educational, vocational, and psychological counseling and support. If only a small group of offenders are in fact responsible for almost all serious crimes, it follows that some personal characteristics must set chronic offenders apart from both noncriminals and nonchronic offenders. Environmental and socialization factors alone cannot explain why one young offender desists from crime, whereas another, living in the same area and experiencing similar environmental conditions, becomes a chronic offender

less than $7,500) are by far the most likely to be victims of violent crimes, and this association occurs across all gender, racial, and age groups. Whereas the poor are almost twice as likely to be the victims of burglary, the wealthy are more likely to be the target of theft crimes, such as pocket picking and purse snatching. Perhaps the affluent, who sport more expensive attire and drive better-make cars, earn the attention of thieves looking for attractive targets.

Victim data suggest that thieves choose their targets carefully, selecting those who seem best able to provide them with a substantial haul. In contrast, the targets of violence are among the nation's poorest people. Although the wealthy face a higher rate of personal theft, the poorest are the most likely to be the victim of burglaries, most likely because they live in close proximity to their attackers.

who escalates the frequency and seriousness of her criminal activity.

A number of criminologists have suggested that chronic offending is caused by some individual trait, genetic condition, or physical characteristic. These conditions may exist before birth or may be a function of birth complications — factors that for all practical purposes are uncontrollable. Some preliminary research efforts indicate that such factors as limited intelligence (as measured by IQ tests) and impulsive personality predict chronic offending.

Early onset of offending has been associated with chronic offending. Children who are found to be disruptive and antisocial as early as age 5 or 6 are the ones most likely to exhibit stable, long-term patterns of disruptive behavior through adolescence. They have measurable behavior problems in such areas as learning and motor skills, cognitive abilities, family relations, and other areas of social, psychological, and physical functioning. Youthful offenders who persist are more likely to abuse alcohol, get into trouble while in military service, become economically dependent, have lower aspirations, get divorced or separated, and have a weak employment record.

The chronic offender concept has had a great deal of impact on the criminal justice system. If a small group of offenders commits almost all of the serious crime, then it stands to reason that their incarceration might have an appreciable influence on the crime rate. This thought pattern has been responsible for the recent spate of "get-tough" laws designed to put habitual offenders behind bars for long periods of time. As a consequence of these get-tough sentences, the prison population has trended upward as crime rates have fallen.

Critical Thinking

The record number of inmates currently in prison and jail reflects the justice system's efforts to curb career offenders and the "lock 'em up and throw away the key" philosophy. This solution is troubling to civil libertarians since it involves possible errors in the prediction of a person's future behavior. Might not some people be unfairly punished because their background characteristics mistakenly indicate they are chronic offenders? Conversely, might not some serious offenders be overlooked because they have a more conventional background? No prediction method is totally accurate, and error can involve a significant infringement on a person's civil rights. Should people be punished because their past deeds indicate a risk of future criminality? Or should criminal punishment be based on the current criminal act?

InfoTrac College Edition Research

Identifying the cause of chronic offending is the subject discussed in

> Deborah Gorman-Smith, Patrick H. Tolan, Rolf Loeber, and David B. Henry, "Relation of Family Problems to Patterns of Delinquent Involvement among Urban Youth," *Journal of Abnormal Child Psychology* 26 (1998): 319.

Treating and controlling chronic adolescent offenders is discussed in

> Cynthia Cupit Swenson and Wallace A. Kennedy, "Perceived Control and Treatment Outcome with Chronic Adolescent Offenders," *Adolescence* 30 (1995): 565.

SOURCES: Paul Tracy and Kimberly Kempf-Leonard, *Continuity and Discontinuity in Criminal Careers* (New York: Plenum Press, 1996); Elizabeth Kandel and Sarnoff Mednick, "Perinatal Complications Predict Violent Offending," *Criminology* 29 (1991): 519–29; Marvin Wolfgang, Robert Figlio, and Thorsten Sellin, *Delinquency in a Birth Cohort* (Chicago: University of Chicago Press, 1972); Marvin Wolfgang, "Delinquency in Two Birth Cohorts," in *Perspective Studies of Crime and Delinquency*, ed. Katherine Teilmann Van Dusen and Sarnoff Mednick (Boston: Kluwer-Nijhoff, 1983), 7–17.

MARITAL STATUS Marital status also influences victimization risk. The unmarried or never married are victimized more often than married people or widows and widowers. These relationships are probably influenced by age, gender, and lifestyle. Many of the young people who have the highest victim risk are actually too young to have been married. Younger, unmarried people also go out in public more often and interact with high-risk peers, increasing their exposure to victimization. In contrast, widows, who are more likely to be older women, suffer much lower victimization rates because they interact with older people, are more likely to stay home at night, and avoid public places. These data are further evidence of the relationship between lifestyle and victimization risk.

RACE One of the most important distinctions found in the NCVS data is the racial differences in the victim rate. African Americans experience violent crimes at a higher rate than other groups. NCVS data show that African Americans have strikingly higher rates of violent personal crimes than do whites. Although the race-specific risk of theft victimization is more similar, African Americans are still more likely to be victimized than whites.

Crimes committed against African Americans tend to be more serious than those committed against whites. For example, African Americans experience higher rates of aggravated assault, whereas whites are more often the victims of simple assault. The most striking difference recorded by the NCVS is in the incidence of robberies: African Americans are about three times as likely to become robbery victims as whites.

Young African-American males are also at great risk for homicide victimization. They face a murder risk four or five times greater than that of young African-American females, five to eight times higher than that of young white males, and sixteen to twenty-two times higher than that of young white females. A longitudinal analysis conducted by the Centers for Disease Control indicates that the murder victimization rate of African-American males is increasing at a much faster pace than for these other groups.[52]

Why do these discrepancies exist? Young black males tend to live in the largest U.S. cities in areas beset by alcohol and drug abuse, poverty, racial discrimination, and violence. Forced to live in the most dangerous areas, their lifestyle places them in the highest at-risk population group.

ECOLOGICAL FACTORS The NCVS data parallel the crime patterns found in the UCR. Most victimizations occur in large urban areas; rural and suburban victim rates are far lower. Most incidents occur during the evening hours (6 P.M. to 6 A.M.). Generally, more serious crimes take place after 6 P.M.; less serious, before 6 P.M. For example, aggravated assaults occur at night, whereas simple assaults are more likely to take place during the daytime. The most likely site for a victimization — especially a violent crime such as rape, robbery, and aggravated assault — is an open, public area such as a street, park, or field. Sadly, one of the most dangerous public places is a public school building. About 10 percent of all U.S. youth ages 12–19 (approximately 2 million) are crime victims while on schoolgrounds each year. It seems that the best way to avoid victimization is to stay home at night with doors and windows locked!

An overwhelming number of victimizations involve a single person. Most victims report that their assailant was not armed (except for the crime of robbery, where about half the offenders carry weapons). In the robberies and assaults involving injury, however, a majority of the assailants are reported as armed. The use of guns and knives is about equal, and there does not seem to be a pattern of a particular weapon being used for a particular crime.

VICTIM–OFFENDER RELATIONSHIPS The NCVS can tell us something about the characteristics of people who commit crime. This information is available only on criminals who actually came in contact with the victim through such crimes as rape, assault, or robbery.

Most offenders and victims do not know each other; about 50 percent of all violent crimes are committed by strangers. However, women seem much more likely than men to be victimized by acquaintances; a majority of female assault victims know their assailants. In all, about 50 percent of all violent crimes are committed by people who were known to the victim, including family members, spouses, parents, children, and siblings.

African Americans experience violent crimes at a higher rate than other groups. NCVS data show that African-American citizens have strikingly higher rates of violent personal crimes than do whites. Here, Margaret Ensley, President of Mothers Against Violence in Schools stands with a photo of her son Michael, a victim of gun violence.

A majority of victims report that the crime was committed by a single offender over the age of 20. About 25 percent of victims indicate that their assailant was a young person 12–20 years of age. This may reflect the criminal activities of youth gangs and groups in the United States.

Whites are the offenders in a majority of single-offender rapes and assaults; there is no racial pattern in single-offender robberies. However, multiple-offender robberies are more likely committed by African Americans.

The NCVS has recently begun to ask victims if their assailants were under the influence of drugs or alcohol. In response, victims report that substance use was involved in 30 percent of the violent crime incidents, including 40 percent of the rapes and 30 percent of the assaults.

The NCVS data suggest that the risk of becoming a crime victim over one's lifetime is a function of personal characteristics and lifestyle. Victimization risk can be increased by being in public places in urban areas late at night. Victimization can be reduced by moving to a suburb and avoiding public places in the evening. The NCVS, then, seems to be indicating that the likelihood of a crime occurring depends to some extent on victim behavior.

REPEAT VICTIMIZATION Does prior victimization enhance or reduce the chances of future victimization? Stable patterns of behavior may encourage victimization, and a few people who maintain them may become "chronic victims," constantly the target of predatory crimes.

Most research does in fact show that individuals who have had prior victimization experiences have a significantly higher chance of repeat victimization than do people who have been nonvictims.[53] Research also shows that households that have experienced victimization are the ones most likely to experience it again.[54] Repeat victimizations are most likely to occur in areas with high crime rates; one study found that during a four-year period, 40 percent of all trauma patients in an urban medical center in Ohio were repeat victims.[55]

What factors predict chronic victimizations? Some combination of personal and social factors may possibly encourage victimization risk. Most revictimizations happen soon after a previous crime, suggesting that repeat victims share some personal characteristics that make them a magnet for predators.[56]

If you want to keep updated on the hot issues in criminology, go to the homepage of the American Society of Criminology's Critical Criminology Division at www.soci.niu.edu/~critcrim/

CAUSES OF CRIME AND VICTIMIZATION

Although the various sources of criminal statistics can tell us about the nature of crime patterns and trends, knowing why an individual commits crime in the first place is also important. Such knowledge is critical if programs are to be devised to deter or prevent crime. If, for example, people commit crime because they are poor and desperate, the key to crime prevention might be a job program and government economic aid. If, however, the root cause of crime is a poor family life marked by conflict and abuse, then providing jobs will not help lower the crime rate; family counseling and parenting skills courses would prove to be more effective.

There is still a great deal of uncertainty about the "real" cause of crime. Some of the more popular explanations are discussed in the following sections.

choice theory
The school of thought holding that people will engage in delinquent and criminal behavior after weighing the consequences and benefits of their actions. Delinquent behavior is a rational choice made by a motivated offender who perceives the chances of gain outweigh any perceived punishment or loss.

Choice Theory: Because They Want To

One prominent view of criminality is that people choose to commit crime after weighing the potential benefits and consequences of their criminal acts. According to **choice theory,** people commit crime if they believe it will provide immediate benefits without the threat of long-term risks. For example, before concluding a drug sale, experienced traffickers will mentally balance the chances of making a large profit with the consequences of being apprehended and punished for drug dealing. They know that most drug deals are not detected and that the potential for enormous, untaxed profits is great. They evaluate their lifestyle and determine how much cash they need to maintain their standard of living, which is usually extravagant. They may have borrowed to finance the drug deal, and their creditors are not usually reasonable if loans cannot be repaid promptly. They also realize that they could be the target of a "sting" operation by undercover agents and, if caught, will get a long mandatory sentence in a forbidding federal penitentiary. If they conclude that the potential for profits is great enough, their need for cash urgent, and the chances of apprehension minimal, they will carry out the deal. If, however, they believe that the transaction will bring them only a small profit and a large risk of apprehension and punishment, they may forgo the deal as too risky. Crime, then, is a matter of personal choice.

According to this view, crimes are events that occur when offenders decide to risk crime after considering personal needs (a desire for money, excitement, experience, or revenge), situational factors (how well a target is protected, the risk of apprehension, the chance for hurting bystanders), and legal factors (the efficiency of police, the threat of legal punishment, the effect of a prior criminal record on future punishment). The decision to commit a specific crime is thus a matter of personal decision making based on a weighing of available information.[57]

The main principles of choice theory are the following:

1. All people of their own free will can choose between conventional or criminal behaviors.
2. For some people, criminal solutions are more attractive because they require less effort for greater gain.
3. People will refrain from antisocial acts if they believe that the punishment or pain they will receive for their actions will be greater than any potential gain.
4. The punishments threatened by the existing criminal law are the primary deterrent to crime.

biological theory
The school of thought holding that certain biochemical, neurological, and genetic factors cause people to commit crime.

Biological Theory: It's in Their Blood

In recent years, there has been interest in finding a biological basis of crime. **Biological theories** can be divided into three broad areas of focus: biochemical factors, neurological problems, and genetic abnormalities.

BIOCHEMICAL FACTORS Crime and violence are possibly functions of biochemical abnormality. Such biochemical factors as vitamin and mineral deficiencies, improper diet, environmental contaminants, and allergies have been linked to antisocial behavior.[58]

A great deal of research has linked hormonal activity to aggressive behavior. Some criminologists argue that gender differences in the crime rate can be linked to the male hormone testosterone and its assumed effect on behavior.[59]

In sum, biochemical studies suggest that some criminal offenders have abnormal levels of organic or inorganic substances that influence their behavior and in some way make them prone to antisocial behavior.

NEUROLOGICAL PROBLEMS Another area of interest to biocriminologists is the relationship of brain activity to behavior. Biocriminologists have used the electroencephalogram to record the electrical impulses given off by the brain. Preliminary studies indicate that 50 to 60 percent of those with behavior disorders display abnormal recordings.[60]

People with an abnormal cerebral structure, referred to as minimal brain dysfunction, may experience periods of explosive rage.[61] Brain dysfunction is sometimes manifested as an attention deficit disorder, another suspected cause of antisocial behavior. About 3 percent of all U.S. children, primarily boys, are believed to suffer from this disorder, and it is the most common reason children are referred to mental health clinics. The condition usually results in poor school performance, bullying, stubbornness, and a lack of response to discipline.[62]

GENETIC ABNORMALITIES Violent behavior is possibly inherited and a function of a person's genetic makeup. One approach has been to evaluate the behavior of adopted children. If an adopted child's behavior patterns run parallel to those of his or her biological parents, it would be strong evidence to support a genetic basis for crime. Preliminary studies conducted in Europe have indicated that the criminality of the biological father is a strong predictor of a child's antisocial behavior.[63] The probability that a youth will engage in crime is significantly enhanced when both biological and adoptive parents exhibit criminal tendencies.

Is it possible that criminal traits are inherited? Though some may scoff at the notion, one of the leading experts in this field, David Rowe, reviewed the available research and concluded that individuals who share genes are alike in personality regardless of how they are reared; in contrast, environment induces little or no personality resemblance in twin pairs.[64]

Psychological Theory: It's in Their Heads

Sometimes when we hear of a particularly gruesome crime, we say of the criminal, "That guy must be crazy." It comes as no surprise, then, that some experts believe that the onset of criminality is caused by psychological factors.

PSYCHOSES There are actually a number of views on this subject. According to the **psychoanalytic view,** some people encounter problems during their early development that cause an imbalance in their personality. Some may become psychotics who cannot restrain their impulsive behavior. One type of psychosis is schizophrenia, a condition marked by incoherent thought processes, a lack of insight, hallucinations, feelings of persecution, and so on. Schizophrenics may suffer delusions and feel persecuted, worthless, and alienated.[65] Examples of people suffering from severe psychological disorders are David Berkowitz, known as the "Son of Sam"; John Hinckley, Jr., who attempted to assassinate President Ronald Reagan; and Milwaukee cannibal Jeffrey Dahmer.

psychoanalytic view of crime
This position holds that criminals are driven by unconscious thought patterns, developed in early childhood, that control behaviors over the life course.

social learning
The view that behavior patterns are modeled and learned in interactions with others.

SOCIAL LEARNING Another psychological view is that criminal behavior is learned through interactions with others. According to **social learning** theorists, people act aggressively because as children they modeled their behavior after the violent acts of adults.

One area of particular interest to social learning is whether the media can influence violence. Studies have shown that youths exposed to aggressive, antisocial behavior on television and in movies are likely to copy that violent behavior. Laboratory studies generally conclude that violence on television can lead to aggressive behavior by children and teenagers who watch such programs.[67] Whether the evidence obtained in controlled laboratory studies can be applied to the real world is still being debated.[68] Considering that the average child watches more than twenty hours of TV a week, any link between TV violence and criminal behavior is important. This issue is discussed further in the Criminal Justice and the Media feature on pages 68–69.

People with psychopathic or antisocial personalities are believed to be dangerous, aggressive individuals who act in a callous manner. Although they may appear charming and have at least average intelligence, psychopaths lack emotional depth and are incapable of caring for others. Aaron Mckinney, convicted of the 1999 murder of Matthew Shepard, a gay college student, is shown here in police custody. Is it possible that such irrational acts of violence are the product of a psychopathic personality structure?

PSYCHOPATHIC PERSONALITY Psychologists have explored the link between personality and crime. Evidence shows that aggressive youth have unstable personality structures often marked by hyperactivity, impulsiveness, and instability.

One area of particular interest to criminology is the identification of the psychopathic (sometimes referred to as the antisocial or sociopathic) personality. Psychopaths are believed to be dangerous, aggressive, antisocial individuals who act in a callous manner. They neither learn from their mistakes nor are deterred by punishment. [69] Although they may appear charming and have at least average intelligence, psychopaths lack emotional depth, are incapable of caring for others, and maintain an abnormally low level of anxiety. They are likely to be persistent alcohol and drug abusers.[70]

The concept of the psychopathic personality is important for criminology, because it has been estimated that somewhere between 10 and 30 percent of all prison inmates can be classified as psychopaths or sociopaths or as having similar character disorders.[71]

Psychopathy has also been linked to the phenomenon of serial murder.[72] Although psychologists are still not certain of its cause, a number of factors are believed to contribute to the development of a psychopathic personality. They include having a psychopathic parent, parental rejection and lack of love during childhood, and inconsistent discipline.[73] Some psychologists suspect that psychopathy is a function of physical abnormality, especially the activity of the autonomic nervous system. Studies measuring the physical makeup of clinically diagnosed psychopaths indicate that such persons react differently to pain and have lower arousal levels to noise and environmental stimuli than do control subjects.[74] Another view is that the psychopathic personality is imprinted at birth and is relatively unaffected by socialization.[75] These people are among the most disturbed offenders who may be at risk for chronic offending.

Social Structure Theory: Because They're Poor

There seems to be an economic bias in the crime rate: Prisons are filled with the poor and hopeless, not the rich and famous. Because crime patterns have a decidedly social orientation, sociological explanations of crime have predominated in criminology.

social structure theory
The view that a person's position in the social structure controls behavior. Those in the lowest socioeconomic tier are more likely to succumb to crime-promoting elements in their environment society, whereas those in the highest tier enjoy social and economic advantages that insulate them from crime-producing forces.

According to **social structure theory,** the United States is a stratified society. The contrast between the lifestyles of the wealthiest members of the upper class and the poorest segment of the lower class is striking. The gap between the richest and the poorest Americans seems to be growing wider; the number of families living in poverty doubled in the past decade. About 20 million high school dropouts face dead-end jobs, unemployment, and social failure. Because of their meager economic resources, lower-class citizens are often forced to live in slum areas marked by substandard housing, inadequate health care, poor educational opportunities, underemployment, and despair. Many families are fatherless and husbandless, headed by a woman who is the sole breadwinner and who is often forced to go on welfare.

The problems of lower-class culture are particularly acute for racial and ethnic minorities who have an income level significantly lower than that of whites and an unemployment rate almost twice as high. They now face the deterioration of the manufacturing economy in the urban United States. Hundreds of thousands of jobs have been lost, further weakening the economic future of young minority men and women.

The crushing burden of urban poverty results in the development of a culture of poverty.[76] This subculture is marked by apathy, cynicism, helplessness, and distrust. The culture is passed from one generation to another so that slum dwellers become part of a permanent underclass, "the truly disadvantaged."[77] Considering the social disability suffered by lower-class slum dwellers, it is not surprising that they turn to crime as a means of support and survival. Forced to endure substandard housing and schools in deteriorated inner-city, socially disorganized neighborhoods and cut off from conventional society, lower-class slum dwellers are faced with a constant assault on their self-image and sense of worth. Criminal acts and drug dealing provide a means of survival in an otherwise bleak existence. In these areas the forces of social control have broken down; this is referred to as *social disorganization.*

Because of low income, some people may be forced to live in neighborhoods with much higher rates of poverty, unemployment, and social disorder than surrounding areas. The crushing burden of poverty makes some people vulnerable to criminal behavior.

Social Process Theory: Socialized to Crime

Not all criminologists agree that the cause of crime can be found solely within the culture of poverty.[78] Some argue that people commit crime as a result of the experiences they have while they are being socialized by the various organizations, institutions, and processes of society. People are most strongly influenced toward criminal behavior by poor family relationships, destructive peer-group relations, educational failure, and labeling by agents of the justice system. Although lower-class citizens have the added burdens of poverty and strain, even middle-class or upper-class citizens may turn to crime if their socialization is poor or destructive.

social process theory
The view that an individual's interactions with key social institutions — family, school, peer group — shapes behavior.

Social process theory points to research efforts linking family problems to crime as evidence that **socialization,** not social structure, is the key to understanding the onset of criminality. The quality of family life is considered to be a significant determining factor in adolescent development.[79] Among the most important research efforts are those showing that inconsistent discipline, poor supervision,

Criminal Justice and the Media

THE MEDIA AND VIOLENCE

Young TV and film viewers are constantly barraged with media depictions of demented and crazed killers who use grotesque violence to dispatch their victim. Depicted in gory detail are the violent acts of crazed baby-sitters *(The Hand That Rocks the Cradle)*; deranged roommates *(Single, White Female)*; unhinged police officers *(Kiss the Girls)*; doctors *(Silence of the Lambs)*, and cab drivers *(The Bone Collector)*; abnormal girlfriends *(Fatal Attraction)* and boyfriends *(Fear)*; unstable husbands *(Sleeping with the Enemy)* and wives *(Black Widow)*; loony fathers *(The Stepfather)*, mothers *(Friday the 13th, Part 1)*, and grandmothers *(Hush)*; unbalanced crime victims *(I Know What You Did Last Summer)*, and unsound high school friends *(Scream)* who grow into murderous college classmates *(Scream II)*. Has viewing this collection of gore on TV, in film rentals, or in move theaters created a generation of violence-prone adolescents? Does the media influence behavior?

If there is in fact a TV–violence link, the problem is indeed alarming. Systematic viewing of TV begins at age 2½ and continues at a high level during the preschool and early school years. It has been estimated that children aged 2 to 5 watch TV for 27.8 hours each week; children aged 6 to 11, 24.3 hours per week; and teens, 23 hours per week. Marketing research indicates that adolescents aged 11 to 14 rent violent horror movies at a higher rate than any other age group. Children this age use older peers and siblings and apathetic parents to gain access to R-rated films. More than 40 percent of U.S. households now have cable TV, which features violent films and shows. Even children's programming is saturated with violence.

The fact that children watch so much violent TV is not surprising, considering the findings of a well-publicized 1995 study conducted by UCLA researchers. They found that of the 161 made-for-TV movies that year, 23 raised concerns about their use of violence, violent theme, violent title, or inappropriate portrayals of a scene; of the 118 theatrical films shown that season, 50 raised concerns about their use of violence. Even some children's TV programming has worrisome signs featuring "sinister combat" as the theme of the show. The characters are usually happy to fight and frequently do so with little provocation. A University of Pennsylvania study found that children's TV programming contained an average of thirty-two violent acts per hour, 56 percent had violent characters, and 74 percent had characters who became the victims of violence (though "only 3.3 percent had characters who were actually killed"). In all, the average child views 8,000 TV murders before finishing elementary school.

Numerous anecdotal cases of violence have been linked to TV and films.

- In 1977 Ronald Zamora killed an elderly woman and then plead guilty by reason of insanity. His attorney claimed Zamora was addicted to TV violence and could no longer differentiate between reality and fantasy; the jury did not buy the defense, and Zamora was found guilty as charged.
- John Hinckley, Jr., shot President Ronald Reagan due to his obsession with actress Jodie Foster, which developed after he watched her play a prostitute in the film *Taxi Driver.* Hinckley viewed the film at least fifteen times.
- In October 1993 a five-year-old Ohio boy set a fire that caused the death of his two-year-old sister. The boy's mother charged that the youth was influenced by the MTV show *Beavis and Butthead,* whose cartoon heroes regularly start fires and chant "Fire is good." MTV responded to the public outcry over the incident by moving the show's broadcast time from 7 P.M. to 10:30 P.M.

A national survey conducted in the wake of the MTV controversy found that almost 80 percent of the general public believes that violence on TV can cause violence in real life. Psychologists, however, believe that media violence does not in itself *cause* violent behavior because if it did there would be millions of daily incidents in which viewers imitated the aggression they watched on TV or in the movies. Most psychologists agree, however, that media violence *contributes* to aggression. Several explanations are offered for the effects of TV and film violence on behavior:

- Media violence can provide aggressive "scripts" that children store in memory. Repeated exposure to these scripts can increase their retention and lead to changes in attitudes.
- Children learn from what they observe. In the same way they learn cognitive and social skills from their parents and friends, children learn to be violent from television.
- Television violence increases the arousal levels of viewers and makes them more prone to act aggressively. Studies measuring the galvanic skin response of subjects — a physical indication of arousal based on the amount of electricity conducted across the palm of the hand — show that viewing violent TV shows led to increased arousal levels in young children.
- Watching TV violence promotes such negative attitudes as suspiciousness and the expectation that the viewer will become involved in violence. Those who watch TV frequently come to view aggression and violence as common and socially acceptable behavior.

socialization
The process in which a person learns to adapt to the cultural and social institutions in society.

and a lack of warm parent–child relationships are closely related to a child's deviant behavior.[80] Educational experience has also been found to have a significant impact on behavioral choices. Youths who fail at school and eventually drop out are the ones most likely to engage in criminal behavior; academic performance is a significant predictor of crime and delinquency.[81]

- Television violence allows aggressive youths to justify their behavior. It is possible that, instead of causing violence, television helps violent youths rationalize their behavior as a socially acceptable and common activity.
- Television violence may disinhibit aggressive behavior, which is normally controlled by other learning processes. Disinhibition takes place when adults are viewed as being rewarded for violence and when violence is seen as socially acceptable. This contradicts previous learning experiences in which violent behavior was viewed as wrong.

Such distinguished bodies as the American Psychological Association, the National Institute of Mental Health, and the National Research Council support the TV–violence link. They base their conclusion on research efforts indicating that watching violence on TV leads to increased levels of violence in both laboratory and natural settings.

Most evaluations of experimental data indicate that watching violence on TV is correlated to aggressive behaviors or at least has a short-term impact on behavior. Subjects who view violent TV shows are likely to exhibit aggressive behavior almost immediately.

A number of critics argue that the evidence simply does not support the claim that watching TV or movies is related to antisocial behavior. There is also little evidence that regional areas experiencing the highest levels of violent TV viewing also have violent crime rates above the norm. Millions of children watch violence every night but do not become violent criminals. If violent TV shows did indeed cause interpersonal violence, then there should be few ecological and regional patterns in the crime rate, of which there are many. Put another way, how can regional differences in the violence rate be explained considering the fact that people all across the nation watch the same TV shows and films?

In the end, experiments that show a correlation between aggression and TV fail to link the association with actual criminal behaviors, such as rape or assault. The weight of the experimental results, then, indicates that violent media have an immediate impact on people with a *preexisting* tendency toward crime and violence.

Although the evidence linking TV violence to aggression is still unclear, concern has caused the TV industry to join with the film industry to place advisory warnings (e.g., PG-13) on shows that have objectionable content. Such practices may help guide some parents but they do little to restrict TV watching when children are home alone (although it may soon be possible to equip television sets with computer chips that prevent the reception of shows designated as having violent themes). Critics charge that such policies run afoul of First Amendment guarantees of free speech; who is to judge that a TV show is too violent?

Critical Thinking

Should the government control the content of TV shows and limit the amount of weekly violence? How could the national news be shown if violence were omitted? What about boxing matches or hockey games?

How can we explain the fact that millions of children watch violent TV shows and remain nonviolent? If there is a TV–violence link, how can we explain the fact that violence rates may have been higher in the Old West than they are today? Do you think violent gang youths stay home and watch violent TV shows?

InfoTrac College Edition Research

Does the media cause violence? To research the debate, see

L. Rowell Huesmann and Jessica Moise, "Media Violence: A Demonstrated Public Health Threat to Children," *Harvard Mental Health Letter* 12 (1996): 5.

Jonathan L. Freedman, "Violence in the Mass Media and Violence in Society: The Link Is Unproven," *Harvard Mental Health Letter* 12 (1996): 4.

SOURCES: UCLA Center for Communication Policy, Television Violence Monitoring Project (Los Angeles 1995); Associated Press, "Hollywood Is Blamed in Token Booth Attack," *Boston Globe,* 28 November 1995, 30; Garland White, Janet Katz, and Kathryn Scarborough, "The Impact of Professional Football Games upon Violent Assaults on Women," *Violence and Victims* 7 (1992): 157–71; Simon Singer, "Rethinking Subcultural Theories of Delinquency and the Cultural Resources of Youth" (Paper presented at the annual meeting of the American Society of Criminology, Phoenix, November 1993); Albert Reiss and Jeffrey Roth, eds., *Understanding and Preventing Violence* (Washington, D.C.: National Academy Press, 1993); Reuters, "Seventy-Nine Percent in Survey Link Violence on TV and Crime," *Boston Globe,* 19 December 1993, 17; Scott Snyder, "Movies and Juvenile Delinquency: An Overview," *Adolescence* 26 (1991): 121–31; Steven Messner, "Television Violence and Violent Crime: An Aggregate Analysis," *Social Problems* 33 (1986): 218–35; Candace Kruttschnitt, Linda Heath, and David Ward, "Family Violence, Television Viewing Habits, and Other Adolescent Experiences Related to Violent Criminal Behavior," *Criminology* 243 (1986): 235–67; Jonathan Freedman, "Television Violence and Aggression: A Rejoinder," *Psychological Bulletin* 100 (1986): 372–78; Wendy Wood, Frank Wong, and J. Gregory Chachere, "Effects of Media Violence on Viewers' Aggression in Unconstrained Social Interaction," *Psychological Bulletin* 109 (1991): 371–83.

conflict theory
The view that human behavior is shaped by interpersonal conflict and that those who maintain social power will use it to further their own needs.

Conflict Theory: It's a "Dog-Eat-Dog World"

Conflict theory views the economic and political forces operating in society as the fundamental causes of criminality. The criminal law and criminal justice system are viewed as vehicles for controlling the poor members of society. The criminal justice system is believed to help the powerful and rich impose their particular morality and standards of good behavior on the entire society, while it protects their property and physical safety from the have-nots, even though the cost may be the legal rights of the lower class. Those in power control the content and direction of the law and legal system.

Crimes are defined in a way that meets with the needs of the ruling classes. The theft of property worth $5 by a poor person can be punished much more severely than the misappropriation of millions by a large corporation. Those in the middle class are drawn into this pattern of control because they are led to believe that they too have a stake in maintaining the status quo and should support the views of the upper-class owners of production.[82]

An important aspect of conflict theory, radical feminist theory, tries to explain how capitalism places particular stress on women and to explicate the role of male dominance in female criminality.[83] Radical feminists view female crime as originating with the onset of male supremacy (patriarchy), the subsequent subordination of women, male aggression, and efforts of men to control women sexually.[84] They focus on the social forces that shape women's lives and experiences to explain female criminality. For example, they attempt to show how the sexual victimization of females is a function of male socialization because so many young males learn to be aggressive and exploitive of women. Exploited at home, female victims try to cope by running away and by engaging in premarital sex and substance abuse. The double standard means that female adolescents still have a much narrower range of acceptable behavior than male adolescents. Any sign of misbehavior is viewed as a substantial challenge to authority that requires immediate control. Feminist scholars view the female criminal as a victim of gender inequality.

developmental theory
The view that social interactions developed over the life course shape behavior. Some interactions, such as involvement with deviant peers, encourage law violations, whereas others, such as marriage and military service, may help people desist from crime.

Developmental Theory: Things Change

According to **developmental theory,** even as toddlers, people begin relationships and behaviors that will determine their adult life course.[85] These transitions are expected to take place in order — beginning with finishing school, entering the workforce, getting married, and having children. Some individuals, however, are incapable of maturing in a reasonable and timely fashion because of family, environmental, or personal problems. In some cases, transitions can occur too early — for example, when adolescents engage in precocious sex. In other cases, transitions may occur too late, such as when a student fails to graduate on time because of bad grades. Sometimes disruption of one trajectory can harm another. For example, teenage childbirth will most likely disrupt educational and career development. Because developmental theories focus on the associations between life events and deviant behaviors, they are sometimes referred to as *life-course theories.*

Disruptions in life's major transitions can be destructive and ultimately can promote criminality. Those who are already at risk because of socioeconomic problems or family dysfunction are the most susceptible to these awkward transitions. The cumulative impact of these disruptions sustains criminality from childhood into adulthood.

Because a transition from one stage of life to another can be a bumpy ride, the propensity to commit crimes is neither stable nor constant; it is a developmental process. A positive life experience may help some criminals desist from crime for a while, whereas a negative one may cause them to resume their activities. Criminal careers are said to be developmental because people are influenced by the behavior of those around them and in turn influence others' behavior. For example, a youth's antisocial behavior may turn his more conventional friends against him; their rejection solidifies and escalates his antisocial behavior.

Developmental theory also recognizes that as people mature the factors that influence their behavior change.[86] At first, family relations may be most influential; in later adolescence, school and peer relations predominate; in adulthood, vocational achievement and marital relations may be the most critical influences. For example, some antisocial children who are in trouble throughout their adolescence may manage to find stable work and maintain intact marriages as adults; these life events help them desist from crime. In contrast, the less fortunate adolescents who develop arrest records and get involved with the wrong crowd may find themselves limited to menial jobs and at risk for criminal careers.

A Final Word There are probably so many views of crime causation because there are so many types of crimes. It is possible that all explanations are partially correct: Some people commit crime because they are poorly socialized; some succumb to the obstacles placed in their path by lower-class life; others have psychological or biological problems; some are victims of class conflict. The various forms of crime theory are summarized in Table 2.2.

SUMMARY

We get our information on crime from a number of sources. One of the most important is the Uniform Crime Report compiled by the FBI. This national survey of serious criminal acts reported to local police departments indicates that more than 12 million index (Part I) crimes (murder, rape, burglary, robbery, assault, larceny/theft, and motor vehicle theft) occurred in 1998. Questioning the validity of the UCR, critics point out that many people fail to report crime to police because of fear, apathy, or lack of respect for law enforcement. Many crime victims also do not report criminal incidents to the police because they believe that nothing can be done or that they should not get involved. However, evidence indicates that the crimes not reported to the police are less serious than reported crimes.

Questions have also been raised about the accuracy of police records and reporting practices. To remedy this situation, the federal government sponsors a massive victim survey designed to uncover the true amount of annual crime. The National Crime Victimization Survey (NCVS) reveals that more than 30 million serious personal crimes are committed every year and that the great majority are not reported to police. A third form of information is self-report surveys, which ask offenders themselves to tell about their criminal behaviors.

The various sources of criminal statistics tell us much about the nature and patterns of crime. Rate increases have been attributed to the influence of drugs, the economy, the age structure, social decay, and other factors. Except for a recent upsurge in teen drug use, all three data sources indicate that crime rates have declined in the 1990s.

The crime patterns found in all three data sources may be more similar than some critics believe. Crime occurs more often in large cities during the summer and at night. Some geographic areas (the South and the West) have higher crime rates than others (the Midwest and New England). Arrest and victim data indicate that males, minorities, the poor, and the young have relatively high rates of criminality. Victims of crime have many of the same demographic characteristics as criminals. They tend to be poor, young, male, and members of a minority group. However, households that experience crime tend to have a higher relative income than those that avoid victimization.

Unfortunately, the police cannot do much about crime; about 20 percent of all reported crimes are solved by police. However, a positive relationship exists between crime seriousness and the probability of a successful clearance; that is, murders and rapes are much more often solved than car thefts or larcenies.

Diverse schools of criminological theory approach the understanding of the cause of crime and its consequences. Some focus on the individual, whereas others view social factors as the most important element in producing crime.

Table 2.2
Concepts and Theories of Criminology: A Review

Theory	Major Premise
Choice Theory	People commit crime when they perceive that the benefits of law violation outweigh the threat and pain of punishment.
Biosocial Theory	
Biochemical	Crime, especially violence, is a function of diet, vitamin intake, hormonal imbalance, or food allergies.
Neurological	Criminals and delinquents often suffer brain impairment. Attention deficit disorder and minimum brain dysfunction are related to antisocial behavior.
Genetic	Delinquent traits and predispositions are inherited. The criminality of parents can predict the delinquency of children.
Psychological Theory	
Psychoanalytic	The development of personality early in childhood influences behavior for the rest of a person's life. Criminals have weak egos and damaged personalities.
Social learning	People commit crime when they model their behavior after others whom they see being rewarded for the same acts. Behavior is enforced by rewards and extinguished by punishment.
Social Structure Theory	
Social disorganization	The conflicts and problems of urban social life and communities control the crime rate. Crime is a product of transitional neighborhoods that manifest social disorganization and value conflict.
Strain	People who adopt the goals of society but lack the means to attain them seek alternatives, such as crime.
Social Process Theory	
Learning theory	People learn to commit crime from exposure to antisocial behaviors. Criminal behavior depends on the person's experiences with rewards for conventional behaviors and punishments for deviant ones. Being rewarded for deviance leads to crime.
Social control theory	A person's bond to society prevents him or her from violating social rules. If the bond weakens, the person is free to commit crime.
Self-control theory	Crime and criminality are separate concepts. People choose to commit crime when they lack self-control. People lacking self-control will seize criminal opportunities.
Conflict Theory	
Conflict theory	People commit crime when the law, controlled by the rich and powerful, defines their behavior as illegal. The immoral actions of the powerful go unpunished.
Radical feminist theory	The capital system creates patriarchy, which oppresses women. Male dominance explains gender bias, violence against women, and repression.
Developmental Theory	
Developmental theory	Early in life people begin relationships that determine their behavior through their life course. Life transitions control the probability of offending.

KEY TERMS

consensus view
criminal law
social control
critical view of crime
crime
National Crime Victimization Survey (NCVS)
official crime statistics
Uniform Crime Report (UCR)
life history
index (Part I) crimes
nonindex (Part II) crimes
self-report survey
chronic offender
choice theory
biological theory
psychoanalytic view
social learning
social structure theory
social process theory
socialization
conflict theory
developmental theory

INFOTRAC COLLEGE EDITION EXERCISES

Do early childhood factors predetermine one's chances of becoming a victim? Some researchers believe that behavior problems appear to play an important role in determining victimization within the peer group later in life. For more on this provocative concept, read the following article, using *InfoTrac College Edition:*

David Schwartz, Steven McFayden-Ketchum, Kenneth A. Dodge, Gregory S. Pettit, and John E. Bates, "Early Behavior Problems as a Predictor of Later Peer Group Victimization: Moderators and Mediators in the Pathways of Social Risk," *Journal of Abnormal Child Psychology* 27 (1999): 191.

Victims need a great deal of support from family and friends after their traumatic experiences. Without support they may begin to suffer depression and low self-esteem. To find out more about this topic, read

Adriaan Denkers, "Factors Affecting Support after Criminal Victimization: Needed and Received Support from the Partner, the Social Network, and Distant Support Providers," *Journal of Social Psychology* 139 (1999): 191.

Some people may be at greater risk for victimization than others. To find out about the concept of *victimization risk,* search *InfoTrac College Edition.*

QUESTIONS

1. Why are crime rates higher in the summer than during other seasons?
2. What factors account for crime rate trends?
3. What factors are present in poverty-stricken urban areas that produce high crime rates?
4. It seems logical that biological and psychological factors might explain why some people commit crime. How would a biologist or a psychologist explain the fact that crime rates are higher in the West than in the Midwest? That there is more crime in the summer than in the winter?
5. If crime is a routine activity, what steps should you take to avoid becoming a crime victim?

NOTES

1. Jayson Blair, "Youth Is Killed on Subway for a Gold-Plated Necklace," *New York Times,* 10 October 1999, B2.

2. Howard Becker, *Outsiders,* 2d ed. (New York: Macmillan, 1972).

3. For a general discussion of Marxist thought on the criminal law, see Michael Lynch and W. Byron Groves, *A Primer in Radical Criminology,* 2d ed. (New York: Harrow and Heston, 1990), 6–26.

4. See, for example, Lloyd Bachman, Patrick O'Malley, and Jerald Bachman, *Monitoring the Future,* 1998 (Ann Arbor: University of Michigan, Institute for Social Research, 1999).

5. Callie Marie Rennison, *Criminal Victimization 1998 Changes 1997–98 with Trends 1993–98* (Washington, D.C.: Bureau of Justice Statistics, 1999); herein cited as NCVS 1998.

6. The arrest data used in this chapter, updated with preliminary 1999 data, come from FBI, *Crime in the United States, 1998* (Washington, D.C.: Government Printing Office, 1999); herein cited as UCR 1999.

7. Claire Sterck-Elifson, "Just for Fun? Cocaine Use among Middle-Class Women," *Journal of Drug Issues* 26 (1996): 63–76.

8. Ibid., 63.

9. Carl Klockars, *The Professional Fence* (New York: Free Press, 1976); Darrell Steffensmeier, *The Fence: In the Shadow of Two Worlds* (Totowa, N.J.: Rowman and Littlefield, 1986).

10. Federal Bureau of Investigation, *Crime in the United States, 1998* (Washington, D.C.: Government Printing Office, 1999). Herein cited in notes as FBI, Uniform Crime Report, and referred to in text as Uniform Crime Report, or UCR.

11. Duncan Chappell, Gilbert Geis, Stephen Schafer, and Larry Siegel, "Forcible Rape: A Comparative Study of Offenses Known to the Police in Boston and Los Angeles," in *Studies in the Sociology of Sex,* ed. James Henslin (New York: Appleton-Century-Crofts, 1971), 169–93.

12. Lawrence Sherman and Barry Glick, "The Quality of Arrest Statistics," *Police Foundation Reports* 2 (1984): 1–8.

13. David Seidman and Michael Couzens, "Getting the Crime Rate Down: Political Pressure and Crime Reporting," *Law and Society Review* 8 (1974): 457.

14. Callie Marie Rennison, *Criminal Victimization 1998 Changes 1997–98 with Trends 1993–98* (Washington, D.C.: Bureau of Justice Statistics, 1999).

15. L. Edward Wells and Joseph Rankin, "Juvenile Victimization: Convergent Validation of Alternative Measurements," *Journal of Research in Crime and Delinquency* 32 (1995): 287–307.

16. A pioneering effort in self-report research is A. L. Porterfield, *Youth in Trouble* (Fort Worth, Tex.: Leo Potishman Foundation, 1946); for a review, see Robert Hardt and George Bodine, *Development of Self-Report Instruments in Delinquency Research: A Conference Report* (Syracuse, N.Y.: Syracuse University Youth Development Center, 1965). See also Fred Murphy, Mary Shirley, and Helen Witner, "The Incidence of Hidden Delinquency," *American Journal of Orthopsychology* 16 (1946): 686–96.

17. Franklyn Dunford and Delbert Elliott, "Identifying Career Criminals Using Self-Reported Data," *Journal of Research in Crime and Delinquency* 21 (1983): 57–86.

18. For example, the following studies have noted the great discrepancy between official statistics and self-report studies: Martin Gold, "Undetected Delinquent Behavior," *Journal of Research in Crime and Delinquency* 3 (1966): 27–46; James Short and F. Ivan Nye, "Extent of Undetected Delinquency, Tentative Conclusions," *Journal of Criminal Law, Criminology and Police Science* 49 (1958): 296–302; Michael Hindelang, "Causes of Delinquency: A Partial Replication and Extension," *Social Problems* 20 (1973): 471–87.

19. D. Wayne Osgood, Lloyd Johnston, Patrick O'Malley, and Jerald Bachman, "The Generality of Deviance in Late Adolescence and Early Adulthood," *American Sociological Review* 53 (1988): 81–93.

20. Lloyd Johnston, Patrick O'Malley, and Jerald Bachman, *Monitoring the Future, 1990* (Ann Arbor: University of Michigan, Institute for Social Research, 1991); Timothy Flanagan and Kathleen Maguire, *Sourcebook of Criminal Justice Statistics, 1989* (Washington, D.C.: Government Printing Office, 1990), 290–91.

21. Michael Hindelang, Travis Hirschi, and Joseph Weis, *Measuring Delinquency* (Beverly Hills: Sage, 1981).

22. Leonore Simon, "Validity and Reliability of Violent Juveniles: A Comparison of Juvenile Self-Reports with Adult Self-Reports" (Paper presented at the meeting of the American Society of Criminology, Boston, November 1995), 26.

23. Stephen Cernkovich, Peggy Giordano, and Meredith Pugh, "Chronic Offenders: The Missing Cases in Self-Report Delinquency," *Criminology* 76 (1985): 705–32.

24. Eric Wish, Thomas Gray, and Eliot Levine, *Recent Drug Use in Female Juvenile Detainees: Estimates from Interviews, Urinalysis and Hair Analysis* (College Park, Md.: Center for Substance Abuse Research, 1996); Thomas Gray and Eric Wish, *Maryland Youth at Risk: A Study of Drug Use in Juvenile Detainees* (College Park, Md.: Center for Substance Abuse Research, 1993).

25. Alfred Blumstein, Jacqueline Cohen, and Richard Rosenfeld, "Trend and Deviation in Crime Rates: A Comparison of UCR and NCVS Data for Burglary and Robbery," *Criminology* 29 (1991): 237–48. See also Hindelang, Hirschi, and Weis, *Measuring Delinquency.*

26. Clarence Schrag, *Crime and Justice: American Style* (Washington, D.C.: Government Printing Office, 1971), 17.

27. FBI, UCR 1999, "Preliminary Report," press release, 21 November 1999.

28. Thomas Bernard, "Juvenile Crime and the Transformation of Juvenile Justice: Is There a Juvenile Crime Wave?" *Justice Quarterly* 16 (1999): 336–56.

29. James A. Fox, *Trends in Juvenile Violence: A Report to the United States Attorney General on Current and Future Rates of Juvenile Offending* (Boston: Northeastern University, 1996).

30. Steven Levitt, "The Limited Role of Changing Age Structure in Explaining Aggregate Crime Rates," *Criminology* 37 (1999): 581–99.

31. Darrell Steffensmeier and Miles Harer, "Making Sense of Recent U.S. Crime Trend Composition Effects and Other Explanations," *Journal of Research in Crime and Delinquency* 36 (1999): 235–74.

32. Ibid., 265.

33. Ralph Weisheit and L. Edward Wells, "The Future of Crime in Rural America," *Journal of Criminal Justice* 22 (1999): 1–22.

34. Daniel Mears, Matthew Ploeger, and Mark Warr, "Explaining the Gender Gap in Delinquency: Peer Influence and Moral Evaluations of Behavior," *Journal of Research in Crime and Delinquency* 35 (1998): 251–66.

35. Freda Adler, *Sisters in Crime* (New York: McGraw-Hill, 1975); Rita James Simon, *The Contemporary Woman and Crime* (Washington, D.C.: Government Printing Office, 1975).

36. Finn-Aage Esbensen and Elizabeth Piper Deschenes, "A Multisite Examination of Youth Gang Membership: Does Gender Matter?" *Criminology* 36 (1998): 799–828.

37. Daniel Georges-Abeyie, "Race, Ethnicity, and the Spatial Dynamic: Toward a Realistic Study of Black Crime, Crime Victimization, and the Criminal Justice Processing of Blacks," *Social Justice* 16 (1989): 35–54.

38. Ibid.

39. David Jacobs and Katherine Woods, "Interracial Conflict and Interracial Homicide: Do Political and Economic Rivalries Explain White Killings of Blacks and Black Killings of Whites?" *American Journal of Sociology* 105 (1999): 157–90.

40. Eric Lotke, "Hobbling a Generation: Young African-American Men in Washington, D.C.'s Criminal Justice System — Five Years Later," *Crime and Delinquency* 44 (1998): 355–66.

41. Alexander Weiss and Steven Chermak, "The News Value of African-American Victims: An Examination of the Media's Presentation of Homicide," *Journal of Crime and Justice* 21 (1998): 71–84.

42. Emilie Andersen Allan and Darrell Steffensmeier, "Youth, Underemployment and Property Crime: Differential Effects of Job Availability and Job Quality on Juvenile and Young Adult Arrest Rates," *American Sociological Review* 54 (1989): 107–23.

43. For a general view, see James Byrne and Robert Sampson, *The Social Ecology of Crime* (New York: Springer-Verlag, 1985).

44. Douglas Smith and G. Roger Jarjoura, "Social Structure and Criminal Victimization," *Journal of Research in Crime and Delinquency* 25 (1988): 27–52; Janet Heitgerd and Robert Bursik, Jr., "Extracommunity Dynamics and the Ecology of Delinquency," *American Journal of Sociology* 92 (1987): 775–87; Ora Simcha-Fagan and Joseph Schwartz, "Neighborhood and Delinquency: An Assessment of Contextual Effects," *Criminology* 24 (1986): 667–703.

45. Rodney Stark, "Deviant Places: A Theory of the Ecology of Crime," *Criminology* 25 (1987): 893–910.

46. Judith Blau and Peter Blau, "The Cost of Inequality: Metropolitan Structure and Violent Crime," *American Sociological Review* 47 (1982): 114–29.

47. For a comprehensive review of crime and the elderly, see Kyle Kercher, "Causes and Correlates of Crime Committed by the Elderly," in *Critical Issues in Aging Policy,* ed. E. Borgatta and R. Montgomery (Beverly Hills: Sage, 1987), 254–306; Darrell Steffensmeier, "The Invention of the 'New' Senior Citizen Criminal," *Research on Aging* 9 (1987): 281–311.

48. Herman Schwendinger and Julia Schwendinger, "The Paradigmatic Crisis in Delinquency Theory," *Crime and Social Justice* 18 (1982): 70–78.

49. Michael Gottfredson and Travis Hirschi, "The True Value of Lambda Would Appear to Be Zero: An Essay on Career Criminals, Criminal Careers, Selective Incapacitation, Cohort Studies and Related Topics," *Criminology* 24 (1986): 213–34; further support for their position can be found in Lawrence Cohen and Kenneth Land, "Age Structure and Crime," *American Sociological Review* 52 (1987): 170–83.

50. Alfred Blumstein, Jacqueline Cohen, and David Farrington, "Criminal Career Re-

search: Its Value for Criminology," *Criminology* 26 (1988): 1–35.

51. Arnold Barnett, Alfred Blumstein, and David Farrington, "Probabilistic Models of Youthful Criminal Careers," *Criminology* 25 (1987): 83–107; David Greenberg, "Age, Crime, and Social Explanation," *American Journal of Sociology* 91 (1985): 1–21.

52. Centers for Disease Control, "Homicide among Young Black Males — United States, 1978–1987," *Morbidity and Mortality Weekly Report* 39 (1990): 869–73.

53. Janet Lauritsen and Kenna Davis Quinet, "Repeat Victimizations among Adolescents and Young Adults," *Journal of Quantitative Criminology* 11 (1995): 143–63.

54. Denise Osborn, Dan Ellingworth, Tim Hope, and Alan Trickett, "Are Repeatedly Victimized Households Different?" *Journal of Quantitative Criminology* 12 (1996): 223–45.

55. Terry Buss and Rashid Abdu, "Repeat Victims of Violence in an Urban Trauma Center," *Violence and Victims* 10 (1995): 183–87.

56. Graham Farrell, "Predicting and Preventing Revictimization," in *Crime and Justice: An Annual Review of Research,* Vol. 20, ed. Michael Tonry and David Farrington (Chicago: University of Chicago Press, 1995), 61–126.

57. Lawrence Cohen and Richard Machalek, "A General Theory of Expropriative Crime: An Evolutionary Ecological Approach," *American Journal of Sociology* 94 (1988): 465–501.

58. Leonard Hippchen, "Some Possible Biochemical Aspects of Criminal Behavior," *Journal of Behavioral Ecology* 2 (1981): 1–6.

59. Alan Booth and D. Wayne Osgood, "The Influence of Testosterone on Deviance in Adulthood: Assessing and Explaining the Relationship," *Criminology* 31 (1993): 93–118.

60. D. Williams, "Neural Factors Related to Habitual Aggression — Consideration of Differences Between Habitual Aggressives and Others Who Have Committed Crimes of Violence," *Brain* 92 (1969): 503–20.

61. R. R. Monroe, *Brain Dysfunction in Aggressive Criminals* (Lexington, Mass.: Heath, 1978); L. T. Yeudall, *Childhood Experiences as Causes of Criminal Behavior,* Senate of Canada, issue no. 1, Thirteenth Parliament, Ottawa, Canada, 1977.

62. Terrie Moffitt and Phil Silva, "Self-Reported Delinquency, Neuropsychological Deficit, and History of Attention Deficit Disorder," *Journal of Abnormal Child Psychology* 16 (1988): 553–69.

63. B. Hutchings and S. A. Mednick, "Criminality in Adoptees and Their Adoptive and Biological Parents: A Pilot Study," in *Biosocial Bases of Criminal Behavior,* ed. S. A. Mednick and Karl O. Christiansen (New York: Gardner Press, 1977).

64. David Rowe, *The Limits of Family Influence: Genes, Experiences and Behavior* (New York: Guilford Press, 1995), 64.

65. August, Aichorn, *Wayward Youth* (New York: Viking Press, 1965).

66. This discussion is based on three works by Albert Bandura: *Aggression: A Social Learning Analysis* (Englewood Cliffs, N.J.: Prentice-Hall, 1973); *Social Learning Theory* (Englewood Cliffs, N.J.: Prentice-Hall, 1977); and "The Social Learning Perspective: Mechanisms of Aggression," in *The Psychology of Crime and Criminal Justice,* ed. H. Toch (New York: Holt, Rinehart and Winston, 1979), 198–326.

67. U.S. Department of Health and Human Services, *Television and Behavior* (Washington, D.C.: Government Printing Office, 1982).

68. Richard Kania, "T.V. Crime and Real Crime: Questioning the Link" (Paper presented at the annual meeting of the American Society of Criminology, Chicago, November 1988).

69. David Lykken, "Psychopathy, Sociopathy, and Crime," *Society* 34 (1996): 30–38.

70. Steven Smith and Joseph Newman, "Alcohol and Drug Abuse–Dependence Disorders in Psychopathic and Nonpsychopathic Criminal Offenders," *Journal of Abnormal Psychology* 99 (1990): 430–39.

71. Ibid.

72. Jack Levin and James Alan Fox, *Mass Murder* (New York: Plenum, 1985).

73. Spencer Rathus and Jeffrey Nevid, *Abnormal Psychology* (Englewood Cliffs, N.J.: Prentice-Hall, 1991), 310–16.

74. Ibid.

75. Samuel Yochelson and Stanton Samenow, *The Criminal Personality* (New York: Jason Aronson, 1977).

76. Oscar Lewis, "The Culture of Poverty," *Scientific American* 215 (1966): 19–25.

77. William Julius Wilson, *The Truly Disadvantaged* (Chicago: University of Chicago Press, 1987).

78. Charles Tittle, Wayne Villemez, and Douglas Smith, "The Myth of Social Class and Criminality: An Empirical Assessment of the Evidence," *American Sociological Review* 43 (1978): 643–56.

79. Rolf Loeber and Magda Stouthamer-Loeber, "Family Factors as Correlates and Predictors of Juvenile Conduct Problems and Delinquency," in *Crime and Justice,* vol. 7, eds. Michael Tonry and Norval Morris (Chicago: University of Chicago Press, 1986), 29–151.

80. Ibid.

81. Eugene Maguin and Rolf Loeber, "Academic Performance and Delinquency," in *Crime and Justice: An Annual Review of Research,* vol. 20, eds. Michael Tonry and David Farrington (Chicago: University of Chicago Press, 1996), 145–264.

82. W. Byron Groves and Robert Sampson, "Critical Theory and Criminology," *Social Problems* 33 (1986): 58–80.

83. Kathleen Daly and Meda Chesney-Lind, "Feminism and Criminology," *Justice Quarterly* 5 (1988): 438–97.

84. For a general review of this issue, see Sally Simpson, "Feminist Theory, Crime and Justice," *Criminology* 27 (1989): 605–32; Daly and Chesney-Lind, "Feminism and Criminology"; James Messerschmidt, *Capitalism, Patriarchy and Crime* (Totowa, N.J.: Rowman and Littlefield, 1986).

85. Marvin Krohn, Alan Lizotte, and Cynthia Perez, "The Interrelationship between Substance Use and Precocious Transitions to Adult Sexuality," *Journal of Health and Social Behavior* 38 (1997): 88.

86. G. R. Patterson, Barbara DeBaryshe, and Elizabeth Ramsey, "A Developmental Perspective on Antisocial Behavior," *American Psychologist* 44 (1989): 329–35.

chapter 3

Criminal Law: Substance and Procedure

In August 1999 Raffi Kodikian claimed he and his friend, David Coughlin, had been lost for days and were dying of thirst when his friend asked him to end his misery in a remote canyon in Carlsbad Caverns National Park, New Mexico. Kodikian, age 25, told park rangers that he and Coughlin, age 26, had gotten lost in the park and had run out of water. Desperate and dehydrated, Kodikian said he killed his long-time friend by stabbing him twice in the chest after Coughlin begged for an end to his pain from lack of water.

Coughlin and Kodikian had been best of friends since 1994. Both were college graduates. Their latest trip had taken them from Boston through Pennsylvania, where Kodikian's parents lived, through Virginia to Nashville, New Orleans, and Austin, Texas, before arriving in Carlsbad, New Mexico. Their destination was Santa Barbara, California, where Coughlin was to attend graduate school.

According to park rangers, Kodikian was found dehydrated and resting under a tarp near his friend's shallow grave. The campers were about 250 feet from the trail out of the canyon and their parked car a mile and half away. Kodikian had written in a journal of "killing my best friend," along with farewell notes to family and friends. Subsequent autopsy results on the body of Coughlin bolstered Kodikian's claims that his best friend was dehydrated and believed he was going to die. But the reports also indicated that Coughlin may have been only moderately dehydrated, that his blood levels were not deficient to the point of death, and that his bladder contained adequate fluid. According to the authorities, Coughlin was nowhere near death when he was killed.

Did Kodikian commit a crime? On May 7, 2000, Kodikian plead guilty to a charge of manslaughter and received a sentence of fifteen years in prison, all but two years being suspended, followed by five years of probation.

Kodikian's behavior shares some important similarities with an ordeal over a century ago. In 1884 two British sailors, desperate after being shipwrecked for days, made the decision to kill and eat a suffering cabin boy. Four days later, they were rescued by a passing ship and returned to England. English authorities, wanting to end the practice of shipwreck cannibalism, tried and convicted the two men for murder. Clemency was considered and a reluctant Queen Victoria commuted the death sentences to six months.[1] In both cases, the killers believed the person they killed would die soon anyway. On the other hand, Coughlin requested Kodikian to kill him, whereas the cabin boy sought survival. ■

Raffi Kodikian, shown here being escorted by local sheriffs in Carlsbad, New Mexico. Is Raffi responsible for the death of his companion, or are his actions legally excusable? Under what circumstances might it be possible legally to take a life?

Considering the climate of our times, it is not surprising that medical and legal experts question the legal recognition of the sanctity of life and the role of the criminal law in our society. In the best interests of society, can there ever be a good reason to take a life? Even the high-profile crusade for euthanasia of Dr. Jack Kevorkian forced prosecutors to try him and eventually convict him of murder when he actually administered a fatal dose of drugs to a dying patient.

Legal scholars believe that the justice system has found a way to lessen criminal responsibility by taking a person's motive into account. Kodikian claims he killed his close friend in what was a mercy killing in the New Mexico desert.[2] Although he could be convicted as a murderer just as the English sailors were, he would not be punished like one. Oftentimes, it is not the quality of the criminal act that is most important but the way society defines and reacts to it.

This chapter focuses on the basic principles of the substantive criminal law, which regulates conduct in our society, such as the nature of Kodikian's behavior. In addition, the chapter also discusses constitutional criminal procedure, showing how the rules of procedure, laid out in the U.S. Constitution and interpreted over time by the Supreme Court, control the operations of the justice system.

substantive criminal law
A body of specific rules that declare what conduct is criminal and prescribe the punishment to be imposed for such conduct.

criminal procedure
The rules and laws that define the operation of the criminal proceedings. Procedural law describes the methods that must be followed in obtaining warrants, investigating offenses, effecting lawful arrests, conducting trials, introducing evidence, sentencing convicted offenders, and reviewing cases by appellate courts.

civil law
All law that is not criminal, including torts (personal wrongs), contract, property, maritime, and commercial law.

The **substantive criminal law** defines crime and punishment in U.S. society. Each state government and the federal government has its own criminal code, developed over many generations and incorporating moral beliefs, social values, and political, economic, and other societal concerns. The criminal law is a living document, constantly evolving to keep pace with society and its needs. The rules designed to implement the substantive law are known as *procedural law.* It is concerned with the criminal process — the legal steps through which an offender passes — commencing with the initial criminal investigation and concluding with release of the offender. Some elements of the law of **criminal procedure** are the rules of evidence, the law of arrest, the law of search and seizure, questions of appeal, and the right to counsel. Many of the rights that have been extended to offenders over the past two decades lie within procedural law.

A working knowledge of the law is critical for the criminal justice practitioner. In our modern society, the rule of law governs almost all phases of human enterprise, including commerce, family life, property transfer, and the regulation of interpersonal conflict. It contains elements that control personal relationships between individuals and public relationships between individuals and the government. The former is known as **civil law,** while the latter is called criminal law; both concepts are distinguished later in this chapter. Because the law defines crime, punishment, and procedure, which are the basic concerns of the criminal justice system, it is essential for students to know something of the nature, purpose, and content of the substantive and procedural criminal law.

THE HISTORICAL DEVELOPMENT OF THE CRIMINAL LAW

The roots of the criminal codes used in the United States can be traced back to such early legal charters as the Babylonian Code of Hammurabi (2000 B.C.), the Mosaic Code of the Israelites (1200 B.C.), and the Roman Twelve Tables. During the sixth century, under the leadership of Byzantine Emperor Justinian, the first great codification of law in the Western world was prepared. Justinian's *Corpus Juris Civilis,* or body of civil law, summarized the system of Roman law that had developed over a thousand years. Rules and regulations to ensure the safety of the state and the individual were organized into a code and served as the basis for future civil and criminal legal classifications. Centuries later, French Emperor Napoleon I created the French civil code, using Justinian's code as a model. France and the other countries that have modeled their legal systems on French and Roman law have what are known as *civil law systems.* Thus, the concept of law and crime has evolved over thousands of years.[3]

Before the Norman Conquest in 1066, the legal system among the early Anglo-Saxons was decentralized. The law often varied from county to county, and very little was written, except for laws covering crimes. Before A.D. 1000, crimes were viewed as personal wrongs, and compensation was often paid to the victim. Major violations of custom and law included violent acts, theft, and disloyalty to the lord. For certain actions, such as treason, the penalty was often death. For other crimes, such as theft, compensation could be paid to the victim. Thus, to some degree, the early criminal law sought to produce an equitable solution to both private and public disputes.[4]

The Common Law

A more immediate source for much U.S. law is the English system of jurisprudence that developed after the Norman Conquest. Prior to the ratification of the U.S. Constitution in 1788 and the development of the first state legal codes, formal law in the original colonies was adopted from existing English law, which is known today as **common law.** Common law first came into being during the reign of King Henry II (1154–1189), when royal judges were appointed to travel to specific jurisdictions to hold court and represent the Crown. Known as circuit judges, they followed a specific route (circuit) and heard cases that had been under the jurisdiction of local courts.[5] The royal judges began to replace local custom with a national law that was followed in courts throughout the country; thus, the law was "common" to the entire nation. The common law developed when English judges actually created many crimes by ruling that certain actions were subject to state control and sanction. The most serious offenses — such as murder, rape, treason, arson, and burglary, which had been viewed largely as personal wrongs (torts for which the victim received monetary compensation from the offender) — were redefined by the judges as offenses against the state, or crimes. Thus, common-law crimes are actions defined by judges as crimes (judge-made crimes).

common law
Early English law, developed by judges, that incorporated Anglo-Saxon tribal custom, feudal rules and practices, and the everyday rules of behavior of local villages. Common law became the standardized law of the land in England and eventually formed the basis of the criminal law in the United States.

English common law evolved constantly to fit specific incidents that the judges encountered. In fact, legal scholars have identified specific cases in which judges created new crimes, some of which exist today. For example, in the ***Carriers* case** (1473), an English court ruled that a merchant who had been hired to transport merchandise was guilty of larceny (theft) if he kept the goods for his own purposes.[6] Before the *Carriers* case, the common law had not recognized a crime when people kept something that was voluntarily placed in their possession, even if the rightful owner had only given them temporary custody of the merchandise. Breaking with legal tradition, the court recognized that the com-

***Carriers* case**
A fifteenth-century case that defined the law of theft and reformulated the concept of taking the possessions of another.

"Wager of Battel," from *Le Coutume de Normandie,* an illuminated manuscript (1450–1470). Before the trial by jury, legal disputes could be settled by a duel in which the survivor was considered the "innocent" party. It was believed that God intervened on behalf of the victor. The wager of battel was introduced in England by the Normans and was used in both civil and criminal disputes.

For an overview of criminal law and links to an extensive number of documents relating to criminal justice, go to the Web site at Cornell University's Legal Information Institute at www.law.cornell.edu/topics/criminal.html

mercial system could not be maintained unless the laws of theft were changed. Thus, larcenies defined by separate and unique criminal laws — such as embezzlement, extortion, and false pretenses — came into existence.

Over time, such common-law decisions made by English judges produced a body of rules and legal principles about crime and punishment that formed the basis of our early American legal system.

Prior to the American Revolution, this common law was the law of the land in the colonies. The original colonists abided by the various common-law rulings and adopted them to fit their needs, making extensive changes in them when necessary. After the War of Independence, most state legislatures incorporated the common law into standardized legal codes. Over the years, some of the original common-law crimes have changed considerably due to revisions. For example, the common-law crime of rape originally applied only to female victims. This has been replaced in a number of jurisdictions by general sexual assault statutes that condemn sexual attacks against any person, male or female. Similarly, statutes prohibiting such offenses as the sale and possession of narcotics or the pirating of videotapes have been passed to control human behavior unknown at the time the common law was formulated. Today, criminal behavior is defined primarily by statute. With few exceptions, crimes are removed, added, or modified by the legislature of a particular jurisdiction.

law of precedent
The legal principle by which the decision or holding in an earlier case becomes the standard with which subsequent similar cases are judged.

stare decisis
To stand by decided cases. The legal principle by which the decision or holding in an earlier case becomes the standard by which subsequent similar cases are judged.

The Principle of Stare Decisis

One of the principal components of the common law was its recognition of the **law of precedent.** Once a decision had been made by a court, that judicial decision was generally binding on other courts in subsequent cases. This principle is based on judge-made law, or case law created by judicial decisions. For example, if a homeowner who killed an unarmed intruder was found not guilty of murder on the ground that he had a right to defend his property, that rule would be applied in subsequent cases involving the same set of facts. In other words, a decision on the issue of self-defense in that case would be followed in that jurisdiction by the same court or a lesser court in future cases presenting the same legal problem. Since the common law represented decisions handed down by judges, as distinguished from law that is determined by statutes, it was essential that the rule of precedent be followed. This legal principle, known as **stare decisis,** originated in England and is still used as the basis for deciding future cases.[7] Stare decisis is firmly rooted in the U.S. system of jurisprudence and serves to furnish the courts with a clear guide for the adjudication of similar issues. The courts are generally bound by the principle of stare decisis to follow criminal law as it has been judicially determined in prior cases. This rule helps promote fairness and reliability in judicial decision making. The Latin term *stare decisis* means "let the decision stand, or precedent."

tort
The law of personal wrongs and damage. Tort-type actions include negligence, libel, slander, assault, and trespass.

intent
An action that on its face indicates a criminal purpose — for example, breaking into a locked building or trespassing on someone's property; a guilty mind.

Criminal Law and Civil Law

In modern U.S. society, law can be divided into two broad categories: criminal law and civil law. All law other than criminal law is known as civil law; it includes tort law (personal wrongs and damages), property law (the law governing the transfer and ownership of property), and contract law (the law of personal agreements).

The differences between criminal law and civil law are significant because, in the U.S. legal system, criminal proceedings are completely separate from civil actions.

The major objective of the criminal law is to protect the public against harm by preventing criminal offenses. The primary concern of the civil law — in the area of private wrongs, or **torts,** for example — is that the injured party be compensated for any harm done. The aggrieved person usually initiates proceedings to recover monetary damages. In contrast, when is a crime is committed, the state initiates the legal process and imposes a punishment in the form of a criminal sanction. Furthermore, in criminal law, the emphasis is on the **intent** of the individual committing the crime; a civil proceeding gives primary attention to affixing the blame each party deserves for producing the damage or conflict.

Despite these major differences, criminal and civil law share certain features. Both seek to control people's behavior by preventing them from acting in an undesirable manner, and both impose sanctions on those who commit violations of the law. The payment of damages to the victim in a tort case, for example, serves some of the same purposes as the payment of a fine in a criminal case. The criminal law sentences offenders to prison, whereas the civil law imposes confinement on such individuals as the mentally ill, alcoholic, and mentally defective. In addition, many actions, such as assault and battery, various forms of larceny, and negligence, are the basis for criminal as well as civil actions.

Table 3.1 summarizes the major similarities and differences between criminal law and tort law. The widely publicized case of O. J. Simpson provides a good example, as the same case went through both criminal and civil proceedings. In the so-called Trial of the Century — Part I, the famous athlete was tried by the state of California and acquitted of the murder of his ex-wife, Nicole, and her friend, Ron Goldman, in a criminal prosecution. As a defendant, Simpson was required to be in court but did not have to testify during the trial. The standard of proof "beyond a reasonable doubt" was used to assess the evidence, and the verdict had to be unanimous. A conviction would have brought a sentence of life in prison.

In the Trial of the Century — Part II, the Estate of Nicole Simpson and the family of Ron Goldman sued O. J. Simpson for the wrongful deaths of his ex-wife and her friend in a civil trial. This was a lawsuit brought by the family of the deceased against the person believed to have caused the death. Simpson was not required to be in court, but when called by either side he had to provide testimony. No television cameras were allowed in the courtroom, whereas the criminal trial was televised on a court TV network. The burden of proof in the civil case was "preponderance of the evidence," or which side had the most convincing case before the jury. In addition, only nine of the twelve jurors had to agree on a general verdict, and any judgment involved money and not imprisonment.

SOURCES OF THE CRIMINAL LAW

The three major sources of the criminal law are (1) common law, statutes, and case decisions; (2) administrative rules and regulations; and (3) constitutional laws.[8]

Table 3.1
A Comparison of Criminal and Tort Law

Similarities	
Both criminal and tort law seek to control behavior.	
Both laws impose sanctions.	
Similar areas of legal action exist, such as personal assault and control of white-collar offenses (for instance, environmental pollution).	
Differences	
Criminal Law	**Tort Law**
Crime is a public offense.	Tort is a civil or private wrong.
The sanction associated with criminal law is incarceration or death.	The sanction associated with a tort is monetary damages.
The right of enforcement belongs to the state.	The individual brings the action.
The government ordinarily does not appeal.	Both parties can appeal.
Fines go to the state	The individual receives damages as compensation for harm done.

Common Law, Statutes, and Case Decisions The common-law crimes adopted into state codes form one major source of the substantive criminal law today. As common law, crimes had a general meaning, and everyone basically understood the definition of such actions as murder, larceny, and rape. Today, statutes enacted by state and federal legislative bodies have built on these common-law meanings and often contain more detailed and specific definitions of the crimes. *Statutes* are thus a way in which the criminal law is created, modified, or expunged. They reflect existing social conditions and deal with issues of morality, such as gambling and sexual activity, as well as traditional common-law crimes, such as murder, burglary, and arson.

Case law and judicial decision making also change and influence laws. For example, a statute may define murder as the "unlawful killing of one human being by another with malice." Court decisions might help explain the meaning of the term *malice* or clarify whether *human being* includes a fetus. A judge may rule that a statute is vague, deals with an act no longer of interest to the public, or is an unfair exercise of state control over an individual. Conversely, some judges may interpret the law so that behaviors that were previously acceptable become outlawed. For example, judges in a particular jurisdiction might find all people who sell magazines depicting nude men and women guilty of the crime of selling obscene material, whereas in the past obscenity was interpreted much more narrowly. Or some courts might consider drunken driving a petty crime, whereas others might interpret the statute on driving under the influence more severely.

Many state criminal codes are now online. To find your state's code, go to www.findlaw.com **and select "State Codes."**

Administrative Rule Making Administrative agencies with rule-making authority also develop measures to control conduct in our society.[9] Some agencies regulate taxation, health, environment, and other public functions; others control drugs, illegal gambling, or pornographic material. The listing of prohibited drugs by various state health boards, for example, is an important administrative control function. Parole boards are administrative agencies that implement the thousands of regulations governing the conduct of criminal offenders after their release from prison. Such rules are called *administrative rules with criminal sanctions,* and agency decisions about these rules have the force and authority of law.

Constitutional Law and Its Limits Regardless of its source, all criminal law in the United States must conform to the rules and dictates of the U.S. Constitution.[10] In other words, any criminal law that conflicts with the various provisions and articles of the Constitution will eventually be challenged in the appellate courts and stricken from the legal code by judicial order (or modified to adhere to constitutional principles). As Chief Justice John Marshall's opinion in *Marbury v. Madison* indicated, "If the courts are to regard the Constitution and the Constitution is superior to any ordinary act of the legislature, the Constitution and not such ordinary act must govern the case to which they apply."[11] This landmark case of 1803 established the concept of judicial review. All laws, including criminal statutes, must therefore meet constitutional standards or be declared invalid.

Among the general limitations set by the Constitution are those that forbid the government to pass *ex post facto laws.* Such laws make an action a crime that was not a crime at the time it was done; they create crimes (or penalties) that could be enforced retroactively (though civil penalties, such as those set in

Timothy Boomer is shown holding a copy of the ticket he received for using obscene language. Boomer's troubles began when he fell out of a canoe while heading down the Rifle River in Arenac County, Michigan. Children nearby were able to hear when Boomer came up cursing his fate. He was found to be in violation of Michigan's 101-year-old ban on using obscene language if women and children are within earshot. Is this a violation of the Constitution's protection of free speech? Can a state pass laws that infringe on a person's Constitutionally protected rights?

tax laws, can be retroactive). The Constitution also forbids *bills of attainder:* legislative acts that inflict punishment without a judicial trial. In addition, criminal laws have been interpreted as violating constitutional principles if they are too vague or overbroad to give clear meaning of their intent. For example, a law forbidding adults to engage in "immoral behavior" could not be enforced because it does not use clear and precise language or give adequate notice as to which conduct is forbidden.[12] The Constitution also forbids laws that make a person's status a crime. For example, addiction to narcotics cannot be made a crime, though laws can forbid the sale, possession, and manufacture of dangerous drugs.

In general, the Constitution has been interpreted to forbid any criminal law that violates a person's right to be treated fairly and equally; this principle is referred to as *substantive due process.* Usually, this means that before a new law can be created, the state must show that there is a compelling need to protect public safety or morals. The Law in Review feature discusses the *Kansas v. Hendricks* case, which deals with the constitutionality of the Kansas Sexually Violent Predator Act, and the *Chicago v. Morales* case, which deals with the legality of a gang-loitering ordinance.[13]

CRIMES AND CLASSIFICATIONS

The decision of how a crime should be classified rests with the individual jurisdiction. Each state has developed its own body of criminal law and consequently determines its own penalties for the various crimes. Thus, the criminal law of a given state defines and grades offenses, sets levels of punishment, and classifies crimes into categories. Over the years, crimes have been generally grouped into (1) felonies, misdemeanors, and violations and (2) other statutory classifications, such as juvenile delinquency, sex-offender categories, and multiple- or first-offender classifications. In general terms, felonies are considered serious crimes, misdemeanors are seen as less serious crimes, and violations may be noncriminal offenses such as traffic offenses and public drunkenness. Some states consider violations civil matters, whereas others classify them as crimes.

Felonies and Misdemeanors

The most common classification in the United States is the division between felonies and misdemeanors.[14] This distinction is based primarily on the degree of seriousness of the crime. Distinguishing between a felony and a misdemeanor is sometimes difficult. Simply put, a **felony** is a serious offense, and a **misdemeanor** is a less serious one.

felony
A more serious offense that carries a penalty of incarceration in a state prison, usually for one year or more. Persons convicted of felony offenses lose such rights as the rights to vote, hold elective office, or maintain certain licenses.

misdemeanor
A minor crime usually punished by less than one year's imprisonment in a local institution, such as a county jail.

Black's Law Dictionary defines the two terms as follows:

> A felony is a crime of a graver or more atrocious nature than those designated as misdemeanors. Generally it is an offense punishable by death or imprisonment in a penitentiary. A misdemeanor is lower than a felony and is generally punishable by fine or imprisonment otherwise than in a penitentiary.[15]

Each jurisdiction in the United States determines by statute what types of conduct constitute felonies or misdemeanors. The most common definition of a felony is that it is a crime punishable in the statute by death or by imprisonment in a state or federal prison. In Massachusetts, for example, any crime that a statute punishes by imprisonment in the state prison system is considered a felony, and all other crimes are misdemeanors.[16] Another way of determining what category an offense falls into is by providing in the statute that a felony is any crime punishable by imprisonment for more than one year. In the former method, the place of imprisonment is critical; in the latter, the length of the prison sentence distinguishes a felony from a misdemeanor.

In the United States today, felonies include serious crimes against the person, such as criminal homicide, robbery, and rape, as well as such crimes against property as burglary and larceny. Misdemeanors include petit (or petty) larceny, assault and battery, and the unlawful possession of marijuana. The least serious, or petty, offenses, which often involve criminal traffic violations, are called *infractions* or *violations*.

Kansas v. Hendricks

Facts

Leroy Hendricks, an admitted pedophile, has a forty-year history of sexually molesting children. In 1984 Hendricks was convicted in Kansas of sexually abusing two thirteen-year-old boys.

Shortly before his scheduled release in 1994, Kansas enacted the Sexually Violent Predator Act. The act defines a sexually violent predator as someone who (1) has been convicted or charged with committing a sexually violent act (rape, sexual assault, or sexual exploitation of a child) and (2) has a mental abnormality. The act defines *mental abnormality* as the inability to control one's sexual conduct to a degree that the person constitutes a menace to the health and safety of others.

The act provides for the involuntary and indeterminate commitment of any person classified as a sexually violent predator. If committed under the statute, the person is placed in a mental health institution, not a prison. It also provides for a number of procedural safeguards to protect the due process rights of any offender committed under the statute: (1) The state must prove beyond a reasonable doubt that the individual is a sexually deviant predator; (2) the individual is entitled to the right to counsel and a jury trial; and (3) the individual is entitled to an annual judicial review where the state must prove again beyond a reasonable doubt that he continues to meet the definition of a sexually dangerous individual.

In 1994, after serving his ten-year prison sentence, Hendricks was involuntarily committed to a mental hospital as a sexually deviant predator after a jury trial under the Kansas statute. Hendricks appealed his civil conviction, and the Kansas Supreme Court struck down the act as a violation of the due process clause. The Kansas court said that a person must be dangerous and mentally ill before being committed involuntarily.

Decision

The U.S. Supreme Court reversed the Kansas court in a 5-to-4 decision written by Justice Thomas. Thomas ruled that (1) the act did not violate substantive due process and was not punitive in nature and (2) the act did not violate the double jeopardy clause of the U.S. Constitution, rejecting the defendant's claim that the civil commitment constituted a second punishment. The Court said that Hendrick's diagnosis as a pedophile qualifies as a mental abnormality under the Kansas statute and plainly satisfies due process of law. According to the Court, a finding of dangerousness, standing alone, is ordinarily not a sufficient ground on which to justify indefinite involuntary commitment. But the Kansas law links that finding to the existence of a mental abnormality that makes it difficult, if not impossible, for the person to control his behavior. Defendants like Hendricks can be held indefinitely if considered mentally abnormal. Therefore, the Court ruled that violent sexual predators who are believed to be dangerous can be locked up indefinitely in mental hospitals against their wills after completing their sentence even if not mentally ill. The Kansas Sexually Violent Predator Act did not violate the due process and double jeopardy clauses and was determined to be constitutional.

Significance of the Case

This case — although decided on narrow grounds — will serve as a powerful impetus for states to adopt sexual predator statutes. Five other states already have similar laws. According to law enforcement officials, the case represents a major victory for crime control in dealing with the problem of recidivist sexual offend-

The felony–misdemeanor classification has a direct effect on the offender charged with the crime. A person convicted of a felony may be barred from certain fields of employment or some professions, such as law and medicine. A felony offender's status as an alien in the United States might also be affected, or the offender might be denied the right to hold public office, vote, or serve on a jury.[17] These and other civil liabilities exist only when a person is convicted of a felony offense, not a misdemeanor.

Whether the offender is charged with a felony or a misdemeanor also makes a difference at the time of arrest. Normally, the law of arrest requires that if the crime is a misdemeanor and has not been committed in the presence of a police officer, the officer cannot make an arrest. This is known as the *in-presence requirement*. However, the police officer does have the legal authority to arrest a suspect for a misdemeanor at a subsequent time by the use of a validly obtained arrest warrant. In contrast, an arrest for a felony may be made regardless of whether the crime was committed in the officer's presence, as long as the officer has reasonable grounds to believe that the person has committed the felony.

ers. On the other hand, libertarians believe that the ruling opens a Pandora's box over the question of what constitutes a "mental abnormality." For example, could an alcoholic who drives drunk be subject to involuntary civil commitment? How far does this ruling go?

Chicago v. Morales (1999)

Facts

Because of an epidemic of gang violence, Chicago passed the Gang Congregation Ordinance in 1997. Under the ordinance, if a police officer observes a person whom she believes to be a gang member loitering in a public place with one or more persons, she can order them to disperse; failure to do so was a violation of the ordinance and grounds for arrest.

The ordinance also limited officers' enforcement discretion by confining arrest authority to designated officers, establishing criteria for defining street gangs and their membership, and providing for designated enforcement areas.

In 1998, after a number of arrests of gang members by the police, the Illinois Supreme Court found that the statute violated due process of law because it was vague and an arbitrary restriction on personal liberty.

Decision

In a 6-to-3 decision, the U.S. Supreme Court affirmed the Illinois court and ruled that the ordinance's broad sweep violates the requirement that the legislature establish minimal guidelines to govern law enforcement activities. The Court said the ordinance encompasses too much harmless behavior: In any public place in Chicago, persons in the company of a gang member shall be ordered to disperse if their purpose is not apparent to an officer. State courts had interpreted the statutory language "to remain in any one place with no apparent purpose" as giving officers absolute discretion to determine what activities constitute loitering. They ruled the three features of the ordinance that limit the officer's discretion — it does not permit issuance of a dispersal order to anyone who is moving along or who has an apparent purpose; it does not permit an arrest if individuals obey a dispersal order; and no order can be issued unless the officer reasonably believes that one of the loiterers is a gang member — were insufficient to limit police discretion.

Significance of the Case

This case reinforces the constitutional principle that criminal laws with unlimited discretion and vagueness will be struck down. The problem with the statute was that it covered a broad range of innocent conduct and delegated too much discretion to the police. On the other hand, the Court said that the statute could be "made constitutional by requiring that loiterers have some harmful purpose before being arrested, or making it clear that only gang members could be arrested rather than people standing nearby." This language has been taken by legal scholars as a cue that a properly drafted ordinance could be constitutional. Chicago intended to try this approach to gang control again.

InfoTrac College Edition Research

Historically, society's response to crime has been almost exclusively punitive. The two cases above represented the use of punitive responses in areas of sexual deviancy and juvenile delinquency.

See, Tag Evers, "A healing approach to crime," *The Progressive*, September 1998 v.62 NJ p30, for a mediation and restorative justice approach rather than a criminal law approach to antisocial behavior.

Other Statutory Classifications

In addition to the felony–misdemeanor classifications, crimes may be classified according to the characteristics of the offender. All states, for example, have juvenile delinquency statutes that classify children under a certain age as juvenile delinquents if they commit acts that would constitute crimes if committed by adults. Some states have special statutory classifications for sex offenders, multiple offenders, youthful offenders, and first offenders. Generally, no special statutory classification exists for white-collar crimes, such as embezzlement, fraud, and income tax violation, which usually involve nonviolent conduct.

THE LEGAL DEFINITION OF A CRIME

There is no single universally accepted legal definition of a crime. Because the determination of what constitutes a crime rests with the individual jurisdiction, the federal government and each state have their own body of criminal law. Most general legal definitions of a crime are basically similar, however. A crime can be defined as follows:

crime
A violation of societal rules of behavior as interpreted and expressed by a criminal legal code created by people holding social and political power. Individuals who violate these rules are subject to sanctions by state authority, social stigma, and loss of status.

> A **crime** is (1) a legal wrong (2) prohibited by the criminal law (3) prosecuted by the state (4) in a formal court proceeding (5) in which a criminal sanction or sentence may be imposed.

As determined by most legal systems, crime can result from the commission of an act in violation of the law or from the omission of a required legal act. For example, a crime can be an intentional act of striking another person or of stealing someone else's property. But it can also involve the failure of a person to act, such as the failure to file an income tax return, parental failure to care for a child, or failure to report a crime or an automobile accident.

The legal definition of a crime involves the elements of the criminal acts that must be proven in a court of law if the defendant is to be found guilty. For the most part, common criminal acts have both mental and physical elements, both of which must be present if the act is to be considered a legal crime. The following definition of the crime of burglary in the nighttime, as stated in the Massachusetts General Laws, is an example of the mental and physical elements of the substantive criminal law:

> Whoever breaks and enters a dwelling house in the nighttime, with intent to commit a felony, or whoever, after having entered with such intent, breaks such dwelling house in the nighttime, any person being lawfully therein, and the offender being armed with a dangerous weapon at the time of such breaking or entry, or so arming himself in such house or making an actual assault on a person lawfully therein, [commits the crime of burglary].[18]

corpus delecti
The body of the crime, made up of the actus reus and mens rea.

Certain basic elements are required for an act to be considered a crime. For the crime of burglary, the state must prove that the defendant actually entered a home by force and was not invited in, that the defendant carried an identifiable weapon, that the crime occurred after sundown, and that the act was intentional. These elements form what is known as the **corpus delicti**, or "body of the crime." The term *corpus delicti* is often misunderstood. Some people, for instance, wrongly believe that it refers to the body of the deceased in a homicide. Corpus delicti describes all the elements that together constitute a crime; it includes (1) the actus reus, (2) the mens rea, (3) the combination of actus reus and mens rea.

actus reus
An illegal act. The actus reus can be an affirmative act, such as taking money or shooting someone, or a failure to act, such as failing to take proper precautions while driving a car.

Actus Reus and Mens Rea

The term **actus reus,** which translates as "guilty act," refers to the forbidden act itself. The criminal law uses it to describe the physical crime and the commission of the criminal act (or omission of the lawful act). In *Criminal Law,* Wayne LaFave and Austin Scott state:

> Bad thought alone cannot constitute a crime, there must be an act, or an omission to act where there is a legal duty to act. Thus, the common-law crimes are defined in terms of act or omission to act and statutory crimes are unconstitutional unless so defined. A bodily movement, to qualify as an act forming the basis of criminal liability, must be voluntary.[19]

The physical act in violation of the criminal statute is usually clearly defined within each offense. For example, in the crime of manslaughter, the unlawful killing of a human being is the physical act prohibited by a statute; in burglary, it is the actual breaking and entering into a dwelling house or other structure for the purpose of committing a felony.

Regarding an omission to act, many jurisdictions hold a person accountable if a legal duty exists and the offender avoids it. In most instances, the duty to act is based on a defined relationship, such as parent–child, or on a contractual duty, such as lifeguard–swimmer. The law, for example, recognizes that a parent has a legal duty to protect a child. When a parent refuses to obtain medical attention for the child and the child dies, the parent's actions constitute an omission to act, and that omission is a crime.

mens rea
Guilty mind. The mental element of a crime or the intent to commit a criminal act.

The second element basic to the commission of any crime is the establishment of the **mens rea,** translated as "guilty mind." Mens rea is the element of the crime that deals with the defendant's intent to commit a criminal act and includes such states of mind as concealing criminal knowledge (scienter), recklessness, negligence, and criminal purpose.[20] A person ordinarily cannot be convicted of a crime unless it is proven that he intentionally, knowingly, or willingly committed the criminal act.

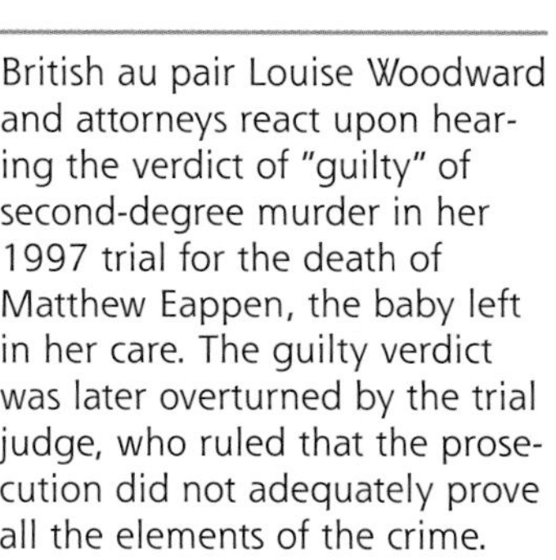

British au pair Louise Woodward and attorneys react upon hearing the verdict of "guilty" of second-degree murder in her 1997 trial for the death of Matthew Eappen, the baby left in her care. The guilty verdict was later overturned by the trial judge, who ruled that the prosecution did not adequately prove all the elements of the crime.

The following case illustrates the absence of mens rea. A student at a university took home some books, believing them to be her own, and subsequently found that the books belonged to her classmate. When she realized that the books did not belong to her, she returned them to their proper owner. The student could not be prosecuted for theft because she did not intend to steal the books in the first place; she did not knowingly take someone else's books and therefore lacked sufficient knowledge that her act was unlawful.

The Relationship of Mens Rea and Actus Reus

The third element needed to prove the corpus delicti of a crime is the relationship of the act to the criminal intent or result. The law requires that the offender's conduct must be the approximate cause of any injury resulting from the criminal act. If, for example, a man chases a victim into the street intending to assault him and the victim is struck and killed by a car, the accused could be convicted of murder if the court felt that his actions made him responsible for the victim's death. If, however, a victim dies from a completely unrelated illness after being assaulted, the court must determine whether the death was a probable consequence of the defendant's illegal conduct or whether it would have resulted even if the assault had not occurred. The New York State Penal Code, Section 120.00 (1), demonstrates these elements. Assault in the third degree states: A person is guilty of such a crime when with intent to cause physical injury to another person (mens rea), he or she causes injury to that person or a third person (actus reus) and there is a concurrence of these elements (relationship of mens rea and actus reus).

Strict Liability

strict liability crime
An illegal act whose elements do not contain the need for intent or mens rea; usually, acts that endanger the public welfare, such as illegal dumping of toxic wastes.

Existence of a criminal intent and a wrongful act must both be proved before an individual can be found guilty of committing a crime. However, certain statutory offenses exist in which mens rea is not essential. These offenses fall within a category known as public welfare, or **strict liability, crimes.** A person can be held responsible for such a violation independent of the existence of intent to commit the offense. Strict liability criminal statutes generally include narcotics control laws, traffic laws, health and safety regulations, sanitation laws, and other regulatory statutes. For example, a driver could not defend herself against a speeding ticket by claiming that she was unaware of how fast she was going and did not intend to speed, nor could a bartender claim that a juvenile to whom he sold liquor looked quite a bit older. No state of mind is generally required where a strict liability statute is violated.[21] These laws are generally an exception to the requirement that all crimes include a mens rea, or guilty mind. Ordinarily, only a wrongful act is needed for a conviction under a strict liability statute.

You can gain some insights into criminal law and procedures, including some of the defenses that can be raised to avoid criminal liability, by looking at some of the famous criminal law cases included on Court TV's Web site. Go to www.courttv.com/index.html

CRIMINAL RESPONSIBILITY

The idea of criminal responsibility is also essential to any discussion of criminal law. The law recognizes that certain conditions of a person's mental state might excuse her from acts that otherwise would be considered criminal. These factors have been used in legal defenses to negate the intent required for the commission of the crime. For example, a person who kills another while insane may argue in court that he was not responsible for criminal conduct. Similarly, a child who violates the law may not be treated as an adult offender. These types of "excuses" are defenses in which the defendant is not considered responsible or blameworthy for having engaged in criminal conduct. Three major types of criminal defense are detailed in this section: insanity, intoxication, and age.

insanity
A legal defense that maintains a defendant was incapable of forming criminal intent because he or she suffers from a defect of reason or mental illness.

M'Naghten rule
A legal definition of insanity. According to M'Naghten, people are insane if they either do not know what they are doing or cannot distinguish between right and wrong.

The Legal Definition of Insanity

Over the years, the legal system has struggled to define the rules relating to the use of **insanity** as a defense in a criminal trial. The tests for criminal responsibility involving insanity followed by U.S. courts are the M'Naghten rule, the irresistible impulse test, the Durham rule, and the substantial capacity test.

The **M'Naghten rule,** or the right–wrong test, is based on the decision in the M'Naghten case. In 1843 Daniel M'Naghten shot and killed Edward Drummond, believing Drummond to be Sir Robert Peel, the British prime minister. M'Naghten was prosecuted for murder. At his trial, he claimed that he was not criminally responsible for his actions because he suffered from delusions at the time of the killing. M'Naghten was found not guilty by reason of insanity. Because of the importance of the case and the unpopularity of the decision, the House of Lords reviewed the decision and asked the court to define the law with respect to crimes committed by persons suffering from insane delusions. The court's answer became known as the M'Naghten rule and has subsequently become the primary test for criminal responsibility in the United States. The M'Naghten rule can be stated as follows:

> A defendant may be excused from criminal responsibility if at the time of the committing of the act the party accused was labouring under such a defect of reason, from a disease of the mind, as not to know the nature and quality of the act he was doing, or if he did know it, that he did not know that he was doing what was wrong.[22]

Thus, according to the M'Naghten rule, a person is basically insane if she is unable to distinguish between right and wrong as a result of some mental disability.

irresistible impulse test
A test of criminal insanity where a person loses control and cannot stop from committing a crime because of mental illness.

Durham rule
A definition of insanity used in New Hampshire that required that the crime be excused if it was a product of a mental illness.

Over the years, the courts have become critical of the M'Naghten rule. Many insane individuals are able to distinguish between right and wrong. Also, clear determinations by the courts of such terms as *disease of the mind, know,* and *the nature and quality of the act* have never been made. As a result, many jurisdictions that follow the M'Naghten rule have supplemented it with the **irresistible impulse test.** This rule excuses from criminal responsibility a person whose mental disease makes it impossible to control personal conduct. The criminal may be able to distinguish between right and wrong but may be unable to exercise self-control because of a disabling mental condition. Almost half of the states use a combined M'Naghten rule–irresistible impulse test.

Another rule for determining criminal insanity is the **Durham rule.** Originally created in New Hampshire in 1871, the Durham rule was reviewed and subsequently adopted by the Court of Appeals for the District of Columbia in 1954, in the case of *Durham v. United States.*[23] In that opinion, the court rejected the M'Naghten formula and stated that an accused is not criminally responsible if the unlawful act was the product of mental disease or defect. This rule, also known as the *products test,* is based on the contention that insanity represents many personality factors, not all of which may be present in every case.

The Durham rule has been viewed with considerable skepticism, primarily because the problem of defining *mental disease, defect,* and *product* does not give the jury a reliable standard by which to make its judgment. Consequently, it has been dropped in the jurisdictions that experimented with it.

substantial capacity test
A test of criminal insanity where the lack of substantial capacity impairs the defendant's ability to conform his or her conduct to the dictates of law.

Another test for criminal insanity, which has become increasingly popular in many courts, is the **substantial capacity test.** In summary, as presented in Section 4.01 of the American Law Institute's Model Penal Code, this test states:

> A person is not responsible for criminal conduct if at the time of such conduct as a result of mental disease or defect he lacks substantial capacity whether to appreciate his criminality (wrongfulness) of his conduct or to conform his conduct to the requirements of the law.[24]

This rule is basically a broader restatement of the M'Naghten rule–irresistible impulse test. It rejects the Durham rule because of its lack of standards and its inability to define the term *product.* The most significant feature of this test is that it requires only a lack of "substantial capacity" rather than complete impairment of the defendant's ability to know and understand the difference between right and wrong. Twenty-four states use the substantial capacity test as defined by the American Law Institute.[25]

Table 3.2 summarizes various rules for determining criminal insanity. In reality, only a small number of offenders actually use the insanity defense because many cases involving insane offenders are processed through civil commitment proceedings.

The insanity defense has been controversial for many years. In the early 1980s the debate intensified when John Hinckley, Jr., was acquitted on insanity grounds in the assassination attempt on President Ronald Reagan. Congress responded with the Insanity Defense Reform Act of 1984, which weakened the defense.

Because many states have rewritten their insanity laws to severely limit the availability of the defense and some have abolished it outright, defendants are finding that insanity pleas are failing as the public grows impatient with violent crime. Studies show that, nationwide, the insanity defense is raised in only about 1 percent of all felony crimes and succeeds in only a small fraction of these cases.[26]

Table 3.2
Insanity Defense Standards

SOURCE: National Institute of Justice. *Crime Study Guide: Insanity Defense,* by Norval Morris (Washington, D.C.: Department of Justice, 1986), 3.

Test	Legal Standard Because of Mental Illness	Final Burden of Proof	Who Bears Burden of Proof
M'Naghten	"Don't know what he was doing or didn't know it was wrong"	Varies from proof by a balance of probabilities on the defense to proof beyond a reasonable doubt on the prosecutor.	
Irresistible impulse	"Could not control his conduct"	Beyond reasonable doubt	Prosecutor
Durham rule	"The criminal act was caused by his mental illness"	Beyond reasonable doubt	Prosecutor
Substantial capacity	"Lacks substantial capacity to appreciate the wrongfulness of his conduct or to control it"	Beyond reasonable doubt	Prosecutor
Current federal law	"Lacks capacity to appreciate the wrongfulness of his conduct"	Clear and convincing evidence	Defense

Intoxication As a general rule, intoxication, which may include drunkenness or being under the influence of drugs, is not considered a defense. However, a defendant who becomes involuntarily intoxicated under duress or by mistake may be excused for crimes committed. Involuntary intoxication may also lessen the degree of the crime. For example, a judgment may be decreased from first- to second-degree murder because the defendant uses intoxication to prove the lack of the critical element of mens rea, or mental intent. Thus, the effect of intoxication on criminal liability depends on whether the defendant uses alcohol or drugs voluntarily. For example, a defendant who enters a bar for a few drinks, becomes intoxicated, and strikes someone can be convicted of assault and battery. On the other hand, if the defendant ordered a nonalcoholic drink that was spiked by someone else, the defendant may have a legitimate legal defense.

Because of the frequency of crime-related offenses involving drugs and alcohol, the impact of intoxication on criminal liability is a persistent issue in the criminal justice system. The connection between drug use, alcoholism, and violent street crime has been well documented. Although those in law enforcement and the judiciary tend to emphasize the use of the penal process in dealing with problems of chronic alcoholism and drug use, others in corrections and crime prevention favor approaches that depend more on behavioral theories and the social sciences. For example, in the case of *Robinson v. California,* the U.S. Supreme Court struck down a California statute making addiction to narcotics a crime, on the ground that it violated the defendant's rights under the Eighth and Fourteenth Amendments to the Constitution.[27] On the other hand, the landmark decision in *Powell v. Texas* placed severe limitations on the behavioral science approach in *Robinson* when it rejected the defense of chronic alcoholism of a defendant charged with the crime of public drunkenness.[28]

Age The law holds that a child is not criminally responsible for actions committed at an age that precludes a full realization of the gravity of certain types of behavior. Under common law, there is generally a conclusive presumption of incapacity for a child under age 7, a reliable presumption for a child between the ages of 7 and 14, and no presumption for a child over the age of 14. This generally means that a child under age 7 who commits a crime will not be held criminally responsible for these actions and that a child between ages 7 and 14 may be held responsible. These common-law rules have been changed by statute in most jurisdictions. Today, the maximum age of criminal responsibility for children ranges from ages 14 to 17 or 18, while the minimum age may be set by statute at age 7 or under age 14.[29] In addition, every jurisdiction has established a juvenile court system to deal with juvenile offenders and children in need of court and societal supervision. Thus, the mandate of the juvenile justice system is to provide for the care and protection of children under a given age, established by state statute. In certain situations, a juvenile court may transfer a more serious chronic youthful offender to the adult criminal court.

CRIMINAL DEFENSE: JUSTIFICATION OR EXCUSE

Criminal defenses may also be based on the concept of justification or excuse. In other words, certain defenses allow for the commission of a crime to be justified or excused on grounds of fairness and public policy. In these instances, defendants normally acknowledge that they committed the act but claim that they cannot be prosecuted because they were justified in doing so. The following major types of criminal defenses involving justification or excuse are explained in this section: consent, self-defense, entrapment, and mistake, compulsion, and necessity.

Consent As a general rule, the victim's consent to a crime does not justify or excuse the defendant who commits the action. The type of crime involved generally determines the validity of consent as an appropriate legal defense. Such crimes as common-law rape and larceny require lack of consent on the part of the victim. In other words, a rape does not occur if the victim consents to sexual relations. In the same way, a larceny cannot occur if the owner voluntarily consents to the taking of property. Consequently, in such crimes consent is an essential element of the crime, and it is a valid defense where it can be proven or shown that it existed at the time the crime was committed. In statutory rape, however, consent is not an element of the crime and is considered irrelevant because the state presumes that young people are not capable of providing consent.

self-defense
A legal defense in which defendants claim that their behavior was legally justified by the necessity to protect their own lives and property or that of another victim from potential harm.

Self-Defense In certain instances, the defendant who admits to the acts that constitute a crime may claim to be not guilty because of an affirmative **self-defense.** To establish the necessary elements to constitute self-defense, the defendant must have acted under a reasonable belief that he was in danger of death or great harm and had no means of escape from the assailant.

As a general legal rule, however, a person defending herself may use only such force as is reasonably necessary to prevent personal harm. A person who is assaulted by another with no weapon is ordinarily not justified in hitting the assailant with a baseball bat. A person verbally threatened by another is not justified in striking the other party. If a woman hits a larger man, generally speaking the man would not be justified in striking the woman and causing her physical harm. In other words, to exercise the self-defense privilege, the danger to the defendant must be immediate. In addition, the defendant is obligated to look for alternative means of avoiding the danger, such as escape, retreat, or assistance from others.

The famous case of Bernhard Goetz, the celebrated "subway shooter," is a well-known example of legal self-defense versus unlawful vigilantism in an urban setting.[30] Goetz, a thirty-seven-year-old businessman, shot four black teenagers on a New York City subway train after being asked for $5. Three of the teens were carrying sharpened screwdrivers and had prior arrest records; they had allegedly threatened Goetz. New York state law allows a victim to shoot in self-defense only if there is reasonable belief that the assailant will use deadly force and if the victim cannot escape.

After a much publicized refusal by a first grand jury to indict Goetz for attempted murder, Goetz was subsequently indicted, tried and acquitted in 1987 of attempted murder and assault but was convicted of illegal possession of an unlicensed concealed handgun. Goetz claimed he shot the four youths in self-defense because he feared he was about to be robbed. This bitter and controversial case finally came to an end in January 1989, when Goetz was given a one-year jail sentence for the illegal handgun charge. According to the prosecution, Goetz had taken the law into his own hands. Goetz maintained that society needs to be protected from criminals. Today, there is a good deal of debate over the application of self-defense to a woman who is battered by her husband and then kills him. This is known as battered-wife syndrome (or in cases involving child abuse, the battered-child syndrome). Self-defense here often requires the presence of imminent danger and the inability to escape from the assailant.

entrapment
A criminal defense that maintains the police originated the criminal idea or initiated the criminal action.

Entrapment

The term **entrapment** refers to an affirmative defense in the criminal law that excuses a defendant from criminal liability when law enforcement agents use traps, decoys, and deception to induce criminal action. It is generally legitimate for law enforcement officers to set traps for criminals by getting information about crimes from informers, undercover agents, and codefendants. Police officers are allowed to use ordinary opportunities for defendants to commit crime and to create these opportunities without excessive inducement and solicitation to commit and involve a defendant in a crime. However, when the police instigate the crime, implant criminal ideas, and coerce individuals into bringing about crime, defendants have the defense of entrapment available to them. Entrapment is not a constitutional defense but has been created by court decision and statute in most jurisdictions.

The degree of government involvement in a criminal act leading to the entrapment defense has been defined in a number of Supreme Court decisions beginning in 1932. The majority view of what constitutes entrapment can be seen in the 1932 case of *Sorrells v. United States.*[31] During Prohibition, a federal officer passed himself off as a tourist while gaining the defendant's confidence. The federal agent eventually enticed the defendant to buy illegal liquor for him. The defendant was then arrested and prosecuted for violating the National Prohibition Act. The Court held that the officer used improper inducements that amounted to entrapment. In deciding this case, the Court settled on the *subjective* view of entrapment, which means that the predisposition of the defendant to commit the offense is the determining factor in entrapment. Following the *Sorrells* case, the Court stated in *Sherman v. United States* that the function of law enforcement is to prevent crime and to apprehend criminals, not to implant a criminal design, originating with officials of the government, in the mind of an innocent person.[32]

In the latest entrapment case, in which a defendant ordered magazines depicting nude boys and was pursued by the government for over two and a half years for violating a new law relating to minors, the Court held that the defendant was entrapped. A predisposition to break the law was held to be the result of government coaxing (see *Jacobson v. United States*).

Consequently, the major legal rule today considers entrapment primarily in light of the defendant's predisposition to commit a crime. A defendant with a criminal record would have a tougher time using this defense successfully than one who had never been in trouble before.

Mistake, Compulsion, and Necessity

Mistake or ignorance of the law is generally no defense to a crime. According to the great legal scholar William Blackstone, "Ignorance of the law, which everyone is bound to know, excuses no man."[33] Consequently, a defendant cannot present a legitimate defense by saying he was unaware of a criminal law, had misinterpreted the law, or believed the law to be unconstitutional.

On the other hand, mistakes of fact, such as taking someone else's coat that is similar to your own, may be a valid defense. If the jury or judge as trier of fact determines that criminal intent was absent, such an honest mistake may remove the defendant's criminal responsibility.

Compulsion or coercion may also be a criminal defense under certain conditions. In these cases, the defendant has been forced into committing a crime. For this defense to be upheld, a defendant must show that the actions were the only means of preventing death or serious harm to self or others. For example, a bank employee might be excused from taking bank funds if she can prove that her family was being threatened and that consequently she was acting under duress. But there is widespread general agreement that duress is no defense for an intentional killing.

One legal defense to crime is to maintain that the action was committed out of necessity in order to avoid injury or even death. Although six states including California have passed laws legalizing marijuana use for medical purposes, it still remains a Federal crime to possess "pot." However, some officers, such as Police Chief Mel Brown of Arcata, California, are willing to let people smoke pot if they register with local authorities and have a legitimate medical need.

Closely connected to the defense of compulsion is that of necessity. According to the Model Penal Code (a substantive model of the criminal code used as a guide by states), "Necessity may be an acceptable defense, provided the harm to be avoided is greater than the offense charged."[34] In other words, the defense of necessity is justified when the crime was committed because the circumstances could not be avoided. For example, a husband steals a car to bring his pregnant wife to the hospital for an emergency delivery, or a hunter shoots an animal of an endangered species that was about to attack her child. The defense has been found inapplicable, however, in cases where defendants sought to shut down nuclear power plants or abortion clinics or to destroy missile components under the belief that the action was necessary to save lives or prevent a nuclear war. Even those who use a controlled substance such as marijuana for medicinal purposes often cannot claim vindication based on medical necessity, although some courts have viewed this as a legitimate defense.[35]

In recent years, mental distress seems to be a favorite maneuver in high-profile criminal cases. Remember Lorena Bobbitt? She was acquitted by convincing a jury that physical and sexual abuse removed responsibility for her mutilation of her husband by cutting off his penis. The first trial of the Menendez brothers who used a childhood abuse defense for killing their parents resulted in a hung jury, but they were subsequently convicted in a second trial and given a life sentence.

Rage and anger are not proof of mental illness, and jealousy is no defense or excuse for murder. Such defenses are often known as *abuse excuses,* or soft defenses. They might also include such excuses as premenstrual syndrome, post-traumatic stress, black rage, cocaine-induced psychosis, XYY chromosome pattern, and many others. For example, in a case involving a man who had bilked senior citizens in a driveway-paving scheme, the defense lawyer argued that the man's "Gypsy" upbringing — a culture where deception and lying is a survival strategy — had caused the criminal behavior. And in a hit-and-run accident, another attorney argued that the defendant had a long family history of alcoholism and that three generations of biological and psychological problems genetically influenced him to commit the crime. All these conditions boil down to one issue: an effort by the defense attorney to limit individual responsibility. These bizarre defenses are generally unacceptable in a criminal case.

SUBSTANTIVE CRIMINAL LAW REFORM

In recent years, many states and the federal government have been examining and revising their substantive and procedural criminal codes. An ongoing effort has been made to update legal codes so that they provide an accurate reflection of public opinion, social change, technological innovation, and other important social issues. What kinds of criminal statutes do we need today? Should it be a crime to aid and abet a suicide? What about a stalking statute that would make it a crime to harass or follow someone? In many jurisdictions, it is still a crime to have sexual relations with any person other than your spouse. What about new gun control regulations?

The most popular criminal law statutes passed by state legislatures include:

1. Domestic or family violence laws
2. Tough recidivist and truth-in-sentencing laws
3. Community notification laws
4. Laws transferring juveniles to adult courts
5. Gun control laws

The Policy, Programs, and Issues in Criminal Justice feature discusses some of these issues and others in detail.

What was a crime thirty years ago — such as performing an abortion — may no longer be a crime today. In this instance, clouds of protest continue to surround the issue as pro- and antiabortion groups argue the merits of such decisions by the government. Conversely, what was unregulated behavior in the past, such as using children to pose for adult sex publications, may be outlawed because of public concern and outrage.[36]

One aspect of criminal law reform involves weeding out laws that seem archaic in light of what is now known about human behavior. For example, alcoholism is now considered a disease that should be treated, not an offense that should be punished. Many experts believe that such offenses as drunkenness, disorderly conduct, vagrancy, gambling, and minor sexual violations are essentially social problems and should not be dealt with by the criminal justice system.

Other criminal law revisions reflect increasing awareness about problems that confront American society. As mentioned previously, a number of states have eliminated traditional rape laws and replaced them with sexually neutral assault statutes that recognize that men as well as women can be the victims of rape. Most jurisdictions have adopted laws that require people in certain occupations, such as teachers and doctors, to report suspected cases of child abuse to the proper authorities.

Racketeer Influenced and Corrupt Organization Act (RICO) Federal legislation that enables prosecutors to bring additional criminal or civil charges against people whose multiple criminal acts constitute a conspiracy. RICO features monetary penalties that allow the government to confiscate all profits derived from criminal activities. Originally intended to be used against organized criminals, RICO also has been used against white-collar crime.

The RICO Act

In an effort to control organized crime, Congress passed the **Racketeer Influenced and Corrupt Organization (RICO) Act** in 1978. This law prevents people from acquiring or maintaining an interest in an ongoing enterprise, such as a union or legitimate business, with funds derived from illegal enterprises and racketeering activities.[37]

RICO did not create new categories of crime, but it did create new categories of offenses in racketeering activity, which it defined as involvement in two or more acts prohibited by twenty-four existing federal statutes and eight state statutes. The offenses listed in RICO include such state-defined crimes as murder, kidnapping, gambling, arson, robbery, bribery, extortion, and narcotic violations and such federally defined crimes as bribery, counterfeiting, transmission of gambling information, prostitution, and mail fraud.

Individuals convicted under RICO are subject to long prison terms and huge fines. The accused also must forfeit to the U.S. government any interest in a business in violation of RICO. These penalties are much more potent than simple conviction and imprisonment. In addition, a separate civil provision of the law permits private parties to sue for racketeering and obtain triple damages. The major purpose of RICO was to address the infiltration of legitimate businesses by organized crime.

Federal Crime Legislation, 1984–1999 One of the most significant criminal law revisions in the last two decades was the 1984 federal Comprehensive Crime Control Act.[38] This legislation reformed a code that was criticized for its complexity and inconsistency. Among the most important changes was the treatment of the insanity defense. In the past, federal prosecutors had the burden of proving that a defendant was sane. Now the burden of proof for insanity has shifted to the defendant. In addition, the 1984 federal code eliminated parole and required that criminal punishments be imposed more fairly and evenhandedly. Another important provision allowed judges to detain

Policy, Programs, and Issues in Criminal Justice

CRIMINAL LAW REFORM

One of the most dramatic developments in the criminal law on state and federal levels has been the enactment of new legislation. With heightened public concern over the nation's crime problem, lawmakers are increasingly disposed to prevent and control antisocial behavior by passing criminal statutes implemented by new and often tougher programs.

According to criminal justice experts, the general public is obsessed with safety. Of all the industrialized nations, the United States has one of the highest rates of violent crime. Consequently, numerous anticrime measures and state laws have been the top priority of legislators. The liberal perception of criminals as those simply in need of sympathy, education, and treatment is basically unacceptable today to a majority of Americans. A judiciary that appears unresponsive to enforcing responsibility and punishment has forced policymakers to develop legislation to address the needs of a society concerned about public safety and punishment.

A summary of measures includes the following:

1. *Domestic or family violence legislation* Abusing family members has become a major public issue; in most states today it is a criminal offense. In 1993 alone nearly one hundred related bills became law. Courts have expanded sentencing powers in domestic abuse cases, and the new legislation often defines more broadly the victims and the crimes against them. Experts believe that omnibus family statutes are essential and will strengthen and support individuals and families at risk from domestic violence and abuse.
2. *Tough recidivist statutes* In 1997 a number of jurisdictions enacted "three-strikes" laws to increase significantly the period of imprisonment for persons previously convicted of two felony offenses. There are even "two-strikes" measures that impose life without parole for a second violent offense. Such criminal laws, often enacted through both legislation and voter initiative, express the intent to abrogate a judge's authority in the interest of justice and public safety. Such statutes are often attacked as being in violation of the cruel and unusual punishment clause of the state and federal constitutions.
3. *Gun laws* Although legislators often shy away from laws dealing with banning guns, particularly because of the gun lobby led by the National Rifle Association, the federal government has made progress in restricting and regulating gun use in the last few years, as have many states. There is now a five-day waiting period on handgun purchases as a result of the Brady Handgun Control Law and a ten-year ban on the manufacture, trade, and possession of nineteen semiautomatic assault weapons, mandated by the Federal Crime Control Act of 1994. In addition, the Supreme Court has ruled on numerous occasions that gun restrictions do not violate individual rights.
4. *Community notification laws* Because legislators often care about children's needs, innovative criminal statutes are being passed requiring that residents be made aware of ex-felony offenders, such as convicted sex offenders who may move into a neighborhood. One such law, "Megan's Law," was passed in New Jersey after the killing of a child by a convicted sex offender who, unknown to the community, moved in across the street from the victim.
5. *Drug laws* Congress and state legislators keep passing laws dealing with possession, use, and sale of illegal drugs. More individuals are incarcerated today for drug offenses than for all violent crimes, and today's prisons are filled wall to wall with drug dealers and addicts. Legalizing drugs

The RICO statute allows law enforcement agents to seize the instrumentalities of crime if they have been used as part of an on-going criminal conspiracy. Seizing valuable items such as cars or boats can be a significant deterrent to crime.

does not appear to be in the future, so it is likely that conservative legislators will use the criminal laws to incarcerate even more drug violators while providing only marginal treatment and aftercare. In addition, the majority of states have instituted unusual statutes against HIV-positive people who don't take precautions or don't tell sex partners about the risks of the AIDS infection.

6. *Stalking statutes* According to the National Conference of State Legislatures, twenty-seven states have enacted stalking statutes. Such laws create and coin *stalking* as a criminal offense and set penalties. States typically define stalking as the willful, malicious, and repeated following and harassing of another person. Although many of these new laws were passed to apply to women terrorized by former boyfriends or husbands, the laws also often apply to women or men stalked by casual acquaintances or even strangers.
7. *Software piracy* Computers and technology play a significant role in our society. Although technology is viewed as an increasingly important development in the fight against crime (fingerprinting analysis, DNA profiling, etc.), defendants are being charged with violating laws against illegal software use for commercial gain. Consequently, the federal government and states are passing statutes against illegally distributing software and infringing copyrighted software programs. In recent years indictments for illegally copying software have been prosecuted under wire fraud statutes, but this often means that home computer users who copy a single software program for their own use would be subject to criminal prosecution. This underscores the development of criminal statutes allowing for the prosecution of software theft by computer, as well as Internet violations on a global basis.

Critical Thinking

Crime control was a major issue in state legislatures in 1995 and 1996. Policymakers concentrated heavily on laws crafted to deal with violent crime and family abuse with punishment as the theme. Might not some people be unfairly punished under such statutes? What really distinguishes the three-strikes acts from other laws involving chronic offenders? With regard to family violence laws, ought not such complex laws require treatment responses and assistance to families in addition to incarceration? Ensuring the right to due process is an issue in virtually all new criminal law regulation. What are the constitutional issues in antistalking legislation, recidivism statutes, gun control laws, and family violence codes?

InfoTrac College Edition Research

One of the many new areas of statutory changes has been in domestic abuse cases.

How can domestic violence laws be effective? One statutory approach is to intervene early in the domestic dispute. To read more about this method, see Linda Dakis, Dade County's Domestic Violence Plan, *Trial Magazine*, Feb. 1996 31 N.2 p4.

SOURCES: Donna Hunzeker, "Significant State Anti-Crime Legislation," *National Conference of State Legislatures* 19 (1994): 1–90; Joseph Califano, "It's Drugs, Stupid," *New York Times Magazine*, 29 January 1995, 41; National Conference of State Legislatures, *1997 State Legislative Summary* (Denver: National Conference, 1997); Michael Higgins, "Is Capital Punishment for Killers Only?" *American Bar Association Journal* 83 (1997): 30; U.S. Department of Justice, *Stalking and Domestic Violence* (Washington, D.C.: Office of Justice Programs, 1998); *Newsweek*, "America under the Gun — Special Report," 23 August 1999.

offenders in jail before their trials if they were considered a danger to the community and themselves. Preventive detention was a significant change in the nation's bail system. Despite these changes, in comparison with the revisions that have taken place in many states, the federal criminal law has not been extensively overhauled.

Amid much national concern about drugs, Congress also passed the Omnibus Drug Law of 1988.[39] Earmarking billions for antidrug activities, the law called for increased drug education and treatment programs and broader federal drug interdiction efforts. This legislation is the basis for U.S. drug enforcement policy today.

Under the Bush administration, Congress passed the Crime Control Act of 1990. Some significant changes were part of this legislation, including improvements in public defender services, the implementation of "shock incarceration" programs in federal and state correctional systems, reforms for the investigation of child abuse cases, efforts to aid crime victims through the Victims Rights and Restitution Act of 1990, authorization for a study of mandatory sentencing by the U.S. Sentencing Commission, provisions dealing with drugs, and the development of new offenses and penalties relating to the savings and loan scandals.[40]

The desire to be tough on crime is often one of the top priorities for politicians. Recent federal crime legislation under the Clinton administration has included the Brady Handgun Control Law of 1993, requiring a five-business-day waiting period before an individual can buy a handgun, and the Violent Crime Control and Law Enforcement Act of 1994, expanding the scope of the death penalty and authorizing billions of dollars for more police officers, prisons, and crime prevention programs.[41] The Crime Control Act of 1994 is the largest crime bill in U.S. history. President Clinton considered this legislation one of the crowning achievements of his first term.

One of the most significant recent pieces of crime legislation is the Antiterrorism and Effective Death Penalty Act of 1996. The "Terrorism Law" was passed as a direct result of the 1995 bombing of the federal building in Oklahoma City. Many of the new law's provisions relate to terrorist activity as well as revisions to federal habeas corpus proceedings. Known as the *great writ,* this is a procedure for obtaining judicial determination of the legality of an individual's custody. The emphasis is on reducing the delay often attributable to habeas corpus proceedings in capital cases.[42]

CONSTITUTIONAL CRIMINAL PROCEDURE

Whereas substantive criminal law primarily defines crimes, the law of criminal procedure consists of the rules and procedures that govern the pretrial processing of criminal suspects and the conduct of criminal trials. The principles that govern criminal procedure flow from the relationship between the individual and the state and include (1) a belief in the presumption of innocence, (2) the right to a defense against criminal charges, and (3) the requirement that the government should act in a lawful manner. In general, these policies are mandated by the provisions of state constitutions. A sound understanding of criminal procedure requires an awareness of constitutional law.

The U.S. Constitution

The U.S. Constitution has played and continues to play a critical role in the development of the criminal law used in the criminal justice system. The forerunner of the Constitution was the Articles of Confederation, adopted by the Continental Congress in 1781. This document was found to be generally inadequate as the foundation for effective government because it did not create a proper balance of power between the states and the central government. As a result, in 1787 the Congress of the Confederation adopted a resolution calling for a convention of delegates from the original states. Meeting in Philadelphia, the delegates' express purpose was to revise the Articles of Confederation. The work of that convention culminated in the drafting of the Constitution; it was ratified by the states in 1788 and put into effect in 1789. In its original form, the Constitution consisted of a preamble and seven articles. The Constitution divided the powers of government into three independent but equal parts: the executive, the legislative, and the judicial branches. The purpose of the separation of powers was to ensure that no single branch of the government could usurp power for itself and institute a dictatorship. The measures and procedures initiated by the framers of the Constitution have developed over time into our present form of government.

How does the Constitution, with its formal set of rights and privileges, affect the operations of the criminal justice system? One way is to guarantee that no one branch of government can in and of itself determine the fate of those accused of crimes. The workings of the criminal justice process illustrate this principle. A police officer, who represents the executive branch of government, makes an arrest on the basis of laws passed by the legislative branch, and the accused is subsequently tried by the judiciary. In this way, citizens are protected from the arbitrary abuse of power by any single element of the law.

The Bill of Rights Besides providing protection by ensuring a separation of powers within the government, the Constitution controls the operations of the criminal justice system. It does so by guaranteeing individual freedoms in the ten amendments added to it on December 15, 1791, collectively known as the **Bill of Rights.**[43]

Bill of Rights
The first ten amendments to the U.S. Constitution.

The Bill of Rights was added to the Constitution to prevent government from usurping the personal freedoms of citizens In its original form, the Constitution contained few specific guarantees of individual rights. The Founding Fathers, aware of the past abuses perpetrated by the British government, wanted to ensure that the rights of U.S. citizens would be safe. The Bill of Rights was adopted only to protect individual liberties from being abused by the national government, however, and did not apply to the actions of state or local officials. This oversight resulted in abuses that have been rectified only with great difficulty and even today remain the subject of court action.

Over the last four decades, the U.S. Supreme Court's interpretation of the Constitution has served as the basis for the creation of legal rights of the accused. The principles that govern criminal procedure are required by the Constitution and Bill of Rights. Of primary concern are the Fourth, Fifth, Sixth, and Eighth Amendments, which limit and control the manner in which the federal government operates the justice system. In addition, the due process clause of the Fourteenth Amendment has helped define the nature and limits of governmental action against the accused on a state level.

- The *Fourth Amendment* is especially important for the criminal justice system because it means that police officers cannot indiscriminately use their authority to investigate a possible crime or arrest a suspect unless either or both actions are justified by the law and the facts of the case. Stopping, questioning, or searching an individual without legal justification represents a serious violation of the Fourth Amendment right to personal privacy.

self-incrimination
Personal utterances or statements that can be used as evidence in a criminal matter. The Fifth Amendment prohibits law enforcement officials from using force or coercion to obtain incriminating statements from suspects in criminal cases.

- Limiting the admissibility of confessions that have been obtained unfairly is another method of controlling police behavior. The right against **self-incrimination** is frequently asserted by a defendant in an effort to exclude confessions or admissions that might be vital to the government's case. In such instances, the application of the *Fifth Amendment* to the Constitution is critical to the criminal justice system.

  The Fifth Amendment has in fact had a tremendous impact on the criminal justice system. In 1966 in the landmark case of *Miranda v. Arizona,* the Supreme Court held that a person accused of a crime has the right to refuse to answer questions when placed in police custody.[44]

- The *Sixth Amendment* guarantees the defendant the right to a speedy and public trial by an impartial jury, the right to be informed of the nature of the charges, and the right to confront any prosecution witnesses. This amendment has had a profound effect on the treatment of persons accused of crimes and has been the basis for numerous significant Supreme Court decisions that have increased the rights of criminal defendants.

  Many Court decisions regarding the Sixth Amendment have also concerned the individual's right to counsel. The right of a defendant to be represented by an attorney has been extended to numerous stages of the criminal justice process, including pretrial custody, identification and lineup procedures, preliminary hearing, submission of a guilty plea, trial, sentencing, and postconviction appeal.

- According to the *Eighth Amendment,* "Excessive bail shall not be required, nor excessive fines imposed, nor cruel and unusual punishments inflicted." Bail is a money bond put up by the accused to attain freedom between arrest and trial. Bail is meant to ensure a trial appearance, since the bail money is forfeited if the defendant misses the trial date. The Eighth Amendment does not guarantee a constitutional right to bail but rather prohibits the exactment of excessive bail. Nevertheless, since many state statutes place no precise limit on the amount of bail a judge may impose, many defendants who cannot make bail are often placed in detention while awaiting trial.

  Another goal of the framers of the Constitution was to curtail the use of torture and excessive physical punishment. Consequently, the prohibition against cruel and unusual punishment was added to the Eighth Amendment. This prohibition has affected the imposition of the death penalty and other criminal dispositions and has become a guarantee that serves to protect both the accused and convicted offenders from actions regarded as unacceptable by a civilized society.

These key amendments furnish the basis for our system of criminal procedure.

THE STATE CRIMINAL JUSTICE SYSTEM UNDER THE CONSTITUTION

The Fourteenth Amendment has been the vehicle most often used to apply the protection of the Bill of Rights to the states. The most important aspect of this amendment is the clause that says no state shall "deprive any person of life, liberty, or property, without due process of law." This meant that the same general constitutional restrictions previously applicable to the federal government were to be imposed on the states. It is essential to keep the following constitutional principles in mind:

administration's activities in the 1980s. In the Bush and Clinton administrations of the 1990s, efforts have been made to prosecute such diverse crimes as those in the scandals involving savings and loan associations and the alleged infiltration of legitimate businesses by organized crime. The criminal law system has demonstrated amazing resilience in its ability to prosecute public officials and private citizens whose behavior has damaged the government.

Both an expansion and a contraction of the criminal law itself can also be anticipated. Areas of expansion will probably include a greater emphasis on controlling career criminals. Laws making it easier for states to punish serious juvenile offenders and incarcerate them in secure adult institutions will probably be passed. More attention will be given to white-collar crimes, as well as to drug-related crimes and terrorism. Corporations are almost certainly going to be held accountable for their illegal acts, especially those that result in physical as well as economical harm. Stock market and computer activities will receive close scrutiny by law enforcement agencies, as will child abuse and family violence.

Software piracy in particular is receiving greater emphasis as computers and technology play an ever-increasing role in our society. This will lead to the development of criminal statutes allowing for the prosecution of software theft by computer, as well as Internet violations on a global basis.

Finally, the legal system will continue to be faced with difficult challenges involving AIDS. Some criminal laws specifically attempt to control the activities of prisoners, prostitutes, drug users, and criminal defendants who are HIV positive to protect others from contracting the disease.

Regardless of what changes occur in the future, the criminal law system will continue to deal with four fundamental problems: (1) defining and classifying antisocial behavior; (2) establishing appropriate criminal sanctions or punishments; (3) applying the proper degree of criminal responsibility; and (4) determining what departures from due-process-of-law safeguards may require the reversal of a conviction.

Lastly, more than any other factor, the role of the Supreme Court will dominate the future direction of criminal law and procedure in the United States. The Court has been the setting for some of the important recent events in the administration of criminal justice. For example, the Court took a decidedly liberal turn in granting individual rights for the accused during the Earl Warren era of the 1960s. In the 1970s and 1980s, Nixon's conservatives — Justices Warren Burger and William Rehnquist — curbed the growth of criminal procedure rights. With the replacement of liberal Justice William Brennan by conservative David Souter of New Hampshire in 1990 and the controversial appointment of Clarence Thomas to replace Thurgood Marshall in 1991, the Court continues to hand down legally conservative opinions favoring state law enforcement over criminal defendants. (see Chapter 7).

But the philosophical direction of the Court now seems to be veering toward a middle road. President Clinton's appointment of Judge Ruth Bader Ginsburg to the Court in 1993 to succeed Justice Byron White tempered the Court's conservatism. In 1994, Clinton appointed Stephen Breyer, a Boston federal appellate court judge, to replace Justice Harry Blackmun. Because Breyer does not have a distinct ideology, his addition adds to the moderate bent of the Court.[50]

Today, the nine-member Court is made up of competing blocs of four liberal-to-moderate judges (John Paul Stevens, Ruth Bader Ginsberg, Stephen Breyer, and David Souter) and three conservative justices (Antonin Scalia, Clarence Thomas, and Chief Justice William Rehnquist). In the middle are Sandra Day O'Connor and Anthony Kennedy, who often are the deciding votes on the criminal law and procedure cases.

SUMMARY

The criminal justice system is basically a legal system. Its foundation is the criminal law, which is concerned with people's conduct. The purpose of criminal law is to regulate behavior and maintain order in society. What constitutes a crime is defined primarily by the state and federal legislatures and reviewed by the courts.

What is considered criminal conduct changes from one period to another. Social norms, values, and community beliefs play major roles in determining what conduct is antisocial. Crimes are generally classified as felonies or misdemeanors, depending on their seriousness. Since a crime is a public wrong against the state, the criminal law imposes sanctions in the form of fines, probation, or imprisonment on a guilty defendant.

Under the criminal law, all adults are presumed to be aware of the consequences of their actions, but the law does not hold an individual blameworthy unless that person is capable of intending to commit the crime of which he is accused. Such factors as insanity, a mental defect, or age mitigate a person's criminal responsibility.

States periodically revise and update the substantive criminal law and the procedural laws in their penal codes; the latter deal with the rules for processing the offender from arrest through trial, sentencing, and release. An accused must be provided with the guarantees of due process under the Fifth and Fourteenth Amendments to the U.S. Constitution.

KEY TERMS

substantive criminal law
criminal procedure
civil law
common law
Carriers case
law of precedent
stare decisis
tort
intent
felony
misdemeanor
crime
corpus delicti
actus reus
mens rea
strict liability crime
insanity
M'Naghten rule
irresistible impulse test
Durham rule
substantial capacity test
self-defense
entrapment
Racketeer Influenced and Corrupt Organization (RICO) Act
Bill of Rights
self-incrimination
due process

 INFOTRAC COLLEGE EDITION EXERCISE

The jury in the 1997 Massachusetts murder trial of British au pair Louise Woodward (accused of killing the baby she was caring for) had four choices:

1. first-degree murder — intent to kill, cause harm or injury or atrocity and extreme cruelty.
2. second-degree murder — defendant acted with malice.
3. acquittal — innocent because the prosecution failed to prove Woodward's guilt beyond a reasonable doubt.
4. hung jury — a verdict where the jury is divided between Woodward's guilt and innocence.

After the jury found her guilty of second-degree murder, the judge reduced Woodward's sentence to manslaughter because the intent to do bodily harm or act with malice was not present. Involuntary manslaughter is a killing with no intention to cause serious bodily harm, such as acting without proper caution.

Suppose you work in the prosecutor's office and you have been assigned the task of coming up with information on criminal homicide to assist the government in its appeal. Search for articles using *InfoTrac College Edition* regarding the distinction between murder and manslaughter. Use key words such as: "malice," "intent to kill," and "provocation."

QUESTIONS

1. What are the specific aims and purposes of the criminal law? To what extent does the criminal law control behavior?
2. What kinds of activities should be labeled *criminal* in contemporary society? Why?
3. What is a criminal act? What is a criminal state of mind? When are individuals liable for their actions?
4. Discuss the various kinds of crime classifications. To what extent or degree are they distinguishable?
5. Numerous states are revising their penal codes. Which major categories of substantive crimes do you think should be revised?
6. Entrapment is a defense when the defendant was entrapped into committing the crime. To what extent should law enforcement personnel induce the commission of an offense?
7. What legal principles can be used to justify self-defense? As the law seeks to prevent, not promote, crime, are such principles sound?
8. What are the minimum standards of criminal procedure required in the criminal justice system?

NOTES

1. *Regina v. Dudley and Stephens,* 14 Q.B.D. 273 (1884).

2. Scott Lehigh, "Mercy or Murder," *Boston Globe,*15 August 1999, F1.

3. Some of the historical criminal law concepts discussed here are a synthesis of those contained in Fred Inbua, James Thompson, and James Zagel, *Criminal Law and Its Administration* (Mineola, N.Y.: Foundation Press, 1974); Jerome Hall, *General Principles of Criminal Law* (Charlottesville, Va.: Michie, 1961); Richard Singer and Martin Gardner, *Crimes and Punishment: Cases, Materials and Readings in Criminal Law* (New York: Matthew Bender, 1989).

4. See, generally, Sanford Kadish and Monrad Paulsen, *Criminal Law and Its Processes* (Boston: Little, Brown, 1975); see also J. Dressler, *Understanding Criminal Law* (New York: Matthew Bender, 1987).

5. See T. F. Pluckett, *A Concise History of Common Law* (Boston: Little, Brown, 1956); see also E. Allan Farnworth, *An Introduction to the Legal System of the United States* (New York: Oceana Publications, 1963).

6. *Carriers Case Yearbook,* 13 Edward IV 9.pL.5 (1473).

7. 372 U.S. 335, 83 S.Ct. 792, 9 L.Ed.2d 799 (1963).

8. See, generally, Wayne R. LaFave and Austin W. Scott, *Criminal Law* (St. Paul: West Publishing Horn Book Series, 1986).

9. E. Gellhorn, *Administrative Law and Process* (St. Paul: West Publishing Nutshell Series, 1981).

10. See John Weaver, *Warren — The Man, The Court, the Era* (Boston: Little, Brown, 1967); see also "We the People," *Time,* 6 July 1987, 6.

11. *Marbury v. Madison,* 5 U.S. (1 Cranch) 137, 2 L.Ed. 60 (1803).

12. Thomas Gardner, *Criminal Law* (St. Paul: West, 1985), 15–18.

13. *Kansas v. Hendricks,* 117 S.Ct. 2072 (1997); *Chicago v. Morales,* 119 S.Ct. 246 (1999).

14. See American Law Institute, Model Penal Code, sec. 104.

15. Henry Black, *Black's Law Dictionary,* rev. 5th ed. (St. Paul: West, 1979), 744, 1150.

16. Mass. Gen. Laws, chap. 274, sec. 1.

17. Sheldon Krantz, *Law of Corrections and Prisoners' Rights, Cases and Materials,* 3d ed. (St. Paul: West, 1986), 702; Barbara Knight and Stephen Early, Jr., *Prisoners' Rights in America* (Chicago: Nelson-Hall, 1986), Chap 1; see also Fred Cohen, "The Law of Prisoners' Rights — An Overview," *Criminal Law Bulletin* 24 (188): 321–49.

18. See Mass. Gen. Laws Ann., chap. 266, sec. 14.

19. LaFave and Scott, *Criminal Law,* 177; see, generally, Frank Miller, Robert Dawson, George Dix, and Raymond Parnas, *Cases and Materials on Criminal Justice Administration,* 3d ed. (New York: Foundation Press, 1988).

20. See American Law Institute, Model Penal Code, sec. 2.02; see also *United States v. Bailey,* 444 U.S. 394, 100 S.Ct. 624, 62 L.Ed.2d 575 (1980).

21. See *United States v. Balint,* 258 U.S. 250, 42 S.Ct. 301, 66 L.Ed. 604 (1922); see also *Morissette v. United States,* 342 U.S. 246, 72 S.Ct. 240, 96 L.Ed. 288 (1952).

22. 8 English Reporter 718 (1943).

23. 94 U.S. App. D.C. 228, 214 F.2d 862 (1954).

24. American Law Institute, Model Penal Code, sec. 4.01.

25. Bureau of Justice Statistics, *Report to the Nation on Crime and Justice,* 2d ed. (Washington, D.C.: Bureau of Justice Statistics, 1988), 87.

26. Richard Schmitt, "Defenses Down — Insanity Pleas Fail a Lot of Defendants," *Wall Street Journal,* 29 February 1996, A1.

27. 370 U.S. 660, 82 S.Ct. 1417, 8 L.Ed.2d 758 (1962).

28. 392 U.S. 514, 88 S.Ct. 2145, 20 L.Ed.2d 1254 (1968).

29. Samuel M. Davis, *Rights of Juveniles: The Juvenile Justice System* (New York: Boardman, 1974; update 1993), chap. 2; Larry Siegel and Joseph Senna, *Juvenile Delinquency: Theory, Practice, and Law* (St. Paul: West, 1996).

30. *People v. Goetz,* 68 N.Y.2d 96, 497 N.E.2d 41, 506 N.Y.S.2d 18 (1986); see also "New York Court Upholds Goetz Gun Conviction," *Boston Globe,* 23 November 1988, 5.

31. 287 U.S. 435, 53 S.Ct. 210, 77 L.Ed. 413 (1932).

32. 356 U.S. 369, 78 S.Ct. 819, 2 L.Ed.2d 848 (1958); see also *Jacobson v. United States,* 503 U.S. 540, 112 S.Ct. 1535, 118 L.Ed.2d 174 (1992).

33. William Blackstone, *Commentaries on the Law of England,* vol. 1, ed. Thomas Cooley (Chicago: Callaghan, 1899), 4, 26. Blackstone was an English barrister who lectured on the English common law at Oxford University in 1753.

34. American Law Institute, Model Penal Code, sec. 2.04.

35. *Commonwealth v. Berrigan,* 509 Pa. 118, 501 A.2d 226 (1985); see also *State v. Tate,* 102 N.J. 64, 505 A.2d 941 (1986).

36. In *New York v. Ferber,* 458 U.S. 747, 102 S.Ct. 3348, 73 L.Ed.2d 1113 (1982), the Supreme Court upheld state laws that ban the use of children in sexually explicit publications even if they are not legally obscene.

37. 18 U.S.C.A., sec. 1961–1968 (amended in 1978, 1984, and 1986). "Enterprise" includes both legitimate and illegitimate associations.

38. *Comprehensive Crime Control Act of 1984,* Title 18, U.S.C.; see also Albert P. Melone, "The Politics of Criminal Code Revision," *Capital U.S. Review* 15 (1986): 191.

39. *Omnibus Drug Law,* H5210, *Congressional Quarterly,* 29 October 1988, 3145.

40. Tom Smith, "Legislative and Legal Developments in Criminal Justice," *Journal on Criminal Justice* 5 (1991): 36–37; see also Gary Weiss, "The Mob on Wall Street," *Business Week,* 16 December 1996, 92–93.

41. For an intensive summary of the Violent Crime Control and Law Enforcement Act of 1994, see *Criminal Law Reporter,* Bureau of National Affairs, 55 (1994): 2305–2430; see also Tom Smith, "Legislative and Legal Developments," *American Bar Association Journal on Criminal Justice* 11 (1996): 50–52.

42. *Antiterrorism and Effective Death Penalty Act of 1996,* Public Law No. 104-132 (1996).

43. For a real-world application and the impact of the Bill of Rights on criminal justice in particular, see Ellen Alderman and Caroline Kennedy, *In Our Defense — The Bill of Rights in Action* (New York: Morrow, 1991).

44. 384 U.S. 436, 86 S.Ct. 1602, 16 L.Ed.2d 694 (1966).

45. See "Essay," *Time,* 26 February 1973, 95; also, for a tribute to the Bill of Rights and due process, see James MacGregor Burns and Steward Burns, *The Pursuit of Rights in America* (New York: Knopf, 1991).

46. Black, *Black's Law Dictionary,* 449.

47. See, generally, Joseph J. Senna, "Changes in Due Process of Law," *Social Work* 19 (1974): 319; see also the interesting student rights case *Goss v. Lopez,* 419 U.S. 565, 95 S.Ct. 729, 42 L.Ed.2d 725 (1975).

48. 342 U.S. 165, 72 S.Ct. 205, 95 L.Ed. 183 (1952).

49. Ibid., at 172, 72 S.Ct. at 209.

50. Erwin Chemerinsky, "The Supreme Court—The Crowded Center," *American Bar Association Journal* 180 (1994): 79–81.

chapter 4

Police in Society: History and Organization

A few years ago, the Richmond, Virginia, homicide rate was the second highest in the nation; gun toting had become a way of life.[1] Then the local police, in cooperation with the U.S. Bureau of Alcohol, Tobacco, and Firearms, created Project Exile. This innovative program was designed to combat gun crime in a simple and direct fashion. Any time Richmond police found a gun on a drug dealer, user, convicted felon, or suspect in a violent crime, the case would be tried under federal statutes that carry mandatory sentences of at least five years without parole — and longer for repeated or aggravated offenses. To publicize the program, its slogan, "An Illegal Gun Gets You 5 Years in Federal Prison," was splashed across billboards in high-crime neighborhoods and on city buses. A TV campaign spread the word over the airwaves. More than 250 armed criminals were arrested and sent to prison. Much to the program creators' delight, murders in Richmond dropped sharply, from 140 in 1997 to 94 in 1998 and 32 in the first six months of 1999. Armed robberies showed a similar decline. Because of its success, Project Exile programs are being adopted in Atlanta; Birmingham, Alabama; Fort Worth, Texas; New Orleans; Norfolk, Virginia; Philadelphia; Rochester, New York; and San Francisco. In Texas, the program's motto is "Gun Crime Means Hard Time"; in Rochester, billboards on the side of city buses read, "You + Illegal Gun = Federal Prison." ■

Programs such as Project Exile typify the effort of modern police agencies to take an aggressive stance against crime. Rather than simply react after a crime occurs, local police are now cooperating with other governmental agencies and working in partnership with the general public to reduce area crime rates. Cracking down on gun crimes, patrolling crime-ridden schools, and acting as community change agents are but a few of the roles of the modern police.

The changing police role is of critical importance for the criminal justice system. The police are the *gatekeepers* of the criminal justice process. They initiate contact with law violators and decide whether to formally arrest them and start their journey through the criminal justice system, to settle the issue in an informal way (such as by issuing a warning), or to simply take no action at all. The strategic position of law enforcement officers, their visibility and contact with the public, and their use of weapons and arrest power have kept them in the forefront of public thought for most of the twentieth century.

Critics charge that police use "racial profiling" in making routine stops, searches, and arrests. In racial profiling, officers would suspect all people of color of being potential criminals. Some commentators have even suggested that there is a new, unofficial crime on the books—"DWB," Driving While Black!

The public may applaud police efforts that have brought the crime rate down, but they are also concerned by media reports of police officers who abuse their power by either using unnecessary force and brutality or routinely violating the civil rights of suspects. Such concern may be warranted. For example, some critics charge that police officers routinely induce or force confessions from criminal suspects. Later at trial, these false confessions may influence jurors even if they seem inconsistent with the facts of the case.[2] Another concern is that police are racially and ethnically biased and use *racial profiling* to routinely stop African Americans and search their cars. Some cynics suggest that police have created a new form of crime: "DWB," driving while black.[3]

Despite these concerns, the majority of citizens give their police force high marks. Though African Americans were believed to hold less positive attitudes toward police, recent research finds that racial differences are actually slight.[4] Citizens are especially likely to give police high marks if they view their neighborhood as safe and that police efficiency is a key to its protection.[5] Metropolitan police departments are attracting applicants who value an exciting, well-paid job that also holds the opportunity to provide valuable community service. So, although police agencies are still trying to define their role and effectively marshal their resources, they continue to be held in high esteem by the public they serve.

In this and the following three chapters, we will evaluate the history, role, organizational issues, and procedures of police agents and agencies and discuss the legal rules that control police behavior.

tithing
In medieval England, a group of ten families who collectively dealt with minor disturbances and breaches of the peace.

hue and cry
A call for assistance in medieval England. The policy of self-help used in villages demanded that everyone respond if a citizen raised a hue and cry to get their aid.

hundred
In medieval England, a group of one hundred families that had the responsibility to maintain the order and try minor offenses.

constable
In medieval England, an appointed official who administered and supervised the legal affairs of a small community.

shire reeve
In medieval England, the senior law enforcement figure in a county, the forerunner of today's sheriff.

watch system
During the Middle Ages in England, men were organized in church parishes to guard at night against disturbances and breaches of the peace under the direction of the local constable.

justice of the peace
Established in 1326 England, the office was created to help the shire reeve in controlling the county and later took on judicial functions.

THE HISTORY OF POLICE

The origin of U.S. police agencies, like that of the criminal law, can be traced to early English society.[6] Before the Norman Conquest, there was no regular English police force. Every person living in the villages scattered throughout the countryside was responsible for aiding neighbors and protecting the settlement from thieves and marauders. This was known as the *pledge system.* People were grouped in collectives of ten families, called **tithings,** and were entrusted with policing their own minor problems. When trouble occurred, the citizen was expected to make a **hue and cry.** Ten tithings were grouped into a **hundred,** whose affairs were supervised by a constable appointed by the local nobleman. The **constable,** who might be considered the first real police officer, dealt with more serious breaches of the law.[7]

Shires, which resembled the counties of today, were controlled by the **shire reeve** appointed by the Crown or local landowner to supervise the territory and ensure that order would be kept. The shire reeve, a forerunner of today's sheriff, soon began to pursue and apprehend law violators as part of his duties.

In the thirteenth century, the **watch system** was created to help protect property in England's larger cities and towns. Watchmen patrolled at night and helped protect against robberies, fires, and disturbances. They reported to the area constable, who became the primary metropolitan law enforcement agent. In larger cities, such as London, the watchmen were organized within church parishes and were usually members of the parish they protected.

In 1326 the office of **justice of the peace** was created to assist the shire reeve in controlling the county. Eventually, these justices took on judicial functions in addition to their primary role as peacekeeper. The local constable became the operational assistant to the justice of the peace, supervising the night watchmen, investigating offenses, serving summonses, executing warrants, and securing prisoners. This system helped delineate the relationship between police and the judiciary, which has continued for more than 670 years.

Eighteenth-Century Developments

At the eighteenth century began, rising crime rates encouraged a new form of private *monied police* who were able to profit both legally and criminally from the lack of formal police departments. These private police agents, referred to as *thief takers,* were universally corrupt, taking profits not only from catching and informing on criminals but also from receiving stolen property, theft, intimidation, perjury, and blackmail. They often relieved their prisoners of money and stolen goods and made more income by accepting hush money, giving perjured evidence, swearing false oaths, and operating extortion rackets. Petty debtors were especially easy targets for those who combined thief taking with the keeping of alehouses and taverns. While incarcerated, the health and safety of prisoners were entirely at the whim of the keepers/thief takers who were virtually free to charge what they wanted for board and other necessities. Court bailiffs who also acted as thief takers were the most passionately detested legal profiteers. They seized debtors and held them in small lockups where they forced their victims to pay exorbitant prices for food and lodging.

The thief takers' use of violence was notorious. They went armed and were prepared to maim or kill in order to gain their objectives. Before he was hung in 1725, Jack Wild, the most notorious thief taker, "had two fractures in his skull and his bald head was covered with silver plates. He had seventeen wounds in various parts of his body from swords, daggers and gunshots, [and] . . . his throat had been cut in the course of his duties."

Henry Fielding, the famed author of *Tom Jones,* along with Saunders Welch and Sir John Fielding, sought to clean up the thief-taking system. Appointed a city magistrate in 1748, Fielding operated his own group of monied police out of Bow Street in London, directing and deploying them throughout the city and its environs, deciding which cases to investigate and what streets to protect. His agents were carefully instructed on their legitimate powers and duties. Fielding's Bow Street Runners were a marked improvement over the earlier monied police because they actually had an administrative structure that improved record-keeping and investigative procedures. Although an improvement, Fielding's forces were not adequate, and by the nineteenth century, state police officers were needed.

In 1829 Sir Robert Peel, England's home secretary, guided through Parliament an "Act for Improving the Police in and near the Metropolis." The Metropolitan Police Act established the first organized police force in London. Composed of over 1,000 men, the London police force was structured along military lines; its members would be known from then on as *bobbies,* after their creator. They wore a distinctive uniform and were led by two magistrates, who were later given the title of commissioner. However, the ultimate responsibility for the police fell to the home secretary and consequently the Parliament.

The early bobbies suffered many of the same problems that have befallen their heirs. Many were corrupt, they were unsuccessful at stopping crime, and they were influenced by the wealthy. Owners of houses of ill repute who in the past had guaranteed their undisturbed operations by bribing watchmen now turned their attention to the bobbies. Metropolitan police administrators fought constantly to terminate cowardly, corrupt, and alcoholic officers, dismissing in the beginning about one-third of the bobbies each year.

Despite its recognized shortcomings, the London experiment proved a vast improvement over what had come before. It was considered so successful that the metropolitan police soon began providing law enforcement assistance to outlying areas that requested it. Another act of Parliament allowed justices of the peace to establish local police forces, and by 1856 every borough and county in England was required to form its own police force.

Law Enforcement in Colonial America

Law enforcement in colonial America paralleled the British model. In the colonies, the county **sheriff** became the most important law enforcement agent. In addition to keeping the peace and fighting crime, sheriffs collected taxes, supervised elections, and handled a great deal of other legal business.

sheriff
The chief law enforcement officer in a county.

The colonial sheriff did not patrol or seek out crime. Instead, he reacted to citizens' complaints and investigated crimes that had occurred. His salary, related to his effectiveness, was paid on a fee system. Sheriffs received a fixed amount for every arrest made. Unfortunately, their tax-collecting chores were more lucrative than fighting crime, so law enforcement was not one of their primary concerns.

In the cities, law enforcement was the province of the town marshal, who was aided, often unwillingly, by a variety of constables, night watchmen, police justices, and city council members. However, local governments had little power of administration, and enforcement of the criminal law was largely an individual or community responsibility.

In rural areas in the South, "slave patrols" charged with recapturing escaped slaves were an early if loathsome form of law enforcement.[8] In the western territories, individual initiative was encouraged by the practice of offering rewards for the capture of felons. If trouble arose, the town *vigilance committee* might form a posse to chase offenders. These **vigilantes** were called on to eradicate such social problems as theft of livestock, through force or intimidation; the San Francisco Vigilance Committee actively pursued criminals in the mid-nineteenth century.

vigilante
A citizen group who tracked down wanted criminals in the Old West.

As cities grew, it became exceedingly difficult for local leaders to organize ad hoc citizen vigilante groups. Moreover, the early nineteenth century was an era of widespread urban unrest and mob violence. Local leaders began to realize that a more structured police function was needed to control demonstrators and keep the peace.

Early Police Agencies

The modern police department was born out of urban mob violence that wracked the nation's cities in the nineteenth century. Boston created the first formal U.S. police department in 1838. New York formed its police department in 1844; Philadelphia in 1854. The new police departments replaced the nightwatch system and relegated constables and sheriffs to serving court orders and running jails.

At first, the urban police departments inherited the functions of the institutions they replaced. For example, Boston police were charged with maintaining public health until 1853, and in New York, the police were responsible for street sweeping until 1881. Politics dominated the departments and determined the recruitment of new officers and promotion of supervisors. An individual with the right connections could be hired despite a lack of qualifications. Early police agencies were corrupt, brutal, and inefficient.[9]

In the late nineteenth century, police work was highly desirable because it paid more than most other blue-collar jobs. By 1880 the average factory worker earned $450 a year, while a metropolitan police officer made $900 annually. For immigrant groups, having enough political clout to be appointed to the police department was an important step up the social ladder.[10] However, job security was uncertain because it depended on the local political machine's staying in power.

Police work itself was primitive. There were few of even the simplest technological innovations common today, such as call boxes or centralized record keeping. Most officers patrolled on foot, without backup or the ability to call for help. Officers were commonly taunted by local toughs and responded with force and brutality. The long-standing conflict between police and the public was born in the difficulty that untrained, unprofessional officers had in patrolling the streets of nineteenth-century U.S. cities and in breaking up and controlling labor disputes. Police were not crime fighters as we know them today. Their major role was maintaining order, and their power was almost unchecked. The average officer had

At the turn of the century, big-city police were still unrespected by the public, unsuccessful in their role as crime stoppers, and uninvolved in progressive activities. The control of police departments by local politicians impeded effective law enforcement and fostered an atmosphere of graft and corruption. This photo of a police officer guiding schoolchildren across train tracks in an urban community, circa 1920, belies the negative image of police officers of the era.

little training, no education in the law, and a minimum of supervision, yet the police became virtual judges of law and fact with the ability to exercise unlimited discretion.[11]

At mid-nineteenth century, the detective bureau was set up as part of the Boston police. Until then, thief taking had been the province of amateur bounty hunters, who hired themselves out to victims for a price. When professional police departments replaced bounty hunters, the close working relationships that developed between police detectives and their underworld informants produced many scandals and, consequently, high personnel turnover.

Police during the nineteenth century were regarded as incompetent and corrupt and were disliked by the people they served. The police role was only minimally directed at law enforcement. Its primary function was serving as the enforcement arm of the reigning political power, protecting private property, and keeping control of the ever-rising numbers of foreign immigrants.

Police agencies evolved slowly through the second half of the nineteenth century. Uniforms were introduced in 1853 in New York. The first technological breakthroughs in police operations came in the area of communications. The linking of precincts to central headquarters by telegraph began in the 1850s. In 1867 the first telegraph police boxes were installed; an officer could turn a key in a box, and his location and number would automatically register at headquarters. Additional technological advances were made in transportation. The Detroit Police Department outfitted some of its patrol officers with bicycles in 1897. By 1913 the motorcycle was being used by departments in the eastern part of the nation. The first police car was used in Akron, Ohio, in 1910, and the police wagon became popular in Cincinnati in 1912.[12] Nonpolice functions, such as care of the streets, began to be abandoned after the Civil War.

Big-city police were still unrespected by the public, unsuccessful in their role as crime stoppers, and uninvolved in progressive activities. The control of police departments by local politicians impeded effective law enforcement and fostered an atmosphere of graft and corruption.

Twentieth-Century Reform In an effort to reduce police corruption, civic leaders in a number of jurisdictions created police administrative boards to reduce local officials' control over the police. These tribunals were responsible for appointing police administrators and controlling police affairs. In many instances, these measures failed because the private citizens appointed to the review boards lacked expertise in the intricacies of police work.

Another reform movement was the takeover of some big-city police agencies by state legislators. Although police budgets were financed through local taxes, control of police was usurped by rural politicians in the state capitals. New York City temporarily lost authority over its police force in 1857. It was not until the first decades of the twentieth century that cities regained control of their police forces.

The Boston police strike of 1919 heightened interest in police reform. The strike came about basically because police officers were dissatisfied with their status in society. Other professions were unionizing and increasing their standards of living, but police salaries lagged behind. The Boston police officers' organization, the Boston Social Club, voted to become a union affiliated with the American Federation of Labor. The officers struck on September 9, 1919. Rioting and looting broke out, resulting in Governor Calvin Coolidge's mobilization of the state militia to take over the city. Public support turned against the police, and the strike was broken. Eventually, all the striking officers were fired and replaced by new recruits. The Boston police strike ended police unionism for decades and solidified power in the hands of reactionary, autocratic police administrators. In the aftermath of the strike, various local, state, and federal crime commissions began to investigate the extent of crime and the ability of the justice system to deal with it effectively and made recommendations to improve police effectiveness.[13] However, with the onset of the Depression, justice reform became a less important issue than economic revival, and for many years, little changed in the nature of policing.

The Emergence of Professionalism Around the turn of the century, a number of nationally recognized leaders called for measures to help improve and professionalize the police. In 1893 the *International Association of Chiefs of Police* (IACP), a professional society, was formed. Under the direction of its first president (District of Columbia Chief of Police Richard Sylvester), the IACP became the leading voice for police reform during the first two decades of the twentieth century. The IACP called for creating a civil service police force and for removing political influence and control. It also advocated centralized organizational structure and record keeping to curb the power of politically aligned precinct captains. Still another professional reform the IACP fostered was the creation of specialized units, such as delinquency control squads.

The most famous police reformer of the time was August Vollmer. While serving as police chief of Berkeley, California, Vollmer instituted university training for young officers. He also helped develop the School of Criminology at the University of California at Berkeley, which became the model for justice-related programs around the United States. Vollmer's disciples included O. W. Wilson, who pioneered the use of advanced training for officers when he took over and reformed the Wichita (Kansas) Police Department in 1928. Wilson was also instrumental in applying modern management and administrative techniques to policing. His text, *Police Administration,* became the single most influential work on the subject.

During this period, police professionalism was equated with an incorruptible, tough, highly trained, rule-oriented department organized along militaristic lines. The most respected department was that in Los Angeles, which emphasized police as incorruptible crime fighters who would not question the authority of the central command.

THE MODERN ERA OF POLICING: 1960–2000

The modern era of policing can be traced from 1960 to 2000. What are the major events that occurred during this period?

Policing in the 1960s

Turmoil and crisis were the hallmarks of policing during the 1960s. Throughout this decade, the Supreme Court handed down a number of decisions designed to control police operations and procedures. Police officers were now required to obey strict legal guidelines when questioning suspects, conducting searches and wiretapping, and so on. As the civil rights of suspects were significantly expanded, police complained they were being "handcuffed by the courts."

Also during this time, civil unrest produced a growing tension between police and the public. African Americans, who were battling for increased rights and freedoms in the civil rights movement, found themselves confronting police lines. When riots broke out in New York, Detroit, Los Angeles, and other cities between 1964 and 1968, the spark that ignited conflict often involved the police. When students across the nation began marching in anti-Vietnam war demonstrations, local police departments were called on to keep order. Police forces were ill-equipped and poorly trained to deal with these social problems; it is not surprising that the 1960s were marked by a number of bloody confrontations between the police and the public.

Confounding these problems was a rapidly growing crime rate. The number of violent and property crimes increased dramatically. Drug addiction and abuse grew to be national concerns, common in all social classes. Urban police departments could not control the crime rate, and police officers resented the demands placed on them by dissatisfied citizens.

Policing in the 1970s

The 1970s witnessed many structural changes in police agencies themselves. The end of the Vietnam War significantly reduced tensions between students and police. However, the relationship between police and minorities was still rocky. Local fears and distrust, combined with conservative federal policies, encouraged police departments to control what was perceived as an emerging minority group "threat."[14]

Increased federal government support for criminal justice greatly influenced police operations. During the decade, the Law Enforcement Assistance Administration (LEAA) devoted a significant portion of its funds to police agencies. Although a number of police departments used this money to purchase little-used hardware, such as antiriot gear, most of it went to supporting innovative research on police work and advanced training of police officers. Perhaps most significant, LEAA's Law Enforcement Education Program helped thousands of officers further their college education. Hundreds of criminal justice programs were developed on college campuses around the country, providing a pool of highly educated police recruits. LEAA funds were also used to import or transfer technology originally developed in other fields into law enforcement. Technological innovations involving computers transformed the way police kept records, investigated crimes, and communicated with one another. State training academies improved the way police learn to deal with such issues as job stress, community conflict, and interpersonal relations.

More women and minorities were recruited to police work. Affirmative action programs helped, albeit slowly, alter the ethnic, racial, and gender composition of U.S. policing.

Policing the 1980s As the 1980s began, the police role seemed to be changing significantly. A number of experts acknowledged that the police were not simply crime fighters and called for police to develop a greater awareness of community issues, which resulted in the emergence of the community policing concept.[15]

Police unions, which began to grow in the late 1960s, continued to have a great impact on departmental administration in the 1980s. Unions fought for and won increased salaries and benefits for their members; starting salaries of more than $30,000 are not uncommon in metropolitan police agencies. In many instances, unions eroded the power of the police chief to make unquestioned policy and personnel decisions. During the decade, chiefs of police commonly consulted with union leaders before making major decisions concerning departmental operations.

While police operations improved markedly during this time, police departments were also beset by problems that impeded their effectiveness. State and local budgets were cut back during the Reagan administration, while federal support for innovative police programs was severely curtailed with the demise of the LEAA.

Police–community relations continued to be a major problem. Riots and incidents of urban conflict occurred in some of the nation's largest cities.[16] They triggered continual concern about what the police role should be, especially in inner-city neighborhoods.

Policing in the 1990s As the 1990s began, several police experts decreed that the nation's police forces should be evaluated not on their crime-fighting ability but on their courteousness, deportment, and helpfulness. Interest renewed in reviving an earlier style of police work featuring foot patrols and increased citizen contact. Police departments began to embrace new forms of policing that stressed cooperation with the community and problem solving. Ironically, urban police departments began to shift their focus to becoming community organizers at a time when technological improvements increased the ability to identify suspects.

Police corruption continued to be an issue, and the rogue cops of the 1990s were even more brazen and violent than the corrupt cops of twenty years earlier. New York, Philadelphia, Los Angeles, and other large cities continued to experience incidence of police corruption and abuse of power. Even in smaller cities, police procedures have been questioned because overenforcement may occur in minority communities.[17] Minority citizens seemed to be the target of incidents of extreme violence and misconduct.[18]

Abner Louima, the victim of a vicious attack by rogue New York City police officers, stands with Rev. Al Sharpton (left). Justin Volpe, the New York City police officer found guilty of sodomizing Louima, received a life sentence. The Louima case was a shocking reminder that the nation's police forces must work closely with the community to end violence and brutality.

exhibit 4.1

The Most Notable Achievement of American Police, 1960–2000

1. The intellectual caliber of the police has risen dramatically. American police today at all ranks are smarter, better informed, and more sophisticated than police in the 1960s.
2. Senior police managers are more ambitious for their organizations than they used to be. Chiefs and their deputies want to leave their own distinctive stamp on their organizations. Many recognize that management is an important, specialized skill that must be developed.
3. An explicit scientific mind-set has taken hold in American policing that involves an appreciation of the importance of evaluation and the timely availability of information.
4. The standards of police conduct have risen. Despite recent well-publicized incidents of brutality and corruption, American police today treat the public more fairly, more equitably, and less venally then police did thirty years ago.
5. Police are remarkably more diverse in terms of race and gender than a generation ago. This amounts to a revolution in American policing, changing both its appearance and, more slowly, its behavior.
6. The work of the police has become intellectually more demanding, requiring an array of new specialized knowledge about technology, forensic analysis, and crime. This has had profound effects on recruitment, notably civilianization, organizational structure, career patterns, and operational coordination.
7. Civilian review of police discipline had gradually become accepted by police. Although the struggle is not yet over, expansion is inevitable as more and more senior police executives see that civilian review reassures the public and validates their own favorable opinion of the overall quality of police performance.

SOURCE: David H. Bayley, "Policing in America," *Society* 36 (1998): 16–20.

Although these incidents are troubling, police experts such as David Bayley believe that the police have made many notable strides over the past three decades, some of the most important of which are listed in Exhibit 4.1.

LAW ENFORCEMENT TODAY

Law enforcement today is divided into four broad categories: federal, state, county, and local policing agencies (and many subcategories within). There is no real hierarchy, and each branch has its own sphere of operations, though overlap may exist.

Federal Law Enforcement Agencies

The federal government has a number of law enforcement agencies designed to protect the rights and privileges of U.S. citizens; no single agency has unlimited jurisdiction, and each has been created to enforce specific laws and cope with particular situations. Federal police agencies have no particular rank order or hierarchy of command or responsibility, and each reports to a specific department or bureau.

THE JUSTICE DEPARTMENT/FEDERAL BUREAU OF INVESTIGATION The U.S. *Department of Justice* is the legal arm of the federal government. Headed by the attorney general, it is empowered to (1) enforce all federal laws, (2) represent the United States when it is party to court action, and (3) conduct independent investigations through its law enforcement services.

The Department of Justice maintains several separate divisions that are responsible for enforcing federal laws and protecting U.S. citizens. The Civil Rights Division proceeds legally against violations of federal civil rights laws that protect citizens from discrimination on the basis of their race, creed, ethnic background, age, or sex. Areas of greatest concern include discrimination in education, housing, and employment, including affirmative action cases. The Tax Division brings legal actions against tax violators. The Criminal Division prosecutes violations of the Federal Criminal Code. Its responsibility includes enforcing statutes relating to bank robbery (since bank deposits are federally insured), kidnapping, mail fraud, interstate transportation of stolen vehicles, and narcotics and drug trafficking.

The Justice Department first became involved in law enforcement when the attorney general hired investigators to enforce the Mann Act (forbidding the transportation of women between states for immoral purposes). These investigators were formalized in 1908 into a distinct branch of the government, the Bureau of Investigation; the agency was later reorganized into the **Federal Bureau of Investigation (FBI)**, under the direction of J. Edgar Hoover (1924–1972).

Federal Bureau of Investigation (FBI)
The arm of the U.S. Justice Department that investigates violations of federal law, gathers crime statistics, runs a comprehensive crime laboratory, and helps train local law enforcement officers.

Today's FBI is not a police agency but an investigative agency with jurisdiction over all matters in which the United States is or may be an interested party. It limits its jurisdiction, however, to federal laws, including all federal statutes not specifically assigned to other agencies. Areas covered by these laws include espionage, sabotage, treason, civil rights violations, murder and assault of federal officers, mail fraud, robbery and burglary of federally insured banks, kidnapping, and interstate transportation of stolen vehicles and property.

The FBI offers a number of important services to local law enforcement agencies. Its identification division, established in 1924, collects and maintains a vast fingerprint file that can be used by local police agencies. Its sophisticated crime laboratory, established in 1932, aids local police in testing and identifying such evidence as hairs, fibers, blood, tire tracks, and drugs. The Uniform Crime Reports (UCR) is another service of the FBI. The UCR is an annual compilation of crimes reported to local police agencies, arrests, police killed or wounded in action, and other information. Finally, the FBI's National Crime Information Center is a computerized network linked to local police departments that provides ready information on stolen vehicles, wanted persons, stolen guns, and so on.

The FBI mission has been evolving to keep pace with world events. With the end of the cold war and the reduction of East–West tension, the FBI's counterintelligence mission has diminished. In some offices, agents have been reassigned to antigang and drug control efforts.[19]

DRUG ENFORCEMENT ADMINISTRATION Government interest in drug trafficking can be traced back to 1914, when the Harrison Act established federal jurisdiction over the supply and use of narcotics. A number of drug enforcement units, including the Bureau of Narcotics and Dangerous Drugs, were charged with enforcing drug laws. In 1973 these agencies were combined to form the **Drug Enforcement Administration (DEA)**.

Drug Enforcement Administration (DEA)
The federal agency that enforces federal drug control laws.

DEA agents assist local and state authorities in investigating illegal drug use and carrying out independent surveillance and enforcement activities to control the importation of narcotics. For example, DEA agents work with foreign governments in cooperative efforts aimed at destroying opium and marijuana crops at their source, hard-to-find fields tucked away in the interiors of Latin America, Asia, Europe, and Africa. Undercover DEA agents infiltrate drug rings and simulate buying narcotics to arrest drug dealers.

The Bureau of Alcohol, Tobacco, and Firearms helps control sales of untaxed liquor and cigarettes, and, through the Gun Control Act of 1968 and the Organized Crime Control Act of 1970, it has jurisdiction over the illegal sales, importation, and criminal misuse of firearms and explosives. Here ATF officers undergo rigorous training as part of a special response team.

TREASURY DEPARTMENT The U.S. Treasury Department maintains the following enforcement branches:

1. *Bureau of Alcohol, Tobacco, and Firearms* The BATF helps control sales of untaxed liquor and cigarettes and, through the Gun Control Act of 1968 and the Organized Crime Control Act of 1970, has jurisdiction over the illegal sales, importation, and criminal misuse of firearms and explosives.
2. *Internal Revenue Service* The IRS, established in 1862, enforces violations of income, excise, stamp, and other tax laws. Its Intelligence Division actively pursues gamblers, narcotics dealers, and other violators who do not report their illegal financial gains as taxable income. For example, the career of Al Capone, the famous 1920s gangster, was brought to an end by the efforts of IRS agents.
3. *Customs Service* The Customs Service guards points of entry into the United States and prevents smuggling of contraband into (or out of) the country. It ensures that taxes and tariffs are paid on imported goods and helps control the flow of narcotics into the country.
4. *Secret Service* The Secret Service was originally charged with enforcing laws against counterfeiting. Today it is also accountable for the protection of the president and the vice-president and their families, presidential candidates, and former presidents. The Secret Service maintains the White House Police Force, which is responsible for protecting the executive mansion, and the Treasury Guard, which protects the mint.

The Del Rio Sector of the United States Border Patrol is responsible for controlling 205 miles of the Rio Grande River, the natural border between the U.S. and Mexico. Go to www.ins.usdoj.gov

OTHER JUSTICE DEPARTMENT AGENCIES Other federal law enforcement agencies under the direction of the Justice Department include the U.S. Marshals, the Immigration and Naturalization Service, and the Organized

Crime and Racketeering Unit. The U.S. Marshals are court officers who help implement federal court rulings, transport prisoners, and enforce court orders. The Immigration and Naturalization Service is responsible for the administration of immigration laws governing the exclusion and deportation of illegal aliens and the naturalization of aliens lawfully present in the United States. This service also maintains border patrols to prevent illegal aliens from entering the United States. The Organized Crime and Racketeering Unit, under the direction of the U.S. attorney general, coordinates federal efforts to curtail organized crime primarily through the use of federal racketeering laws.

State Law Enforcement Agencies Unlike municipal police departments, state police were legislatively created to deal with the growing incidence of crime in nonurban areas, a consequence of the increase in population mobility and the advent of personalized mass transportation in the form of the automobile. County sheriffs — elected officials with occasionally corrupt or questionable motives — had proven to be ineffective in dealing with the wide-ranging criminal activities that developed during the latter half of the nineteenth century. In addition, most local police agencies were unable to effectively protect against highly mobile lawbreakers who randomly struck at cities and towns throughout a state. In response to citizens' demands for effective and efficient law enforcement, state governors began to develop plans for police agencies that would be responsible to the state, instead of being tied to local politics and possible corruption.

The Texas Rangers, created in 1835, was one of the first state police agencies formed. Essentially a military outfit that patrolled the Mexican border, it was followed by the Massachusetts state constables in 1865 and the Arizona Rangers in 1901. Pennsylvania formed the first truly modern state police in 1905.[20]

Today about twenty-three state police agencies have the same general police powers as municipal police and are territorially limited in their exercise of law enforcement regulations only by the state's boundaries. In some jurisdictions, state police are also given special police powers; for example, Maryland employs its state police to serve civil process, and Arizona's Department of Public Safety provides emergency medical services. The remaining state police agencies are primarily responsible for highway patrol and traffic law enforcement. Some state police, such as those in California, direct most of their attention to the enforcement of traffic laws, whereas those in Georgia, Arkansas, and South Dakota are not responsible for traffic control.

Nearly every state law enforcement agency hosts a Web site. To see two of the more interesting ones, go to the Pennsylvania State Police's home page at www.state.pa.us/PA_Exec/State Police/index.htm **and the Washington State Patrol's home page at** www.wa.gov/wsp/wsphome.htm

Most state police organizations are restricted by legislation from becoming involved in the enforcement of certain areas of the law. For example, in some jurisdictions, state police are prohibited from becoming involved in strikes or other labor disputes, unless violence erupts.

The nation's 80,000 state police employees (55,000 officers and 25,000 civilians) are not only involved in law enforcement and highway safety but also carry out a variety of functions, including maintaining a training academy and providing emergency medical services. State police crime laboratories aid local departments in investigating crime scenes and analyzing evidence. State police also provide special services and technical expertise in such areas as bomb-site analysis and homicide investigation. Other state police departments, such as California's, are involved in highly sophisticated traffic and highway safety programs, including the use of helicopters for patrol and rescue, the testing of safety devices for cars, and the conducting of postmortem examinations to determine the causes of fatal accidents.

County Law Enforcement Agencies Most of the nation's county police departments, with their 265,000 employees (including 175,000 sworn officers), are independent agencies whose senior officer, the sheriff, is usually an elected political official (in all states except Rhode Island and Hawaii).[21] The county sheriff's role has evolved from that of the early English shire reeve, whose primary duty was to assist the royal judges in trying prisoners and enforcing sentences. From the time of the westward expansion in the United States until municipal departments were developed, the sheriff was often the sole legal authority over vast territories.

The duties of a county sheriff's department vary according to the size and degree of development of the county. The standard tasks of a typical sheriff's department are serving civil process (summons and court orders), providing court security, operating the county jail, and investigating crimes. Less commonly, sheriff's departments may serve as coroners, tax collectors, overseers of highways and bridges, custodians of the county treasury, and providers of fire, animal control, and emergency medical services; in years past, sheriffs' offices also conducted executions. Typically, a sheriff department's law enforcement functions are restricted to unincorporated areas within a county, unless a city or town police department requests its help.

Some sheriffs' departments are exclusively law enforcement oriented; some carry out court-related duties only; some are involved solely in correctional and judicial matters and not in law enforcement. However, a majority are full-service programs that carry out judicial, correctional, and law enforcement activities. As a rule, agencies serving large population areas (over 1 million) are devoted to maintaining county correctional facilities, while those in smaller population areas are focused on law enforcement.

In the past, sheriffs' salaries were almost always based on the fees they received for the performance of official acts. They received fees for every summons, warrant, subpoena, writ, or other process they served; they were also compensated for summoning juries or locking prisoners in cells. Today, sheriffs are salaried to avoid conflict of interest.

Metropolitan Law Enforcement Agencies Local police comprise the majority of the nation's authorized law enforcement personnel. Metropolitan police departments range in size from the New York City Police Department with more than 30,000 sworn officers and 10,000 civilian employees, to rural police departments, which may have a single officer. In all, local police departments have an estimated 530,000 full-time employees, including 420,000 sworn personnel and more than 100,000 civilian employees. Local police employment was up by an average of about 3 percent per year since 1993, compared with about 1 percent per year from 1987 to 1993. Racial and ethnic minorities comprised 21.5 percent of full-time sworn officers in local police departments in 1997. This compares with 19.1 percent in 1993, 17.0 percent in 1990, and 14.6 percent in 1987 (Table 4.1).[22]

Most TV police shows feature the trials of big-city police officers, but the overwhelming number of departments actually have fewer than fifty officers and serve a population of under twenty-five thousand. Seventy agencies employed one thousand or more full-time sworn personnel, including forty-one local police, fifteen state police, twelve sheriffs, and two special police agencies. In contrast, 2,245 agencies had just one full-time officer, and 1,164 relied solely on part-time officers.[23] The cost of maintaining these police forces is high. The

	Local Law Enforcement Agencies				Primary State Law Enforcement Agencies
Item description	**Total**	**County police**	**Municipal police**	**Sheriff**	
Number of agencies by number of full-time sworn personnel					
1,000 or more	55	7	34	14	15
550-999	68	4	39	25	17
250-499	133	11	74	48	11
100-249	395	8	307	80	6
Average number of					
Full-time employees per 10,000 residents	25	17	29	17	4
Full-time sworn officers per 10,000 residents	19	13	23	12	2
Median percent change in number of full-time employees 1993-97					
Total employees	10%	9%	9%	15%	7%
Sworn officers	9	9	9	13	4
Civilian employees	10	8	8	13	6

Table 4.1
Personnel in State and Local Law Enforcement Agencies with 100 or More Officers

SOURCE: *Law Enforcement Management and Administrative Statistics, 1997* (Washington, D.C.: Bureau of Justice Statistics, 1999), p. 1.

average police officer costs taxpayers about $62,000 per year, including salary, benefits, and other costs; this amounts to an annual cost of over $130 for every resident in the jurisdiction. Residents in larger jurisdictions who want and receive greater police protection pay more than 40 percent more each year for police services than those living in small towns.

Regardless of their size, most individual metropolitan police departments perform a standard set of functions and tasks and provide similar services to the community. These include the following:

traffic enforcement
accident investigation
patrol and peacekeeping
property and violent crime investigation
death investigation
narcotics and vice control
radio communications
crime prevention
fingerprint processing
search and rescue

The police role is expanding, so procedures must be developed to aid special-needs populations, including AIDS-infected suspects, the homeless, and victims of domestic and child abuse.[24]

These are only a few examples of the multiplicity of roles and duties assumed today in some of the larger urban police agencies around the nation. Smaller agencies can have trouble effectively carrying out these tasks; the hundreds of small police agencies in each state often provide duplicative services. Whether unifying smaller police agencies into "superagencies" would improve services is often debated among police experts. Smaller municipal agencies can provide important specialized services that might have to be relinquished if they were combined and incorporated into larger departments. Another approach has been to maintain smaller departments but to link them via computerized information-sharing and resource management networks.[25]

THE FUTURE OF LAW ENFORCEMENT

One view is that police departments will be reshaping their role, de-emphasizing crime fighting and stressing community organization and revitalization.[26] Around the country, citizens are demanding that police departments reconsider their image as disinterested outsiders. Community leaders are asking that, instead of riding around anonymously in patrol cars, police officers become actively involved in neighborhood affairs. Programs that do this include neighborhood-based ministations and foot patrols. Departments are also increasing their use of civilian employees, thereby freeing sworn officers for law enforcement tasks.

Police departments are evolving because leaders recognize that traditional models have not been effective. In the future, the police role may shift further away from a legalistic style that isolates officers from the public to a service orientation that holds officers accountable to the community and encourages them to learn from the people they serve. This means that the police must actively create a sense of community where none has existed and recruit neighborhood cooperation for crime control and prevention activities.

Another change that police agencies will continue to emphasize is the decentralization of command through the creation of specialized units, substations, and direct response teams. Although decentralization does not automatically ensure greater citizen cooperation, it is believed to increase sensitivity to citizen needs, create special knowledge of and commitment to the area served, and foster heightened community trust in the police.

Another innovation that will probably mushroom in the future is the employment of civilians for tasks that are now carried out by sworn officers. As police salaries and benefits increase, civilian employees will become an economic necessity. In addition, employing citizens from the community can help police departments become sensitive to the cultural environment they serve.[27]

Police departments will become increasingly more proactive and focus their attention on solving particular community problems. These problems will include domestic abuse, drug dealing, and drunk driving, because police administrators believe that arrests for these crimes may help reduce recidivism and because vocal community groups demand action against violators. There will be new categories of "high-tech" crimes with which police agencies will have to deal, ranging from theft of information and data to electronic counterfeiting. Police officers now trained to prevent burglaries may someday have to learn to create high-tech forensic labs that can identify suspects who are involved in theft of genetically engineered cultures from biomedical labs.[28]

Criminal Investigation

Criminal investigation will be enhanced by the application of sophisticated electronic gadgetry: computers, cellular phones, and digital communication devices.[29] It is now recognized that there are geographic "hot spots" where a majority of predatory crimes are concentrated. Computer mapping programs that can translate addresses into map coordinates now allow departments to identify problem areas for particular crimes, such as drug dealing. Computer maps allow police to identify the location, time of day, and linkage among criminal events and to concentrate their forces accordingly.[30] Crime mapping is discussed in the following Criminal Justice and Technology feature.

The demographic structure of policing will also evolve. The numbers of minority and female police officers should continue to grow. In the past, white males followed their fathers into a police career. A new generation of minorities and women will now be able to follow their parents into police work.

Information Technology Crime mapping is not the only way technology will be used to improve the effectiveness of police resources.[31] Budget realities demand that police leaders make the most effective use of their forces, and technology seems to be an important method of increasing productivity at a relatively low cost. The introduction of technology has already been explosive. In 1964, for example, only one city, St. Louis, had a police computer system; by 1968, ten states and fifty cities had state-level criminal justice information systems; today, almost every city of more than fifty thousand people has some sort of computer-support services.[32] Figure 4.1 shows that a significant number of law enforcement agencies now use mobile computer terminals.

One of the most important computer-aided tasks is the identification of criminal suspects. Computers now link neighboring agencies so that they can share information on cases, suspects, and warrants. One such system is the Police Information Network, which electronically links the ninety-three independent law enforcement agencies in the San Francisco area to allow them to share information. In addition, local departments now use computerized databases to record not only crime-related information but also motor vehicle and business data, workers' compensation files, and other public records that can be used to locate and track wanted felons.[33] On a broader jurisdictional level, the FBI implemented the National Crime Information Center in 1967. This system provides rapid collection and retrieval of data about persons wanted for crimes anywhere in the fifty states.

Computers are also being used to expedite the analysis of evidence. Los Angeles police can instantly cross-reference computer databases (e.g., compare files on suspects who own brown Chevrolets with those who have facial scars).[34]

Some police departments are using computerized imaging systems to replace mug books. Photos or sketches are stored in computer memory and easily retrieved for viewing. Several software companies have developed identification programs that help witnesses create a composite picture of the perpetrator (Figure 4.2). A vast library of photographed or drawn facial features can be stored in computer files and accessed on a terminal screen. Witnesses can scan through thousands of noses, eyes, and lips until they find those that match the suspect's. Eyeglasses, mustaches, and beards can be added; skin tones can be altered. When the composite is created, an attached camera makes a hard copy for distribution.[35]

Figure 4.1
Percent of law enforcement agencies using mobile computers or terminals, 1993 and 1997

SOURCE: *Local Police Departments, 1997* (Washington, D.C.: Bureau of Justice Statistics, 1999), 3.

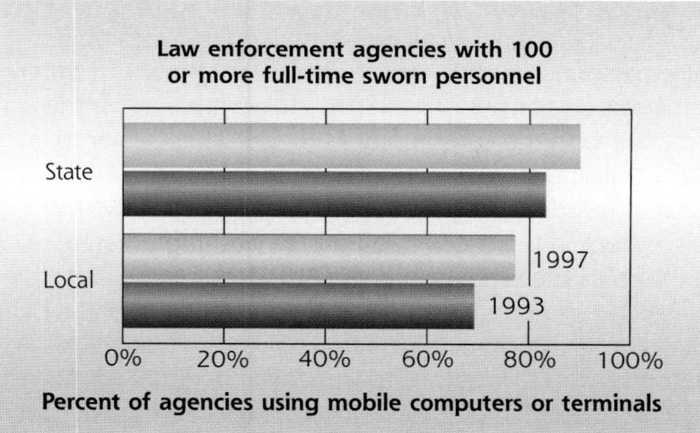

Criminal Identification Computer systems now used in the booking process can also help in the suspect identification process. During booking, a visual image of the suspect is stored in a computer's memory, along with other relevant information. By calling up color photos on the computer monitor, police can then easily create a "photo lineup" of all suspects having a particular characteristic described by a witness.

New techniques are constantly being developed. Soon, through the use of genetic algorithms (mathematical models), a computerized composite image of a suspect's face will be constructed from relatively little information.[36] Digitization of photographs will enable the reconstruction of blurred images. Videotapes of bank robbers or blurred photos of license plates, even bite marks, can be digitized using highly advanced mathematical models.

Criminal Justice and Technology

CRIME MAPPING

Crime maps offer police administrators graphic representations of where crimes are occurring in their jurisdictions. Computerized crime mapping gives the police the power to analyze and correlate a wide array of data to create immediate, detailed visuals of crime patterns. The most simple maps (such as Figure A, which shows the occurrence of Part I crimes in Tempe, Arizona, during the month of August 1999) display crime locations or concentrations and can be used to help direct patrols to places they are most needed. More complex maps can be used to chart trends in criminal activity and have even proven valuable in solving individual criminal cases. For example, serial rapists may be caught by observing and understanding the patterns of their crime so that detectives may predict where they will strike next and stake out the area with police decoys.

Crime mapping makes use of the new computer technology. Instead of archaic pin maps, computerized crime maps let the police detect patterns of crimes and pathologies or related problems. It enables them to work with multiple layers of information and scenarios, thus identifying far more successfully the emerging hot spots of criminal activity and appropriate target resources.

A survey conducted by the National Institute of Justice found that 36 percent of agencies with one hundred or more sworn officers are now using some form of computerized crime mapping.

A number of the nation's largest departments are now using mapping techniques. The New York City Police Department's CompStat process relies on computerized crime mapping to identify crime hot spots and hold officers accountable for crime reduction along the department's chain of command. The department credits CompStat for dramatic and continuing reductions in crime in New York City. The Chicago Police Department has developed ICAM (Information Collection for Automated Mapping), designed to help police officers in analyzing and solving neighborhood crime problems. ICAM, operational in all twenty-five police districts, lets beat officers and other police personnel quickly and easily generate maps of timely, accurate crime data for their beats and larger units. ICAM makes it easier for the police to share crime information with the community as they work together to support Chicago's community policing strategy.

Some mapping efforts cross jurisdictional boundaries. Examples include the Regional Crime Analysis System in the greater Baltimore–Washington area and the multijurisdictional efforts of the Greater Atlanta PACT Data Center. The Charlotte–Mecklenburg Police Department (North Carolina) uses data collected by other city and county agencies in its crime-mapping efforts. By coordinating the tax assessor's, public works, planning, and sanitation departments, Charlotte–Mecklenburg departmental analysts have made links between disorder and crime that have been instrumental in supporting the department's community policing.

Crime mapping represents one of the latest technological advances in the allocation of police resources to fight crime effectively.

New computer software is being created that allows two-dimensional mug shots to be re-created on a three-dimensional basis. This technology has the human face divided into sixty-four features. For each of the 64 features, such as noses, mouths, and chins, there are 256 different types of each feature to choose from within the program. The result is that virtually anyone's face can be re-created according to a witness or victim's description. Once re-created, the image can be compared with over 1 million mug shots in less than a second to search for a match. Rather than relying on an artist's sketch based on a victim's description of a suspect, investigators can work with a victim on a computer to

Figure A
Crime map of Tempe, Arizona, August 1999

SOURCE: Courtesy of Tempe (Arizona) Police Department.

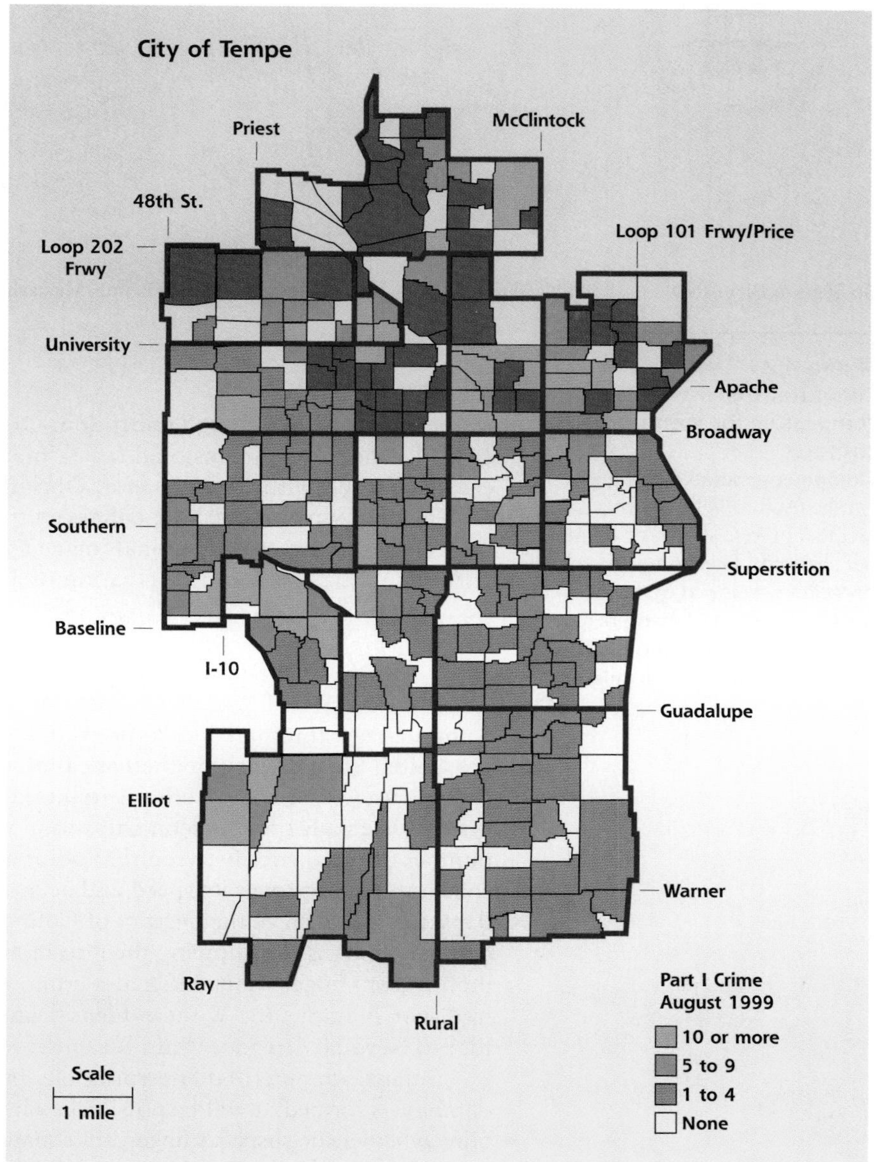

Mapinfo and Vertical Mapping are computer programs used by law enforcement agencies to determine "hot spots." To see how this technology works, go to www.tetrad.com/new/crime.html

SOURCES: William W. Bratton and Peter Knobler, *Turnaround: How America's Top Cop Reversed the Crime Epidemic* (New York: Random House, 1998) 289; Jeremy Travis, *Computerized Crime Mapping, NIJ News* (Washington, D.C.: National Institute of Justice, January 1999).

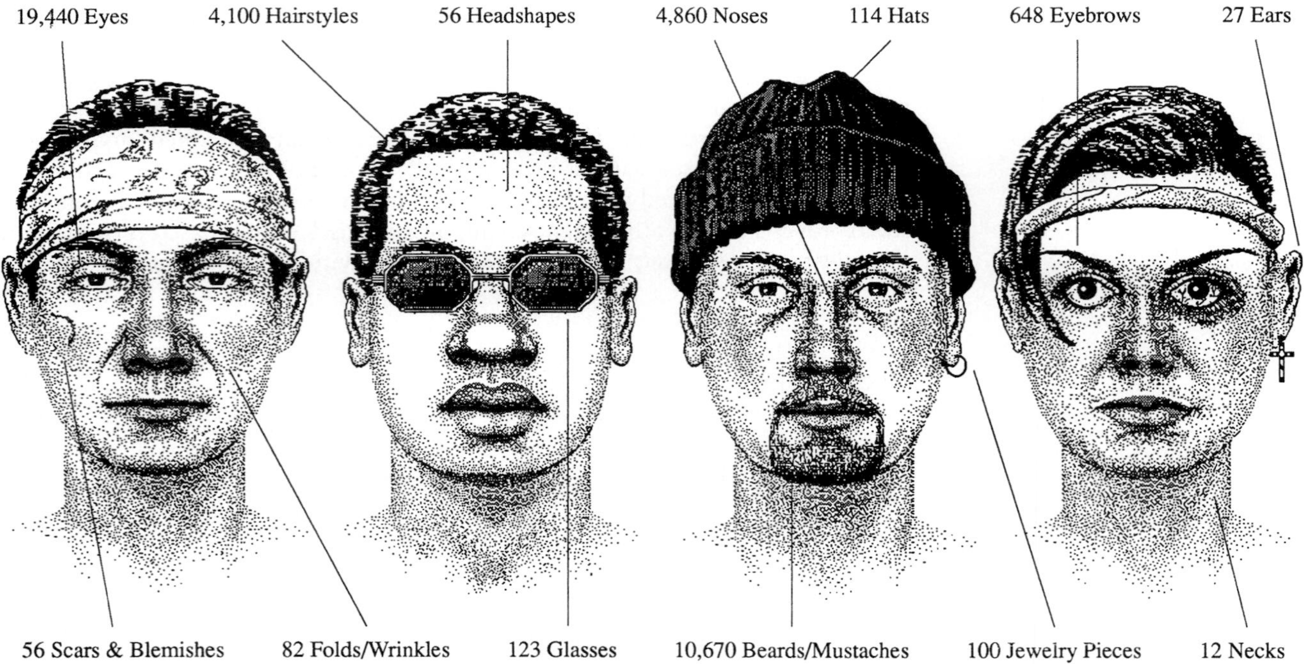

Figure 4.2
Computer-generated composites for identifying suspects
Computer-generated composites can be used to help a witness create a precise sketch of criminal suspects. The Compusketch© program developed by the Visatex Corporation of Campbell, California, contains thousands of facial features and details.

come up with a matching description. Once detectives have mug shots, they can take the three-dimensional facial images contained in the software and create a match with the mug shot. Once this is done for all 64 features, a two-dimensional mug shot can be enhanced to make a three-dimensional head. Effects on the three-dimensional image such as lighting and angles can also be changed to make a better re-creation of an environment in which a crime has taken place.[37]

Automated Fingerprint Identification Systems The use of computerized automated fingerprint identification systems (AFIS) is growing in the United States. Using mathematical models, AFIS can classify fingerprints and identify up to 250 characteristics (minutiae) of the print.[38] These automated systems use high-speed silicon chips to plot each point of minutiae and count the number of ridge lines between that point and its four nearest neighbors, which substantially improves its speed and accuracy over earlier systems. Some police departments, such as the District of Columbia's, report that computerized fingerprint systems are allowing them to make over one hundred identifications a month from fingerprints taken at a crime scene. AFIS files have been regionalized. For example, the Western Identification Network serves Alaska, California, Idaho, Nevada, Oregon, Utah, Washington, and Wyoming.[39]

If these computerized fingerprint files become standardized and a national database is formed, it will be possible to check records in all fifty states to determine whether the suspect's fingerprints match those taken at the crime scene of previously unsolved cases. A national fingerprint identification system should become an even more effective tool in 2000 because laser technology should vastly improve fingerprint analysis. Investigators will soon be able to recover prints that in the past were too damaged to be used as evidence. New breeds of fingerprint analysis will soon be available. The FBI plans to create an integrated AFIS that will allow local departments to scan fingerprints, send them electronically to a national depository, and receive back identification and criminal history of suspects.[40]

DNA profiling
The identification of criminal suspects by matching DNA samples taken from their person with specimens found at crime scenes.

DNA Testing Advanced technology is also spurring new forensic methods of identification and analysis.[41] The most prominent technique is **DNA profiling**, a procedure that has gained national attention because of the O. J. Simpson case. This technique allows suspects to be identified on the basis of the genetic material found in hair, blood, and other bodily tissues and fluids. When DNA is used as evidence in a rape trial, DNA segments are taken from the victim, the suspect, and blood and semen found on the victim. A DNA match indicates a 4 billion-to-1 chance that the suspect is the offender.

Two methods of DNA matching are used. The most popular technique, known as *RFLP* (restriction fragment length polymorphism), uses radioactive material to produce a DNA image on an X-ray film. The second method, *PCR* (polymerase chain reaction), amplifies DNA samples through molecular photocopying.[42]

DNA fingerprinting is now used as evidence in criminal trials in more than twenty states.[43] The use of DNA evidence to gain convictions has also been upheld on appeal.[44] The use of DNA evidence in criminal trials received a boost in 1997 when the FBI announced that the evidence has become so precise that experts no longer have to supply a statistical estimate of accuracy while testifying at trial (i.e., "The odds are one in a billion that this is the culprit"); they can now state in court that there exists "a reasonable degree of scientific certainty" that evidence came from a single suspect.[45]

Leading the way in the development of the most advanced forensic techniques is the Forensic Science Research and Training Center operated by the FBI in Washington, D.C., and Quantico, Virginia. The lab provides information and services to hundreds of crime labs throughout the United States. The National Institute of Justice is also sponsoring research to identify a wider variety of DNA segments for testing and is involved in developing a PCR-based DNA-profiling examination, using fluorescent detection, that will reduce the time required for DNA profiling. The FBI is now operating the DNA Index System (NDIS), a computerized database

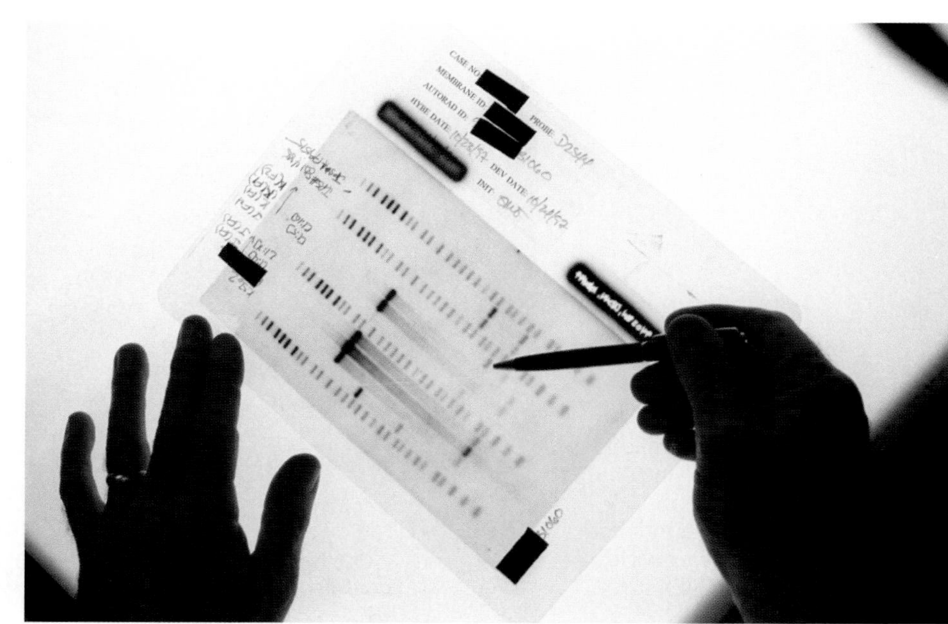

The use of DNA evidence has become widespread. On March 15, 2000, Manhattan prosecutors indicted a man known as the East Side rapist, even though police investigators had not been able to identify the culprit. Based on a DNA signature alone, the indictment will prevent the statute of limitations from expiring in three of the seven rapes the man is suspected of committing between 1994 and 1998. If the DNA is matched by police, the suspect can be brought to justice.

that will allow DNA taken at a crime scene to be searched electronically to find matches against samples taken from (1) convicted offenders and (2) other crime scenes. The first database will allow sus-pects to be identified, and the second will allow investigators to establish links between crimes, such as those involving serial killers or rapists. In 1999 the FBI announced the system made its first "cold hit" by linking evidence taken from crime scenes in Jacksonville, Florida, to ones in Washington, D.C., thereby tying nine crimes to a single offender.[46] When Timothy Spence was executed in Virginia on April 27, 1994, he was the first person convicted and executed almost entirely on the basis of DNA evidence.[47]

Communications Computer technology will enhance communications and information dissemination. For example, the St. Petersburg (Florida) Police Department has equipped all its officers with portable computers, which has significantly cut down on the time needed to write and duplicate reports.[48] Police can now use terminals to draw accident diagrams, communicate with city traffic engineers, and merge their incident reports into other databases. Pen computing, in which officers write directly on a computer screen, eliminates paperwork and increases the accuracy of reports.[49] To make this material more accessible to the officer on patrol, head-up display (HUD) units now project information onto screens located on patrol car windshields; police officers can now access computer readouts without taking their eyes off the road![50]

Future police technology will involve more efficient communications systems. Officers are now using cellular phones in their cars to facilitate communications with victims and witnesses.[51] Departments that cover wide geographical areas and maintain independent precincts and substations are experimenting with **teleconferencing** systems that provide both audio and video linkages. Police agencies may use advanced communications gear to track stolen vehicles. Car owners will be able to buy transmitters that give off a signal to a satellite or other listening device that can then be monitored and tracked by the specially equipped patrol cars; this system is being tested.[52] Finally, some departments are linking advanced communications systems with computers, making use of elec-

teleconferencing
Using audio and video linkups to allow people to communicate from distant locations.

Technology helps police officers increase their crime solving abilities. This police car in New York is equipped with a monitor that can identify stolen vehicles supplied with the LOJACK tracking device.

tronic bulletin boards that link officers in an active on-line system, enabling them to communicate faster and more easily.[53]

PRIVATE SECURITY

Because police forces alone can have only a limited influence on controlling crime and protecting victims, alternative methods of policing have been developed. In the next decade, *private security forces* should significantly affect law enforcement.

The emergence of the private security industry has been dramatic, increasing at a much greater pace than public policing.[54] In fact, as Figure 4.3 shows, it is estimated that more money is spent on private protection than on state-sponsored law enforcement agencies; by 2000 over $100 billion will have been spent on private security.[55] Today, more than 1.5 million people work in private security—far more than the total number of sworn police officers.

Much of what is known about the national trends in private policing comes from the **Hallcrest Report,** a government-financed survey of the industry that found that the use of private security falls into two major areas.[56] **Proprietary security** is undertaken by an organization's own employees and includes both plainclothes and uniformed agents directed by the organization's head of security. The second type of private security is **contractual services,** such as guards, investigators, and armored cars, provided by private companies, such as Wackenhut and Pinkerton's. Also included within the category of contractual security is the wide variety of security products such as safes, electronic access-control devices, and closed-circuit television.

The Hallcrest Report estimated that by 2000 there will have been 750,000 contract guards and 410,000 proprietary security forces. The technology that supports the field will grow rapidly, with more sophisticated alarm systems, access control, and closed-circuit television.

The expanded role of private security is not without its perils. Many law enforcement executives are critical of the quality of private security and believe it has little value as a crime control mechanism. One complaint heard by the Hallcrest researchers was the lack of training and standards in the profession. Still another source of contention between private security and local police agencies is the increasing number of police calls that are a function of private security measures.

The Hallcrest Report recommended a number of strategies to improve the quality of private security: upgrade employee quality; create statewide regulatory bodies and statutes for controlling security firms; require mandatory training; increase police knowledge of private security; expand the interaction between police and private security providers, such as the sharing of information; and transfer some police functions, such as burglar alarm checking, to the private sector. The report recommended that the industry create its own standards similar to those adopted by the British Security Industry Association to professionalize the trade.

Figure 4.3
Private security versus law enforcement and spending

SOURCE: William Cunningham, John Strauchs, and Clifford Van Meter, *Private Security: Patterns and Trends* (Washington, D.C.: National Institute of Justice, 1991), p. 3.

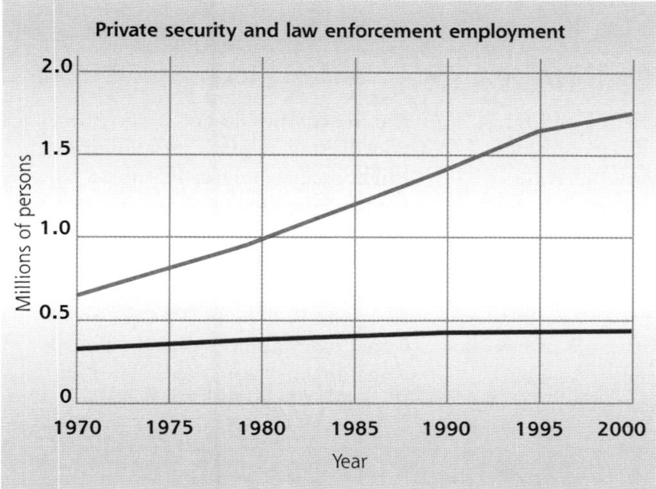

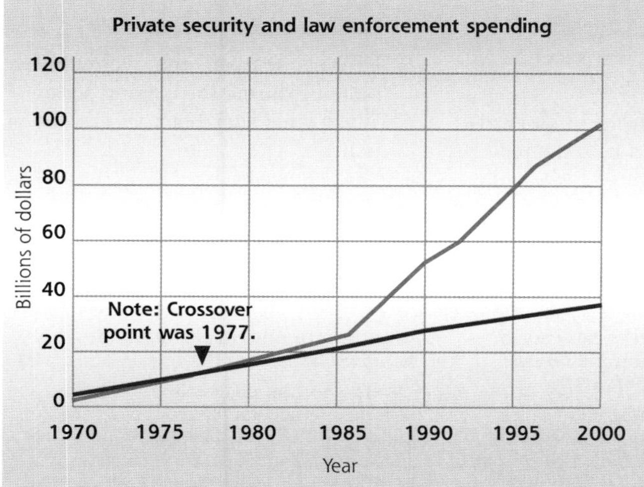

SUMMARY

Present-day police departments evolved out of early European and colonial American crime control forces.

Many types of organizations are involved in law enforcement activities on the local, state, and federal levels of government. The most visible law enforcement agencies are local police departments, which carry out patrol, investigative, and traffic functions, as well as many support activities.

By 2000 police departments will have begun to rely on advanced computer-based technology to identify suspects and collate evidence. Automated fingerprint systems and computerized identification systems will have become widespread. There is danger that technology may make police overly intrusive and interfere with civil liberties.

KEY TERMS

tithings
hue and cry
hundred
constable
shire reeve
watch system
justice of the peace
sheriff
vigilante
Federal Bureau of Investigation (FBI)
Drug Enforcement Administration (DEA)
DNA profiling
teleconferencing

INFOTRAC COLLEGE EDITION EXERCISE

InfoTrac College Edition provides some important research on the private security industry. Do a search using the key words "private security" and "private police."

Private security service has become a multibillion-dollar industry with ten thousand firms and 1.5 million employees. Even federal police services have been privatized to cut expenses, a move that was opposed by the American Federation of Government Employees. To learn more about this growth, see

Gayle M. B. Hanson, "Private Protection is Secure Industry," *Insight on the News* 13 (1997): 19.

There will be more legal scrutiny as the private security business blossoms. For example, are security guards subject to the same search-and-seizure standards as police officers? The Supreme Court has repeatedly stated that purely private search activities do not violate the Fourth Amendment's prohibitions. Might security guards be subject to Fourth Amendment requirements if they are performing services that are traditionally reserved for the police, such as guarding communities? To find out, read

John B. Owens, "Westec Story: Gated Communities and the Fourth Amendment," *American Criminal Law Review* 34 (1997): 127–160.

QUESTIONS

1. List the problems faced by today's police departments that were also present during the early days of policing.
2. Distinguish between the duties of the state police, sheriffs' departments, and local police departments.
3. Why has the private security industry blossomed? What factors will influence the role of private policing during the coming decade?
4. What are some of the technological advances that should help the police solve more crimes? What are the dangers of these advances?
5. Discuss the trends that will influence policing during the coming decade. What other social factors may affect police?

NOTES

1. "Have Gun? Will Travel: Criminals Are Afraid to Arm Themselves in a Virginia City That Simply Enforced the Law," *Time,* 16 August 1999, 30.

2. Richard A. Leo and Richard J. Ofshe, "The Consequences of False Confessions: Deprivations of Liberty and Miscarriages of Justice in the Age of Psychological Interrogation," *Journal of Criminal Law and Criminology* 88 (1998): 429–96.

3. "Law Enforcement Seeks Answers to 'Racial Profiling' Complaints," *Criminal Justice Newsletter* 29 (1998): 5.

4. Liqun Cao, James Frank, and Francis Cullen, "Race, Community Context and Confidence in the Police," *American Journal of Police* 15 (1996): 3–15.

5. Thomas Priest and Deborah Brown Carter, "Evaluations of Police Performance in an African American Sample," *Journal of Criminal Justice* 27 (1999): 457–65.

6. This section relies heavily on such sources as Malcolm Sparrow, Mark Moore, and David Kennedy, *Beyond 911, A New Era for Policing* (New York: Basic Books, 1990); Daniel Devlin, *Police Procedure, Administration, and Organization* (London: Butterworth, 1966); Robert Fogelson, *Big City Police* (Cambridge, Mass.: Harvard

University Press, 1977); Roger Lane, *Policing the City, Boston 1822–1885* (Cambridge, Mass.: Harvard University Press, 1967); J. J. Tobias, *Crime and Industrial Society in the Nineteenth Century* (New York: Schocken Books, 1967); Samuel Walker, *A Critical History of Police Reform: The Emergence of Professionalism* (Lexington, Mass.: Lexington Books, 1977); Samuel Walker, *Popular Justice* (New York: Oxford University Press, 1980); John McMullan, "The New Improved Monied Police: Reform Crime Control and Commodification of Policing in London, *British Journal of Criminology* 36 (1996): 85–108.

7. Devlin, *Police Procedure, Administration, and Organization,* 3.

8. Phillip Reichel, "Southern Slave Patrols as a Transitional Type," *American Journal of Police* 7 (1988): 51–78.

9. Walker, *Popular Justice,* 61.

10. Ibid., 8.

11. Dennis Rousey, "Cops and Guns: Police Use of Deadly Force in Nineteenth-Century New Orleans," *American Journal of Legal History* 28 (1984): 41–66.

12. Law Enforcement Assistance Administration, *Two Hundred Years of American Criminal Justice* (Washington, D.C.: Government Printing Office, 1976).

13. National Commission on Law Observance and Enforcement, *Report on the Police* (Washington, D.C.: Government Printing Office, 1931), 5–7.

14. Pamela Irving Jackson, *Minority Group Threat, Crime, and Policing* (New York: Praeger, 1989).

15. James Q. Wilson and George Kelling, "Broken Windows," *Atlantic Monthly* 249 (1982): 29–38.

16. Frank Tippett, "It Looks Just like a War Zone," *Time,* 27 May 1985, 16–22; "San Francisco, New York Police Troubled by Series of Scandals," *Criminal Justice Newsletter* 16 (1985): 2–4; Karen Polk, "New York Police: Caught in the Middle and Losing Faith," *Boston Globe,* 28 December 1988, 3.

17. John Klofas, "Drugs and Justice: The Impact of Drugs on Criminal Justice in a Metropolitan Community," *Crime and Delinquency* 39 (1993): 204–24.

18. Steven Tuch and Ronald Weitzer, "The Polls-Trends, Racial Differences in Attitudes toward the Police," *Public Opinion Quarterly* 61 (1997): 642–63.

19. Kathleen Grubb, "Cold War to Gang War," *Boston Globe,* 22 January 1992, 1.

20. Bruce Smith, *Police Systems in the United States* (New York: Harper & Row, 1960), 72.

21. *Sheriffs' Departments,* 1997 Bureau of Justice Statistics Executive Summary, October 1999.

22. *Local Police Departments, 1997* (Washington, D.C.: Bureau of Justice Statistics, 1999).

23. Brian A. Reaves and Andrew L. Goldberg, *Census of State and Local Law Enforcement Agencies, 1997* (Washington, D.C.: Bureau of Justice Statistics, 1998).

24. See, for example Susan Martin and Edwin Hamilton, "Police Handling of Child Abuse Cases: Policies, Procedures and Issues," *American Journal of Police* 9 (1990).

25. See, for example, Robert Keppel and Joseph Weis, *Improving the Investigation of Violent Crime: The Homicide Investigation and Tracking System* (Washington, D.C.: National Institute of Justice, 1993).

26. This section leans heavily on Jerome Skolnick and David Bayley, *The New Blue Line* (New York: Free Press, 1986), 210–30.

27. See Stephen Matrofski, "The Prospects of Change in Police Patrol: A Decade in Review," *American Journal of Police* 9 (1990): 1–69.

28. Larry Coutorie, "The Future of High-Technology Crime, A Parallel Delphi Study," *Journal of Criminal Justice* 23 (1995): 13–27.

29. Bill Clede, "Cellular Digital Packet Data: CDPD," *Law and Order* 43 (1995): 36–37.

30. J. Thomas McEwen and Faye Taxman, *Applications of Computerized Mapping to Police Operations* (Alexandria, Va.: Institute for Law and Justice, 1994).

31. Lois Pliant, "Information Management," *Police Chief* 61 (1994): 31–35.

32. Mark Birchler, "Computers in a Small Police Agency," *FBI Law Enforcement Bulletin* 58 (1989): 7–9.

33. John Schmitz, "Criminals Versus Computers," *Law and Order* 42 (1994): 80–84.

34. Kristen Olson, "LAPD's Newest Investigative Tool," *Police Chief* 55 (1988): 30.

35. See Judith Blair Schmitt, "Computerized ID Systems," *Police Chief* 59 (1992): 33–45.

36. Richard Rau, "Forensic Science and Criminal Justice Technology: High-Tech Tools for the 90s," *NIJ Reports* 224 (1991): 6–10.

37. Spotlight on Computer Imaging," *Police Chief* 66 (1999): 6–8.

38. William Stover, "Automated Fingerprint Identification — Regional Application of Technology," *FBI Law Enforcement Bulletin* 53 (1984): 1–4.

39. Schmitt, "Computerized ID Systems," 35.

40. Lois Pliant, "Exploiting Fingerprint Technology," *Police Chief* 61 (1994): 29–34.

41. See, generally, Ryan McDonald, "Juries and Crime Labs: Correcting the Weak Links in the DNA Chain," *American Journal of Law and Medicine* 24 (1998): 345–63; "DNA Profiling Advancement," *FBI Law Enforcement Bulletin* 67 (1998): 24.

42. Rau, "Forensic Science and Criminal Justice Technology."

43. "California Attorney General Endorses DNA Fingerprinting," *Criminal Justice Newsletter* 1 (1989): 1.

44. *State v. Ford,* 301 S.C. 485, 392 S.E.2d 781 (1990).

45. "Under New Policy, FBI Examiners Testify to Absolute DNA Matches," *Criminal Justice Newsletter* 28 (1997): 1–2.

46. "FBI's DNA Profile Clearinghouse Announce First 'Cold Hit,'" *Criminal Justice Newsletter* 16 March 1999, 5.

47. "South Side Strangler's Execution Cited as DNA Evidence Landmark," *Criminal Justice Newsletter,* 2 May 1994, 3.

48. Brewer Stone, "The High-Tech Beat in St. Pete," *Police Chief* 55 (1988): 23–28.

49. "Pen Computing: The Natural 'Next Step' for Field Personnel," *Law and Order* 43 (1995): 37.

50. Miller McMillan, "High Tech Enters the Field of View," *Police Chief* 62 (1994): 29.

51. Ibid., 24.

52. Mark Thompson, "Police Seeking Radio Channel for Stolen Auto Tracking System," *Criminal Justice Newsletter,* 15 March 1989, 1.

chapter 5

The Police: Role and Function

In July 1996 the elite antigang unit from the Los Angeles Police Department's Rampart Division raided gang-infested apartments at Shatto Place; their target was the notorious 18th Street Gang, one of Los Angeles's most violent gangs. During the raid, police officers killed one gang member and wounded another. A departmental investigation found nothing wrong and exonerated the police involved. Then in 1999, Rafael A. Perez, an officer who took part in the raid was caught stealing eight pounds of cocaine from police evidence lockers. After pleading guilty in September 1999, he bargained for a lighter sentence by telling departmental investigators about police brutality, perjury, planted evidence, drug corruption, and attempted murder within the Rampart Division and its antigang unit, known as CRASH (Community Resources Against Street Hoodlums). Perez told authorities that during the Shatto raid, the victims may have been unarmed so that the raiding officers resorted to a "throwdown" — slang for a weapon being planted to make a shooting legally justifiable. Perez's testimony resulted in at least twelve Rampart cops being fired or relieved from duty. But Perez was not done. He also said he and his partner, Officer Nino Durden, shot an unarmed 18th Street Gang member named Javier Ovando, then planted a semiautomatic rifle on the unconscious suspect and claimed that Ovando had tried to shoot them during a stakeout. Their testimony helped get Ovando, confined to a wheelchair for life because of the shooting, a twenty-three-year sentence for assault. Now Ovando has been freed from prison and is suing the city for more than $20 million.[1] ■

The Los Angeles scandal illustrates the difficulty some police officers have in carrying out their role. They are told to be enforcers of the law in some of the toughest areas in urban America, yet they are criticized or even jailed when their tactics become too aggressive. Is it unrealistic to expect police officers to fulfill society's demand for order while maintaining a tight grip on their behavior and emotions?

This chapter describes the organization of police departments and their various operating branches: patrol, investigation, service, and administration. It discusses the realities and ambiguities of the police role and how the concept of the police mission has been changing radically. The chapter concludes with a brief overview of some of the most important administrative issues confronting U.S. law enforcement agencies.

THE POLICE ORGANIZATION

Most municipal police departments in the United States are independent agencies within the executive branch of government and operating without specific administrative control from any higher governmental authority. On occasion, police agencies will cooperate and participate in mutually beneficial enterprises, such as sharing information on known criminals, or they may help federal agencies investigate interstate criminal cases. Aside from such cooperative efforts, police departments tend to be functionally independent organizations with unique sets of rules, policies, procedures, norms, budgets, and so on. The unique structure of police agencies greatly influences their function and effectiveness.

Although many police agencies are in the process of rethinking their organization and goals, the majority are still organized in a militaristic, hierarchical manner, as illustrated in Figure 5.1. Within this organizational model, each element of the department normally has its own chain of command. For example, in a large municipal department, the detective bureau might have a captain who serves as the director of a particular division (such as homicide), a lieutenant who oversees individual cases and acts as liaison with other police agencies, and sergeants and inspectors who carry out the actual field work. Smaller departments may have a captain as head of all detectives, while lieutenants supervise

Figure 5.1
Organization of a metropolitan police department

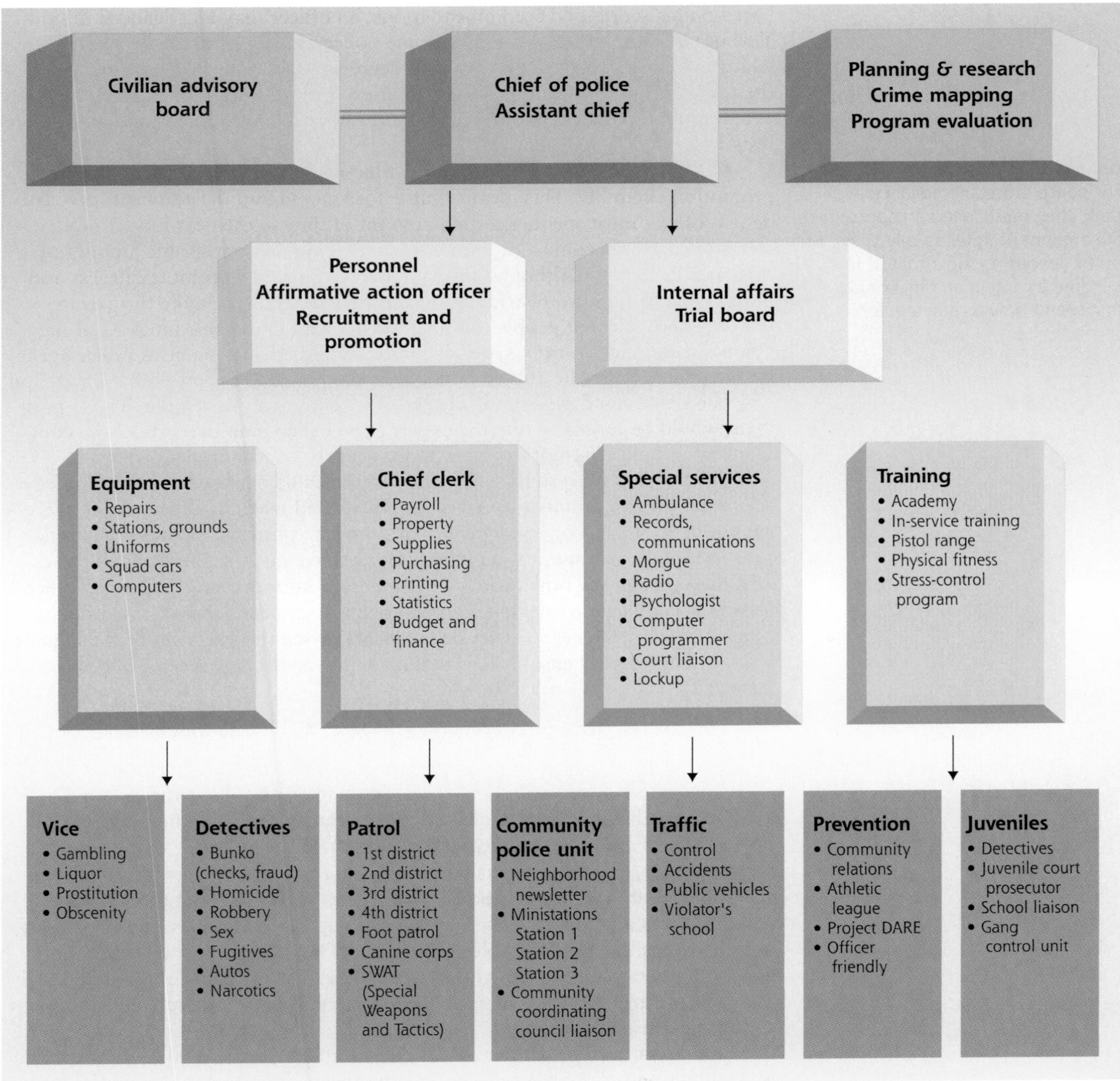

police chief
The top administrator of the police department, who sets policy and has general control over all operating branches.

individual subsystems (such as robbery or homicide). At the head of the organization is the **police chief,** who sets policy and has general administrative control over all the department's various operating branches.

The typical police department's organizational structure has several problems. First, citizens often have difficulty in determining who is actually responsible for the department's policies and operations. Second, the large number of operating divisions and the lack of any clear relationship among them almost guarantee that the decision-making practices of one branch will be unknown to another; two divisions may unknowingly compete with each other over jurisdiction on a particular case.

Most departments also follow a military-like system in promoting personnel within the ranks; at an appropriate time, a promotion test may be given and, based on his scores and recommendations, an officer may be advanced in rank. This organizational style frustrates some police officers from furthering their education, since a college or advanced degree may have little direct impact on their promotion potential or responsibilities. Furthermore, some otherwise competent police officers cannot increase their rank because of their inability to take tests well.

time-in-rank system
For police officers to advance in rank, they must spend an appropriate amount of time, usually years, in the preceding rank; that is, to become a captain an officer must first spend time as a lieutenant.

Most police departments employ a **time-in-rank system** for determining promotion eligibility. This means that before moving up the administrative ladder, an officer must spend a certain amount of time in the next lowest rank; a sergeant cannot become a captain without serving an appropriate amount of time as a lieutenant. Although this system is designed to promote fairness and limit favoritism, it also restricts administrative flexibility. Unlike the private sector, where talented people can be pushed ahead in the best interests of the company, the time-in-rank system prohibits rapid advancement. A police agency would probably not be able to hire a computer systems expert with a Ph.D. and give her a command position in charge of its data-analysis section. The department would be forced to hire the expert as a civilian employee under the command of a ranking senior officer who may not be as technically proficient.

Under this rank system, a title can rarely be taken away or changed once it is earned. Police administrators become frustrated when qualified junior officers cannot be promoted or reassigned to appropriate positions because they lack time in rank or because less qualified officers have more seniority. Inability to advance through the ranks convinces numerous educated and ambitious officers to seek private employment. The rank system also means that talented police officers cannot transfer to other departments or sell their services to the highest bidder. Time in rank ensures the stability — for better or worse — of police agencies.

THE POLICE ROLE

In countless books, movies, and TV shows, the public has been presented with a view of policing that romanticizes police officers as fearless crime fighters who think little of their own safety as they engage in daily shoot-outs with Uzi-toting drug runners, psychopathic serial killers, and organized crime hit men. Occasionally, but not often, fictional patrol officers and detectives seem aware of departmental rules, legal decisions, citizen groups, civil suits, or physical danger. They are rarely faced with the economic necessity of moonlighting as security guards, caring about an annual pay raise, or griping when someone less deserving gets promoted ahead of them for political reasons.

How close is this portrayal of a selfless crime fighter to real life? Not very, according to most research efforts. Police officers are asked to deal with hundreds of incidents each year. For example, the Los Angeles Police Department receives over 3.5 million calls for service each year, or 593 per officer; police in Dallas receive over 1.6 million calls, or 665 per officer. This seems to be a staggering load, but some departments — such as Lawrence, Massachusetts — receive over 1,500 calls for service per officer each year![2]

Most research efforts show that a police officer's crime-fighting efforts are only a small part of his overall activities. Studies of police work indicate that a significant portion of an officer's time is spent handling minor disturbances, service calls, and administrative duties. Studies conducted over the past two decades have found that social service and administrative tasks consume more than half a police officer's time and account for more than half of her calls. Police work, then, involves much more than "catching criminals."[3]

These results are not surprising when UCR (Uniform Crime Reports) arrest data are considered. Each year, about 600,000 local, county, and state police officers make about 15 million arrests, or about twenty-five each. Of these, about 2.5 million are for serious index crimes (Part I), or less than five yearly per officer. Given an even distribution of arrests, it is evident that the average police officer makes two arrests per month and less than one felony arrest every two months.

These figures should be interpreted with caution because not all police officers are engaged in activities that allow them to make arrests, such as patrol or detective work. About one-third of all sworn officers in the nation's largest police departments are in such units as communications, antiterrorism, administration, and personnel and are therefore unlikely to make arrests. Even if the number of arrests per officer were adjusted by one-third, it would still amount to only nine or ten serious crime arrests per officer per year. So, though police handle thousands of calls each year, relatively few result in an arrest for a serious crime, such as a robbery and burglary; in suburban and rural areas, years may go by before a police officer arrests someone for a serious crime.

The U.S. State Department's Office of the Coordinator for Counterterrorism hosts a Web site. Go to www.state.gov/www/global/terrorism/

The evidence, then, shows that the police role involves a preponderance of noncrime-related activities and is similar in both large and small departments. Although officers in large urban departments may be called on to handle more felony cases than those in small towns, they, too, will probably find that the bulk of their daily activities are not crime related. In the future, police officers will probably spend even more of their time learning to deal with the social problems exploding across the United States, ranging from women who have been battered in domestic disputes to runaway children. More attention will be paid to **special-needs populations:** substance abusers, the homeless, the mentally ill, and the disabled.[4]

special-needs population
A group of people whose personal problems need to be addressed by human services organizations — for example, the disabled, mentally ill, or substance abusers.

Metropolitan police departments carry out a wide variety of tasks and maintain a number of highly specialized roles. The most important of these, the patrol and investigation functions, are described in the next sections.

THE PATROL FUNCTION

Regardless of style of policing, uniformed patrol officers are the backbone of the police department, usually accounting for about two-thirds of a department's personnel.[5] Patrol officers are the most highly visible components of the entire criminal justice system. They are charged with supervising specific areas of their jurisdiction, called **beats,** whether on foot, in a patrol car, or by motorcycle, horse, helicopter, or even boat. Each beat, or patrol area, is covered twenty-four hours a day by different shifts. The major purpose of patrol is to

beat
A defined patrol area.

1. Deter crime by maintaining a visible police presence.
2. Maintain public order (peacekeeping) within the patrol area.

3. Enable the police department to respond quickly to law violations or other emergencies.
4. Identify and apprehend law violators.
5. Aid individuals and care for those who cannot help themselves.
6. Facilitate the movement of traffic and people.
7. Create a feeling of security in the community.[6]

order maintenance (peacekeeping)
The order-maintenance aspect of the police role involves peacekeeping, maintaining order and authority without the need for formal arrest, "handling the situation," and keeping things under control by using threats, persuasion, and understanding.

Patrol officers' responsibilities are immense; they may suddenly be faced with an angry mob, an armed felon, or a suicidal teenager and be forced to make split-second decisions on what action to take. At the same time, they must be sensitive to the needs of citizens who are often of diverse racial and ethnic backgrounds.

Most experts agree that the great bulk of police patrol efforts is devoted to what has been described as order maintenance or peacekeeping, an activity that falls on the borderline between criminal and noncriminal behavior. For instance, police may decide to stop teenagers in order to determine if they are operating a stolen vehicle, and, if the registration proves valid, warn them about the consequences of careless driving.

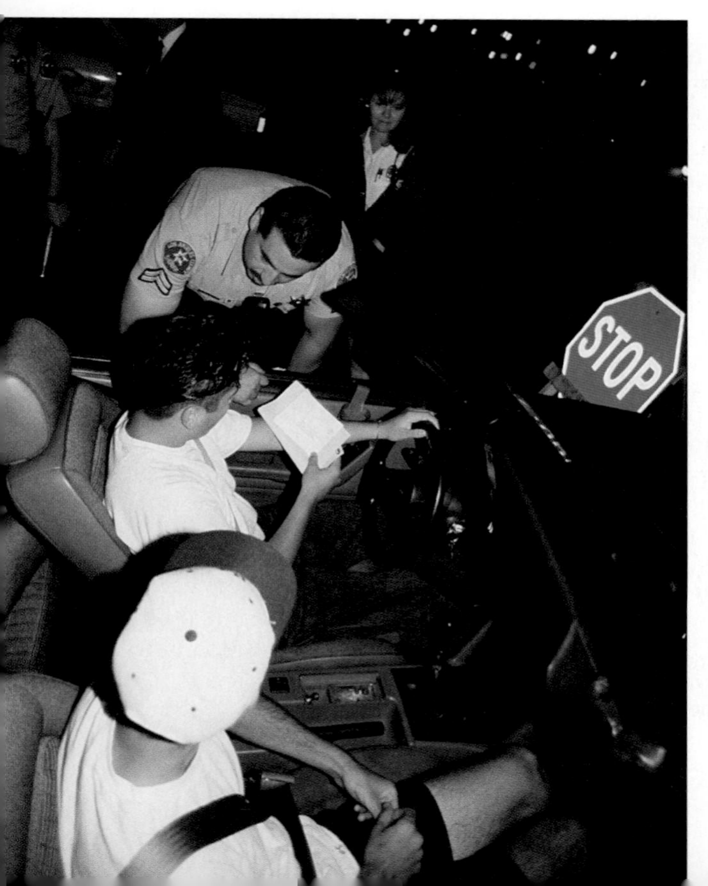

Patrol Activities

Most experts agree that the great bulk of patrol efforts is devoted to what has been described as **order maintenance, or peacekeeping:** maintaining order and civility within their assigned jurisdiction.[7] Order-maintenance functions fall on the border between criminal and noncriminal behavior. The patrol officer's discretion often determines whether a noisy neighborhood dispute involves the crime of disturbing the peace or whether it can be controlled with street-corner diplomacy and the combatants sent on their way. Similarly, teenagers milling around in the shopping center parking lot can be brought in and turned over to the juvenile authorities or handled in a less formal and often more efficient manner.

The major role of police seems to be "handling the situation." Police encounter many troubling incidents that need some sort of "fixing up."[8] Enforcing the law might be one tool a patrol officer uses; threat, coercion, sympathy, understanding, and apathy might be others. Most important is keeping things under control so that there are no complaints that the officer is doing nothing or doing too much. The real police role, then, may be as a community problem solver.

Police officers actually practice a policy of selective enforcement, concentrating on some crimes but handling the majority in an informal manner. A police officer is supposed to know when to take action and when not to, whom to arrest and whom to deal with by issuing a warning or some other informal action. If a mistake is made, the officer can come under fire from his peers and superiors, as well as the general public. Consequently, the patrol officer's job is extremely demanding and often unrewarding and unappreciated. It is not surprising that the attitudes of police officers toward the public are sometimes characterized as being ambivalent and cynical.[9]

Does Patrol Deter Crime?

For many years, preventive police patrol has been considered one of the greatest deterrents to criminal behavior. The visible presence of patrol cars on the street and the rapid deployment of police officers to the scene of the crime were viewed as particularly effective law enforcement techniques. However, research efforts have questioned the basic assumptions of patrol. The most widely heralded attempt at measuring patrol effectiveness was undertaken during the early 1970s in Kansas City, Missouri, under sponsorship of the Police Foundation, a private institute that studies police behavior.[10]

To evaluate the effectiveness of patrol, the researchers divided fifteen separate police districts into three groups: One group retained normal patrol; the second (proactive) set of districts were supplied with two to three times the normal amount of patrol forces; the third (reactive) group had its preventive patrol eliminated, and police officers responded only when summoned by citizens to the scene of a particular crime.

The Los Angeles Police Department, Dallas Police Department, and New York Police Department broadcast radio reports from patrol officers live on the Web. To listen, go to www.policescanner.com/

Data from the Kansas City study indicated that these variations in patrol techniques had little effect on the crime patterns in the fifteen districts. The presence or absence of patrol did not seem to affect residential or business burglaries, motor vehicle thefts, larcenies involving auto accessories, robberies, vandalism, or other criminal behavior.[11] Moreover, variations in patrol techniques appeared to have little influence on citizens' attitudes toward the police, their satisfaction with police, or their fear of future criminal behavior.[12]

Although the Kansas City study found little evidence that police patrol could deter crime, police in a number of jurisdictions have attempted to test the effectiveness of patrol by targeting areas for increased police presence. For example, a police task force might target street-level narcotics dealers by using undercover agents and surveillance cameras in known drug-dealing locales. Or they may actively enforce public nuisance laws in an effort to demonstrate the department's crime-fighting resolve. These efforts have not proven to be successful mechanisms for lowering crime rates.[13] In addition, there is the problem of **displacement:** Criminals move from an area targeted for increased police presence to another that is less well protected; when the police leave, they return to "business as usual."

displacement
The process by which the presence of police officers in one area causes criminals to move to another, less well-guarded neighborhood.

Proactive Patrol The Kansas City study, although subject to criticism because of its research design, greatly influenced the way police experts viewed the effectiveness of patrol. Its rather lukewarm findings set the stage for community and problem-oriented policing models, which stress social service over crime deterrence. However, it may be too soon to dismiss police patrol as a crime-fighting technique. Although the mere presence of police may not be sufficient to deter crime, the manner in which they approach their task may make a difference. Evidence shows that cities with larger police departments, which have more officers per capita than the norm, also experience lower levels of violent crimes.[14] Police departments that use a **proactive,** aggressive law enforcement style may help reduce crime rates. Jurisdictions that encourage patrol officers to stop motor vehicles to issue citations and to aggressively arrest and detain suspicious persons also experience lower crime rates than jurisdictions that do not follow such proactive policies.[15] Departments that more actively enforce minor regulations, such as disorderly conduct and traffic laws, are also more likely to experience lower felony rates.[16]

proactive policing
A police department policy emphasizing stopping crimes before they occur rather than reacting to crimes that have already occurred.

Pinpointing why proactive policing works so effectively is difficult. It may have a **deterrent effect:** Aggressive policing increases community perception that police arrest many criminals and that most violators get caught; criminals are scared to commit crimes in a town that has such an active police force! Proactive policing may also help control crime because it results in conviction of more criminals. Because aggressive police arrest more suspects, there are fewer left on the street to commit crime; fewer criminals produce lower crime rates.

deterrent effect
Stopping or reducing crime by convincing would-be criminals that they stand a significant risk of being apprehended and punished for their crimes.

Aggressive police patrol efforts have been a critical success. The downturn in the New York City violent crime rate during the 1990s has been attributed to aggressive police work aimed at lifestyle crimes: vandalism, panhandling, and graffiti.[17] However, as the Policy, Programs, and Issues in Criminal Justice feature shows, aggressive police work may have its downside.

TARGETING CRIMES Evidence also shows that targeting specific crimes can be successful. One aggressive patrol program, known as the Kansas City Gun Experiment, was directed at restricting the carrying of guns in high-risk

Policy, Programs, and Issues in Criminal Justice

ZERO TOLERANCE: AGGRESSIVE POLICING IN NEW YORK CITY

During the 1990s New York City experienced a significant reduction in street crime. Much of the crime reduction has been attributed to the NYPD's (New York Police Department) concerted effort to rid the city of seemingly minor lifestyle offenses such as prostitution, low-level drug dealing, and panhandling. City and law enforcement officials believe that dangerous criminals will be deterred if they get tough on these crimes and maintain a zero-tolerance policy toward any offense. Criminologist Judith Greene has explored whether the NYPD's zero-tolerance approach is truly responsible for the rather impressive reduction in urban crime rates.

When Mayor Rudolph Giuliani took office in 1993, he promised to make New York City a safer place. One of Guiliani's first acts was to hire then Boston Police Chief William Bratton to run the NYPD. At the time of Bratton's appointment, many thought that a significant crime reduction was impossible, believing that the NYPD was too big to manage effectively.

Bratton, however, brought a fresh approach to policing. He helped update the technology of the NYPD by creating the crime-mapping CompStat program, which put crime data into the hands of precinct commanders. Bratton held commanders accountable if crime problems were not taken care of in a timely fashion. He also replaced officers whose performances he deemed inadequate. Finally, Bratton increased the freedom of police officers to stop, search, and question those who have violated the law, even if infractions were not especially serious. Law enforcement officials believed that stopping and questioning a suspect on an unimportant law violation might turn up a weapon or lead to information about a more serious crime that was yet to take place.

The numbers seemed to support the new practices of the police because the city saw dramatic reductions in the number of murders, nonnegligent homicides, robberies, and burglaries from 1993 to 1997. New York also saw its place on the FBI index crimes fall from 87th in 1993 to 150th in 1997.

Although the numbers appear to support a zero-tolerance approach, Greene reports that the city paid a heavy price for adopting an aggressive crime control strategy. Filings of civil rights violations committed by the NYPD climbed 75 percent in four years after the zero-tolerance strategy began. By 1996 citizen complaints filed with New York's Civilian Complaint Review Board had risen by 60 percent. Complaints against the police in cases in which no arrests were made doubled within a year of the implementation; most incidents occurred in minority neighborhoods. Amnesty International claimed that New York had problems with police brutality and the use of unjustifiable force.

Greene also points out that during the early 1990s other urban areas employed less aggressive police tactics to achieve similar results. For example, the San Diego (California) Police Department took a more community-oriented approach to crime prevention by adopting what they refer to as the *neighborhood policing philosophy.* This model has law enforcement personnel work in conjunction with community organizations such as Neighborhood Watch programs to prevent and control crime. The SDPD works closely with citizens and businesses to try to create change in areas where chronic crime problems exist. Information sharing is the norm, and teams work with residents to find solutions to long-term problems.

The crime reduction results achieved by San Diego's neighborhood policing philosophy are similar to those attained with New York City's heralded zero-tolerance program. However, the results were achieved at less cost. New York's 37.4 percent drop in crime from 1990 to 1995 was bolstered by a 39.5 percent increase in personnel; San Diego's 36.8 percent crime rate drop during the same time period was accomplished with only a 6.2 percent increase in staff. Perhaps even more important to the community, San Diego's crime rate decrease was accompanied by a decrease in the number of citizen complaints filed against the police.

InfoTrac College Edition Research

To learn more about the pros and cons of zero-tolerance policing, read

Matt Bai and Gregory Beals, "A Mayor under Siege: How Rudy Giuliani, One of the Nation's Most Successful Officeholders, Got Himself Caught in a Political Cross-Fire over the Death of an Unarmed Man," *Newsweek* 5 April 1999, 40.

Sandra Walklate, "Zero Tolerance: Policing a Free Society," *British Journal of Criminology* 38 (1998): 317.

SOURCE: Judith Greene, "Zero Tolerance: A Case Study of Police Policies and Practices in New York City," *Crime and Delinquency* 45 (1999): 171–88.

Police officers make an arrest outside a Los Angeles laundromat. Some experts believe that strong action on "life style crimes," such as loitering and panhandling, can help reduce the overall crime rate. Although these tactics may work, how do they affect the social climate? How aggressive should police officers be in cracking down on crime?

places at high-risk times. Working with academics from the University of Maryland, the Kansas City Police Department focused extra patrol attention on a "hot spot" high-crime area identified by computer analysis of all gun crimes. Over a twenty-nine-week period, the gun patrol officers made thousands of car and pedestrian checks and traffic stops and made over six hundred arrests. Using frisks and searches, they found twenty-nine guns; an additional forty-seven weapons were seized by other officers in the experimental area. There were 169 gun crimes in the target beat in the twenty-nine weeks prior to the gun patrol but only 86 while the experiment was underway, a decrease of 49 percent. Drive-by shootings dropped significantly, as did homicides, without any displacement to other areas in the city. It is possible that the weapons seized were taken from high-rate offenders who were among the most likely perpetrators of gun-related crimes; their "lost opportunity" to commit violent crimes may have resulted in an overall rate decrease. It is also possible that the gun sweeps caused some of the most violent criminals to be taken off the streets. And as word of the patrol got out, there may have been a general deterrent effect: People contemplating violent crime may have been convinced that apprehension risks were unacceptably high.[18]

MAKING ARRESTS Is it possible that more formal police action, such as an arrest, can reduce crime? A number of experts have expressed doubt that formal police action can have any general deterrent effect or, if it does, that it would be anything but short-lived and temporary.[19] Research studies do show, however, that contact with the police may cause some offenders to forgo repeat criminal behavior; formal police action, such as arrest, may in fact deter future criminality. For example, an arrest for drunk driving reduces the likelihood of further driving while intoxicated. An arrest apparently increases people's belief that they will be rearrested if they drink and drive and heightens their perception of the unpleasantness associated with an arrest.[20] Evidence also points out that many first offenders will forgo criminal activity after arrest.[21] Research conducted in Florida indicates that arrest activity may have an immediate impact on the crime rate; that is, as the number of arrests increase, the number of crimes reported to authorities decreases substantially the following day.[22] It is possible that news of increased and aggressive police activity is rapidly diffused through the population and has an immediate impact that erodes over time. Studies using data collected annually may miss this immediate deterrent effect.

Even if formal action does deter crime, police chiefs may find it difficult to convince patrol officers to make more arrests. Despite a departmental policy requiring officers to be more active, police officers may be reluctant to change their style and tactics.[23] Research efforts indicate that departmental directives to make more arrests may have relatively little effect on police behavior.[24] Influencing actual police activities in the field may prove to be a difficult task.

Adding Patrol Officers

One reason patrol activity may be less effective than desired is the lack of adequate resources. Does adding more police help bring down the crime rate? Comparisons of police expenditures in U.S. cities indicate that cities with the highest crime rates also spend the most on police services.[25] The actual number of law enforcement officers in a jurisdiction seems to have little effect on area crimes, nor does adding officers lower the crime rate.[26]

Adding resources may not bring down the crime rate, but it may improve the overall effectiveness of the justice system. Communities with relatively high crime rates that devote fewer financial resources to police work find that many cases that result in arrest are dropped before they ever get to trial.[27] It is possible that overworked police in high-crime areas may be processing cases with little hope of prosecution to give the public the message that they are trying to "do something." Inadequate resources make it difficult to gather sufficient evidence to ensure a conviction, and prosecutors are likely to drop these cases. Adding resources, in this instance, could possibly improve the quality of police arrests.

THE INVESTIGATION FUNCTION

Since the first independent detective bureau was established by the London Metropolitan Police in 1841,[28] criminal investigators have been romantic figures vividly portrayed in novels, movies such as Eddie Murphy's *Beverly Hills Cop* and Clint Eastwood's *Dirty Harry* series, and television shows such as *Columbo, NYPD Blue,* and *Law & Order.* The fictional police detective is usually depicted as a loner, willing to break departmental rules, perhaps even violate the law, to capture the suspect. The average fictional detective views departmental policies and U.S. Supreme Court decisions as unfortunate roadblocks to police efficiency. Civil rights are either ignored or actively scorned.[29]

Although every police department probably has a few "hell-bent for leather" detectives who take matters into their own hands at the expense of citizens' rights, the modern criminal investigator is most likely an experienced civil servant, trained in investigatory techniques, knowledgeable about legal rules of evidence and procedure, and at least somewhat cautious about the legal and administrative consequences of her actions.[30] Although detectives are often handicapped by limited time, money, and resources, they are certainly aware of how their actions will one day be interpreted in a court of law.

Detectives are probably the elite of the police force: They are usually paid more than patrol officers, engage in more interesting tasks, wear civilian clothes, and are subject to a less stringent departmental control than patrol officers.[31]

Detectives investigate the causes of crime and attempt to identify the individuals or groups responsible for committing particular offenses. They may enter a case after patrol officers have made the initial contact, such as when a patrol car interrupts a crime in progress and the offenders flee before they can be apprehended. They can investigate a case entirely on their own, sometimes by following up on leads provided by informants.

vice squad
Police officers assigned to enforce morality-based laws, such as those on prostitution, gambling, and pornography.

Detective divisions are typically organized into sections or bureaus, such as homicide, robbery, or rape. Some jurisdictions maintain **vice squads,** which are usually staffed by plainclothes officers or detectives specializing in victimless crimes, such as prostitution or gambling. Vice squad officers may set themselves up as customers for illicit activities to make arrests. For example, male undercover detectives may frequent public men's rooms and make advances toward entering men; those who respond are arrested for homosexual soliciting. In other instances, female police officers may pose as prostitutes. These covert police activities have often been criticized as violating the personal rights of citizens, and their appropriateness and fairness have been questioned.

sting operation
An undercover police operation in which police pose as criminals to trap law violators.

Sting Operations

Another approach to detective work, commonly referred to as a **sting operation,** involves organized groups of detectives who deceive criminals into openly committing illegal acts or conspiring to engage in criminal activity. Numerous sting operations have been aimed at capturing professional thieves and seizing stolen merchandise. Undercover detectives pose as "fences," set up ongoing fencing operations, and encourage thieves interested in selling stolen merchandise. Transactions are videotaped to provide prosecutors with strong cases. Sting operations have netted millions of dollars in recovered property and resulted in the arrests of many criminals. These results seem impressive, but sting operations have drawbacks.[32] By its very nature, a sting involves deceit by police agents that often comes close to entrapment. Sting operations may encourage criminals to commit new crimes because they have a new source for fencing stolen goods. Innocent people may hurt their reputations by buying merchandise from a sting operation when they had no idea the items had been stolen. By putting the government in the fencing business, such operations blur the line between law enforcement and criminal activity.

Undercover Work

Sometimes detectives go *undercover* in order to investigate crime.[33] Undercover work can take a number of forms. A lone agent can infiltrate a criminal group or organization to gather information on future criminal activity. For example, a DEA (Drug Enforcement Administration) agent may go undercover to gather intelligence on drug smugglers. Undercover officers can also pose as victims to capture predatory criminals who have been conducting street robberies and muggings.

Undercover work is considered a necessary element of police work, although it can prove dangerous for the agent. Police officers may be forced to engage in illegal or immoral behavior to maintain their cover. They also face significant physical danger in playing the role of a criminal and dealing with mobsters, terrorists, and drug dealers. In far too many cases, undercover officers are mistaken for real criminals and are injured by other law enforcement officers or private citizens trying to stop a crime. Arrest situations involving undercover officers may also provoke violence when suspects do not realize they are in the presence of police and therefore violently resist arrest.

Undercover officers may also experience psychological problems. Being away from home, keeping late hours, and always worrying that their identity will be uncovered all create enormous stress. Officers have experienced postundercover stress, resulting in trouble at work and, in many instances, ruined marriages and botched prosecutions. Hanging around with criminals for a long period of time, making friends, and earning their trust can also have a damaging psychological impact.

Evaluating Investigations Serious criticism has been leveled at the nation's detective forces for being bogged down in paperwork and relatively inefficient in clearing cases. One famous study of 153 detective bureaus found that a great deal of a detective's time was spent in nonproductive work and that investigative expertise did little to solve cases; half of all detectives could be replaced without negatively influencing crime clearance rates.[34]

Although some question remains about the effectiveness of investigations, police detectives do make a valuable contribution to police work because their skilled interrogation and case-processing techniques are essential to eventual criminal conviction.[35] Nonetheless, a majority of cases that are solved are done so when the perpetrator is identified at the scene of the crime by patrol officers. Research shows that if a crime is reported while in progress, the police have about a 33 percent chance of making an arrest; the arrest probability declines to about 10 percent if the crime is reported one minute later, and to 5 percent if more than fifteen minutes has elapsed. As the time between the crime and the arrest grows, the chances of a conviction are also reduced, probably because the ability to recover evidence is lost. Put another way, once a crime has been completed and the investigation is put in the hands of detectives, the chances of identifying and arresting the perpetrator diminish rapidly.[36]

A detailed "handbook" on the ins and outs of the crime scene investigation can be found at www.police.ucr.edu/csi.html

Improving Investigations A number of efforts have been made to revamp and improve investigation procedures. One practice has been to give patrol officers greater responsibility for conducting preliminary investigations at the scene of the crime. In addition, the old-fashioned precinct detective has been replaced by specialized units, such as homicide or burglary squads, that operate over larger areas and can bring specific expertise to bear. Technological advances in DNA and fingerprint identification have also aided investigation effectiveness.

One reason for investigation ineffectiveness is that detectives often lack sufficient resources to carry out a lengthy ongoing probe of any but the most serious cases. Research shows the following:

1. *Unsolved cases* Almost 50 percent of burglary cases are screened out by supervisors before assignment to a detective for a follow-up investigation. Of those assigned, 75 percent are dropped after the first day of the follow-up investigation. Although robbery cases are more likely to be assigned to detectives, 75 percent of them are also dropped after one day of investigation.
2. *Length of investigation* The vast majority of cases are investigated for no more than four hours stretching over three days. An average of eleven days elapses between the initial report of a crime and the suspension of the investigation.
3. *Sources of information* Early in an investigation, the focus is on the victim; as the investigation is pursued, emphasis shifts to the suspect. The most critical information for determining case outcome is the name and description of the suspect and related crime information. Victims are most often the source of information; unfortunately, witnesses, informants, and members of the police department are consulted far less often. However, when these sources are tapped, they are likely to produce useful information.

Investigations can take but a moment or last many years. Boston police found bodies that had been buried for years near some railroad tracks. These victims of mob wars were discovered when an informer told FBI agents their whereabouts.

4. *Effectiveness* Preliminary investigations by patrol officers are critical. In situations where the suspect's identity is not known immediately after the crime is committed, detectives make an arrest in less than 10 percent of all cases.[37]

Considering these findings, detective work may be improved if greater emphasis is placed on collecting physical evidence at the scene of the crime, identifying witnesses, checking departmental records, and using informants. The probability of successfully settling a case is improved if patrol officers gather evidence at the scene of a crime and effectively communicate it to detectives working the case. Police managers should pay more attention to screening cases, monitoring case flow and activity, and creating productivity measures to make sure that individual detectives and detective units are meeting their goals. Also recommended is the use of targeted investigations that direct attention at a few individuals, such as career criminals, who are known to have engaged in the behavior under investigation.

THE CHANGING CONCEPTS OF POLICING

Community Policing Many police officers feel unappreciated by the public they serve, which may be due to the underlying conflicts inherent in the police role. Police may want to be proactive crime fighters who initiate actions against law violators; yet most remain reactive, responding when a citizen calls for service. The desire for direct action is often blunted because police are expected to perform many civic duties that in earlier times were the responsibility of every citizen: keeping the peace, performing emergency medical care, dealing with family problems, and helping during civil emergencies.

Most of us agree that a neighborhood brawl must be stopped, that shelter must be found for the homeless, and that the inebriate must be taken safely home, but few of us want to personally jump into the fray; we would rather "call the cops." The police officer has become a "social handyman" called in to fix up problems that the average citizen wishes would simply go away. Police officers are viewed as the "fire it takes to fight fire."[38] The public needs the police to perform those duties that the average citizen finds distasteful or dangerous, such as breaking up a domestic quarrel. At the same time, the public resents the power the police have to use force, arrest people, and deny people their vices. Put another way, the average citizen wants the police to crack down on undesirable members of society while excluding her own behavior from legal scrutiny.

Because of these natural role conflicts, the relationship between the police and the public has been the subject of a great deal of concern. As you may recall, the respect Americans have for police effectiveness, courtesy, honesty, and conduct seems to be problematic. Citizens may be less likely to go to police for help, to report crimes, to step forward as witnesses, or to cooperate with and aid police. Victim surveys indicate that many citizens have so little faith in the police that they will not report even serious crimes, such as rape or burglary. In some communities, citizen self-help groups have sprung up to supplement police protection.[39] In return, police officers often feel ambivalent and uncertain about the public they are sworn to protect.

Because of this ambivalence and role conflict, more communities are adapting new models of policing that reflect the changing role of the police. Some administrators now recognize that police officers are better equipped to be civic problem solvers than effective crime fighters. Rather than ignore, deny, or fight this reality, police departments are being reorganized to maximize their strengths and minimize their weaknesses. What has emerged is the community policing movement, a new concept of policing designed to bridge the gulf between police agencies and the communities they serve.

BROKEN WINDOWS: THE DEVELOPMENT OF COMMUNITY POLICING

> A quiet revolution is reshaping American policing. — George Kelling[40]

Police agencies have been trying to gain the cooperation and respect of the communities they serve for more than thirty years. At first, efforts at improving the relationships between police departments and the public involved programs with the general title of **police–community relations (PCR)**. Developed at the stationhouse and departmental levels, these initial PCR programs were designed to make citizens more aware of police activities, alert them to methods of self-protection, and improve general attitudes toward policing.

police–community relations (PCR)
Programs developed by police departments to improve relations with the community and develop cooperation with citizens. The forerunner of the community policing model.

Though PCR efforts showed a willingness for police agencies to cooperate with the public, some experts believed that law enforcement agencies must undergo a significant transformation in order to create meaningful partnerships with the public. These views were articulated in a critical 1982 paper by two justice policy experts, George Kelling and James Q. Wilson, who espoused a new approach to improving police relations in the community, which has come to be known as the **broken windows model.**[41] Kelling and Wilson made three points:

broken windows model
The term used to describe the role of the police as maintainers of community order and safety.

1. *Neighborhood disorder creates fear.* Urban areas filled with street people, youth gangs, prostitutes, and the mentally disturbed are the ones most likely to maintain a high degree of crime.

Today the role of police is multifaceted. Police must perform many civic duties that in earlier times were the responsibility of all citizens: keeping the peace, performing emergency medical care, dealing with family problems, helping during civil emergencies. They must be responsive to the community they serve. Here, police help sort things out after a 1999 high school brawl in Decatur, Illinois.

2. *Neighborhoods give out crime-promoting signals.* A neighborhood filled with deteriorated housing, unrepaired broken windows, and untended disorderly behavior gives out crime-promoting signals. Honest citizens live in fear in these areas, and predatory criminals are attracted to them.
3. *Police need citizen cooperation.* If police are to reduce fear and successfully combat crime in these urban areas, they must have the cooperation, support, and assistance of the citizens.

According to the broken windows approach, community relations and crime control effectiveness cannot be the province of a few specialized units housed within a traditional police department. Instead, the core police role must be altered if community involvement is to be won and maintained. To accomplish this goal, urban police departments should return to the earlier style of policing in which officers on the beat had intimate contact with the people they served. Modern police departments generally rely on motorized patrol to cover wide areas, to maintain a visible police presence, and to ensure rapid response time. Although effective and economical, the patrol car removes officers from the mainstream of the community, alienating people who might otherwise be potential sources of information and help to the police.

The broken windows approach holds that police administrators would be well served by deploying their forces where they can encourage public confidence, strengthen feelings of safety, and elicit cooperation from citizens. Community preservation, public safety, and order maintenance — not crime fighting — should become the primary focus of patrol. Put another way, just as physicians and dentists practice preventive medicine and dentistry, police should help maintain an intact community structure rather than simply fight crime.

foot patrol
Police patrols that take officers out of cars and put them on a walking beat in order to strengthen ties with the community.

IMPLEMENTING COMMUNITY POLICING The community policing concept was originally implemented through a number of innovative demonstration projects.[42] Among the most publicized were experiments in **foot patrol,**

which took officers out of cars and set them to walking beats in the neighborhood. Foot patrol efforts were aimed at forming a bond with community residents by acquainting them with the individual officers who patrolled their neighborhood, letting them know that police were caring and available. The first foot patrol experiments were conducted in cities in Michigan and New Jersey. An evaluation of foot patrol indicated that, although it did not bring down the crime rate, residents in areas where foot patrol was added perceived greater safety and were less afraid of crime.[43]

Since the advent of these programs, hundreds of communities have adopted innovative forms of decentralized, neighborhood-based community policing models. Recent surveys indicate that there has been a significant increase in community policing activities in recent years and that certain core programs such as crime prevention activities have become embedded in the police role.[44]

Community-oriented policing (COP) programs have been implemented in large cities, suburban areas, and rural communities.[45] The most successful programs give officers the time to meet with local residents to talk about crime in the neighborhood and to use personal initiative to solve problems (see Exhibit 5.1).

While not all programs work (police–community newsletters and cleanup campaigns do not seem to do much good), the overall impression has been that patrol officers can actually reduce the level of fear in the community. Some COP programs assign officers to neighborhoods, organize training programs for community leaders, and feature a bottom-up approach to deal with community problems: Decision making involves the officer on the scene, not a directive from central headquarters. Others have created programs for juveniles who might ordinarily have little to do but get involved in gangs but are now directed at such activities as neighborhood cleanup efforts.[46] In Spokane, Washington, for example, the community–police effort created a program called COPY Kids,

exhibit 5.1

Residential Police Officer Program

One successful community policing initiative is the Alexandria (Virginia) Residential Police Officer (RPO) program in which veteran police officers are stationed in areas that have such problems as elevated crime levels, nuisance activities, dilapidated buildings, graffiti, and absentee landlords. RPOs work closely with residents to create and implement effective crime and problem reduction strategies. By working with citizens, rather than for them, the police hope to reduce not only the number of crimes but also residents' fear of crime while increasing their quality of life.

To determine its effectiveness, the RPO program was evaluated in one of the city's oldest communities—Arlandria, home to over forty-five hundred people who were concerned about drugs, juvenile gangs, and other crime and nuisance activities. The results of a survey given to the residents in 1992 and 1998 were compared in order to gauge the impact of the program. In addition, reported crimes, nuisance incidents, and calls for service were charted from 1992 when the RPOs first arrived. In the 1992 survey, residents complained about drug dealing in the streets, lack of police presence, and fear of crime. By 1998 citizens were less concerned about crime and gangs and more concerned about quality-of-life issues such as trash and loitering. All three measures of criminal activity indicated a decrease in crime. Between 1992 and 1998, reported crime dropped by 17 percent, the number of reported nuisance incidents declined by almost 19 percent, and the number of calls for service dropped 12 percent.

SOURCE: "Expanding Alexandria's Residential Police Officer Program," *Police Chief* (October 1999): 3–7.

Bonnie Campbell, former Iowa attorney general, heading a federal program, Violence Against Women Act, meets with Seattle police officers. In the future, police officers must become more aware of lingering social problems, such as domestic violence, if they are to gain the cooperation of the general public.

a summer outreach program for disadvantaged youths, that promotes a positive work ethic, emphasizes the values of community involvement, and helps create a positive image of the police department.[47] Washington, D.C.'s Howard University Violence Prevention Project aims to create a safety net that protects youths against social risk factors. The project relies on a team approach that involves parents, teachers, mental health professionals, business owners, and local police. The police component of the project, called the Youth Trauma Team, requires that police officers, along with psychologists, respond to violent incidents that occur at night. They talk to children who have been a part of or have witnessed violence and afterward link them with services as needed. Police officers involved in the project receive training in conflict resolution, cultural sensitivity, and crisis de-escalation. They also have networked or partnered extensively with existing social service providers in the community in a multidisciplinary team effort to provide comprehensive care.[48]

NEIGHBORHOOD POLICING Community policing means more than implementing direct-action programs. It also refers to a philosophy of policing that requires departments to reconsider their recruitment, organization, and operating procedures. What are some of the most important community policing concepts? First, community policing emphasizes results, not bureaucratic process. Rather than react to problems in the community, police departments take the initiative in identifying issues and actively treating their cause. Problem-solving and analysis techniques replace emphasis on bureaucratic detail. There is less concern with "playing it by the book" and more with getting the job done.

To achieve the goals of COP, some agencies have tried to decentralize, an approach sometimes referred to as innovative **neighborhood-oriented policing (NOP).**[49] Problem solving is best done at the neighborhood level where issues originate, not at a far-off central headquarters. Because each neighborhood has its own particular needs, police decision making must be flexible and adaptive. For example, neighborhoods undergoing change in racial composition all experience high levels of racially motivated violence.[50] Police must be able to distinguish these neighborhood characteristics and allocate resources to meet their needs.

neighborhood-oriented policing (NOP)
Community policing efforts aimed at individual neighborhoods.

CHANGING THE POLICE ROLE Community policing also stresses sharing power with local groups and individuals. A key element of the community policing philosophy is that citizens must actively participate with police to fight crime.[51] This participation might involve providing information in areawide crime investigations or helping police reach out to troubled youths.

Community policing also means the eventual redesign of police departments. Management's role must be reordered to focus on the problems of the community, not the needs of the police department. The traditional vertical police organizational chart must be altered so that top-down management gives way to bottom-up decision making. The patrol officer becomes the manager of his beat and a key decision maker. Figure 5.2 shows how one police department is organized for community policing.

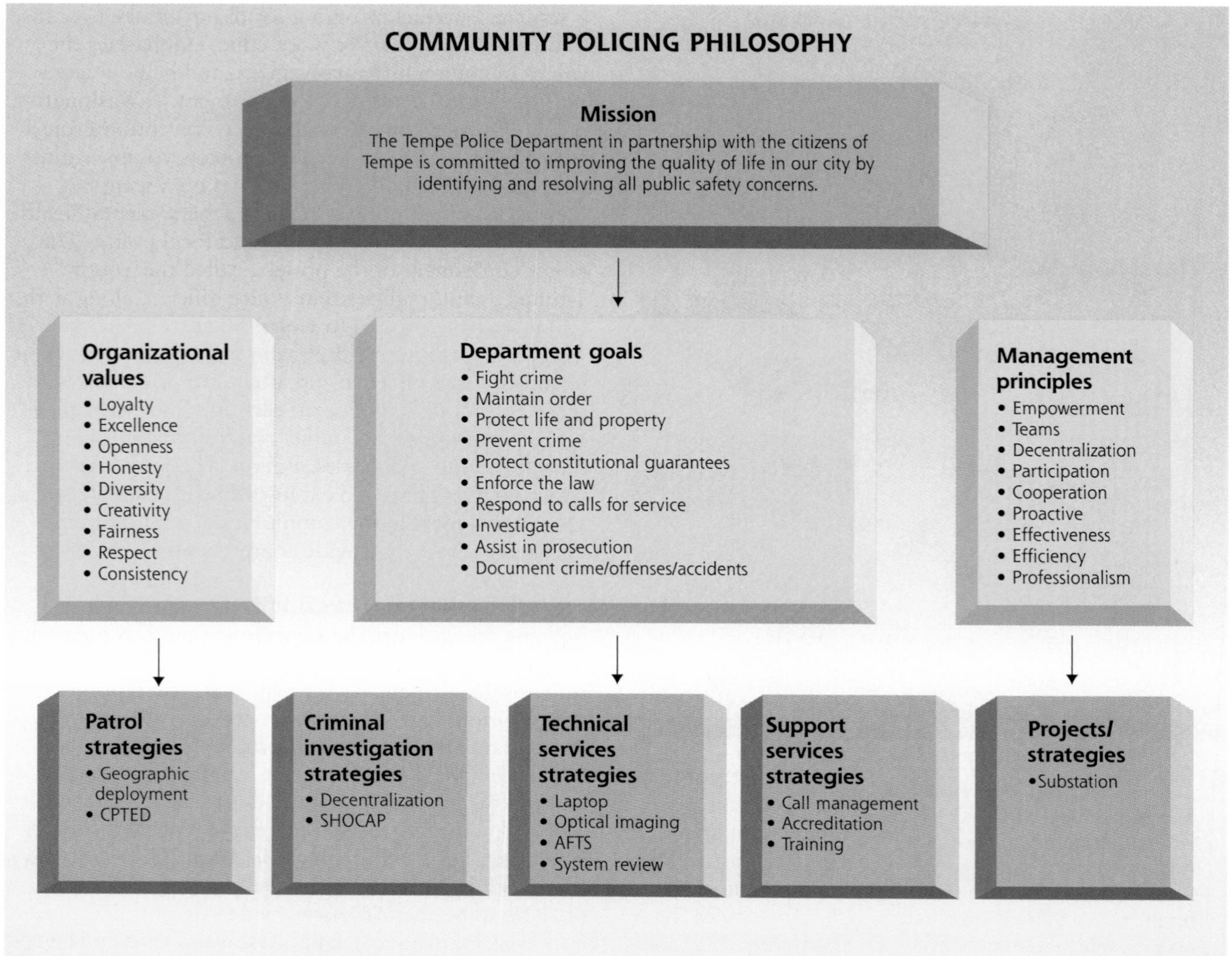

Figure 5.2
Tempe (Arizona) Police Department planning model
SOURCE: Tempe Police Department.

Community policing requires that police departments alter their recruitment and training requirements. Future officers must develop community-organizing and problem-solving skills, along with traditional police skills. Their training must prepare them to succeed less on their ability to make arrests or issue citations and more on their ability to solve problems effectively.

The community policing concept is not only catching on in the United States, but it has also captured the interest of police departments around the world.[52] Community policing is being used in numerous countries, including Denmark, Finland, and Great Britain.

problem-oriented policing
A style of police operations that stresses proactive problem solving, rather than reactive crime fighting.

Problem-Oriented Policing

Closely associated with yet independent from the community policing concept are **problem-oriented policing** strategies. Traditional police models focus on responding to calls for help in the fastest possible time, dealing with the situation, and then getting on the street again as soon as possible.[53] In contrast, the core of problem-oriented policing is a proactive orientation.

Problem-oriented policing strategies require police agencies to identify particular long-term community problems — street-level drug dealers, prostitution rings, gang hangouts — and to develop strategies to eliminate them.[54] As with community policing, being problem solvers requires that police departments rely on local residents and private resources. This means that police managers must learn how to develop community resources, design cost-efficient and effective solutions to problems, and become advocates as well as agents of reform.[55]

A significant portion of police departments are now using special units to confront specific social problems. For example, as Figure 5.3 shows, a significant number of departments now employ special units devoted to youth issues ranging from child abuse to gangs.

Problem-oriented policing models are supported by the fact that a great deal of urban crime is concentrated in a few "hot spots."[56] A significant portion of all police calls in metropolitan areas typically radiate from a relatively few locations: bars, malls, the bus depot, hotels, and certain apartment buildings.[57] By implication, concentrating police resources on these **hot spots of crime** could appreciably reduce crime.[58]

hot spots of crime
Places from which a significant portion of all police calls originate. These hot spots include taverns and housing projects.

The new COP models are essentially problem oriented, and both efforts can be combined. For example, in Vancouver, Canada, community police officers assigned to reduce and control street prostitution actually included prostitutes in their planning activities and were able to reduce neighborhood conflict by mediating between residents and prostitutes. They included both groups to help control collateral problems such as drug dealing and pornography.[59]

Problem-oriented strategies can also be developed within traditional police organizations.[60] The Jersey City (New Jersey) police recently applied a variety of aggressive crime-reducing techniques in some of the city's highest crime areas. Evaluations of the program show that crime rates were reduced when police officers used aggressive problem solving (e.g., drug enforcement) and community improvement (e.g., increased lighting and cleaned vacant lots) techniques in

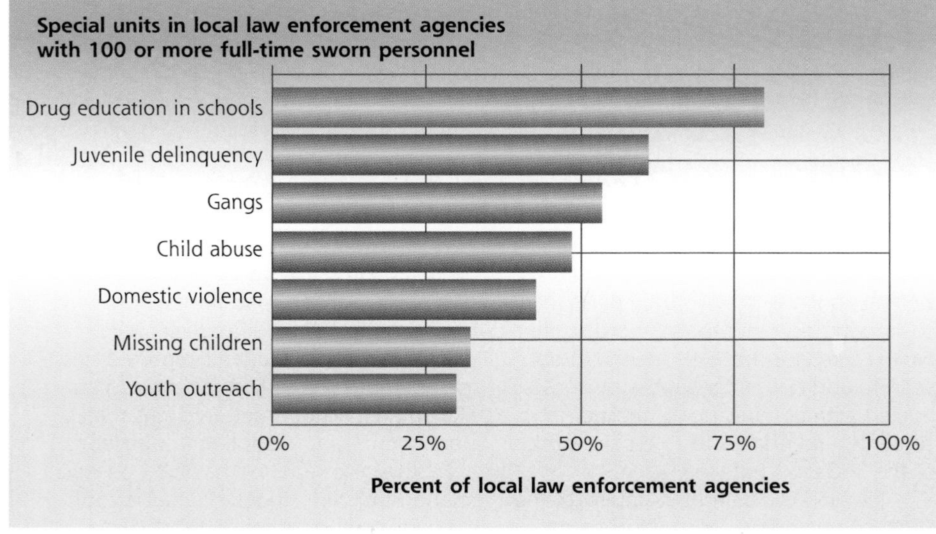

Figure 5.3
Percent of local agencies operating full-time special units for youth and family problems, 1997

SOURCE: *Law Enforcement Management and Administrative Statistics, 1997* (Washington, D.C.: Bureau of Justice Statistics, 1999), 7.

high-crime areas.[61] Another recent initiative by the Dallas Police Department assigned officers to aggressively pursue truancy and curfew enforcement, a tactic that resulted in lower rates of gang violence.[62] The following Policy, Programs, and Issues in Criminal Justice feature describes one municipal program that was designed to reduce a problem of growing national concern, school violence.

While programs such as these seem successful, the effectiveness of any street-level problem-solving efforts must be interpreted with caution.[63] It is possible that the criminals will be displaced to other, "safer" areas of the city and will return shortly after the program is called a success and the additional police forces have been pulled from the area.[64] Nonetheless, evidence shows that merely saturating an area with police may not deter crime, but focusing efforts at a particular problem may have a crime-reducing effect.

Policy, Programs and Issues in Criminal Justice

SCHOOL RESOURCE OFFICERS

Horrific outbursts of school violence, such as the shootings that occurred at Columbine High School in 1999, have prompted school administrators to improve security at schools around the nation. To assist in keeping students safe, some school systems have called upon School Resource Officers (SROs).

The goal of placing SROs in city schools is to create an atmosphere in which students and teachers can focus on learning without fear. SROs are expected to reduce the number of weapons in schools, prohibit drug use, counsel students with problems, and — because of their visible presence — secure school buildings from nonstudents. The SRO is expected to deter offenses from being committed on school grounds even before they happen.

Ida Johnson analyzed the effectiveness of the SRO program in a southern school district. Johnson compared weekly school disciplinary records for 1994–1995, the year before officers were assigned to schools on a permanent basis, with incident reports and disciplinary records for the 1995–1996 school year. In addition, interviews were conducted with administrators, teachers, students, and officers to assess the work of the SROs.

Johnson evaluated the impact of the SROs on three types or levels of student misbehavior. Level 1 offenses included harassment and intimidation of other students, chronic tardiness, use of profanity, and minor disturbances on a school bus. Level 2 offenses included such acts as fighting, larceny, use of tobacco, trespassing, proposition of sexual acts, and leaving school without permission. Level 3 offenses, deemed the most serious, included arson, aggravated battery, possession of firearms or other weapons, grand theft, and burglary.

Evaluation found that 3,760 offenses occurred in the district during the 1995–1996 school year, a drop of nearly 300 from the year before the SRO program was initiated. Taken as a whole, declines were recorded in all three offense levels, and the number of misdemeanor and felony arrests occurring on school grounds decreased.

Interviews with administrators and students indicate support for the presence of SROs in schools. Administrators perceived that the use of weapons had declined and that levels of marijuana, gambling, fighting, and illicit sexual behavior were down since SROs were placed in schools. Students reported feeling more secure and that having an SRO in their schools deterred classmates from committing disciplinary infractions.

SROs also reported having a positive relationship with students. Officers counseled students on career choices and encouraged them to excel academically. SROs made daily contact with the parents of at-risk students. Nearly all the SROs felt parents and teachers responded positively to them.

The SRO concept has great promise as a means of reducing school crime. Efforts should be made to expand officer training, increase the number of officers hired, increase communication between SROs and other community members, and implement regular counseling sessions between SROs and the students, teachers, and parents they serve.

Critical Thinking

Does placing uniformed officers in schools compromise the educational process? Or do they create a positive atmosphere for learning? Explain.

InfoTrac College Edition Research

To learn more about the work of school resource officers, check out

Connie Mulqueen, "School Resource Officers More Than Security Guards," *American School & University* 71 (1999): SS17.

SOURCE: Ida Johnson, "School Violence: The Effectiveness of a School Resource Officer," *Journal of Criminal Justice* 27 (1999): 173–93.

Has Innovative Policing Met Its Goals? The core concepts of police work are changing as administrators recognize the limitations and realities of police work in modern society. The oft-repeated charge that police catch relatively few criminals and have little deterrent effect has had a tremendous influence on police policy. On the one hand, many departments are experimenting with programs designed to bring police officers into closer contact with the community to increase citizen cooperation in the fight against crime. Major cities, such as New York, have made implementing community policing models a priority.

If they are to be successful, community policing strategies must be able to react effectively to some significant administrative problems. Police administrators must be able to define the concept of community in terms of an ecological area defined by common norms, shared values, and interpersonal bonds.[65] After all, the main focus of community policing is to activate the community norms that make neighborhoods more crime resistant. To do so requires a greater identification with ecological areas: If community policing projects cross the boundaries of many different neighborhoods, any hope of learning and accessing community norms, strengths, and standards will be lost.[66]

Besides understanding and identifying actual community areas, police departments must also establish the exact role of community police agents. How should they integrate their activities with those of regular patrol forces? For example, should foot patrols have primary responsibility for policing in an area, or should they coordinate their activities with officers assigned to patrol cars? Should community police officers be solely problem identifiers and neighborhood organizers, or should they also be expected to be law enforcement agents who get to the crime scene rapidly and later do investigative work? Can community police teams and regular patrols work together, or must a department abandon traditional police roles and become purely community policing oriented?

Retraining and reorienting police from their traditional roles into a more social service orientation may also be difficult. Most police officers do not have the social service skills required of effective community agents. Surveys report that, although police officers are generally favorable to community policing, they also suffer ridicule from their peers because of the "cushy" assignment that is not "real" police work, that they are often unsure of what to do, and that their program has little effect on the crime rate.[67]

Because the community policing model calls for a revision of the police role from law enforcer to community organizer, police training must be revised to reflect this new mandate. Midlevel managers who are receptive to and can implement community-change strategies must be recruited and trained.[68] If widescale community policing is to be adopted, a whole new type of police officer must be recruited and trained in a whole new way.

OVERCOMING OBSTACLES Although these are formidable obstacles to overcome, there is growing evidence that community and problem-oriented policing can work and fit well with traditional forms of policing.[69] Many police experts and administrators have embraced the community and problem-oriented policing concepts as revolutionary revisions of the basic police role. Community policing efforts have been credited with helping reduce crime rates in large cities such as New York and Boston. The most professional and highly motivated officers are the ones most likely to support community policing efforts.[70]

These results are encouraging, but there is neither clear-cut evidence that community policing is highly successful at reducing crime nor changing the traditional values and attitudes of police officers involved in the programs.[71] Crime rate reductions in cities that have used COP may be the result of an overall downturn in the nation's crime rate or some other factor such as an improved economy. Research efforts have not shown that Neighborhood Watch or police storefront programs meet their stated goals. Meetings with community groups and going door to door to reduce neighborhood crime rates show mixed results.[72] Also troubling are the results of a recent evaluation of community policing efforts in Indianapolis, Indiana, and St. Petersburg, Florida: COP officers actually spend more time on administrative work than regular patrol officers. Furthermore, when given the opportunity to choose with whom to work, community officers actually spend less time with citizens with the most pressing needs than do patrol officers. The "clientele" of community policing are citizens who are more receptive to police and whose problems may be more easily solved.[73]

There is also evidence that police departments are paying lip service to the community to give the impression they are progressive and dynamic. In reality, they are unwilling to exact real change. For example, one survey of COP programs in Florida found that, although numerous departments consider themselves community oriented, each had its own distinct view of what community policing was all about; no single, definitive model of community policing could be found. What became evident was that the departments were more intent on implementing community policing by changing the officer rather than the organization; that is, officers were expected to change the way they behaved as police officers rather than changing the structure and organization of the police department.[74]

If you want more information on how a police academy operates, go to the home page of the Oakland (Missouri) Police Academy at www.occ.cc.mi.us/police/Home.htm

SUPPORT FUNCTIONS

As the model of a typical police department in Figure 5.1 (page 137) indicates, not all members of a department engage in what the general public regards as "real police work" — patrol, detection, and traffic control. Even in departments that are embracing community and problem-oriented policing, a great deal of police resources are actually devoted to support and administrative functions. There are too many tasks to mention in detail, but the most important include those discussed next.

Many police departments maintain their own personnel service, which carries out such functions as recruiting new police officers, creating exams to determine the most qualified applicants, and handling promotions and transfers. Innovative selection techniques are constantly being developed and tested. For example, the Behavioral-Personnel Assessment Device (B-PAD) requires police applicants to view videotaped scenarios and respond as if they were officers handling the situation; reviews indicate that this procedure may be a reliable and unbiased method of choosing new recruits.[75]

internal affairs
The branch of the police department that investigates charges of corruption or misconduct made against police officers.

Larger police departments often maintain an **internal affairs** branch, which is charged with policing the police. Internal affairs process citizen complaints of police corruption, investigate what may be the unnecessary use of force by police officers, and even probe police participation in actual criminal activity, such as burglaries or narcotics violations. In addition, internal affairs divisions may assist police managers when disciplinary action is brought against individual officers. Internal affairs is a controversial function since investigators are feared and distrusted by fellow police officers. Nonetheless, rigorous self-scrutiny is the only way police departments can earn the respect of citizens.

Most police departments are responsible for the administration and control of their own budgets. This task includes administering payroll, purchasing equipment and services, planning budgets for future expenditures, and auditing departmental financial records.

Police departments maintain separate units that are charged with maintaining and disseminating information on wanted offenders, stolen merchandise, traffic violators, and so on. Modern data management systems enable police to

Police departments provide emergency aid to the ill, counseling for youngsters, speakers for school and community agencies on safety and drug abuse, and countless other services designed to improve citizen-police interactions. Here a community service officer establishes a bond with youngsters on a local playground.

use their records in a highly sophisticated fashion. For example, officers in a patrol car who spot a suspicious-looking vehicle can instantly receive a computerized rundown on whether it has been stolen. Or, if property is recovered during an arrest, police using this sort of system can determine who reported the loss of the merchandise and arrange for its return.

Another important function of police communication is the effective and efficient dispatching of patrol cars. Again, modern computer technologies have been used to make the most of available resources.[76]

In many departments, training is continuous throughout an officer's career. Training usually begins at a police academy, which may be run exclusively for larger departments or be part of a regional training center servicing smaller and varied governmental units. More than 90 percent of all police departments require preservice training, including almost all departments in larger cities (population over one hundred thousand). The average officer receives more than five hundred hours of preservice training, including four hundred hours in the classroom and the rest in field training. Police in large cities receive over one thousand hours of instruction divided almost evenly between classroom and field instruction.[77] Among the topics usually covered are law and civil rights, firearms handling, emergency medical care, and restraint techniques.[78]

After assuming their police duties, new recruits are assigned to field-training officers who break them in on the job. However, training does not stop here. On-the-job training is a continuous process in the modern police department and covers such areas as weapons skills, first aid, crowd control, and community relations. Some departments use roll call training, in which superior officers or outside experts address police officers at the beginning of the workday. Other departments allow police officers time off to attend annual training sessions to sharpen their skills and learn new policing techniques.

Police departments provide emergency aid to the ill, counsel youngsters, speak to school and community agencies on safety and drug abuse, and provide countless other services designed to improve citizen–police interactions.

Larger police departments maintain specialized units that help citizens protect themselves from criminal activity. For example, they advise citizens on effective home security techniques or conduct Project ID campaigns — engraving valuables with an identifying number so that they can be returned if recovered after a burglary; police also work in schools teaching kids how to avoid drug use.[79]

Police agencies maintain (or have access to) forensic laboratories that enable them to identify substances to be used as evidence and to classify fingerprints.

Planning and research functions include designing programs to increase police efficiency and strategies to test program effectiveness. Police planners monitor recent technological developments and institute programs to adapt them to police services.

police productivity
The amount of order, crime control, and other law enforcement activities provided by an individual officer and consequently by the department as a whole.

IMPROVING POLICE PRODUCTIVITY

Police administrators have sought to increase the productivity of their line, support, and administrative staff. As used today, the term **police productivity** refers to the amount of actual order, maintenance, crime control, and other law enforcement activities provided by individual police officers and concomitantly by police departments as a whole. By improving police productivity, a department can keep the peace, deter crime, apprehend criminals, and provide useful public services without necessarily increasing its costs. This goal is accomplished by having each police officer operate with greater efficiency, thus using fewer resources to achieve greater effectiveness.

Despite the emphasis on increasing police effectiveness, serious questions have been raised about how the police accomplish their assigned tasks.[80] One basic complaint has been that the average patrol officer spends relatively little time on what is considered real police work. More often than not, highly skilled police officers can be found writing reports, waiting in court corridors, getting involved in domestic disputes, and handling what are generally characterized as "miscellaneous noncriminal matters." Police departments are now experimenting with cost-saving reforms that maximize effectiveness while saving taxpayer dollars. For example, J. David Hirschel and Charles Dean describe how a program to summon offenders to court via a "field citation" is considerably cheaper than a formal arrest. Factoring in the cost of rearresting offenders who fail to appear in court, a citation program would save about $72 per case. Considering the millions of arrests made each year, the adoption of a citation policy could produce considerable savings, not to mention the cost-saving effect on the overcrowded jail system.[81] Other cost-saving productivity measures include consolidation, informal arrangements, sharing, pooling, contracting, police service districts, use of civilian employees, multiple tasking, special-assignment programs, budget supplementation, and differential police responses.[82]

Consolidation and Informal Arrangements

One way to increase police efficiency is to *consolidate* police services. This means combining small departments (usually under ten employees) in adjoining areas into a superagency that services the previously fragmented jurisdictions. Consolidation has the benefit of creating departments large enough to use expanded services — such as crime labs, training centers, communications centers, and emergency units — that are not cost effective in smaller departments. This procedure is controversial since it demands that existing lines of political and administrative authority be drastically changed. Nonetheless, consolidation of departments or special services (such as a regional computer center) has been attempted in California (the Los Angeles Sheriff's Department), Massachusetts, New York, and Illinois.[83]

To increase productivity, some agencies have formed mutual aid pacts to share infrequently used emergency services such as SWAT and Emergency Response Teams. Sometimes Federal or state agencies will be called upon to provide assistance.

Unwritten, cooperative, *informal agreements* may be made between localities to perform a task collectively that would be mutually beneficial (such as monitoring neighboring radio frequencies so that needed backup can be provided). An example is the Metro Task Force program implemented in New Jersey that commits state troopers to help local police officers in urban areas for limited times and assignments.[84]

Sharing, Pooling, and Contracting

Sharing is the provision or reception of services that aid in the execution of a law enforcement function (such as the sharing of a communications system by several local agencies). Some agencies form mutual-aid pacts so that they can share infrequently used emergency services such as SWAT and Emergency Response Teams.[85] Some states have gone as far as setting up centralized data services that connect most local police agencies into a statewide information net.[86]

Some police agencies *pool* resources by two or more agencies to perform a specified function under a predetermined, often formalized arrangement with direct involvement by all parties. An example is the use of a city–county law enforcement building or training academy or the establishment of a crime task force.

Another productivity measure is a limited and voluntary approach in which one government enters into a *contract,* a formal binding agreement to provide all or certain specified law enforcement services (such as communications or patrol service) to another government for an established fee. Many communities that contract for full law enforcement service do so at the time they incorporate, to avoid the costs of establishing their own police capability. For example, some small towns in Florida contract with the Broward County Sheriff's Department to provide law enforcement for their communities; contracting saves each town millions of dollars.[87]

Police Service Districts Some jurisdictions have set aside areas, usually within an individual county, where a special level of service is provided and financed through a special tax or assessment. In California, residents of an unincorporated portion of a county may petition to form such a *police service district* to provide more intensive patrol coverage than is available through existing systems. Such service may be provided by a sheriff, another police department, or a private person or agency. This system is used in Contra Costa and San Mateo Counties in California and Suffolk and Nassau Counties in New York.

Civilian Employees One common cost-saving method is to use *civilian employees* in administrative support or even in some line activities. Their duties have included operating communications gear; performing clerical work, planning and researching; and staffing traffic control (meter monitors). Using civilian employees can be a considerable savings to taxpayers, since their salaries are considerably lower than those of regular police officers. In addition, it allows trained, experienced officers to spend more time on direct crime control and enforcement activities.

Another form of civilian help comes in the form of COP programs that use civilian volunteers to supplement police services. For example, the "code blue" program in Fort Worth, Texas, is designed to organize neighborhood watch groups that supplement police patrol while providing the delivery of on-site services unavailable before the program was instituted.[88]

Multiple Tasking Some police officers are trained to *multiple tasking*, carrying out other functions of municipal government. For example, in a number of smaller departments, the roles of firefighters and police officers have been merged into a job called a public safety officer. The idea is to increase the number of people trained in both areas to have the potential for putting more police at the scene of a crime or more firefighters at a blaze than was possible when the two tasks were separated. The system provides greater coverage at far less cost.[89]

Special-Assignment Programs Some departments train officers for *special-assignment programs* that are required only occasionally. For example, the Special Enforcement Team in Lakewood, Colorado, is trained in a variety of police tasks, such as radar operation, surveillance, traffic investigation, and criminal investigations, but specializes in tactical operations, such as crowd control and security.[90]

Budget Supplements Municipal agencies commonly seek out *budget supplements* — innovative sources of income to supplement the department's limited resources. For example, Chicago police instituted a private fund drive that raised over $1.5 million to purchase protective clothing, and other departments have created private foundations to raise funds to support police-related activities. Additional budget-supplementing activities include conducting fund-raising events, using traffic fines for police services, enacting special taxes that go directly for police services, and auctioning goods forfeited by crime-involved individuals.

Differential Police Response *Differential police response* strategies maximize resources by separating police requests for services in terms of the form the police response takes. Some calls will result in the dispatch of a sworn officer, others in the dispatching of a less highly trained civilian; calls considered low priority are handled by asking citizens to walk in or to mail in their requests.[91]

SUMMARY

Today's police departments operate in a military-like fashion; policy generally emanates from the top of the hierarchy. Most police officers therefore use a great deal of discretion when making on-the-job decisions.

The most common law enforcement agencies are local police departments, which carry out patrol and investigative functions, as well as many support activities. Many questions have been raised about the effectiveness of police work, and some research efforts seem to indicate that police are not effective crime fighters. However, indications exist that aggressive police work, the threat of formal action, and cooperation between departments can have a measurable impact on crime. To improve effectiveness, police departments have developed new methods of policing that stress community involvement and problem solving. They have also been concerned with developing more effective and productive methods for using their resources.

KEY TERMS

police chief
time-in-rank system
special-needs population
beat
order maintenance (peacekeeping)
displacement
proactive policing
deterrent effect
vice squad
sting operation
police–community relations
broken windows model
foot patrol
neighborhood-oriented policing (NOP)
problem-oriented policing
hot spots of crime
internal affairs
police productivity

INFOTRAC COLLEGE EDITION EXERCISES

There are numerous sources in *InfoTrac College Edition* to research the topic of community-oriented policing (COP). First, do a search on the concept of "problem-oriented policing." Then to find out what COP means to various police departments in terms of strategies, philosophy, and officer skills, check out

Michael G. Breci and Timothy E. Erickson, "Community Policing: The Process of Transitional Change," *FBI Law Enforcement Bulletin* 67 (1998): 16.

To check out the effectiveness of citizen participation in community policing, read

Eli Lehrer, "Communities and Cops Join Forces," *Insight on the News* 15 (1999): 16.

This paper finds that communities in which the residents watch out for one another and take active steps in crime prevention have a crime rate that is 40 percent lower than equivalent communities that do not take such measures.

For a more critical look at COP, see

Gerasimos A. Gianakis and G. John Davis III, "Reinventing or Repackaging Public Services? The Case of Community-Oriented Policing," *Public Administration Review* 58 (1998): 485.

QUESTIONS

1. Should the primary police role be law enforcement or community service? Explain.
2. Should a police chief be permitted to promote an officer with special skills to a supervisory position, or should all officers be forced to spend "time in rank"? Why or why not?
3. Do the advantages of proactive policing outweigh the disadvantages? Explain.
4. Should all police recruits take the same physical tests, or are different requirements permissible for male and female applicants? Explain.
5. Can the police and the community ever form a partnership to fight crime? Why or why not? Does the community policing model remind you of early forms of policing? Explain.

NOTES

1. John Cloud, "L.A. Confidential, for Real: Street Cops Accused of Frame-ups in Widening Scandal," *Time,* 27 September 1999, 44; "L.A.'s Dirty War on Gangs: A Trail of Corruption Leads to Some of the City's Toughest Cops," *Newsweek,* 11 October 1999, 72.

2. Brian Reaves and Andrew Goldberg, *Law Enforcement Management and Administrative Statistics, 1997: Data for Individual State and Local Law Enforcement Agencies with 100 or More Officers* (Washington, D.C.: Bureau of Justice Statistics, 1999).

3. Velmer Burton, James Frank, Robert Langworthy, and Troy Barker, "The Prescribed Roles of Police in a Free Society: Analyzing State Legal Codes," *Justice Quarterly* 10 (1993): 683–95.

4. David Carter and Allen Sapp, "Police Experiences and Responses Related to the Homeless," *Journal of Criminal Justice* 16 (1993): 87–96; Peter Finn and Monique Sullivan, *Police Response to Special Populations* (Washington, D.C.: National Institute of Justice, 1988).

5. Brian Reaves and Pheny Smith, *Law Enforcement Management and Administrative Statistics, 1993: Data for Individual State and Local Agencies with 100 or More Officers* (Washington, D.C.: Bureau of Justice Statistics, 1995).

6. American Bar Association, *Standards Relating to Urban Police Function* (New York: Institute of Judicial Administration, 1974), standard 2.2.

7. Albert J. Reiss, *The Police and the Public* (New Haven, Conn.: Yale University Press, 1971), 19.

8. James Q. Wilson, *Varieties of Police Behavior: The Management of Law and Order in Eight Communities* (Cambridge, Mass.: Harvard University Press, 1968).

9. See Harlan Hahn, "A Profile of Urban Police," in *The Ambivalent Force,* ed. A. Niederhoffer and A. Blumberg (Hinsdale, Ill.: Dryden Press, 1976), 59.

10. George Kelling, Tony Pate, Duane Dieckman, and Charles Brown, *The Kansas City Preventive Patrol Experiment: A Summary Report* (Washington, D.C.: Police Foundation, 1974).

11. Ibid., 3–4.

12. Ibid.

13. Kenneth Novak, Jennifer Hartman, Alexander Holsinger, and Michael Turner, "The Effects of Aggressive Policing of Disorder on Serious Crime," *Policing* 22 (1999): 171–90.

14. David Jacobs and Katherine Woods, "Interracial Conflict and Interracial Homicide: Do Political and Economic Rivalries Explain White Killings of Blacks or Black Killings of Whites?" *American Journal of Sociology* 105 (1999): 157–90.

15. James Q. Wilson and Barbara Boland, "The Effect of Police on Crime," *Law and Society Review* 12 (1978): 367–84.

16. Robert Sampson, "Deterrent Effects of the Police on Crime: A Replication and Theoretical Extension," *Law and Society Review* 22 (1988): 163–91.

17. For a thorough review of this issue, see Andrew Karmen, *Why Is New York City's Murder Rate Dropping So Sharply?* (New York: John Jay College, 1996).

18. Lawrence Sherman, James Shaw, and Dennis Rogan, *The Kansas City Gun Experiment* (Washington, D.C.: National Institute of Justice, 1994).

19. H. Lawrence Ross, *Deterring the Drunk Driver: Legal Policy and Social Control* (Lexington, Mass.: Heath, 1982); Samuel Walker, *Sense and Nonsense about Crime* (Belmont, Calif.: Wadsworth, 1985), 82–85.

20. Perry Shapiro and Harold Votey, "Deterrence and Subjective Probabilities of Arrest: Modeling Individual Decisions to Drink and Drive in Sweden," *Law and Society Review* 18 (1984): 111–49.

21. Mitchell Chamlin, "Crime and Arrests: An Autoregressive Integrated Moving Average (ARIMA) Approach," *Journal of Quantitative Criminology* 4 (1988): 247–55.

22. Stewart D'Alessio and Lisa Stolzenberg, "Crime, Arrests and Pretrial Jail Incarceration: An Examination of the Deterrence Thesis," *Criminology* 36 (1998): 735–61.

23. Frances Lawrenz, James Lembo, and Thomas Schade, "Time Series Analysis of the Effect of a Domestic Violence Directive on the Number of Arrests per Day," *Journal of Criminal Justice* 17 (1989): 493–99.

24. Kathleen Ferraro, "Policing Woman Battering," *Social Problems* 36 (1989): 61–74.

25. Craig Uchida and Robert Goldberg, *Police Employment and Expenditure Trends* (Washington, D.C.: Bureau of Justice Statistics, 1986).

26. Colin Loftin and David McDowall, "The Police, Crime, and Economic Theory: An Assessment," *American Sociological Review* 47 (1982): 393–401.

27. Joan Petersilia, Allan Abrahamse, and James Q. Wilson, "A Summary of Rand's Research on Police Performance, Community Characteristics and Case Attrition," *Journal of Police Science and Administration* 17 (1990): 219–29.

28. See Belton Cobb, *The First Detectives* (London: Faber & Faber, 1957).

29. See, for example, James Q. Wilson, "Movie Cops — Romantic vs. Real," *New York Magazine,* 19 August 1968, 38–41.

30. For a view of the modern detective, see William Sanders, *Detective Work: A Study of Criminal Investigations* (New York: Free Press, 1977).

31. James Ahern, *Police in Trouble* (New York: Hawthorn Books, 1972), 83–85.

32. Robert Langworthy, "Do Stings Control Crime? An Evaluation of a Police Fencing Operation," *Justice Quarterly* 6 (1989): 27–45.

33. Mark Porgebin and Eric Poole, "Vice Isn't Nice: A Look at the Effects of Working Undercover," *Journal of Criminal Justice* 21 (1993): 385–96; Gary Marx, *Undercover: Police Surveillance in America* (Berkeley: University of California Press, 1988).

34. Peter Greenwood and Joan Petersilia, *Summary and Policy Implications,* vol. 1 of *The Criminal Investigation Process* (Santa Monica, Calif.: Rand Corp., 1975).

35. Mark Willman and John Snortum, "Detective Work: The Criminal Investigation Process in a Medium-Size Police Department," *Criminal Justice Review* 9 (1984): 33–39.

36. Police Executive Research Forum, *Calling the Police: Citizen Reporting of Serious Crime* (Washington, D.C.: Police Executive Research Forum, 1981).

37. John Eck, *Solving Crimes: The Investigation of Burglary and Robbery* (Washington, D.C.: Police Executive Research Forum, 1984).

38. Egon Bittner, *The Functions of Police in Modern Society* (Cambridge, Mass.: Oelgeschlager, Gunn & Hain, 1980), 8; see also James Q. Wilson, "The Police in the Ghetto," in *The Police and the Community,* ed. Robert F. Steadman (Baltimore: Johns Hopkins University Press, 1974), 68.

39. George Kelling, *Police and Communities: The Quiet Revolution* (Washington, D.C.: National Institute of Justice, 1988).

40. Ibid.

41. George Kelling and James Q. Wilson, "Broken Windows: The Police and Neighborhood Safety," *Atlantic Monthly* 249 (1982): 29–38.

42. For a general review, see Robert Trojanowicz and Bonnie Bucqueroux, *Community Policing: A Contemporary Perspective* (Cincinnati: Anderson, 1990).

43. Police Foundation, *The Newark Foot Patrol Experiment* (Washington, D.C.: Police Foundation, 1981).

44. Jihong Zhao, Nicholas Lovrich, and Quint Thurman, "The Status of Community Policing American Cities," *Policing* 22 (1999): 74–92.

45. Albert Cardarelli, Jack McDevitt and Katrina Baum, "The Rhetoric and Reality of Community Policing in Small and Medium-Sized Cities and Towns," *Policing* 21 (1998): 397–415.

46. Quint Thurman, Andrew Giacomazzi, and Phil Bogen, "Research Note: Cops, Kids, and Community Policing — An Assessment of a Community Policing Demonstration

Project," *Crime and Delinquency* 39 (1993): 554–64.

47. Quint Thurman and Phil Bogen, "Research Note: Spokane Community Policing Officers Revisited," *American Journal of Police* 15 (1996): 97–114.

48. Diana Fishbein, "The Comprehensive Care Model," *FBI Law Enforcement Bulletin* 67 (1998): 1–5.

49. Susan Sadd and Randolph Grinc, *Implementation Challenges in Community Policing* (Washington, D.C.: National Institute of Justice, 1996).

50. Donald Green, Dara Strolovitch, and Janelle Wong, "Defended Neighborhoods, Integration and Racially Motivated Crime," *American Journal of Sociology* 104 (1998): 372–403.

51. Walter Baranyk, "Making a Difference in a Public Housing Project," *Police Chief* 61 (1994): 31–35.

52. Jerome Skolnick and David Bayley, *Community Policing: Issues and Practices around the World* (Washington, D.C.: National Institute of Justice, 1988).

53. Ibid., 17.

54. Herman Goldstein, "Improving Policing: A Problem-Oriented Approach," *Crime and Delinquency* 25 (1979): 236–58.

55. Skolnick and Bayley, *Community Policing,* 12.

56. Lawrence Sherman, Patrick Gartin, and Michael Buerger, "Hot Spots of Predatory Crime: Routine Activities and the Criminology of Place," *Criminology* 27 (1989): 27–55.

57. Ibid., 45.

58. Dennis Roncek and Pamela Maier, "Bars, Blocks, and Crimes Revisited: Linking the Theory of Routine Activities to the Empiricism of 'Hot Spots,'" *Criminology* 29 (1991): 725–53.

59. E. Nick Larsen, "Community Policing and the Control of Street Prostitution," (Paper presented at the annual meeting of the American Society of Criminology, Chicago, November 1996).

60. Herman Goldstein, "Toward Community-Oriented Policing: Potential Basic Requirements, and Threshold Questions," *Crime and Delinquency* 33 (1987): 6–30.

61. Anthony Braga, David Weisburd, Elin Waring, Lorraine Green Mazerolle, William Spelman, and Francis Gajewski, "Problem-Oriented Policing in Violent Crime Places: A Randomized Controlled Experiment," *Criminology* 37 (1999): 541–80.

62. Eric Fritsch, Tory Caeti, and Robert Taylor, "Gang Suppression through Saturation Patrol, Aggressive Curfew, and Truancy Enforcement: A Quasi-Experimental Test of the Dallas Anti-Gang Initiative," *Crime and Delinquency* 45 (1999): 122–39.

63. Bureau of Justice Assistance, *Problem-Oriented Drug Enforcement: A Community-Based Approach for Effective Policing* (Washington, D.C.: National Institute of Justice, 1993).

64. Ibid., 64–65.

65. Jack R. Greene, "The Effects of Community Policing on American Law Enforcement: A Look at the Evidence" (Paper presented at the International Congress on Criminology, Hamburg, Germany, September 1988).

66. Roger Dunham and Geoffrey Alpert, "Neighborhood Differences in Attitudes toward Policing: Evidence for a Mixed-Strategy Model of Policing in a Multi-Ethnic Setting," *Journal of Criminal Law and Criminology* 79 (1988): 504–22.

67. "Community Policing Officers See Benefits in Citizen Relations," *Criminal Justice Newsletter* 27 (1986): 4–5.

68. Ellen Cohn, "The Citizen Police Academy: A Recipe for Improving Police–Community Relations," *Journal of Criminal Justice* 24 (1996): 265–71.

69. David Kessler, "Integrating Calls for Service with Community- and Problem-Oriented Policing: A Case Study," *Crime and Delinquency* 39 (1993): 485–508.

70. L. Thomas Winfree, Gregory Bartku, and George Seibel, "Support for Community Policing versus Traditional Policing among Nonmetropolitan Police Officers: A Survey of Four New Mexico Police Departments," *American Journal of Police* 15 (1996): 23–47.

71. Jihong Zhao, Ni He, and Nicholas Lovrich, "Value Change among Police Officers at a Time of Organizational Reform: A Follow-up Study of Rokeach Values," *Policing* 22 (1999): 152–70.

72. See, for example, Lawrence Sherman, "Policing for Crime Prevention," in *Preventing Crime: What Works, What Doesn't, What's Promising* (Washington, D.C.: Bureau of Justice Program, 1997).

73. Roger Parks, Stephen Mastrofski, Christina DeJong, and M. Kevin Gray, "How Officers Spend Their Time with the Community," *Justice Quarterly* 16 (1999): 483–519.

74. Gerasimos Gianakis and G. John Davis, "Reinventing or Repackaging Public Services? The Case of Community-Oriented Policing," *Public Administration Review* 58 (1998): 485–505.

75. William Doerner and Terry Nowell, "The Reliability of the Behavioral-Personnel Assessment Device (BPAD) in Selecting Police Recruits," *Policing* 22 (1999): 343–52.

76. See, for example, Richard Larson, *Urban Police Patrol Analysis* (Cambridge, Mass.: MIT Press, 1972).

77. Brian Reaves, *State and Local Police Departments, 1990* (Washington, D.C.: Bureau of Justice Statistics, 1992), 6.

78. Philip Ash, Karen Slora, and Cynthia Britton, "Police Agency Officer Selection Practices," *Journal of Police Science and Administration* 17 (1990): 258–69.

79. Dennis Rosenbaum, Robert Flewelling, Susan Bailey, Chris Ringwalt, and Deanna Wilkinson, "Cops in the Classroom: A Longitudinal Evaluation of Drug Abuse Resistance Education (DARE)," *Journal of Research in Crime and Delinquency* 31 (1994): 3–31.

80. Greenwood and Petersilia, *Summary and Policy Implications;* Peter Greenwood et al., *Observations and Analysis,* vol. 3 of *The Criminal Investigation Process* (Santa Monica, Calif.: Rand Corp., 1975).

81. J. David Hirschel and Charles Dean, "The Relative Cost-Effectiveness of Citation and Arrest," *Journal of Criminal Justice* 23 (1995): 1–12.

82. Adapted from Terry Koepsell and Charles Gerard, *Small Police Agency Consolidation: Suggested Approaches* (Washington, D.C.: Government Printing Office, 1979).

83. Thomas McAninch and Jeff Sanders, "Police Attitudes toward Consolidation in Bloomington/Normal, Illinois: A Case Study," *Journal of Police Science and Administration* 16 (1988): 95–105.

84. James Garofalo and Dave Hanson, *The Metro Task Force: A Program of Intergovernmental Cooperation in Law Enforcement* (Washington, D.C.: National Institute of Justice, 1984).

85. Mike D'Alessandro and Charles Hoffman, "Mutual Aid Pacts," *Law and Order* 43 (1995): 90–93.

86. Leonard Sipes, Jr., "Maryland's High-Tech Approach to Crime Fighting," *Police Chief* 61 (1994): 18–20.

87. Nick Navarro, "Six Broward County Cities Turn to the Green and Gold," *Police Chief* 59 (1992): 60.

88. Greg Givens, "A Concept to Involve Citizens in the Provision of Police Services," *American Journal of Police* 12 (1993): 1–9; for a review, see Stephen Mastrofski, "Varieties of Community Policing," *American Journal of Police* 12 (1993): 65–75.

89. For a detailed review of this issue, see John Crank, "Patterns of Consolidation among Public Safety Departments, 1978–1988," *Journal of Police Science and Administration* 17 (1990): 277–88.

90. Kenneth Perry, "Tactical Units Reduce Overtime Costs," *Police Chief* 52 (1985): 57–58.

91. Robert Worden, "Toward Equity and Efficiency in Law Enforcement: Differential Police Response," *American Journal of Police* 12 (1993): 1–24.

chapter 6

Issues in Policing

On a warm August morning in 1997, Sammy Velez, a transvestite with a crack habit, took advantage of the rush-hour commotion near Penn Station to snatch a purse. Tripping in his high-heeled boots, he couldn't make a clean getaway, so he threw the purse back. Two New York police officers were soon in pursuit. They chased Velez in and out of traffic until he stumbled and fell. Velez curled up on the ground at the feet of the officers and raised his arms to protect a body weakened by AIDS and weighing barely one hundred pounds. In the ensuing struggle, Velez's left eyeball was ruptured, and his collarbone and many facial bones fractured. Velez later told authorities that he was pummeled by the officers, kicked in the face until his eye dangled from its socket. The officers denied beating him; they suggested he hurt himself when he fell. The city of New York paid Velez $75,000 to settle his claim that police used excessive force in blinding his left eye for a botched purse snatching.[1] ■

The Velez case was one among a number of highly publicized incidents of violence involving big-city police departments. These incidents highlight the critical and controversial role police play in the justice system and the need for developing a professional, competent police force. The police are the gatekeepers of the criminal justice process. They initiate contact with law violators and decide whether to formally arrest them and start their journey through the criminal justice system, settle the issue in an informal way (such as by issuing a warning), or simply take no action at all. The strategic position of law enforcement officers, their visibility and contact with the public, and their use of weapons and arrest power have kept them in the forefront of public thought for most of the twentieth century.

In the late 1960s and early 1970s, great issue was taken with the political and social roles of the police. Critics viewed police agencies as biased organizations that harassed minority citizens, controlled political dissidents, and generally seemed out of touch with the changing times. The major issues appeared to be controlling the abuse of police power and making police agencies more responsible to public control. During this period, major efforts were undertaken in the nation's largest cities to curb police power.

Since the mid-1970s, the relationship between police and the public has changed. Police departments have become more sensitive to their public image. Programs have been created to improve relations between police and community — to help police officers on the beat to be more sensitive to the needs of the public and to cope more effectively with the stress of their jobs.[2] For the past three decades, much public interest has focused on the function of the police. The U.S. public seems genuinely concerned today about the quality and effectiveness of local police. Most citizens seem to approve of their local law enforcement agents; 60 percent say they have a "great deal of confidence" in the police.[3] While this is encouraging, approval is often skewed along racial lines: Police procedures have been questioned because overenforcement may be present in minority communities.[4] Minority citizens also seem to be more adversely affected than whites when well-publicized incidents of police misconduct occur.[5] It may not be surprising then that 26 percent of African-American citizens report having little confidence in the police compared with 8 percent of whites.[6]

The general public is not the only group concerned about police attitudes and behavior. Police administrators and other law enforcement experts have focused their attention on issues that may influence the effectiveness and efficiency of police performance in the field. Some of their concerns are outgrowths of the development of policing as a profession: Does an independent police culture exist, and what are its characteristics? Do police officers develop a unique working personality, and if so, does it influence their job performance? Are there police officer styles that make some police officers too aggressive and others inert and passive? Is policing too stressful an occupation?

Another area of concern is the social composition of police departments: Who should be recruited as police officers? Are minorities and women being attracted to police work, and what have their experiences been on the force? Should police officers have a college education?

Important questions are also being raised about the problems police departments face interacting with the society they are entrusted with supervising: Are police officers too forceful and brutal, and do they discriminate in their use of deadly force? Are police officers corrupt, and how can police deviance be controlled?

THE POLICE PROFESSION

All professions have unique characteristics that distinguish them from other occupations and institutions. Policing is no exception. Police experts have long sought to understand the unique nature of the police experience and to determine how the challenges of police work shape the field and its employees. In this section, some of the factors that make policing unique are discussed in detail. The accompanying Criminal Justice and the Media feature discusses how the media portrays police work and the police profession.

The Police Culture

Police experts have found that the experience of becoming a police officer and the nature of the job itself cause most officers to band together in a police subculture, characterized by cynicism, clannishness, secrecy, and insulation from others in society — the so-called **blue curtain.** Police officers tend to socialize together and believe that their occupation cuts them off from relationships with civilians. Joining the police subculture means always having to stick up for fellow officers against outsiders, maintaining a tough, macho exterior personality, and distrusting the motives and behavior of outsiders.[7] Six core beliefs are viewed as being the heart of the police culture today:

blue curtain
The secretive, insulated police culture that isolates officers from the rest of society.

1. Police are the only real crime fighters. The public wants the police officer to fight crime; other agencies, both public and private, only play at crime fighting.
2. No one else understands the real nature of police work. Lawyers, academics, politicians, and the public in general have little concept of what it means to be a police officer.
3. Loyalty to colleagues counts above everything else. Police officers have to stick together because everyone is out to get the police and make the job more difficult.
4. It is impossible to win the war against crime without bending the rules. Courts have awarded criminal defendants too many civil rights.
5. Members of the public are basically unsupportive and unreasonably demanding. People are quick to criticize police unless they need police help themselves.
6. Patrol work is the pits. Detective work is glamorous and exciting.[8]

These cultural beliefs make it difficult for police to accept new ideas and embrace innovative concepts, such as community policing. The forces that support a police culture generally are believed to develop out of on-the-job experiences. Most officers, both male and female, originally join police forces because they want to help people, fight crime, and have an interesting, exciting, prestigious career with a high degree of job security.[9] Recruits often find that the social reality of police work does not mesh with their original career goals. They are unprepared for the emotional turmoil and conflict that accompany police work today.

Membership in the police culture helps recruits adjust to the rigors of police work and provides the emotional support needed for survival.[10] The culture

NYPD BLUE

Hard-charging police officers have long been the focus of films and TV shows. Representative of the genre is the gritty police drama *NYPD Blue*, which presents the ongoing saga of a group of streetwise New York detectives assigned to the One-Five precinct. The show's core figure is Detective Andy Sipowicz (Dennis Franz), a recovering alcoholic who lost both his family and his self-respect after battling the bottle for decades. Now sober, Sipowicz is easily enraged by the deadbeats he meets on the job. He exhibits multiple personality traits, at times a coarse racist and at other times a kind, good-hearted man with high morals.

Over the lifetime of the show, a number of detectives have been paired with Sipowicz — most recently Danny Sorenson (Rick Schroder), who although young has street smarts and heart. Among other detectives in the precinct is Diane Russell, also a recovering alcoholic and the widow of Sipowicz's former partner. Russell's traumatic childhood with a sexually abusive father has left her emotionally scarred. Lieutenant Arthur Fancy (James McDaniel), an African American who leads the squad, is acutely aware of the scrutiny he's placed under by his superiors.

Rounding out the cast is Detective Baldwin Jones, who transferred into the 15th squad from a bias crimes unit to replace the departed Dt. James Martinez (Nicholas Turturro); and Detective Greg Medavoy (Gordon Clapp) who, despite being a walking bundle of neuroses and insecurity, is a good investigator who has managed to earn the respect of his coworkers.

NYPD Blue aims for authenticity by using New York street scenes and characters. Unlike so many other cop shows and movies, few criminals are affluent, highly educated society folk. The detectives rarely use their weapons, engage in high-speed chases, or pursue criminals by jumping from one rooftop to another. They rarely sustain injury or get beaten to a pulp by criminals only to be on the job an hour later. In other words, *NYPD Blue* avoids the ludicrous vision of police officer as action hero that is the stock in trade of the Bruce Willis (*Die Hard*) and Mel Gibson (*Lethal Weapon*) series. In fact, the thought of Sipowicz jumping from one rooftop to another or pursuing a criminal down the street is ludicrous: It is doubtful whether he can bend over to lace up his own shoes.

Like their real-life counterparts, the detectives have a myriad of social and personal problems, including obesity and alcoholism, conditions that rarely afflict superheroes (Medavoy and Sipowicz are always dieting; Sipowicz and Russell are members of Alcoholics Anonymous). Sipowicz has to confront his racist attitudes, which constantly entangle him with African Americans both on the job and off. During the last few seasons, he has lost his former partners Detective John Kelly (David Caruso) to an internal affairs investigation and Bobby Simone (Jimmy Smits) to a fatal heart infection. Sipowicz's oldest son — Andy, Jr. — was killed by a pair of armed robbers, and his wife, Sylvia, dies after being shot by a stray bullet in a courthouse shootout. There is little question that Sipowicz has faced the personal and job-related stress that plagues all too many police officers.

Although *NYPD Blue* aims for realism, the plots often stray into a media version of police work. The squad almost always solve their cases, get the bad guys to talk, and can concentrate on a single case for days on end until it is solved. If every arrestee was willing to confess, as they are when captured by detectives of the fifteenth squad, then we would have no need for the prosecutors who appear regularly on the competing show *Law & Order.*

Some experts believe there is a police subculture, referred to as the "blue curtain," characterized by cynicism, clannishness, secrecy, and insulation from others in society. Members of the police subculture stick up for fellow officers against outsiders and distrust the motives and behavior of outsiders.

encourages decisiveness in the face of uncertainty and the ability to make split-second judgments that may later be subject to extreme criticism. Hard-core officers who view themselves as crime fighters are the ones most likely to value solidarity and depend on the support and camaraderie of their fellow officers.[11] The police subculture encourages its members to draw a sharp distinction between good and evil. Officers, more than mere enforcers of the law, are warriors in the age-old battle between right and wrong.[12] In contrast, criminals are referred to as "terrorists" and "predators," terms that convey the fact that they are evil individuals ready to prey upon the poor and vulnerable. Because the predators represent a real danger, the police culture demands that its members be both competent and concerned with the safety of their peers and partners. Competence is often translated into respect and authority, and citizens must obey lest they face "payback."[13]

In sum, the police culture has developed in response to the insulated, dangerous lifestyle of police officers. Policing is a dangerous occupation, and the availability of unquestioned support and loyalty of their peers is not something officers could readily do without.[14]

cynicism
The belief that most people's actions are motivated solely by personal needs and selfishness.

The Police Personality

Police officers develop a unique set of personality traits that distinguish them from the average citizen. The typical police personality has been described as dogmatic, authoritarian, suspicious, racist, hostile, insecure, conservative, and cynical.[15] **Cynicism** has been found on all levels of policing, including chiefs of police, and throughout all stages of a police career.[16] Maintenance of these negative values and attitudes is believed to cause police officers to be secretive and isolated from the rest of society, producing the blue curtain.[17]

The police officer's working personality is shaped by constant exposure to danger and the need to use force and authority to reduce and control threatening situations.[18] Police feel suspicious of the public they serve and defensive about the actions of their fellow officers. There are two opposing viewpoints on the cause of this phenomenon. One position holds that police departments attract recruits who are by nature cynical, authoritarian, secretive, and so on.[19] Other experts maintain that socialization and experience on the police force itself cause these character traits to develop in police officers.

Since the first research measuring police personality was published, numerous efforts have been made to determine whether the typical police recruit does indeed possess a unique personality that sets her apart from the average citizen. The results have been mixed.[20] While some research concludes that police values are different from those of the general adult population, other efforts reach an opposing conclusion; some have found that police officers are actually more psychologically healthy than the general population, less depressed and anxious, and more social and assertive.[21] Still other research on police personality found that police officers highly value such personality traits as warmth, flexibility, and emotion; these traits are far removed from rigidity and cynicism.[22] Since research has found evidence supportive of both viewpoints, no one position dominates on the issue of how the police personality develops, or even if one actually exists.

In what is probably the most well-known study of police personality, *Behind the Shield* (1967), Arthur Neiderhoffer examined the assumption that most police officers develop into cynics as a function of their daily duties.[23] Among his most important findings were that police cynicism did increase with length of service, that patrol officers with college educations become quite cynical if they are denied promotion, and that military-like police academy training caused new recruits to quickly become cynical about themselves. For example, Niederhoffer found that nearly 80 percent of first-day recruits believed that the police department was an "efficient, smoothly operating organization"; two months later less than 33 percent professed that belief. Similarly, 50 percent of the new recruits believed that a police superior was "very interested in the welfare of his subordinates"; two months later that number had declined to 13 percent.[24]

The development of negative attitudes by police officers may have an extremely damaging effect on their job performance. A police officer's feelings of cynicism seem to intensify the need to maintain respect and exert authority over others.[25] As police escalate their use of authority, citizens learn to distrust and fear them. These feelings of hostility and anger in turn create feelings of potential danger among police officers, resulting in "police paranoia."[26] Cynical attitudes make police very conservative and resistant to change, factors that interfere with the efficiency of police work.[27]

police officer style
The belief that the bulk of police officers can be classified into ideal personality types. Popular types include *supercops,* who desire to enforce only serious crimes, such as robbery and rape; *professionals,* who use a broad definition of police work; *service-oriented officers,* who see their job as a helping profession; and *avoiders,* who do as little as possible. The actual existence of ideal police officer types has been much debated.

Policing Style

Policing encompasses a multitude of diverse tasks, including peacekeeping, criminal investigation, traffic control, and providing emergency medical service. Part of the socialization as a police officer is developing a working attitude, or **style,** through which he approaches policing. For example, some police officers may view their job as a well-paid civil service position that stresses careful compliance with written departmental rules and procedures. Other officers may see themselves as part of the "thin blue line" that protects the public from wrongdoers. They will use any means to get the culprit, even if it involves such cheating as planting evidence on an obviously guilty person who so far has escaped arrest. Should the police bend the rules to protect the public? This has been referred to as the "Dirty Harry problem," after the popular Clint Eastwood movie character who routinely (and successfully) violated all known standards of police work.[28]

Several studies have attempted to define and classify police styles into behavioral clusters. These classifications, called *typologies,* attempt to categorize law enforcement agents by groups, each of which has a unique approach to police work. The purpose of such classifications is to demonstrate that the police are not a cohesive, homogeneous group, as many believe, but rather are individuals with differing approaches to their work.[29] The way police approach their task and their attitude toward the police role, as well as their peers and superior officers, have been shown to affect police work. Somewhat surprisingly, officers who have the most negative attitudes toward peers and superiors may be the most likely to be aggressive and quick to make formal arrests.[30]

An examination of the literature suggests that four styles of police work seem to fit the current behavior patterns of most police agents: the crime fighter, the social agent, the law enforcer, and the watchman.

crime fighter
The police style that stresses dealing with hard crimes and arresting dangerous criminals.

THE CRIME FIGHTER To the **crime fighter,** the most important police work is investigating serious crimes and apprehending criminals. This type of police officer believes that murder, rape, and other major personal crimes should be the primary concerns of police agencies. They consider property crimes to be less significant, while such matters as misdemeanors, traffic control, and social service functions would be better handled by other agencies of government. This type of police officer believes that the ability to investigate criminal behavior posing a serious threat to life and safety, combined with the power to arrest criminals, separates a police department from other municipal agencies. They see diluting these functions with minor social service and nonenforcement duties as harmful to police efforts to create a secure society.[31]

social agent
The police style that believes that police should be involved in a wide range of activities without regard to their connection to law enforcement.

THE SOCIAL AGENT Strongly opposed to the crime fighter is the sort of police officer described as the social agent. The **social agent** believes that police should be involved in a wide range of activities without regard for their connection to law enforcement. Rather than viewing themselves as criminal catchers, social agents consider themselves problem solvers. They are troubleshooters who patch the holes that appear where the social fabric wears thin. They are happy to work with special-needs populations such as the homeless, schoolchildren, and those in need of emergency services. The social agent fits well within a community policing unit.

law enforcer
The police style that emphasizes the detection and apprehension aspects of police work. Law enforcers see the police role as one of enforcing all statutes and ordinances. According to this officer's view, duty is clearly set out in law, and the law enforcer stresses playing it "by the book."

THE LAW ENFORCER Like the crime fighter, the **law enforcer** tends to emphasize the detection and apprehension aspects of police work. Unlike the crime fighter, this police officer does not distinguish between major and minor crimes. Although a law enforcer may prefer working on serious crimes — they are more intriguing and rewarding in terms of achievement, prestige, and status — she sees the police role as one of enforcing all statutes and ordinances. According to this officer's view, duty is clearly set out in law, and the law enforcer stresses playing it "by the book." Since the police are specifically charged with apprehending all types of lawbreakers, they see themselves as generalized law enforcement agents. They do not perceive themselves as lawmakers or as judges of whether existing laws are fair; quite simply, legislators legislate, courts judge, and police officers perform the functions of detecting violations, identifying culprits, and taking the lawbreakers before a court. The law enforcer is devoted to the profession of police work and is the officer most likely to aspire to command rank.

watchman
A police style that stresses reacting to calls for service rather than aggressively pursuing crime.

THE WATCHMAN The **watchman** style is characterized by an emphasis on the maintenance of public order as the police goal, rather than on law enforcement or general service.[32] Watchmen choose to ignore many infractions and requests for service unless they believe that the social or political order is jeopardized. Juveniles are "expected" to misbehave and are best ignored or treated informally. Motorists will often be left alone if their driving does not endanger or annoy others. Vice and gambling are problems only when the currently accepted standards of public order are violated.[33] The watchman is the most passive officer, more concerned with retirement benefits than crime rates.

DO POLICE STYLES ACTUALLY EXIST? As you may recall, the police role involves a great deal of time spent in noncrime service-related activities, ranging from providing emergency medical care to directing traffic. Although officers who admire one style of policing may emphasize one area of law enforcement over another, their daily activities will likely require them to engage in police duties they consider trivial or unimportant. While some pure types exist, an officer probably cannot specialize in one area of policing while ignoring the others.[34]

It is possible that today's police officer is more of a generalist than ever before and that future police recruits will be required to engage in a great variety of police tasks. Figure 6.1 summarizes the four police styles.

POLICE DISCRETION

Style and role orientation may influence how police officers carry out their duties and the way they may use their **discretion.**[35] Police have the ability to deprive people of their liberty, arrest them and take them away in handcuffs, and even use deadly force to subdue them. A critical aspect of this professional responsibility is the personal discretion each officer has in carrying out his daily activities. Discretion can involve the selective enforcement of the law, as when a vice squad plainclothes officer decides not to take action against a tavern that is serving drinks after hours. Patrol officers use discretion when they decide to arrest one suspect for disorderly conduct but escort another home.

discretion
The use of personal decision making and choice in carrying out operations in the criminal justice system. For example, police discretion can involve the decision to make an arrest; prosecutorial discretion can involve the decision to accept a plea bargain.

The majority of police officers use a high degree of personal discretion in carrying out daily tasks, sometimes referred to as *low-visibility decision making* in criminal justice[36] This terminology suggests that, unlike members of almost every other criminal justice agency, police are neither regulated in their daily procedures by administrative scrutiny nor subject to judicial review (except when their behavior clearly violates an offender's constitutional rights). As a result, the exercise of discretion by police may sometimes deteriorate into discrimination, violence, and other abusive practices. The following sections describe the factors that influence police discretion and review suggestions for its control.

Figure 6.1
Four styles of policing

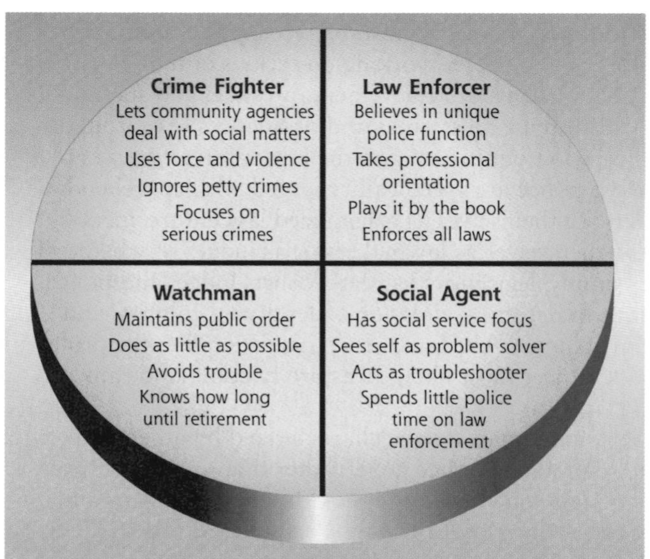

Legal Factors

Police discretion is inversely related to the severity of the offense. There is far less personal discretion available when police confront a suspect in a case involving murder or rape than there is with a simple assault or trespass. The likelihood of a police officer taking legal action then may depend on how the individual views offense severity. The relationship between the parties involved influences decision making. An altercation between two friends or relatives may be handled differently than an assault on a stranger. A case in point is policing domestic violence cases. Research indicates that police are reluctant to even respond to these kinds of cases because they are a constant source of frustration and futility. Victims, they believe, often fail to get help or change their abusive situation.[37] Even when they are summoned, police are likely to treat domestic violence cases more casually than other assault cases.[38] Evidence shows that police intentionally delay responding to domestic disputes, hoping that by the time they get there the problem will be settled.[39] Yet, when domestic abuse involves extreme violence, especially if a weapon is brandished or used, then police are more likely to respond with a formal arrest.[40]

Environmental Factors The degree of discretion an officer will exercise is at least partially defined by the living and working environment.[41] Police officers may work or dwell within a community culture that either tolerates eccentricities and personal freedoms or expects extremely conservative, professional, no-nonsense behavior on the part of its civil servants. Communities that are proactive and contain progressive governmental institutions also may influence the direction of a police officer's discretion. For example, police in communities that provide training in domestic violence prevention and maintain local shelters are more likely to take action in cases involving spousal abuse.[42]

An officer who lives in the community she serves is probably strongly influenced by and shares a large part of the community's beliefs and values and is likely to be sensitive to and respect the wishes of neighbors, friends, and relatives. Conflict may arise, however, when the police officer commutes to an assigned area of jurisdiction, as is often the case in inner-city precincts. The officer who holds personal values in opposition to those of the community can exercise discretion in ways that conflict with the community's values and result in ineffective law enforcement.[43]

Another environmental factor affecting the police officer's performance is his perception of community alternatives to police intervention. A police officer may exercise discretion to arrest an individual in a particular circumstance if it seems that nothing else can be done, even if the officer does not believe that an arrest is the best possible example of good police work. In an environment that has a proliferation of social agencies — detoxification units, drug control centers, and childcare services, for example — a police officer will obviously have more alternatives to choose from in deciding whether to make an arrest. In fact, referring cases to these alternative agencies saves the officer both time and effort — records do not have to be made out and court appearances can be avoided. Thus, social agencies provide greater latitude in police decision making.

Departmental Factors The policies, practices, and customs of the local police department are another influence on discretion. These conditions vary from department to department and strongly depend on the judgment of the chief and others in the organizational hierarchy. For example, departments can issue directives aimed at influencing police conduct. Patrol officers may be asked to issue more tickets and make more arrests or to refrain from arresting under certain circumstances. Occasionally, a directive will instruct officers to be particularly alert for certain types of violations or to make some sort of interagency referral when specific events occur. For example, the department may order patrol officers to crack down on street panhandlers or to take formal action in domestic violence cases.[44] These factors affect the decisions of the police officer, who has to produce appropriate performance statistics by the end of the month or be prepared to offer justification for following a course of action other than that officially prescribed.

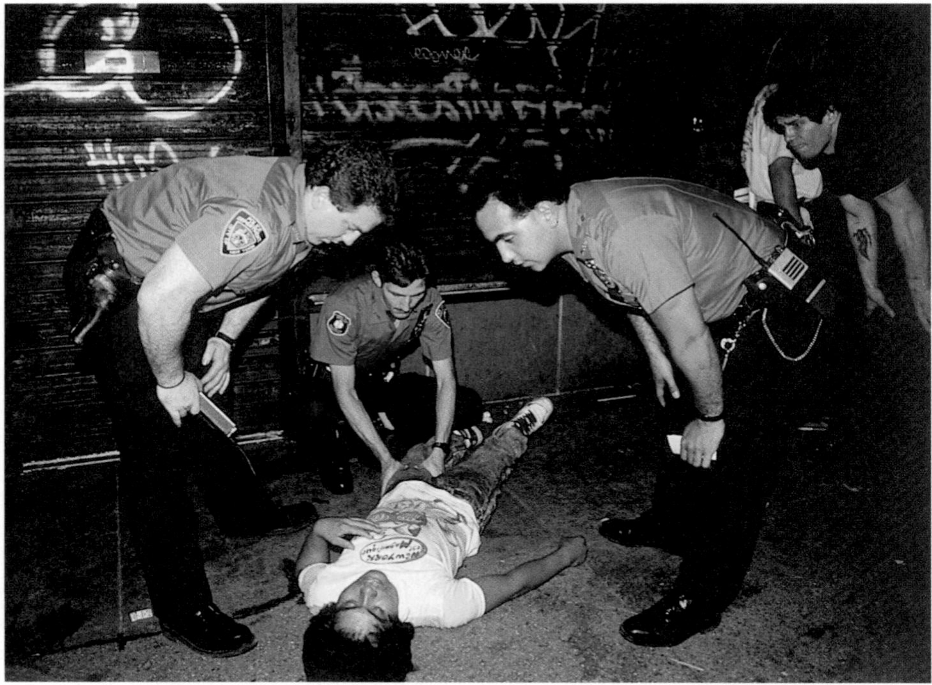

Police officers in New York are seen here giving aid to a youth. The police role involves numerous tasks. Although one style of policing may be emphasized over another, their daily activities may make it impossible for the "average" officer to forgo all aspects of the police role.

The ratio of supervisory personnel to subordinates may also influence discretion: Departments with a high ratio of sergeants to patrol officers may experience fewer officer-initiated actions than one in which fewer eyes are observing the action in the streets. The size of the department may also determine the level of officer discretion. In larger departments, looser control by supervisors seems to encourage a level of discretion unknown in smaller, more tightly run police agencies.

PEER PRESSURE Police discretion is also subject to peer pressure.[45] Police officers suffer a degree of social isolation because the job involves strange working conditions and hours, including being on twenty-four-hour call, and their authority and responsibility to enforce the law may cause embarrassment during social encounters. At the same time, officers must handle irregular and emotionally demanding encounters involving the most personal and private aspects of people's lives. As a result, police officers turn to their peers for both on-the-job advice and off-the-job companionship, essentially forming a subculture to provide a source of status, prestige, and reward.

The peer group affects how police officers exercise discretion on two distinct levels. In an obvious, direct manner, other police officers dictate acceptable responses to street-level problems by displaying or withholding approval in office discussions. Second, the officer who takes the job seriously and desires the respect and friendship of others will take their advice, abide by their norms, and seek out the most experienced and most influential patrol officers on the force and follow their behavior models.

Situational Factors

The situational factors attached to a particular crime provide another extremely important influence on police actions and behavior. Regardless of departmental or community influences, the officer's immediate interaction with a criminal act, offender, citizen, or victim will weigh heavily on the use of discretionary powers. Some early research efforts found that

demeanor
The way in which a person outwardly manifests his or her personality.

police officers rely heavily on **demeanor** (the attitude and appearance of the offender) in making decisions. If an offender is surly, talks back, or otherwise challenges the officer's authority, formal action is more likely to be taken.[46] Research by David Klinger has challenged the influence of demeanor on police decision making, suggesting that it is criminal behavior and actions that occur during police detention and not negative attitude that influence the police decision to take formal action.[47] For example, a person who struggles or touches police during a confrontation is a likely candidate for arrest; merely having a "bad attitude" is not enough to generate police retaliation. Although Klinger's data are persuasive, the weight of the evidence seems to show that in many police–citizen interactions, a negative demeanor will result in formal police action.[48]

Another set of situational influences on police discretion concerns the manner in which a crime or situation is encountered. If, for example, a police officer stumbles on an altercation or break-in, the discretionary response may be different from a situation in which the officer is summoned by police radio. If an act has received official police recognition, such as the dispatch of a patrol car, police action must be taken, or an explanation made as to why it was not. Or if a matter is brought to an officer's attention by a citizen observer, the officer can ignore the request and risk a complaint or take discretionary action. When an officer chooses to become involved in a situation, without benefit of a summons or complaint, maximum discretion can be used. Even in this circumstance, however, the presence of a crowd or of witnesses may influence the officer's decision making.

And, of course, the officer who acts alone is also affected by personal matters — physical condition, mental state, police style, and whether she has other duties to perform.

Other factors that might influence police are the use of a weapon, seriousness of injury, and the presence of alcohol or drugs.

Figure 6.2
Influences on police discretion

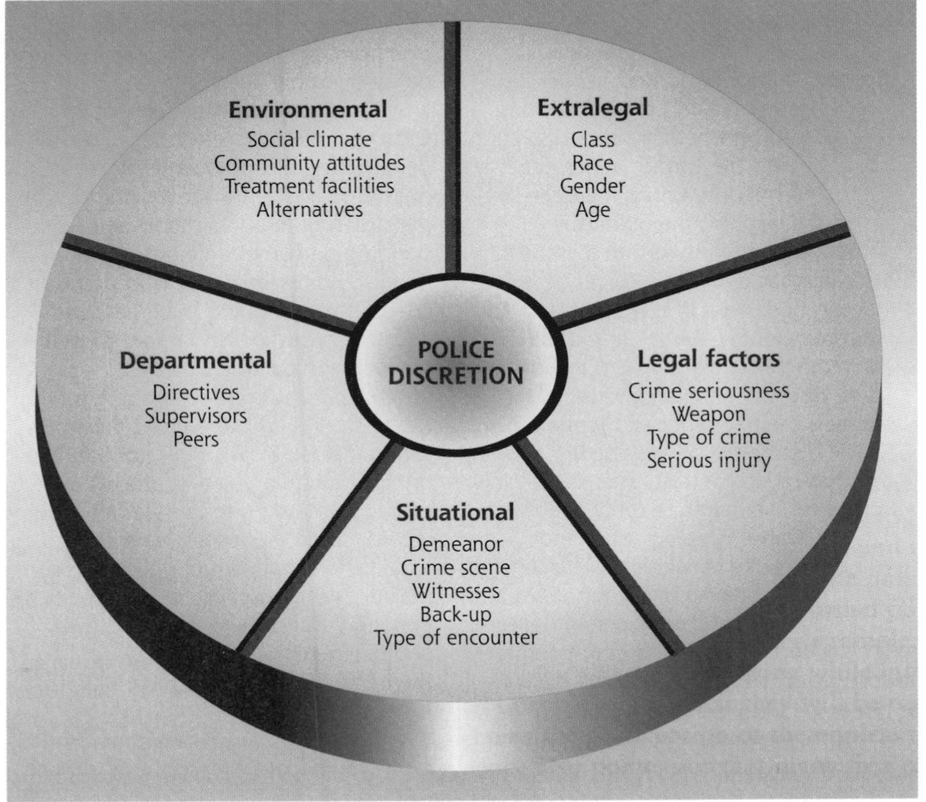

Extralegal Factors

One often-debated issue is whether police take race, class, and gender into account when making arrest decisions. For example, research shows that police are less likely to make arrests in cases of elder mistreatment than in other assaults; the age of the victim influences their decision making.[49] The question then is whether police discretion is shaped by such extralegal factors as age, gender, income, and race. Because this issue is so important, it is the topic of the Race, Culture, and Gender feature.

Police discretion is one of the most often debated issues in criminal justice (see Figure 6.2). On its face, the unequal enforcement of the law smacks of unfairness and violates the Constitution's doctrines of due process and equal protection. Yet if some discretion were not exercised, police would be forced to function as robots merely following the book. Administrators have sought to control discretion so that its exercise may be both beneficial to citizens and nondiscriminatory.[50]

WHO ARE THE POLICE?

The composition of the nation's police forces is changing. Traditionally, police agencies were composed of white males with a high school education who viewed policing as a secure position that brought them the respect of family and friends and a step up the social ladder. It was not uncommon to see police families in which one member of each new generation would enter the force. This picture has been changing and will continue to change. As criminal justice programs turn out thousands of graduates every year, an increasing number of police officers have at least some college education. In addition, affirmative action programs have helped slowly change the racial and gender composition of police depart-

Race, Culture, and Gender

DOES RACE INFLUENCE THE POLICE USE OF DISCRETION?

In the late summer of 1997, New Yorkers were shocked as an astounding case of police brutality began to unfold in the daily newspapers. Abner Louima, age 33, a Haitian immigrant, had been arrested on August 9 outside Club Rendez-vous, a Brookyn nightclub, after a fight had broken out. Louima later claimed that the arresting officers had become furious when he protested his arrest, twice stopping the patrol car to beat him with their fists. When they arrived at the station house, two officers, apparently angry because some of the club-goers had fought with the police, led Louima to the men's room, removed his trousers, and attacked him with the handle of a toilet plunger, first shoving it into his rectum and then into his mouth, breaking teeth, while Louima screamed, "Why are you doing this to me? Why? Why?" The officers also shouted racial slurs at Louima who was rushed to a hospital for emergency surgery to repair a puncture in his small intestine and injuries to his bladder. Louima, who witnesses said had no bruises or injuries when officers took him into custody, arrived at the hospital three hours later bleeding profusely.

In the aftermath of the case, New York Police Department investigators granted departmental immunity to nearly one hundred officers, in order to gain information. By cracking the blue curtain of silence, a number of police officers were given long prison sentences on charges of sexual abuse and first-degree assault.

One often-debated issue is whether police take race, class, and gender into account when making arrest decisions. The question is whether police discretion works against the young, males, the poor, and minority group members and favors the wealthy, the politically connected, and majority group members. Research has uncovered evidence supporting both sides of this argument. For example, Ronald Weitzer found that, although police are involved in at least some discrimination against racial minorities, the frequency and scope of police discrimination may be less than anticipated. In contrast, after thoroughly reviewing the literature on police bias, Samuel Walker, Cassia Spohn, and Miriam DeLone conclude that police discriminate against racial minorities and that significant problems persist between the police and racial and ethnic communities in the United States. The Walker research concludes that, despite progress, significant racial and ethnic disparities remain the norm.

These two polar positions on race discrimination by police is reflected in the research literature, which yields research reflecting both sides of the issue. A number of studies have found that race does in fact play an important role in police discretion. For example, a significant body of literature shows that police are more likely to "hassle" or arrest poor, African-American males. Darlene Conley's research found evidence that police frequently stop and question youths of color walking down the streets of their neighborhoods or standing on corners. Neighborhood youths told her how suspicion produces crime: If you're going to be harassed and "messed with," you might as well not care and commit crime.

In contrast to these findings, a number of studies have produced data indicating that racial bias does not influence the decision to arrest and process a suspect. According to this view, it is prior record, crime seriousness, and other legal factors that control police decision making, not a suspect's race, ethnicity, or gender. Suspects who are intoxicated and belligerent are more likely to invoke the ire of police officers, regardless of their race or ethnicity.

One reason for this dilemma is that racial influences on police decision mak-

ments to reflect community makeup. The following sections explore these changes in detail.

Police Education In recent years, many police experts have argued that police recruits should have a college education. This development is not unexpected, considering that higher education for police officers has been recommended by national commissions since 1931.[51]

Although education is valued, most law enforcement agencies do not require recruits to have an advanced degree. Today 16 percent of state police agencies require a two-year college degree, and 4 percent require a four-year degree. Among large municipal police agencies, 9 percent have a degree requirement, with 2 percent requiring a four-year degree. Among sheriff's departments, 6 percent require a degree, including 1 percent with a four-year degree requirement.[52]

What are the benefits of higher education for police officers? Better communication with the public, especially minority and ethnic groups, is believed to be

ing are often subtle and hard to detect. For example, it may be that the victim's race, and not the criminal's, is the key to racial bias: Police officers are more likely to take formal action when the victim of crime is white than when the victim is a minority group member. These data suggest that any study of police discretion must take into account both victim and offender characteristics if it is to be truly valid.

Police bias may possibly be a function of administrative policy and not individual officer bias. Research by Carole Wolff Barnes and Rodney Kingsnorth, conducted in California, shows that African-American drug offenders have a far greater chance of getting their cases dismissed by prosecutors than white offenders. They reason that the highly political nature of the "war on drugs" pressures law enforcement agencies to produce a high number of arrests. Targeting African Americans who conduct drug sales in open markets like parks and crack houses produces a large number of "easy" arrests. Because drug sweeps and crackdowns often violate civil rights, many cases later get tossed out by prosecutors. However, when the charges stick, offenders usually get long prison sentences. Should one racial group be targeted by police because their modus operandi makes them easier to arrest?

Regardless of which position is correct, all police officers do not operate in an unfair and unjust manner, nor can all police departments be accused of operating with a racial bias. Evidence exists that the influence of race on police discretion varies from jurisdiction to jurisdiction and may be a function of the professionalism of the individual department.

Critical Thinking

What, if anything, can be done to reduce racial bias on the part of police? Would adding minority officers help? Why or why not? Would it be a form of racism to assign minority officers to minority neighborhoods? Explain.

Would research showing that police are more likely to make arrests in interracial incidents than in intraracial incidents constitute evidence of racism? Explain.

InfoTrac College Edition Research

Do police discriminate against African Americans? To read more about this controversial issue, go to

Michael Foote, "Do Traffic Cops Discriminate?" *State Legislatures* 25 (1999): 33.

"Is Crime 'Profiling' a Reasonable Premise?" *USA Today* 12 August 1999, 12.

SOURCES: David Kocieniewski, "Man Says Officers Tortured Him after Arrest," *New York Times*, 13 August 1997, 1; Dan Barry, "Second Officer Faces Charges in Torture," *New York Times*, 16 August 1997, 1; Dan Barry, "Officers' Silence Still Thwarting Torture," *New York Times*, 5 September 1997; John Kavanagh, "The Occurrence of Resisting Arrest in Arrest Encounters: A Study of Police–Citizen Violence," *Criminal Justice Review* 22 (1997): 16–29; Ronald Weitzer, "Racial Discrimination in the Criminal Justice System: Findings and Problems in the Literature," *Journal of Criminal Justice* 24 (1996): 309–22. Samuel Walker, Cassia Spohn, and Miriam DeLone, *The Color of Justice, Race, Ethnicity, and Crime in America* (Belmont, Calif.: Wadsworth, 1996), 115; Sandra Lee Browning, Francis Cullen, Liqun Cao, Renee Kopache, and Thomas Stevenson, "Race and Getting Hassled by the Police: A Research Note," *Police Studies* 17 (1994): 1–10; Dale Dannefer and Russell Schutt, "Race and Juvenile Justice Processing in Court and Police Agencies," *American Journal of Sociology* 87 (1982): 1113–32; Darlene Conley, "Adding Color to a Black and White Picture: Using Qualitative Data to Explain Racial Disproportionality in the Juvenile Justice System," *Journal of Research in Crime and Delinquency* 31 (1994): 135–48. See, generally, William Wilbanks, *The Myth of a Racist Criminal Justice System* (Monterey, Calif.: Brooks/Cole, 1987); Carole Wolff Barnes and Rodney Kingsnorth, "Race, Drugs and Criminal Sentencing: Hidden Effects of the Criminal Law," *Journal of Criminal Justice* 24 (1996): 549–61.

one benefit. Educated officers write better and more clearly and are more likely to be promoted. Police administrators believe that education enables officers to perform more effectively, generate fewer citizen complaints, show more initiative in performing police tasks, and generally act more professionally.[53] In addition, educated officers are less likely to have disciplinary problems and are viewed as better decision makers.[54] Studies have shown that college-educated police officers generate fewer citizen complaints and have better behavioral and performance characteristics than their less-educated peers.[55] Research by John Krimmel indicates that educated officers are more likely to rate themselves higher on most performance indicators, indicating that if nothing else higher education is associated with greater self-confidence and assurance.[56]

Little evidence shows, however, that educated officers are more effective crime fighters; education appears to have relatively little influence on police officer behavior.[57] The diversity of the police role, the need for split-second decision making, and the often boring and mundane tasks police are required to do are all considered reasons why some experts believe that formal education for police officers may be a waste of time.[58] However, superiors find educated officers to be more reliable employees and better report writers, and citizens find them to be exceptional in the use of good judgment and problem solving.[59]

Although perhaps not requiring officers to have a college education, most police departments seem to value academic experience. A national survey of police education requirements found that 62 percent had at least one formal policy in support of officers pursuing higher education and 58 percent required course work to be job related.[60] Although the scope of job-related education included a variety of subjects, about half of the surveyed departments expressed a preference for criminal justice majors, most often because of their enhanced knowledge of the entire criminal justice system and issues in policing. Another promising trend: Although not requiring college credits for promotion, 82 percent of the departments recognized that college education is an important element in promotion decisions.

Minorities in Policing

For the past two decades, U.S. police departments have made a concerted effort to attract minority police officers, and there have been some impressive gains. As might be expected, cities with large minority populations are the ones having a higher proportion of minority officers in their police departments.[61]

The reasons for this effort are varied. Viewed in its most positive light, police departments recruit minority citizens to field a more balanced force that truly represents the communities they serve. African Americans generally have less confidence in the police than whites and are skeptical of their ability to protect them from harm.[62] A heterogeneous police force can be instrumental in gaining the public's confidence by helping dispel the view that police departments are generally bigoted or biased organizations. Furthermore, minority police officers possess special qualities that can serve to improve police performance. For example, Spanish-speaking officers can help with investigations in Hispanic neighborhoods, while Asian officers are essential for undercover or surveillance work with Asian gangs and drug importers. Figure 6.3 shows the racial and gender breakdown of the nation's largest police departments.

MINORITY POLICE OFFICERS

The earliest known date of when an African American was hired as a police officer was 1861 in Washington, D.C.; Chicago hired its first black officer in 1872.[63] By 1890 an estimated 2,000 minority police officers were employed in the United States. At first, black officers suffered a great deal of discrimination. Their work assignments were restricted, as were their chances for promotion. Minority officers were often assigned solely to the patrol of black neighborhoods, and in some cities they were required to call a white officer to make an arrest. White officers held highly prejudicial attitudes, and as late as the 1950s some refused to ride with blacks in patrol cars.[64]

The experience of African-American police officers has not been an easy one. In his classic 1969 book, *Black in Blue,* Nicholas Alex pointed out that black officers of the time suffered from what he called **double marginality.**[65] On the one hand, black officers had to deal with the expectation that they would give members of their own race a break. On the other hand, they often experienced overt racism from their police colleagues. Alex found that black officers' adaptation to these pressures ranged from denying that black suspects should be treated differently from whites to treating black offenders more harshly than white offenders, to prove their lack of bias. Alex offered several reasons for some black officers being tougher on black offenders: They desired acceptance from their white colleagues; they were particularly sensitive to any disrespect given them by black teenagers; and they viewed themselves as protectors of the black community. Evidence of this effect was found by criminologist Kim Michelle Lersch who in her study of complaints against police officers found that minority citizens were actually more likely to accuse a minority officer of misconduct than a white officer.[66]

double marginality
According to Alex, the social burden African-American police officers carry by being both minority group members and law enforcement officers.

These conflicts have become more muted as minority representation has increased. As Figure 6.3 shows, racial and ethnic minorities now make up about 22 percent of full-time sworn officers in local police departments, up from 15 percent in 1987.[67]

Minority police officers now seem more aggressive and self-assured, less willing to accept any discriminatory practices by the police department.[68] They now appear to be experiencing some of the same problems and issues encountered by white officers.[69] For example, minority officers report feeling similar if somewhat higher rates of job-related stress and strain than white officers.[70] However, they may deal with stress in a somewhat different fashion. Minority officers are more likely to deal with stress by seeking aid from fellow minority officers, whereas white officers are more likely to try to express their feelings to others, form social bonds, and try to get others to like them more.[71]

African-American and white police officers share similar attitudes toward community policing (although minority officers report being even more favorable toward it than white officers).[72] African-American officers may today be far less detached and alienated from the local community than white or Hispanic officers.[73] Also helping is the fact that the number of African-American officers in some of the nation's largest cities is now proportionate to minority representation in the population. For example, Los Angeles, Washington, D.C., Boston, and Pittsburgh, among other cities, now have police forces that represent their population.[74] So although minority officers report feeling somewhat more job-related stress and strain than white officers do, it appears that they are on the path to overcoming the problems of double marginality.[75]

Figure 6.3
Minority local police officers, 1987, 1990, 1993, and 1997

SOURCE: *Bureau of Justice Statistics, Local Police Departments, 1997* (Washington, D.C.: Bureau of Justice Statistics, 1999), 1.

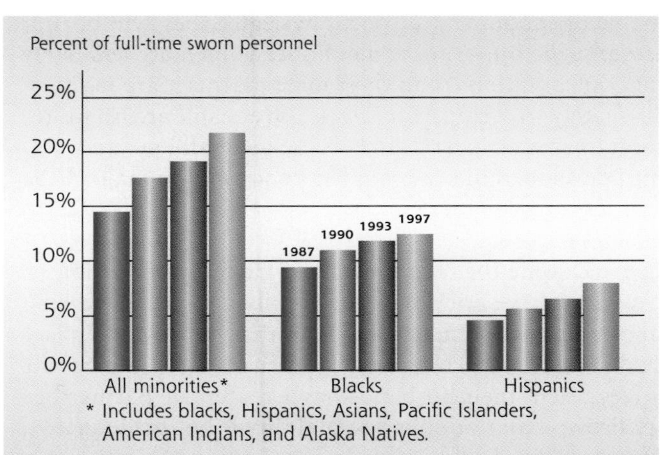

Women in Policing

In 1910 Alice Stebbins Wells became the first woman to hold the title of police officer (in Los Angeles) and to have arrest powers.[76] For more than half a century, female officers endured

A Miami police officer carries the belongings of serial killer Andrew Cunanan off a boat in Miami, where he had killed himself on July 24, 1997. Because much police work is strenuous, most departments require recruits to have the physical strength and agility to successfully fill everyday job demands.

separate criteria for selection, were given menial tasks, and were denied the opportunity for advancement.[77] Some relief was gained with the passage of the 1964 Civil Rights Act and its subsequent amendments. Courts have consistently supported the addition of women to police forces by striking down entrance requirements that eliminated almost all female candidates but could not be proven to predict job performance (such as height and upper-body strength).[78] Women do not do as well as men on strength tests and are much more likely to fail the entrance physical than male recruits; critics contend that many of these tests do not reflect the *actual* tasks police do on the job.[79] Nonetheless, the role of women in police work is still restricted by social and administrative barriers that have been difficult to remove. Today, about 6 percent of all sworn officers are women.

Women continue to be underrepresented in the senior administrative ranks, and many believe they are assigned duties that underutilize their skills and training.[80] Policewomen become frustrated if they aspire to rise in police organizations when they begin to recognize that few women get promoted to command positions. Female recruits often lack successful female role models on which to shape their career aspirations.[81] It may not be surprising then that research by Robin Haarr and Merry Morash found that female officers report significantly higher levels of job-related stress than male officers.[82]

JOB PERFORMANCE Gender bias is certainly not supported by existing research indicating that female officers are highly successful police officers.[83] In an important study of recruits in the Metropolitan Police Department of Washington, D.C., policewomen were found to display extremely satisfactory work performances.[84] Compared with male officers, women were found to respond to similar types of calls, and the arrests they made were as likely to result in conviction. Women were more likely then their male colleagues to receive support from the community and were less likely to be charged with improper conduct. Policewomen seem to be more understanding and sympathetic to crime victims than male officers and are more likely to offer them treatment.[85]

Research has also debunked another enduring myth about female officers: Because they are less capable of subduing a suspect physically, they will be more likely to use firearms. Actually, the opposite is true: Policewomen are less likely to use a firearm in violent confrontations than their male partners, are more emotionally stable, are less likely to seriously injure a citizen, and are no more likely to suffer injuries than their male partners.[86] These generally positive results are similar to findings developed in other studies conducted in major U.S. cities.[87]

GENDER CONFLICTS Despite the overwhelming evidence supporting their performance, policewomen have not always been fully accepted by their male peers or the general public. Male officers complain that policewomen lack the emotional and physical strength to perform well in situations involving violence.[88] Some officers' wives resent their husbands having a female partner because they consider the policewoman not only a sexual threat but inadequate support in a violent encounter.[89] Studies of policewomen indicate that they are still struggling for acceptance, believe that they do not receive equal credit for their job performance, and report that it is common for them to be sexually harassed by their co-workers.[90] Surveys of male officers show that only one-third actually accept a woman on patrol and that more than half do not think that women can handle the physical requirements of the job as well as men.[91] This form of bias is not unique to the United States. Research shows that police-women working in northern England report being excluded from full membership in the force, based on gender inequality. Though policewomen in England are enthusiastic for crime-related work, their aspirations are frequently frustrated in favor of male officers.[92]

Gender conflict, jealousy, and stereotyping may be responsible in part for the spate of sexual harassment incidents involving some of the nation's largest police departments. In 1994, for example, the FBI compensated two female agents who had brought charges of being verbally harassed and physically assaulted by their supervisor.[93]

If evidence of gender equality could be proven beyond a doubt, it would be a blow to some male officers who have long been schooled in a macho police culture that is disrespectful of women; they could no longer regard police work as the "manly" profession they entered.[94] It is ironic that research now indicates that, despite gender conflict, both male and female officers share similar attitudes toward their role and occupational duties.[95]

Those female officers who fail to catch on to the unwritten police subculture are often written off as "bad police material."[96] Women who prove themselves tough enough to gain respect as police officers are then labeled as "lesbians," or "bitches" to neutralize their threat to male dominance, a process referred to as **defeminization.**[97] Male officers also generally assume that female officers who adopt an aggressive style of policing will be quicker to use deadly force than their male counterparts. Women working in this male-dominated culture can experience stress and anxiety.[98] It is not surprising, then, that significantly more female than male officers report being the victim of discrimination on the job. And the male officers who claim to have experienced gender-based discrimination suggest that it comes at the hands of policewomen who use their "sexuality" for job-related benefits.[99]

defeminization
The process by which policewomen become enculturated into the police profession at the expense of their feminine identity.

The International Association of Women Police (at www.iawp.org/**) and the National Center for Women and Policing (at** www.feminist.org/police/ncwp.html**) both offer Web sites with information and advice for women police officers.**

These perceptions of female officers are often based on gender stereotypes and are consequently incorrect.[100] Nonetheless, female officers are frequently caught in the classic catch-22 dilemma: If they are physically weak, male partners view them as a risk in street confrontations; if they are actually more powerful and aggressive than their male partners, they are regarded as an affront to the male officer's manhood.

MINORITY FEMALE OFFICERS African-American women, who account for only about 2 percent of police officers, occupy a unique status. In a study of African-American policewomen serving in five large municipal departments, Susan Martin found that they do in fact perceive significantly more racial discrimination than both other female officers and African-American male officers.[101] However, white policewomen were significantly more likely to perceive sexual discrimination than African-American policewomen were.

Martin found that black policewomen often incur the hostility of both white women and African-American men who feel threatened that they will take their place. On patrol, black policewomen are treated differently than white police-women by male officers: Neither group of women are viewed as equals: White policewomen are protected and coddled, whereas black policewomen are viewed as passive, lazy, and unequal. In the station house, male officers show little respect for black women, who face "widespread racial stereotypes as well as outright

Atlanta police chief Beverly Harvard was the first woman to head a big-city police department.

racial harassment."[102] Black women also report having difficult relationships with black male officers, their relationships strained by tensions and dilemmas "associated with sexuality and competition for desirable assignments and promotions."[103] Surprisingly, there was little unity among the female officers. Martin concludes: "Despite changes in the past two decades, the idealized image of the representative of the forces of 'law and order' and protector who maintains 'the thin blue line' between 'them' and 'us' remains white and male."[104]

THE FUTURE OF WOMEN IN POLICING What does the future hold for policewomen? One of the main concerns is the low number of female officers in supervisory positions. So far, women, especially African-American officers, have been woefully underrepresented in the police command hierarchy. A number of lawsuits have been filed to reverse this situation.[105] However, change in this area continues to be slow. Male officers may find it difficult to take orders from female supervisors; some female officers may not seek promotion because they fear rejection from their male colleagues.[106]

Another area of concern is the development of an effective maternity policy. Most departments do not have policies that identify when pregnant officers are unfit for patrol or other duties and whether they should be reassigned to lighter duties and what these duties should entail. If the number of women on police forces continues to grow, maternity issues are bound to become an important staffing issue for police administrators.[107]

Despite these problems, the future of women in policing grows continually brighter.[108] Female officers want to remain in policing because it pays a good salary, offers job security, and is a challenging and exciting occupation.[109] These factors should continue to bring women to policing for years to come.

PROBLEMS OF POLICING

Law enforcement is not an easy job. The role ambiguity, social isolation, and threat of danger present in "working the street" are the police officer's constant companions. What effects do these strains have on police? This section discusses three of the most significant problems: job stress, violence, and corruption.

Job Stress

The complexity of their role, the need to exercise prudent discretion, the threat of using violence and having violence used against them, and isolation from the rest of society all take a toll on law enforcement officers. It is not surprising, then, that police officers experience tremendous stress, a factor that leads to alcoholism, divorce, depression, and even suicide. Even civilian employees, such as dispatchers, have been found to exhibit elevated stress levels.[110] Stress may not be constant, but at some time during their career (usually the middle years), most officers will feel the effects of stress.[111]

CAUSES OF STRESS A number of factors have been associated with job stress.[112] The pressure of being on duty twenty-four hours a day leads to stress and emotional detachment from both work and public needs. Stress has been related to internal conflict with administrative policies that deny officers support and a meaningful role in decision making. For example, stress may occur when officers are forced to adapt to a department's new methods of policing, such as community-oriented policing, and they are skeptical about the change in policy.[113] In addition, police suffer stress in their personal lives when they bring the job home or when their work hours are shifted, causing family disruptions.[114] Other stressors include poor training, substandard equipment, inadequate pay, lack of opportunity, job dissatisfaction, role conflict, exposure to brutality, and fears about competence, success, and safety.[115] Some officers may feel stress because they believe that the court system favors the rights of the criminal and "handcuffs" the police; others might be sensitive to a perceived lack of support from governmental officials and the general public.[116] Some officers believe that their superiors care little about their welfare.[117]

Police psychologists have divided these stressors into four distinct categories:

1. *External stressors,* such as verbal abuse from the public, justice system inefficiency, and liberal court decisions that favor the criminal. What are perceived to be antipolice judicial decisions may alienate police and reduce their perceptions of their own competence.[118]
2. *Organizational stressors,* such as low pay, excessive paperwork, arbitrary rules, and limited opportunity for advancement
3. *Duty stressors,* such as rotating shifts, work overload, boredom, fear, and danger
4. *Individual stressors,* such as discrimination, marital difficulties, and personality problems[119]

Police Stressline, which provides law enforcement officers with tips on managing stress, also offers a window into the challenges of police work. Go to www.geocities.com/HotSprings/Spa/7762/index.html

The effects of stress can be shocking. Police work has been related to both physical and psychological ailments. Police have a significantly high rate of premature death caused by such conditions as heart disease and diabetes. They also experience a disproportionate number of divorces and other marital problems. Research indicates that police officers in some departments, but not all, have higher suicide rates than the general public.[120] Police who feel stress may not be open to adopting new ideas and programs such as community policing.[121]

COMBATING STRESS Research efforts have shown that the more support police officers get in the workplace, the lower their feelings of stress and anxiety.[122] Consequently, departments have attempted to fight job-related stress by training officers to cope with its effects. Today, stress training includes diet information, biofeedback, relaxation and meditation, and exercise. Many departments include stress management as part of an overall "wellness" also designed to promote physical and mental health, fitness, and good nutrition.[123] Some programs have included family members: They may be better able to help the officer cope if they have more knowledge about the difficulties of police work. Still other efforts promote *total wellness programming,* which enhances the physical and emotional well-being of officers by emphasizing preventive physical and psychological measures.[124] Research also shows that since police perceive many benefits of their job and enjoy the quality of life it provides, stress reduction programs might help officers focus on the positive aspects of police work.[125]

Stress is a critically important aspect of police work. Further research is needed to create valid methods of identifying police officers under considerable stress and to devise effective stress reduction programs.[127]

Violence

Since their creation, U.S. police departments have wrestled with the charge that they are brutal, physically violent organizations. Early police officers resorted to violence and intimidation to gain the respect that was not freely given by citizens. In the 1920s, the Wickersham Commission detailed numerous instances of police brutality, including the use of the third degree to extract confessions.

Police violence first became a major topic for discussion in the 1940s, when rioting provoked serious police backlash. Retired Supreme Court Justice Thurgood Marshall, when he was chief counsel of the National Association for the Advancement of Colored People's Legal Defense Fund, referred to the Detroit police as a "gestapo" after a 1943 race riot left thirty-four people dead.[127] Twenty-five years later, excessive police force was again an issue when television cameras captured police violence against protestors at the Democratic National Convention in Chicago.

Today, police brutality continues to be a concern, especially when police use excessive violence against members of the minority community. The nation looked on in disgust when a videotape was aired on network newscasts showing members of the Los Angeles Police Department beating, kicking, and using electric stun guns on Rodney King. Earlier, Los Angeles police stopped using a restraining choke hold, which cuts off blood circulation to the brain, after minority citizens complained that it caused permanent damage and may have killed as many as seventeen people. It is not surprising that three-quarters of all complaints filed against the police for misconduct tend to be by nonwhite males under the age of 30.[128]

The question of police use of force has two main aspects: (1) Are typical police officers generally brutal, violent, and disrespectful to the citizens with whom they come in daily contact? (2) Are the police overzealous and discriminatory in their use of deadly force when apprehending suspected felons? Let's examine each of these issues separately.

police brutality
Usually involves such actions as the use of abusive language, unnecessary use of force or coercion, threats, prodding with nightsticks, stopping and searching people to harass them, and so on.

POLICE BRUTALITY

Police brutality usually involves such actions as using abusive language, unnecessarily using force or coercion, making threats, prodding with nightsticks, stopping and searching people to harass them, and so on. Charges of generalized police brutality were common between the 1940s and 1960s. Surveys undertaken by the President's Commission on Law Enforcement and the Administration of Justice and other national commissions found that many citizens believed that police discriminated against minorities when they used excessive force in handling suspects, displayed disrespect to innocent bystanders, and so on.[129] However, by 1967 the President's Commission concluded that the police use of physical brutality had somewhat abated.[130]

Although charges of police brutality continue to be made in many jurisdictions, the evidence suggests that actual instances of physical abuse of citizens by police officers are less frequent than commonly imagined.[131] Numerous studies have found that violent interactions are actually atypical.[132] Studies of individual police departments have found that when force is used, it usually involves grabbing and restraining; weapons are rarely used.[133] For example, one study of the Phoenix, Arizona, police found that physical force was used in only 22 percent of arrests and that when force was used it was typically at a minimal level; weapons of any kind, such as flashlights, were used in only 2 percent of arrests. When force was used, it typically involved situations where suspects used force themselves.[134]

National surveys on police use of force have also found that the police use of force is rare.[135] For example, the International Association of Chiefs of Police (IACP), a national organization devoted to professional policing, is now conducting an ongoing survey of the police use of violence in 150 police departments. Some preliminary findings from the project include:

- The police use-of-force rate is 4.19 per 10,000 responded-to calls for service, or 0.0419 percent.
- About 87 percent of use-of-force incidents involve officers using physical force. Officers use chemical force in 7 percent of the incidents and firearms in about 5 percent.
- About 10 percent of officers using force sustained injuries, less than 1 percent serious. About 38 percent of subjects in force incidents were injured, with 1.5 percent sustaining major injuries.[136]

Research by the federal government estimates that 144 million contacts occur between the police and the public each year, and of these only 500,000 involve some force (Figure 6.4). Other research indicates that the use of force appears to be unrelated to an officer's personal characteristics, such as age, gender, and ethnicity. A situational factor is more likely; for example, an officer is

Figure 6.4
Police–community contact and the use of force

*Figures may not add to 100% because of rounding and the exclusion of those persons classified as "other" from the presentation. **Most of the 500,000 also said they were handcuffed.

SOURCE: Lawrence Greenfield, Patrick Langan, and Steven Smith, *Police Use of Force* (Washington, D.C.: Bureau of Justice Statistics, 1997), 3.

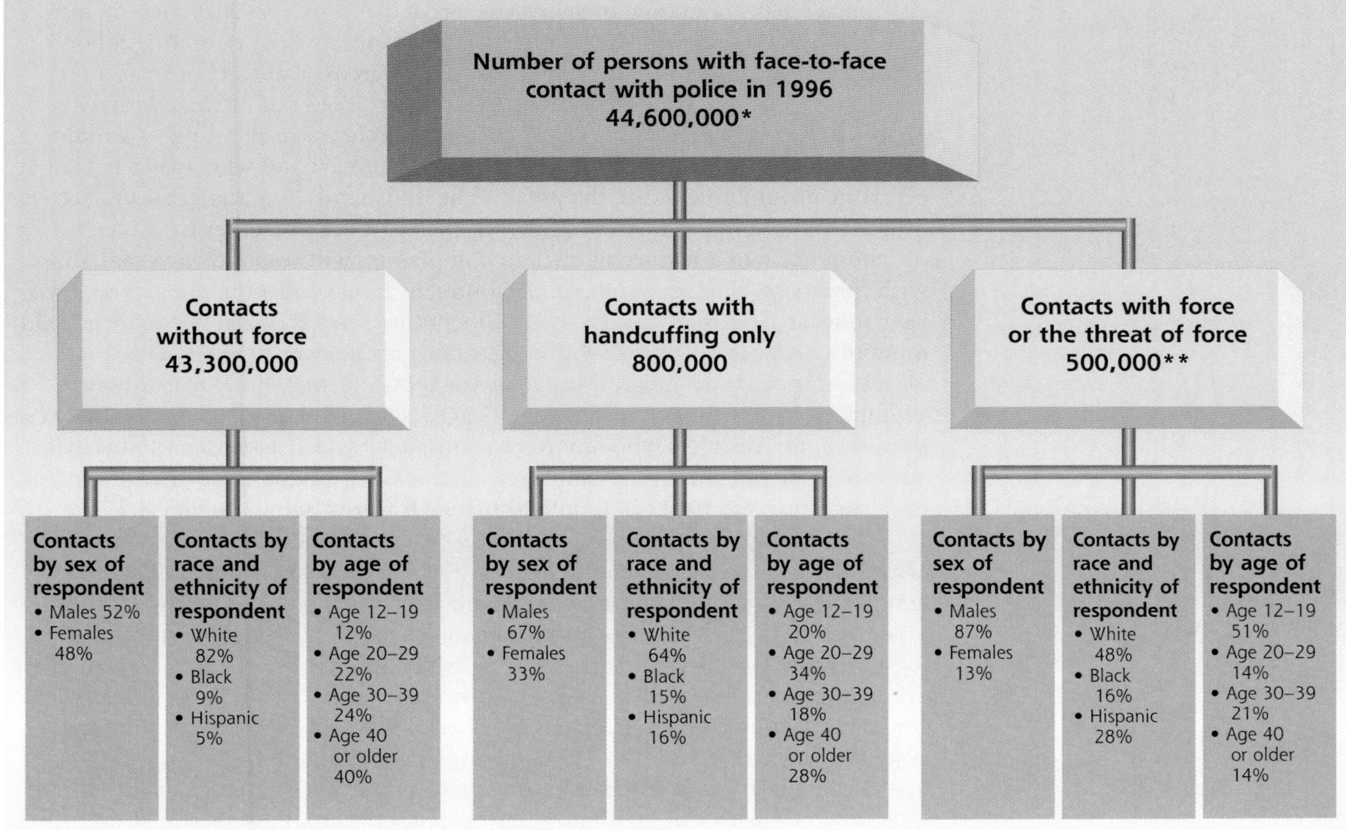

trying to make an arrest, and the suspect is resisting. Force is also more likely to be used with special populations, such as people under the influence of alcohol or drugs or with mentally ill patients.

WHO ARE THE PROBLEM COPS? There is also evidence that a small proportion of officers are disproportionately involved in use-of-force incidents.[137] What kind of police officer gets involved in problem behavior? Are some officers "chronic offenders"? Research conducted in a southeastern city by Kim Michelle Lersch and Tom Mieczkowski found that a few officers (7%) were in fact chronic offenders who accounted for a significant portion of all citizen complaints (33%). Those officers receiving the bulk of the complaints tended to be younger and less experienced and had been accused of harassment or violence after a proactive encounter that they had initiated. Although repeat offenders were more likely to be accused of misconduct by minority citizens, there was little evidence that attacks were racially motivated.[138]

CURBING BRUTALITY Because incidents of brutality undermine efforts to build a bridge between police and the public, police departments around the United States have instituted specialized training programs to reduce them. Urban police departments are now implementing or considering implementing neighborhood and community policing models to improve relations with the public. In addition, detailed rules of engagement that limit the use of force are now common in major cities. However, the creation of departmental rules limiting behavior is often haphazard and is usually a reaction to a crisis situation (e.g., a citizen is seriously injured) rather than part of a systematic effort to improve police–citizen interactions.[139]

Some cities are taking an aggressive proactive stance to curb violent cops. Since 1977 the New York City Police Department has been operating a Force-Related Integrity Testing program in which undercover officers pose as angry citizens in elaborate sting operations intended to weed out officers with a propensity for violence. In a typical encounter, officers responding to a radio call on a domestic dispute confront an aggressive husband who spews hatred at everyone around, including the police. The "husband" is actually an undercover officer from the Internal Affairs Bureau, who is testing whether the officers, one of whom has had a history of civilian complaints, will respond to verbal abuse with threats or violence. The NYPD conducts about 600 sting operations each year to test the integrity of its officers, including several dozen devoted to evaluating the conduct of officers with a history of abuse complaints.[140]

What may be the greatest single factor that can control the use of police brutality is the threat of civil judgments against individual officers who use excessive force, police chiefs who ignore or condone violent behavior, and the cities and towns in which they are employed. This issue is discussed further in the Policy, Programs, and Issues in Criminal Justice feature "Suing the Police."

deadly force
The ability of the police to kill suspects if they resist arrest or present a danger to the officer or the community. The police cannot use deadly force against an unarmed fleeing felon.

DEADLY FORCE As commonly used, the term **deadly force** refers to the actions of a police officer who shoots and kills a suspect who is fleeing from arrest, assaulting a victim, or attacking an officer.[141] The justification for the use of deadly force can be traced to English common law, in which almost every criminal offense was a felony and bore the death penalty. The use of deadly force in the course of arresting a felon was considered expedient, saving the state the burden of trial (the "fleeing felon" rule).[142]

Although the media depict hero cops in a constant stream of deadly shootouts in which scores of "bad guys" are killed, the actual number of people killed by the police each year is most likely between 250 and 300.[143] Although these data are encouraging, some researchers believe that the actual number of police shootings is far greater and may be hidden or masked by a number of factors. For example, coroners may be intentionally or accidentally underreporting police homicides by almost half.[144]

FACTORS RELATED TO POLICE SHOOTINGS Is police use of deadly force a random occurrence, or are there social, legal, and environmental factors associated with its use? The following patterns have been related to police shootings.

1. *Exposure to violence* Most police shootings involve suspects who are armed and who either attack the officer or are engaged in violent crimes. A number of studies have found that fatal police shootings were closely related to reported violent crime rates and criminal homicide rates; police officers kill civilians at a higher rate in years when the general level of violence in the nation is higher.[145] The perception of danger may contribute to the use of violent means for self-protection.[146]

   Police officers may become exposed to violence when they are forced to confront the emotionally disturbed. Some distraught people attack police as a form of suicide.[147] This tragic event has become so common that the term *suicide by cop* has been coined to denote victim-precipitated killings by police. For example, over the past decade more than 10 percent of the shootings by police officers in Los Angeles involved suicidal people intentionally provoking police.[148]

2. *Workload* A relationship exists among police violence and the number of police on the street, the number of calls for service, the number and nature of police dispatches, the number of arrests made in a given jurisdiction, and police exposure to stressful situations.

3. *Firearms availability* Cities that experience a large number of crimes committed with firearms are also likely to have high police-violence rates. A strong association has been found between police use of force and "gun density" (the proportion of suicides and murders committed with a gun).[149]

4. *Social variables* Research suggests that many individuals shot by police are transients or nonresidents caught at or near the scenes of robberies or burglaries of commercial establishments.[150] The greatest number of police shootings occur in areas that have great disparities in economic opportunity and a resulting high level of income inequality.[151]

5. *Administrative policies* The philosophy, policies, and practices of individual police chiefs and departments significantly influence the police use of deadly force.[152] Departments that stress restrictive policies on the use of force generally have lower shooting rates than those that favor tough law enforcement and encourage officers to shoot when necessary. Poorly written or ambivalent policies encourage shootings because they allow the officer at the scene to decide when deadly force is warranted, often under conditions of high stress and tension.

6. *Race and police shootings* No other issue is as important to the study of the police use of deadly force as that of racial discrimination. A number of critics have claimed that police are more likely to shoot and kill minority offenders than they are whites. In a famous statement, Paul Takagi charged that police have "one trigger finger for whites and another for blacks."[153] Takagi's complaint was supported by a number of research studies that showed that a

Policy, Programs, and Issues in Criminal Justice

SUING THE POLICE

There is perhaps no sizable police department in the country that has not been sued in state or federal court for damages or injunctive relief. — Rolando del Carmen (1993)

An estimated thirty thousand-plus civil suits are now being brought annually, and about 1 in every 30 officers is sued each year. For example, in the 1998–1999 fiscal year, New York City paid out a record $40 million to settle lawsuits that accused its police officers of misconduct. Increasing 40 percent in a single year, the payments reflected both the sharp rise in the number of cases settled and the fact that media publicity about police misconduct made it difficult for the city to negotiate from strength. Not only did the amount paid out in settlements rise, but the number of new brutality claims also increased by 10 percent, to 2,324, the highest number in a decade. Several large settlements helped push the total paid to record levels.

One such case involved Anthony Baez, who was playing touch football in the street with his brothers in December 1994 when an errantly thrown ball struck New York City police officer Francis Livoti's patrol car. The officer tried to stop the game, and Baez, age 29, of Orlando, Florida, died in the ensuing struggle. A police department investigation found that Livoti had used an illegal choke hold to subdue Baez. Though Livoti was acquitted in 1996 of negligent homicide, he was fired from the force and in June 1998 was convicted of violating Baez's civil rights in federal court. On October 1, 1998, the city agreed to pay nearly $3 million to settle lawsuits filed by the Baez family. In another case, the city agreed to pay $2.75 million to an African-American electrician who, while walking to work in Greenwich Village in 1996, was beaten by police officers because he fit the profile of a black suspect they were seeking.

Why Police Are Sued

In a number of areas of police behavior, legal action has been common. Officers have been sued when, while in "hot pursuit" of a vehicle, they use excessive speed and their negligent behavior results in the death or injury of the suspects or innocent bystanders. Police may be sued for false arrest because a reasonable officer should have known there were no legal grounds.

People may sue the police if they believe that excessive force was used during their arrest or custody. They may collect damages if they can show that the force used was unreasonable, considering all circumstances known to the officer at the time he acted. Excessive force suits commonly occur when police use a weapon, such as a gun or baton, to subdue an unarmed person who is protesting her treatment.

A suit can also be brought if the police fail to act in a matter — for example, despite a (court) restraining order, they fail to arrest a husband who is battering his wife, or they fail to give aid to the victim of a crime.

The police can be sued for abandonment. This occurs when individuals who should be taken into police custody are left to fend for themselves and consequently suffer injuries. For example, police have been held liable when a parent is taken into custody and minor children, left at the scene of the crime without care, suffer injury. The police have also been found liable when they have taken a drunk driver into custody while leaving an obviously intoxicated passenger in possession of the car and the passenger becomes a drunk driver. Liability has also been attached when law enforcement officers abandon an individual who is in the process of being assaulted, especially when the victim pleads for the officers' help. Courts seem willing to assess damages if an officer's actions (or inaction) enhanced or created the danger or if departmental policies contributed to the injuries.

Suits are now being brought when police officers take sexual advantage of people falling under their control. Police departments are liable for the sexual misconduct of their employees when the activity is committed under the guise of agency authority or to further its activities and objectives.

Legal Rights

Civil suits became common after the Supreme Court ruled in 1978 (*Monell v. Department of Social Services*) that local agencies could be held liable under the federal 1983 Civil Rights Act for actions of their employees if it was part of an official custom or practice. Before *Monell*, attorneys were reluctant to file civil actions against police officers because even if the case could be won, there was often no way to collect damages from individuals who in most instances were without attachable financial resources. After *Monell*, police agencies, with their "deep pockets," could be held liable if in some way the officer's behavior could be attributed to an official policy or behavior. Liability increases if the policy or behavior is sanctioned by a high-ranking official, such as the chief.

A victim can seek redress against the department and the municipality it serves if he can show that the incident stemmed from a practice that, although not necessarily an official policy, was so widespread that it had become a "custom" that fairly represented official policy. To make the department liable under this standard, the victim might show that the actions that led to his injury were practices accepted by supervisors, that many police officers frequently engaged in these practices, that the police department failed to investigate or discipline officers involved in similar incidents, and that the department knew about such practices and did little to prohibit them. For example, a municipality could be held liable under the Civil Rights Act if police officers made it a custom to use excessive force in making arrests, police officials ignored the problem despite many complaints and incidents, brutality complaints were rarely investigated, and neither rules to limit force nor special training programs to aid police in making arrests were created.

Training

One area of particular concern has been the failure of police departments to properly train officers. Municipalities have been held liable if an officer uses excessive force and that officer has not been trained in the use of force or the training was forgotten, obsolete, and inadequate. The Supreme Court in *Canton v. Harris* ruled that to be liable for their failure to train, police departments must be "deliberately indifferent" to the needs of people injured by the untrained officers. Some commentators believe that *Harris* made suing police more difficult because of the need to prove *deliberate indifference* and not mere negligence or misconduct. Although it is difficult to define deliberate indifference, it would most likely include situations in which the need for training was so obvious that its absence seems a clear-cut violation of constitutional rights, as when police are not given any firearms training after they leave the police academy, even though the department has switched its standard weapon from the .38-caliber revolver to the 9-mm automatic. Deliberate indifference might also involve failure to train officers in dealing with a particular crime problem, such as domestic abuse, even though police officials should recognize it as a significant area of concern.

The Threat of Civil Litigation

The threat to police departments posed by civil litigation is significant. Not only are they liable for large dollar awards to victims, but they must also pay hefty legal fees. It is not uncommon for a plaintiff in a civil rights case to be awarded a nominal amount of damages, with ten times that amount going to her attorney in legal fees. Research by Victor Kappeler and his associates found that litigation filed against the police in federal courts is on the increase. In addition, this research found that plaintiffs are more successful when they sue the police than previously thought, winning just about half the cases brought to court. Awards ranged from $1 to $1,650,000; findings of liability based on claims of excessive force averaged $187,503.

Today relatively few citizen complaints against the police are sustained by internal police investigations. A study conducted by the Police Foundation, an organization that does research on policing, found that fewer than 13 percent of citizen complaints about excessive force were sustained by the departments themselves. In about one-fourth of the city departments, officers were not required to provide information to investigators. The threat of large civil penalties generated from civilian judges and juries may prove the most effective deterrent yet to the police use of excessive force. It will certainly cause police departments to carefully consider whom they hire, how they train, when they investigate, and what action they take against officers who are brutal or negligent.

Critical Thinking

Policing is a dangerous, stressful job. Is it fair to hold officers and towns liable for the occasional use of excessive force? Why or why not?

Many offenders are disrespectful to officers and provoke violent responses. Even Rodney King, who was brutally beaten by police, resisted being handcuffed and flailed his arms around, rather than meekly consenting to arrest. Would the threat of civil suits prevent officers from taking the necessary steps to subdue dangerous criminals? Explain.

People want police to make neighborhoods safe, even if it means putting their lives at risk. Research has found that many officers have a real fear of lawsuits and maintain an "us versus them" mentality. Will these concerns undermine police–community relations at a time when they are seen as critical to effective policing? Explain. Should officers be immune from punishment if they use too much force in this dangerous undertaking? Why or why not?

InfoTrac College Edition Research

When can the police be sued for using excessive force? To learn more, review

> John C. Hall, "Deadly Force: A Question of Necessity," *FBI Law Enforcement Bulletin* 64 (1995): 27.

SOURCES: Associated Press, "NY pays $3M to Police Victim Kin," *New York Times*, 2 October 1998; Kevin Flynn, Record Payouts in Settlements of Lawsuits; Michael Vaughn, "Police Sexual Violence: Civil Liability under State Tort Law," *Crime and Delinquency* 45 (1999): 334–57. Against the New York City Police Are Set for Year, *New York Times*, 1 October 1999, 12; David Griswold, "Complaints against the Police: Predicting Dispositions," *Journal of Criminal Justice* 22 (1994): 215–21; Michael Vaughn, "Police Civil Liability for Abandonment in High-Crime Areas and Other High-Risk Situations," *Journal of Criminal Justice* 22 (1994): 407–24; Victor Kappeler, Stephen Kappeler, and Rolando Del Carmen, "A Content Analysis of Police Civil Liability Cases: Decisions of the Federal District Courts, 1978–1990," *Journal of Criminal Justice* 21 (1993): 325–37; Police Foundation, *Police Use of Force: Official Reports, Citizen Complaints, and Legal Consequences* (Washington, D.C.: Police Foundation, 1993).

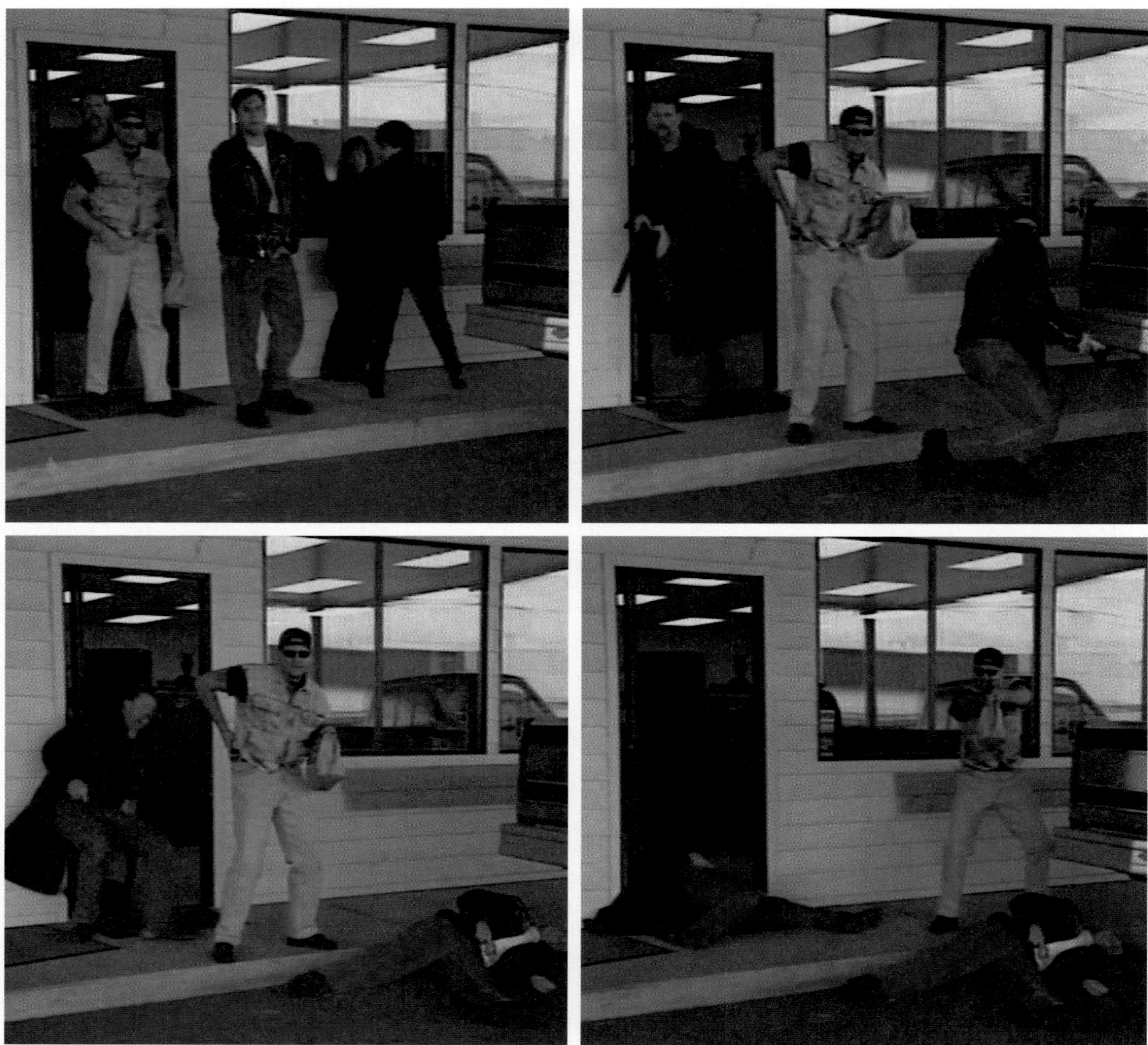

A police officer, in training to control the use of deadly force, may be presented with an interactive film that requires him to make split-second decisions. Here, three robbers emerge from a store. When they fail to yield to a command to "halt!" and one reaches inside his coat for a weapon, the officer fires rubber bullets at the screen, bringing down two of the robbers while the third is prepared to shoot back.

disproportionate number of police killings involved minority citizens — almost 80 percent in some of the cities surveyed.[154]

Do these findings alone indicate that police discriminate in the use of deadly force? Some pioneering research by James Fyfe helps provide an answer to this question. In his study of New York City shootings over a five-year period, Fyfe found that police officers were most likely to shoot suspects who were armed and with whom they became involved in violent confrontations. Once such factors as being armed with a weapon, being involved in a violent crime, and attacking an officer were considered, the racial differences in the police use of force ceased to be significant. In fact, Fyfe found that black officers were almost twice as likely as white officers to have shot citizens. Fyfe attributes this finding to the fact that (1) black officers work and live in high-crime, high-violence areas where shootings are more common and (2) black officers hold proportionately more line positions and fewer administrative posts than white officers, which would place them more often on the street and less often behind a desk.[155]

CONTROLLING DEADLY FORCE Since the police use of deadly force is such a serious problem, ongoing efforts have been made to control its use.

One of the most difficult problems that influenced its control was the continued use of the fleeing felon rule in a number of states. However, in 1985 the Supreme Court outlawed the indiscriminate use of deadly force with its decision in the case of *Tennessee v. Garner.* In this case, the Court ruled that the use of deadly force against apparently unarmed and nondangerous fleeing felons is an illegal seizure of their person under the Fourth Amendment. Deadly force may not be used unless it is necessary to prevent the escape and the officer has probable cause to believe that the suspect poses a significant threat of death or serious injury to the officer or others. The majority opinion stated that where the suspect poses no immediate threat to the officer and no threat to others, the harm resulting from failing to apprehend the suspect does not justify the use of deadly force to do so: "A police officer may not seize an unarmed, nondangerous suspect by shooting him dead."[156]

With *Garner,* the Supreme Court effectively put an end to any local police policy that allowed officers to shoot unarmed or otherwise nondangerous offenders if they resisted arrest or attempted to flee from police custody. However, the Court did not ban the use of deadly force or otherwise control police shooting policy. Consequently, in *Graham v. Connor,* the Court created a reasonableness standard for the use of force: Force is excessive when, considering all the circumstances known to the officer at the time he acted, the force used was unreasonable.[157] For example, an officer is approached in a threatening manner by someone wielding a knife. The assailant fails to stop when warned and is killed by the officer. The officer would not be held liable if it turns out that the shooting victim was deaf and could not hear the officer's command and if the officer at the time of the incident had no way of knowing the person's disability.

Individual state jurisdictions still control police shooting policy. Some states have adopted statutory policies that restrict the police use of violence. Others have upgraded training in the use of force. The Federal Law Enforcement Training Center has developed the FLETC use-of-force model, illustrated in Figure 6.5, to teach officers the proper method to escalate force in response to the threat they face. As the figure shows, resistance ranges from compliant and cooperative to assaultive with the threat of serious bodily harm or death. Officers are taught via lecture, demonstration, computer-based instruction, and training scenarios to assess the suspect's behavior and apply an appropriate and corresponding amount of force.[158]

Another method of controlling police shootings is through internal review and policymaking by police administrative review boards. For example, New York's Firearm Discharge Review Board was established to investigate and adjudicate all police firearm discharges. Among the dispositions available to the board are the following:

1. The discharge was in accordance with law and departmental policy.
2. The discharge was justifiable, but the officer should be given additional training in the use of firearms or in the law and departmental policy.

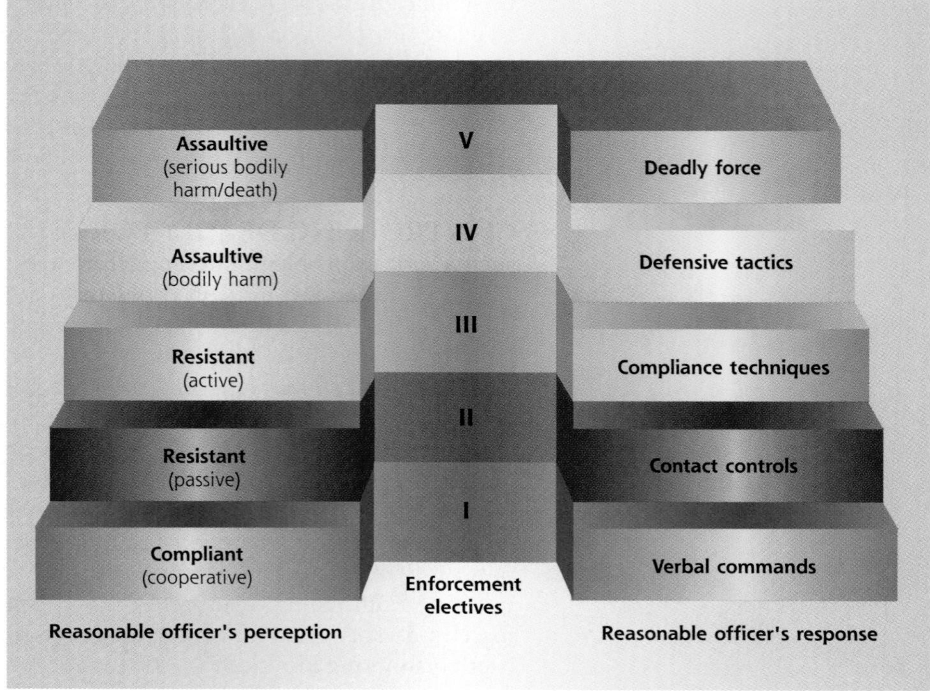

Figure 6.5
The Federal Law Enforcement Training Center's use-of-force model

SOURCE: Franklin Graves and Gregory Connor, The Federal Law Enforcement Training Center, Glynco, Georgia.

3. The shooting was justifiable under law but violated departmental policy and warrants departmental disciplinary action.
4. The shooting was in apparent violation of law and should be referred to the appropriate prosecutor if criminal charges have not already been filed.
5. The officer involved should be transferred (or offered the opportunity to transfer) to a less sensitive assignment.
6. The officer involved should receive testing or alcoholism counseling.[159]

The review board approach is controversial because it can mean that the department recommends that one of its own officers be turned over for criminal prosecution, an outcome with which some legal scholars disagree.[160]

POLICE AS VICTIMS Although police officers are often taken to task for being too violent, the public sometimes forgets that police are all too often injured and killed by armed assailants. More than sixty-five thousand are attacked and twenty-three thousand seriously injured each year.[161] Data suggest that officers are significantly at risk for injury when they use force, particularly when they strike a suspect with their fists (48% chance) or use their hands and arms to control a suspect (43% chance).[162]

A long-held belief has been that police officers who answer domestic violence calls are at risk of violence against them; when confronted, one of the two battling parties turns on the outsider who dares interfere in a "private matter." Research conducted in Charlotte, North Carolina, however, indicates that domestic violence calls may be no more dangerous than many other routine police interactions.[163] So while police officers should be on their guard when investigating a call for assistance from an abused spouse, the risk of violence against them may be no greater than when they answer a call for a burglary or car theft. The issue of when police are injured or killed in the line of duty is further explored in the Policy, Programs, and Issues in Criminal Justice feature.

Corruption From their creation, U.S. police departments have wrestled with the problem of controlling illegal and unprofessional behavior by their officers. Corruption pervaded the American police when the early departments were first formed. In the nineteenth century, police officers systematically ignored violations of laws related to drinking, gambling, and prostitution in return for regular payoffs. Some actually entered into relationships with professional criminals, especially pickpockets. Illegal behavior was tolerated in return for goods or information. Police officers helped politicians gain office by allowing electoral fraud to flourish; some senior officers sold promotions to higher rank within the department.[164]

Policy, Programs, and Issues in Criminal Justice

IN THE LINE OF FIRE: SHOOTINGS OF POLICE

Professional criminals and drug dealers armed with automatic weapons, such as Uzi machine guns, pose a significant hazard to law enforcement officers. Every year, between fifty and one hundred law enforcement and public safety officers are feloniously killed in the line of duty; about two-thirds of these are shooting victims. For example, in 1997 seventy law enforcement officers were slain feloniously in the line of duty; in 1998 sixty-one were slain. Most officers were slain during arrest situations, such as attempting to prevent robberies or apprehend robbery suspects. In addition, officers were slain while answering disturbance calls, encountering ambush situations, enforcing traffic laws, investigating suspicious persons or circumstances, and while handling prisoners. Another seventy to eighty officers are killed each year in job-related incidents, such as traffic accidents.

What are the factors that predict the shooting of police officers? The majority of incidents were initiated by the officers themselves, as opposed to an unexpected attack by a hidden assailant; black officers had a greater risk of getting killed than white officers and by black assailants. Officers faced the greatest danger when they were attempting to arrest an armed assailant. Ecological patterns may also be present when an officer becomes the victim of violent crime. Southern cities, with high violence and gun-ownership rates, experience the highest numbers of officer fatalities.

Research also shows that off-duty police and plainclothes officers are very likely to be shot. One reason is that off-duty officers, who are usually armed, are expected to take appropriate action yet suffer tactical disadvantages, such as a lack of communication and backup. Plainclothes officers are often mistaken for perpetrators or unwanted interveners.

An FBI report shows that police officers may get killed because they failed to follow proper procedures, perhaps because they were too trusting and let their "guard down." They failed to call for backup, acted alone, failed to search the suspect completely, and in an effort to make the suspect more comfortable failed to secure handcuffs properly. When interviewed by the FBI, the slain officers' peer described them as friendly to everyone and quick to look for good in people. In contrast, their slayers suffered personality disorders that rendered them incapable of obeying social norms and having a conscience or feelings of remorse.

The FBI report has been criticized by William King and Beth Sanders for being methodologically flawed. It is possible, they suggest, that the difference between fatal and nonfatal shooting incidents is actually "luck, a bullet-proof vest or closer medical facilities." Clearly, more research is needed to understand the circumstances of why police get killed in the line of duty.

InfoTrac College Edition Research

Is it possible to train police to protect themselves and civilians in deadly force encounters? The following articles discuss this critical issue:

John McCormick, "On a High-Tech Firing Line: Simulators That Shoot Back Are Helping Cops Learn How to Use Deadly Force. A *Newsweek* Reporter Takes the Test of Deciding Who Lives — and Who Dies," *Newsweek*, 6 December 1999, 64.

Chris Whitcomb, "Scenario-Based Training at the F.B.I.," *Training & Development* 53 (1999): 42.

SOURCES: FBI National Press Office, Press Release, 10 May 1999; Anthony Pinizzotto, Edward F. Davis, and Charles E. Miller III, "In the Line of Fire: Learning from Assaults on Law Enforcement Officers," *FBI Law Enforcement Bulletin* 67 (1998): 15–24; FBI, *Killed in the Line of Duty: A Study of Selected Felonious Killings of Law Enforcement Officers* (Washington, D.C.: Government Printing Office, 1992); William King and Beth Sanders, "Nice Guys Finish Last: A Critical Review of Police Officers Killed in the Line of Duty," *Policing* 20 (1997): 392–408.

The U.S. Supreme Court has prohibited police from shooting unarmed felons unless they are considered to be a significant threat to society. Thus, it would be illegal for the police to shoot at the unarmed suspect shown here, even if he tried to escape.

Since the early nineteenth century, scandals involving police abuse of power have occurred in many urban cities, and elaborate methods had been devised to control or eliminate the problem. Although most police officers are not corrupt, the few who are dishonest bring discredit to the entire profession.

Knapp Commission
A public body that led an investigation into police corruption in New York and uncovered a widespread network of payoffs and bribes.

meat eater
A term used to describe a police officer who actively solicits bribes and vigorously engages in corrupt practices.

grass eater
A term used to describe a police officer who accepts payoffs when everyday duties place him or her in a position to be solicited by the public.

Mollen Commission
An investigatory body formed in New York City in 1993 to scrutinize police misconduct.

VARIETIES OF CORRUPTION Police deviance can include a number of activities. In a general sense, it involves misuse of authority by police officers in a manner designed to produce personal gain for themselves or others.[165] However, debate continues over whether a desire for personal gain is an essential part of corruption. Some experts argue that police misconduct also involves such issues as the unnecessary use of force, unreasonable searches, or an immoral personal life and that these should be considered as serious as corruption devoted to economic gain.

Scholars have attempted to create typologies categorizing the forms that the abuse of police powers can take. For example, when investigating corruption among police officers in New York, the **Knapp Commission** classified abusers into two categories: meat eaters and grass eaters.[166] **Meat eaters** aggressively misuse police power for personal gain by demanding bribes, threatening legal action, or cooperating with criminals. Across the country, police officers have been accused, indicted, and convicted of shaking down club owners and other businesspeople.[167] In contrast, **grass eaters** accept payoffs when their everyday duties place them in a position to be solicited by the public. For example, police officers have been investigated for taking bribes to look the other way while neighborhood bookmakers ply their trade.[168] The Knapp Commission concluded that the vast majority of police officers on the take are grass eaters, although the few meat eaters who are caught capture all the headlines. In 1993 another police scandal prompted formation of the **Mollen Commission,** which found that some New York cops were actively involved in violence and drug dealing.

Other police experts have attempted to create models to better understand police corruption. It may be possible to divide police corruption into four major categories:[169]

1. *Internal corruption* This corruption takes place among police officers themselves, involving both the bending of departmental rules and the outright performance of illegal acts. For example, Chicago police officers conspired to sell relatively new police cars to other officers at cut-rate prices, forcing the department to purchase new cars unnecessarily. In Boston a major scandal hit the police department when a captain was indicted in an exam tampering-and-selling scheme. Numerous officers bought promotion exams from the captain, while others had him lower the scores of rivals who were competing for the same job.[170]
2. *Selective enforcement or nonenforcement* This form occurs when police abuse or exploit their discretion. If an officer frees a drug dealer in return for valuable information, that is considered a legitimate use of discretion; if the officer did so for money, that is an abuse of police power.
3. *Active criminality* This is participation by police in serious criminal behavior. Police may use their positions of trust and power to commit the very crimes they are entrusted with controlling. For example, a police burglary ring in Denver was so large that it prompted one commentator to coin the phrase "burglars in blue." During the past twenty years, police burglary rings have been uncovered in Chicago, Reno, Nashville, Cleveland, and Burlington, Vermont, among other cities.[171] Another disturbing trend has been police use of drugs and alcohol. Police departments have been active in referring officers to treatment programs when substance abuse problems are detected. [172]
4. *Bribery and extortion* This includes practices in which law enforcement roles are exploited specifically to raise money. Bribery is initiated by the citizen; extortion is initiated by the officer. Bribery or extortion can be a one-shot transaction, as when a traffic violator offers a police officer $20 to forget about issuing a summons. Or the relationship can be an ongoing one, in which the officer solicits (or is offered) regular payoffs to ignore criminal activities, such as gambling or narcotics dealing. This is known as "being on the pad."

Sometimes police officers accept routine bribes and engage in petty extortion without considering themselves corrupt; they consider these payments as some of the unwritten "benefits" of police work. For example, *mooching* involves receiving free gifts of coffee, cigarettes, meals, and so on in exchange for possible future acts of favoritism. *Chiseling* occurs when officers demand admission to entertainment events or price discounts; *shopping* involves taking small items, such as cigarettes, from a store whose door was accidentally left unlocked after business hours.[173]

CORRUPT DEPARTMENTS It has also been suggested that entire police departments can be categorized on the basis of the level and type of corruption existing within them.[174] Three types of departments may exist:

1. *"Rotten apples" and "rotten pockets"* This type of police department has a few corrupt officers ("rotten apples") who use their position for personal gain. When these corrupt officers band together, they form a "rotten pocket." Robert Daley described the activities of such a group in his book *Prince of the City*.[175] Agents of New York City's Special Investigations Unit kept money they confiscated during narcotics raids and used illegal drugs to pay off informers. *Prince of the City* tells the story of New York Detective Frank

Leuci, whose testimony against his partners before investigating committees made him an outcast in the police department. Rotten pockets help institutionalize corruption because their members expect newcomers to conform to their illegal practices and to a code of secrecy.

2. *Pervasive unorganized corruption* This type of department contains a majority of personnel who are corrupt but have little relationship to one another. Though many officers are involved in taking bribes and extortion, they are not cooperating with one another for personal gain.

3. *Pervasive organized corruption* This describes a department in which almost all members are involved in systematic and organized corruption. The Knapp Commission found this type of relationship in New York City's vice divisions, where payoffs and bribes were an organized and accepted way of police life.

THE CAUSES AND CONTROL OF CORRUPTION No single explanation satisfactorily accounts for the various forms the abuse of power takes. One view puts the blame on the type of person who becomes a police officer. This position holds that policing tends to attract lower-class individuals who do not have the financial means to maintain a coveted middle-class lifestyle. As they develop the cynical, authoritarian police personality, accepting graft seems an all-too-easy method of achieving financial security.

A second view is that the wide discretion police enjoy, coupled with low visibility they maintain with the public and their own supervisors, makes them likely candidates for corruption. In addition, the "code of secrecy" maintained by the police subculture helps insulate corrupt officers from the law. Similarly, police managers, most of whom have risen through the ranks, are reluctant to investigate corruption or punish wrongdoers. Thus, corruption may also be viewed as a function of police institutions and practices.[176]

A third position holds that corruption is a function of society's ambivalence toward many forms of vice-related criminal behavior that police officers are sworn to control. Unenforceable laws governing moral standards promote corruption because they create large groups with an interest in undermining law enforcement. These include consumers — people who gamble, wish to drink after the legal closing hour, or patronize a prostitute — who do not want to be deprived of their chosen form of recreation. Even though the consumers may not actively corrupt police officers, their existence creates a climate that tolerates active corruption by others.[177] Since vice cannot be controlled and the public apparently wants it to continue, the officer may have little resistance to inducements for monetary gain offered by law violators.

How can police misconduct be controlled? One approach is to strengthen the internal administrative review process within police departments. A strong and well-supported internal affairs division has been linked to lowered corruption rates.[178] However, asking police to police themselves is not a simple task. Officers are often reluctant to discipline their peers. For example, a 1999 review of disciplinary files found that hundreds of New York City police officers escaped punishment when their cases were summarily dismissed by the police department without ever interviewing victims or witnesses or making any other efforts to examine the strength of the evidence.[179]

accountability system
Dealing with police corruption by making superiors responsible for the behavior of their subordinates.

Another approach, instituted by then New York Commissioner Patrick Murphy in the wake of the Knapp Commission, is the **accountability system.** This holds that supervisors at each level are directly accountable for the illegal behaviors of the officers under them. Consequently, a commander can be demoted or forced to resign if one of her command is found guilty of corruption.[180] Close scrutiny by a department, however, can lower officer morale and create the suspicion that the officers' own supervisors distrust them.

Some departments have set up guidelines to help reduce corruption. In 1996 the city of Philadelphia agreed to implement a set of reforms to combat corruption in order to settle a lawsuit brought by civil rights organizations. The following were among the measures taken to reduce corruption:

- A policy mandating that all citizens' complaints be forwarded for investigation by the internal affairs division.
- Development of computer files that contain all types of complaints and suits against individual officers that could be easily accessed during investigations
- A policy requiring that internal affairs give a high priority to any officer's claim that another officer was corrupt or used excessive force
- Mandatory reporting and recording of all incidents in which an officer used more than incidental force
- Training of officers to treat citizens without racial bias; assigning a deputy commissioner to monitor charges of race discrimination
- Reviewing all policies and practices to ensure they do not involve or have the potential for race bias.[181]

Another approach is to create outside review boards or special prosecutors, such as the Mollen Commission in New York and the Christopher Commission in Los Angeles, to investigate reported incidents of corruption. However, outside investigators and special prosecutors are often limited by their lack of intimate knowledge of day-to-day operations. As a result, they depend on the testimony of a few officers who are willing to cooperate, either to save themselves from prosecution or because they have a compelling moral commitment. Outside evaluators also face the problem of the blue curtain, which is quickly closed when police officers feel their department is under scrutiny.

A more realistic solution to corruption, albeit a difficult one, might be to change the social context of policing. Police operations must be made more visible, and the public must be given freer access to controlling police operations. All too often, the public finds out about police problems only when a scandal hits the newspaper. Some of the vice-related crimes the police now deal with might be decriminalized or referred to other agencies. Although decriminalization of vice cannot in itself end the problem, it could lower the pressure placed on individual police officers and help eliminate their moral dilemmas.

SUMMARY

Police departments today are faced with many critical problems in their development and relationship with the public. Police are believed to be insulated from the rest of society. Some experts hold that police officers have distinct personality characteristics marked by authoritarianism and cynicism. It is also alleged that police maintain a separate culture with distinct rules and loyalties. A police personality also influences their working style. Four distinct police styles have been identified, and each influences police decision making. The complexity and danger of the police role produce an enormous amount of stress that harms police effectiveness.

Social concerns also affect police operations. Today, many police officers are seeking higher education. The jury is still out on whether educated officers are actually more effective. Women and minorities are now being recruited into the police in increasing numbers. Research indicates that, with few exceptions, they perform as well or even better than other officers. The percentage of minorities on police forces reflects their representation in the general population, but the number of female officers still lags behind. Of greater importance is increasing the number of women and minorities in supervisory positions.

Police departments have also been concerned about limiting police stress and improving police–community relations. One critical concern is the police use of deadly force. Research indicates that antishooting policies can limit deaths resulting from police action. Another effort has been to identify and eliminate police corruption, which still mars the reputation of police forces.

KEY TERMS

blue curtain
cynicism
police officer style
crime fighter
social agent
law enforcer
watchman
discretion
demeanor
double marginality
defeminization
police brutality
deadly force
Knapp Commission
meat eater
grass eater
Mollen Commission
accountability system

INFOTRAC COLLEGE EDITION EXERCISES

There have been ongoing cases of police corruption despite the efforts of law enforcement managers to control it and weed out "dirty cops." The issue of corruption can be researched using *InfoTrac College Edition.* To find out about some recent cases in Philadelphia and Los Angeles, read

John Cloud, "L.A. Confidential, for Real: Street Cops Accused of Frame-ups in Widening Scandal," *Time,* 27 September 1999, 44.

Michael Kramer, "How Good Cops Go Bad: Brutality, Racism, Cover-ups, Lies: A Guilty Police Officer Tells How the Process Works," *Time,* 15 December 1997, 78.

"L.A.'s Dirty War on Gangs: A Trail of Corruption Leads to Some of the City's Toughest Cops," *Newsweek,* 11 October 1999, 72.

The United States is not alone in experiencing police corruption. For a view of the international scene, read the following papers on corruption in Russia and England:

Robert Chesshyre, "The Most Dangerous Tribe in London," *New Statesman* 127 (1998): 28.

John Lloyd, "100 Dollars? That Will Do Nicely," *New Statesman* 128 (1999): 21.

QUESTIONS

1. Should male and female officers have exactly the same duties in a police department? Explain.
2. Do you think that an officer's working the street will eventually produce a cynical personality and distrust for civilians? Explain.
3. How can education help police officers?
4. Should a police officer who accepts a free meal from a restaurant owner be dismissed from the force? Why or why not?
5. A police officer orders an unarmed person running away from a burglary to stop; the suspect keeps running and is shot and killed by the officer. Has the officer committed murder? Explain.
6. Would you like to live in a society that abolished police discretion and used a full enforcement policy? Why or why not?

NOTES

1. Deborah Sontag and Dan Barry, "Using Settlements to Measure Police Abuse," *New York Times,* 17 September 1997.

2. Bernie Patterson, "Job Experience and Perceived Job Stress among Police, Correctional and Probation/Parole Officers," *Criminal Justice and Behavior* 19 (1992): 260–85.

3. Kathleen Maguire and Ann Pastore, *Sourcebook of Criminal Justice Statistics, 1995* (Washington, D.C.: Bureau of Justice Statistics, 1996), 133.

4. John Klofas, "Drugs and Justice: The Impact of Drugs on Criminal Justice in a Metropolitan Community," *Crime and Delinquency* 39 (1993): 204–24.

5. Steven Tuch and Ronald Weitzer, "The Polls-Trends, Racial Differences in Attitudes toward the Police," *Public Opinion Quarterly* 61 (1997): 642–63.

6. Kathleen Maguire and Ann L. Pastore, eds. (1999) *Sourcebook of Criminal Justice Statistics* [online]. Available: http://www.albany.edu/sourcebook.

7. See, for example, Richard Harris, *The Police Academy: An Inside View* (New York: Wiley, 1973); John Van Maanen, "Observations on the Making of a Policeman," in *Order Under Law,* ed. R. Culbertson and M. Tezak (Prospect Heights, Ill.: Waveland Press, 1981), 111–26; Jonathan Rubenstein, *City Police* (New York: Ballantine Books, 1973); John Broderick, *Police in a Time of Change* (Morristown, N.J.: General Learning Press, 1977).

8. Malcolm Sparrow, Mark Moore, and David Kennedy, *Beyond 911, A New Era for Policing* (New York: Basic Books, 1990), 51.

9. M. Steven Meagher and Nancy Yentes, "Choosing a Career in Policing: A Comparison of Male and Female Perceptions," *Journal of Police Science and Administration* 16 (1986): 320–27.

10. Michael K. Brown, *Working the Street* (New York: Russell Sage, 1981), 82.

11. Stan Shernock, "An Empirical Examination of the Relationship between Police Solidarity and Community Orientation," *Journal of Police Science and Administration* 18 (1988): 182–98.

12. Ibid., 360.

13. Ibid., 359.

14. Egon Bittner, *The Functions of Police in Modern Society* (Cambridge, Mass.: Oelgeschlager, Gunn & Hain, 1980), 63.

15. Richard Lundman, *Police and Policing* (New York: Holt, Rinehart & Winston, 1980); see also Jerome Skolnick, *Justice without Trial* (New York: Wiley, 1966).

16. Robert Regoli, Robert Culbertson, John Crank, and James Powell, "Career Stage and Cynicism among Police Chiefs," *Justice Quarterly* 7 (1990): 592–614.

17. William Westly, *Violence and the Police: A Sociological Study of Law, Custom, and Morality* (Cambridge, Mass.: MIT Press, 1970).

18. Skolnick, *Justice without Trial,* 42–68.

19. Milton Rokeach, Martin Miller, and John Snyder, "The Value Gap between Police and Policed," *Journal of Social Issues* 27 (1971): 155–71.

20. Bruce Carpenter and Susan Raza, "Personality Characteristics of Police Applicants: Comparisons across Subgroups and with Other Populations," *Journal of Police Science and Administration* 15 (1987): 10–17.

21. Larry Tifft, "The 'Cop Personality' Reconsidered," *Journal of Police Science and Administration* 2 (1974): 268; David Bayley and Harold Mendelsohn, *Minorities and the Police* (New York: Free Press, 1969); Robert Balch, "The Police Personality: Fact or Fiction?" *Journal of Criminal Law, Criminology, and Police Science* 63 (1972): 117.

22. Lowell Storms, Nolan Penn, and James Tenzell, "Policemen's Perception of Real and Ideal Policemen," *Journal of Police Science and Administration* 17 (1990): 40–43.

23. Arthur Niederhoffer, *Behind the Shield: The Police in Urban Society* (Garden City, N.Y.: Doubleday, 1967).

24. Ibid., 216–20.

25. Robert Regoli and Eric Poole, "Measurement of Police Cynicism: A Factor Scaling Approach," *Journal of Criminal Justice* 7 (1979): 37–52.

26. Ibid., 43.

27. Ibid., 44.

28. Carl Klockars, "The Dirty Harry Problem," *Annals* 452 (1980): 33–47.

29. Jack Kuykendall and Roy Roberg, "Police Manager's Perceptions of Employee Types: A Conceptual Model," *Journal of Criminal Justice* 16 (1988): 131–35.

30. Stephen Matrofski, R. Richard Ritti, and Jeffrey Snipes, "Expectancy Theory and Police Productivity in DUI Enforcement," *Law and Society Review* 28 (1994): 113–38.

31. William Muir, *Police: Streetcorner Politicians* (Chicago: University of Chicago Press, 1977).

32. James Q. Wilson, *Varieties of Police Behavior* (Cambridge, Mass.: Harvard University Press, 1968), chap. 7.

33. Ibid., 141.

34. Ellen Hochstedler, "Testing Types: A Review and Test of Police Types," *Journal of Criminal Justice* 9 (1981): 451–66.

35. For a thorough review, see Eric Riksheim and Steven Chermak, "Causes of Police Behavior Revisited," *Journal of Criminal Justice* 21 (1993): 353–83.

36. Skolnick, *Justice without Trial.*

37. Peter Sinden and B. Joyce Stephens, "Police Perceptions of Domestic Violence: The Nexus of Victim, Perpetrator, Event, Self and Law," *Policing* 22 (1999): 313–26.

38. Helen Eigenberg, Kathryn Scarborough, and Victor Kappeler, "Contributory Factors Affecting Arrest in Domestic and Nondomestic Assaults," *American Journal of Police* 15 (1996): 27–51.

39. Leonore Simon, "A Therapeutic Jurisprudence Approach to the Legal Processing of Domestic Violence Cases," *Psychology, Public Policy and Law* 1 (1995): 43–79.

40. Robert Kane, "Patterns of Arrest in Domestic Violence Encounters: Identifying a Police Decision-Making Model," *Journal of Criminal Justice* 27 (1999): 65–79.

41. Gregory Howard Williams, *The Law and Politics of Police Discretion* (Westport, Conn.: Greenwood Press, 1984).

42. Dana Jones and Joanne Belknap, "Police Responses to Battering in a Progressive Pro-Arrest Jurisdiction," *Justice Quarterly* 16 (1999): 249–73.

43. Douglas Smith and Jody Klein, "Police Control of Interpersonal Disputes," *Social Problems* 31 (1984): 468–81.

44. Jones and Belknap, "Police Responses to Battering," 249–73.

45. Westly, *Violence and the Police.*

46. Nathan Goldman, *The Differential Selection of Juvenile Offenders for Court Appearance* (New York: National Council on Crime and Delinquency, 1963).

47. David Klinger, "Demeanor or Crime? Why 'Hostile' Citizens Are More Likely to Be Arrested," *Criminology* 32 (1994): 475–93.

48. Richard Lundman, "Demeanor or Crime? The Midwest City Police–Citizen Encounters Study," *Criminology* 32 (1994): 631–53; Robert Worden and Robin Shepard, "On the Meaning, Measurement, and Estimated Effects of Suspects' Demeanor toward the Police" (Paper presented at the American Society of Criminology meeting, Miami, November 1994).

49. R. Steven Daniels, Lorin Baumhover, William Formby, and Carolyn Clark-Daniels, "Police Discretion and Elder Mistreatment: A Nested Model of Observation, Reporting and Satisfaction," *Journal of Criminal Justice* 27 (1999): 209–25.

50. Brown, *Working the Street,* 290.

51. See Larry Hoover, *Police Educational Characteristics and Curricula* (Washington, D.C.: Government Printing Office, 1975).

52. Brian Reaves and Andrew Goldberg, *Law Enforcement Management and Administrative Statistics, 1997: Data for Individual State and Local Law Enforcement Agencies with 100 or More Officers* (Washington, D.C.: Bureau of Justice Statistics, 1999).

53. Bruce Berg, "Who Should Teach Police: A Typology and Assessment of Police Academy Instructors," *American Journal of Police* 9 (1990): 79–100.

54. David Carter and Allen Sapp, *The State of Police Education: Critical Findings* (Washington, D.C.: Police Executive Research Forum, 1988), 6.

55. See, for example, B. E. Sanderson, "Police Officers: The Relationship of a College Education to Job Performance," *Police Chief* 44 (1977): 62.

56. John Krimmel, "The Performance of College-Educated Police: A Study of Self-Rated Police Performance Measures," *American Journal of Police* 15 (1996): 85–95.

57. Robert Worden, "A Badge and a Baccalaureate: Policies, Hypotheses, and Further Evidence," *Justice Quarterly* 7 (1990): 565–92.

58. See Lawrence Sherman and Warren Bennis, "Higher Education for Police Officers: The Central Issues," *Police Chief* 44 (1977): 32.

59. Worden, "A Badge and a Baccalaureate," 587–89.

60. Carter and Sapp, *The State of Police Education.*

61. Jihong Zhao and Nicholas Lovrich, "Determinants of Minority Employment in American Municipal Police Agencies: The Representation of African American Officers," *Journal of Criminal Justice* 26 (1998): 267–78.

62. David Murphy and John Worrall, "Residency Requirements and Public Perceptions of the Police in Large Municipalities," *Policing* 22 (1999): 327–42.

63. Jack Kuykendall and David Burns, "The Black Police Officer: An Historical Perspective," *Journal of Contemporary Criminal Justice* 1 (1980): 4–13.

64. Ibid.

65. Nicholas Alex, *Black in Blue: A Study of the Negro Policeman* (New York: Appleton-Century-Crofts, 1969).

66. Kim Michelle Lersch, "Predicting Citizen's Race in Allegations of Misconduct against the Police," *Journal of Criminal Justice* 26 (1998): 87–99.

67. *Local Police Departments, 1997, Executive Summary* (Washington, D.C.: Bureau of Justice Statistics, 1999).

68. Nicholas Alex, *New York Cops Talk Back* (New York: Wiley, 1976).

69. Stephen Leinen, *Black Police, White Society* (New York: New York University Press, 1984).

70. Donald Yates and Vijayan Pillai, "Frustration and Strain among Fort Worth Police Officers," *Sociology and Social Research* 76 (1992): 145–49.

71. Robin Haarr and Merry Morash, "Gender, Race, and Strategies of Coping with Occupational Stress in Policing," *Justice Quarterly* 16 (1999): 303–36.

72. Donald Yates and Vijayan Pillai, "Race and Police Commitment to Community Policing," *Journal of Intergroup Relations* 19 (1993): 14–23.

73. Bruce Berg, Edmond True, and Marc Gertz, "Police, Riots, and Alienation," *Journal of Police Science and Administration* 12 (1984): 186–90.

74. Samuel Walker and K. B. Turner, "A Decade of Modest Progress: Employment of Black and Hispanic Police Officers, 1983–1992" (Omaha: Department of Criminal Justice, University of Nebraska, 1993, mimeographed).

75. Yates and Pillai, "Frustration and Strain among Fort Worth Police Officers."

76. For a review of the history of women in policing, see Dorothy Moses Schulz, "From Policewoman to Police Officer: An Unfinished Revolution," *Police Studies* 16 (1993): 90–99; Cathryn House, "The Changing Role of Women in Law Enforcement," *Police Chief* 60 (1993): 139–44.

77. Susan Martin, "Female Officers on the Move? A Status Report on Women in Policing," in *Critical Issues in Policing,* ed. Roger Dunham and Geoffery Alpert (Grove Park, Ill.: Waveland Press, 1988), 312–31.

78. *Le Bouef v. Ramsey,* 26 FEP Cases 884 (9/16/80).

79. Michael Birzer and Delores Craig, "Gender Differences in Police Physical Ability Test Performance," *American Journal of Police* 15 (1996): 93–106.

80. Carole Garrison, Nancy Grant, and Kenneth McCormick, "Utilization of Police Women," *Police Chief* 55 (1988): 32–33.

81. Eric Poole and Mark Pogrebin, "Factors Affecting the Decision to Remain in Policing: A Study of Women Officers," *Journal of Police Science and Administration* 16 (1988): 49–55.

82. Haarr and Morash, "Gender, Race, and Strategies of Coping," 303–36.

83. Merry Morash and Jack Greene, "Evaluating Women on Patrol: A Critique of Contemporary Wisdom," *Evaluation Review* 10 (1986): 230–55.

84. Peter Bloch and Deborah Anderson, *Policewomen on Patrol: Final Report* (Washington, D.C.: Police Foundation, 1974).

85. Robert Homant and Daniel Kennedy, "Police Perceptions of Spouse Abuse: A Comparison of Male and Female Officers," *Journal of Criminal Justice* 13 (1985): 49–64.

86. Sean Grennan, "Findings on the Role of Officer Gender in Violent Encounters with Citizens," *Journal of Police Science and Administration* 15 (1988): 78–85.

87. See, for example, Jack Molden, "Female Police Officers: Training Implications," *Law and Order* 33 (1985): 62–63.

88. Joseph Balkin, "Why Policemen Don't Like Policewomen," *Journal of Police Science and Administration* 16 (1988): 29–38.

89. Anthony Bouza, "Women in Policing," *FBI Law Enforcement Bulletin* 44 (1975): 2–7.

90. James Daum and Cindy Johns, "Police Work from a Woman's Perspective," *Police Chief* 61 (1994): 46–49.

91. Mary Brown, "The Plight of Female Police: A Survey of NW Patrolmen," *Police Chief* 61 (1994): 50–53.

92. Simon Holdaway and Sharon K. Parker, "Policing Women Police: Uniform Patrol, Promotion and Representation in the CID," *British Journal of Criminology* 38 (1998): 40–48.

93. Associated Press, "Two Female Agents Settle FBI Suit," *Boston Globe,* 19 May 1994, 8.

94. Balkin, "Why Policemen Don't Like Policewomen," 36.

95. Alissa Pollitz Worden, "The Attitudes of Women and Men in Policing: Testing Conventional and Contemporary Wisdom," *Criminology* 31 (1993): 203–43.

96. Adriane Kinnane, *Policing* (Chicago: Nelson-Hall, 1979), 58.

97. Bruce Berg and Kimberly Budnick, "Defeminization of Women in Law Enforcement: A New Twist in the Traditional Police Personality," *Journal of Police Science and Administration* 14 (1986): 314–19.

98. Curt Bartol, George Bergen, Julie Seager Volckens, and Kathleen Knoras, "Women in Small-Town Policing, Job Performance and Stress," *Criminal Justice and Behavior* 19 (1992): 245–59.

99. Susan Martin, "Outsider within the Station House: The Impact of Race and Gender on Black Women Police," *Social Problems* 41 (1994): 383–400.

100. Michael Charles, "Women in Policing: The Physical Aspects," *Journal of Police Science and Administration* 10 (1982): 194–205.

101. Martin, "Outsider within the Station House," 387.

102. Ibid., 392.

103. Ibid., 394.

104. Ibid., 397.

105. Roi Dianne Townsey, "Black Women in American Policing: An Advancement Display," *Journal of Criminal Justice* 10 (1982): 455–68.

106. J. G. Wexler and V. Quinn, "Considerations in the Training and Development of Women Sergeants," *Journal of Police Science and Administration* 13 (1985): 98–105.

107. Martin, "Female Officers on the Move?" 325–26.

108. Ibid.

109. Poole and Pogrebin, "Factors Affecting the Decision to Remain in Policing," 54–55.

110. Roy Roberg, David Hayhurst, and Harry Allen, "Job Burnout in Law Enforcement Dispatchers: A Comparative Analysis," *Journal of Criminal Justice* 16 (1988): 385–94.

111. Yates and Pillai, "Frustration and Strain among Fort Worth Police Officers."

112. For an impressive review, see Richard Farmer, "Clinical and Managerial Implication of Stress Research on the Police," *Journal of Police Science and Administration* 17 (1990): 205–17.

113. Lawrence Travis III and Craig Winston, "Dissension in the Ranks: Officer Resistance to Community Policing and Support for the Organization," *Journal of Crime and Justice* 21 (1998): 139–55.

114. Francis Cullen, Terrence Lemming, Bruce Link, and John Wozniak, "The Impact of Social Supports on Police Stress," *Criminology* 23 (1985): 503–22.

115. Farmer, "Clinical and Managerial Implications"; Nancy Norvell, Dale Belles, and Holly Hills, "Perceived Stress Levels and Physical Symptoms in Supervisory Law Enforcement Personnel," *Journal of Police Science and Administration* 16 (1988): 75–79.

116. Donald Yates and Vijayan Pillai, "Attitudes toward Community Policing: A Causal Analysis," *Social Science Journal* 33 (1996): 193–209.

117. Harvey McMurray, "Attitudes of Assaulted Police Officers and Their Policy Implications," *Journal of Police Science and Administration* 17 (1990): 44–48.

118. Robert Ankony and Thomas Kelly, "The Impact of Perceived Alienation of Police Officers' Sense of Mastery and Subsequent Motivation for Proactive Enforcement," *Policing* 22 (1999): 120–32.

119. John Blackmore, "Police Stress," in *Policing Society,* ed. Clinton Terry (New York: Wiley, 1985), 395.

120. Rose Lee Josephson and Martin Reiser, "Officer Suicide in the Los Angeles Police Department: A Twelve-Year Follow-up," *Journal of Police Science and Administration* 17 (1990): 227–30.

121. Yates and Pillai, "Attitudes toward Community Policing," 205–06.

122. Ibid.

123. Rosanna Church and Naomi Robertson, "How State Police Agencies Are Addressing the Issue of Wellness," *Policing* 22 (1999): 304–12.

124. Farmer, "Clinical and Managerial Implications," 215.

125. Peter Hart, Alexander Wearing, and Bruce Headey, "Assessing Police Work Experiences: Development of the Police Daily Hassles and Uplifts Scales," *Journal of Criminal Justice* 21 (1993): 553–73.

126. Vivian Lord, Denis Gray, and Samuel Pond, "The Police Stress Inventory: Does It Measure Stress?" *Journal of Criminal Justice* 19 (1991): 139–49.

127. Samuel Walker, *Popular Justice* (New York: Oxford University Press, 1980), 197.

128. Richard R. Johnson, "Citizen Complaints: What the Police Should Know," *FBI Law Enforcement Bulletin* 67 (1998): 1–6.

129. See, for example, President's Commission on Law Enforcement and the Administration of Justice, *Task Force Report: The Police* (Washington, D.C.: Government Printing Office, 1967), 181–82; *National Advisory Commission on Civil Disorders, Police and the Community* (Washington, D.C.: Government Printing Office, 1968), 158–59.

130. President's Commission, *Task Force Report,* 181–82.

131. Lawrence Sherman, "Causes of Police Behavior: The Current State of Quantitative Research," *Journal of Research in Crime and Delinquency* 17 (1980): 80–81.

132. David Bayley and James Garofalo, "The Management of Violence by Police Patrol Officers," *Criminology* 27 (1989): 1–27.

133. Joel Garner, John Buchanan, Tom Schade, and John Hepburn, *Understanding the Use of Force by and against the Police* (Washington, D.C.: National Institute of Justice, 1996).

134. Ibid.

135. Antony Pate and Lorie Fridell, *Police Use of Force: Official Reports, Citizen Complaints, and Legal Consequences* (Washington, D.C.: Police Foundation, 1993).

136. Kenneth Adams, Geoffrey P. Alpert, Roger G. Dunham, Joel H. Garner, Lawrence A. Greenfield, Mark A. Henriquez, Patrick A. Langan, Christopher D. Maxwell, and Steven K. Smith, *Use of Force by Police: Overview of National and Local Data* (Washington, D.C.: National Institute of Justice/Bureau of Justice Statistics, 1999).

137. Ibid.

138. Kim Michelle Lersch and Tom Mieczkowski, "Who Are the Problem-Prone Officers? An Analysis of Citizen Complaints," *American Journal of Police* 15 (1996): 23–42.

139. Samuel Walker, "The Rule Revolution: Reflections on the Transformation of American Criminal Justice, 1950–1988," Working Papers, Series 3 (Madison: Institute for Legal Studies, University of Wisconsin Law School, December 1988).

140. Kevin Flynn, "New York Police Sting Tries to Weed Out Brutal Officers," *New York Times,* 24 September 1999, 2.

141. Lawrence Sherman and Robert Langworthy, "Measuring Homicide by Police Officers," *Journal of Criminal Law and Criminology* 4 (1979): 546–60.

142. Ibid.

143. James Fyfe, "Police Use of Deadly Force: Research and Reform," *Justice Quarterly* 5 (1988): 165–205.

144. Sherman and Langworthy, "Measuring Homicide by Police Officers."

145. Richard Kania and Wade Mackey, "Police Violence as a Function of Community Characteristics," *Criminology* 15 (1977): 27–48.

146. John MacDonald, Geoffrey Alpert, and Abraham Tennenbaum, "Justifiable Homicide by Police and Criminal Homicide: A Research Note," *Journal of Crime and Justice* 22 (1999): 153–64.

147. Richard Parent and Simon Verdun-Jones, "Victim-Precipitated Homicide: Police Use of Deadly Force in British Columbia," *Policing* 21 (1998): 432–49.

148. "10% of Police Shootings Found to Be 'Suicide by Cop,'" *Criminal Justice Newsletter* 29 (1998): 1.

149. Sherman and Langworthy, "Measuring Homicide by Police Officers."

150. Ibid.

151. David Lester, "Predicting the Rate of Justifiable Homicide by Police Officers," *Police Studies* 16 (1993): 43; Jonathan Sorenson, James Marquart, and Deon Brock, "Factors Related to Killings of Felons by Police Officers: A Test of the Community Violence and Conflict Hypotheses," *Justice Quarterly* 10 (1993): 417–40; David Jacobs and David Britt, "Inequality and Police Use of Deadly Force: An Empirical Assessment of a Conflict Hypotheses," *Social Problems* 26 (1979): 403–12.

152. Fyfe, "Police Use of Deadly Force," 181.

153. Paul Takagi, "A Garrison State in a 'Democratic' Society," *Crime and Social Justice* 5 (1974): 34–43.

154. Mark Blumberg, "Race and Police Shootings: An Analysis in Two Cities," in *Contemporary Issues in Law Enforcement,* ed. James Fyfe (Beverly Hills, Calif.: Sage, 1981), 152–66.

155. James Fyfe, "Shots Fired" (Ph.D. diss., State University of New York, Albany, 1978).

156. *Tennessee v. Garner,* 471 U.S. 1, 105 S.Ct. 1694, 85 L.Ed.2d 889 (1985).

157. *Graham v. Connor,* 490 U.S. 386, 109 S.Ct. 1865, 104 L.Ed.2d 443 (1989).

158. Franklin Graves and Gregory Connor, "The FLETC Use-of-Force Model," *Police Chief* 59 (1992): 56–58.

159. See James Fyfe, "Administrative Interventions on Police Shooting Discretion: An Empirical Examination," *Journal of Criminal Justice* 7 (1979): 313–25.

160. Frank Zarb, "Police Liability for Creating the Need to Use Deadly Force in Self-Defense," *Michigan Law Review* 86 (1988): 1982–2009.

161. National Law Enforcement Officers Memorial Fund, Press Release, Washington, D.C., 7 February 1996.

162. Adams et al., *Use of Force by Police.*

163. J. David Hirschel, Charles Dean, and Richard Lumb, "The Relative Contribution of Domestic Violence to Assault and Injury of Police Officers," *Justice Quarterly* 11 (1994): 99–118.

164. Walker, *Popular Justice,* 64.

165. Herman Goldstein, *Police Corruption* (Washington, D.C.: Police Foundation, 1975), 3.

166. Knapp Commission, *Report on Police Corruption* (New York: Braziller, 1973), 1–34.

167. Elizabeth Neuffer, "Seven Additional Detectives Linked to Extortion Scheme," *Boston Globe,* 25 October 1988, 60.

168. Kevin Cullen, "U.S. Probe Eyes Bookie Protection," *Boston Globe,* 25 October 1988.

169. Michael Johnston, *Political Corruption and Public Policy in America* (Monterey, Calif.: Books/Cole, 1982), 75.

170. William Doherty, "Ex-Sergeant Says He Aided Bid to Sell Exam," *Boston Globe,* 26 February 1987, 61.

171. Anthony Simpson, *The Literature of Police Corruption,* vol. 1 (New York: John Jay Press, 1977), 53.

172. Peter Kraska and Victor Kappeler, "Police On-Duty Drug Use: A Theoretical and Descriptive Examination," *American Journal of Police* 7 (1988): 1–28.

173. Ellwyn Stoddard, "Blue Coat Crime," in *Thinking about Police,* ed. Carl Klockars (New York: McGraw-Hill, 1983), 338–49.

174. Lawrence Sherman, *Police Corruption: A Sociological Perspective* (Garden City, N.Y.: Doubleday, 1974).

175. Robert Daley, *Prince of the City* (New York: Houghton Mifflin, 1978).

176. Sherman, *Police Corruption,* 40–41.

177. Samuel Walker, *Police in Society* (New York: McGraw-Hill, 1983), 181.

178. Sherman, *Police Corruption,* 194.

179. Kevin Flynn, "Police Dept. Routinely Drops Cases of Officer Misconduct, Report Says," *New York Times,* 15 September 1999, 1.

180. Barbara Gelb, *Tarnished Brass: The Decade after Serpico* (New York: Putnam, 1983); Candace McCoy, "Lawsuits against Police: What Impact Do They Have?" *Criminal Law Bulletin* 20 (1984): 49–56.

181. "Philadelphia Police Corruption Brings Major Reform Initiative," *Criminal Justice Newsletter* 27 (1996): 4–5.

chapter 7

Police and the Rule of Law

Sandra Houghton and two other individuals were in an automobile stopped for speeding and a faulty brake light in the early morning hours of July 23, 1995. The driver, David Young, had a syringe in his shirt pocket. When asked about it, the driver, with refreshing candor, replied that he used it to take drugs. The officer then checked inside the car, saw Houghton's purse on the seat, searched it, and found a vial of liquid methamphetamine. She was arrested, tried, and convicted of drug possession.

It took four years for Houghton's case to reach the U.S. Supreme Court for review. The state appeals court overturned the conviction, but the Supreme Court upheld it, ruling that the police officer had probable cause (reason to believe a crime was committed) to search the purse of a presumably innocent passenger. According to the Court, effective law enforcement would be impaired without the ability to search a passenger's personal belongings when there is reason to believe contraband is hidden. ■

Thousands of incidents like the *Houghton* case occur each year. Traditional police power to strictly enforce traffic laws is often used as a way to search for drugs on the roadway. The U.S. Supreme Court has given police officers greater leeway to stop cars, to detain drivers and their passengers, and to search vehicles — often with the intent of finding illegal drugs. The *Houghton* case illustrates the complex Fourth Amendment issues that the police and courts face in modern society. Should privacy rights be secondary to public safety? Should the Fourth Amendment be a check on police power? The question presented to the Supreme Court in *Houghton* was whether the so-called automobile exception to the Fourth Amendment allows the police to conduct a warrantless search of a passenger's belongings where there is no apparent evidence that the passenger is involved in a crime.[1] This is one example of many different types of cases involving the law of search and seizure regarding automobiles, which is discussed in this chapter.

The police are charged with both preventing crime and arresting criminals who have broken the law. To carry out these tasks, as in the *Houghton* case, police officers need to be able to search for evidence, to seize items such as guns and drugs, and to question suspects, witnesses, and victims. For trial, they need to provide sufficient evidence to prove guilt "beyond a reasonable doubt." Therefore, soon after the crime is committed, they must make every effort to gather physical evidence, obtain confessions, and take witness statements that will stand up in court. Police officers also realize that evidence such as the testimony of a witness or coconspirator may evaporate before the trial begins. Then the case outcome may depend on some piece of physical evidence or a suspect's statement taken early during the investigation.

The need for police officers to gather evidence can conflict with the constitutional rights of citizens. For example, although police might prefer a free hand to search homes and cars for evidence, the Fourth Amendment restricts police activities by limiting searches and/or seizures to only those deemed "reasonable." When police wish to vigorously interrogate a suspect, they must honor the Fifth Amendment's prohibition against forcing people to incriminate themselves.

COURT REVIEW OF POLICE OPERATIONS

Over the years, police handling of criminal suspects has been moderated by the courts. At one time, the U.S. Supreme Court did little to curb police. In the 1960s the Warren Court moved vigorously to restrict police activities, going so far as to "punish" police by excluding from trial any evidence obtained in violation of the suspect's constitutional rights (the so-called exclusionary rule). Some critics charged that Supreme Court decisions "handcuffed" the police while giving criminal suspects free rein to continue their law-violating activities; the rising crime rate in the 1960s and 1970s was also blamed on the Warren Court's "submissiveness." Since then, under the leadership of the Court by Chief Justices Warren Burger (1969–1985) and William Rehnquist (1985 to present), the balance has shifted: Criminal suspects receive fewer protections, and police officers find it easier to obtain search warrants, interrogate suspects, and conduct lineups. Also, many appellate courts reverse a smaller percentage of convictions appealed to them than they did a few decades ago. Getting tough with criminals has generally been the trend in the 1990s.

Some experts believe that search-and-seizure rules are too complex for the police to execute properly. The search warrant requirement, for example, has more than a dozen exceptions; when the police apply the wrong rules, the search could be deemed illegal, and a guilty defendant could go free. However, some studies show that prosecutions are lost because of suppression rulings less than 1 percent of the time.[2] (See the discussion of the exclusionary rule at the end of this chapter.)

After a crime has been committed, the police may use various means to collect evidence. Police must decide how best to investigate each crime. Should surveillance techniques be used to secure information? Is there reasonable suspicion to justify stopping and frisking a suspect? Has the investigation shifted from a general inquiry and begun to focus on a particular suspect so that the police can start a legally appropriate interrogation? Depending on the circumstances, one investigative technique may be more appropriate than another.

Criminal detection, apprehension, and arrest are the primary investigative functions performed by law enforcement officers.[3] Proper police investigations involve collecting facts and information that will lead to the identification, arrest, and conviction of the criminal. Many police operations are informational — such as referring an alcoholic to a hospital or resolving a family dispute — and based on agency policy or police discretion. In contrast, the primary techniques of investigation — such as stopping and questioning people or interrogating a suspect — are controlled by statute and constitutional case law and are subject to review by the courts.

For a handy summary of the many laws regarding police procedure that can be traced to the Fourth Amendment, go to caselaw.findlaw.com/data/Constitution/amendment04/

The U.S. Supreme Court has taken an active role in reviewing police operations. The Supreme Court has considered numerous appeals charging that police violated a suspect's rights during the investigation, arrest, and custody stages of the justice process. Of primary concern has been police conduct in obtaining and serving search and arrest warrants and in conducting postarrest interrogations and lineups. In some instances, the Court has expanded police power — for example, by increasing the occasions when police can search without a warrant. In other cases, the Court has restricted police operations — for example, by ruling that every criminal suspect has a right to an attorney when being interrogated by police. Changes in the law often reflect such factors as the justices' legal philosophy, their emphasis on the ability of police to control crime, their views on public safety, and their commitment to the civil liberties of criminal defendants. The issues and cases discussed in the following sections reflect the endless ebb and flow of judicial decision making and its impact on the law enforcement process.

search and seizure
The legal term, contained in the Fourth Amendment to the U.S. Constitution, that refers to the searching for and carrying away of evidence by police during a criminal investigation.

Fourth Amendment
The U.S. constitutional amendment that forbids unreasonable searches and seizures and requires probable cause for search warrants.

SEARCH AND SEIZURE

Evidence collected by the police is governed by the **search-and-seizure** requirements of the Fourth Amendment of the U.S. Constitution.[4] The **Fourth Amendment** protects the defendant against unreasonable searches and seizures. Thus, any search or seizure undertaken without a search warrant is unlawful. Also, no warrant will be issued unless there is probable cause to believe that an offense has been or is being committed.

search warrant
An order issued by a judge, directing officers to conduct a search of specified premises for specified objects or persons and bring them before the court.

A **search warrant** is an order from a court authorizing and directing the police to search a designated place for the property stated in the order. The order must be based on the sworn testimony of the police officer that the facts on which the request for the search warrant is made are trustworthy.

Search Warrant Requirements

Three critical concepts in the Fourth Amendment are directly related to the search warrant: unreasonableness, probable cause, and particularity.

unreasonableness
A broad term often used in search-and-seizure law to make certain that a decision is based on reasonable facts and results in a fair and rational decision.

probable cause
The evidentiary criterion necessary to sustain an arrest or the issuance of an arrest or search warrant; less than absolute certainty or "beyond a reasonable doubt" but greater than mere suspicion or "hunch." Probable cause consists of a set of facts, information, circumstances, or conditions that would lead a reasonable person to believe that an offense was committed and that the accused committed that offense. An arrest made without probable cause may be susceptible to prosecution as an illegal arrest under "false imprisonment" statutes.

particularity
The requirement that a search warrant state precisely where the search is to take place and what items are to be seized.

Unreasonableness in searches and seizures generally refers to when a police officer exceeds the scope of police authority. Most unreasonable actions are those in which the officer did not have sufficient information to justify the search. Concerning **probable cause,** the Fourth Amendment provides that a search warrant cannot be obtained unless it is supported by facts that convince the court that a crime has been or is being committed. Regarding **particularity,** the Fourth Amendment requires that a search warrant specify the place to be searched and the reasons for searching it.

In practice, law enforcement officers rarely use a search warrant to enter a home or search a person. But in certain kinds of cases — such as investigations of organized crime, gambling, drug, and pornography cases — search warrants are particularly useful.

Use of Informers

The U.S. Supreme Court has played an active role in interpreting the legal requirements of a search warrant. One of the major issues has been the reliability of the evidence used to support a warrant request. In many instances, the source of the supporting evidence is a police informer. Such information is normally referred to as **hearsay evidence.**

hearsay evidence
Testimony that is not firsthand but relates information told by a second party.

The Supreme Court has determined that such hearsay evidence must be supported by additional evidence. In *Illinois v. Gates* (1983), the Court established that to obtain a warrant the police must prove to a judge that, considering the "totality of the circumstances," there is a fair probability of a crime.[5]

To obtain a search warrant, the following procedural requirements must be met: (1) The police officer must request the warrant from the court; (2) the officer must submit an affidavit establishing the proper grounds for the warrant; and (3) the affidavit must state the place to be searched and the property to be seized.

WARRANTLESS SEARCHES

The courts have established some significant exceptions to the search warrant requirement of the Fourth Amendment. Two critical exceptions are searches incident to a lawful arrest and field interrogations. Other specialized warrantless searches include automobile searches, consent searches, and drug courier profiles. These exceptions, as well as the doctrine of plain view and the law of electric surveillance, are discussed next.

Searches Incident to a Lawful Arrest

search incident to a lawful arrest
An exception to the search warrant rule; limited to the immediate surrounding area.

Traditionally, a search without a search warrant is permissible if it is a **search incident to a lawful arrest.** For example, if shortly after the armed robbery of a grocery store, officers arrest a suspect with a briefcase who is hiding in the basement, a search of the

Chimel v. California
The 1969 U.S. Supreme Court decision that limited the scope of a search made by a police officer to the immediate area under the defendant's control.

Law enforcement officers are permitted to "frisk" a person for weapons if he or she is acting in a suspicious manner. Because the officers have less than probable cause to arrest, the search must be brief and restricted to the person's outer garments.

suspect and of the briefcase would be lawful without a warrant. The legality of this type of search depends almost entirely on the lawfulness of the arrest. The arrest will be upheld if the police officer observed the crime being committed or had probable cause to believe that the suspect committed the offense. If the arrest is found to have been invalid, then any warrantless search made incident to the arrest would be considered illegal, and the evidence obtained from the search would be excluded from trial.

The police officer who searches an arrested suspect must generally observe two rules: (1) Search the suspect at the time of or immediately following the arrest; (2) search only the suspect and the area within the suspect's immediate control, about arm's length from the suspect. Thus, a search may not legally go beyond the area where the suspect can reach for a weapon or destroy evidence. The U.S. Supreme Court dealt with the problem of the permissible scope of a search incident to a lawful arrest in the important case of ***Chimel v. California***.[6] According to the *Chimel* doctrine, the police can search a suspect without a warrant after a lawful arrest to protect themselves from danger and to secure evidence.

On the afternoon of September 13, 1965, three police officers arrived at the Santa Ana, California home of Ted Chimel, with a warrant authorizing his arrest for the burglary of a coin shop. The officers knocked on the door, identified themselves to Chimel's wife, and asked if they could come inside. She admitted the officers into the house, where they waited ten or fifteen minutes until Chimel returned home from work. When he entered the house, one of the officers handed him the arrest warrant and asked for permission to look around. Chimel objected but was advised that the officers could conduct a search on the basis of the lawful arrest. No search warrant had been issued.

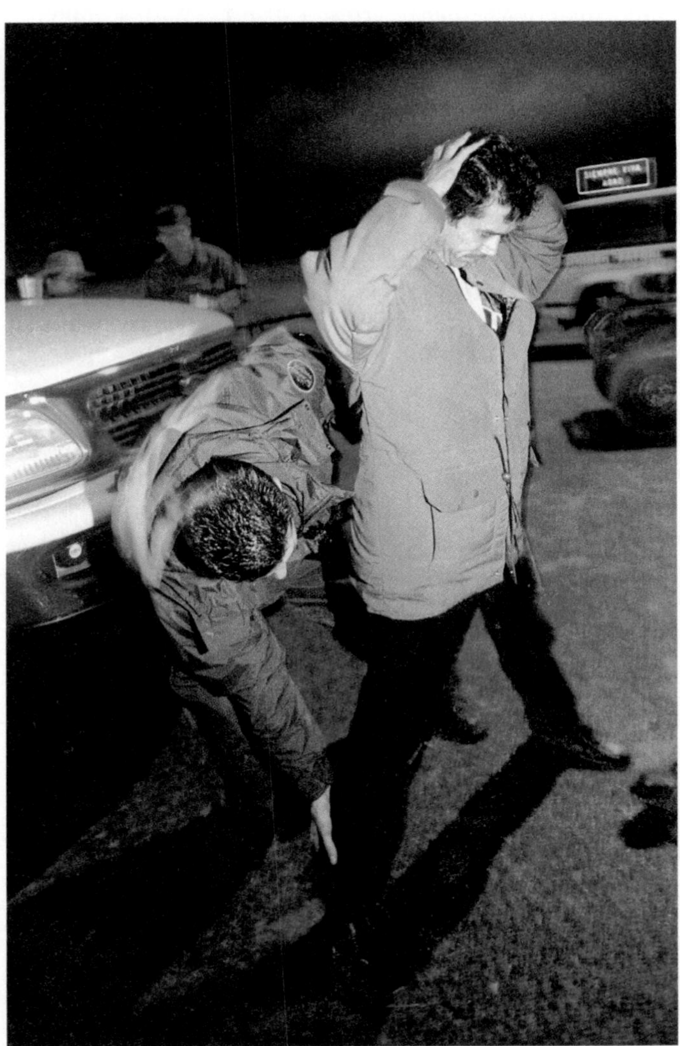

Accompanied by Chimel's wife, the officers then looked through the entire three-bedroom house. The officers told Chimel's wife to open drawers in the master bedroom and sewing room and "to physically move contents of the drawers from side to side so that [they] might view any items that would have come from [the] burglary." After completing the search, the officers seized numerous items, including some coins. The entire search took between forty-five minutes and an hour.

At the defendant's subsequent state trial on two charges of burglary, the coins taken from his house were admitted into evidence against him over his objection that they had been unconstitutionally seized. He was convicted and the judgment was affirmed by the California Supreme Court.

The U.S. Supreme Court decided that the search of Chimel's house went far beyond any area where he might conceivably have obtained a weapon or destroyed any evidence and that no constitutional basis existed for extending the search to all areas of the house. The Court concluded that the scope of the search was unreasonable under the Fourth Amendment as applied through the Fourteenth Amendment, and Chimel's conviction was overturned.

The *Chimel* case changed the policy with regard to the scope of a search made by an officer incident to a lawful arrest. In the past, a police officer was permitted to search all areas under the control of the defendant. The Court's ruling in *Chimel* allows the officer to search only the defendant and the immediate physical surroundings under the defendant's control, generally interpreted as an arm's length distance around the defendant. No longer can a police officer who arrests a person in that person's home search the entire house without a valid search warrant.

threshold inquiry
A term used to describe a stop and frisk.

stop and frisk
The situation in which police officers who are suspicious of an individual run their hands lightly over the suspect's outer garments, to determine whether the person is carrying a concealed weapon. Also called a *patdown* or *threshold inquiry,* a stop and frisk is intended to stop short of any activity that could be considered a violation of Fourth Amendment rights.

Terry v. Ohio
The 1968 U.S. Supreme Court decision upholding the right of the police to conduct a brief inquiry of a suspicious person when they believe such person may be dangerous.

field interrogation
The questioning by police of a person suspected of a crime at the time of apprehension and arrest.

Field Interrogation: Stop and Frisk

Another important exception to the rule requiring a search warrant is the **threshold inquiry,** or the **stop-and-frisk** procedure. Police officers frequently stop people behaving in a suspicious manner or about whom complaints are being made. Ordinarily, police are not required to have enough evidence for an arrest in order to stop a person for brief questioning. If police could stop a person only when making an arrest, they would be prevented from investigating many potentially criminal situations. For this reason, the courts have given the police the authority to stop a person, ask questions, and search the person in a limited way, such as frisking for a concealed weapon. The courts have concluded that it is unreasonable to expect a police officer to decide immediately whether to arrest a suspect. With a limited power to stop and frisk, the officer can investigate suspicious persons and situations without having to meet the probable cause standard for arrest. If the officer did not have this authority, many innocent individuals would probably be arrested.

In the 1968 landmark case of ***Terry v. Ohio,*** the U.S. Supreme Court established the standard for police to stop and frisk a suspect based on reasonable suspicion. That is, police can stop someone when they have reason to believe that she may be armed and dangerous to the police or others.[7] The Court's intention was to allow the officer, who interacts with members of the community many times each day, to conduct proper investigations where necessary, while keeping invasions of personal rights to a minimum and protecting the officer from harm.[8]

The **field interrogation** process is based primarily on the police officer's ability to determine whether suspicious conduct exists that gives the officer reason to believe that a crime is about to be committed. Some jurisdictions have enacted legislation authorizing the stop-and-frisk procedure, thereby codifying the standard established in *Terry v. Ohio*. Courts have ruled that frisking must be limited to when the police officer determines that his safety or that of others is at stake. The stop-and-frisk exception cannot be used to harass citizens or conduct exploratory searches.

Motor Vehicle Searches

The U.S. Supreme Court has also established that certain situations justify the warrantless search of a motor vehicle on a public street or highway. In *Carroll v. United States,* the Supreme Court ruled that distinctions should be made between searches of motor vehicles, persons, and homes. The Court also concluded that a warrantless search of a motor vehicle is valid if the police have probable cause to believe that it contains evidence they are seeking.[9]

The legality of searching motor vehicles without a warrant has always been a trouble spot for police and the courts. Should the search be limited to the interior, or can the police search the trunk? What about a suitcase in the trunk? What about the glove compartment? Does a traffic citation give the police the

Police search a vehicle incident to an arrest. In *United States v. Ross,* the U.S. Supreme Court ruled such searches could be conducted without a warrant if there was probable cause that the vehicle had been involved in a crime and contained criminal evidence.

right to search a motor vehicle? These questions have produced significant litigation over the years. To clear up the matter, the Supreme Court decided the landmark case of ***United States v. Ross*** in 1982.[10] The *Ross* case held that police officers who legitimately stop a vehicle and who have probable cause to believe that contraband is concealed within it may conduct a warrantless search of the vehicle. In sum, the most important requirement for a warrantless search of a motor vehicle is that it must be based on the legal standard of probable cause that a crime related to the vehicle has been or is being committed. Police who undertake the search of a vehicle must have reason to believe that it contains evidence pertaining to the crime. Of special concern are the major constitutional cases and rules regarding traffic stops, described in the Policy, Programs, and Issues in Criminal Justice feature.

United States v. Ross
The 1982 U.S. Supreme Court decision upholding that a warrantless search of an automobile is permissible if probable cause exists to believe that the vehicle contains criminal evidence.

Consent Searches

Police officers may also undertake warrantless searches when the suspect consents to the search. Those who agree to a **consent search** essentially waive their constitutional rights under the Fourth Amendment. Ordinarily, courts are reluctant to accept such waivers and require the state to prove that the consent was voluntarily and intelligently given. In some jurisdictions, consent searches are valid only after the suspect is informed of the option to refuse consent.

consent search
A voluntary agreement to allow a search with the knowledge that any evidence may be used at the defendant's trial.

The major legal issue in most consent searches is whether the police can prove that consent was given voluntarily. For example, in the 1968 case of *Bumper v. North Carolina,* police officers searched the home of an elderly woman after informing her that they possessed a search warrant.[11] At the trial, the prosecutor informed the court that the search was valid because the woman had given her consent. When the government could not produce the warrant, the court decided that the search was invalid because the woman's consent was not given voluntarily. On appeal, the U.S. Supreme Court upheld the lower-court finding that the consent had been illegally obtained by the false claim of the police.

In most consent searches, however, voluntariness is a question of fact to be determined from all circumstances of the case. In *Schneckloth v. Bustamonte*, for example, where the defendant actually helped the police by opening the trunk and glove compartment of the car, the Supreme Court said this demonstrated that the consent was voluntarily given.[12] Furthermore, the police are usually under no obligation to inform a suspect of the right to refuse consent. Failure to

Policy, Programs, and Issues in Criminal Justice

TRAFFIC STOPS: UNDERCUTTING THE FOURTH AMENDMENT

Of special concern to the police and the public are the constitutional rules regarding traffic stops. In 1977 the U.S. Supreme Court ruled in *Pennsylvania v. Mimms* that officers could order drivers out of their cars during routine traffic stops; officers' safety outweighed the intrusion on individual rights. It came as no surprise in 1997 when the Supreme Court held in *Maryland v. Wilson* that the police had the same authority with respect to passengers. In the *Wilson* case, a state patrol officer lawfully stopped a vehicle for speeding. While the driver was producing his license, the front-seat passenger, Wilson, was ordered out of the vehicle. As he exited, crack cocaine dropped to the ground. Wilson was arrested and convicted of drug possession. His attorney moved to suppress the evidence, and the Maryland Appeals Court agreed. But the Supreme Court disagreed and extended the *Mimms* rule to passengers. The decision means that passengers must comply when ordered out of a lawfully stopped vehicle.

In other decisions, the Court further bolstered police powers in traffic stops. The legality of *pretext stops* (those where police use traffic violations as an exercise to stop a vehicle) was challenged in *Whren v. United States* (1996). Two black defendants claimed that plainclothes police officers used traffic violations as an exercise to stop their vehicle because the officers lacked objective evidence that they were drug couriers. The Court said, however, that if probable cause exists to stop a person for a traffic violation, the motivation of the officers is irrelevant.

In *Ohio v. Robinette* (1996), the key issue was whether police officers must inform detained drivers that they are "free to go" before asking consent to search the vehicle. The Court concluded that no such warning is needed to make consent to search reasonable. Robinette was stopped for speeding. After checking his license, the officer asked if Robinette was carrying any illegal contraband in the car. When the defendant answered in the negative, the officer asked and received permission to search the car. The search turned up illegal drugs. The Court said that the Ohio rule that an officer may not obtain consent to search in a valid traffic stop situation without first notifying the defendant that she is free to go is illegal. According to the Court, the touchstone of the Fourth Amendment is reasonableness, and it is assessed by examining the totality of the circumstances, not by applying rigid rules.

In 1999 the Supreme Court ruled that a police officer could also search the property of any passenger in a suspect's car. (See the chapter-opening vignette, which describes the facts of the *Wyoming v. Houghton* case.) But in a surprise decision, *Knowles v. Iowa* (1998), the Court rejected a search incident to the issuance of a traffic citation. When a police officer stopped a defendant for speeding and then searched a car without probable cause or consent, finding drugs, the Court said the search violated the Fourth Amendment. The search was not justified by either of the two bases relied upon by the Court in past decisions — the protection of the officer or the need to discover or preserve evidence.

Critical Thinking

The U.S. Supreme Court has decided that police are allowed to make pretextual stops without knowing that a search will produce drugs. They can order drivers and passengers out of cars during routine traffic stops. Further, they are not required to tell drivers that they are free to go before asking for consent to search a vehicle. What is the impact of these Court decisions?

Legal experts believe that the public interest in protecting an officer's safety outweighs the intrusion on a driver's rights. Do you agree? Explain.

Think about how many thousands of innocent passengers are involved in traffic stops every day. Is the risk to the police outweighed by the intrusion on the privacy rights of so many citizens? Explain.

One of the major issues with this line of cases is whether it will be easier for the police to target minority motorists for traffic stops. Do you think it will be? Explain.

InfoTrac College Edition Research

Use *InfoTrac College Edition* to read more about automobile searches. Look under "probable cause," "search warrant," and "electronic surveillance" to broaden your understanding of Fourth Amendment law.

SOURCES: *Maryland v. Wilson*, 65 U.S.L.W. 4124, February 19, 1997; *Ohio v. Robinette*, 117 S.Ct. 417 (1996); *Whren v. United States*, 116 S.Ct. 1769 (1996); Mark Hansen, "Rousting Miss Daisy?" *American Bar Association Journal* 83 (1997): 22; *Knowles v. Iowa*, 119 S.Ct. 507 (1998); *Wyoming v. Houghton*, 119 S.Ct. 1297 (1999).

tell a suspect of this right does not make the search illegal, but it may be a factor used by courts to decide whether the suspect gave consent voluntarily.

The Bus Sweep Today, consent searches have additional significance because of their use in drug control programs. On June 20, 1991 the U.S. Supreme Court, in ***Florida v. Bostick,*** upheld the police technique of boarding buses and, without suspicion of illegal activity, questioning passengers, asking for identification, and requesting permission to search luggage.[13] Using what is known as the **bus sweep,** police in the *Bostick* case boarded a bus during a stopover in Fort Lauderdale. The officers picked out the defendant and asked to inspect his ticket and identification. After identifying themselves as narcotics officers looking for illegal drugs, they asked to inspect the defendant's luggage. Although it is not clear whether the defendant consented to the search in which contraband was found and whether he was informed of his right to refuse to consent to the search, he was convicted.

Florida v. Bostick
The 1991 U.S. Supreme Court decision upholding the police investigation technique known as the *bus sweep,* where without probable cause the police can search a person's luggage.

bus sweep
Police investigation technique where the police board a bus or train without suspicion of illegal activity and question passengers, asking for identification and seeking permission to search their baggage.

The Supreme Court was faced with deciding whether consent was freely given or whether the nature of the bus sweep search negated the defendant's consent. Justice Sandra Day O'Connor, writing for the majority, said that police asking questions and requesting to search luggage does not constitute a "seizure" in every instance.[14] In other words, drug enforcement officers, after obtaining consent, may search luggage on a crowded bus without a search warrant or probable cause.

This case raises fundamental questions about the legality of new techniques used to discourage drug trafficking. Law enforcement officials are concerned about intercepting large amounts of drugs and money. Bus sweeps are one answer to the drug menace. But is the Supreme Court compromising individual Fourth Amendment rights when it considers these encounters between police and citizens to be consensual in nature?

A similar issue involves expanding police officers' searches in public housing projects. Supporters of "gun sweeps" argue that the danger of gun violence in the projects constitutes an emergency circumstance in which the Supreme Court may uphold such a warrantless search.

The Doctrines of Plain View and Curtilage Another instance in which police can seize evidence without benefit of a warrant is if it is in plain view. For example, if a police officer notices that one person in a group that he is legally questioning has drugs in her pocket, the officer could seize the evidence and arrest the suspect. Or if the police are conducting a search under a warrant for narcotics and they come upon a gun in the home, they can seize the gun, even though it is not mentioned in the warrant. The 1986 case of *New York v. Class* illustrates the **plain-view doctrine.**[15] A police officer stopped a car for a traffic violation. Wishing to check the vehicle identification number on the dashboard, he reached into the car to clear away material that was obstructing his view and noticed a gun under the seat — "in plain view." The U.S. Supreme Court upheld the seizure of the gun because the police officer had the right to check the vehicle number.

plain-view doctrine
The doctrine that evidence in plain view to police officers may be seized without a search warrant.

The plain-view doctrine was applied and further developed in *Arizona v. Hicks* in 1987.[16] Here, the Supreme Court held that moving a stereo component in plain view a few inches in order to record the serial number constituted a search under the Fourth Amendment. When a check with police headquarters revealed the item had been stolen, the equipment was seized and offered for evidence at Hicks's trial. The Court held that a plain-view search and seizure could only be justified by probable cause, not reasonable suspicion, and suppressed the

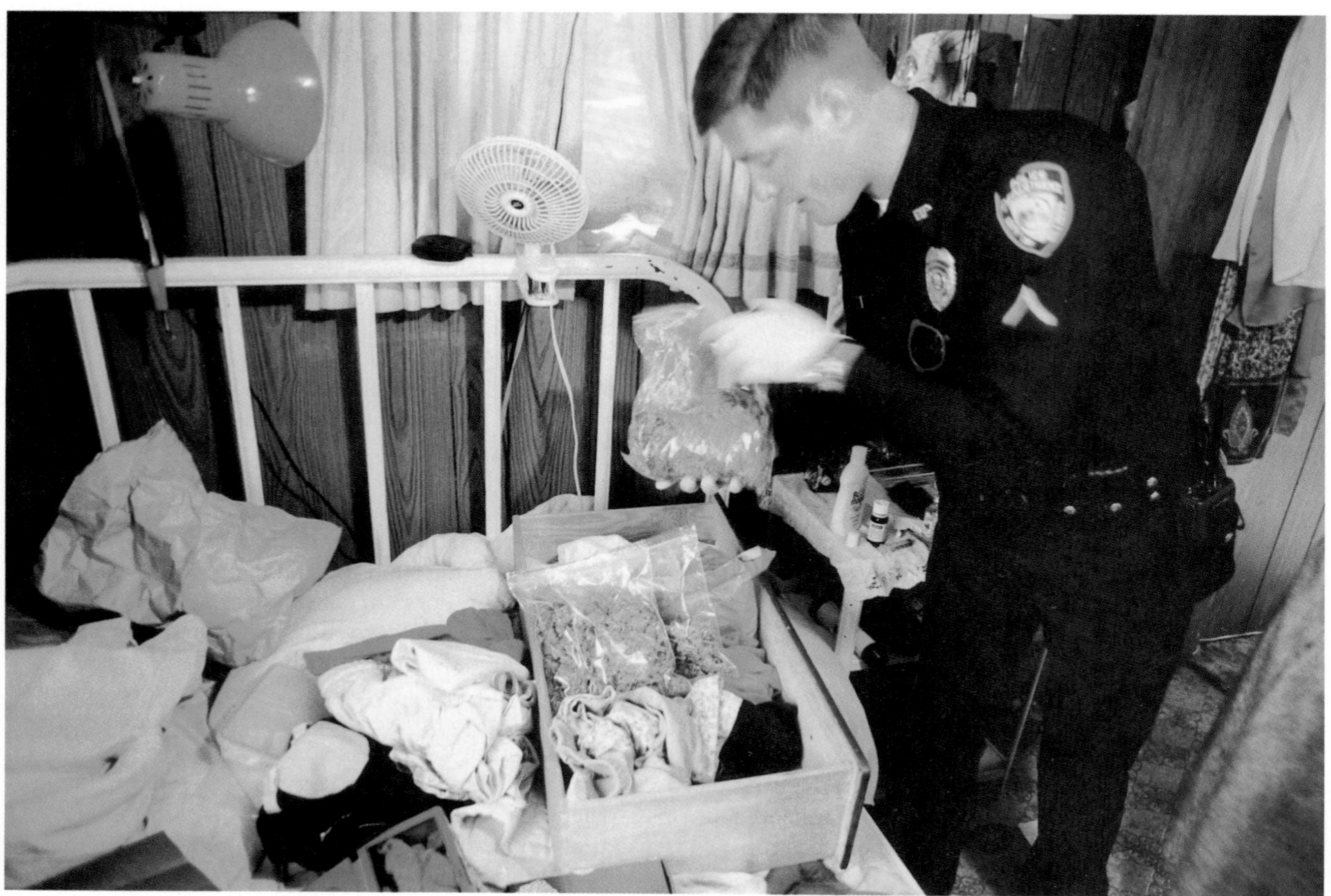

The Supreme Court has allowed police officers who see contraband or evidence in plain view to seize it without a warrant. For example, if they stop a car for a traffic violation and see drugs on the seat, they are allowed to seize the drugs. Here, an officer seizes drugs that were found in "plain view" during a routine investigation.

evidence against the defendant. In this case, the Court decided to take a firm stance on protecting Fourth Amendment rights. The standard of reasonable suspicion, as opposed to probable cause, was not enough in this case. The *Hicks* decision is uncharacteristic in an era when most decisions have tended to expand the exceptions to the search warrant requirement.

By way of analogy, the concept of the plain-view doctrine has been extended to the *plain-feel doctrine*. In *Minnesota v. Dickerson*, a police officer patting down a suspect who had been validly stopped under *Terry v. Ohio* may seize an object whose contour and mass make it apparent it is a sizable object.[17] The patdown must be limited to a search for weapons. The case in effect expands the idea of plain view to embrace all senses, not merely that of sight.

An issue long associated with plain view is whether police can search open fields, which are fenced in but are otherwise open to view. In *Oliver v. United States* (1984), the U.S. Supreme Court distinguished between the privacy granted persons in their own home or its adjacent grounds (**curtilage**) and a field. The Court ruled that police can use airplane surveillance to spot marijuana fields and then send in squads to seize the crops, or they can peer into fields from cars for the same purpose.[18]

curtilage
The fields attached to a house.

These cases illustrate how the concepts of curtilage, plain feel, and open fields have added significance in defining the scope of the Fourth Amendment in terms of the plain-view doctrine.

wiretapping
The use of a concealed listening or recording device, done with judicial approval for the purpose of obtaining evidence of criminal activity.

Court TV hosts a useful Web site on search and seizure law. The site offers FAQs and links to other sites that deal with this issue. Go to www.courttv.com/legalcafe/home/search/

Electronic Surveillance

The use of wiretapping to intercept secret conversations between parties has significantly affected police investigative procedures. Electronic devices allow people to listen to and record the private conversations of others over telephones, through walls and windows, and even over long-distance phone lines.

The earliest and most widely used form of electronic surveillance is **wiretapping.** With approval from the court and a search warrant, law enforcement officers place listening devices that allow them to tap into private telephone conversations. Such devices are often placed in homes and automobiles.

Electronic eavesdropping represents an invasion of an individual's privacy, unless a court gives prior permission to intercept conversations in this manner. Police can obtain criminal evidence by eavesdropping only if such activities are controlled under rigid guidelines established under the Fourth Amendment, and they must normally request a court order based on probable cause before using electronic eavesdropping equipment.

Many citizens believe that electronic eavesdropping through hidden microphones, radio transmitters, and telephone taps and bugs represents a grave threat to privacy.[19] Although the use of such devices is controversial, the police are generally convinced of their value in investigating criminal activity. Others, however, believe that these techniques are often used beyond their lawful intent, to monitor political figures, harass suspects, or investigate cases involving questionable issues of national security.

In response to concerns about invasions of privacy, the U.S. Supreme Court has increasingly limited the use of electronic eavesdropping in the criminal justice system. *Katz v. United States* (1967) is an example of a case in which the government failed to meet the requirements necessary to justify electronic surveillance.[20] The *Katz* doctrine is usually interpreted to mean that the government must obtain a court order if it wishes to listen into conversations in which the parties have a reasonable expectation of privacy, such as in their own homes or on the telephone; public utterances or actions are fair game. *Katz* concluded that electronic eavesdropping is a search, even though there is no actual trespass. Therefore, a warrant is needed.

Congress has also passed legislation to control the interception of oral communications. The Omnibus Crime Control Act (Title III) of 1968 prohibited lawful interceptions except by warrant or with consent.[21] The federal electronic surveillance law was modified by the Electronic Communications Privacy Act of 1986.[22] In light of technological changes, Title III of the new act was expanded to include not only all forms of wire and oral communications but also virtually all types of electronic communication. The law added new offenses to the previous list of crimes for which electronic surveillance could be used and liberalized court procedures for permitting such surveillance.

The United States has over 80 million people on the Internet. The advent of e-commerce, for instance, endangers our privacy and gives criminals the opportunity to steal Social Security and credit card numbers and passwords, wage cyberwar, and commit software piracy. Since almost 50 percent of Americans send or receive e-mail everyday, new legislation will be needed in the future to deal with crimes unheard of today.[23]

The basic principle of the law of electronic surveillance is that wiretapping and other devices that violate privacy are contrary to the Fourth Amendment. As a result of technological advances, such devices probably pose a greater threat to personal privacy than physical searches. The U.S. Supreme Court has permitted only narrow exceptions, such as court-ordered warrants and consensual monitoring.[24]

ARREST

The arrest power of the police involves taking a person into custody in accordance with lawful authority and holding that person to answer for a violation of the criminal law. For all practical purposes, the authority of the police to arrest a suspect is the basis for crime control; without such authority, the police would be powerless to implement the criminal law.

The arrest power is used primarily by law enforcement officers. Generally, law enforcement personnel are employed by public police agencies, derive their authority from statutory laws, and take an oath to uphold the laws of their jurisdiction. Most police officers have complete law enforcement responsibility and unrestricted powers of arrest in their jurisdictions; they carry firearms, and they give evidence in criminal trials.

arrest
The taking of a person into the custody of the law, the legal purpose of which is to restrain the accused until he or she can be held accountable for the offense at court proceedings. The legal requirement for an arrest is probable cause. Arrests for investigation, suspicion, or harassment are improper and of doubtful legality. The police have the responsibility to use only the reasonable physical force necessary to make an arrest. The summons has been used as a substitute for arrest.

An **arrest,** the first formal police procedure in the criminal justice process, occurs when a police officer takes a person into custody or deprives a person of freedom for having allegedly committed a criminal offense. Because the police stop large numbers of people each day for a variety of reasons, the time when an arrest actually occurs may be hard to pinpoint. Some people are stopped for brief periods of questioning, others are informally detained and released, and still others are formally placed under arrest. An arrest occurs when the following conditions exist:

1. The police officer believes that there is sufficient evidence of a crime to restrain the suspect.
2. The officer deprives the individual of freedom.
3. The suspect believes that she is in the custody of the officer and cannot voluntarily leave.

The police officer is not required to exclaim "You're under arrest!" as usually presented in TV dramas, nor does the officer first have to haul the suspect to the station house. Basically, a person who has been deprived of liberty is under arrest.

The *arrest warrant,* an order issued by the court, determines that an arrest should be made and directs the police to bring the named person before the court. An arrest warrant must be based on probable cause that the person to be arrested has committed or is attempting to commit a crime. The police will ordinarily go before a judge and obtain a warrant where no danger exists that the suspect will leave the area, where a long-term investigation of organized crime is under way, or where probable cause exists to arrest the suspect.

Most arrests are made without a warrant. The decision to arrest is often made by the police officer during contact with the suspect. However, an arrest may be made without a warrant only in the following two circumstances:

1. The arresting officer can establish probable cause that a crime has been committed and that the defendant is the person who committed it.
2. The law of a given jurisdiction allows for arrest without a warrant.

In the case of a felony, most jurisdictions provide that police officers may arrest a suspect without a warrant where probable cause exists, even if the officers did not see the crime being committed. In the case of a misdemeanor, officers need to observe the crime firsthand, but many states have eliminated this requirement. This is important for such crimes as domestic violence, shoplifting, or cases where the suspect will escape if not arrested immediately.

As a general rule, if the police make an arrest without a warrant, the person arrested must be brought promptly before a magistrate, for a probable cause

In order for a legal arrest to occur, the police must have sufficient evidence to restrain suspects and deprive them of their liberty. An arrest can be initiated with a court ordered warrant or if the police officer on his or her own initiative develops "probable cause" that a suspect has been involved in a serious crime.

hearing. The U.S. Supreme Court dealt with the meaning of *promptness* in the 1991 case of *Riverside County v. McLaughlin.*[25] The Court said that the police may detain an individual arrested without a warrant for up to forty-eight hours without a court hearing. This decision takes into account the state's interest in taking suspects into custody and the individual's concern about prolonged custody affecting employment and family relations.

Interrogation of a Suspect: The *Miranda* Case Prior to the 1966 landmark case *Miranda v. Arizona,* suspects might make statements to police without knowing they could remain silent to avoid self-incrimination (a Fifth Amendment right). Also, police could take confessions from suspects who had not consulted with an attorney (a Sixth Amendment right). In the *Miranda* case, which is described in the Law in Review feature, the U.S. Supreme Court held that the police must give the ***Miranda* warning** to a person in custody before questioning begins.[26] Suspects in custody must be told that they have the following rights:

***Miranda* warning**
The result of two U.S. Supreme Court decisions (*Escobedo v. Illinois* and *Miranda v. Arizona*) that require police officers to inform individuals under arrest that they have a constitutional right to remain silent, that their statements can later be used against them in court, that they can have an attorney present to help them, and that the state will pay for an attorney if they cannot afford to hire one. Although aimed at protecting an individual during in-custody interrogation, the warning must also be given when the investigation shifts from the investigatory to the accusatory stage — that is, when suspicion begins to focus on an individual.

1. They have the right to remain silent.
2. If they decide to make a statement, the statement can and will be used against them in a court of law.
3. They have the right to consult with an attorney before questioning and to have an attorney present at the time of the interrogation.
4. If they cannot afford an attorney, one will be appointed for them by the state.

Most suspects choose to remain silent, and since oral as well as written statements are admissible in court, police officers often do not elicit any statements without making certain a defense attorney is present. If an accused decides to answer any questions, he may also stop at any time and refuse to answer further questions. A suspect's constitutional rights under *Miranda* can be

Law in Review

MIRANDA V. ARIZONA (1966)

Miranda v. Arizona is a landmark decision that climaxed a long line of self-incrimination cases in which the police used unreasonable methods to obtain confessions from suspects accused of committing a crime.

Facts

Ernesto Miranda, a twenty-five-year-old mentally retarded man, was arrested in Phoenix, Arizona, and charged with kidnapping and rape. Miranda was taken from his home to a police station, where he was identified by a complaining witness. After about two hours of interrogation, he signed a written confession. Miranda was subsequently convicted and sentenced to twenty to thirty years in prison. His conviction was affirmed by the Arizona Supreme Court, and he appealed to the U.S. Supreme Court, claiming that he had not been warned that any statement he made would be used against him and that he had not been advised of any right to have counsel present at his interrogation.

The *Miranda* case was one of four cases heard simultaneously by the U.S. Supreme Court, which dealt with the legality of confessions obtained by the police from a suspect in custody. In *Vignera v. New York* (1966), the defendant was arrested in connection with a robbery and taken to two different detective headquarters, where he was interrogated and subsequently confessed after eight hours in custody. In *Westover v. United States* (1966), the suspect was arrested by the Kansas City police, placed in a lineup and booked on a felony charge. He was interrogated by the police during the evening and the morning and by the FBI in the afternoon, when he signed two confessions. In *California v. Steward* (1966), the defendant was arrested at his home for being involved in a robbery. He was taken to a police station and placed in a cell, where over a period of five days he was interrogated nine times. The Supreme Court in *Miranda* described the common characteristics of these four cases:

> In each, the defendant was questioned by the police in a room in which he was cut off from the outside world. In none of these cases was the defendant given a full and effective warning of his rights at the outset of the interrogation process. In all the cases, the questioning elicited oral admissions, and in three of them, signed statements as well which were admitted at their trials. They all thus share salient features — incommunicado interrogation of individuals in a police-dominated atmosphere, resulting in self-incriminating statements without full warnings of constitutional rights.

Decision

The major constitutional issue in *Miranda,* as in the other three cases, was the admissibility of statements obtained from a defendant questioned while in custody or while otherwise deprived of his freedom. The Fifth Amendment provides that no person shall be compelled to be a witness against herself. This means that a defendant cannot be required to testify at her trial and that a suspect who is questioned before trial cannot be subjected to any physical or psychological pressure to confess.

In the opinion of Chief Justice Earl Warren in the *Miranda* case, "the third degree method was still 'sufficiently widespread to be the object of concern.'" Of greater concern, he believed, was the increased use of sophisticated psychological pressures on suspects during interrogation. Thus, in a 5-to-4 decision, Miranda's conviction was overturned, and the Court established specific procedural guidelines for police to follow before eliciting statements from persons in police custody.

The Court's own summary of its decision is as follows:

> Our holding will be spelled out with some specificity in the pages which follow but briefly it is this: the prosecution may not use statements, whether exculpatory or inculpatory, stemming from custodial interrogation of the defendant unless it demonstrates the use of procedural safeguards effective to secure the privilege against self-incrimination. By custodial interrogation, we mean questioning initiated by law enforcement officers after a person has been taken into custody or otherwise deprived of his freedom of action in any significant way. As for the procedural safeguards to be employed, unless fully effective means are devised to inform accused persons of their right of silence and to assure a continuous opportunity to exercise it, the following measures are required. Prior to any questioning the person must be warned that he has the right to remain silent, that any statement he does make may be used as evidence against him, and that he has a right to the presence of an attorney, either retained or appointed. The defendant may waive effectuation of these rights, provided the waiver is made voluntarily, knowingly, and intelligently. If, however, he indicates in any manner and at any stage of the process that he wishes to consult with an attorney before speaking, there can be no questioning. Likewise, if the individual is alone and indicates in any manner that he does not wish to be interrogated, the police may not question him. The mere fact that he may have answered some questions or volunteered some statements on his own does not deprive him of the right to refrain from answering any further inquiries until he has consulted with an attorney and thereafter consents to be questioned.

Significance of the Case

The *Miranda* decision established that the Fifth Amendment privilege against self-incrimination requires that a criminal suspect in custody or in any other manner deprived of freedom must be informed of his rights. If the suspect is not warned, then any evidence given is not admissible by the government to prove its case. It also established that the Sixth Amendment right to counsel applied to a suspect.

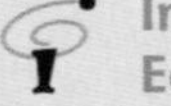

InfoTrac College Edition Research

Many experts consider the *Miranda* case the hallmark decision of the Warren Court. Go to *InfoTrac College Edition* to read more about this landmark case. See

> Richard Leo, "*Miranda* Re-visited," *Journal of Criminal Law and Criminology* 86 (1996): 621.

A *Miranda* card, spelling out the famous warning, has become a routine element of police paraphernalia.

given up *(waived)*, however. Consequently, a suspect should give careful consideration before abrogating any custodial rights under the *Miranda* warning.

Over thirty years have passed since this warning was established by the Warren Court. During this time, U.S. appellate courts have heard literally thousands of cases involving alleged violations of *Miranda* rights, custodial interrogation, right to counsel, and statements made to persons other than the police, among others. Some experts believe felons have been freed because of the *Miranda* decision.

Escobedo v. Illinois
The 1964 U.S. Supreme Court decision upholding that the Sixth Amendment, which guarantees the right to counsel, applies to preindictment interrogations when the accused asks to consult with an attorney.

As previously indicated, prior to the *Miranda* safeguards, confessions could be obtained from a suspect. An early ruling in *Brown v. Mississippi* (1936) held that statements obtained by physical coercion were inadmissible evidence, but it also limited the use of counsel to aid the accused at this early stage of the criminal process.[27] Not until 1964 in ***Escobedo v. Illinois*** was the groundwork laid for the *Miranda* decision. The U.S. Supreme Court finally recognized the critical relationship between the Fifth Amendment privilege against self-incrimination and the Sixth Amendment right to counsel. Danny Escobedo was a convicted murderer who maintained that the police questioning forced him to make statements that were regarded as a voluntary confession. In *Escobedo*, the Court recognized that he had been denied the assistance of counsel, which was critical during police interrogation. With this decision, the Court made clear its concern a suspect should be permitted certain due process rights during interrogation.[28]

Two years later came the *Miranda* decision, which has had an historic impact on police interrogation practices at the arrest stage of the criminal justice process. Now, suspects are read their *Miranda* rights before questioning. In fact, police commonly carry a card listing these rights.

If the accused is not given the *Miranda* warning, any evidence obtained during interrogation is not admissible. It is important to note, however, that the *Miranda* decision does not deny the police the opportunity to ask questions of a witness at the scene of the crime, as long as the person is not in custody and the questioning is nonaccusatory. In addition, a suspect can still offer a voluntary confession after the *Miranda* warning has been read.

After the *Miranda* decision, many people became concerned that the U.S. Supreme Court under Chief Justice Earl Warren had gone too far in providing protections to suspects. Some public figures even warned that the Court was emptying the prisons of criminals, and law enforcement officers throughout the nation expressed concern that *Miranda* would seriously hamper their efforts to obtain confessions and other self-incriminating statements from defendants. Early research indicated, however, that the decision had little or no effect on the number of confessions obtained by the police and that it has not affected the rate of convictions.[29] Since *Miranda,* little empirical evidence has been produced showing that the decision has had a detrimental impact on law enforcement efforts.

In conclusion, *Miranda,* one of the best known U.S. Supreme Court decisions of the twentieth century could be on its way back to the court for reconsideration as one of the nation's legal fixtures for over three decades. The impetus is a U.S. Circuit Court of Appeals decision, *United States v. Dickerson* (1999), which ruled that a bank robbery suspect's voluntary confession is valid even if the police have not informed the suspect of his *Miranda* rights.[30] The court's reason: The U.S. Department of Justice has declined to enforce a law passed by Congress in 1968 essentially reversing *Miranda.* Incorporated into the U.S. Code as 18 U.S.C.A., section 3501, it restored the pre-*Miranda* voluntary standards, declaring that a confession "shall be admissible if it is voluntarily given." For over three decades, the Justice Department has maintained that 18 U.S.C.A., section 3501, was unconstitutional. But *Miranda* was never overturned.

Table 7.1 summarizes some of the most significant Fourth and Fifth Amendment Supreme Court decisions that have had an impact on law enforcement practices and individual rights.

THE PRETRIAL IDENTIFICATION PROCESS

After someone accused is arrested, she is ordinarily brought to the police station, where the police list the possible criminal charges. At the same time, they obtain other information, such as a description of the offender and the circumstances of the offense, for booking purposes. The **booking process** is a police administrative procedure in which generally the date and time of the arrest are recorded; arrangements are made for bail, detention, or removal to court; and any other information needed for identification is obtained. The defendant may be fingerprinted, photographed, and required to participate in a lineup. In a lineup, a suspect is placed in a group for the purpose of being viewed and identified by a witness. In accordance with the U.S. Supreme Court decisions in *United States v. Wade* (1967)[31] and *Kirby v. Illinois* (1972),[32] the accused has the right to have counsel present at this postindictment lineup or identification procedure.

booking process
The administrative record of an arrest, listing the offender's name, address, physical description, date of birth, and employer; the time of arrest; the offense; and the name of the arresting officer. Photographing and fingerprinting of the offender are also part of the booking process.

In the *Wade* case, the Supreme Court held that a defendant has a right to counsel if the lineup takes place after the suspect has been formally charged. The Court believed that the lineup is a critical stage of the criminal justice process. If this right to counsel is violated, the evidence of the lineup identification must be excluded from the trial.

One of the most difficult legal issues is determining whether the identification procedure is "suggestive" and consequently violates the due process clause of the Fifth and Fourteenth Amendments. In *Simmons v. United States* (1968), the U.S. Supreme Court said, "The primary evil to be avoided is a very substantial likelihood of irreparable misidentification."[33] In its decision in *Neil v. Biggers* (1972), the Court established the following general criteria to judge the suggestiveness of a pretrial identification procedure: (1) the opportunity of the witness to view the criminal at the time of the crime, (2) the degree of attention by the witness and the accuracy of the prior description by the witness, (3) the

During the booking process, police identify suspects, take their fingerprints, bring in witnesses for purposes of identification, and interrogate suspects about their suspected criminal activities.

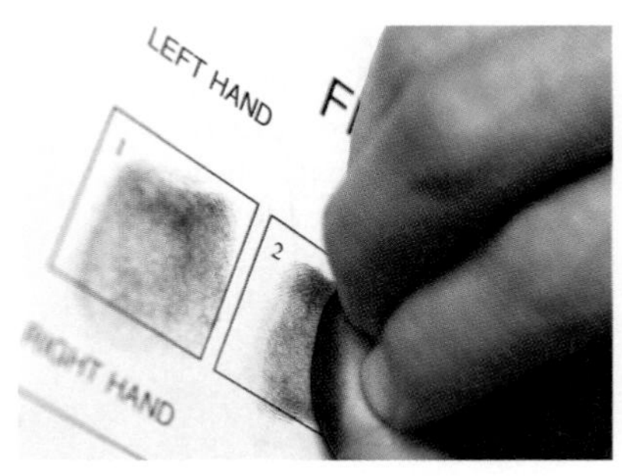

level of certainty demonstrated by the witness, and (4) the length of time between the crime and the confrontation.[34]

THE EXCLUSIONARY RULE

No review of the legal aspects of policing would be complete without a discussion of the exclusionary rule, the principal means used to restrain police conduct. As previously mentioned, the Fourth Amendment guarantees individuals the right to be secure in their persons, homes, papers, and effects against unreasonable searches and seizures. The **exclusionary rule** provides that all evidence obtained by *unreasonable* searches and seizures is inadmissible in criminal trials. Similarly, it excludes the use of illegal confessions under Fifth Amendment prohibitions.

exclusionary rule
The principle that prohibits using evidence illegally obtained in a trial. Based on the Fourth Amendment "right of the people to be secure in their persons, houses, papers, and effects, against unreasonable searches and seizures," the rule is not a bar to prosecution because legally obtained evidence may be available that may be used in a trial.

For many years, evidence obtained by unreasonable searches and seizures was admitted by state and federal governments in criminal trials. The only criteria for admissibility were whether the evidence was incriminating and whether it would assist the judge or jury in reaching a verdict. How the evidence was obtained was unimportant; its admissibility was determined by its relevance to the criminal case.

In 1914, however, the U.S. Supreme Court established the exclusionary rule in the case of *Weeks v. United States*.[35] The defendant, Freemont Weeks, was accused of using the mail for illegal purposes. After his arrest, his home was searched without a valid search warrant. Letters and other materials found in his room were admitted as evidence at the trial, and Weeks was convicted based on incriminating evidence. On appeal, the Supreme Court held that evidence obtained by unreasonable search and seizure must be excluded in a federal criminal trial.

Thus, for the first time, the Court held that the Fourth Amendment barred the use, in a federal prosecution, of evidence obtained through illegal search and seizure. With this ruling, the Court established the exclusionary rule. The rule was based not on legislation but on judicial decision making. Can the criminal go free because the constable blunders? That became the question.

Mapp v. Ohio
The 1961 U.S. Supreme Court decision that applied the exclusionary rule to state criminal cases where evidence acquired through an unreasonable search and seizure must be excluded.

In 1961 the Supreme Court made the exclusionary rule applicable to state courts in the landmark decision of ***Mapp v. Ohio***.[36] Because of the importance of the *Mapp* case, it is discussed in the Law in Review feature.

Table 7.1
Notable Case Doctrines and Exceptions to the Fourth Amendment (Search and Seizure) and Fifth Amendment (Self-Incrimination) Clauses: Balancing Individual Rights and Law Enforcement

Fourth Amendment Doctrine on Privacy	Cases	Decisions
Exigent or emergency	*Mincey v. Arizona* (1978)	There is no murder-scene exception to the requirement for a search warrant unless there is an emergency, which usually refers to a life-threatening emergency.
Expectation of privacy	*Katz v. United States* (1967)	Electronic eavesdropping is a search.
Open fields	*Oliver v. United States* (1984)	To what extent can police search a field and curtilage?
Plain view	*Arizona v. Hicks* (1987)	Fourth Amendment may not apply when object is in plain view.
Search Warrant Requirements		
Probable cause	*Brinegar v. United States* (1949)	Probable cause exists where the facts and circumstances within the officers' knowledge and of which they have trustworthy information are sufficient for a person of reasonable caution to believe that an offense has been committed. This is the best definition of probable cause.
Exceptions to the Search Warrant Requirement		
Federal requirement of of exclusionary rule	*Weeks v. United States* (1914)	U.S. Supreme Court applied the exclusionary rule to federal prosecutions.
State application	*Mapp v. Ohio* (1961)	U.S. Supreme Court applied the exclusionary rule to state prosecutions.
Search incident to arrest	*Chimel v. California* (1969)	Permissible scope for a search is only the area "within the immediate control," meaning about arm's length.
Automobile search	*United States v. Ross* (1982)	Warrantless search of a car is permissible when it is based on probable cause.

Table 7.1 (Continued)

Doctrine on Searches	Cases	Decisions
Stop and frisk	*Terry v. Ohio* (1968)	Police are authorized to stop and frisk suspicious persons.
Consent	*Schneckloth v. Bustamonte* (1973)	Consent to search must be voluntarily given.
Bus sweep	*Florida v. Bostick* (1991)	Police, after obtaining consent, may conduct a search of luggage without a search warrant or probable cause.
Exceptions to the Exclusionary Rule for Search Warrants		
Good faith	*United States v. Leon* (1984)	When police rely on good faith in a warrant, the evidence seized is admissible even if the warrant is subsequently deemed defective.
Warrant error	*Arizona v. Evans* (1995)	Evidence seized incident to an arrest, based on a patrol car's computer showing an outstanding arrest warrant that was in error due to court-employee mistake, need not be excluded from trial.
Fifth Amendment Doctrine on Self-Incrimination		
Self-incrimination	*Miranda v. Arizona* (1966)	Defendant must be given the *Miranda* warning before questioning begins. (For details of case, see Law in Review on page 216.)

Current Status and Controversy The U.S. Supreme Court, with its conservative bent of recent years, has been diminishing the scope of the exclusionary rule. In *Illinois v. Gates* (1983), the Court made it easier for police to search a suspect's home by allowing an anonymous letter to be used as evidence in support of a warrant.[37] In another critical case, *United States v. Leon* (1984), the Court ruled that evidence seized by police relying on a warrant issued by a detached and neutral magistrate can be used in a court proceeding, even if the judge who issued the warrant may have relied on less than sufficient

According to the exclusionary rule, evidence, such as a crime weapon seized by police using tactics that violate Constitutional protections against illegal searches and seizures, cannot be used in a court of law. Such evidence must be excluded from trial.

good faith exception
The principle of law holding that evidence may be used in a criminal trial even though the search warrant used to obtain it is technically faulty, if the police acted in good faith and to the best of their ability when they sought to obtain it from a judge.

Arizona v. Evans
The 1995 U.S. Supreme Court case that added computer errors to the list of valid reasons that a search warrant might be issued in error but in good faith.

evidence.[38] In this case, the Court articulated a **good faith exception** to the exclusionary rule: Evidence obtained with less than an adequate search warrant may be admissible in court if the police officers acted in good faith in obtaining court approval for their search and there was no police misconduct. However, deliberately misleading a judge or using a warrant that the police know is deficient would be grounds to invoke the exclusionary rule. A 1988 study of the effects of the *Leon* decision found no impact on the judicial suppression of evidence.[39] Although prosecutors initially applauded the decision and defense lawyers feared that the police would be inclined to secure warrants from sympathetic judges, both groups agree that *United States v. Leon* has had little practical effect on the processing of criminal cases.

In 1995 the Supreme Court in ***Arizona v. Evans*** added computer errors to the list of valid reasons that an officer might mistakenly apply a search warrant in good faith, so evidence collected under the faulty warrant would still be admissible.[40] The case raised the question again about whether the rule is appropriate when the police act in good faith, believing they are in conformity with the Fourth Amendment.

The facts in *Evans* were relatively simple. Phoenix police officers stopped the defendant for a vehicular violation and in so doing ran a computer check that showed an outstanding arrest warrant. As Evans was being arrested, he dropped a marijuana cigarette, and more of the drug was found in the car. There was one problem with the seizure of the marijuana. Seventeen days earlier, the Phoenix Justice Court had quashed the arrest warrant, but the change did not appear in the computer records. The U.S. Supreme Court ruled that the evidence did not have to be suppressed under the exclusionary rule. The rule was designed as a means of deterring police misconduct, not mistakes by employees, and it doesn't apply where the police acted in reasonable reliance on an apparently valid warrant.

The exclusionary rule has long been a controversial subject in the administration of criminal justice. It was conceived to control illegal searches and seizures by police, and that remains its primary purpose today. It is justified on the basis that it deters illegal searches and seizures. Yet most experts believe that no impartial data exist to prove that the rule has a direct impact on police behavior. This is by far the most significant criticism of the rule. By excluding evidence, the rule apparently has had a more direct effect on the criminal trial than on the police officer on the street. Furthermore, the rule is powerless when the police have no interest in prosecuting the accused or in obtaining a conviction. In addition, it does not control the harassment of individuals by law enforcement officials, bent on disregarding constitutional rights, especially when the police are not interested in prosecuting them.

The most widely voiced criticism of the exclusionary rule, however, is that it allows guilty defendants to go free. Because courts frequently decide in many types of cases (particularly those involving victimless offenses, such as gambling and drug use) that certain evidence should be excluded, the rule is believed to result in excessive court delays and to negatively affect plea-bargaining negotiations. In fact, however, the rule appears to result in relatively few case dismissals.

Suggested approaches to dealing with violations of the exclusionary rule include (1) criminal prosecution of police officers who violate constitutional rights, (2) internal police control, (3) civil lawsuits against state or municipal police officers, and

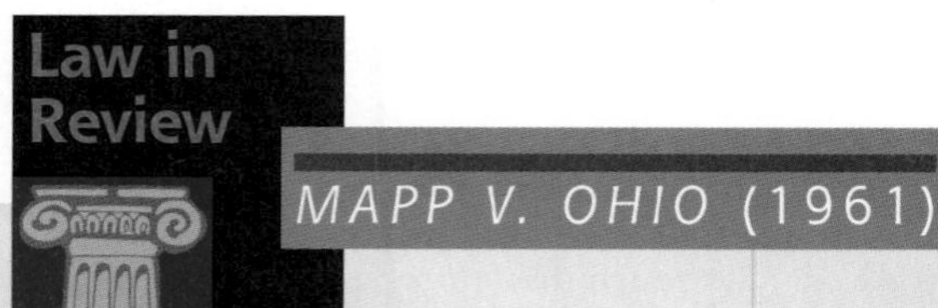

Facts

On May 23, 1957, three police officers arrived at Dolree Mapp's home, after receiving a tip that "a person [was] hiding out in the home, who was wanted for questioning in connection with a recent bombing and that there was a large amount of police paraphernalia being hidden in the home." Mapp and her daughter lived on the top floor of the two-family dwelling. The officers knocked on the door and demanded entrance, but Mapp, after telephoning her attorney, refused to admit them without a search warrant.

Three hours later, the officers returned along with four or more additional officers. When Mapp did not immediately come to the door, the police forced open one of the doors. Meanwhile, Mapp's attorney arrived, but the officers would not permit him to see Mapp or to enter the house. Mapp was halfway down the stairs from the upper floor to the front door when the officers burst into the hall. She demanded to see the search warrant. A paper, claimed to be a search warrant, was held up by one of the officers. She grabbed the "warrant" and placed it in her bosom. A struggle ensued in which the officers recovered the paper and handcuffed Mapp because she had ostensibly been belligerent.

Mapp was then forcibly taken upstairs to her bedroom, where the officers searched a dresser, a chest of drawers, a closet, and some suitcases. They also looked into a photo album and through her personal papers. The search spread to the rest of the second floor. In the course of the search, the police officers found pornographic literature. Mapp was arrested and subsequently convicted in an Ohio court of possessing obscene materials.

Decision

The question of the *Mapp* case was whether the evidence was seized in violation of the search-and-seizure provisions of the Fourth Amendment and therefore inadmissible in the state trial, which resulted in an obscenity conviction. The Supreme Court of Ohio found the conviction valid. However, the U.S. Supreme Court overturned it, stating that the Fourth Amendment prohibition against unreasonable searches and seizures, enforceable against the states through the due process clause, had been violated by the police. Justice Tom Clark, delivering the majority opinion of the Court, made clear the importance of this constitutional right in the administration of criminal justice when he stated:

> There are those who say, as did Justice [then Judge] Cardozo, that under our constitutional exclusionary doctrine "[t]he criminal is to go free because the constable has blundered." In some cases this will undoubtedly be the result. But . . . there is another consideration — the imperative of judicial integrity. . . . The criminal goes free, if he must, but it is the law that sets him free. Nothing can destroy a government more quickly than its failure to observe its own laws, or worse its disregard of the charter of its own existence.

Significance of the Case

In previous decisions the U.S. Supreme Court had refused to exclude evidence in state court proceedings based on Fourth Amendment violations of search and seizure. The *Mapp* case overruled such decisions, including that of *Wolf v. Colorado,* and held that evidence gathered in violation of the Fourth Amendment would be inadmissible in a state prosecution. For the first time, the Court imposed federal constitutional standards on state law enforcement personnel.

The exclusionary rule operates to exclude from admission in a trial evidence determined to be the product of an unconstitutional search or seizure. It was with the *Mapp* case that the Supreme Court applied the exclusionary rule to the states.

For more on this controversial rule, go to *InfoTrac College Edition* and check under such terms as "search and seizure," "Fourth Amendment," and "exclusionary rule."

(4) federal lawsuits against the government under the Federal Tort Claims Act. An individual using any of these alternatives, however, would be faced with such obstacles as the cost of bringing a lawsuit, proving damages, and dealing with a bureaucratic law enforcement system. In the end, of all the civilized countries in the world, only the United States applies an exclusionary rule to protect individuals from illegal searches and seizures.[41] Whether the U.S. Supreme Court or legislative bodies adopt any more significant changes to the rule will depend largely on efforts by police to discipline themselves. It will also depend on a tough civil tort remedy that allows lawsuits and claims for damages against offending police officers.

The fate of the exclusionary rule will remain difficult to predict. Although it is a simple rule of evidence, it involves complex issues of fairness, justice, and crime control.[42] Many legal experts believe the time has come again to reexamine and reform the rule. Modifications to the exclusionary rule are a perennial issue before the U.S. Congress.

SUMMARY

Law enforcement officers use many investigatory techniques to detect and apprehend criminal offenders. These include searches, electronic eavesdropping, interrogation, the use of informants, surveillance, and witness identification procedures. Over the past three decades, in particular through U.S. Supreme Court decisions, serious constitutional limitations have been placed on the pretrial process. Under interpretations of the Fourth Amendment, for example, police are required to use warrants to conduct searches, except in some clearly defined situations. The exceptions to the search warrant rule include searches of automobiles used in a crime, stop and frisk, searches incident to an arrest, searches of material in plain view, and some instances of electronic eavesdropping.

Police interrogation procedures have also been reviewed extensively. Through the *Miranda* rule, the Supreme Court established an affirmative procedure as a requirement for all custodial interrogations. The *Miranda* case is arguably the best-known Supreme Court ruling in history.

The exclusionary rule continues to be one of the most controversial issues in the criminal justice system. Even though the courts have curtailed its application in recent years, it still generally prohibits the admission of evidence that violates the defendant's constitutional rights. Curtailing the use of the exclusionary rule might widen the scope of the justice system's crime control efforts but reduce due process protections for the defendant.

KEY TERMS

search and seizure
Fourth Amendment
search warrant
unreasonableness
probable cause
particularity
hearsay evidence
search incident to a lawful arrest
Chimel v. California
threshold inquiry
stop and frisk
Terry v. Ohio
field interrogation
United States v. Ross
consent search
Florida v. Bostick
bus sweep
plain-view doctrine
curtilage
wiretapping
arrest
Miranda warning
Escobedo v. Illinois
booking process
exclusionary rule
Mapp v. Ohio
good faith exception
Arizona v. Evans

INFOTRAC COLLEGE EDITION EXERCISES

A number of legal experts have commented on the likelihood that the *Miranda v. Arizona* case would be overturned by the U.S. Supreme Court over the next few years. In fact, the Court has agreed to revisit the *Miranda* warning in the 1999–2000 term. The basis for this speculation is that the Court is far more conservative today than when the rule was established in 1966.

Explore *InfoTrac College Edition* for articles on *Miranda v. Arizona.* Based on what you find, does it appear that the predictions for overturning *Miranda* might be accurate? To search for information, use key words such as "voluntary confessions," "right to an attorney," and "police interrogations."

QUESTIONS

1. Should obviously guilty persons go free because police originally arrested them with less than probable cause? Explain.
2. Should illegally seized evidence be excluded from trial, even though it is conclusive proof of a person's criminal acts? Explain.
3. Should police be personally liable if they violate a person's constitutional rights? Why or why not? How might this influence their investigations? Explain.
4. Should a person be put in a lineup without the benefit of counsel? Explain.
5. What is the purpose of the *Miranda* warnings?
6. Have criminals been given too many rights? Explain. Should courts be more concerned with the rights of victims or the rights of offenders? Why or why not?
7. Does the exclusionary rule effectively deter police misconduct? Explain.
8. Do you agree or disagree with the *Mapp v. Ohio* decision? Explain.
9. What is a pretextual traffic stop?

NOTES

1. *Wyoming v. Houghton,* 119 S.Ct. 1297 (1999).

2. William Greenhalgh, *The Fourth Amendment Handbook: A Chronological Survey of Supreme Court Decisions* (Chicago: American Bar Association Section on Criminal Justice, 1995).

3. See, generally, American Bar Association, *Standards Relating to the Urban Police Function,* 2d ed. (Chicago: ABA, 1988).

4. See classic works of Wayne R. LaFave, *Arrest: The Decision to Take a Suspect into Custody* (Boston: Little, Brown, 1965); Lawrence P. Tiffany, Donald McIntyre, and Daniel Rotenberg, *Detection of Crime: Stopping and Questioning, Search and Seizure* (Boston: Little, Brown, 1967); Wayne R. LaFave, *Search and Seizure: A Treatise on the Fourth Amendment* (St. Paul: West, 1978).

5. *Illinois v. Gates,* 462 U.S. 213, 103 S.Ct. 2317, 76 L.Ed.2d 527 (1983).

6. *Chimel v. California,* 395 U.S. 752, 89 S.Ct. 2034, 23 L.Ed.2d 685 (1969).

7. *Terry v. Ohio,* 392 U.S. 1, 88 S.Ct. 1868, 20 L.Ed.2d 889 (1968).

8. Ibid., at 20–27, 88 S.Ct. at 1879–83.

9. *Carroll v. United States,* 267 U.S. 132, 45 S.Ct. 280, 69 L.Ed. 543 (1925).

10. *United States v. Ross,* 20.456 U.S. 798, 102 S.Ct. 2157, 72 L.Ed.2d 572 (1982); see also Barry Latzer, "Searching Cars and Their Contents: *U.S. v. Ross,*" *Criminal Law Bulletin* 6 (1982): 220; Joseph Grano, "Rethinking the Fourth Amendment Warrant Requirements," *Criminal Law Review* 19 (1982): 603.

11. *Bumper v. North Carolina,* 391 U.S. 543, 88 S.Ct. 1788, 20 L.Ed.2d 797 (1968).

12. *Schneckloth v. Bustamonte,* 412 U.S. 218, 93 S.Ct. 2041, 36 L.Ed.2d 854 (1973).

13. *Florida v. Bostick,* 500 U.S. 167, 111 S.Ct. 2382, 115 L.Ed.2d 389 (1991).

14. Joseph Cronin, "Working the Buses: Leave the Searching to Us," *Suffolk University Law School Journal* 22 (1991): 31–37; see also Edward Felsenthal, "High Court May Back Gun Sweeps," *Wall Street Journal,* 21 April 1994, B12.

15. *New York v. Class,* 475 U.S. 106, 106 S.Ct. 960, 89 L.Ed.2d 81 (1986).

16. *Arizona v. Hicks,* 480 U.S. 321, 107 S.Ct. 1149, 94 L.Ed.2d 347 (1987); see also Note, "Fourth Amendment Requires Probable Cause for Search and Seizure Under Plain View Doctrine," *Journal of Criminal Law and Criminology* 78 (1988): 763.

17. *Minnesota v. Dickerson,* 508 U.S. 366, 113 S.Ct. 2130, 124 L.Ed.2d 334 (1993).

18. *Oliver v. United States,* 466 U.S. 170, 104 S.Ct. 1735, 80 L.Ed.2d 214 (1984).

19. Gary T. Marx, *Undercover: Police Surveillance in America* (Berkeley: University of California Press, 1988).

20. *Katz v. United States,* 389 U.S. 347, 88 S.Ct. 507, 19 L.Ed.2d 576 (1967).

21. *Omnibus Crime Control Act,* Title III, 90th Congress (1968); 18 U.S.C., sec. 2511–2520.

22. *Electronic Communications and Privacy Act of 1986,* Public Law No. 99–508, Title 18 U.S.C., sec. 2510.

23. See *Newsweek,* "E-Life — How the Internet Is Changing America," 30 September (1999), 38–78.

24. See Michael Goldsmith, "The Supreme Court and Title III: Rewriting the Law of Electronic Surveillance," *Journal of Criminal Law and Criminology* 74 (1983): 76–85.

25. *Riverside County v. McLaughlin,* 500 U.S. 44, 111 S.Ct. 1661, 114 L.Ed.2d 49 (1991).

26. *Miranda v. Arizona,* 384 U.S. 436, 86 S.Ct. 1602, 16 L.Ed.2d 694 (1966).

27. *Brown v. Mississippi,* 297 U.S. 278, 56 S.Ct. 461, 80 L.Ed.2d 682 (1936).

28. *Escobedo v. Illinois,* 378 U.S. 478, 84 S.Ct. 1758, 12 L.Ed.2d 977 (1964).

29. Michael Wald, "Interrogations in New Haven: The Impact of *Miranda,*" *Yale Law Journal* 76 (1967): 1519.

30. Alexandra McDonald, "Mixing It Up with *Miranda,*" *American Bar Association Journal* 85 (1999): 30–31; Tony Mauro, "The Case against *Miranda* — Undoing Tradition," *USA Today,* 19 March 1999, 1; Roger Parloff, "*Miranda* on the Hot Seat," *New York Times Magazine,* 26 September 1999, 84–88.

31. *United States v. Wade,* 388 U.S. 218, 87 S.Ct. 1926, 18 L.Ed.2d 1149 (1967).

32. *Kirby v. Illinois,* 406 U.S. 682, 92 S.Ct. 1877, 32 L.Ed.2d 411 (1972).

33. *Simmons v. United States,* 390 U.S. 377, 88 S.Ct. 967, 19 L.Ed.2d 1247 (1968).

34. *Neil v. Biggers,* 409 U.S. 188, 93 S.Ct. 375, 34 L.Ed.2d 401 (1972).

35. *Weeks v. United States,* 232 U.S. 383, 34 S.Ct. 341, 58 L.Ed. 652 (1914).

36. *Mapp v. Ohio,* 367 U.S. 643, 81 S.Ct. 1684, 6 L.Ed.2d 1081 (1961).

37. *Illinois v. Gates,* 462 U.S. 213, 103 S.Ct. 2317, 76 L.Ed.2d 527 (1983).

38. *United States v. Leon,* 468 U.S. 897, 104 S.Ct. 3405, 82 L.Ed.2d 677 (1984).

39. Craig V. Chida, *The Effects of* United States v. Leon *on Police Search Warrant Practices* (Washington, D.C.: Government Printing Office, 1988).

40. *Arizona v. Evans,* 514 U.S. 115 S.Ct. 1185, 131 L.Ed.2d 34 (1995).

41. See "The Exclusionary Rule," *American Bar Association Journal* 19 (1983): 3; "Rule Prohibiting Illegal Evidence Faces Limitation," *Wall Street Journal,* 30 November 1982, 42; Bradford Wilson, *Exclusionary Rule* (Washington, D.C.: Government Printing Office, 1986); Jana Nestlerode, "Distinguishing the Exclusionary Rule Exceptions," *Journal of National Association of District Attorneys* 24 (1991): 29–35; Lawrence Crocker, "Can the Exclusionary Rule Be Saved?" *Journal of Criminal Law and Criminology* 84 (1993): 310; Harold Rothwax, *The Collapse of Criminal Justice* New York: Random House, 1996); Tom Smith, "Legislative and Legal Developments," *American Bar Association Journal of Criminal Justice* 11 (1996): 46–47.

chapter 8

Courts, Prosecution, and the Defense

On an August night in Altoona, Iowa, the local McDonald's was filled with customers when a man walked in, looking for cash. He forced the manager to open the safe and give him the money. Before the police arrived, the gunman fled the scene. Initial descriptions were contradictory, but with the help of store employees, an artist drew a composite picture that led to the arrest of Terry Schutz. Eyewitnesses said he was the thief, even though his girlfriend insisted they were together at the time of the crime. Schutz was tried, convicted, and sentenced to twenty years in prison.

In another case, a university student in Boston was very confident that the stranger who had broken into her apartment and raped her was Calvin Johnson. So was a neighboring student, who had been raped two weeks earlier. On the basis of their testimony, a jury convicted Johnson of rape, and he was sentenced to life in prison. ■

How accurate are eyewitness identifications? In Schutz's case, the defense attorney wanted to tell the jury about research into human memory. For instance, mistakes are more likely when the witness and suspect are of different races. Extreme stress, especially when violence or the threat of violence exists, also interferes with recall. The court, however, was unwilling to accept such testimony. Today, some jurisdictions will set aside a conviction and order a new trial on the ground that memory experts should have been allowed to give such testimony to a jury.

In the rape case, DNA evidence indicated that the semen in the rape victim was not Johnson's and he was released from prison. There is mounting evidence through DNA science that innocent people have been convicted because of faulty identification. Since its introduction in American courts in 1987, DNA has been used to exonerate sixty-two wrongfully convicted men. In 1999 a federal commission recommended also permitting convicts to use DNA evidence to file appeals at any time, even if the deadline for such appeals has passed.[1]

The criminal court is the setting in which many of the most important decisions in the criminal justice system are made: Eyewitness identification, bail, trial, plea negotiations, and sentencing all involve court-made decisions. Within the confines of the court, those accused of crime (defendants) call on the tools of the legal system to provide them with a fair and just hearing, with the burden of proof resting on the state; crime victims ask the government to provide them with justice for the wrongs done them and the injuries they have suffered; and agents of the criminal justice system attempt to find solutions that benefit the victim, the defendant, and society in general. The court process is designed to provide an open and impartial forum for deciding the truth of the matter and reaching a solution that, although punitive, is fairly arrived at and satisfies the rule of law.

As we already know, in today's crowded court system, such abstract goals are often impossible to achieve. In reality, the U.S. court system is often the scene of accommodation and "working things out," rather than an arena for a vigorous criminal defense. Plea negotiations and other nonjudicial alternatives, such as diversion, are far more common than the formal trial process.

In this chapter, we examine the structure and function of the court system, as well as the roles of the judge, the prosecutor, and the defense attorney in the criminal process. Each state, like the federal government, has an independent judicial branch. The prosecutor, to a great extent, is the person who single handedly controls the "charging" decision in the judicial system. To charge or not, and for what offense, is the prosecutor's great discretionary authority. The defense attorney acts in a different capacity. Although defendants have a right to defend themselves, most are represented by a lawyer who is knowledgeable about the criminal law. The criminal lawyer has a legal obligation to make every effort to provide a competent and adequate defense.

THE CRIMINAL COURT PROCESS

The court is a complex social agency with many independent but interrelated subsystems, each of which has a role in the court's operation: police, prosecutor, defense attorney, judge, and probation department. It is also the scene of many important elements of criminal justice decision making: bail, detention, charging, jury selection, trial, and sentencing.

As you may recall, there are two ways to view the criminal court process. In the traditional model, the court is seen as a setting for an adversarial procedure that pits the defendant against the state, the defense counsel against the prosecutor. Procedures are fair and formalized, controlled by the laws of criminal procedure and the rules of evidence.

In the second model, the court is viewed as a system that encourages settling matters in the simplest, quickest, and most efficient manner possible. Rather than being adversaries, prosecutors and defense attorneys form a work group with the judge and other court personnel that tries to handle the situation with as little fuss as possible. This usually involves dropping the case if the defendant agrees to make restitution or enter a treatment or diversion program, plea bargaining, or using some other "quick fix." In Malcolm Feeley's early study of a lower court in Connecticut, not one defendant in 1,640 cases analyzed insisted on having a jury trial, and only half made use of legal counsel. Because cases dragged on endlessly, people were encouraged to plea-bargain. The haphazard nature of justice produced a situation in which the defendant's prior criminal record and the seriousness of the current charge had little influence on case outcome. Felons with prior records fared as well as first-time misdemeanants.[2]

The Washtenaw County (Michigan) Trial Court Web site takes you inside the operating procedure of a trial court, as well as introducing you to the people that work there. Go to www.co.washtenaw.mi.us/depts/courts/index.htm

The U.S. court system has evolved over the years into an intricately balanced legal process, which has recently come under siege because of the sheer numbers of cases it must consider and the ways in which it is forced to handle such overcrowding. Overloaded court dockets have given rise to charges of "assembly-line justice," in which a majority of defendants are induced to plead guilty, jury trials are rare, and the speedy trial is highly desired but unattainable.

Overcrowding causes the poor to languish in detention, while the wealthier go free on bail. The possibility increases that an innocent person may be frightened into pleading guilty and, conversely, a guilty person released because a trial has been delayed too long.[3] Whether providing more judges or new or enlarged courts will solve the problem of overcrowding remains to be seen. Meanwhile, diversion programs, decriminalization of certain offenses, and bail reform provide other avenues of possible relief. More efficient court management and administration is also seen as a step that might ease the congestion of the courts. The introduction of professional trial court managers — administrators, clerks, and judges with management skills — is one of the more significant waves of change in the nation's courts in recent decades.

Another emphasis today is on the jury. The role of the grand jury has diminished in favor of the preliminary hearing in felony court cases. Trial court juries have changed in how they are selected, as have size and verdict rules. The U.S. Supreme Court has relaxed the requirements that verdicts be unanimous and be

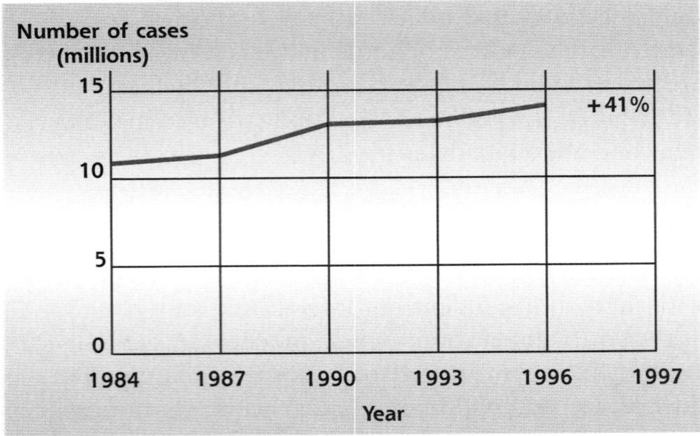

(a)

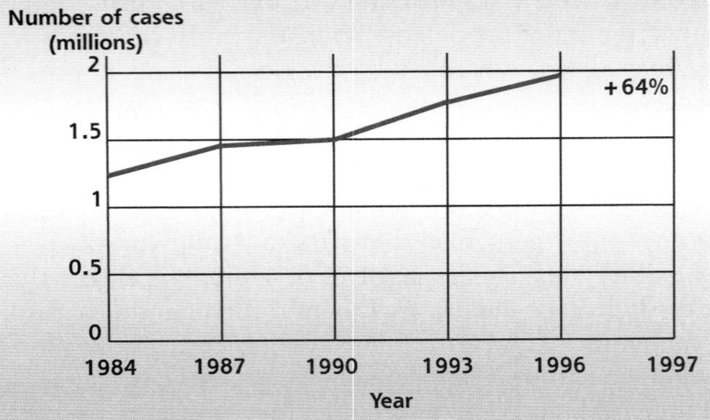

(b)

Figure 8.1
Criminal (a) and juvenile (b) cases filed in state courts, 1984–1997

SOURCE: Brian Ostrom and Neal Kauder, *Examining the Work of State Courts, 1997: A National Perspective from the Court Statistics Project* (Williamsburg, Va.: National Center for State Courts, 1998).

rendered by twelve-person juries (see Chapter 10). A major effort is also under way to increase the representativeness of jury pools.

Lastly, advanced technology is spurring new scientific methods of criminal identification. No area is questioned more than DNA profiling, where evidence is used to link defendants to the crime. Today, many states allow DNA evidence to be admitted during both the trial and appellate proceedings.

These issues are extremely important if defendants are going to view their experience as a fair one in which they could present their side of the case and influence its outcome. Ironically, evidence shows that the informal justice system, which is often deplored by experts, may provide criminal suspects a greater degree of satisfaction than the more formal criminal trial.[4]

To house this rather complex process, each state maintains its own state court organization and structure. American courts basically have two systems: state and federal. There are fifty state trial and appellate systems and separate courts for the District of Columbia and the Commonwealth of Puerto Rico. Usually three (or more) separate court systems exist within each state jurisdiction. These are described next.

STATE COURTS

The state court system alone handled 86 million new cases in 1997. That total included nearly 20 million civil and domestic cases, over 13 million criminal cases, almost 2 million juvenile cases, and 51 million traffic and ordinance violations. Significant growth characterized the states' criminal caseloads, which rose about 40 percent from 1984 to 1997; juvenile delinquency and status offense cases were up 64 percent during the same period[5] (Figure 8.1). (See Chapter 15.)

Courts of Limited Jurisdiction

There are approximately 14,000 courts of limited jurisdiction in the United States. Most are organized along town, municipal, and county lines of government; the rest are controlled by state governments. Limited jurisdiction courts outnumber general jurisdiction courts approximately 5 to 1 (14,000 to 3,000).[6]

lower court
A generic term referring to a court that has jurisdiction over misdemeanors and conducts preliminary investigations of felony charges.

Courts of limited jurisdiction (sometimes called municipal courts, or **lower courts**) are restricted in the types of cases they may hear. Usually, they will handle misdemeanor criminal infractions, violations of municipal ordinances, traffic violations, and civil suits where the damages involve less than a certain amount of money (usually $10,000). These courts also conduct preliminary hearings for felony criminal cases.

The lower criminal courts are restricted in the criminal penalties they can impose. Most can levy a fine of $1,000 or less and incarcerate a person for twelve months or less in the local jail.

Included within the category of courts of limited jurisdiction are special courts, such as juvenile, family, and probate (divorce, estate issues, and custody) courts. Some states separate limited courts into those that handle civil cases only

Two youths wait in a juvenile court docket. Most underage suspects are tried in a specialized court for children. The juvenile court is covered more fully in Chapter 15.

and those that settle criminal cases. A particular problem, such as drug use, may cause states to even create specialized juvenile and adult drug courts. These newest types of specialty courts are discussed in the Policy, Programs, and Issues in Criminal Justice feature.

The nation's lower courts are the ones most often accused of providing assembly-line justice. Because the matters they decide involve minor personal confrontations and conflicts — family disputes, divorces, landlord–tenant conflicts, barroom brawls — the rule of the day is "handling the situation" and resolving the dispute.

Courts of General Jurisdiction

Approximately three thousand courts of general jurisdiction, or **felony courts,** exist in the United States. They process about 1.5 million felony cases each year and convict over 1 million adults of felonies.[7] Courts of general jurisdiction handle the more serious felony cases (e.g., murder, rape, robbery), whereas courts of limited jurisdiction handle misdemeanors (e.g., simple assault, shoplifting, bad checks). About 90 percent of the general courts are state administered, and the remainder are controlled by counties or municipalities. The overwhelming majority of general courts hear both serious civil and criminal matters (felonies). A general jurisdiction trial court is the highest state trial court where felony criminal cases are adjudicated.

felony court
A state or federal court that has jurisdiction over felony offenses — serious crimes that carry a penalty of incarceration in a state or federal prison for one year or more.

Courts of general jurisdiction may also be responsible for reviewing cases on appeal from courts of limited jurisdiction. In some cases, they will base their decision of a review of the transcript of the case, whereas in others they can actually grant a new trial; this latter procedure is known as the *trial de novo* process. Changes in the courts of general jurisdiction, such as increases in felony filing rates, are watched closely because serious crime is of great public concern.

Appellate Courts

If defendants believe that the procedures used in their case were in violation of their constitutional rights, they may appeal the outcome of their case. For example, defendants can file an appeal if they believe that the law they were tried under violates constitutional standards (e.g., it was too vague) or if the procedures used in the case contravened principles of due process and equal protection or were in direct opposition to a constitutional guarantee (e.g., defendants were denied the right to have competent legal representation). **Appellate courts** do not try cases; they review the procedures of the case to determine whether an error was made by judicial authorities. Judicial error can include admitting into evidence illegally seized material, improperly charging a jury, allowing a prosecutor to ask witnesses improper questions, and so on. The appellate court can order a new trial, allow the defendant to go free, or uphold the original verdict.

appellate court
A court that reconsiders a case that has already been tried in order to determine whether the measures used complied with accepted rules of criminal procedure and were in line with constitutional doctrines.

Most criminal appeals are limited to trial convictions, sentences, and guilty plea convictions. The most basic feature of the appellate system is the distinction between mandated appeals by right and discretionary review of certain cases. For example, appeals of trial convictions are ordinarily under the courts' mandatory jurisdiction. The most famous appellate court with discretionary jurisdiction is the U.S. Supreme Court, the nation's highest court.

court of last resort
A court that handles the final appeal on a matter. The U.S. Supreme Court is the official court of last resort for criminal matters.

State criminal appeals are heard in one of the appellate courts in the fifty states and the District of Columbia. Each state has at least one **court of last resort,** usually called a state supreme court, which reviews issues of law and fact appealed from the trial courts; a few states have two high courts, one for civil appeals and the other for criminal cases. In addition, many states have estab-

Policy, Programs, and Issues in Criminal Justice

SPECIALTY COURTS

A growing phenomenon in the United States is the creation of specialty courts that focus on one type of criminal act — for example, *gun courts* and *drug courts.* All cases within the jurisdiction that involve this particular type of crime are funneled to the specialty court, where presumably they will get prompt resolution.

One well-known example is the gun court in Providence, Rhode Island. All felony cases in Bristol and Providence Counties are automatically routed to the gun court, where once a preliminary hearing has begun the cases must be heard within sixty days. The purpose is to make sure that violent felons are not lost in the shuffle of crowded urban courts, where witnesses disappear and offenders are free to abscond.

Another specialty court is the drug court, which has jurisdiction over the burgeoning number of cases involving substance abuse and trafficking. The aim is to place nonviolent first offenders into intensive treatment programs rather than jail or prison.

The movement toward specialized drug courts began in the late 1980s in response to rising rates of drug-related court cases and to the inability of traditional law enforcement and justice policies to reduce the supply of and demand for illegal drugs. Since the first drug court was created in Miami in 1989, these courts have focused on providing, through the court system, treatment to drug-involved criminal justice populations, with judges having primary authority over case handling.

One such court, the Drug Night Court program in Cook County, Illinois, was set up as an emergency measure to deal with the rapidly expanding number of narcotics cases being filed. Evaluations have praised the drug court program, indicating that it is an efficient method for processing cases, dramatically reducing the processing time of drug cases. The main difficulty is finding quality staff who want to work evening hours and maintaining their morale and efficiency. Similar drug courts have been developed in other jurisdictions (e.g., New Jersey) with varying degrees of success.

There are also *juvenile courts,* which specialize in cases of underage minors who violate the criminal law (called juvenile delinquents), who are uncontrollable or unmanageable (called status offenders, who may be truants and runaways), or who are not provided with adequate care by their parents (called neglected children). Some states have created comprehensive family courts, which handle all problems involving youths and their families, including custody issues. (The juvenile court will be discussed more fully in Chapter 15.)

Critical Thinking

What are the key operational features of the drug court? Do they include early intervention, frequent drug testing, and judicial involvement in the defendants' progress?

Individual judges, trial courts, and entire state court systems are adopting a new, problem-solving orientation to their work, one well removed from the traditional model of the "dispassionate, disinterested magistrate." In doing so, courts are taking a path previously cut by other components of the criminal justice system, where a problem-solving orientation first emerged as a reaction to the management-dominated concept of police reform of the 1970s and 1980s. In the new model, *problem* is defined expansively to include "a wide range of behavioral and social problems that arise in a community." This new idea is called *therapeutic jurisprudence.* Do you agree with this concept? Why or why not? What kind of programs can evolve from achieving court and community collaboration?

InfoTrac College Edition Research

One of the most significant specialized court systems is the juvenile court, which has jurisdiction over juvenile offenders as well as children in need of supervision. Read the following article from *InfoTrac College Edition:*

> Barry C. Feld, "Symposium Issue on the Future of the Juvenile Court," *Journal of Criminal Law and Criminology* (fall 1997).

SOURCES: John Larrabee, "You're Going to Jail Fast in Nation's First Gun Court," *USA Today,* 19 December 1994, 3; Bureau of Justice Assistance, *Drug Night Courts: The Cook County Experience* (Washington, D.C.: National Institute of Justice, 1994); John Krimmel, "New Jersey's Drug Court Project," *Criminal Justice Policy Review* 6 (1992): 333–42; Adele Harrell, *Drug Courts and Graduated Sanctions* (Washington, D.C.: National Institute of Justice, 1998), 1; David Rottman and Pamela Casey, "Therapeutic Jurisprudence and Problem-Solving Courts," *National Institute of Justice Journal* (July 1999): 13–18.

The criminal court is the central stage of the justice system. Here, prosecution and defense attorneys in the Paul Allen murder case discuss matters with Judge Glen Dawson of the Second District Court in Farmington, Utah. On February 18, 2000, Allen was charged with the 1996 killing of his wife in order to collect on her $250,000 life insurance policy.

The Office of Justice Program's Drug Court Clearinghouse and Technical Assistance Project offers information, FAQs, and sample materials for those interested in drug courts. Go to www.american.edu/academic.depts/spa/justice/dcclear.htm

lished intermediate appellate courts to review decisions by trial courts and administrative agencies before they reach the supreme court stage. A great deal of diversity exists in the organizational features of the state appellate court system.

Many people believe that criminal appeals clog the nation's court system because so many convicted criminals try to "beat the rap" on a technicality. Actually, criminal appeals represent a small percentage of the total number of cases processed by the nation's appellate courts. All types of appeals, including criminal ones, continue to inundate the courts, so most courts are having problems processing cases expeditiously.

State courts have witnessed an increase in the number of appellate cases each year. In the meantime, the number of judges and support staff has not kept pace. The resulting imbalance has led to the increased use of intermediate courts to screen cases.

Figure 8.2 illustrates the interrelationship of appellate and trial courts in a model state court structure. Each state's court organization of course varies from this standard pattern. All states have a tiered court organization (lower, upper, and appellate courts), but they vary somewhat in the way they have delegated responsibility to a particular court system.

In sum, most states have at least two trial courts and two appellate courts, but they differ about where jurisdiction over such matters as juvenile cases and felony versus misdemeanor offenses is found. Such matters vary from state to state and between the state courts and the federal system. According to the National Center for State Courts, there is no single uniform court system in the United States.[8]

FEDERAL COURTS

The legal basis for the federal court system is contained in ARTICLE 3, SECTION 1, of the U.S. Constitution, which provides that "the judicial power of the United States shall be vested in one Supreme Court, and in such inferior courts as Congress may from time to time ordain and establish." The important clauses in ARTICLE 3 indicate that the

Figure 8.2
A model of a state judicial system

SOURCES: American Bar Association, *Law and the Courts* (Chicago: ABA, 1974), 20; Bureau of Justice Statistics, *State Court Organization—1993* (Washington, D.C.: Department of Justice, 1995).

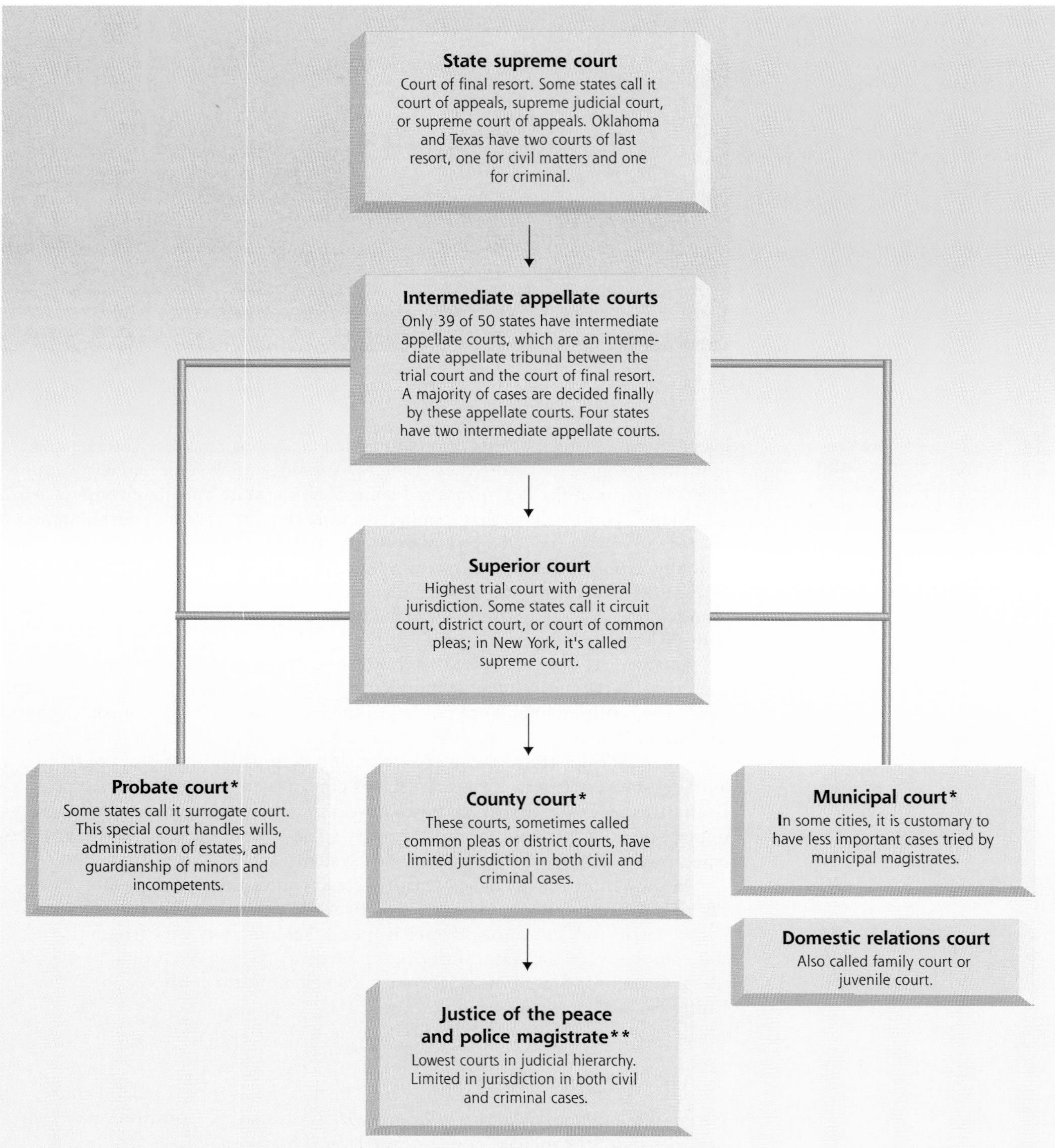

*Courts of special jurisdiction, such as probate, family, or juvenile courts, and the so-called inferior courts, such as common pleas or municipal courts, may be separate courts or part of the trial court of general jurisdiction.

**Justices of the peace do not exist in all states. Where they do exist, their jurisdictions vary greatly from state to state.

federal courts have jurisdiction over the laws of the United States and treaties and cases involving admiralty and maritime jurisdiction, as well as over controversies between two or more states and citizens of different states.[9] This complex language generally means that state courts have jurisdiction over all legal matters, unless they involve a violation of a federal criminal statute or a civil suit between citizens of different states or between a citizen and an agency of the federal government.

Within this authority, the federal government has established a three-tiered hierarchy of court jurisdiction that, in order of ascendancy, consists of the (1) U.S. district courts, (2) U.S. courts of appeals (circuit courts), and (3) the U.S. Supreme Court (Figure 8.3).

District Courts U.S. district courts are the trial courts of the federal system. They have jurisdiction over cases involving violations of federal laws, including civil rights abuses, interstate transportation of stolen vehicles, and kidnappings. They may also hear cases on questions involving citizenship and the rights of aliens. The jurisdiction of the U.S. district court will occasionally overlap that of state courts. For example, citizens who reside in separate states

Figure 8.3
The federal judicial system

SOURCE: American Bar Association *Law and the Courts* (Chicago: ABA, 1974), 21. Updated information provided by the Federal Courts Improvement Act of 1982 and West Publishing Company, St. Paul, Minnesota.

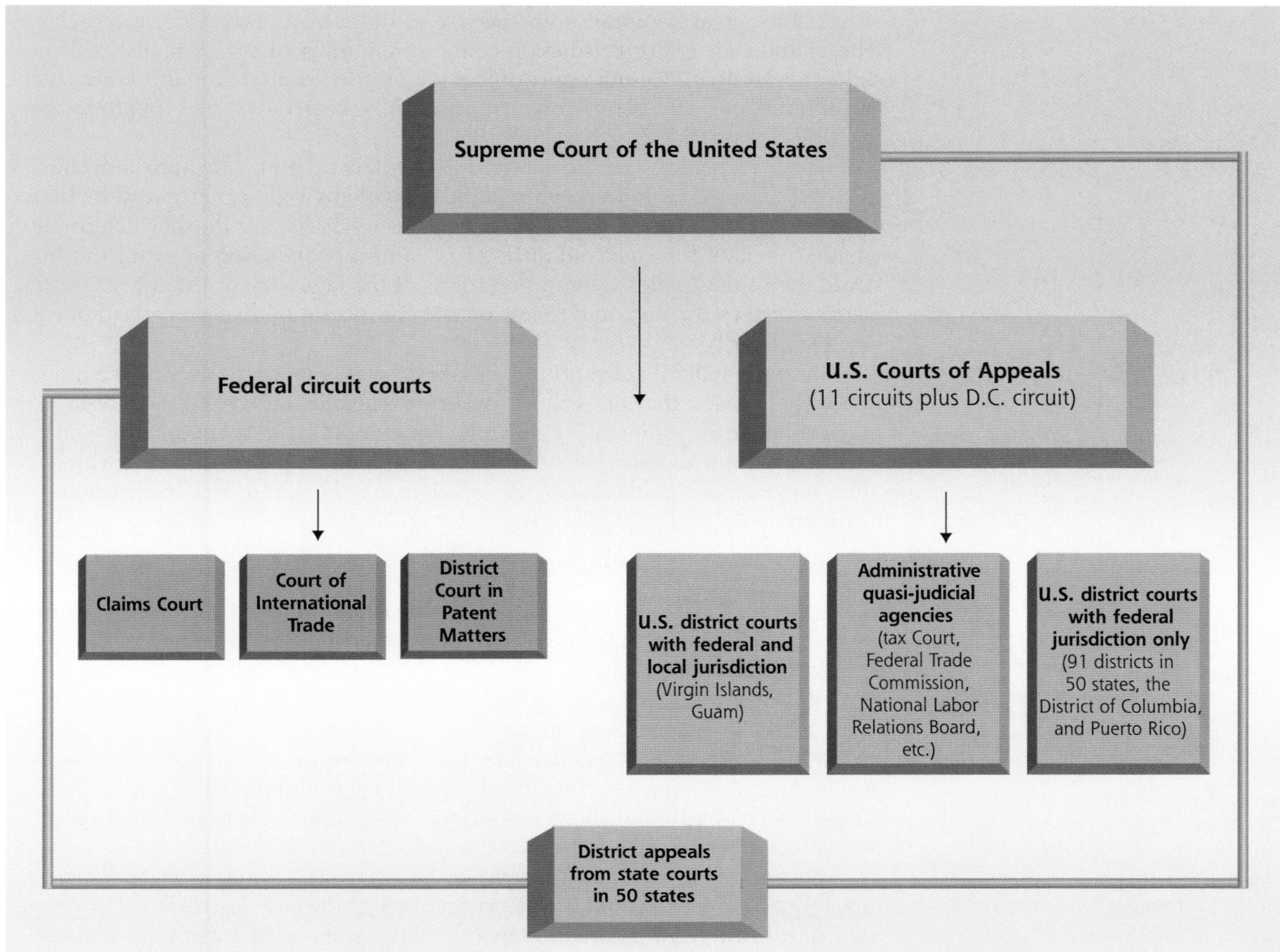

and are involved in litigation of an amount in excess of $10,000 may choose to have their cases heard in either of the states or the federal court. Finally, federal district courts hear cases in which one state sues a resident (or firm) in another state, where one state sues another, or where the federal government is a party in a suit. A single judge ordinarily presides over criminal trials; a defendant may also request a jury trial.

Federal district courts were organized by Congress in the Judicial Act of 1789, and today ninety-four independent courts are in operation. Originally, each state was allowed one court; as the population grew, however, so did the need for courts. Now each state has from one to four district courts, and the District of Columbia has one for itself. The generally stable federal criminal trial caseload reached a low in 1980 of about thirty thousand cases, down from forty thousand in 1972. Since that time, criminal filings have increased, to about forty-five thousand in 1997. The number of drug cases has contributed to the upward trend in criminal filings.

Federal Appeals Courts

Approximately forty thousand appeals from the district courts are heard each year in the twelve federal courts of appeals, sometimes referred to as U.S. circuit courts. This name is derived from the historical practice of having judges ride the circuit and regularly hear cases in the judicial seats of their various jurisdictions. Today, appellate judges are not required to travel (although some may sit in more than one court), and each federal appellate court jurisdiction contains a number of associate justices who share the caseload. Circuit court offices are usually located in major cities, such as San Francisco and New York, and cases to be heard must be brought to these locations by attorneys.

The circuit court is empowered to review federal and state appellate court cases on substantive and procedural issues involving rights guaranteed by the Constitution. Circuit courts do not actually retry cases, nor do they determine whether the facts brought out during trial support conviction or dismissal. Instead, they analyze judicial interpretations of the law, such as the charge (or instructions) to the jury, and reflect on the constitutional issues involved in each case they hear.

Although federal court criminal cases do make up only a small percentage of appellate cases, they are still of concern to the judiciary. Steps have been taken to make appealing more difficult. For example, the U.S. Supreme Court has tried to limit the number of appeals being filed by prison inmates, which often represent a significant number of cases appealed in the federal criminal justice system.

The U.S. Supreme Court

The U.S. Supreme Court is the nation's highest appellate body and the court of last resort for all cases tried in the various federal and state courts.

The Supreme Court is composed of nine members appointed for lifetime terms by the president, with the approval of Congress. The Court has discretion over most of the cases it will consider and may choose to hear only those it deems important, appropriate, and worthy of its attention. The Court chooses around three hundred of the five thousand cases that are appealed each year; only half of these receive full opinions.

writ of certiorari
An order of a superior court requesting that the record of an inferior court (or administrative body) be brought forward for review or inspection.

When the Supreme Court decides to hear a case, it grants a **writ of certiorari,** requesting a transcript of the proceedings of the case for review. However, the Court must grant jurisdiction in a few instances, such as decisions from a three-judge federal district court on reapportionment or cases involving the Voting Rights Act.

When the Supreme Court rules on a case, usually by majority decision (at least five votes), its rule becomes a precedent that must be honored by all lower courts. For example, if the Court grants a particular litigant the right to counsel at a police lineup, all similarly situated clients must be given the same right. This type of ruling is usually referred to as a **landmark decision.** The use of precedent in the legal system gives the Supreme Court power to influence and mold the everyday operating procedures of the police, trial courts, and corrections agencies. This influence became particularly pronounced during the tenure of Chief Justices Earl Warren and Warren Burger, who greatly amplified and extended the power of the Court to influence criminal justice policies. Under current Chief Justice William Rehnquist, the Court has continued to influence criminal justice matters, ranging from the investigation of crimes to the execution of criminals. The personal legal philosophy of the justices and their orientation toward the civil and personal rights of victims and criminals significantly affect the daily operations of the justice system.

landmark decision
A decision handed down by the U.S. Supreme Court that becomes the law of the land and serves as a precedent for similar legal issues.

Four of the justices of the Supreme Court on their way to discuss a case. Although thousands of appeals are filed each year, only one hundred or so receive a full opinion.

HOW A CASE GETS TO THE SUPREME COURT The Supreme Court is unique in several ways. First, it is the only court established by constitutional mandate, rather than federal legislation. Second, it decides basic social and political issues of grave consequence and importance to the nation. Third, the Court's nine justices shape the future meaning of the U.S. Constitution. Their decisions identify the rights and liberties of citizens throughout the United States.

When the nation was first established, the Supreme Court did not review state court decisions involving issues of federal law. Even though Congress had given the Supreme Court jurisdiction to review state decisions, much resistance and controversy surrounded the relationship between the states and the federal government. However, in a famous decision, *Martin v. Hunter's Lessee* (1816), the Court reaffirmed the legitimacy of its jurisdiction over state court decisions when such courts handled issues of federal or constitutional law.[10] This decision allowed the Court to actively review actions by states and their courts and reinforced the Court's power to make the supreme law of the land. Since that time, a defendant who indicates that governmental action — whether state or federal — violates a constitutional law is in a position to have the Court review such action.

To carry out its responsibilities, the Supreme Court had to develop a method for dealing with the large volume of cases coming from the state and federal courts for final review. In the early years of its history, the Court sought to review every case brought before it. Since the middle of the twentieth century, however, the Court has used the writ of certiorari to decide what cases it should hear. (*Certiorari* is a Latin term meaning "to bring the record of a case from a lower court up to a higher court for immediate review.") When applied, it means that an accused in a criminal case is requesting the U.S. Supreme Court to hear the case. More than 90 percent of the cases heard by the Court are brought by petition for a writ of certiorari. Under this procedure, the justices have discretion to select the cases they will review for a decision. Of the thousands of cases filed before the Court every year, only 100 to 150 receive a full opinion. Four of the nine justices sitting on the Court must vote to hear a case brought by a writ of certiorari for review. Generally, these votes are cast in a secret meeting attended only by the justices.

After the Supreme Court decides to hear a case, it reviews written and oral arguments. The written materials are referred to as *legal briefs,* and oral arguments are normally presented to the justices at the Court in Washington, D.C.

After the material is reviewed and the oral arguments heard, the justices normally meet in what is known as a *case conference.* At this case conference, they discuss the case and vote to reach a decision. The cases voted on by the Court generally come from the judicial systems of the various states or the U.S. courts of appeals, and they represent the entire spectrum of law.

In reaching a decision, the Supreme Court reevaluates and reinterprets state statutes, the U.S. Constitution, and previous case decisions. Based on a review of the case, the Court either affirms or reverses the decision of the lower court. When the justices reach a decision, the chief justice of the Court assigns someone of the majority group to write the opinion. Another justice normally writes a dissent, or minority, opinion. When the case is finished, it is submitted to the public and becomes the law of the land. The decision represents the legal precedents that add to the existing body of law on a given subject, change it, and guide its future development.

In the area of criminal justice, the decisions of the U.S. Supreme Court have had the broadest impact on the reform of the system. The Court's action is the final step in settling constitutional criminal disputes throughout the nation. By discretionary review through a petition for certiorari, the Court requires state courts to accept its interpretation of the Constitution. In doing so, the Court has changed the day-by-day operations of the criminal justice system. (See the Law in Review feature for an example of the Court's role in the federal and state partnership.)

FEDERAL AND STATE COURT CASELOADS

The nation's courts handle over 100 million civil, criminal, and traffic cases each year, resulting in backlogs, delays, and assembly-line justice.[11] Of these cases, approximately 13 million are criminal matters, an all-time high in 1997. In addition, the federal district courts hear approximately 45,000 criminal and 200,000 civil cases a year. While these figures seem overwhelming, they are even more disturbing because of the sharp increase in both civil and criminal litigation in the past few years. For example, in 1980 federal district courts disposed of 29,000 criminal cases; by 1990 the number had increased to 42,000; in 1997 the number had risen to about 45,000. In 1980 about 19,000 appeals were heard in federal circuit courts; by 1990 the number had grown to almost 35,000 and to 40,000 in 1997.[12] In state courts, the number of felony case filings increased from 690,000 in 1984 to more than 1 million by 1990 and 1.17 million in 1992, an increase of almost 65 percent in six years. In 1997 the figure stood at 1.5 million (Figure 8.4). As noted previously, the state criminal court caseload rose 38 percent between 1984 and 1997, while the U.S. population increased by only 10 percent during the same period. The increasing volume of criminal court cases filed in state courts is one important measure of the amount of criminal activity in our society (see Chapter 2).

Criminal cases are clearly on the rise. The significant increases in both criminal and civil litigation has forced state and local governments to seek ever greater resources for the courts. Court services — including the judiciary, prosecution, legal services such as public defenders, and other court-related matters (juries, stenographers, clerks, bailiffs, maintenance) — continue to run in the billions of dollars each year.

What causes court caseloads to overflow? In a survey of judges and trial court administrators, two factors that stood out were the excessive number of continuances demanded by attorneys and the increasing number of pretrial motions on evidence and procedural issues. As the law becomes more complex and involves such issues as computer crimes, the need for a more involved court

Law in Review

THE ROLE OF THE HIGH COURT AND STATES' RIGHTS

In 1993 the U.S. Congress passed the Brady Handgun Violence Prevention Act. One requirement of the law was that local officials check the backgrounds of handgun purchasers. As a result, the law has been credited with keeping thousands of convicted criminals from purchasing handguns in the intervening years. President Clinton considered this legislation one of the most important accomplishments of his first term in office.

In 1997, however, the U.S. Supreme Court struck down the use of background checks by ruling that Congress does not have the power to order the states to conduct such checks on prospective gun buyers. While not addressing the other main provision of the law — the requirement that gun buyers face a five-day waiting period — the Court affirmed the principle of states' rights over federal regulatory power. In a 5-to-4 decision, the Court said the federal gun law violated the Tenth Amendment of the Constitution. The Tenth Amendment gives states all powers that are not specifically given to the federal government by the Constitution. The Court ruled that Congress went too far in passing a law that required local law enforcement to carry out a federal mandate.

In recent years the Supreme Court has been sympathetic to the states' rights argument. In 1997 the Court declared unconstitutional a federal law that prohibited the possession of guns near schools because it believed that states, not Congress, had the power to enact such a law. The Brady Law ruling marks another case in which law enforcement is viewed as a state and local function.

As a practical matter, by striking down the handgun check, the Supreme Court used its power to press the federal government to complete a national computerization system for gun checks. The Brady Law required the federal government to establish a national computer bank containing criminal records for each state so that local police can have access to information to block felons from buying handguns. However, the Court's decision is not expected to change substantially the way checks are conducted since the majority of states already require their own handgun checks.

What about the role of the Court in policing the relationships among the three branches of government? It appears that the Court is more skeptical of federal authority than any Court in recent history. The decision represented the Court's recognition that Congress cannot infringe on state powers and that the Brady Law was a major encroachment on state's rights. Underlying this decision is the fear that the Brady Law ruling could threaten federal domestic abuse laws. This ruling highlights the role of the Supreme Court in balancing power between the federal government and the states. According to Justice Antonin Scalia, "The federal government may neither issue directives requiring states to address particular problems, nor command state officials to administer or enforce a federal regulatory program."

Critical Thinking

Is it fair for the Supreme Court to strike down a key provision of the Brady Law? Do you think this ruling seems like constitutional common sense to the average person? Explain.

How do we continue to keep handguns out of the hands of criminals?

InfoTrac College Edition Research

Gun control advocates view the Brady Law as a good first step in curbing gun violence. One method of reducing gun violence may be to make guns safer. Using *InfoTrac College Edition*, read more about this plan in

> Krista D. Robinson, Stephen P. Teret, Susan DeFrancesco, and Stephen W. Hargaten, "Making Guns Safer," *Issues in Science and Technology, Summer* 14 (1998): 37.

SOURCE: *Prince v. United States*, 95–103, July 28, 1997; *United States v. Lopez*, 115 S.Ct. 1624 (1995).

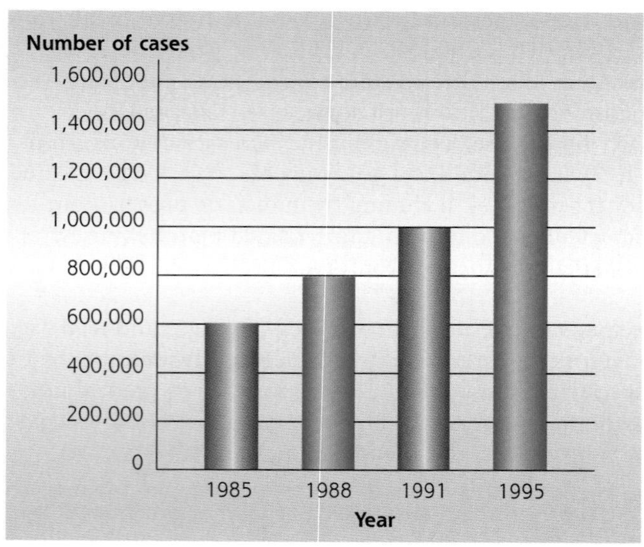

Figure 8.4
Total felony case filings from thirty-three states

SOURCES: B. Ostrom and N. Kauder, *Examining the Work of State Courts, 1997* (Williamsburg, Va.: National Center for State Courts, 1998).

process has escalated. Ironically, efforts being made to reform the criminal law may also be helping to overload the courts. For example, the increase of mandatory prison sentences for some crimes may reduce the use of plea bargaining and increase the number of jury trials because defendants fear that a conviction will lead to incarceration and thus must be avoided at all costs. Second, the recent explosion in civil litigation has added to the backlog because most courts handle both criminal and civil matters.

Some courts give criminal cases priority. The National Center for State Courts still reports, however, that many states do not keep up with the flow of criminal cases since their clearance rates are less than 100 percent. A state court's clearance rate is a key measure of the adequacy of the court's resources. A clearance rate of 100 percent means that cases are disposed of by the court at the same rate that new cases are filed. The processing of felony cases poses considerable problems for general jurisdiction courts because the offenses (1) often involve violent or drug crimes, (2) receive a great deal of public attention, (3) generate substantial prosecutorial cost, (4) impose tremendous burdens on the victims, and (5) involve serious evidentiary issues, such as DNA or blood analysis.

If relief is to be found, it will probably be in the form of better administrative and management techniques that improve the use of existing resources. Most courts, however, are not keeping pace with increasing numbers of criminal trial and appellate cases.[13] Another possible method of creating a more efficient court system is to unify existing state courts into a single administrative structure using modern management principles. A third solution would be the appointment of additional judges to the court. The Clinton administration has been criticized for its slow pace in filling vacancies on the federal bench.

THE JUDICIARY

The *judge* is the senior officer in a court of criminal law. His duties are quite varied and far more extensive than might be expected. During trials, the judge rules on the appropriateness of conduct, settles questions of evidence and procedure, and guides the questioning of witnesses. In a **jury trial** the judge must instruct jurors on which evidence is proper to examine and which should be ignored. The judge also formally charges the jury by instructing its members on what points of law and evidence they must consider to reach a decision of either guilty or not guilty. When a jury trial is waived, the judge must decide whether to hold for the complainant or the defendant. Finally, if a defendant is found guilty, the judge must decide on the sentence (in some cases, this is legislatively determined), which includes choosing the type of sentence, its length, and in the case of probation the conditions under which it may be revoked.

jury trial
The process of deciding a case by a group of persons selected and sworn in to serve as jurors at a criminal trial, often as a six- or twelve-person jury.

Other Judicial Functions

Beyond these stated duties, the trial judge has extensive control and influence over the other agencies of the court: probation, the court clerk, the police, and the district attorney's office. Probation and the clerk may be under the judge's explicit control. In some courts, the operations, philosophy, and procedures of these agencies are within the magistrate's administrative domain. In others — for example, where a state agency controls the probation department — the attitudes of the county or district court judge greatly influence the way a probation department is run and how its decisions are made. Judges often consult with probation staff on treatment decisions, and many judges are interested in providing the most innovative and up-to-date care possible.

Police and prosecutors are also directly influenced by the judge, whose sentencing discretion affects the arrest and charging processes. For example, if a judge usually chooses minimal sentences — such as a fine for a particular offense — the police may be reluctant to arrest offenders for that crime, knowing that doing so will basically be a waste of time. Similarly, if a judge is known to have a liberal attitude toward police discretion, the local department may be more inclined to engage in practices that border on entrapment or to pursue cases through easily obtained wiretaps. However, a magistrate oriented toward strict use of due process guarantees would stifle such activities by dismissing all cases involving apparent police abuses of personal freedoms. The district attorney's office may also be sensitive to judicial attitudes. The district attorney might forgo indictments in cases that the presiding magistrate expressly considers trivial or quasi-criminal and in which the judge has been known to take only token action, such as the prosecution of pornographers.

Finally, the judge considers requests by police and prosecutors for leniency (or severity) in sentencing. The judge's reaction to these requests is important if the police and the district attorney are to honor the bargains they may have made with defendants to secure information, cooperation, or guilty pleas. For example, when police tell informers that they will try to convince the judge to go easy on them to secure required information, they will often discuss the terms of the promised leniency with representatives of the court. If a judge ignores police demands, the department's bargaining power is severely diminished, and communication within the criminal justice system is impaired.

Judicial Qualifications

The qualifications for appointment to one of the existing 30,000 judgeships vary from state to state and court to court. Most typically, the potential judge must be a resident of the state, licensed to practice law, a member of the state bar association, and at least twenty-five and less than seventy years of age. However, a significant degree of diversity exists in the basic qualification, depending on the level of court jurisdiction. While almost every state requires judges to have a law degree if they are to serve on appellate courts or courts of general jurisdiction, it is not uncommon for municipal or town court judges to lack a legal background, even though they maintain the power to incarcerate criminal defendants.

Many methods are used to select judges, depending on the level of court jurisdiction. In some jurisdictions, the governor simply appoints judges. In others, the governor's recommendations must be confirmed by (1) the state senate, (2) the governor's council, (3) a special confirmation committee, (4) an executive council elected by the state assembly, or (5) an elected review board. Some states employ a judicial nominating commission that submits names to the governor for approval.

Another form of judicial selection is popular election. In some jurisdictions, judges run as members of the Republican, Democratic, or other parties, whereas in others they run without party affiliation. In thirteen states, partisan elections are used for selecting judges in courts of general jurisdiction; in seventeen states, nonpartisan elections are used; and in the remainder, upper–trial court judges are appointed by the governor or the legislature.

In the adversary process, the prosecutor is responsible for focusing the power of the state on those who disobey the law by charging them with a crime, releasing them from prosecution, or eventually bringing them to trial. Here Los Angeles prosecutor Pamela Bozanich is shown cross-examining Lyle Menendez, who was on trial for murdering his parents.

Missouri Plan
A way of picking judges through nonpartisan elections as a means of ensuring judicial performance standards.

Many states have adopted some form of what is known as the **Missouri Plan** to select appellate court judges, and six states also use it to select trial court judges. This plan consists of three parts: (1) a judicial nominating commission to nominate candidates for the bench, (2) an elected official (usually from the executive branch) to make appointments from the list submitted by the commission, and (3) subsequent nonpartisan and noncompetitive elections in which incumbent judges run on their records and voters can choose either their retention or dismissal.[14]

The quality of the judiciary is a concern. Although merit plans, screening committees, and popular elections are designed to ensure a competent judiciary, it has often been charged that many judicial appointments are made to pay off political debts or to reward cronies and loyal friends. Also not uncommon are charges that those desiring to be nominated for judgeships are required to make significant political contributions.

prosecutor
Representative of the state (executive branch) in criminal proceedings; advocate for the state's case — the charge — in the adversary trial, for example, the attorney general of the United States, U.S. attorneys, attorneys general of the states, district attorneys, and police prosecutors. The prosecutor participates in investigations both before and after arrest, prepares legal documents, participates in obtaining arrest or search warrants, decides whether to charge a suspect and, if so, with which offense. The prosecutor argues the state's case at trial, advises the police, participates in plea negotiations, and makes sentencing recommendations.

THE PROSECUTOR

In 1994 about twenty-four hundred chief state court prosecutors employed about sixty-five thousand attorneys, investigators, and support staff to handle felony cases in the state trial courts. Hundreds of municipal and county attorneys prosecute criminal cases in courts of limited jurisdiction, while others work in the federal court system. The personnel and workload of prosecutors' offices (county-state-federal) has increased by 20 percent since 1996.[15]

Depending on the level of government and the jurisdiction in which she functions, the **prosecutor** may be known as a district attorney, a county attorney, a state's attorney, or a U.S. attorney. Whatever the title, the prosecutor is ordinarily a member of the practicing bar who has been appointed or elected to be a public prosecutor.

Although the prosecutor participates with the judge and defense attorney in the adversary process, the prosecutor is responsible for bringing the state's case against the accused. The prosecutor focuses the power of the state on those who are accused of disobeying the law by charging them with a crime, releasing them from prosecution, or eventually bringing them to trial.

Although the prosecutor's primary duty is to enforce the criminal law, his fundamental obligation as an attorney is to seek justice, as well as to convict those who are guilty. For example, if the prosecutor discovers facts suggesting that the accused is innocent, he must bring this information to the attention of the court.

The senior prosecutor must make policy decisions on the exercise of prosecutorial enforcement powers in a wide range of cases in criminal law, consumer protection, housing, and other areas of the law. In so doing, the prosecutor determines and ultimately shapes the manner in which justice is exercised in society.

Many individual prosecutors are caught between being compelled by their supervisors to do everything possible to obtain a guilty verdict and acting as a concerned public official to ensure that justice is done. Sometimes this conflict can lead to *prosecutorial misconduct*. According to some legal authorities, unethical prosecutorial behavior is often motivated by the desire to obtain a conviction and by the fact that prosecutorial misbehavior is rarely punished by the courts.[16] Some prosecutors may conceal evidence or misrepresent it or influence juries by impugning the character of opposing witnesses. Even where a court may instruct a jury to ignore certain evidence, a prosecutor may attempt to sway the jury or the judge by simply mentioning the tainted evidence. Since appellate courts generally uphold convictions in cases where such misconduct is not considered serious (the harmless error doctrine), prosecutors are not penalized for their misbehavior, nor are they personally liable for their conduct. Overzealous, excessive, and even cruel prosecutors, motivated by a desire for political gain or notoriety, produce wrongful convictions, thereby abusing their office and the public trust.[17] According to legal expert Stanley Fisher, prosecutorial excesses appear when the government (1) always seeks the highest charges, (2) interprets the criminal law expansively, (3) wins as many convictions as possible, and (4) obtains the severest penalties.[18]

Duties of the Prosecutor

The prosecutor is the chief law enforcement officer of a particular jurisdiction. Her participation spans the entire gamut of the justice system, from the time search and arrest warrants are issued or a grand jury is empaneled to the final sentencing decision and appeal. The general duties of a prosecutor include (1) enforcing the law, (2) representing the government, (3) maintaining proper standards of conduct as an attorney and court officer, (4) developing programs and legislation for law and criminal justice reform, and (5) being a public spokesperson for the field of law. Of these, representing the government while presenting the state's case to the court is the prosecutor's most frequent task. In this regard, the duties of the prosecutor are highlighted in Exhibit 8.1

exhibit 8.1

Duties of the Prosecutor

1. Investigates possible violations of the law
2. Cooperates with police in investigating a crime
3. Determines what the charge will be
4. Interviews witnesses in criminal cases
5. Reviews applications for arrest and search warrants
6. Subpoenas witnesses
7. Represents the government in pretrial hearings and in motion procedures
8. Enters into plea-bargaining negotiations
9. Tries criminal cases
10. Recommends sentences to courts upon convictions
11. Represents the government in appeals

Many jurisdictions have also established special prosecution programs aimed at seeking indictments and convictions of those committing major felonies, violent offenses, rapes, and white-collar crimes. In a recent national survey of prosecutorial practices, Michael Benson and his colleagues found an apparent increase in the local prosecution of corporate offenders.[19] According to Benson, the federal government historically played the dominant role in controlling white-collar crime. But there appears to be an increased willingness to prosecute corporate misconduct on a local level if an offense causes substantial harm. The National District Attorneys Association (NDAA) has responded to the concerns of prosecutors faced with the need to enforce complex environmental laws by creating the National Environmental Crime Prosecution Center. This center, modeled after the National Center for Prosecution of Child Abuse, lends assistance to district attorneys who are prosecuting environmental crimes.

In addition, a form of priority prosecutions commonly known as the career criminal prosecution program is popular in many jurisdictions. This program involves identifying dangerous adult and juvenile offenders who commit a high number of crimes so that prosecutors can target them for swift prosecution. In 1999 the NDAA developed a National Traffic Law Center to focus on improving the quality of justice in traffic safety prosecutions.[20]

Types of Prosecutors In the federal system, prosecutors are known as U.S. attorneys and are appointed by the president. They are responsible for representing the government in federal district courts. The chief prosecutor is usually an administrator, and assistants normally handle the actual preparation and trial work. Federal prosecutors are professional civil service employees with reasonable salaries and job security.

On the state and county levels, the attorney general and the district attorney, respectively, are the chief prosecutorial officers. Again, the bulk of the criminal prosecution and staff work is performed by scores of full- and part-time attorneys, police investigators, and clerical personnel. Most attorneys who work for prosecutors on the state and county levels are political appointees who earn low salaries, handle many cases, and, in some jurisdictions, maintain private law practices. Many young lawyers take these staff positions to gain the trial experience that will qualify them for better opportunities. In most state, county, and municipal jurisdictions, however, the office of the prosecutor can be described as having the highest standards of professional skill, personal integrity, and working conditions.

In urban jurisdictions, the structure of the district attorney's office is often specialized, with separate divisions for felonies, misdemeanors, and trial and appeal assignments. In rural offices, chief prosecutors handle many of the criminal cases themselves. Where assistant prosecutors are employed, they often work part time, have limited professional opportunities, and depend on the political patronage of chief prosecutors for their positions.

The personnel practices, organizational structures, and political atmospheres of many prosecutors' offices often restrict the effectiveness of individual prosecutors in investigating and prosecuting criminal offenses. For many years, prosecutors have been criticized for bargaining justice away, using their position as a stepping stone to higher political office, and often failing to investigate or simply dismissing criminal cases. Lately, however, the prosecutor's public image has improved. Violations of federal laws, such as white-collar crime, drug peddling, and corruption, are being more aggressively investigated by the ninety-four U.S. attorneys and the nearly two thousand assistant U.S. attorneys. The National Drug Prosecution Center of the NDAA, for instance, is assisting state and federal prosecutors in enforcing complex drug laws.

Aggressive federal prosecutors have also made extraordinary progress in the war against insider trading and security fraud on Wall Street, using informants, wiretaps, and federal racketeering laws. Through RICO (Racketeer Influenced and Corrupt Organization Act, detailed in Chapter 3), the government has successfully obtained convictions of important Mafia gangsters.[21]

State crimes ranging from murder to larceny are prosecuted in state courts by district attorneys, who are stepping up their efforts against career criminals, shortening the time it takes to bring serious cases to trial, and addressing the long-neglected problems of victims and witnesses. With such actions, the prosecutor will continue to be one of the most powerful and visible professionals in the justice system. Table 8.1 identifies the special categories of felony prosecutions today involving some newly defined crimes.

PROSECUTORIAL DISCRETION One might expect that after the police arrest and bring a suspect to court, the entire criminal court process would be mobilized. This is often not the case, however. For a variety of reasons, a substantial percentage of defendants are never brought to trial. The prosecutor decides whether to bring a case to trial or to dismiss it outright. Even if the prosecutor decides to pursue a case, the charges may later be dropped if conditions are not favorable for a conviction, in a process called nolle prosequi.

Even in felony cases, the prosecutor ordinarily exercises much discretion in deciding whether to charge the accused with a crime.[22] After a police investigation, the prosecutor may be asked to review the sufficiency of the evidence to determine whether a criminal complaint should be filed. In some jurisdictions, this may involve presenting the evidence at a preliminary hearing. In other cases, the prosecutor may decide to seek a criminal complaint through the grand jury or other information procedure.

Table 8.1
Special Types of High-Priority Offenses

Case Type
Domestic violence
Stalking
Elder abuse
Hate crime
Environmental pollution
Gang membership
HIV exposure
Child Related
Juvenile delinquency
Nonpayment of child support
Parental abduction of children
Fraud
Bank/thrift fraud
Health-care fraud
Computer fraud/tampering

There is little question that prosecutors exercise a great deal of discretion in even the most serious cases. Barbara Boland studied the flow of felony cases through three jurisdictions in the United States: Golden, Colorado; Manhattan, New York; and Salt Lake City, Utah.[23] Although procedures were different in the three districts, prosecutors used their discretion to dismiss a high percentage of the cases before trial. When cases were forwarded for trial, very few defendants were actually acquitted, indicating that the prosecutorial discretion was exercised to screen out the weakest cases. In addition, of those cases accepted for prosecution, a high percentage ended with the defendant pleading guilty. All the evidence here points to the conclusion that prosecutorial discretion is used to reduce potential trial cases to a minimum.

The prosecutor may also play a limited role in exercising discretion in minor offenses. This role may consist of simply consulting with the police after their investigation results in a complaint being filed against the accused. In such instances, the decision to charge a person with a crime may be left primarily to the discretion of the law enforcement agency. The prosecutor may decide to enter this type of case after an arrest has been made and a complaint has been filed with the court, and he may subsequently determine whether to adjust the matter or proceed to trial. In some minor crimes, the prosecutor may not even appear until the trial stage of the process (or not at all); the police officer sometimes handles the entire case, including its prosecution.

The power to institute formal charges against the defendant is the key to the prosecutorial function. The ability to initiate or discontinue charges against a defendant is the control and power the prosecutor has over an individual's liberty. Almost seventy years ago, Newman Baker commented on the problems of prosecutorial decision making:

> "To prosecute or not to prosecute?" is a question which comes to mind of this official scores of times each day. A law has been contravened and the statute says he is bound to commence proceedings. His legal duty is clear. But what will be the result? Will it be a waste of time? Will it be expensive to the state? Will it be unfair to the defendant (the prosecutor applying his own ideas of justice)? Will it serve any good purpose to society in general? Will it have good publicity value? Will it cause a political squabble? Will it prevent the prosecutor from carrying the offender's home precinct when he, the prosecutor, runs for Congress after his term as prosecutor? Was the law violated a foolish piece of legislation? If the offender is a friend, is it the square thing to do to reward friendship by initiating criminal proceedings? These and many similar considerations are bound to come to the mind of the man responsible for setting the wheels of criminal justice in motion.[24]

Because they are ultimately responsible for deciding whether to prosecute, prosecutors must be aware of the wide variety of circumstances that affect their decisions. Frank Miller has identified a number of factors that affect discretion and the charging decision. Some of these include (1) the attitude of the victim, (2) the cost of prosecution to the criminal justice system, (3) the avoidance of undue harm to the suspect, (4) the availability of alternative procedures, (5) the use of civil sanctions, and (6) the willingness of the suspect to cooperate with law enforcement authorities.[25]

The Role of Prosecutorial Discretion

Regardless of its source, the proper exercise of prosecutorial discretion can improve the criminal justice process. For example, its use can prevent unnecessarily rigid implementation of the criminal law. Discretion allows the prosecutor to consider alternative decisions and humanize the operation of the criminal justice system. If prosecutors had little or no discretion, they would be forced to prosecute all cases brought to their attention. Judge Charles Breitel has stated, "If every policeman, every prosecutor, every court, and every postsentence agency performed his or its responsibility in strict accordance with rules of law, precisely and narrowly laid down, the criminal law would be ordered but intolerable."[26]

On the other hand, too much discretion can lead to abuses that result in the abandonment of law. One of the nation's most eminent legal scholars, Roscoe Pound, has defined *discretion* as "an authority conferred by law to act in certain conditions or situations in accordance with an official's or an official agency's considered judgment and conscience. It is an idea of morals, belonging to the twilight between law and morals."[27] In terms of prosecutorial practices, this definition implies the need to select and choose among alternative decisions — to remove cases from the criminal process, to modify criminal charges, or to prosecute to the fullest intent of legal authority. Because there is no easy way to make these decisions, it has been recommended that the prosecutor establish standards for evaluating whether criminal proceedings should be brought against an accused.

Prosecutorial discretion is also influenced by the types of problems that exist in serious felony cases. The main reasons for not prosecuting a defendant include (1) search or seizure problems, (2) unavailability of prosecution's witness, (3) speedy trial restrictions, and (4) victim reluctance.

Town of Newton v. Rumery The 1987 U.S. Supreme Court case that grants the prosecutor wide discretion in negotiating plea bargains as long as the defendant's legal rights are guaranteed.

Judicial Restraints The prosecutor's charging discretion has been considered and examined by the U.S. Supreme Court. For example, in ***Town of Newton v. Rumery*** (1987), a defendant entered into an agreement with a prosecutor under which the criminal charges against him would be dropped in exchange for his agreeing not to file a civil suit against the town police. The defendant later filed the suit anyway, maintaining that the original agreement was coercive and interfered with his right to legal process. He lost the case when the trial court ruled that his earlier agreement not to file suit against the town was binding. On appeal, the Supreme Court found for the town. It upheld the legality of the prosecutor's actions because the idea for the bargain had originated with the defense and therefore was not inherently coercive. *Rumery* illustrates that prosecutors maintain significant discretion to work out bargains and deals as long as they do not deprive defendants of their legal rights.[28]

The courts have also reviewed such prosecutorial behavior issues as (1) disciplining a prosecutor for making disruptive statements in court, (2) the failure of a prosecutor to adhere to sentence recommendations pursuant to a plea bargain, (3) disqualifying a prosecutor who represented a criminal defendant currently under indictment, (4) removing a prosecutor for making public statements harmful to the office of the district attorney that are not constitutionally protected under the First Amendment, and (5) removing a prosecutor for withholding evidence that might exonerate a defendant.

Prosecutors need to exercise control and discretion. In accordance with the national prosecution standards of the NDAA and the American Bar Association, the broad discretion given to the prosecutor necessitates that the greatest effort be made to use this power fairly.[29]

Courts have also been more concerned about prosecutors who use their discretion in a vindictive manner to punish defendants who exercise their legal rights. For example, in *North Carolina v. Pearce* (1969), the U.S. Supreme Court held that a judge in a retrial cannot impose a sentence more severe than that originally imposed. In other words, a prosecutor cannot seek a stricter sentence for a defendant who succeeds in getting her first conviction set aside.[30] In *Blackledge v. Perry* (1974), the Court dealt with the issue of vindictiveness on the part of the prosecutor and found that imposing a penalty on a defendant for having successfully pursued a statutory right of appeal is a violation of due process of

Attorney Stephen Jones, who represented Timothy McVeigh in the Oklahoma City bombing trial, reads headlines about his client. Jones is a professional legal advocate, who, by his zealous preparation of facts and law, hopes to get his client a fair and impartial judgment. The duty of a lawyer to his client and his duty to the legal system are the same: to represent his client zealously within the boundaries of the law.

law.[31] But in *Bordenkircher v. Hayes* (1978), the Court allowed the prosecutor to carry out threats of increased charges made during plea negotiations when the defendant refused to plead guilty to the original charge.[32]

These decisions provide the framework of the "prosecutorial vindictiveness" doctrine: Due process of law may be violated if the prosecutor retaliates against a defendant and there is proof of actual vindictiveness. The prosecutor's legitimate exercise of discretion must be balanced against the defendant's legal rights.

public defender
An attorney generally employed by the government to represent poor persons accused of a crime at no cost to the accused.

THE DEFENSE ATTORNEY

The defense attorney is the counterpart of the prosecuting attorney in the criminal process. The accused has a constitutional right to counsel, and when the defendant cannot afford an attorney, the state must provide one. The accused may obtain counsel from the private bar if he can afford to do so; if the defendant is indigent, private counsel or a **public defender** may be assigned by the court (see the discussion on the defense of the indigent later in this chapter).

defense counsel. At a time when society is tough on crime, the conduct of the defense attorney is subject to heightened scrutiny. This guide assists lawyers in making ethical choices without compromising the defendants' right to competent and zealous representation under the Sixth Amendment.

THE RIGHT TO COUNSEL

Over the past decade, the rules and procedures of criminal justice administration have become extremely complex. Bringing a case to court involves a detailed investigation of a crime, knowledge of court procedures, the use of rules of evidence, and skills in criminal advocacy. Both the state and the defense must have this specialized expertise, particularly when an individual's freedom is at stake. Consequently, the right to the assistance of counsel in the criminal justice system is essential if the defendant is to have a fair chance of presenting a case in the adversary process.

indigent
Person who is needy and poor or who lacks the means to hire an attorney.

Sixth Amendment
The U.S. constitutional amendment containing various criminal trial rights, such as the right to public trial, right to trial by jury, and the right to confrontation of witnesses.

Gideon v. Wainwright
The 1963 U.S. Supreme Court case that granted counsel to indigent defendants in felony prosecutions.

One of the most critical issues in the criminal justice system has been whether an **indigent** defendant has the right to counsel. Can the accused who is poor and cannot afford an attorney have a fair trial without the assistance of counsel? Is counsel required at preliminary hearings? Should the convicted indigent offender be given counsel at state expense in appeals of the case? Questions such as these have arisen constantly in recent years. The federal court system has long provided counsel to the indigent defendant on the basis of the **Sixth Amendment** to the U.S. Constitution, unless she waived this right.[37] This constitutional mandate clearly applies to the federal courts, but its application to state criminal proceedings has been less certain.

In the 1963 landmark case of ***Gideon v. Wainwright,*** the U.S. Supreme Court took the first major step on the issue of right to counsel by holding that state courts must provide counsel to indigent defendants in felony prosecutions.[38] Almost ten years later, in the 1972 case of *Argersinger v. Hamlin,* the Court extended the obligation to provide counsel to all criminal cases where the penalty includes imprisonment — regardless of whether the offense is a felony or misdemeanor.[39] These two major decisions relate to the Sixth Amendment right to counsel as it applied to the presentation of a defense at the trial stages of the criminal justice system.

In numerous Supreme Court decisions since *Gideon v. Wainwright,* the states have been required to provide counsel for indigent defendants at virtually all other stages of the criminal process, beginning with arrest and concluding with the defendant's release from the system. Today, the Sixth Amendment right to counsel and the Fifth and Fourteenth Amendment guarantee of due process of law have been judicially interpreted together to provide the defendant with counsel by the state in all types of criminal proceedings.

In addition to guaranteeing the right of counsel at the earliest stages of the justice system, as well as at trials, the Supreme Court has moved to extend the right to counsel to postconviction and other collateral proceedings, such as probation and parole revocation and appeal. When, for example, the court intends to revoke a defendant's probation and impose a sentence, the probationer has a right to counsel at the deferred sentence hearing.[40] Where the state provides for an appellate review of the criminal conviction, the defendant is entitled to the assistance of counsel for this initial appeal.[41] The defendant does not have the right to counsel for an appellate review beyond the original appeal or for a discretionary review to the U.S. Supreme Court. The Supreme Court has also required the states to provide counsel in other proceedings that involve the loss of personal liberty, such as juvenile delinquency hearings[42] and mental health commitments.[43]

Areas still remain in the criminal justice system where the courts have not required assistance of counsel for the accused. These include (1) preindictment lineups; (2) booking procedures, including the taking of fingerprints and other forms of identification; (3) grand jury investigations; (4) appeals beyond the first review; (5) disciplinary proceedings in correctional institutions; and (6) postrelease revocation hearings. Nevertheless, the general rule of thumb is that no person can be deprived of freedom or lose a "liberty interest" without representation by counsel.

The right to counsel can also be spelled out in particular federal or state statutes. For example, beyond abiding by current constitutional requirements, a state may provide counsel by statute at all stages of juvenile proceedings, in dealing with inmate prison infractions or pretrial release hearings, or when considering temporary confinement of drug or sex offenders for psychiatric examination.

Today, the scope of representation for the indigent defendant is believed to cover virtually all areas of the criminal process and most certainly those critical points at which a person's liberty is at stake. Table 8.2 summarizes the major U.S. Supreme Court decisions granting defendants counsel throughout the criminal justice system.

The Private Bar

Today, the lawyer whose practice involves a substantial proportion of criminal cases is often considered a specialist in the field. Since most lawyers are not prepared in law school for criminal work, their skill often results from their experience in the trial courts. Such famous lawyers as Robert Shapiro, Alan Dershowitz, John Cochran, F. Lee Bailey, and Gerry Spence are the elite of the private criminal bar; they are nationally known criminal defense attorneys who often represent defendants for large fees in celebrated and widely publicized cases. Attorneys like these are relatively few in number and do not regularly handle the ordinary criminal defendant.

Besides this limited group of well-known criminal lawyers, some lawyers and law firms serve as house counsel for such professional criminals as narcotics dealers, gamblers, prostitutes, and even big-time burglars. These lawyers, however, constitute a very small percentage of the private bar practicing criminal law.

A large number of criminal defendants are represented by lawyers who often accept many cases for small fees. These lawyers may belong to small law firms or work alone, but a sizable portion of their practice involves representing those accused of crime. Other private practitioners occasionally take on criminal matters as part of their general practice.

Associated with the private practice of criminal law is the fact that the fee system can create a conflict of interest. Because private attorneys are usually paid in advance and do not expect additional funds if their client is convicted and because many are aware of the guilt of their clients before the trial begins, they earn the greatest profit if they get the case settled as quickly as possible. This usually means bargaining with the prosecutor rather than going to trial. Even if attorneys win the case at trial, they may lose personally, since the time expended will not be compensated by more than the gratitude of their client. And, of course, many criminal defendants cannot afford even a modest legal fee and therefore cannot avail themselves of the services of a private attorney. For these reasons, an elaborate, publicly funded legal system has developed.

Legal Services for the Indigent

To satisfy the constitutional requirements that indigent defendants be provided with the assistance of counsel at various stages of the criminal process, the federal government and the states have had to evaluate and expand criminal defense services. Prior to the Supreme Court's mandate in *Gideon v. Wainwright,* public defendant services were provided mainly by local private attorneys appointed and paid for by the court — called **assigned counsels** — or by limited public defendant programs. In 1961,

assigned counsel
A lawyer appointed by the court to represent a defendant in a criminal case because the person is too poor to hire counsel.

for example, public defender services existed in only 3 percent of the counties in the United States, serving only about one-quarter of the country's population.[44] The general lack of defense services for indigents traditionally stemmed from these causes, among others:

1. Until fairly recently, the laws of most jurisdictions did not require the assistance of counsel for felony offenders and others.
2. Only a few attorneys were interested in criminal law practice.
3. The organized legal bar was generally indifferent to the need for criminal defense assistance.
4. The caseloads of lawyers working in public defender agencies were staggering.
5. Financial resources for courts and defense programs were limited.

Today, virtually all jurisdictions have public defender systems in one form or another.

However, beginning with the *Gideon* case in 1963 and continuing through the *Argersinger* decision in 1972, the criminal justice system has been forced to increase public defender services. Today, about three thousand state and local agencies are providing indigent legal services in the United States.

Providing legal services for the indigent offender is a huge undertaking. Almost 5 million offenders are given free legal services annually. And although most states have a formal set of rules to signify who is an indigent and many require indigents to repay the state for at least part of their legal services (known as *recoupment*), indigent legal services still cost over $1.5 billion annually.

Programs providing counsel assistance to indigent defendants can be divided into three major categories: public defender systems, assigned counsel systems, and contract systems. In addition, other approaches to the delivery of legal services include the use of mixed systems, such as representation by both the public defender and the private bar, law school clinical programs, and prepaid legal services. Of the three major approaches, assigned counsel systems dominate defender programs, with the majority of U.S. courts using this method; 34 percent use public defenders, and 6 percent contract attorneys.[45] Although many jurisdictions have a combination of these programs, statewide public defender programs seem to be on the increase.

PUBLIC DEFENDERS Public defender offices are located in the majority of counties in the United States. The first public defender program in the United States opened in 1913 in Los Angeles. Over the years, primarily as a result of efforts by judicial leaders and bar groups, the public defender program has become the model for the delivery of legal services to indigent defendants in criminal cases throughout the country.

Most public defender offices can be thought of as law firms whose only clients are criminal offenders. However, there is a major division in the administration of public defender services. Many states have a statewide public defender's office headed by a chief public defender who administers the operation. In some of these states, the chief defender establishes offices in all counties around the state; in others, the chief defender relies on part-time private attorneys to provide indigent legal services in rural counties. Statewide public defenders are organized as part of the judicial branch, as part of the executive branch, as an independent state agency, or even as a private, nonprofit organization.

In the majority of states, the public defender's office is organized on the county level of government, and each office is autonomous. For example, in Florida elected public defenders operate separately in each of the judicial circuits

Table 8.2
Major U.S. Supreme Court Cases Granting Right to Counsel

Case	Holding
Powell v. Alabama, 287 U.S. 45 (1932)	A defendant has the right to counsel at his trial in a state capital case
Townsend v. Burke, 334 U.S. 736 (1948)	A convicted offender has a right to counsel at the time of sentencing
Moore v. Michigan, 355 U.S. 155 (1957)	A defendant has the right to counsel when submitting a guilty plea to court.
Hamilton v. Alabama, 368 U.S. 52 (1961)	The arraignment is a critical stage in the criminal process, so denial of the right to counsel is a violation of due process of law.
Douglas v. California, 372 U.S. 353 (1963)	An indigent defendant granted a first appeal from a criminal conviction has the right to be represented by counsel on appeal.
Gideon v. Wainwright, 372 U.S. 335 (1963)	An indigent defendant charged in a state court with a noncapital felony has the right to the assistance of free counsel at trial under the due process clause of the Fourteenth Amendment.
Escobedo v. Illinois, 378 U.S. 478 (1964)	A defendant has the right to counsel during the course of any police interrogation.
Massiah v. United States, 377 U.S. 201 (1964)	A defendant has the right to counsel during postindictment interrogation.
Miranda v. Arizona, 384 U.S. 436 (1966)	Procedural safeguards, including the right to counsel, must be followed at custodial interrogation to secure the privilege against self-incrimination.
In re Gault, 387 U.S. 1 (1967)	Procedural due process, including the right to counsel, applies to juvenile delinquency adjudication that may lead to a child's commitment to a state institution.
Mempa v. Rhay, 389 U.S. 128 (1967)	A convicted offender has the right to assistance of counsel at probation revocation hearings where the sentence has been deferred.
United States v. Wade, 388 U.S. 218 (1967)	A defendant in a pretrial, postindictment lineup for identification purposes has the right to assistance of counsel.
Brady v. United States, 397 U.S. 742 (1970)	Counsel is required during the plea-bargaining process.
Coleman v. Alabama, 399 U.S. 1 (1970)	The preliminary hearing is a critical stage in a criminal prosecution, requiring the state to provide the indigent defendant with counsel.

Table 8.2
(continued)

Argersinger v. Hamlin, 407 U.S. 25 (1972)	A defendant has the right to counsel at trial whenever she may be imprisoned for any offense, even for one day, whether classified as a misdemeanor or a felony.
Morrissey v. Brewer, 408 U.S. 471 (1972) *Gagnon v. Scarpelli,* 411 U.S. 778 (1973)	A defendant has a right to counsel in the court's discretion at probation revocation and parole board revocation hearings.
Faretta v. California, 422 U.S. 806 (1975)	A defendant has a constitutional right to defend himself if his waiver of right to counsel is knowing and intelligent.

in the state. In Pennsylvania, a local public defender is legislatively mandated in each of the state's counties. In Illinois, each county with a population above a certain level has a legislatively mandated public defender's office.

ASSIGNED COUNSEL SYSTEM In contrast to the public defender system, the assigned counsel system involves the use of private attorneys appointed by the court to represent indigent defendants. The private attorney is selected from a list of attorneys established by the court and is reimbursed by the state for any legal services rendered to the client. Assigned counsels are usually used in rural areas, which do not have sufficient criminal caseloads to justify a full-time public defender staff.

There are two main types of assigned counsel systems. In the first, which makes up about 75 percent of all assigned counsel systems, the presiding judge appoints attorneys on a case-by-case basis; this is referred to as an *ad hoc assigned counsel system.* In a *coordinated assigned counsel system,* an administrator oversees the appointment of counsel and sets up guidelines for the administration of indigent legal services. The fees awarded to assigned counsels can vary widely, ranging from a low of $10 per hour for handling a misdemeanor out of court to over $100 per hour for a serious felony handled in court. Some jurisdictions may establish a maximum allowance per case of $750 for a misdemeanor and $1,500 for a felony. Average rates seem to be between $40 and $80 per hour, depending on the nature of the case. Restructuring the attorney fee system is undoubtedly needed to maintain fair standards for the payment of such legal services.

The assigned counsel system, unless organized properly, suffers from such problems as unequal assignments, inadequate legal fees, and the lack of supportive or supervisory services. Other disadvantages are the frequent use of inexperienced attorneys and the tendency to use the guilty plea too quickly. Some judicial experts believe the assigned counsel system is still no more than an ad hoc approach that presents serious questions about the quality of representation. However, the system is simple to operate. It also offers the private bar an important role in providing indigent legal services, since most public defender systems cannot represent all needy criminal defendants. Thus, the appointed counsel system gives attorneys the opportunity to do criminal defense work.

contract system (attorney)
Providing counsel to indigent offenders by having attorneys under contract to the county handle all (or some) such cases.

CONTRACT SYSTEM The **contract system** is a relative newcomer to providing legal services to the indigent. In this system, a block grant is given to a lawyer or law firm to handle indigent defense cases. In some instances, the attorney is

Lawyers doing criminal defense work have discovered an increasing need for their services, not only at trial but also at the pretrial and postjudicial stages of the criminal justice system. Public defenders may be called on to provide a variety of services to their clients. Here a public defender meets with a client at the client's home.

given a set amount of money and is required to handle all cases assigned. In other jurisdictions, contract lawyers agree to provide legal representation for a set number of cases at a fixed fee. A third system involves representation at an estimated cost per case until the dollar amount of the contract is reached. At that point, the contract may be renegotiated, but the lawyers are not obligated to take new cases.

The contract system is used often in counties that also have public defenders. Such counties may need independent counsel when a conflict of interest arises or when there is a constant overflow of cases. It is also used in sparsely populated states that cannot justify the structure and costs of full-time public defender programs. Pauline Houlden and Steven Balkin found that contract attorneys were at least as effective as assigned counsel and were most cost effective.[46] The per case cost in any jurisdiction for indigent defense services is determined largely by the type of program offered. In most public defender programs, funds are obtained through annual appropriations; assigned counsel costs relate to legal charges for appointed counsel; and contract programs negotiate a fee for the entire service. No research currently available indicates which method is the most effective way to represent the indigent on a cost-per-case basis. Advantages of the contract system include the provision of comprehensive legal services, controlled costs, and improved coordination in counsel programs.[47]

MIXED SYSTEMS A mixed system uses both public defenders and private attorneys in an attempt to draw on the strengths of both. In this approach, the public defender system operates simultaneously with the assigned counsel system or contract system to offer total coverage to the indigent defendant. This need occurs when the caseload increases beyond the capacity of the public defender's office. In addition, many counties supply independent counsel to all codefendants in a single case to prevent a conflict of interest. In most others, separate counsel will be provided if a codefendant requests it or if the judge or public defender perceives a conflict of interest. Because all lawyers in a public defender's office are considered to be working for the same firm, outside counsel is required if codefendants are in conflict with one another. Many counties having public defenders also have a program to assign counsel in overflow and conflict-of-interest cases. Public defender services supplemented by contract programs and an assigned counsel system often provide the best model to uphold the Sixth Amendment right to counsel for indigent defendants.

Other methods of providing counsel to the indigent include the use of law school students and prepaid legal service programs (similar to comprehensive medical insurance). Most jurisdictions have a student practice rule of procedure; third-year law school students in clinical programs provide supervised counsel to defendants in nonserious offenses. In *Argersinger v. Hamlin,* Supreme Court Justice William Brennan suggested that law students are an important resource in fulfilling constitutional defense requirements. [48]

COSTS OF DEFENDING THE POOR Over the past decade, the justice system has been faced with extreme pressure to provide counsel for all indigent criminal defendants. Inadequate funding has made implementation of this Sixth Amendment right an impossible task. The chief reasons for underfunded defender programs are (1) caseload problems, (2) lack of available attorneys, and (3) legislative restraints. Increasing numbers of drug cases, mandatory sentencing, and even overcharging have put tremendous stress on defender services. The system is also overloaded with appeals by indigent defendants convicted at the trial level whose representation involves filing complex briefs and making oral arguments. Such postconviction actions often consume a great deal of time and result in additional backlog problems. Death penalty litigation is another area where legal resources for the poor are strained.

In some jurisdictions, attorneys are just not available to provide defense work. Burnout due to heavy caseloads, low salaries, and poor working conditions is generally the major cause for the limited supply of attorneys interested in representing the indigent defendant. Some attorneys even refuse to accept appointments in criminal cases because the fees are too low.

Lack of government funding is the most significant problem today. While the entire justice system is often underfunded, the prosecutor–defense system is usually in the worst shape. Ordinarily, providing funding for indigent criminal defendants is not the most politically popular thing to do.

Obviously, the Sixth Amendment means little without counsel. The constitutional mandate that calls for legal representation requires adequate funding for these services. The National Center for State Courts, the National Legal Aid and Defenders Association, the American Bar Association, and many other legal and citizen groups believe that the public defender system is losing the battle for funding to the enormous increase in drug cases.

Funding for defender programs is ordinarily the responsibility of state and local government. As a result of an amendment to the Crime Control Act of 1990, however, federal funds are also available through the Drug Control Act of 1988.[49] According to most experts on defense funding, jurisdictions whose legislatures have been relatively generous in funding such programs in the past have continued to do so, while underfunded programs have become more seriously hampered. The Anti-Terrorism Act of 1996 authorizes over $300 million to improve the federal judiciary's defender program.[50]

Over the years, the quality of legal representation for indigent defendants has often been criticized by criminal justice experts. Yet, despite that assertion, a study of felony dispositions in nine state trial courts by the National Center for State Courts proves otherwise.[51] The study found that public defenders are consistently as successful as private counsel in resolving cases expeditiously and providing effective representation. There are few differences in conviction rates, charge reduction rates, incarceration rates, and lengths of prison sentences in cases represented by different types of criminal defense attorneys. Other implications of the study included (1) defenders of the indigent constituted an experienced group of attorneys who were part of an emerging subprofession, (2) financial resources are essential to effective public defense work, and (3) the type of organizational structure (public defender, contract attorney, assigned counsel, or private counsel) must be based on the circumstances of each jurisdiction. Exhibit 8.3 describes the key developments of defense services over the past decade.

The Competence of Defense Attorneys

The presence of competent and effective counsel has long been a basic principle of the adversary system. With the Sixth Amendment guarantee of counsel for virtually all defendants, the performance of today's attorneys has come into question.

Inadequacy of counsel may occur in a variety of instances. The attorney may refuse to meet regularly with her client, fail to cross-examine key government witnesses, or fail to investigate the case properly. A defendant's plea of guilty may be based on poor advice, where the attorney may misjudge the admissibility of evidence. When codefendants have separate counsel, conflicts of interest between the defense attorneys may arise. On an appellate level, the lawyer may decline to file a brief, instead relying on a brief submitted for one of the coappellants. Such problems as these are being raised with increasing frequency.

Strickland v. Washington
The 1984 U.S. Supreme Court decision upholding that defendants have the right to reasonably effective assistance of counsel (i.e., competent representation).

The concept of attorney competence was defined by the U.S. Supreme Court in the 1984 case of ***Strickland v. Washington.***[52] Strickland had been arrested for committing a string of extremely serious crimes, including murder, torture, and kidnapping. Against his lawyer's advice, Strickland pleaded guilty and threw himself on the mercy of the trial judge at a capital sentencing hearing. He also ignored his attorney's recommendation that he exercise his right to have an advisory jury at his sentencing hearing.

In preparing for the hearing, the lawyer spoke with Strickland's wife and mother but did not otherwise seek character witnesses. Nor was a psychiatric examination requested since, in the attorney's opinion, Strickland did not have psychological problems. The attorney also did not ask for a presentence investigation because he felt such a report would contain information damaging to his client.

Although the presiding judge had a reputation for leniency in cases where the defendant confessed, he sentenced Strickland to death. Strickland appealed

exhibit 8.3

Significant Achievements in Defense Services for the Poor

1990–2000

- New defense services in many southern states, including Louisiana, Arkansas, and Mississippi
- Renewed interest by the U.S. Justice Department to support the need for more resources for indigent defense
- Creation of a state commissioner office to oversee indigent defense systems
- Increased fees for assigned counsel
- Expansion of staff attorney public defender programs
- Rise of mixed funding where low-income criminal defendants pay for part of their defense

SOURCE: John Aranga, "Defense Services for the Poor," *American Bar Association Journal on Criminal Justice* 13 (1999): 45–46.

on the grounds that his attorney had rendered ineffective counsel, citing his failure to seek psychiatric testimony and present character witnesses.

The case eventually went to the Supreme Court, which upheld Strickland's sentence. The justices found that a defendant's claim of attorney incompetence must have two components. First, the defendant must show that the counsel's performance was deficient and that such serious errors were made as to eliminate the presence of counsel guaranteed by the Sixth Amendment. Second, the defendant must also show that the deficient performance prejudiced the case to an extent that the defendant was deprived of a fair trial. In the case at hand, the Court found insufficient evidence that the attorney had acted beyond the boundaries of professional competence. The *Strickland* case established the two-pronged test for determining effectiveness of counsel.

Burger v. Kemp
The 1987 U.S. Supreme Court decision upholding that no conflict of interest results when a defense attorney represents two defendants charged with the same crime as long as counsel acts competently and effectively.

The U.S. Supreme Court dealt with the issue of conflict of interest between defense lawyers in ***Burger v. Kemp*** (1987).[53] Two defendants charged with murder were represented by law partners. Each defendant was tried separately, but the attorneys conferred and assisted each other in the trial process. One defendant, who was found guilty and sentenced to death, claimed ineffective legal representation because he believed his attorney failed to present mitigating circumstances to show that he was less culpable than the codefendant. But the Supreme Court said this view was unfounded because the defendant claiming the conflict of interest actually perpetrated the crime. The Court also said it is not per se a violation of constitutional guarantees of effective assistance of counsel when a single attorney represents two defendants or when two partners supplement each other in the trial defense.

The key issue is the level of competence that should be required of defense counsel in criminal cases. This question concerns appointed counsel, as well as counsel chosen by the accused. Some appellate court decisions have overturned lower-court convictions when it was judged that the performance of counsel had reduced the trial to a farce or a mockery. Other appellate courts have held that there was ineffective counsel where gross incompetence had the effect of eliminating the basis for a substantial defense.

reasonable competence standard
The standard by which legal representation is judged: Did the defendant receive a reasonable level of legal aid?

In recent years, the courts have adopted a **reasonable competence standard,** but differences exist on the formulation and application of this standard. For example, is it necessary for defense counsel to answer on appeal every nonfrivolous issue requested by his convicted client? What if counsel does not provide the court with all the information at the sentencing stage and the defendant feels counsel's performance is inadequate? Whether any of these instances is an appropriate situation for stating that counsel is incompetent requires court review.

COURT ADMINISTRATION

In addition to qualified personnel, there is a need for efficient management of the judiciary system. Former Chief Justice Warren Burger wrote:

> The days are . . . past when a chief judge, with the help of a secretary and the clerk of the court, can manage the increasingly complex tasks required of them to keep courts functioning effectively. We must be constantly alert to new ideas, new methods, new ways of looking at the judiciary.[54]

The need for efficient management techniques in an ever-expanding criminal court system has led to the recognition of improved court administration as a way to relieve court congestion. Management goals include improving organization and scheduling of cases, devising methods to allocate court resources efficiently, administering fines and monies due the court, preparing budgets, and overseeing personnel.

The federal courts have led the way in creating and organizing court administration. In 1939 Congress passed the Administrative Office Act, which established the Administrative Office of the United States Courts. Its director was charged with gathering statistics on the work of the federal courts and preparing the judicial budget for approval by the Conference of Senior Circuit Judges. One clause of the act created a judicial council with general supervisory responsibilities for the district and circuit courts.

Unlike the federal government, the states have experienced a slow and uneven growth in the development and application of court management principles. The first state to establish an administrative office was North Dakota in 1927. Today, all states employ some form of central administration.

The federal government has encouraged the development of state court management through funding assistance to court managers. In addition, the federal judiciary has provided the philosophical impetus for better and more effective court management. A court system is an extremely complex organization that is far more difficult to manage than the typical business enterprise or government agency because

1. Its key people are accustomed to working as individuals and do not take kindly to regimentation.
2. A very high value is placed on judicial independence, and this severely limits the pressures that can be brought to bear to produce desired administrative results.
3. Many persons involved in the judicial process — attorneys, jurors, witnesses, litigants — are not employed by the judiciary.
4. Participants in the judicial process often have conflicting goals.[55]

Another obstacle facing court administration is the generally low profile of the courts themselves. Except in times of unusual stress, judicial performance is hidden from public view, and mismanagement is rarely noted by taxpayers. Despite increased efforts to manage courts efficiently, successes have been rare. For example, a survey of the nation's state and local courts revealed that many have fragmented and overlapping jurisdictions, lack sufficiently trained personnel, and have no consistent procedures for handling various types of proceedings. The study concluded: Each court in each county in each state is different. Each has its own set of challenges. They are closely tied to the experience and temperament of the judge, the size and quality of the bar, the people who live in the area, and the kind of justice they demand.[56]

Despite the multitude of problems in reforming court management, some progress is being made. In most jurisdictions today, centralized court administrative services perform numerous functions with the help of sophisticated computers that free the judiciary to fulfill their roles as arbiters of justice.

Technology and Court Management

Computers are becoming an important aid in the administration and management of courts. Rapid retrieval and organization of data can be used for such functions as

- Maintaining case histories and statistical reporting.
- Monitoring and scheduling of cases.
- Preparing documents.
- Indexing cases.

- Issuing summonses.
- Notifying witnesses, attorneys, and others of required appearances.
- Selecting and notifying jurors.
- Preparing and administering budgets and payrolls.[57]

The federal government has encouraged the states to experiment with computerized information systems. Federal funds were used to begin a fifty-state consortium for the purpose of establishing a standardized crime-reporting system called SEARCH (Systems for the Electronic Analysis and Retrieval of Criminal Histories).

Computer technology is also being applied in the courts in such areas as videotaped testimonies, new court-reporting devices, information systems, and data-processing systems to handle such functions as court docketing and jury management. In 1968 only ten states had state-level automated information systems; today, all states employ such systems for a mix of tasks and duties.

Another modern technology being used for court administration is the facsimile machine. Fax machines allow the courts to relay criminal arrest or search warrants, juvenile warrants, and temporary restraining orders instantly to police officers.

Court jurisdictions are also cooperating with police departments in the installation of communication gear that allows defendants to be arraigned via closed-circuit TV while they are in police custody. Closed-circuit TV has been used for judicial conferences and scheduling meetings. Courts are also using voice-activated cameras to record all testimony during trials; these are the sole means of keeping trial records.

The computer cannot replace the judge, but it can be used as an ally to help speed the trial process by identifying backlogs and bottlenecks that can be eradicated by applying intelligent managerial techniques. Just as a manager must know the type and quantity of goods on hand in a warehouse, so an administrative judge must have available information concerning those entering the judge's domain, what happened to them once they were in it, and how they have fared since judgment has been rendered.

SUMMARY

The U.S. court system is a complex social institution. There is no set pattern of court organization. Courts are organized on federal, state, county, and local levels of government. The judge, the prosecutor, and the defense attorney are the major officers of justice in the judicial system. The judge approves plea bargains, tries cases, and determines the sentence given the offender. The prosecutor, who is the people's attorney, has discretion to decide the criminal charge and disposition. The prosecutor's daily decisions significantly affect police and court operations.

The role of the defense attorney in the criminal justice system has grown dramatically during the past thirty years. Today, providing defense services to the indigent criminal defendant is an everyday practice. Under landmark decisions of the U.S. Supreme Court, particularly *Gideon v. Wainwright* and *Argersinger v. Hamlin,* all defendants who may be imprisoned for any offense must be afforded counsel at trials. Methods of providing counsel include systems for assigned counsel, where an attorney is selected by the court to represent the accused, and public defender programs, where public employees provide legal services. Lawyers doing criminal defense work have discovered an increasing need for their services, not only at trial but also at the pre- and postjudicial stages of the criminal justice system.

In sum, criminal trials need to be better engineered for the truth. The justice system cannot condone prosecutorial over defense misconduct. There is also the urgent need to merge the judiciary in an efficient manner.

KEY TERMS

lower court
felony court
appellate court
court of last resort
writ of certiorari
landmark decision
jury trial
Missouri Plan
prosecutor
Town of Newton v. Rumery
public defender
adversarial procedure
indigent
Sixth Amendment
Gideon v. Wainwright
assigned counsel
contract system
Strickland v. Washington
Burger v. Kemp
reasonable competence standard

 INFOTRAC COLLEGE EDITION EXERCISES

The role of counsel for the accused is complex, involving multiple obligations. Toward the client, the defense lawyer is a counselor and advocate; toward the prosecutor, the lawyer is a professional adversary; and toward the court, the lawyer is both advocate for the client and officer of the court. The defense attorney advocates the use of due process perspective because it provides fair and equitable treatment to those accused of a crime. Public defenders use hearings, notices, motions, and other legal devices in gaining outcomes for their clients (acquittals, charge reductions, and short sentences to prison).

Search for articles using *InfoTrac College Edition* regarding the role of the criminal defense attorney in the justice system. Use key terms like "public defenders," "indigency," and "right to counsel."

QUESTIONS

1. Should attorneys disclose information given them by their clients concerning participation in an earlier unsolved crime? Explain.
2. Should defense attorneys cooperate with a prosecutor if it means that their clients will go to jail? Explain.
3. Should a prosecutor have absolute discretion over which cases to proceed on and which to drop? Explain.
4. Should clients be made aware of an attorney's track record in court? Explain.
5. Does the assigned counsel system present an inherent conflict of interest, since attorneys are hired and paid by the institution they are to oppose? Explain.
6. Do you believe prosecutors have a great deal of discretion? Why or why not?
7. Was independent counsel Ken Starr's pursuit of President Clinton an example of prosecutorial abuse? Explain.

NOTES

1. Richard Willing, "DNA Tests Cast Doubt on Justice System," *USA Today,* 28 September 1999, 3A.
2. Malcolm Feeley, *The Process Is the Punishment* (New York: Russell Sage, 1979), 9–11.
3. Thomas Henderson, *The Significance of Judicial Structure: The Effect of Unification on Trial Court Operations* (Washington, D.C.: National Institute of Justice, 1984).
4. Johnathan Casper, Tom Tyler, and Bonnie Fisher, "Procedural Justice in Felony Cases," *Law and Society Review* 22 (1988): 497–505.
5. Brian Ostrom and Neal Kauder, *Examining the Work of State Courts, 1997: A National Perspective from the Court Statistics Project* (Williamsburg, Va.: National Center for State Courts, 1998).
6. This section relies heavily on Conference of State Court Administrators and National Center for State Courts, *State Court Caseload Statistics, Annual Report, 1990* (Williamsburg, Va.: National Center for State Courts, 1992); and Brian J. Ostrom, *State Court Caseload Statistics, Annual Report, 1995* (Williamsburg, Va.: National Center for State Courts, 1996), herein cited as State Court Statistics.
7. Patrick Langan, *State Felony Courts and Felony Laws* (Washington, D.C.: Bureau of Justice Statistics, 1987). See also Ostrom, *State Court Statistics,* 1995; and Ostrom and Kauder, *Examining the Work of State Courts, 1997;* Jodi Brown, and Patrick Langan, *Felony Sentences in the United States, 1996* (Washington, D.C.: Bureau of Justice Statistics, 1999), 1.
8. David B. Rottman et al., *State Court Organization, 1993* (Washington, D.C.: Bureau of Justice Statistics, 1995).
9. U.S. Constitution, ART. 3, SECS. 1 and 2.
10. 1 Wharton 304, 4 L.Ed. 97 (1816).
11. See Ostrom and Kauder, *Examining the Work of State Courts, 1997.*
12. Ibid.
13. American Bar Association, *The State of Criminal Justice, Annual Report, 1993* (Chicago: ABA), 13.
14. Sari Escovitz with Fred Kurland and Nan Gold, *Judicial Selection and Tenure* (Chicago: American Judicature Society, 1974), 3–16.
15. *Bureau of Justice Statistics Bulletin,* "Prosecutors in State Courts — 1996"

(Washington, D.C.: Office of Justice Programs, 1999).

16. See Bennett Gershman, "Why Prosecutors Misbehave," *Criminal Law Bulletin* 22 (1986): 131–43; Editorial debate, "Prosecutor Conduct," *USA Today*, 1 April 1999, 14A.

17. American Bar Association, *Model Rules of Professional Conduct* (Chicago: ABA, 1983), rule 3.8; see also Stanley Fisher, "In Search of the Virtuous Prosecutor: A Conceptual Framework," *American Journal of Criminal Law* 15 (1988): 197.

18. Stanley Fisher, "Zealousness and Overzealousness: Making Sense of the Prosecutor's Duty to Seek Justice," *Prosecutor* 22 (1989): 9; see also Bruce Green, "The Ethical Prosecutor and the Adversary System," *Criminal Law Bulletin* 24 (1988): 126–45.

19. Michael Benson, Francis Cullen, and William Maakestad, "Local Prosecutors and Corporate Crime," *Crime and Delinquency* 36 (1990): 356–72; see also Neil Weiner, "Priority Prosecution of Juveniles," *NIJ Journal* (November 1993).

20. "NDAA Establishes Environmental Center," *National District Attorneys Association Bulletin* 10 (1991): 1; Marcia Chaiken and Jan Chaiken, *Priority Prosecutors of High-Rate Dangerous Offenders* (Washington, D.C.: National Institute of Justice, 1991); also National Traffic Law Center, *Prosecutor* 33 (1999): 37–39.

21. "Litigator's Legacy," *Wall Street Journal*, 11 January 1989, 1; Selwyn Raab, "A Battered and Ailing Mafia Is Losing Its Grip on America," *New York Times*, 22 October 1990, 1.

22. Kenneth C. Davis, *Discretionary Justice* (Baton Rouge: Louisiana State University Press, 1969), 180; see also James B. Stewart, *The Prosecutor* (New York: Simon & Schuster, 1987).

23. Barbara Boland, *The Prosecution of Felony Arrests* (Washington, D.C.: Government Printing Office, 1983).

24. Newman Baker, "The Prosecutor — Initiation of Prosecution," *Journal of Criminal Law, Criminology, and Police Science* 23 (1993): 770–71; see also Joan Jacoby, *The American Prosecutor: A Search for Identity* (Lexington, Mass.: Lexington Books, 1980).

25. Frank W. Miller, *Prosecution: The Decision to Charge a Suspect with a Crime* (Boston: Little, Brown, 1970).

26. Charles D. Breitel, "Controls in Criminal Law Enforcement," *University of Chicago Law Review* 27 (1960): 427.

27. Roscoe Pound, "Discretion, Dispensation, and Mitigation: The Problem of the Individual Special Case," *New York University Law Review* 35 (1960): 925; "Unleashing the Prosecutor's Discretion: *United States v. Goodwin*," *American Criminal Law Review* 20 (1983): 507.

28. *Town of Newton v. Rumery*, 480 U.S. 386, 107 S.Ct. 1187, 94 L.Ed.2d 405 (1987); see also American Bar Association, *Standards for Prosecution and Defense Function*, 3d ed. (Washington, D.C.: ABA Criminal Justice Project, 1993).

29. National District Attorneys Association, *National Prosecution Standards* (Alexandria, Va.: NDAA, 1991).

30. *North Carolina v. Pearce*, 395 U.S. 711, 89 S.Ct. 2072, 23 L.Ed.2d 656 (1969).

31. *Blackledge v. Perry*, 417 U.S. 21, 94 S.Ct. 2098, 40 L.Ed.2d 628 (1974).

32. *Bordenkircher v. Hayes*, 434 U.S. 357, 98 S.Ct. 663, 54 L.Ed.2d 604 (1978).

33. President's Commission on Law Enforcement and the Administration of Justice, *The Challenge of Crime in a Free Society* (Washington, D.C.: Government Printing Office, 1968), 150; American Bar Association, *Report of Standing Committee on Legal Aid and Indigent Defendants* (Chicago: ABA, 1991).

34. *American Bar Association Model Rules of Professional Conduct* (Chicago: ABA, 1983), rule 3.8.

35. Monroe H. Freedman, "Professional Responsibility of the Criminal Defense Lawyer: The Three Hardest Questions," *Michigan Law Review* 64 (1966): 1468.

36. Rodney Uphoff, ed., "Ethical Problems Facing the Criminal Defense Lawyer: Practical Answers to Tough Questions" (Chicago: American Bar Association, 1995).

37. The Sixth Amendment provides: "In all criminal prosecutions, the accused shall enjoy the right . . . to have the assistance of counsel for his defense."

38. *Gideon v. Wainwright*, 372 U.S. 335, 83 S.Ct. 792, 9 L.Ed.2d 799 (1963).

39. *Argersinger v. Hamlin*, 407 U.S. 25, 92 S.Ct. 2006, 32 L.Ed.2d 530 (1972).

40. *Mempa v. Rhay*, 389 U.S. 128, 88 S.Ct. 254, 19 L.Ed.2d 336 (1967).

41. *Douglas v. California*, 372 U.S. 353, 83 S.Ct. 814, 9 L.Ed.2d 811 (1963).

42. *In re Gault*, 387 U.S. 1, 875 S.Ct. 1428, 18 L.Ed.2d 527 (1967).

43. *Specht v. Patterson*, 386 U.S. 605, 87 S.Ct. 1209, 18 L.Ed.2d 326 (1967).

44. See F. Brownell, *Legal Aid in the United States* (Chicago: National Legal Aid and Defender Association, 1961); for an interesting study of the Cook County, Illinois, Office of Public Defenders, see Lisa McIntyre, *Public Defenders — Practice of Law in Shadows of Dispute* (Chicago: University of Chicago Press, 1987).

45. Carla Gaskins, *Criminal Defense for the Poor — 1986* (Washington, D.C.: Bureau of Justice Statistics, 1988), 2; see also Robert L. Spangenberg and Tessa Schwartz, "The Indigent Defense Crisis Is Chronic," *American Bar Association Journal on Criminal Justice* 9 (1994): 12.

46. Pauline Houlden and Steven Balkin, "Quality and Cost Comparisons of Private Bar Indigent Defense Systems: Contract vs. Ordered Assigned Counsel," *Journal of Criminal Law and Criminology* 76 (1985): 176–200.

47. Lawrence Spears, "Contract Counsel: A Different Way to Defend the Poor — How It's Working in North Dakota," *American Bar Association Journal on Criminal Justice* 6 (1991): 24–31.

48. *Argersinger v. Hamlin*, 407 U.S. 25, 92 S.Ct. 2006, 32 L.Ed.2d 530 (1972).

49. See *Drug Control Act of 1988*, 42 U.S.C., sec. 375(G)(10).

50. *Anti-Terrorism Act of 1996*, Public Law No. 104-132 (1996).

51. Roger Hanson et al., "Indigent Defenders — Get the Job Done and Done Well" (Williamsburg, Va.: National Center for State Courts, 1992).

52. *Strickland v. Washington*, 466 U.S. 668, 104 S.Ct. 2052, 80 L.Ed.2d 674 (1984).

53. *Burger v. Kemp*, 483 U.S. 776, 107 S.Ct. 3114, 97 L.Ed.2d 638 (1987).

54. Warren Burger, "Rx for Justice: Modernize the Courts," *Nation's Business* (September 1974): 62.

55. Cited in National Advisory Commission on Criminal Justice Standards and Goals, *Courts* (Washington, D.C.: Government Printing Office, 1973), 171.

56. Edward McConnell, *Justice in the States* (Williamsburg, Va.: National Center for State Courts, n.d.).

57. National Center for State Courts, *Report on Trends in the State Courts* (Williamsburg, Va.: National Center for State Courts, 1988).

chapter 9

Pretrial Procedures

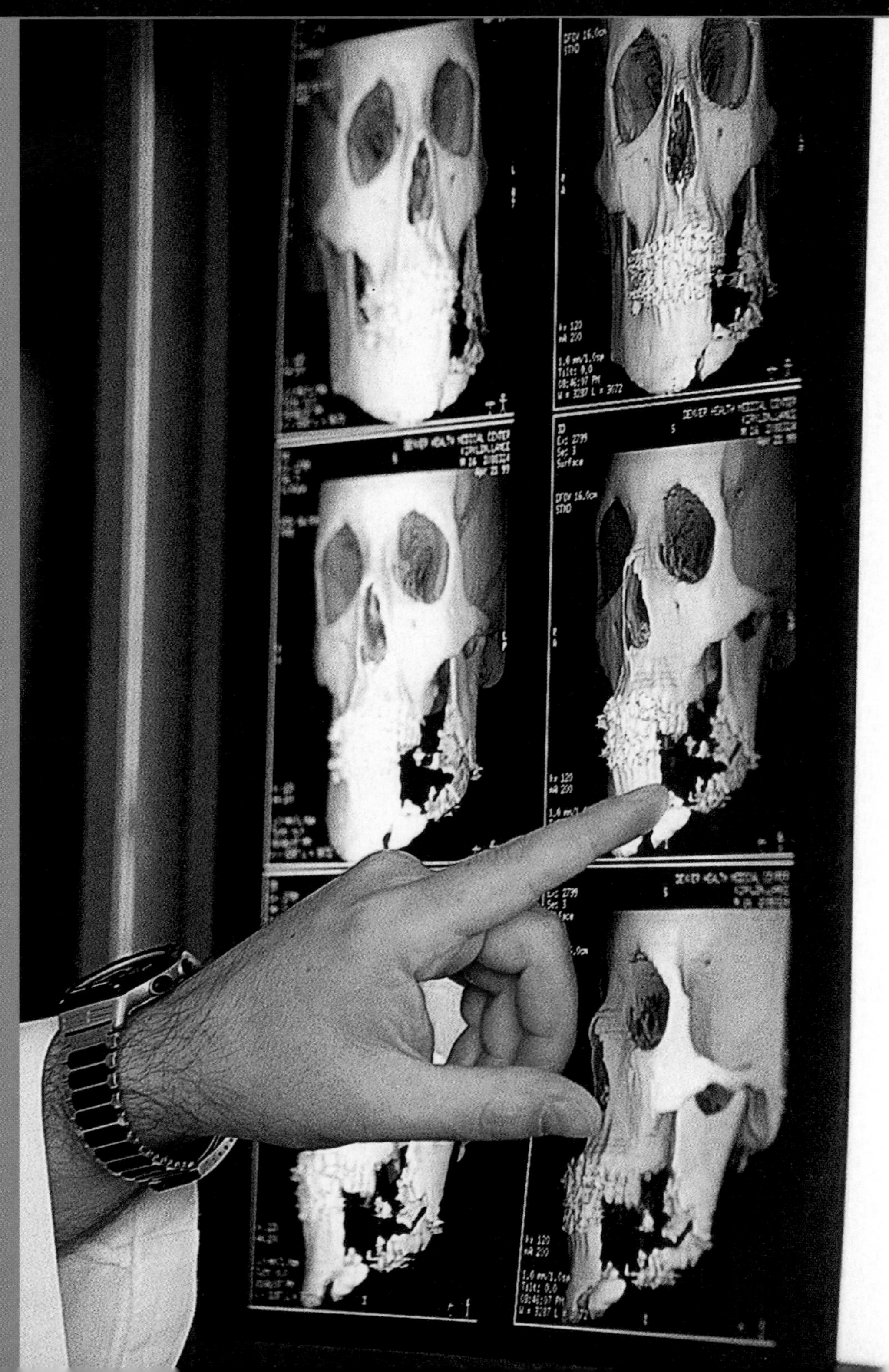

Many legal experts believe that the Ted Kaczynski case is one of the most bizarre criminal cases in this century. Other crimes have been more horrible or deadlier, but few crimes have taken twenty years to solve. The case began when a bomb went off at Northwestern University in 1978. More bombs were sent to universities and airlines in the early 1980s. The FBI subsequently came up with the nickname, Unabomber, partly because it appeared that all attacks looked to be the work of one man and partly because he solely targeted university and airline personnel. By the time he was captured in 1996, Ted Kaczynski had committed sixteen

Unabomber attacks, killing three people and injuring twenty-two others. The FBI reviewed more than two hundred suspects and received many thousands of phone calls, eventually leading to his arrest.

Who was Ted Kaczynski? Born in Chicago in 1942, Kaczynski was a brilliant student who became a mathematics professor at the University of California after graduating from Harvard and receiving his master's and Ph.D. degrees at the University of Michigan. After resigning from teaching, Kaczynski dropped out of society, built a small cabin in rural Lincoln, Montana, and lived off the land. He then began his crusade to disrupt industrial society.

Kaczynski's downfall occurred when he sent a 35,000-word manifesto against modern civilization to the *New York Times* and *Washington Post.* After publication, David Kaczynski, Ted's brother, recognized the similarity between the manifesto and some of his brother's letters and alerted the FBI that his brother could be the Unabomber. When the FBI searched Kaczynski's house, they found bomb parts, chemicals, wires, and hand-drawn diagrams for bombs.

Kaczynski was charged with being the antitechnology killer known as the Unabomber. Lengthy negotiations followed between the prosecution and the defense over whether Kaczynski was competent to stand trial. In addition, Kaczynski feuded with his lawyers over their plans to use the insanity defense and to have the jury know he was a paranoid schizophrenic. When Kaczynski attempted suicide and then sought to handle his defense, the court conducted a competency examination. Even though Kaczynski was a paranoid schizophrenic and lived like a hermit, the court psychiatrist said he was competent to stand trial despite his illness. The only legal standard for competency is whether a defendant is able to understand the charges and help in his defense. The psychiatric report became the turning point in whether Kaczynski would be brought to trial. Prosecutors knew they would have a difficult time persuading a jury to execute a mentally ill person.

In exchange for the government dropping its demand for a trial and death sentence, Kaczynski agreed to enter a guilty plea where he received a life sentence without parole. Thus, the longest and most expensive manhunt for a serial killer in U.S. history ended — in a plea bargain. The plea bargain avoided the trial process, eliminated the cost of the trial, and shortened the time required for resolving the case. ■

pretrial procedure
A proceeding held before an official trial, such as a pretrial hearing, bail review, and pretrial diversion to a noncriminal program.

The plea bargain is just one of a series of events that are critical links in the chain of justice. These include arraignments, grand jury investigations, bail hearings, plea-bargaining negotiations, and predisposition treatment efforts. These **pretrial procedures** are critically important components of the justice process because the great majority of all criminal cases are resolved informally at this stage and never come before the courts. Although the media like to focus on the elaborate jury trial with its dramatic elements and impressive setting, formal criminal trials are relatively infrequent. Consequently, understanding the events that take place during the pretrial period is essential in grasping the reality of criminal justice policy.

Cases are settled during the pretrial stage in a number of ways. Prosecutors can use their discretion to drop cases before formal charges are filed, because of insufficient evidence, office policy, witness conflicts, or similar problems. Even if charges are filed, the prosecutor can decide not to proceed against the defendant (nolle prosequi) because of a change in the circumstances of the case.

In addition, the prosecution and the defense almost always meet to try to arrange a nonjudicial settlement for the case. Plea bargaining, in which the defendant exchanges a guilty plea for some consideration, such as a reduced sentence, is commonly used to terminate the formal processing of the case. The prosecution or the defense may believe, for example, that a trial is not in the best interests of the victim, the defendant, or society because the defendant is incapable of understanding the charges or controlling her behavior. In this instance, the defendant may have a competency hearing before a judge and be placed in a secure treatment facility until ready to stand trial. Or the prosecutor may waive further action so that the defendant can be placed in a special treatment program, such as a detoxification unit at a local hospital.

booking process
The administrative record of an arrest, listing the offender's name, address, physical description, date of birth, and employer; the time of arrest; the offense; and the name of the arresting officer. Photographing and fingerprinting of the offender are also part of the booking process.

PROCEDURES FOLLOWING ARREST

After arrest, the accused is ordinarily taken to the police station, where the police list the possible criminal charges against him and obtain other information for the **booking process.** This may include recording a description of the suspect and the circumstances of the offense. The suspect may then be fingerprinted, photographed, and required to participate in a lineup.

Individuals arrested on a misdemeanor charge are ordinarily released from the police station on their own recognizance to answer the criminal charge before the court at a later date. They are usually detained by the police until it is decided

complaint
A sworn allegation made in writing to a court or judge that an individual is guilty of some designated (complained of) offense. This is often the first legal document filed regarding a criminal offense. The complaint can be "taken out" by the victim, the police officer, the district attorney, or another interested party. Although the complaint charges an offense, an indictment or information may be the formal charging document.

initial hearing
The stage in the justice process during which the suspect is brought before a magistrate for consideration of bail. The suspect must be taken for an initial hearing within a "reasonable time" after arrest. For petty offenses, this step often serves as the final criminal proceeding, either by adjudication by a judge or the offering of a guilty plea.

arraignment
The step at which accused offenders are read the charges against them and are asked how they plead. In addition, the accused are advised of their rights. Possible pleas are guilty, not guilty, nolo contendere, and not guilty by reason of insanity.

indictment
A written accusation returned by a grand jury charging an individual with a specified crime after determination of probable cause; the prosecutor presents enough evidence (a prima facie case) to establish probable cause.

grand jury
A group (usually consisting of twenty-three citizens) chosen to hear testimony in secret and to issue formal criminal accusations (indictments). It also serves an investigatory function.

whether a criminal complaint will be filed. The **complaint** is the formal written document identifying the criminal charge, the date and place where the crime occurred, and the circumstances of the arrest. The complaint is sworn to and signed under oath by the complainant, usually a police officer. The complaint will request that the defendant be present at an **initial hearing** held soon after the arrest is made; in some jurisdictions, this may be referred to by other names, such as **arraignment.** The defendant may plead guilty at the initial hearing, and the case may be disposed of immediately. Defendants who plead not guilty to a minor offense have been informed of the formal charge, provided with counsel if they are unable to afford a private attorney, and asked to plead guilty or not guilty as charged. A date in the near future is set for trial, and the defendant is generally released on bail or on her own recognizance to await trial.

Where a felony or a more serious crime is involved, the U.S. Constitution requires an intermediate step before a person can be tried. This involves proving to an objective body that there is probable cause to believe that a crime has taken place and that the accused should be tried on the matter. This step of the formal charging process is ordinarily an indictment from a grand jury or an information issued by a lower court.

An **indictment** is a written accusation charging a person with a crime; it is drawn up by a prosecutor and submitted to a **grand jury,** which — after considering the evidence presented by the prosecutor — votes to endorse or deny the indictment. An **information** is a charging document drawn up by a prosecutor in jurisdictions that do not use the grand jury system. The information is brought before a lower-court judge in a **preliminary hearing** (sometimes called a **probable cause hearing**). The purpose of this hearing is to require the prosecutor to present the case so that the judge can determine whether the defendant should be held to answer for the charge in a felony court.

After an indictment or information is filed, the accused is brought before the trial court for arraignment, during which the judge informs the defendant of the charge, ensures that the accused is properly represented by counsel, and determines whether he should be released on bail or some other form of release pending a hearing or trial.

The defendant who is arraigned on an indictment or information can ordinarily plead guilty, not guilty or nolo contendere, which is equivalent to a guilty plea but cannot be used as evidence against the defendant in a civil case on the same matter. In cases where a guilty plea is entered, the defendant admits to all elements of the crime, and the court begins a review of the person's background for sentencing purposes. A not-guilty plea sets the stage for a trial on the merits or for negotiations, known as *plea bargaining,* between the prosecutor and the defense attorney.

Before discussing these issues, it is important to address the question of pretrial release and bail, which may arise at the police station, at the initial court appearance in a misdemeanor, or at the arraignment in most felony cases.

PRETRIAL SERVICES

As we have described, many jurisdictions today are faced with significant increases in the number of criminal cases, particularly those involving drugs. The police have responded with an unprecedented number of arrests, clogging an already overburdened jail system. Of these arrestees, the justice system must determine which can safely be released pending trial. Pretrial services help courts deal with this problem. At the pretrial stage, the system is required to balance the often conflicting goals of ensuring community safety and respecting the rights of the arrestee.

information
Like the indictment, a formal charging document. The prosecuting attorney makes out the information and files it in court. Probable cause is determined at the preliminary hearing, which, unlike grand jury proceedings, is public and attended by the accused and his or her attorney.

preliminary hearing (probable cause hearing)
The step at which criminal charges initiated by an information are tested for probable cause; the prosecution presents enough evidence to establish probable cause — that is, a prima facie case. The hearing is public and may be attended by the accused and his or her attorney.

Often, there is some confusion about the meaning of *pretrial services.* These are the practices and programs that screen arrestees to provide the bail-setting magistrate with concise summaries of the arrestee's personal background as it relates to bail.[1] This definition is distinguished from *diversion,* in which criminal prosecution is bypassed for alternative measures, such as treatment or counseling; diversion is discussed at the end of this chapter.

Pretrial service programs seek to

1. Improve the release/detention decision process in criminal courts by providing complete, accurate, nonadversarial information to judicial officers.
2. Identify those for whom alternative forms of supervision may be more appropriate than incarceration.
3. Monitor released pretrial arrestees to ensure that they comply with the conditions of release imposed by the judicial officer for the benefit of public safety.[2]

Virtually all jurisdictions in the United States have pretrial release in one form or another. Court-administered programs make up the greatest percentage of pretrial programs (38%), and probation-administered programs constitute the next largest segment (24%). The general criteria used to assess eligibility for release center on the defendant's community ties and prior criminal justice involvement. Many jurisdictions have conditional and supervised release and third-party custody release, in addition to release on a person's own recognizance.

In recent years, many states have also begun to rely on programs to detect illicit drug use by defendants. The aim is to provide a judge with an objective measure of a defendant's drug use for pretrial release determination and to serve as a tool for controlling possible misconduct during the pretrial release period. A recent demonstration program of mandatory drug testing of criminal defendants in eight federal judicial districts revealed that over 31 percent of the defendants who submitted to urinalysis provided positive samples.[3] Judges and magistrates generally believe that pretrial drug testing is a valuable tool in implementing the statutory requirements of any pretrial release program. The validity of judicial predictions of dangerousness of future crimes based on drug testing remains uncertain[4] Recent studies show that urine test results have no consistent power to predict pretrial misconduct.[5]

Effective pretrial release programs benefit the justice system in many ways. Judicial officers can make more effective decisions about whom may be released safely. The compliance of pretrial arrestees with their conditions of release can be monitored. In addition, pretrial programs can operate at different stages of the judicial process, thereby increasing the number of release options available to the courts. Table 9.1 provides a list of such pretrial release mechanisms.

bail
The monetary amount for or condition of pretrial release, normally set by a judge at the initial appearance. The purpose of bail is to ensure the return of the accused at subsequent proceedings. If the accused is unable to make bail, he or she is detained in jail. The Eighth Amendment provides that excessive bail shall not be required.

BAIL

Bail is money or some other security provided to the court to ensure the appearance of the defendant at every subsequent stage of the criminal justice process. Its purpose is to obtain the release from custody of a person charged with a crime. Once the amount of bail is set by the court, the defendant is required to deposit all or a percentage of the entire amount in cash or security (or to pay a professional bonding agent to submit a bond). If the defendant is released on bail but fails to appear in court at the stipulated time, the bail deposit is forfeited. A defendant who fails to make bail is confined in jail until the court appearance.

Table 9.1
Pretrial Release Alternatives

Stage	Release Mechanism
1. Police	**Field citation release:** An arresting officer releases the arrestee on a written promise to appear in court, made at or near the actual time and location of the arrest. This procedure is commonly used for misdemeanor charges and is similar to issuing a traffic ticket.
2. Police	**Station house citation release:** The determination of an arrestee's eligibility and suitability for release and her actual release are deferred until after she has been removed from the scene of an arrest and brought to the station house or police headquarters.
3. Police/ pretrial	**Jail citation release:** The determination of an arrestee's eligibility and suitability for citation release and his actual release are deferred until after he has been delivered by the arresting department to a jail or other pretrial detention facility for screening, booking, and admission.
4. Pretrial/court	**Direct release authority by pretrial program:** To streamline release court processes and reduce the length of stay in detention, courts may authorize pretrial programs to release arrestees without direct judicial involvement. Where court rule delegates such authority, the practice is generally limited to misdemeanor charges, but felony release authority has been granted in some jurisdictions.
5. Police/court	**Bail schedule:** An arrestee can post bail at the station house or jail, according to amounts specified in a bail schedule. The schedule is a list of all bailable charges and a corresponding dollar amount for each. Schedules may vary widely from jurisdiction to jurisdiction.
6. Court	**Judicial release:** Arrestees who have not been released by either the police or the jailer and who have not posted bail appear at the hearing before a judge, magistrate, or bail commissioner within a set period of time. In jurisdictions with pretrial release programs, program staff often interview arrestees detained at the jail prior to the first hearing, verify the background information, and present recommendations to the court at arraignment.

The Legal Right to Bail The Eighth Amendment to the U.S. Constitution does not guarantee a constitutional right to bail but rather prohibits "excessive bail." Since many state statutes place no precise limit on the amount of bail a judge may impose, many defendants who cannot make bail are placed in detention while awaiting trial. It has become apparent over the years that the bail system is discriminatory because defendants who are financially well-off can make bail, whereas indigent defendants languish in pretrial detention in the county jail. In addition, keeping a person in jail imposes serious financial burdens on local and state governments — and, in turn, on taxpayers — who must pay for the cost of confinement. These factors have given rise to bail reform programs that depend on the defendant's personal promise to appear in court for trial (recognizance), rather than on financial ability to meet bail. These reforms have enabled many deserving but indigent offenders to go free, but another trend has been to deny people bail on the grounds that they are a danger to themselves or to others in the community.

The Eighth Amendment restriction on excessive bail may also be interpreted to mean that the sole purpose of bail is to ensure that the defendant returns for trial; bail may not be used as a form of punishment, nor may it be used to co-

Training for bounty hunters in Tombstone, Arizona. Highly criticized, bounty hunters have been retained by bondsmen to track down bail jumpers and return them for trial in order to recover their bond.

erce or threaten a defendant. In most cases, a defendant has the right to be released on reasonable bail. Many jurisdictions also require a bail review hearing by a higher court in cases in which the initial judge set what might be considered excessive bail.

The U.S. Supreme Court's interpretation of the Eighth Amendment's provisions on bail was set out in the 1951 case of *Stack v. Boyle*.[6] In that case, the Supreme Court found bail to be a traditional right to freedom before trial that permits unhampered preparation of a defense and prevents the criminal defendant from being punished prior to conviction. The Court held that bail is excessive when it exceeds an amount reasonably calculated to ensure that the defendant will return for trial. The Court indicated that bail should be in the amount that is generally set for similar offenses. Higher bail can be imposed when evidence supporting the increase is presented at a hearing at which the defendant's constitutional rights can be protected. Although *Stack* did not mandate an absolute right to bail, it did set guidelines for state courts to follow: If a crime is bailable, the amount set should not be frivolous, unusual, or beyond a person's ability to pay.

Receiving Bail Whether a defendant can be expected to appear at the next stage of the criminal proceedings is a key issue in determining bail. Bail cannot be used to punish an accused, nor can it be denied or revoked at the indulgence of the court. Many experts believe that money bail is one of the most unacceptable aspects of the criminal justice system: It is discriminatory because it works against the poor; it is costly because the government must pay to detain those offenders who are unable to make bail but who would otherwise remain in the community; it is unfair because a higher proportion of detainees receive longer sentences than people released on bail; and it is dehumanizing because innocent people who cannot make bail suffer in the nation's deteriorated jail system.[7]

How successful are bail and pretrial release? A 1980s study of bail procedures in eight urban jurisdictions (including Baltimore, Washington, D.C., Miami, Tucson, Louisville, and San Jose) found that about 85 percent of all defendants received bail. Of these, about 15 percent did not return for trial because they had absconded. An additional 15 percent were rearrested for another crime before their trial date. Thus, about 30 percent of those released on bail could be considered failures for one reason or another.[8]

A federal court study found that about 10 percent of the defendants released by trial courts failed to honor their bail; the reasons included rearrest, failure to appear, and violation of the conditions of bail.[9] Those rearrested tended to (1) be on bail longer (nine months or more), (2) have a serious prior record, (3) abuse drugs, (4) have a poor work record, and (5) be disproportionately young, male, and minority group members.

The differences between the state and federal studies may be attributed to the types of offenders who pass through their jurisdictions. The federal courts probably see more white-collar offenders and fewer violent offenders. Thus, although the state statistics are less than encouraging, the 10 percent failure rate recorded by the federal government indicates that pretrial release has been successful in some jurisdictions.

The Professional Bail Agents of the United States Web site is designed to help bail bondspersons to be more competent and effective. You can visit the site at www.pbus.com/pba2.htm **Or, if you want to understand how a bail bond agency operates, go to Action Bail Bond's home page at** www.actionbail.com

A comprehensive 1990 study of the National Pretrial Reporting Program found that about 24 percent of the released defendants failed to appear in court and about 18 percent were rearrested for a felony while on pretrial release.[10] Some of the conclusions resulting from this important study are that (1) significant numbers of defendants are given pretrial release, (2) the failure-to-appear rate varies according to the type of arrest charge and the type of release, and (3) defendants in different age groups and those with different criminal backgrounds are rearrested at different rates. The rates of rearrest and of failure to appear, which range from 18 to 24 percent, respectively, are similar to the results of previous research in the area. The study presents new and convincing evidence that pretrial release continues to be a successful component in the criminal justice system, providing pivotal services at key stages of the criminal process.

One of the most recent Justice Department study of pretrial release programs in the seventy-five largest counties found that nearly 40 percent of defendants failed bail because (1) they didn't appear for scheduled court hearings, (2) they remained fugitives one year after their court date, and (3) they committed new felonies while out on bail.[11] Thus, contradictory data exist about the viability and success of pretrial release programs in America.

bail bonding
The business of providing bail to needy offenders, usually at an exorbitant rate of interest.

deposit bail
The monetary amount set by a judge at a hearing as a condition of pretrial release, ordering a percentage of the total bond required to be paid by the defendant.

Bail Bonding Today

One of the collateral developments of the bail system is the practice of **bail bonding.** For a fee, bonding agents lend money to people who cannot make bail on their own. Powerful ties often exist between bonding agents and the court, with the result that defendants are steered toward particular bonding agents. Charges of kickbacks and cooperation accompany such arrangements. Allegations of corruption associated with the bail-bonding system have long been made. Consequently, many states have abolished bonding agents, replacing them with bail systems in which the state itself acts as a bonding agency. Defendants put up 10 percent of the total bail but are responsible for paying the entire amount if they abscond; this is referred to as the "10 percent cash match," or **deposit bail,** system. The potential for abuse inherent in the system has led many critics to suggest that in many instances the traditional bail system is an unsatisfactory pretrial release procedure.

The History of Bail Reform

Efforts have been made to reform and even eliminate money bail and reduce the importance of bonding agents. Until the early 1960s, the justice system relied primarily on money bonds as the principal form of pretrial release. Many states now allow defendants to be re-

release on recognizance (ROR) A nonmonetary condition for the pretrial release of an accused individual; an alternative to monetary bail that is granted after the court determines that the accused has ties in the community, has no prior record of default, and is likely to appear at subsequent proceedings.

Manhattan Bail Project The innovative experiment in bail reform that introduced and successfully tested the concept of release on recognizance.

Bail Reform Act of 1984 Federal legislation that provides for both greater emphasis on release on recognizance for nondangerous offenders and preventive detention for those who present a menace to the community.

leased on their own recognizance without any money bail. **Release on recognizance (ROR)** was pioneered by the Vera Institute of Justice in an experiment called the **Manhattan Bail Project,** which began in 1961 with the cooperation of the New York City criminal courts and local law students.[12] It came about because defendants with financial means were able to post bail to secure pretrial release, while indigent defendants remained in custody. The project found that if the court had sufficient background information about the defendant, it could make a reasonably good judgment about whether the accused would return to court. When release decisions were based on such information as the nature of the offense, family ties, and employment record, most defendants returned to court when released on their own recognizance. The results of the Vera Institute's initial operation showed a default rate of less than .7 percent. The bail project's experience suggested that releasing a person on the basis of verified information more effectively guaranteed appearance in court than did money bail. Highly successful ROR projects were set up in major cities around the country, including Philadelphia and San Francisco. By 1980 more than 120 formal programs were in operation, and today they exist in almost every major jurisdiction.[13]

The success of ROR programs in the early 1960s resulted in bail reforms that culminated with the enactment of the federal Bail Reform Act of 1966, the first change in federal bail laws since 1789.[14] This legislation sought to ensure that release would be granted in all noncapital cases in which there was sufficient reason to believe that the defendant would return to court. The law clearly established the presumption of ROR that must be overcome before money bail is required, authorized 10 percent deposit bail, introduced the concept of conditional release, and stressed the philosophy that release should be under the least restrictive method necessary to ensure court appearance.

During the 1970s and early 1980s, the pretrial release movement was hampered by public pressure over pretrial increases in crime. As a result, the more recent federal legislation, the **Bail Reform Act of 1984,** mandated that no defendants shall be kept in pretrial detention simply because they cannot afford money bail, established the presumption for ROR in all cases in which a person is bailable, and formalized restrictive preventive detention provisions, which are explained later in this chapter. The 1984 act required that community safety, as well as the risk of flight, be considered in the release decision. Consequently, such criminal justice factors as the seriousness of the charged offense, the weight of the evidence, the sentence that may be imposed upon conviction, court appearance history, and prior convictions are likely to influence the release decisions of the federal court.

A number of innovative alternative bail programs are described in Table 9.2. The most often used are (1) personal recognizance, (2) unsecured or personal bond, (3) surety or cash bond, and (4) percentage or deposit bail. ROR and conditional release have nearly replaced the traditional cash bail system.

Bail reform is considered one of the most successful programs in the recent history of the criminal justice system. Yet it is not without critics who suggest that emphasis should be put on controlling the behavior of serious criminals rather than on making sure that nondangerous defendants are released before their trials. Criminal defendants released without bail and those who commit crimes awaiting trial fuel the constant debate over pretrial release versus community protection.

THE PREVENTIVE DETENTION CONTROVERSY

Those who promote bail reform point to the Eighth Amendment of the Constitution as evidence that bail should be made available to almost all people accused of crime. The presumption of bail is challenged

Table 9.2
Innovative Bail Systems

SOURCE: Adapted from Andy Hall, *Pretrial Release Program Options* (Washington, D.C.: National Institute of Justice, 1984), 32–33.

Program	Description
NONFINANCIAL RELEASE	
Release on recognizance (ROR)	The defendant is released on a promise to appear, without any requirement of money bond. This form of release is unconditional —i.e., without imposition of special conditions, supervision, or specially provided services.
Conditional release	The defendant is released on a promise to fulfill some stated requirements that go beyond those associated with ROR. Four types of conditions are placed on defendants: (1) status quo conditions, such as requiring that the defendant retain residence or employment status; (2) restrictive conditions, such as requiring that the defendant remain in the jurisdiction; (3) contact conditions, such as requiring that the defendant report by telephone or in person to the release program; and (4) problem-oriented conditions, such as requiring that the defendant participate in drug or alchohol treatment programs.
FINANCIAL RELEASE	
Unsecured bail	The defendant is released with no immediate requirement of payment. However, if the defendant fails to appear, he or she is liable for the full amount.
Privately secured bail	A private organization or individual posts the bail amount, which is returned when the defendant appears in court.
Property bail	The defendant may post evidence of real property in lieu of money.
Deposit bail	The defendant deposits a percentage of the bail amount, typically 10%, with the court. When the defendant appears in court, the deposit is returned, sometimes minus an administrative fee. If the defendant fails to appear, he or she is liable for the full amount of the bail.
Surety bail	The defendant pays a percentage of the bond, usually 10%, to a bonding agent who posts the full bail. The fee paid to the bonding agent is not returned to the defendant if he or she appears in court. The bonding agent is liable for the full amount of the bond should the defendant fail to appear. Bonding agents often require posting collateral to cover the full bail amount.
Cash bail	The defendant pays the entire amount of bail set by the judge to secure release. The bail is returned to the defendant when he or she appears in court.

by those who believe that releasing dangerous criminals before trial poses a threat to public safety. They point to evidence showing that many people released on bail commit new crimes while at large and often fail to appear for trial. One response to the alleged failure of the bail system to protect citizens is the adoption of **preventive detention** statutes. These laws require that certain dangerous defendants be confined before trial for their own protection and that of the community. Preventive detention is an important manifestation of the crime control perspective on justice, since it favors the use of incapacitation to control the future behavior of

preventive detention
The practice of holding dangerous suspects before trial without bail.

Inmates in the Los Angeles county jail. People who cannot make bail are not only subject to incarceration before they are tried, but they also suffer higher rates of conviction and incarceration than defendants who had been released on bail. Bail reform has attempted to remedy this problem by reducing the number of detained defendants.

suspected criminals. Often, the key question is whether preventive detention is punishment before trial.

The most striking use of preventive detention can be found in the federal Bail Reform Act of 1984, which contrasted sharply with previous law.[15] Although the act does contain provisions for ROR, it also allows judges to order preventive detention if they determine "that no condition or combination of conditions will reasonably assure the appearance of the person as required and the safety of any other person and the community."[16]

A number of state jurisdictions have incorporated elements of preventive detention into their bail systems. Although most of the restrictions do not constitute outright preventive detention, they serve to narrow the scope of bail eligibility. These provisions include (1) exclusion of certain crimes from bail eligibility; (2) definition of bail to include appearance in court and community safety; and (3) the limitations on right to bail for those previously convicted.

Preventive detention has also been a source of concern for civil libertarians who believe it violates the due process clause of the U.S. Constitution, since it means that a person will be held in custody before proven guilty. In two important cases, the U.S. Supreme Court disagreed with this analysis. In *Schall v. Martin,* the Court upheld the application of preventive detention statutes to juvenile defendants on the grounds that such detention is useful to protect the welfare of the minor and society as a whole.[17] In ***United States v. Salerno,*** the Court upheld the Bail Reform Act's provision on preventive detention.[18] According to Chief Justice William Rehnquist, the statute conforms to the principle that "[i]n our society liberty is the norm, and detention prior to trial or without trial is the carefully limited exception."[19] Because of the importance of this case, it is analyzed in the Law in Review feature.

United States v. Salerno
The 1987 U.S. Supreme Court decision upholding that the practice of detaining dangerous suspects before trial without bail was constitutional.

PRETRIAL DETENTION

The criminal defendant who is not eligible for bail or ROR is subject to **pretrial detention** in the local county jail. The jail has long been a trouble spot for the criminal justice system. Conditions tend to be poor and rehabilitation nonexistent.

pretrial detention
Holding an offender in secure confinement before trial.

In terms of the number of persons affected each year, pretrial custody accounts for more incarceration in the United States than does imprisonment after sentencing. In the 1990s, on any given day in the United States, almost 300,000 people were held in more than thirty-five hundred local jails. Over the course of a year, many times that number pass through these jails. More than 50 percent of those held in local jails have been accused of crimes but not convicted; they are pretrial detainees. In the United States, people are detained at a rate twice that of neighboring Canada and three times that of Great Britain. Hundreds of jails are overcrowded, and many are under court orders to reduce their populations and improve conditions. The national jail-crowding crisis has worsened over the years.

UNITED STATES V. SALERNO (1987)

In this case, the U.S. Supreme Court held that the use of preventive detention is constitutionally permissible.

Facts

On March 21, 1986, Anthony Salerno and codefendant Vincent Cafaro were charged in a twenty-nine-count indictment alleging various racketeering violations, including gambling, wire fraud, extortion, and conspiracy to commit murder. At their arraignment, the government moved to have them detained on the grounds that no condition of release could ensure community safety. At a detention hearing, the prosecution presented evidence that Salerno was the "boss" of the Genovese crime family and that Cafaro was a "captain." Wiretap evidence indicated that the two men had participated in criminal conspiracies, including murder. The court heard testimony from two witnesses who had personally participated in the murder conspiracies. In rebuttal, Salerno provided character statements, presented evidence that he had a heart condition, and challenged the veracity of the government's witnesses. Cafaro claimed the wiretaps had merely recorded "tough talk." The trial court allowed the detention on the grounds that the defendants wanted to use their pretrial freedom to continue their "family" business and "when business as usual involves threats, beatings, and murder, the present danger such people pose to the community is self-evident."

On appeal, the U.S. Court of Appeals for the Second Circuit agreed with the defendants' claim that the government could not detain suspects simply because they were thought to represent a danger to the community. The circuit court found that the criminal law system holds people accountable for their past deeds, not their anticipated future actions. The government then reappealed the case to the U.S. Supreme Court.

Decision

The Supreme Court held that the preventive detention act had a legitimate and compelling regulatory purpose and did not violate the due process clause. Preventive detention was not designed to punish dangerous individuals but to find a solution for the social problem of people committing crimes while on bail; preventing danger to the community is a legitimate societal goal.

The Court also stated that society's need for protection can outweigh an individual's liberty interest: Under some circumstances, individuals can be held without bail. The act provides that only the most serious criminals can be held and mandates careful procedures to ensure that the judgment of future dangerousness is made after careful deliberation. Finally, the Court found that the Eighth Amendment does not limit the setting (or denial) of bail simply to prohibit defendants' flight to avoid trial and held that considerations of dangerousness are a valid reason to deny pretrial release.

Significance of the Case

Salerno legitimizes the use of preventive detention as a crime control method. It permits the limitations on bail already in place in many state jurisdictions to continue. *Salerno* further illustrates the concern for community protection that has developed in the past decade. It is a good example of the recent efforts by the Court to give the justice system greater control over criminal defendants. At this time, it is still unclear how often judges will rely on preventive detention statutes that require a hearing on the facts or whether they will simply continue to set extremely high bail for defendants whom they wish to remain in pretrial custody.

InfoTrac College Edition Research

Read the U.S. Supreme Court case, *Schall v. Martin*, 467 U.S. 253 (1984), which allows for the placement of children in preventive detention before their adjudication.

Use *InfoTrac College Edition* to access articles that compare the use of preventive detention programs for adult offenders with those used to detain juvenile offenders.

An attorney confers with her client, who is being held in pretrial detention. Research shows that defendants held in custody before trial have a higher conviction rate and receive longer sentences than those who make bail.

The latest data indicate that local jails held approximately 450,000 to 500,000 adults awaiting trial or serving a sentence. According to the Bureau of Justice Statistics, the jail population in the United States has increased dramatically in the past decade; the number of inmates on any given day has more than doubled during that period.[20]

Jails are often considered the weakest link in the criminal justice process: They are frequently dangerous, harmful, decrepit, and filled with the poor and friendless. The costs of holding a person in jail range up to more than $100 per day and $36,000 per year. In addition, detainees are often confined with those convicted of crimes and those who have been transferred from other institutions because of overcrowding. Many felons are transferred to jails from state prisons to ease crowding. It is possible to have in close quarters a convicted rapist, a father jailed for nonpayment of child support, and a person awaiting trial for a crime that he did not actually commit. Thus, jails contain a mix of inmates, which can lead to violence, brutality, and suicide.

Why does the jail crisis persist? Societal problems — such as drug use, the needs of the mentally ill, and cutbacks in federal and state social service funding — provide a partial answer. To a large degree, jails are in poor condition because the public does not care about them.

What happens to people who do not get bail or who cannot afford to put up bail money? Traditionally, they find themselves getting a long prison sentence if they are convicted at trial.[21] Data on cases processed through the federal court system indicate that detainees received significantly longer sentences than those who had been released on bail; for some crime categories, the detainees' sentences were double that of bailees.[22]

In sum, the first stage of bail reform began in the 1960s because reformers were critical of the discriminatory setting of unaffordable bail for the urban poor and deplored the conditions of jail confinement. The second stage involved the passage of the federal Bail Reform Act of 1984, which moved the emphasis in bail decisions toward denial of bail for community protection. This transformation was completed with the *Schall* and *Salerno* decisions, which gave approval to the use of preventive detention. Today, most states and the federal system have changed their laws to allow judges to detain suspects who are a danger to the community if released during the pretrial period.[23] The debate on pretrial release versus community safety is discussed in the Policy, Programs, and Issues in Criminal Justice feature.

CHARGING THE DEFENDANT

Charging a defendant with a crime is a process that varies somewhat depending on whether it occurs via a grand jury or a preliminary hearing.

The Indictment Process — The Grand Jury

The grand jury was an early development of the English common law. Under the Magna Carta (1215), no freeman could be seized and imprisoned unless he had been

Policy, Programs, and Issues in Criminal Justice

THE PRETRIAL RELEASE DEBATE

Whereas pretrial release advocates believe that accused individuals should not be incarcerated before their trial just because they can't afford bail, opponents charge that pretrial release programs put too many potentially dangerous people back on the street without supervision. Which position is correct?

The Eighth Amendment of the U.S. Constitution prohibits excessive bail. Even prosecutors and victims' groups agree that bail shouldn't be used to punish suspects. But others argue that defendants who don't have to raise their own bail have no incentive to return for trial.

One-third of defendants accused of violent crimes are often released without paying bail. Of that number, about 25 percent fail to appear in court, and 11 percent commit new felonies while awaiting trial. Possibly half of the defendants released under pretrial release programs have often previously jumped bail, and many others have prior felony convictions.

On the other hand, pretrial release programs, which began during the 1960s, were originally designed for indigent defendants. Based on personal history, prior criminal record, and risk of flight, a judge could set a defendant free on personal recognizance and monitor her until trial. Over the years, caseloads expanded, and court rulings and statutes now provide the opportunity for pretrial release to virtually all defendants. Also, judges use pretrial release to relieve jail overcrowding. As a result, more time elapses before a defendant is brought to trial, which increases the likelihood of trial default and the commission of additional crimes while under pretrial release. Using new monitoring devices such as electronic bracelets and telephone contacts, pretrial release officials still defend their programs as needed for poor defendants and as cost effective for taxpayers.

Critical Thinking

Historically, bail statutes were designed to ensure the defendant's appearance at court proceedings. Bail reform was needed, however, because of unregulated and discriminatory use of pretrial detention, primarily among poor defendants in urban jails. The solution was to establish pretrial release programs. But isn't it true that many people released today often commit crimes while awaiting trial? Why?

United States v. Salerno upheld the federal Bail Reform Act of 1984, which authorized the use of preventive detention in federal criminal prosecutions. Preventive detention is used before trial solely to prevent an accused from committing further crimes during the pretrial period. Can we really predict a person's future behavior? Isn't a prediction of dangerousness so unreliable as to pose due process violations? Should people be punished because their past actions indicate a risk of criminality? Compare preventive detention with money bail.

Despite such reservations, legislatures have increasingly relied on preventive detention as an instrument of social control. According to the *Salerno* case, the detention of dangerous individuals is not punishment but regulation. To civil libertarians, restrictions on liberty and freedom constitute a form of punishment. To what degree does preventive detention further community safety?

InfoTrac College Edition Research

Search for articles using *InfoTrac College Edition* regarding pretrial release programs. Choose any number of articles with programs that you feel are working and discuss why you believe they are successful. When searching, use key words such as "bail," "release on recognizance," and "detention."

SOURCES: Andrea Gerlin, "Criminal Defendants Released without Bail Spark Heated Debate," *Wall Street Journal*, 9 July 1996, A; see also Jeffrey Fagan and Martin Guggenheim, "Preventive Detention and Judicial Prediction of Dangerousness for Juveniles: A Natural Experiment," *Journal of Criminal Law and Criminology* 86 (1996): 415.

judged by his peers. To determine fairly who was eligible to be tried, a group of freemen from the district where the crime was committed would be brought together to examine the facts of the case and determine whether the charges had merit. Thus, the grand jury was created as a check against arbitrary prosecution by a judge who might be a puppet of the government.

The concept of the grand jury was brought to the American colonies by early settlers and later incorporated into the Fifth Amendment of the U.S. Constitution, which states that "no person shall be held to answer for a capital, or otherwise infamous crime, unless on presentment or indictment of a grand jury."

What is the role of the grand jury today? First, the grand jury has the power to act as an independent investigating body. In this capacity, it examines the possibility of criminal activity within its jurisdiction. These investigative efforts are directed toward general rather than individual criminal conduct. After an investigation is completed, a report called a *presentment* is issued. The presentment contains not only information concerning the findings of the grand jury but also usually a recommendation of indictment.

The grand jury's second and better known role is accusatory in nature. In this capacity, the grand jury acts as the community's conscience in determining whether the accusation of the state (the prosecution) justifies a trial. The grand jury relies on the testimony of witnesses called by the prosecution through its subpoena power. After examining the evidence and the testimony of witnesses, the grand jury decides whether probable cause exists for prosecution. If it does, an indictment, or *true bill,* is affirmed. If the grand jury fails to find probable cause, a *no bill* (meaning that the indictment is ignored) is passed. In some states, a prosecutor can present evidence to a different grand jury if a no bill is returned; in other states, this action is prohibited by statute.

charge
In a criminal case, the specific crime the defendant is accused of committing.

The grand jury usually meets at the request of the prosecution. Hearings are closed and secret. The prosecuting attorney presents the **charges** and calls witnesses who testify under oath to support the indictment. Usually, the accused individuals are not allowed to attend the hearing unless they are asked to testify by the prosecutor or grand jury.

The Indictment Process — The Preliminary Hearing

The preliminary hearing is used in about half the states as an alternative to the grand jury. Although the purpose of preliminary and grand jury hearings is the same — to establish whether probable cause is sufficient to merit a trial — the procedures differ significantly.

The preliminary hearing is conducted before a magistrate or inferior court judge and, unlike the grand jury hearing, is open to the public unless the defendant requests otherwise. Present at the preliminary hearing are the prosecuting attorney, the defendant, and the defendant's counsel, if already retained. The prosecution presents its evidence and witnesses to the judge. The defendant or the defense counsel then has the right to cross-examine witnesses and to challenge the prosecutor's evidence.

waiver
The act of voluntarily relinquishing a right or advantage; often used in the context of waiving one's right to counsel (e.g., *Miranda* warning) or waiving certain steps in the criminal justice process (e.g., the preliminary hearing). Essential to waiver is the voluntary consent of the individual.

After hearing the evidence, the judge decides whether there is sufficient probable cause to believe that the defendant committed the alleged crime. If so, the defendant is bound over for trial, and the prosecuting attorney's information (same as an indictment) is filed with the superior court, usually within fifteen days. When the judge does not find sufficient probable cause, the charges are dismissed, and the defendant is released from custody.

A unique aspect of the preliminary hearing is the defendant's right to waive the proceeding. In most states, the prosecutor and the judge must agree to this waiver. A **waiver** has advantages and disadvantages for both the prosecutor and

Vernon Jordan, amidst media cameras and microphones outside U.S. Courthouse with his attorney William Hundley, about to testify before a grand jury, after receiving a subpoena summons from Ken Starr's office in the White House sex scandal probe, March 3, 1998.

the defendant. In most situations, a prosecutor will agree to a waiver because it avoids revealing evidence to the defense before trial. However, if the state believes it is necessary to obtain a record of witness testimony because of the possibility that a witness or witnesses may be unavailable for the trial or unable to remember the facts clearly, the prosecutor might override the waiver. In this situation, the record of the preliminary hearing can be used at the trial.

The defendant will most likely waive the preliminary hearing for one of three reasons: (1) He has already decided to plead guilty; (2) he wants to speed the criminal justice process; or (3) he hopes to avoid the negative publicity that might result from the hearing. On the other hand, the preliminary hearing is of obvious advantage to the defendant who believes that it will result in a dismissal of the charges. In addition, the preliminary hearing gives the defense the opportunity to learn what evidence the prosecution has. Figure 9.1 outlines the significant differences between the grand jury and the preliminary hearing processes.

Arraignment An arraignment takes place after an indictment or information is filed following a grand jury or preliminary hearing. At the arraignment, the judge informs the defendant of the charges against her and appoints

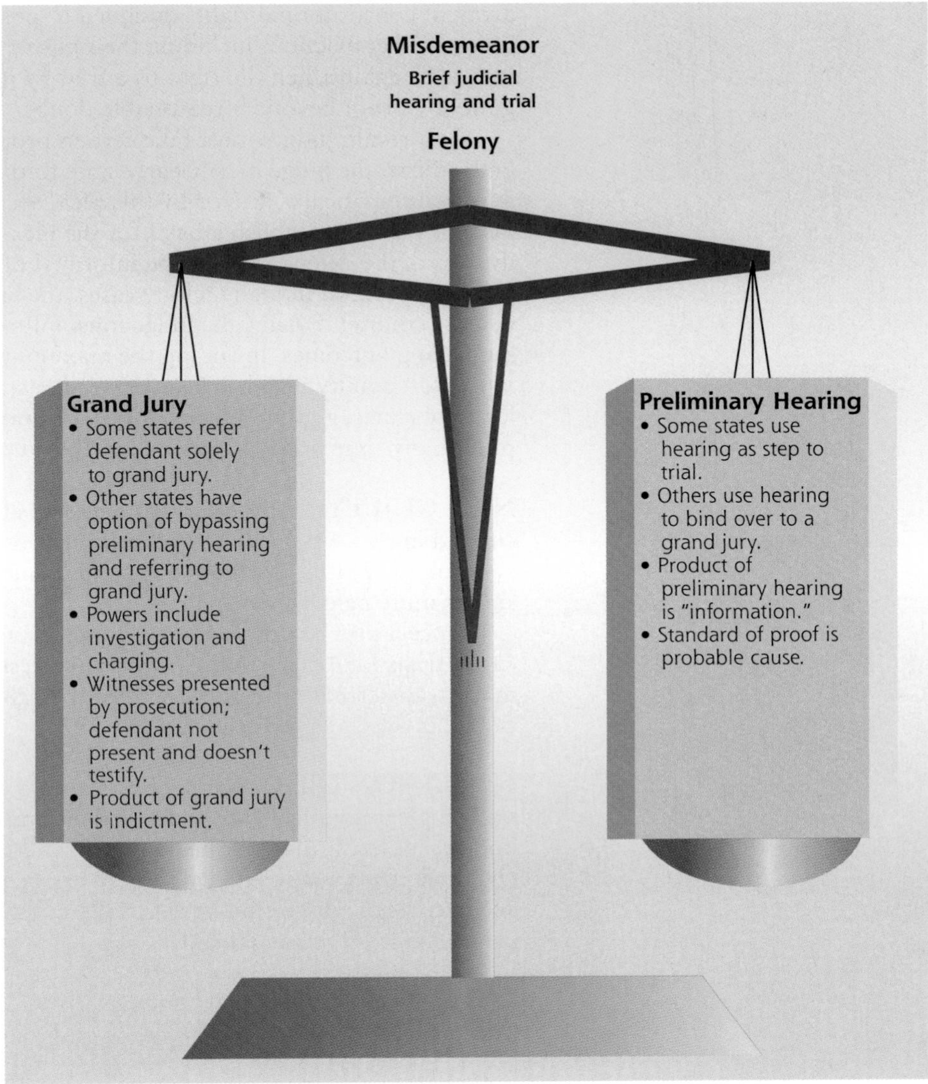

Figure 9.1
Charging the defendant with a crime
Note the differences between the grand jury and preliminary hearing.

counsel if one has not yet been retained. According to the Sixth Amendment of the U.S. Constitution, the accused has the right to be informed of the nature and cause of the accusation; thus, the judge at the arraignment must make sure that the defendant clearly understands the charges.

After the charges are read and explained, the defendant is asked to enter a plea. If a plea of not guilty or not guilty by reason of insanity is entered, a trial date is set. When the defendant pleads guilty or nolo contendere, a date for sentencing is arranged. The magistrate then either sets bail or releases the defendant on personal recognizance.

The Plea Ordinarily, a defendant in a criminal trial will enter one of three pleas: guilty, not guilty, or nolo contendere.

GUILTY More than 90 percent of defendants appearing before the courts plead guilty prior to the trial stage. A guilty plea has several consequences. It functions not only as an admission of guilt but also as a surrender of the entire array of constitutional rights designed to protect a criminal defendant against unjustified conviction, including the right to remain silent, the right to confront witnesses against her, the right to a trial by jury, and the right to be proven guilty by proof beyond a reasonable doubt.

As a result, judges must take certain procedures when accepting a plea of guilty. First, the judge must clearly state to the defendant the constitutional guarantees automatically waived by this plea. Second, the judge must believe that the facts of the case establish a basis for the plea and that the plea is made voluntarily. Third, the defendant must be informed of the right to counsel during the pleading process. In many felony cases, the judge will insist on the presence of defense counsel. Finally, the judge must inform the defendant of the possible sentencing outcomes, including the maximum sentence that can be imposed.

After a guilty plea has been entered, a sentencing date is arranged. In a majority of states, a guilty plea may be withdrawn and replaced with a not-guilty plea at any time prior to sentencing if good cause is shown.

NOT GUILTY At the arraignment or before the trial, a not-guilty plea is entered in two ways: (1) It is verbally stated by the defendant or the defense counsel, or (2) it is entered for the defendant by the court when the defendant stands mute before the bench.

Once a plea of not guilty is recorded, a trial date is set. In misdemeanor cases, trials take place in the lower-court system, whereas felony cases are normally transferred to the superior court. At this time, a continuance or issuance of bail is once again considered.

NOLO CONTENDERE The plea nolo contendere ("no contest") is essentially a plea of guilty. This plea has the same consequences as a guilty plea, with one exception: It may not be held against the defendant as proof in a subsequent civil matter because technically there has been no admission of guilt. This plea is accepted at the discretion of the trial court and must be voluntarily and intelligently made by the defendant.

PLEA BARGAINING

One of the most common practices in the criminal justice system today, and a cornerstone of the "informal justice" system, is **plea bargaining.** More than 90 percent of criminal convictions are estimated to result from negotiated pleas of guilty. Even in serious felony cases, some jurisdictions will have several plea-bargaining arrangements for every trial.

plea bargaining
The discussion between the defense counsel and the prosecution by which the accused agrees to plead guilty for certain considerations. The advantage to the defendant may be a reduction of the charges, a lenient sentence, or (in the case of multiple charges) dropped charges. The advantage to the prosecution is that a conviction is obtained without the time and expense of lengthy trial proceedings.

Plea bargaining has been defined concisely as the exchange of prosecutorial and judicial concessions for pleas of guilty.[24] Normally, a bargain can be made between the prosecutor and the defense attorney in four ways: (1) The initial charges may be reduced to those of a lesser offense, thus automatically reducing the sentence imposed; (2) in cases where many counts are charged, the prosecutor may reduce the number of counts; (3) the prosecutor may promise to recommend a lenient sentence, such as probation; and (4) when the charge imposed has a negative label attached (e.g., child molester), the prosecutor may alter the charge to a more "socially acceptable" one (such as assault) in exchange for a plea of guilty. In a jurisdiction where sentencing disparities exist between judges, the prosecutor may even agree to arrange for a defendant to appear before a lenient judge in exchange for a plea; this practice is known as "judge shopping."

Because of excessive criminal court caseloads and the personal and professional needs of the prosecution and the defense (to get the case over with in the shortest amount of time), plea bargaining has become an essential yet controversial part of the administration of justice. Proponents contend that plea bargaining actually benefits both the state and the defendant in the following ways:

1. The overall costs of the criminal prosecution are reduced.
2. The administrative efficiency of the courts is greatly improved.
3. The prosecution can devote more time to more serious cases.
4. The defendant avoids possible detention and an extended trial and may receive a reduced sentence.[25]

Those who favor plea bargaining believe it is appropriate to enter into plea discussions when the interests of the state in the effective administration of justice will be served. Opponents of the plea-bargaining process believe that the negotiated plea should be eliminated. Some argue that plea bargaining is objectionable because it encourages defendants to waive their constitutional right to trial. In addition, some experts suggest that sentences tend to be less severe when a defendant enters a guilty plea than in actual trials and that plea bargains result in even greater sentencing disparity. Particularly in the eyes of the general public, this allows the defendant to beat the system and further tarnishes the criminal process. Plea bargaining also raises the danger that an innocent person will be convicted of a crime if he is convinced that the lighter treatment from a guilty plea is preferable to the risk of conviction with a harsher sentence following a formal trial.

It is unlikely that plea negotiations will be eliminated or severely curtailed in the near future. Supporters of the total abolition of plea bargaining are in the minority. As a result of abuses, however, efforts are being made to improve plea-bargaining operations. Such reforms include (1) development of uniform plea practices, (2) representation of counsel during plea negotiations, and (3) establishment of time limits on plea negotiations.

Legal Issues in Plea Bargaining

The U.S. Supreme Court has reviewed the propriety of plea bargaining in several decisions, particularly in regard to the voluntariness of guilty pleas. Defendants are entitled to the effective assistance of counsel to protect them from pressure and influence. The Court ruled in *Hill v. Lockhart* (1985) that to prove ineffectiveness the defendant must show a "reasonable probability that, but for counsel's errors, he would not have pleaded guilty and would have insisted on going to trial."[26]

Boykin v. Alabama
The 1969 U.S. Supreme Court decision upholding that a defendant's plea bargain can only be accepted if it is a voluntary affirmative statement in a judicial hearing.

In ***Boykin v. Alabama*** (1969), the Court held that an affirmative action (such as a verbal statement) that the plea was made voluntarily must exist on the record before a trial judge may accept a guilty plea.[27] This is essential because a guilty plea basically constitutes a waiver of the defendant's Fifth Amendment privilege against self-incrimination and Sixth Amendment right to a jury trial. Subsequent to *Boykin,* the Court ruled in *Brady v. United States* (1970) that a guilty plea is not invalid merely because it is entered to avoid the possibility of the death penalty.[28]

When the question arose about whether a guilty plea may be accepted by a defendant maintaining her innocence, the Supreme Court, in *North Carolina v. Alford* (1970), said that such action was appropriate where a defendant was seeking a lesser sentence. In other words, a defendant could plead guilty without admitting guilt.[29]

Santobello v. New York
The 1971 U.S. Supreme Court decision upholding that promises of a prosecutor that are the foundation of a guilty plea must be honored by the government unless voided by a court.

In ***Santobello v. New York*** (1971), the Court held that the promise of the prosecutor must be kept and that a prosecutor's breaking of a plea-bargaining agreement required a reversal for the defendant.[30] In *Ricketts v. Adamson*

(1987), the Court ruled that defendants must also keep their side of a bargain to receive the promised offer of leniency. In this case, the defendant was charged with first-degree murder but was allowed to plead guilty to second-degree murder in exchange for testifying against his accomplices. The testimony was given, but the codefendants' conviction was later reversed on appeal. Ricketts refused to testify a second time, and the prosecutor withdrew the offer of leniency. On appeal, the Supreme Court allowed the recharging and held that Ricketts had to suffer the consequences of his voluntary choice not to testify again.[31]

How far can prosecutors go to convince a defendant to plead guilty? The Supreme Court ruled in the 1978 case of *Bordenkircher v. Hayes* that a defendant's due process rights are not violated when a prosecutor threatens to reindict the accused on more serious charges if the defendant does not plead guilty to the original offense.[32]

United States v. Mezzanatto The 1995 U.S. Supreme Court decision upholding that a defendant's statements in a plea bargain can be used against him or her if he or she goes to trial.

In 1995 the U.S. Supreme Court decided the case of ***United States v. Mezzanatto***, which may cause the plea-bargaining process to change in state courts. In *Mezzanatto,* the Court declared that statements made by the defendant during plea bargaining can be used at trial for impeachment purposes. This means that a prosecutor can refuse to plea-bargain with a defendant unless the defendant agrees that any statements made during the negotiations can be used to impeach him at trial. The Court narrowly interpreted Rule 410 of the Federal Rules of Evidence, which says that statements made during plea bargaining are inadmissible at trial. Although the ruling applies only to federal trials, it is likely to be adopted by many state court systems that watch Supreme Court decisions and follow suit.[33]

From repeated actions by the Supreme Court, we realize that plea bargaining is a constitutionally accepted practice in the United States. Table 9.3 summarizes the major Supreme Court decisions regulating plea-bargaining practices.

Plea-Bargaining Decision Making

Because the plea-bargaining process is largely informal, lacking in guidelines, and discretionary, some effort has been made to determine what kinds of information and how much is used by the prosecutor to make plea-bargaining decisions. Research has found that certain information weighs heavily in the prosecutorial decision to accept a plea negotiation.[34] Such factors as the offense, the defendant's prior record and age, and the type, strength, and admissibility of evidence are considered important in the plea-bargaining decision. The attitude of the complainant is also an important factor in the decision-making process; for example, in victimless cases, such as heroin possession, the police attitude is most often considered, whereas in victim-related crimes, such as rape, the attitude of the victim is a primary concern. The study also revealed that prosecutors in low-population or rural jurisdictions not only use more information while making their decisions but also seem more likely than their urban counterparts to accept bargains. It was suggested that "this finding tends to dispute the notion that plea bargaining is a response to overcrowding in large urban courts."[35] It appears that where caseload pressures are less, the acceptance of a plea bargain is actually more probable.

The Role of the Prosecutor in Plea Bargaining

The major players in the plea negotiations are (1) the prosecutor, (2) the defense attorney, (3) the judge, and (4) the defendant. The prosecutor in the U.S. system of criminal justice has broad discretion in the exercise of his responsibilities. Such discretion includes deciding whether to initiate a criminal prosecution, determining the nature and number of the criminal charges, and choosing whether

Table 9.3
Notable U.S. Supreme Court Cases on the Regulation of Plea Bargaining

Case	Ruling
Boykin v. Alabama (1969)	A defendant must make an affirmative statement that the plea is voluntary before the judge can accept it.
Brady v. United States (1970)	Avoiding the possibility of the death penalty is not grounds to invalidate a guilty plea.
North Carolina v. Alford (1970)	Accepting a guilty plea from a defendant who maintains his or her innocence is valid.
Santobello v. New York (1971)	The promise of a prosecutor that rests on a guilty plea must be kept in a plea-bargaining agreement.
Bordenkircher v. Hayes (1978)	A defendant's constitutional rights are not violated when a prosecutor threatens to reindict the accused on more serious charges if he or she is not willing to plead guilty to the original offense.
Hill v. Lockhart (1985)	To prove ineffectiveness of defense counsel, a defendant needs to show a reasonable probability that, except for counsel's errors, the defendant would not have pleaded guilty.
Ricketts v. Adamson (1987)	A defendant is required to keep his or her side of the bargain to receive the promised offer of leniency, since plea bargaining rests on an agreement between the parties.
United States v. Mezzanatto (1995)	A defendant who wants to plea-bargain in federal court can be required to agree that, if he testifies at trial, his statements during the plea-bargain negotiations can be used against him.

to plea-bargain a case and under what conditions. Plea bargaining is one of the major tools the prosecutor uses to control and influence the criminal justice system (the other two are the decision to initiate a charge and the ability to take the case to trial). Few states have placed limits on the discretion of prosecutors in plea-bargaining situations. Instead, in making a plea-bargaining decision, the prosecutor is generally free to weigh competing alternatives and factors, such as the seriousness of the crime, the attitude of the victim, the police report of the incident, and applicable sentencing provisions. Plea bargaining frequently occurs in cases where the government believes the evidence is weak, as when a key witness seems unreliable or unwilling to testify. Bargaining permits a compromise settlement in a weak case where the criminal trial outcome is in doubt.

On a case-by-case basis, the prosecutor determines the concessions to be offered in the plea bargain and seeks to dispose of each case quickly and efficiently. On the broader scale, however, the role of the chief prosecutor as an administrator also affects plea bargaining. Whereas the assistant prosecutor evaluates and moves individual cases, the chief prosecutor must establish plea-bargaining guidelines for the entire office. In this regard, the prosecutor may be acting as an administrator.[36] Guidelines cover such aspects as avoiding over-indictment and controlling nonprovable indictments, reducing felonies to misdemeanors, and bargaining with defendants.

Some jurisdictions have established guidelines to provide consistency in plea-bargaining cases. For instance, a given office may be required to define the

Most cases are settled with a plea bargain. Here, James LIn-den discusses terms of his sentencing on September 25, 1999, with the county prosecutor and his defense attorney. Accused of being involved in the killing of a 25-year-old California woman, Linden pled guilty to one count of harboring a wanted felon and also to being an accessory to a felony.

kinds and types of cases and offenders that may be suitable for plea bargaining. In other jurisdictions, approval to plea-bargain may be required. Other controls might include procedures for internally reviewing decisions by the chief prosecutor and the use of written memorandums to document the need and acceptability for a plea bargain in a given case. For example, pleas may be offered on a "take it or leave it" basis. In each case, a special prosecutor, whose job it is to screen cases, sets the bargaining terms. If the defense counsel cannot accept the agreement, there is no negotiation, and the case must go to trial. Only if complications arise in the case, such as witnesses changing their testimony, can negotiations be reopened.[37]

The prosecutor's role in plea bargaining is also important on a statewide or systemwide basis because it involves exercising leadership in setting policy. The most extreme example of a chief prosecutor influencing the plea-negotiation process has occurred where the prosecutor has attempted to eliminate plea bargaining. In Alaska such efforts met with resistance from assistant prosecutors and others in the system, particularly judges and defense attorneys.[38]

The Role of the Defense Counsel in Plea Bargaining

Both the U.S. Supreme Court and such organizations as the American Bar Association (ABA) have established guidelines for the court receiving a guilty plea and for the defense counsel representing the accused in plea negotiations.[39] No court should accept a guilty plea unless the defendant has been properly advised by counsel and the court has determined that the plea is voluntary and has a factual basis; the court has the discretion to reject a plea if it is inappropriately offered. The defense counsel — a public defender or a private attorney — is required to play an advisory role in plea negotiations. The defendant's counsel is expected to be aware of the facts of the case and of the law and to advise the defendant of the alternatives available. The defense attorney is basically responsible for making certain that the accused understands the nature of the plea-bargaining process and the guilty plea. This means that the defense counsel should explain to the defendant that by pleading guilty, she is waiving certain rights that would be available on going to trial. In addition, the defense attorney has the duty to keep the defendant informed of developments and discussions with the prosecutor regarding plea bargaining. While doing so, the attorney for the accused cannot misrepresent evidence or mislead the client into making a detrimental agreement.

According to Keith Bystrom, the defense counsel is not only ethically but constitutionally required to communicate all plea-bargaining offers to a client even if counsel believes the offers to be unacceptable.[40]

In reality, most plea negotiations occur in the chambers of the judge, in the prosecutor's office, or in the courthouse hallway. Under these conditions, it is often difficult to assess the actual roles played by the prosecutor and the defense attorney. Even so, it is fundamental that a defendant not be required to plead guilty until advised by counsel and that a guilty plea should not be made unless it is done with the consent of the accused.

The Role of the Judge in Plea Bargaining

One of the most confusing problems in the plea-bargaining process has been the proper role of the judge. Should the judge act only in a supervisory capacity or actually enter into the negotiation process? The leading national legal organization, the ABA, is opposed to judicial participation in plea negotiations.[41] The ABA sets out its position on the role of the judge in the plea-bargaining process by clearly stating that the trial judge should not participate in plea discussions. In addition, the Federal Rules of Criminal Procedure prohibit federal judges from participating in plea negotiations.[42] A few states disallow any form of judicial involvement in plea bargaining, but others permit the judge to participate.

The ABA objects in general to the judge participating in plea negotiations because of his position as chief judicial officer. A judge should not be a party to arrangements for the determination of a sentence, whether as a result of a guilty plea or a finding of guilty based on proof. Furthermore, judicial participation in plea negotiations (1) creates the impression in the mind of the defendant that she could not receive a fair trial, (2) lessens the ability of the judge to make an objective determination of the voluntariness of the plea, (3) is inconsistent with the theory behind the use of presentence investigation reports, and (4) may induce an innocent defendant to plead guilty because he is afraid to reject the disposition desired by the judge.[43]

On the other hand, those who suggest that the judge should participate directly in plea bargaining argue that such an approach would make sentencing more uniform and ensure that the plea-bargaining process would be fairer and more efficient.

The Victim and Plea Bargaining

Related to the issue of the prosecutor's exercise of discretion is the proper role of the victim in influencing plea bargaining. Often defense attorneys criticize prosecutors for treating victims' interests as paramount and oppose the practice of seeking approval for the proposed plea from a victim or family member. Some suggest that the system today is too "victim driven." Others maintain that the victim plays an almost secondary role in the process.

In reality, the victim is not "empowered" at the pretrial stage of the criminal process. Statutes do not require that the prosecutor defer to the victim's wishes, and there are no legal consequences for ignoring the victim in a plea-bargaining decision. Even the ABA's *Model Uniform Victims of Crime Act* only suggests that the prosecutor "confer" with the victim.[44]

Victims are certainly not in a position to veto a plea bargain. Most of the work of the victims' rights movement in the justice system is devoted to securing financial compensation from the state and some restitution when possible from the defendant. At the current time, it is at the trial stage where the victim has the greatest influence. Here, the victim often has the right to offer a victim-impact statement after a guilty determination and before the court imposes a sentence.

There is no question that the prosecutor should consider the impact that a plea bargain may have on the victim or victim's family. Some victims' groups even suggest that the victim's family have statutory authority to approve or disapprove any plea bargain between the prosecutor and defense attorney in criminal homicide cases. Given the volume of plea bargains, it appears that the victim should have greater control and participation.

As we have mentioned, over 90 percent of all criminal cases are generally disposed of without a trial. Plea bargaining is an inevitable result and essential to the continued functioning of the criminal justice process. If that is so, then it must be conducted fairly, and as George Fletcher, a noted legal scholar at Columbia Law School indicates, "with due consideration of the victim whose complaint initiates the action."[45]

Plea-Bargaining Reform Plea bargaining is so widespread that it is recognized as one of the major elements of the criminal justice system. Despite its prevalence, its merits are hotly debated. Those opposed to the widespread use of plea bargaining assert that it is coercive in its inducement of guilty pleas, that is encourages the unequal exercise of prosecutorial discretion, and that it complicates sentencing as well as the job of correctional authorities. Others argue that it is unconstitutional and that it results in cynicism and disrespect for the entire system.

On the other hand, its proponents contend that the practice ensures the flow of guilty pleas essential to administration efficiency. It allows the system the flexibility to individualize justice and inspires respect for the system because it is associated with certain and prompt punishment.[46]

In recent years, efforts have been made to convert plea bargaining into a more visible, understandable, and fair dispositional process. Many jurisdictions have developed safeguards and guidelines to prevent violations of due process and to ensure that innocent defendants do not plead guilty under coercion. Such safeguards include the following: (1) The judge questions the defendant about the facts of the guilty plea before accepting the plea; (2) the defense counsel is present and can advise the defendant of her rights; (3) the prosecutor and the defense attorney openly discuss the plea; and (4) full and frank information about the defendant and the offenses is made available at this stage of the process. In addition, judicial supervision ensures that plea bargaining is conducted in a fair manner.

What would happen if plea bargaining were banned outright, as its critics advocate? Numerous jurisdictions throughout the United States have experimented with bans on plea bargaining. In 1975 Alaska eliminated the practice. Honolulu has also attempted to abolish plea bargaining. Other jurisdictions, including Iowa, Arizona, Delaware, and the District of Columbia, have sought to limit the use of plea bargaining.[47] In theory, eliminating plea bargains means that prosecutors in these jurisdictions give no consideration or concessions to a defendant in exchange for a guilty plea. The no–plea bargaining approach is the subject of Exhibit 9.1.

In reality, however, in these and most jurisdictions, sentence-related concessions, charge-reduction concessions, and alternative methods for prosecution

exhibit 9.1

Instituting a No–Plea–Bargaining Policy in Memphis, Tennessee ("No Deal—Hard Crime Gets All the Time")

Goal: To eliminate plea bargains and indictments for certain violent crimes—murder, aggravated rapes, and aggravated robbery.

Problem: Memphis has been ranked in the top 10% of American cities in its crime rate (especially violent crime). The public was demanding action from its public officials.

Rationale: The no–plea bargaining policy on violent crimes was adapted for two commonsense reasons. First, the government wanted to hold those guilty of violent crimes accountable to the extent possible. Second, it is essential to deter others from committing violent acts.

Program: A special Violent Crimes Prosecution Unit was established to handle the cases. In the first two years of the program, there were over 2,000 indictments, of which 164 were for first-degree murder and 1,646 for aggravated robbery.

Impact: Over 90% of the cases disposed of by 1999 were through guilty verdicts and guilty pleas as indicted. More violent criminals are spending more time in prison than would otherwise be the case. There has been no court case overload. A trend exists toward fewer violent crimes. More public confidence exists in the criminal justice system.

SOURCE: William Gibbons, "Instituting a No Plea Bargaining Policy," *Prosecutor* 40 (1999): 36–40.

continue to be used in one fashion or another.[48] Where plea bargaining is limited or abolished, the number of trials may increase, the sentence severity may change, and more questions regarding the right to a speedy trial may arise. Discretion may also be shifted further up the system. Instead of spending countless hours preparing for and conducting a trial, prosecutors may dismiss more cases outright or decide not to prosecute them after initial action has been taken.

In 1993 Candace McCoy published a well-documented book, *Politics and Plea Bargaining: Victims' Rights in California,* in which she describes legislative efforts to eliminate the plea-bargaining process in California. Instead of achieving a ban on plea bargaining, the process shifted from the superior to the municipal courts. McCoy found that the majority of defendants pled guilty after some negotiations and that the new law actually accelerated the guilty plea process. McCoy's prescription is not to ban plea bargaining but make it better. This includes (1) emphasizing public scrutiny of plea bargaining, (2) adhering to standards of professionalism, and (3) making a greater commitment to due process procedures.[49]

diversion
A noncriminal alternative to trial, usually featuring counseling, job training, and educational opportunities.

PRETRIAL DIVERSION

Another important feature in the early court process is placing offenders into noncriminal **diversion** programs before their formal trial or conviction. Pretrial diversion programs were first established in the late 1960s and early 1970s, when it became apparent that a viable alternative to the highly stigmatized criminal sentence was needed. In diversion programs, formal criminal proceedings against an accused are suspended while that person participates in a community treatment program under court supervision. Diversion helps the offender avoid the stigma of a criminal conviction and enables the justice system to reduce costs and alleviate prison overcrowding.

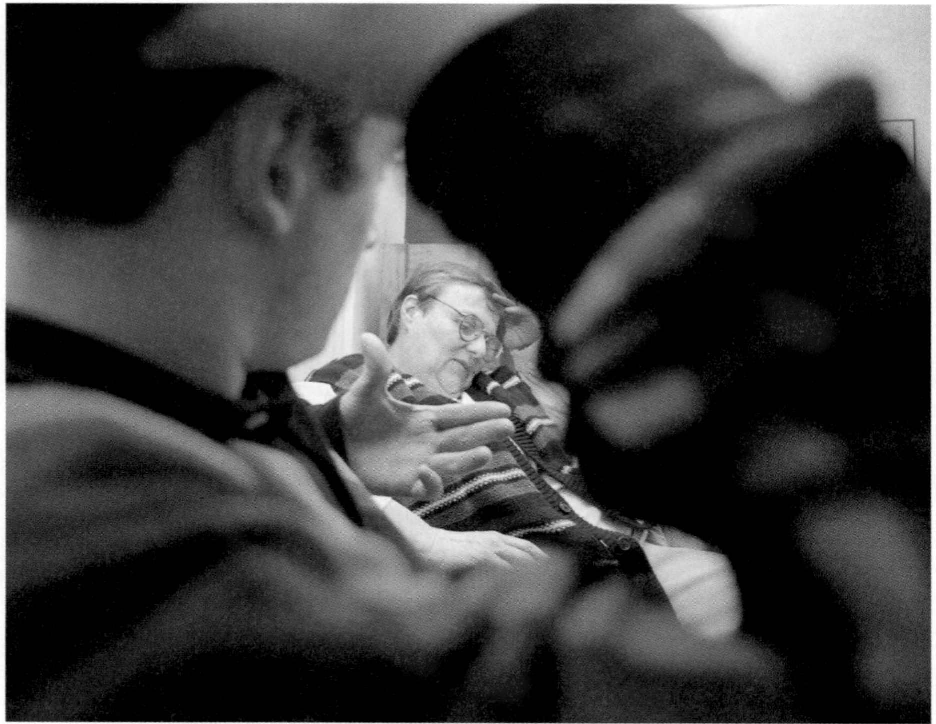

A counselor confers with a problem youth during a counseling session in a program designed to steer youth away from criminal lifestyles. Diversion programs can have both treatment and economic benefits since they are typically far less costly to operate than the traditional prison system.

Many diversion programs exist throughout the United States. These programs vary in size and emphasis but generally pursue the same goal: to constructively bypass criminal prosecution by providing a reasonable alternative in the form of treatment, counseling, or employment programs.

The prosecutor often plays the central role in the diversion process. Decisions about nondispositional alternatives are based on (1) the nature of the crime, (2) special characteristics of the offender, (3) whether the defendant is a first-time offender, (4) whether the defendant will cooperate with a diversion program, (5) the impact of diversion on the community, and (6) consideration for the opinion of the victim.[50]

Diversion programs can take many forms. Some are separate, independent agencies that were originally set up with federal funds but are now being continued with county or state assistance. Others are organized as part of a police, prosecutor, or probation department's internal structure. Still others are a joint venture between the county government and a private, nonprofit organization that actually carries out the treatment process.

First viewed as a panacea that could reduce court congestion and help treat minor offenders, diversion programs have come under fire for their alleged failures. Some national evaluations have concluded that diversion programs are no more successful at avoiding stigma and reducing recidivism than traditional justice processing.[51] The most prominent criticism is that they help **widen the net** of the justice system. By this, critics mean that the people placed in diversion programs are the ones most likely to have otherwise been dismissed after a brief hearing with a warning or small fine.[52]

widening the net
The charge that programs designed to divert offenders from the justice system actually enmesh them further in the process by substituting more intrusive treatment programs for less intrusive punishment-oriented outcomes.

Those who would have ordinarily received a more serious sentence are not eligible for diversion anyway. Thus, rather than limiting contact with the system, the diversion programs actually increase it. Of course, not all justice experts agree with this charge, and some have championed diversion as a worthwhile exercise of the criminal justice system's rehabilitation responsibility. Although diversion may not be a cure-all for criminal behavior, it is an important effort that continues to be made in most jurisdictions across the United States. Originally proposed by the well-known President's Commission on Law Enforcement in 1967 and supported by federal funds, most existing programs are now underwritten with state funds.[53]

SUMMARY

Many important decisions about what happens to a defendant are made prior to trial. Hearings, such as before the grand jury and the preliminary hearing, are held to determine if probable cause exists to charge the accused with a crime. If so, the defendant is arraigned, enters a plea, is informed of his constitutional rights, particularly the right to the assistance of counsel, and is considered for pretrial diversion. The use of money bail and other alternatives, such as release on recognizance, allows most defendants to be free pending their trial. Bail provisions are beginning to be toughened, resulting in the preventive detention of people awaiting trial. Preventive detention has been implemented because many believe that significant numbers of criminals violate their bail and commit further crimes while on pretrial release.

The issue of discretion plays a major role at this stage of the criminal process. Since only a small percentage of criminal cases eventually go to trial, many defendants agree to plea bargains or are placed in diversion programs. Not enough judges, prosecutors, defense attorneys, and courts exist to try every defendant accused of a crime. As a result, such subsystems as plea bargaining and diversion are essential elements in the administration of the criminal justice system. Research indicates that most cases never go to trial but are bargained out of the system. Although plea bargaining has been criticized, efforts to control it have not met with success. Similarly, diversion programs have not been overly successful, yet they continue to be used throughout the United States.

KEY TERMS

pretrial procedure
booking process
complaint
initial hearing
arraignment
indictment
grand jury
information
preliminary hearing (probable cause hearing)
bail
bail bonding
deposit bail
release on recognizance (ROR)
Manhattan Bail Project
Bail Reform Act of 1984
preventive detention
United States v. Salerno
pretrial detention
charge
waiver
plea bargaining
Boykin v. Alabama
Santobello v. New York
United States v. Mezzanatto
diversion
widen the net

 INFOTRAC COLLEGE EDITION EXERCISES

Doesn't preventive detention punish an individual who has not been found guilty of the allegations made by the state? At the same time, aren't justice officials required to protect the community? A preventive detention statute is an example of the crime control perspective and the judicious use of a serious criminal sanction — jail. Denying defendants the right to bail because they are dangerous is the basis of the preventive detention law. Merely accusing a person of a crime and keeping the person incarcerated has caused critics to question the legality of such a practice. Yet, the U.S. Supreme Court upheld the constitutionality of the preventive detention statute in *United States v. Salerno* (1987).

Using *InfoTrac College Edition,* search for articles that argue against the use of preventive detention. Use key words such as "bail," "detention," and "pretrial release."

QUESTIONS

1. Should criminal defendants be allowed to bargain for a reduced sentence in exchange for a guilty plea? Why or why not?
2. Should those accused of violent acts be subjected to preventive detention instead of bail, even though they have not been convicted of a crime? Explain.
3. What purpose does a grand jury or preliminary hearing serve in adjudicating felony offenses?
4. What is the purpose of bail? Of preventive detention?
5. Is plea bargaining constitutional? Explain.
6. Nearly three years after the JonBenet Ramsey murder in Boulder, Colorado, the grand jury was dismissed, and no charges were ever filed. Why?

NOTES

1. D. Alan Henry, "Pretrial Services: Today and Yesterday," *Federal Probation* (June 1991): 54.

2. Bureau of Justice Assistance, *Pretrial Services Program* (Washington, D.C.: Government Printing Office, 1990), 3.

3. Director of Administrative Office of the United States Courts, *The Demonstration Program of Mandatory Drug Testing of Criminal Defendants* (Washington, D.C.: Bureau of Justice Assistance, 1991).

4. U.S. Department of Justice, *Predicting Pretrial Misconduct with Drug Tests of Arrestees* (Washington, D.C.: National Institute of Justice Research in Brief, 1996), 1.

5. William Rhodes, Raymond Hyatt, and Paul Scheiman, "Predicting Pretrial Misconduct with Drug Tests of Arrestees: Evidence from Eight Settings," *Journal of Quantitative Criminology* 12 (1996): 315–47; D. Alan Henry and John Clark, *Pretrial Drug Testing — An Overview* (Washington, D.C.: Bureau of Justice Assistance, 1999).

6. *Stack v. Boyle,* 342 U.S. 1, 72 S.Ct. 1, 96 L.Ed. 3 (1951).

7. Andy Hall, *Pretrial Release Program Options* (Washington, D.C.: National Institute of Justice, 1984), 30–31.

8. Mary Toborg, *Pretrial Release: A National Evaluation of Practices and Outcomes* (Washington, D.C.: National Institute of Justice, 1982).

9. William Rhodes, *Pretrial Release and Misconduct* (Washington, D.C.: Bureau of Justice Statistics, 1985).

10. Bureau of Justice Statistics, *Pretrial Release of Felony Defendants, 1990* (Washington, D.C.: Government Printing Office, 1991), 1.

11. Andrea Gerlin, "Criminal Defendants Released without Bail Spark a Heated Debate," *Wall Street Journal,* 9 July 1996, A1.

12. Vera Institute of Justice, *1961–1971: Programs in Criminal Justice* (New York: Vera Institute of Justice, 1972).

13. Chris Eskridge, *Pretrial Release Programming* (New York: Clark Boardman, 1983), 27.

14. Public Law 89-465, 18 U.S.C., sec. 3146 (1966).

15. 18 U.S.C., sec. 3142 (1984).

16. See, generally, Fred Cohen, "The New Federal Crime Control Act," *Criminal Law Bulletin* 21 (1985): 330–37.

17. *Schall v. Martin,* 467 U.S. 253, 104 S.Ct. 2403, 81 L.Ed.2d 207 (1984).

18. *United States v. Salerno,* 481 U.S. 739, 107 S.Ct. 2095, 95 L.Ed.2d 697 (1987).

19. Ibid. at 742, 107 S.Ct. at 2098 (1987).

20. Bureau of Justice Statistics, *Fiscal Year 1998 at a Glance* (Washington, D.C.: Office of Justice Programs, 1999), 30.

21. Two excellent studies are Caleb Foote, "Compelling Appearance in Court: Administration of Bail in Philadelphia," *University of Pennsylvania Law Review* 102 (1956): 1056; and idem, "A Study of Administration of Bail in New York City," *University of Pennsylvania Law Review* 106 (1960): 693–730.

22. Rhodes, *Pretrial Release and Misconduct;* see also Foote, "A Study of Administration of Bail in New York City"; Ellen Steury and Nancy Frank, "Gender Bias and Pretrial Release," *Journal of Criminal Justice* 18 (1990): 417–32.

23. Michael Corrado, "Punishment and the Wild Beast of Prey: The Problem of Preventive Detention," *Journal of Criminal Law and Criminology* 86 (1996): 778–92.

24. Alan Alschuler, "The Prosecutor's Role in Plea Bargaining," *University of Chicago Law Review* (1968): 50–112.

25. For the most cogent arguments favoring plea bargaining, see John Wheatley, "Plea Bargaining — A Case for Its Continuance," *Massachusetts Law Quarterly* 59 (1974): 31.

26. *Hill v. Lockhart,* 474 U.S. 52, 106 S.Ct. 366, 88 L.Ed.2d 203 (1985).

27. *Boykin v. Alabama,* 395 U.S. 238, 89 S.Ct. 1709, 23 L.Ed.2d 274 (1969).

28. *Brady v. United States,* 397 U.S. 742, 90 S.Ct. 1463, 25 L.Ed.2d 747 (1970).

29. *North Carolina v. Alford,* 400 U.S. 25, 91 S.Ct. 160, 27 L.Ed.2d 162 (1970).

30. *Santobello v. New York,* 404 U.S. 257, 92 S.Ct. 495, 30 L.Ed.2d 427 (1971).

31. *Ricketts v. Adamson,* 483 U.S. 1, 107 S.Ct. 2680, 97 L.Ed.2d 1 (1987).

32. *Bordenkircher v. Hayes,* 434 U.S. 357, 98 S.Ct. 663, 54 L.Ed.2d 604 (1978).

33. *United States v. Mezzanatto,* 116 S.Ct. 1480, 134 L.Ed.2d 687 (1995).

34. Stephen P. Lagoy, Joseph J. Senna, and Larry J. Siegel, "An Empirical Study on Information Usage for Prosecutorial Decision Making in Plea Negotiations," *American Criminal Law Review* 13 (1976): 435–71.

35. Ibid., 462.

36. Alschuler, "The Prosecutor's Role in Plea Bargaining."

37. Barbara Boland and Brian Forst, *The Prevalence of Guilty Pleas* (Washington, D.C.: Bureau of Justice Statistics, 1984), 3; see also Gary Hengstler, "The Troubled Justice System," *American Bar Association Journal* 80 (1994): 44.

38. National Institute of Law Enforcement and Criminal Justice, *Plea Bargaining in the United States* (Washington, D.C.: Georgetown University, 1978), 8.

39. See American Bar Association, *Standards Relating to Pleas of Guilty,* 2d ed. (Chicago: ABA, 1988); see also *North Carolina v. Alford,* 400 U.S. 25, 91 S.Ct. 160, 27 L.Ed.2d 162 (1970).

40. Keith Bystrom, "Communicating Plea Offers to the Client," in *Ethical Problems Facing the Criminal Defense Lawyer,* ed. Rodney Uphoff (Chicago: American Bar Association Section on Criminal Justice, 1995), 84.

41. American Bar Association, *Standards Relating to Pleas of Guilty,* standard 3.3; National Advisory Commission on Criminal Justice Standards and Goals, *Task Force Report on Courts* (Washington, D.C.: Government Printing Office, 1973), 42.

42. Federal Rules of Criminal Procedure, rule 11.

43. American Bar Association, *Standards Relating to Pleas of Guilty,* 73; see also Alan Alschuler, "The Trial Judge's Role in Plea

Bargaining," *Columbia Law Review* 76 (1976): 1059.

44. American Bar Association, *Model Uniform Victims of Crime Act* (Chicago: ABA, 1992).

45. George P. Fletcher, *With Justice for Some — Victims' Rights in Criminal Trials* (New York: Addison-Wesley, 1995), 190–93.

46. *Santobello v. New York,* 404 U.S. 257, 92 S.Ct. 495, 30 L.Ed.2d 427 (1971).

47. National Institute of Law Enforcement and Criminal Justice, *Plea Bargaining in the United States,* 37–40.

48. For a discussion of this issue, see Michael Tonry, "Plea Bargaining Bans and Rules," in *Sentencing Reform Impacts* (Washington, D.C.: Government Printing Office, 1987).

49. Candace McCoy, *Politics and Plea Bargaining: Victims' Rights in California* (Philadelphia: University of Pennsylvania Press, 1993).

50. National District Attorneys Association, *National Prosecution Standards,* 2d ed. (Alexandria, Va.: NDAA, 1991), 130.

51. Franklyn Dunford, D. Wayne Osgood, and Hart Weichselbaum, *National Evaluation of Diversion Programs* (Washington, D.C.: Government Printing Office, 1982).

52. Sharla Rausch and Charles Logan, "Diversion from Juvenile Court, Panacea or Pandora's Box?" in *Evaluating Juvenile Justice,* ed. James Kleugel (Beverly Hills, Calif.: Sage, 1983), 19–30.

53. See Malcolm Feeley, *Court Reform on Trial* (New York: Basic Books, 1983).

chapter 10

The Criminal Trial

In October 1998, Matthew Shepard, age 21, an openly gay student at the University of Wyoming, was beaten savagely and abandoned to die. Tied for eighteen hours to a rural fence, he died five days later in a local hospital. Prosecutors said Aaron McKinney and a friend, who subsequently pled guilty, lured Shepard from a bar and drove him to a remote spot; there, McKinney pistol-whipped him into a coma. The government claimed that robbery was the primary motive but that the victim was singled out because he was gay.

In a case that drew nationwide attention, McKinney was indicted for robbery, kidnapping, and first-degree murder. During the criminal trial before a jury of seven men and five women, the prosecutors

Chastity Pasley waits to be arraigned in Albany County Court in Laramie, Wyoming, on October 9, 1998. She is charged with being an accomplice in the beating death of Matthew Shepard.

portrayed McKinney as a bloodthirsty person intent on killing a gay man in a blind rage, triggered by his own drug addiction. Testimony from the codefendant substantiated the fact that McKinney fatally beat the victim.

The defense attorney argued that Shepard went with the defendant willingly and even sexually groped him, which caused McKinney to explode violently against Shepard and kill him. According to the defense, the criminal homicide was not premeditated murder because Shepard provoked McKinney. The defense attempted to use a "gay panic" strategy, which is based on the theory that a person with latent homosexual tendencies will have an uncontrollable violent reaction when propositioned by a homosexual. This was barred by the court.

After many hours of deliberation, the jury convicted McKinney of felony-murder — that is, a killing while committing other crimes, in this case kidnapping and aggravated robbery. On the charge of first-degree murder, the jury acquitted McKinney and convicted him of second-degree murder, which means they didn't believe the killing was premeditated. McKinney was sentenced to life imprisonment but spared the death penalty.[1] ■

Cases such as McKinney's point out why the criminal trial process remains a matter of vital importance to the criminal justice system. It must render fair, impartial justice in deciding the outcome of a conflict between the state and the accused. The opportunity to go to trial provides the foremost safeguard against abuse of informal processing and serves as the basis for encouraging public faith in the system. To many theorists of jurisprudence, the dynamic center of the criminal trial is the fact-finding process. Did McKinney commit murder with premeditation? Was the defendant provoked by Shepard's sexual advances?

adjudication
The determination of guilt or innocence; a judgment concerning criminal charges. The majority of offenders charged plead guilty; of the remainder, some cases are adjudicated by a judge and a jury, some are adjudicated by a judge without a jury, and others are dismissed.

The **adjudication** stage of the criminal justice process begins with a hearing that seeks to determine the truth of the facts of a case. This process is usually referred to as the criminal *trial,* such as described in the *McKinney* case. As we have mentioned, the classic jury trial of a criminal case is an uncommon occurrence. The greatest proportion of individuals charged with crimes plead guilty. Others have their cases dismissed by the judge for a variety of reasons: The government may decide not to prosecute (nolle prosequi); the accused may be found emotionally disturbed and unable to stand trial; or the court may be unwilling to attach the stigma of a criminal record to a particular defendant.

Still other defendants waive their constitutional right to a jury trial. In this situation, which occurs daily in the lower criminal courts, the judge may initiate a number of formal or informal dispositions, including dismissing the case, finding the defendant not guilty, finding the defendant guilty and imposing a sentence, or even continuing the case indefinitely. The decision the judge makes often depends on the seriousness of the offense, the background and previous record of the defendant, and the judgment of the court about whether the case can be properly dealt with in the criminal process.

In a minor case in some jurisdictions, for example, the *continuance* is a frequently used disposition. In this instance, the court holds a case in abeyance without a finding of guilt to induce the accused to improve her behavior in the community; if the defendant's behavior does improve, the case is ordinarily closed within a specific amount of time.

The number of actual criminal jury trials is small in comparison with all the cases processed through the criminal justice system, since upward of 90 percent of all defendants plead guilty and about 5 percent are dealt with by other methods; it appears that fewer than 5 percent ever reach the trial stage. Those cases that are actually tried before a jury often involve serious crimes. Such crimes require a formal inquiry into the facts to determine the guilt or innocence of the accused.

Even though proportionately few cases are actually tried by juries, the trial process remains a focal point in the criminal justice system. It symbolizes the U.S. system of jurisprudence, in which an accused person can choose to present a defense against the government's charges. The fact that the defendant has the option of going to trial significantly affects the operation of the criminal justice system.

LEGAL RIGHTS DURING TRIAL

Underlying every trial are constitutional principles, complex legal procedures, rules of court, and interpretations of statutes, all designed to ensure that the accused will receive a fair trial. This section discusses the most important constitutional rights of the accused at the trial stage of the criminal justice system and reviews the legal nature of the trial process. Here we examine the major legal decisions and statutes involving the right to confront witnesses and the rights to a jury trial, counsel, self-representation, and a speedy and public trial.

confrontation clause
The constitutional right of a criminal defendant to see and cross-examine all the witnesses against him or her.

The Right to Confront Witnesses

The Sixth Amendment states, "In all criminal prosecutions, the accused shall enjoy the right . . . to be confronted with the witnesses against him."[2] The **confrontation clause** is essential to a fair criminal trial because it restricts and controls the admissibility of hearsay evidence. In other words, secondhand evidence, which depends on a witness not available in court, is ordinarily limited in preference to the personal knowledge of a witness or victim of a crime. The framers of the Constitution sought face-to-face accusations in which the defendant has a right to see and cross-examine all witnesses against him. The idea that it is always more difficult to tell lies about people to their faces than behind their backs illustrates the meaning of the confrontation clause. In other words, a witness in a criminal trial may have more difficulty repeating her testimony when facing the accused in a trial than in providing information to the police during an investigation.

The accused has the right to confront the witnesses and challenge their assertions and perceptions: Did they really see what they believe? Are they biased? Can they be trusted? What about the veracity of their testimony? Generally speaking, the courts have been nearly unanimous in their belief that the right of confrontation and cross-examination is an essential requirement for a fair trial.[3]

This face-to-face presence has been reviewed by the U.S. Supreme Court in matters involving a child as a witness in criminal proceedings. In the 1988 case of *Coy v. Iowa,* the Supreme Court limited the protection available to child sex abuse victims at the trial stage.[4] In *Coy,* two girls were allowed to be cross-examined behind a screen that separated them from the defendant. The Court ruled that the screen violated the defendant's right to confront witnesses and overturned his conviction. However, Justice Sandra Day O'Connor made it clear that ruling out the protective screen did not bar the states from using videotapes or closed-circuit TV.

In *Maryland v. Craig* (1990), the second case in this area, the Supreme Court carved out an exception to the Sixth Amendment confrontation clause by deciding that alleged child abuse victims could testify by closed-circuit TV if face-to-face confrontation would cause them trauma.[5] In allowing the states to take testimony via closed-circuit TV, the Court has found that circumstances exist in child sex abuse cases that override the defendant's right of confrontation.

As a result of these decisions, the confrontation clause does not guarantee criminal defendants the *absolute* right to a face-to-face meeting with witnesses at their trial. This right may be denied when necessary to further an important public policy, such as protecting a child from trauma in a criminal trial.

The Right to a Jury Trial

The defendant has the right to choose whether the trial will be before a judge or a jury. Although the Sixth Amendment to the U.S. Constitution guarantees the right to a jury trial, the defendant can and often does waive this right. A substantial proportion of defendants, particularly those charged with misdemeanors, are tried before the court without a jury.

The major legal issue surrounding jury trial has been the question of whether all offenders, both misdemeanants and felons, have an absolute right to a jury trial. Because the Constitution is silent on this point, the U.S. Supreme Court has ruled that all defendants in felony cases have this right. In *Duncan v. Louisiana* (1968), the Supreme Court held that the Sixth Amendment right to a jury trial is

Jury forewoman Niki Deutchman answers media questions after the trial of Oklahoma City bombing conspirator Terry Nichols.

applicable to the states as well as to the federal government and that it can be interpreted to apply to all defendants accused of serious crimes.[6] The Court in *Duncan* based its holding on the premise that in the American states, as in the federal judicial system, a general grant of jury trial for serious offenses is a fundamental right, essential for preventing miscarriages of justice and for ensuring that fair trials are provided for all defendants.[7]

The *Duncan* decision did not settle whether all defendants charged with crimes in state courts are constitutionally entitled to jury trials. It seemed to draw the line at only those charged with serious offenses, leaving the decision to grand jury trials to defendants in minor cases to the discretion of the individual states.

In the 1970 case of *Baldwin v. New York,* the Supreme Court departed from the distinction of serious versus minor offenses and decided that a defendant has a constitutional right to a jury trial when facing a prison sentence of six months or more, regardless of whether the crime committed was a felony or a misdemeanor.[8] Where the possible sentence is six months or less, the accused is not entitled to a jury trial unless it is authorized by state statute.

In the 1989 case of *Blanton v. North Las Vegas,* the Court ruled unanimously that when a state defines the crime of drunk driving as a petty offense,[9] the U.S. Constitution does not require that the defendant receive a jury trial. If, however, a state treats driving under the influence as a serious crime, a jury trial would be required. This decision upheld a Nevada law classifying drunk driving as a petty offense and similar procedures in at least five other jurisdictions in the United States. In most jurisdictions, the more serious the charge, the greater likelihood of trial — and of a trial by jury.

The latest Supreme Court decision on jury trials occurred in the 1996 case of *Lewis v. United States.*[10] As noted, the Court has used six months' potential imprisonment as the dividing line between petty offenses for which the Sixth Amendment gives no right to jury trial and "serious" offenses that enjoy such a legal right. In the *Lewis* case, the Court faced the unusual problem of multiple petty offenses that had an aggregate potential imprisonment in excess of six months. The defendant argued that he was constitutionally entitled to a jury trial. But the Court said there was no Sixth Amendment right to a jury trial for a string of petty offenses tried together, even where the potential aggregate sentence could exceed six months. The reasons were (1) the Court believed the legislature was responsible for the design of an offense with a maximum possible penalty and (2) the prosecutor has the right to exercise discretion to join different offenses in one trial without defeating the legislative intent to distinguish between petty and serious offenses.

Other important issues related to the defendant's rights in a criminal jury trial include the right to a jury consisting of twelve people or fewer and the right to a unanimous verdict.

JURY SIZE The actual size of the jury has been a matter of great concern. Can a defendant be tried and convicted of a crime by a jury of fewer than twelve persons? Traditionally, twelve jurors have deliberated as the triers of fact in criminal cases involving misdemeanors or felonies. However, the U.S. Constitution does not specifically require a jury of twelve persons. As a result, in *Williams v. Florida* in 1970, the U.S. Supreme Court held that a **six-person jury** in a criminal trial does not deprive a defendant of the constitutional right to a jury trial.[11] The Court made clear that the twelve-person panel is not a necessary ingredient of a trial by jury, and it upheld a Florida statute permitting the use of a six-person jury in a robbery trial.

six-person jury
The criminal trial of a defendant before a jury of six persons as opposed to a traditional jury of twelve persons.

Justice Byron White, writing for the majority, said, "In short, while sometime in the 14th century the size of the jury came to be fixed generally at 12, that particular feature of the jury system appears to have been a historical accident, unrelated to the great purpose which gave rise to the jury in the first place."[12] *Williams v. Florida* has offered a welcome measure of relief to an overburdened crime control system. Today, jury size may be reduced for all but the most serious criminal cases.

UNANIMOUS VERDICT Besides the convention of twelve-person juries in criminal trials, tradition also had been that the jurors' decision must be unanimous. However, in the 1972 case of *Apodica v. Oregon,* the U.S. Supreme Court held that the Sixth and Fourteenth Amendments do not prohibit criminal convictions by less than unanimous jury verdicts in noncapital cases.[13] In the *Apodica* case, the Court upheld an Oregon statute requiring only ten of twelve jurors to convict the defendant of assault with a deadly weapon, burglary, and grand larceny. Such verdicts are not unusual in civil matters, but much controversy remains regarding their place in the criminal process.

The Right to Counsel at Trial

Recall from previous chapters that the defendant has a right to counsel at numerous points in the criminal justice system. Through a series of leading U.S. Supreme Court decisions (*Powell v. Alabama* in 1932,[14] *Gideon v. Wainwright* in 1963,[15] and *Argersinger v. Hamlin* in 1972[16]), the right of a criminal defendant to have counsel in state trials has become a fundamental right in the criminal justice system. Today, state courts must provide counsel at trial to indigent defendants who face the possibility of incarceration.

It is interesting to note the historical development of the law regarding right to counsel, for it shows the gradual process of decision making in the Supreme Court, as well as reiterating the relationship between the Bill of Rights and the Fourteenth Amendment. The Bill of Rights protects citizens against federal encroachment, and the Fourteenth Amendment provides that no state shall deprive any person of life, liberty, and property without due process of law. A difficult

Attorney Karen Ackerson with her client Henry Watson in Los Angeles County Court. The right to counsel has been interpreted to mean that all people who face confinement must be provided with legal assistance at trial.

constitutional question has been whether the Fourteenth Amendment incorporates the Bill of Rights and makes its provisions binding on individual states. In *Powell v. Alabama* (also known as the *Scottsboro Boys case*), for example, nine young black men were charged in an Alabama court with raping two young white women. They were tried and convicted without the benefit of counsel. The U.S. Supreme Court concluded that the presence of a defense attorney is so vital to a fair trial that the failure of the Alabama trial court to appoint counsel was a denial of due process of law under the Fourteenth Amendment. In this instance, due process meant the right to counsel for defendants accused of committing a capital offense.

Then, in the case of *Gideon v. Wainwright* almost thirty years later, the Supreme Court in a unanimous and historic decision stated that, although the Sixth Amendment does not explicitly lay down a rule binding on the states, right to counsel is so fundamental and ethical to a fair trial that states are obligated to abide by it under the Fourteenth Amendment's due process clause. Thus, the Sixth Amendment requirement regarding the right to counsel in the federal court system is also binding on the states. (The Law in Review feature examines the *Gideon* case.)

The *Gideon* decision made it clear that a person charged with a felony in a state court has an absolute constitutional right to counsel. Some states applied the *Gideon* ruling to all criminal trials, but others did not provide a defendant with an attorney in misdemeanor cases. Then, in the momentous 1972 decision of *Argersinger v. Hamlin,* the Supreme Court held that no person can be imprisoned for any offense — whether classified as a petty offense, a misdemeanor, or a felony — unless he is offered representation by counsel at trial. The right to counsel in misdemeanor cases is limited to cases where the defendant is actually sentenced to jail, as decided by *Scott v. Illinois* in 1979.[17] The decision extended this right to virtually all defendants in state criminal prosecutions. The timeline in Figure 10.1 indicates how it has taken over two hundred years to establish what the U.S. Constitution stated in 1791 — namely, "in all criminal prosecutions, the accused shall enjoy the right . . . to have the assistance of counsel for his defense."[18]

The Right to Self-Representation

Another important question regarding the right to counsel is whether criminal defendants are guaranteed the right to represent themselves — that is, to act as their own lawyers. Before the

Facts

Clarence Gideon was charged in a Florida state court with having broken into and entered a poolroom with intent to commit a misdemeanor. This offense is a felony under Florida law. Appearing in court without funds and without a lawyer, the petitioner asked the court to appoint him counsel. The court replied that it could not appoint counsel because under Florida law the only time the court can appoint counsel for a defendant is when that person is charged with a capital offense.

Put to a trial before a jury, Gideon conducted his defense about as well as could be expected from a layperson. He made an opening statement to the jury, cross-examined the state's witnesses, presented witnesses in his own defense, declined to testify himself, and made a short argument emphasizing his innocence of the charge contained in the information filed in the case. The jury returned a verdict of guilty, and Gideon was sentenced to serve five years in the Florida state prison.

Gideon filed a habeas corpus petition in the Florida Supreme Court attacking his conviction and sentence on the ground that the trial court's refusal to appoint counsel for him denied him rights guaranteed by the Constitution and the Bill of Rights. Relief was denied. Gideon then filed an in forma pauperis appeal to the U.S. Supreme Court, which granted certiorari and appointed counsel to represent him.

The issues faced by the Supreme Court were simple but of gigantic importance: (1) Is an indigent defendant charged in a state court with a noncapital felony entitled to the assistance of a lawyer under the due process clause of the Fourteenth Amendment? (2) Should *Betts v. Brady* be overruled?

Decision

Justice Hugo Black delivered the opinion of the Court:

> We accept *Betts v. Brady*'s assumption, based as it was on our prior cases, that a provision of the Bill of Rights which is fundamental and essential to a fair trial is made obligatory upon the States by the Fourteenth Amendment. We think the Court in *Betts v. Brady* was wrong, however, in concluding that the Sixth Amendment's guarantee is not one of the fundamental rights. In our adversary system of criminal justice, any person brought into court, who is too poor to hire a lawyer, cannot be assured a fair trial unless counsel is provided for him. That government hires lawyers to prosecute and defendants who have the money to hire lawyers to defend, are the strongest indications of the widespread belief that lawyers in criminal court are necessities, not luxuries. The right of one charged with crime to counsel may not be deemed essential to fair trial in some countries, but it is in ours.

Significance of the Case

The U.S. Supreme Court unanimously overruled its earlier decision in *Betts v. Brady* and explicitly held that the right to counsel in criminal cases is fundamental and essential to a fair trial and as such applicable to the states by way of the Fourteenth Amendment. The *Gideon* decision thus guarantees the right to counsel in criminal cases in both federal and state proceedings. The refusal to appoint counsel for indigent defendants consequently violates the due process clause of the Fourteenth Amendment and the right to counsel of the Sixth Amendment.

InfoTrac College Edition Research

For a historical study of the origins of the right to counsel movement in constitutional law, read the Supreme Court case of *Powell v. Arizona* (1932). For an amazing account of the *Gideon* case, see

> Anthony Lewis, *Gideon's Trumpet* (New York: Vintage Books, 1966).

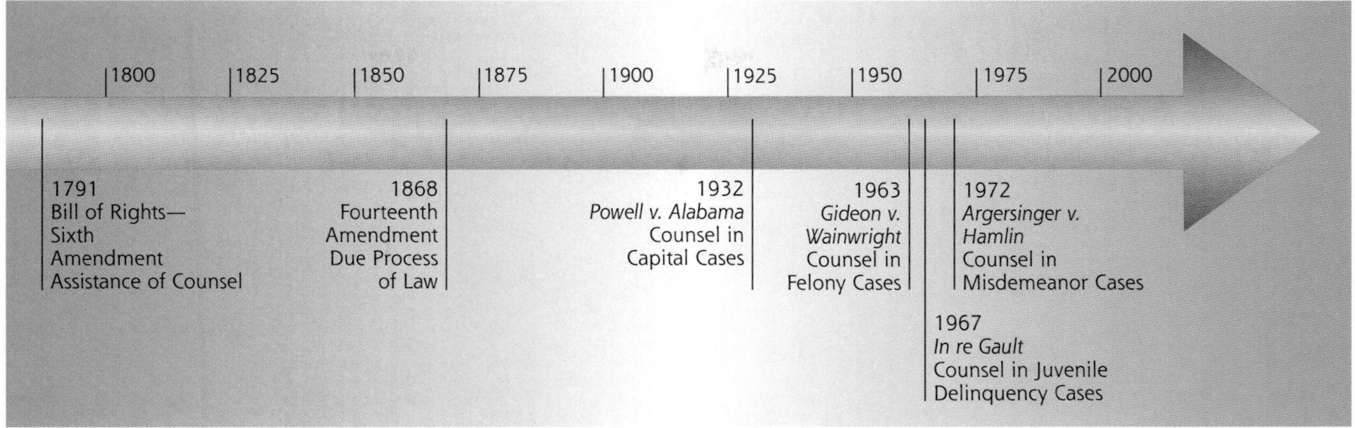

Figure 10.1
Historical timeline of right to counsel
Almost two centuries were needed to establish that adults and juveniles have a right to counsel at trial.

pro se
The defense of self-representation.

1975 U.S. Supreme Court decision in *Faretta v. California,*[19] defendants in most state courts and in the federal system claimed the right to proceed **pro se,** or for themselves, by reason of federal and state statutes and on state constitutional grounds. This permitted defendants to choose between hiring counsel or conducting their own defense. Whether a constitutional right to represent oneself in a criminal prosecution existed remained an open question until the *Faretta* decision.

The defendant, Anthony Faretta, was charged with grand theft in Los Angeles County. Before his trial, he requested that he be permitted to represent himself. The judge told Faretta that he believed this would be a mistake but accepted his waiver of counsel. The judge then held a hearing to inquire into Faretta's ability to conduct his own defense and subsequently ruled that Faretta had not made an intelligent and knowing waiver of his right to the assistance of counsel. As a result, the judge appointed a public defender to represent Faretta, who was brought to trial, found guilty, and sentenced to prison. He appealed, claiming that he had a constitutional right to self-representation.

Upon review, the U.S. Supreme Court recognized Faretta's pro se right on a constitutional basis, while making it conditional on a showing that the defendant could competently, knowingly, and intelligently waive his right to counsel. The Court's decision was based on the belief that the right of self-representation finds support in the structure of the Sixth Amendment, as well as in English and colonial jurisprudence from which the amendment emerged. Thus, in forcing Faretta to accept counsel against his will, the California trial court deprived him of his constitutional right to conduct his own defense.

It is important to recognize that the *Faretta* case dealt only with the constitutional right of self-representation. It did not provide guidelines for administering the right during the criminal process.

Today, a defendant in a criminal trial is able to waive the right to the assistance of counsel; that is, the defendant has a constitutional right to defend herself if her waiver of right to counsel is knowing and intelligent. Generally, however, the courts have encouraged defendants to accept counsel so that criminal trials may proceed in an orderly and fair manner.

There has been no case decided, similar to *Faretta,* that a defendant has a federal constitutional right to prosecute his own criminal appeal. The Supreme Court ruled on this issue in *Martinez v. Court of Appeals of California*[20] and found that historical and practical differences between trials and appeals convinced them that due process does not require a recognition of the right to self-representation in criminal appeals.

Colin Ferguson, accused and later convicted of the Long Island Rail Road shootings, acting in his own behalf in court during closing statement in his trial, February 16, 1995, in the Nassau County courthouse. Can a disturbed person such as Ferguson, who went on a murderous rampage, ever be truly competent to conduct their own defense? During the trial, Ferguson told the jury that he was charged with 93 counts because the attack occurred in 1993.

The Right to a Speedy Trial

The requirement of the right to counsel at trial in virtually all criminal cases often causes delays in the formal processing of defendants through the court system. Counsel usually seeks to safeguard the interests of the accused and in so doing may employ a variety of legal devices — pretrial motions, plea negotiations, trial procedures, and appeals — that require time and extend the decision-making period in a particular case. The involvement of counsel, along with inefficiencies in the court process — such as the frequent granting of continuances, poor scheduling procedures, and the abuse of time by court personnel — has made the problem of delay in criminal cases a serious and constitutional issue. As the American Bar Association's *Standards Relating to Speedy Trial* state, "Congestion in the trial courts of this country, particularly in urban centers, is currently one of the major problems of judicial administration."[21]

The Sixth Amendment guarantees a criminal defendant the right to a speedy trial in federal prosecutions. This right has been made applicable to the states by the 1967 decision in *Klopfer v. North Carolina*.[22] In this case, the defendant Klopfer was charged with criminal trespass. His original trial ended in a mistrial, and he sought to determine whether and when the government intended to retry him. The prosecutor asked the court to take a "nolle prosequi with leave," a legal device discharging the defendant but allowing the government to prosecute him in the future. The U.S. Supreme Court held that the effort by the government to postpone Klopfer's trial indefinitely without reason denied him the right to a speedy trial guaranteed by the Sixth and Fourteenth Amendments.

In *Klopfer,* the Supreme Court emphasized the importance of the speedy trial in the criminal process by stating that this right was "as fundamental as any of the rights secured by the Sixth Amendment."[23] Its primary purposes are to

1. Improve the credibility of the trial by seeking to have witnesses available for testimony as early as possible.
2. Reduce the anxiety for the defendant in awaiting trial, as well as to avoid pretrial detention.

3. Avoid extensive pretrial publicity and questionable conduct of public officials that would influence the defendant's right to a fair trial.
4. Avoid any delay that could affect the defendant's ability to defend herself.

Since the *Klopfer* case in 1967, the Supreme Court has dealt with the speedy trial guarantee on numerous occasions. One such example is the 1992 case of *Doggett v. United States,* in which the Court found that a delay of eight and a half years between indictment and arrest was prejudicial to the defendant and required a dismissal of the charges against the defendant.[24]

The Right to a Fair Trial

Every person charged with a crime also has a fundamental right to a fair trial. What does it mean to have a fair trial in the criminal justice system? A *fair trial* is one before an impartial judge and jury, in an environment of judicial restraint, orderliness, and fair decision making. Although it is not expressly stated in the U.S. Constitution, the right of the accused to a fair trial is guaranteed by the due process clauses of the Fifth and Fourteenth Amendments. This fair trial right may be violated in a number of ways. A hostile courtroom crowd, improper pressure on witnesses, or any behavior that produces prejudice toward the accused, among other things, can preclude a fair trial. When, for example a defendant was required to go to trial in prison clothing, the U.S. Supreme Court found a violation of the due process clause of the Fourteenth Amendment.[25] Adverse pretrial publicity can also deny a defendant a fair trial. The release of premature evidence by the prosecutor, extensive and critical reporting by the news media, and vivid and uncalled for details in indictments can all prejudice a defendant's case.

Recently, one of the controversial issues involving the conduct of a trial has been the apparent conflict between the constitutional guarantees of fair trial and freedom of the press. When there is wide pretrial publicity, whether an accused can have a fair trial as guaranteed by the Fifth, Sixth, and Fourteenth Amendments has been a matter of great concern.

Publicity is essential to preserving confidence in the trial system. This principle may occasionally clash with the defendant's right to a fair trial. Both the prosecution and the defense may use the media to reflect their side. Press conferences, leaked news stories, and daily TV and radio coverage all contribute to a media sideshow. Even jury sequestration may not be successful if many of the jurors have prior knowledge of the case. In the end, the media play a critical role in both the initial conviction and the subsequent acquittal on retrial of the defendant. The sensational and unending TV and press coverage of the *O. J. Simpson* case raised the issue of whether pretrial publicity violated Simpson's constitutional right to a fair trial.

Judges involved in newsworthy criminal cases have attempted to place restraints on media coverage to preserve the defendant's right to a fair trial; at the same time, it is generally believed that the media have a constitutional right to provide news coverage.

The U.S. Supreme Court dealt with the fair trial–free press issue in the 1976 case of *Nebraska Press Association v. Stuart.*[26] The Court ruled unconstitutional a trial judge's order prohibiting the press from reporting the confessions implicating the defendant in the crime. The Court's decision was based primarily on the fact that "prior restraints on speech and publication are the most serious and least tolerable infringement on First Amendment rights."[27]

In *Gannett Co. v. DePasquale* (1979), the Court was asked to decide whether the public had an independent constitutional right of access to a pretrial judicial hearing, even though all the parties had agreed to closure to guarantee a fair trial.[28] Justice Potter Stewart, writing for the Court, said that the trial court was correct in finding that the press had a right of access of constitutional dimensions but that this right was outweighed by the defendant's right to a fair trial.[29] In other words, the Court balanced competing social interests and found that denial of access by the public did not violate the First, Sixth, or Fourteenth Amendment rights of the defendant. The interest of justice requires that the defendant's case not be jeopardized, and the desire for a fair trial far outweighs the public's right of access to a pretrial suppression hearing. The *Gannett* decision is not ordinarily cited as precedent to determine whether a right of access to trials is constitutionally guaranteed, since the Court believes that motion hearings are not trials.

First Amendment
The U.S. constitutional amendment that guarantees freedom of speech, religion, press, and assembly and the right of the people to petition the government for a redress of grievances.

The question of the **First Amendment** right of access to preliminary hearings was raised again in the 1986 case of *Press-Enterprise Co. v. Superior Court.*[30] The defendant, charged with murder, agreed to have the preliminary hearing closed to the press and the public. But the Supreme Court said that closure is permissible under the First Amendment only if there is substantial probability that the defendant's right to a fair trial would be prejudiced by publicity that closed proceedings would prevent. According to the Court, preliminary hearings have traditionally been open to the public and should remain so.

In a 1993 case involving pretrial hearings, a reporter for the largest newspaper in Puerto Rico was denied access to a probable cause hearing because of a rule in the Commonwealth of Puerto Rico requiring that the hearings be held privately. The Supreme Court held that this rule violated the First Amendment to the Constitution based on the *Press-Enterprise* case and indicated that a pretrial hearing cannot be closed to the press except if prejudice will result to the accused.[31]

The Right to a Public Trial

The U.S. Supreme Court has also interpreted the First Amendment to mean that members of the press (and the public) have a right to attend trials. The most important case on this issue is *Richmond Newspapers, Inc. v. Virginia* (1980).[32] Here, the Supreme Court clearly established that criminal trials must remain public. Following the *Richmond Newspapers* case, the Supreme Court extended the right of the press to attend trials involving even highly sensitive, sexually related matters in which the victim is under eighteen years of age.[33]

Although the Court has ruled that criminal trials are open to the press, the right to a public trial is basically for the benefit of the accused. The familiar language of the Sixth Amendment clearly states that "the accused shall enjoy the right to a speedy and public trial." Underlying this provision is the belief that a trial in the criminal justice system must be a public activity. The amendment is rooted in the principle that justice cannot survive behind walls of silence.[34] It was enacted because the framers of the U.S. Constitution distrusted secret trials and arbitrary proceedings. In the 1948 case of *In re Oliver,* for instance, the Supreme Court held that the secrecy of a criminal contempt trial violated the right of the defendant to a public trial under the Fourteenth Amendment.[35] In *Oliver,* the Court recognized the constitutional guarantee of a public trial for the defendant in state and federal courts. Three decades later, the *Richmond Newspapers* decision clearly affirmed the right of the public and the press to attend criminal trials.

Because of the public interest in high-profile criminal cases, whether jury trials should be televised is one of the most controversial questions in the criminal justice system. The legal community is divided over the use of TV cameras in the courtroom. Today, many state courts permit such coverage, often at the judge's discretion, but federal courts prohibit TV coverage altogether. In 1981 the U.S. Supreme Court, in *Chandler v. Florida,* removed any constitutional

Cameras are now allowed in the courtroom in even greater numbers. Here a cameraman focuses on a defense attorney's cross-examination during the O.J. Simpson criminal murder trial. Do cameras in the courtroom change or affect trial outcomes? Do they make it impossible for a defendant to get a fair trial if, for example, the case ends in a hung jury and the person must be retried before a new jury whose members may have watched part or all of the first trial on TV?

obstacles to the use of electronic media coverage and still photography of public criminal proceedings over the objections of a criminal defendant.[36] To be certain, the defendant has a constitutional right to a public trial, but it is equally imperative that the media be allowed to exercise its First Amendment rights. "Media circus" has been used to describe the intense media coverage of the *Simpson* case. If you turned on ABC, CNN, or Court TV, the topic was usually the same: the *People v. O. J. Simpson.* In this type of trial, the Court is required to protect the rights of the accused by providing him with a fair trial by an unbiased jury. Unfortunately, many legal experts feel that the media circus generated by highly publicized cases makes it difficult, if not impossible, to provide famous defendants with an unbiased jury.

In sum, the defendant's right to an impartial trial and jury under the Fifth and Sixth Amendments often runs into direct conflict with the First Amendment's guarantee of freedom of the press and public access. In the Policy, Programs, and Issues in Criminal Justice feature, the matter of televising criminal trials is reviewed. This is one example of the fair trial–free press dilemma.

THE TRIAL PROCESS

The trial of a criminal case is a formal process conducted in a specific and orderly fashion in accordance with rules of criminal law, procedure, and evidence. Unlike what transpires in popular TV programs involving lawyers — where witnesses are often asked leading and prejudicial questions and where judges go far beyond their supervisory role — the modern criminal trial is a complicated and often time-consuming, technical affair. It is a structured adversary proceeding in which both the prosecution and defense follow specific procedures and argue the merits of their cases before the judge and jury. Each side seeks to present its case in the most favorable light. When possible, the prosecutor and the defense attorney will object to evidence they consider damaging to their positions. The prosecutor will use direct testimony, physical evidence, and a confession, if available, to convince the jury that the accused is guilty beyond a reasonable doubt. The defense attorney will rebut the

A group of college students has put together a Web site that addresses the most important aspects of the criminal trial in the United States. To visit this highly informative site, go to http://library.thinkquest.org/2760/homep.htm

government's case with her own evidence, make certain that the rights of the criminal defendant under the federal and state constitutions are considered during all phases of the trial, and determine whether an appeal is appropriate if the client is found guilty.

Although each jurisdiction in the United States has its own trial procedures, all jurisdictions conduct criminal trials in a generally similar fashion. The basic steps of the criminal trial, which proceed in an established order, are described in this section and outlined in Figure 10.2.

Policy, Programs, and Issues in Criminal Justice

GUIDELINES TO TELEVISING CRIMINAL TRIALS

From 1990 to 1999, media-type trials that present popular drama in the criminal justice system have surged. In 1990 Lyle and Erik Menendez were tried for the murder of their parents. In 1991 there were the Rodney King police brutality and the William Kennedy Smith rape trials. In 1992 Mike Tyson was tried for rape, and Pamela Smart was tried for plotting the murder of her husband. In 1993 the federal civil rights trials of the officers accused in the beating of Rodney King and Sheik Omar Rahman's trial for bombing the World Trade Center occurred. In 1994 Lorena Bobbit was tried for maliciously wounding her husband, and Tonya Harding was tried for plotting an attack on her Olympic skating rival, Nancy Kerrigan. In 1994 and 1995, O. J. Simpson was tried for double murder, Colin Ferguson was found guilty for the Long Island murders of commuter train passengers, and Susan Smith was indicted for murdering her two small children. In 1997 Timothy McVeigh was tried and convicted of the Oklahoma federal building bombing, and Louise Woodward was tried and convicted of second-degree murder, but her conviction was reduced to manslaughter. In 1998 and 1999, school shootings occurred in which students killed or injured other students and teachers and raised questions about children and gun control. Also in 1999, one of America's youngest murder defendants, Nathaniel Abraham, age 13, was tried and found guilty of second-degree murder.

Isn't it true that only certain trials, such as those involving the most celebrated cases, are likely to be televised? Do these trials really provide the public with an accurate and fair representation of the criminal justice system? Do they educate the public about how the courts operate?

What are the pros and cons for televising criminal trials? Lawyers who represent the news media often point out valid arguments for using cameras in the courtroom: (1) Public trials would encourage participants to do a better job; (2) in a democratic society, the public should have access to all trials, even those of a scandalous nature; and (3) TV coverage can contribute to educating the public about the justice system. Conversely, some defense lawyers and judges believe that televised trials should be restricted because they are only a form of entertainment and suppress the search for truth. Others question whether the public interest outweighs the defendant's ability to obtain a fair trial.

What are current programs and policies regarding the use of TV cameras in the courtroom?

- Most state courts allow TV cameras in courts, with various restrictions.
- Cameras are not allowed in the federal courts.
- A commercial court TV network offers the most sensationalized criminal trials.
- A noncommercial court TV network has been proposed to focus on educational trials and expose the judicial process to proper public scrutiny.
- Camera advocates have tried to get state and federal legislation to permit cameras in all state and federal courtrooms, to no avail.
- The U.S. Supreme Court has decided that no rule prohibits TV cameras in state court trials, although the decision often is left to the judge's discretion.

Critical Thinking

Three major concerns arise in TV criminal trials: (1) Jurors and potential jurors are exposed to media coverage that may cause prejudgment; (2) in-court media coverage, especially cameras and TV, can increase community and political pressure on participants and even cause grandstanding by participants; (3) media coverage can erode the dignity and decorum of the courtroom. In a democratic society, shouldn't the public have access to all trials through the TV medium, regardless of these concerns?

InfoTrac College Edition Research

Televising courtroom dramas in criminal trials has resulted in a boom of lawyer-centered talk shows, including *Burden of Proof* on CNN, *Cochran & Co.* on Court TV, and *Rivera Live* on CNBC. Does the public actually debate the legal, political, and social issues through these trials? Use *InfoTrac College Edition* to do research on high profile criminal trials such as the O. J. Simpson case. Focus on such issues as a defendant's right to a public trial and the rights of the press under the First Amendment.

SOURCES: *Chandler v. Florida*, 449 U.S. 560, 101 S.Ct. 802, 66 L.Ed.2d 740 (1981); "Rally for Court Cameras Falls Short," *American Bar Association Journal* 81 (1995): 30.

Figure 10.2
The steps in a jury trial

SOURCE: Marvin Zalman and Larry Siegel, *Criminal Procedure: Constitution and Society* (St. Paul: West, 1991), 655.

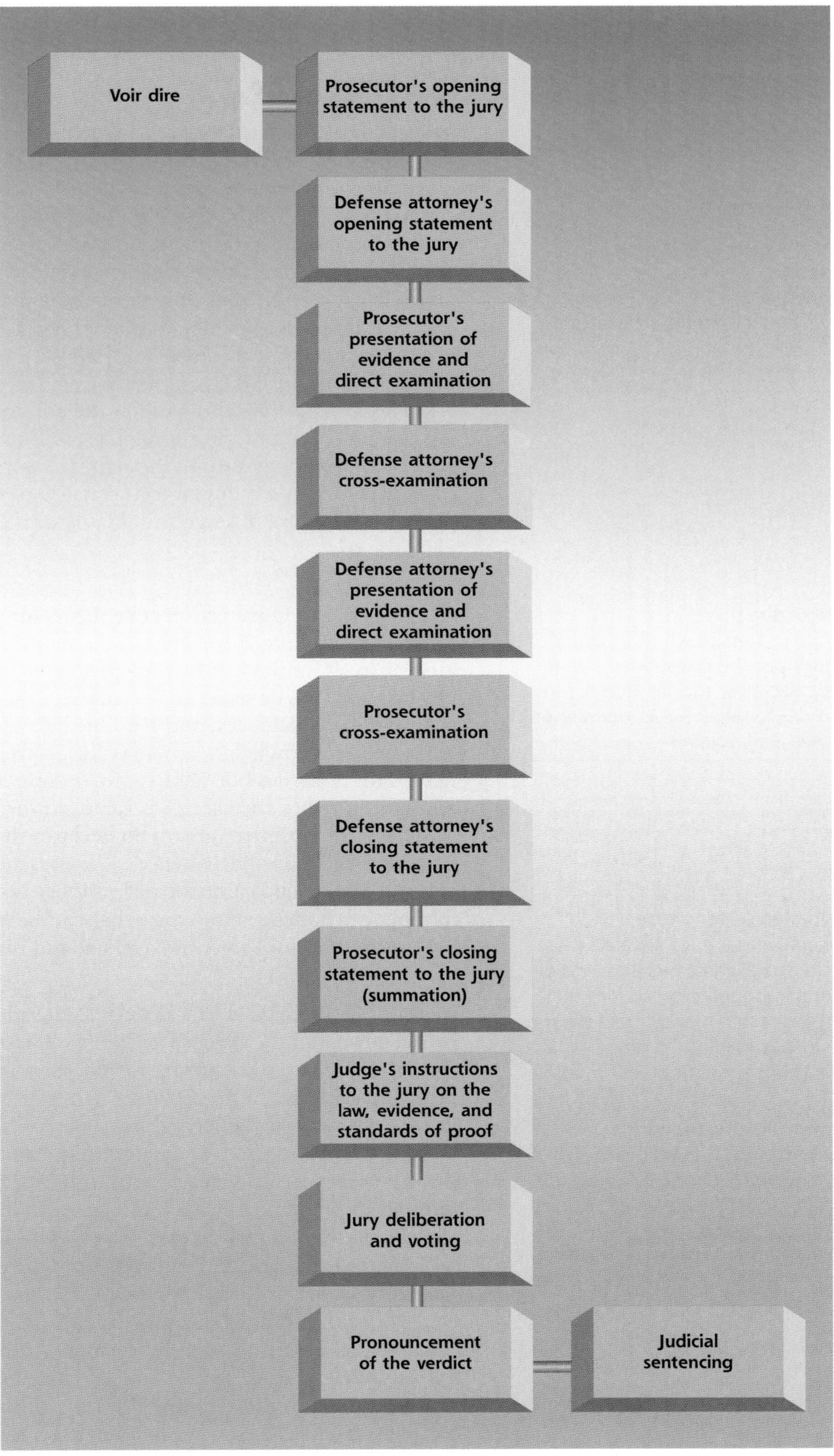

Jury Selection In both civil and criminal cases, jurors are selected randomly from tax assessment or voter registration lists within each court's jurisdiction.

Few states impose qualifications on those called for jury service. Many states mandate a residency requirement.[37] There is also little uniformity in the amount of time served by jurors, with the term ranging from one day to months, depending on the nature of the trial. In addition, most jurisdictions prohibit convicted felons from serving on juries, as well as others exempted by statute, such as public officials, physicians, and attorneys. The initial list of persons chosen, which is called **venire,** or jury array, provides the state with a group of potentially capable citizens able to serve on a jury. Many states, by rule of law, review the venire to eliminate unqualified persons and to exempt those who by reason of their professions are not allowed to be jurors. The actual jury selection process begins with those remaining on the list.

venire
The group called for jury duty from which jury panels are selected.

The court clerk, who handles the administrative affairs of the trial — including the processing of the complaint, evidence, and other documents — randomly selects enough names to fill the required number of places on the jury. In most cases, the jury in a criminal trial consists of twelve persons, with two alternate jurors standing by to serve should any of the regular jurors be unable to complete the trial.

VOIR DIRE Once prospective jurors are chosen, the lengthy process of **voir dire** (from the French for "to tell the truth") starts. To determine their appropriateness to sit on the jury, prospective jurors are examined under oath by the government, the defense, and sometimes the judge about their backgrounds, occupations, residences, and possible knowledge of or interest in the case. A juror who acknowledges any bias for or prejudice against the defendant — if the defendant is a friend or relative, for example, or if the juror has already formed an opinion about the case — is removed for *cause* and replaced with another. Thus, any prospective juror who declares that he cannot be impartial and render a verdict solely on the evidence to be presented at the trial may be removed by either the prosecution or the defense. Because normally no limit is placed on the number of **challenges for cause** that can be exercised, it often takes considerable time to select a jury for controversial and highly publicized criminal cases.

voir dire
The process in which a potential jury panel is questioned by the prosecution and the defense in order to select jurors who are unbiased and objective.

challenge for cause
Removing a juror because he or she is biased or has prior knowledge about a case, or for other reasons that demonstrate the individual's inability to render a fair and impartial judgment in a case.

PEREMPTORY CHALLENGES Besides challenges for cause, both the prosecution and the defense are allowed **peremptory challenges,** which enable the attorneys to excuse jurors for no particular reason or for undisclosed reasons. For example, a prosecutor might not want a bartender as a juror in a drunk-driving case, believing that a person with that occupation would be sympathetic to the accused. Or the defense attorney might excuse a prospective male juror because the attorney prefers to have a predominantly female jury. The number of peremptory challenges permitted is limited by state statute and often varies by case and jurisdiction.

peremptory challenge
The dismissal of a potential juror by either the prosecution or the defense for unexplained, discretionary reasons.

The peremptory challenge has been criticized by legal experts who question the fairness and propriety with which it has been used.[38] The most significant criticism is that it has been used to exclude blacks from hearing cases in which the defendant is also black. In *Swain v. Alabama* (1964), the U.S. Supreme Court upheld the use of peremptory challenges in isolated cases to exclude jurors by reason of racial or other group affiliations.[39] This policy was extremely troublesome because it allowed what seemed to be legally condoned discrimination against minority group members. Consequently, in 1986 the Court struck down the *Swain* doctrine in *Batson v. Kentucky.*[40]

The *Batson* case held that the use of peremptory challenges against potential jurors by prosecutors in criminal cases violated the U.S. Constitution if the challenges were based on race. Since that decision, the issue of race discrimination in the use of peremptory challenges has been raised by defendants in numerous cases. In the 1991 case of *Powers v. Ohio,* for instance, the U.S. Supreme Court was faced with deciding the legality of peremptory challenges involving jurors not of the same race as the defendant.[41] The Supreme Court held that the racial identity of "*Batson*-excluded prospective jurors" and the defendant need not be the same. In other words, the equal protection clause prohibits a prosecutor from using the peremptory challenge to exclude qualified and unbiased persons from a jury solely by reason of race. In so ruling, the Court rejected the government's contention that the jurors be of the same race as the defendant. Similarly, in the 1992 case of *Georgia v. McCollum,* the Court said that criminal defendants may not seek to exclude potential jurors strictly on the basis of race. Race-based peremptory challenges to potential jurors in civil lawsuits have also been declared unconstitutional.[42]

Batson strikes down a legal procedure that was "out of sync" with modern ideas of justice and fairness. It prevents an element of racial discrimination from entering into the trial stage of justice, which is one of the cornerstones of American freedom. Yet it preserves, under controlled circumstances, the use of the peremptory challenge, which is an integral part of the jury selection process. While some argue that the *Batson* rule should be limited to race and ethnicity, the Supreme Court declared in 1994 that the rule also bars gender-based peremptory challenges. In other words, both sides in a civil or criminal case should be required to provide a nondiscriminatory reason for removing a large number of prospective male or female jurors *(J.E.B. v. Alabama).*[43] Although peremptory challenges are often used to discriminate against prospective jurors, these constitutional restraints have made them less discriminatory. Table 10.1 highlights the evolution of the *Batson v. Kentucky* peremptory challenges cases, and the Race, Culture, and Gender feature provides additional information on discrimination in jury selection.

Opening Statements

Once the jury has been selected and the criminal complaint has been read to the jurors by the court clerk, the prosecutor and the defense attorney may each make an opening statement about the case. The purpose of the prosecutor's statement is to introduce the judge and the jury to the particular criminal charges, to outline the facts, and to describe how the government will prove the defendant guilty beyond a reasonable doubt. The defense attorney reviews the case and indicates how the defense intends to show that the accused is not guilty.

Usually, the defense attorney makes an opening statement after the government reads its case. In some jurisdictions, the court in its discretion can permit the defense to make opening remarks before any evidence is introduced. But, for the most part, current rules dictate that the prosecutor is entitled to offer an opening statement first.

The opening statement gives the jury a concise overview of the evidence that is to follow. In the opening statement, neither attorney is allowed to make prejudicial remarks or inflammatory statements or mention irrelevant facts. Both are free, however, to identify what they will eventually prove by way of evidence, which includes witnesses, physical evidence, and the use of expert testimony. As a general rule, the opening statements used in jury trials are important because they provide the fact finders (the jury) with an initial summary of the case. They are infrequently used and less effective in **bench trials**, however, where juries are

bench trial
The trial of a criminal matter by a judge only. The accused waives any constitutional right to trial by jury.

Table 10.1
Evolution of *Batson v. Kentucky* and Its Progeny

Case	Ruling
Batson v. Kentucky (1986)	Under the Fourteenth Amendment, the Supreme Court ruled that prosecutors were barred from using peremptory challenges to remove black jurors because of their race.
Powers v. Ohio (1991)	The Court concluded that a defendant has the standing to object to the race-based exclusion by the use of peremptory challenges of jurors on the grounds of equal protection, even if not of the same race as the challenged jurors.
Edmonson v. Leesville Concrete Co. (1991)	The Batson ruling applies to attorneys in civil lawsuits. In other words, a private party in a civil action may not raise peremptory challenges to exclude jurors on the basis of race.
Georgia v. McCollum (1992)	On the basis of *Batson*, the Georgia decision prohibited the exercise of peremptory challenges on the basis of race by defense attorneys in criminal cases.
J.E.B. v. Alabama (1994)	The Court held that the equal protection clause of the Fourteenth Amendment bars discrimination in jury selection on the basis of sex. Discrimination in jury selection, whether based on race or gender, causes harm to the litigants, the community, and the individual jurors who are wrongfully excluded from participation in the judicial process.

not used. Most lower-court judges have handled hundreds of similar cases and do not need the benefit of an opening statement.

Presentation of the Prosecutor's Evidence

WITNESS TESTIMONY Following the opening statements, the government begins its case by presenting evidence to the court through its witnesses. Those called as witnesses — such as police officers, victims, or experts — provide testimony via **direct examination.** During direct examination, the prosecutor questions the witness to reveal the facts believed pertinent to the government's case. Testimony involves what the witness actually saw, heard, or touched and does not include opinions. However, a witness's opinion can be given in certain situations, such as when describing the motion of a vehicle or indicating whether a defendant appeared to act intoxicated or insane. Witnesses may also qualify to give opinions because they are experts on a particular subject relevant to the case; for example, a psychiatrist may testify about a defendant's mental capacity at the time of the crime.

direct examination
The questioning of one's own (prosecution or defense) witness during a trial.

After the prosecutor finishes questioning a witness, the defense conducts a **cross-examination** of the same witness by asking questions in an attempt to clarify the defendant's role in the crime. The right to cross-examine witnesses is an essential part of a trial, and unless extremely unusual circumstances exist (such as a person's being hospitalized), witness statements will not be considered unless they are made in court and open for question. If desired, the prosecutor

cross-examination
The process in which the defense and the prosecution interrogate witnesses during a trial.

may seek a second direct examination after the defense attorney has completed cross-examination; this allows the prosecutor to ask additional questions about information brought out during cross-examination. Finally, the defense attorney may then question, or recross-examine, the witness once again. All witnesses for the trial are sworn in and questioned in the same basic manner.

TYPES OF EVIDENCE AT A CRIMINAL TRIAL Besides testimonial evidence given by police officers, citizens, and experts, the court also acts on real, or nonverbal, evidence.[44] **Real evidence** often consists of the exhibits taken into the jury room for review by the jury. A revolver that may have been in the defendant's control at a time of a murder, tools in the possession of a suspect charged with a burglary, and a bottle allegedly holding narcotics are all examples of real,

real evidence
Any object produced for inspection at the trial (weapon, photograph).

Race, Culture, and Gender

JURY SELECTION AND PEREMPTORY CHALLENGES

Jury selection often accounts for a large share of criminal trial time, particularly in high-profile cases involving serious crimes. Jury size ordinarily is limited to six or twelve persons. Several jury procedures often have an effect on jury selection. They include (1) the voir dire examination, where prospective jurors are questioned for the purpose of ascertaining their fitness to serve on the jury; (2) the challenge for cause, where jurors are eliminated because of prejudice; and (3) the peremptory challenge, an objection to a juror for no apparent reason.

Of all these procedures, the peremptory challenge poses the greatest actual and potential risk of jury discrimination. The U.S. Supreme Court, in *Batson v. Kentucky,* recognized the widespread abuses of peremptory challenges by deciding that purposeful discrimination in their use is a violation of the defendant's right to an impartial jury. In addition, the court extended the *Batson* rule beyond racial discrimination to the category of gender.

Despite the expansion of the *Batson* rule, other dimensions still exist for evaluating discrimination in peremptory challenges. Often race-neutral explanations can uphold what may be discriminatory peremptory challenges of minorities. For instance, it may be possible to strike Spanish-speaking minorities if a prosecutor claims that they would have difficulty understanding the testimony. There is also the need to determine whether the social class of jurors is as important as race and gender in explaining disproportionate jury representation.

Based on the cases addressing peremptory challenges decided by the U.S. Supreme Court, it is clear that excluding potential jurors from criminal trials because of race or gender violates the defendant's rights under the Fourteenth Amendment. Justice Thurgood Marshall recognized the seriousness of this issue when he suggested in the *Batson* case that peremptory challenges should be eliminated entirely from the criminal justice system.

Charles Ogletree also points out that the seemingly neutral explanations of prosecutors for peremptory challenges undermine the protection against jury discrimination established by the *Batson* case. Ogletree suggests that the following procedural protections be implemented: (1) the dismissal of a criminal case where a prosecutor violates *Batson* and (2) the elimination of prosecution peremptory challenges. However, it seems unlikely that such rules would be established by a state court or legislature.

Critical Thinking

Would criminal trials be more fair without peremptory challenges? Explain.

The number of peremptory challenges available differ in each state and in the federal court system. The American Bar Association has recommended ten peremptory challenges per side in capital cases, five per side when a sentence of imprisonment of more than six months may be imposed, and three per side when a sentence of incarceration is less than six months or when no incarceration is involved. Are these standards reasonable? Explain.

Should social class indicators (income, occupation, and authority position of prospective jurors) be considered in determining jury participation? Why or why not?

InfoTrac College Edition Research

For an interesting analysis of the complex nature of the peremptory challenge, see

Brian Stern and Mark Maney, "Racism, Peremptory Challenges and Democratic Jury — The Jurisprudence of Delicate Balance," *Journal of Criminal Law and Criminology* 79 (1988): 65.

SOURCES: Charles Ogletree, "Just Say No! A Proposal to Eliminate Racially Discriminatory Uses of Peremptory Challenges," *American Criminal Law Review* 31 (1994): 1099–1151; Marvin Zalman and Larry Siegel, *Criminal Procedure — Constitution and Society,* 2d ed. (Belmont, Calif.: Wadsworth, 1997); Hiroshi Fukurai, "Race, Social Class, and Jury Participation: New Dimensions for Evaluating Discrimination in Jury Service," *Journal of Criminal Justice* 24 (1996): 71–78.

The use of experts is an important method of introducing evidence in criminal trials. Here on May 8, 1995, molecular biologist Robin Cotton gives testimony at the Simpson trial stating that "DNA banding patterns" depicted in numerous X-rays matched Simpson's.

or physical, evidence. Photographs, maps, diagrams, and crime scene displays are further types of real evidence. The criminal court judge will also review documentary evidence, such as writings, government reports, public records, business or hospital records, fingerprint identification, and DNA profiling.

In general, the primary test for the admissibility of evidence in either a criminal or civil proceeding is its relevance; that is, the court must ask itself whether the gun, shirt, or photograph, for instance, has relevant evidentiary value in determining the issues in the case. Ordinarily, evidence that establishes an element of the crime is acceptable to the court. For example, in a prosecution for possession of drugs, evidence that shows the defendant to be a known drug user might be relevant. In a prosecution for bribery, monies received in the form of a canceled check identified as the amount received would clearly be found relevant to the case.

circumstantial (indirect) evidence
Evidence not bearing on the fact in dispute but on various indirect circumstances from which the judge or jury might infer the existence of the fact (e.g., the defendant was seen in the house with wet clothing is circumstantial evidence that the person walked in the rain).

Circumstantial (indirect) evidence is also often used in trial proceedings. Such evidence is often inferred or indirectly used to prove a fact in question. On the issue of malice in a criminal murder trial, for instance, it would be appropriate to use circumstantial evidence to prove the defendant's state of mind. Such evidence has often been the controversial issue in many celebrated criminal cases. The Dr. George Parkman case, more than a century ago, attracted national attention when Parkman's colleague at Harvard University, Dr. Webster, was convicted of murder after Parkman disappeared.[45] Because no body was found, Webster's conviction was based on circumstantial evidence.

directed verdict
The right of a judge to direct a jury to acquit a defendant because the state has not proven the elements of the crime or otherwise has not established guilt according to law.

Motion for a Directed Verdict

Once the prosecution has provided all the government's evidence against a defendant, it will inform the court that it rests the people's case. The defense attorney at this point may enter a motion for a **directed verdict.** This is a procedural device by means of which the defense attorney asks the judge to order the jury to return a verdict of not guilty. The judge must rule on the motion and will either sustain it or overrule it, depending on whether she believes that the prosecution proved all elements of the alleged crime. In essence, the defense attorney argues in the directed verdict that the prosecutor's case against the defendant is insufficient to prove the defendant guilty beyond a reasonable doubt. If the motion is sustained, the trial is terminated. If it is rejected by the court, the case continues with the defense portion of the trial.

Presentation of the Defense Attorney's Evidence

The defense attorney has the option of presenting many, some, or no witnesses on behalf of the defendant. In addition, the defense attorney must decide whether the defendant should take the stand and testify in his own behalf. In a criminal trial, the defendant is protected by the Fifth Amendment right to be free from self-incrimination, which means that a person cannot be forced by the state to testify against herself. However, defendants who choose voluntarily to tell their side of the story can be subject to cross-examination by the prosecutor.

After the defense concludes its case, the government may then present rebuttal evidence. This normally involves bringing evidence forward that was not used when the prosecution initially presented the case. The defense may examine the rebuttal witnesses and introduce new witnesses in a process called a *surrebuttal.* After all evidence has been presented to the court, the defense attorney may again submit a motion for a directed verdict. If the motion is denied, both the prosecution and the defense prepare to make closing arguments, and the case on the evidence is ready for consideration by the jury.

Closing Arguments

Closing arguments are used by the attorneys to review the facts and evidence of the case in a manner favorable to each of their positions. At this stage of the trial, both prosecution and defense are permitted to draw reasonable inferences and to show how the facts prove or refute the defendant's guilt. Often both attorneys have a free hand in arguing about the facts, issues, and evidence, including the applicable law. They cannot comment on matters not in evidence, however, or on the defendant's failure to testify in a criminal case. Normally, the defense attorney will make a closing statement first, followed by the prosecutor. Either party can elect to forgo the right to make a final summation to the jury.

Instructions to the Jury

charge
In a criminal trial, the instructions the judge gives to the jury, regarding principles of law that should guide and control their decision.

In a criminal trial, the judge will instruct, or **charge,** the jury members on the principles of law that ought to guide and control their decision on the defendant's innocence or guilt. Included in the charge will be information about the elements of the alleged offense, the type of evidence needed to prove each element, and the burden of proof required to obtain a guilty verdict. Although the judge commonly provides the instruction, he may ask the prosecutor and the defense attorney to submit instructions for consideration; the judge will then use discretion in determining whether to use any of their instructions. The instructions that cover the law applicable to the case are extremely important because they may serve as the basis for a subsequent appeal. Procedurally, in highly publicized and celebrated cases, the judge may have sequestered the jury overnight to prevent them from having contact with the outside world. This process, called *sequestration,* is discretionary with the trial judge, and most courts believe "locking up a jury" is needed only in sensational cases.

verdict
A finding of a jury or a judge on questions of fact at a trial.

The Verdict Once the charge is given to the jury members, they retire to deliberate on a verdict. As previously mentioned, the **verdict** in a criminal case — regardless of whether the trial involves a six- or twelve-person jury — is usually required to be unanimous. Unanimity of twelve is not required by the U.S. Constitution in state cases but is the rule in federal criminal trials. Unanimity is required with six-person juries. A review of the case by the jury may take hours or even days. The jurors are always sequestered during their deliberations, and in certain lengthy and highly publicized cases, they are kept overnight in a hotel until the verdict is reached. In less sensational cases, the jurors may be allowed to go home, but they are cautioned not to discuss the case with anyone.

If a verdict cannot be reached, the trial may result in a *hung jury,* after which the prosecutor must bring the defendant to trial again if the prosecution desires a conviction. If found not guilty, the defendant is released from the criminal process. If the defendant is convicted, the judge will normally order a presentence investigation by the probation department before imposing a sentence. Before sentencing, the defense attorney will probably submit a motion for a new trial, alleging that legal errors occurred in the trial proceedings. The judge may deny the motion and impose a sentence immediately, a practice quite common in most misdemeanor offenses. In felony cases, however, the judge will set a date for sentencing, and the defendant will either be placed on bail or held in custody until that time.

The Sentence The imposition of the criminal sentence is normally the responsibility of the trial judge. In some jurisdictions, the jury may determine the sentence or make recommendations involving leniency for certain offenses. Often, the sentencing decision is based on information and recommendations given to the court by the probation department after a presentence investigation of the defendant. The sentence itself is determined by the statutory requirements for the particular crime as established by the legislature; in addition, the judge ordinarily has a great deal of discretion in reaching a sentencing decision. The different criminal sanctions available include fines, probation, imprisonment, and even commitment to a state hospital. The sentence may be a combination of all these. (Sentencing is discussed in detail in Chapter 11.)

The Appeal Defendants have as many as three possible avenues of *appeal:* the direct appeal, postconviction remedy, and federal court review. Both the direct appeal and federal court review provide the convicted person with the opportunity to appeal to a higher state or federal court on the basis of an error that affected the conviction in the trial court. Extraordinary trial court errors, such as the denial of the right to counsel or the inability to provide a fair trial, are subject to the *plain error rule* of the federal courts.[46] *Harmless errors,* such as the use of innocuous identification procedures or the denial of counsel at a noncritical stage of the proceeding, would not necessarily result in the overturning of a criminal conviction. A postconviction appeal, on the other hand, or what is often referred to as *collateral attack,* takes the form of a legal petition, such as habeas corpus, and is the primary means by which state prisoners have their convictions or sentence reviewed in the federal court. A **writ of habeas corpus** (meaning "you have the body") seeks to determine the validity of a detention by asking the court to release the person or give legal reasons for the incarceration.

writ of habeas corpus
A judicial order requesting that a person detaining another produce the body of the prisoner and give reasons for his or her capture and detention. Habeas corpus is a legal device used to request that a judicial body review the reasons for a person's confinement and the conditions of confinement. Habeas corpus is known as "the great writ."

Rolando Cruz was wrongly imprisoned and spent ten years on death row before a successful appeal earned his release. He is one of eleven men on death row who have been released in Illinois since 1987, proving the importance of the appellate process.

In most jurisdictions, direct criminal appeal to an appellate court is a matter of right. This means that the defendant has an automatic right to appeal a conviction based on errors that may have occurred during the trial proceedings. A substantial number of criminal appeals are the result of disputes over points of law, such as the introduction at the trial of illegal evidence detrimental to the defendant or statements made during the trial that were prejudicial to the defendant. Through objections made at the pretrial and trial stages of the criminal process, the defense counsel will reserve specific legal issues on the record as the basis for appeal. A copy of the transcript of these proceedings will serve as the basis on which the appellate court will review any errors that may have occurred during the lower-court proceedings.

Because an appeal is an expensive, time-consuming, and technical process involving a review of the lower-court record, the research and drafting of briefs, and the presentation of oral arguments to the appellate court, the defendant has been granted the right to counsel at this stage of the criminal process. In the 1963 case of *Douglas v. California,* the U.S. Supreme Court held that an indigent defendant has a constitutional right to the assistance of counsel on a direct first appeal.[47] If the defendant appeals to a higher court, the defendant must have private counsel or apply for permission to proceed **in forma pauperis** (meaning "in the manner of a pauper"); that is, the defendant may be granted counsel at public expense if the court believes the appeal has merit. There is no constitutional right to free counsel beyond the first appeal.[48]

in forma pauperis
"In the manner of a pauper." A criminal defendant granted permission to proceed in forma pauperis is entitled to assistance of counsel at state expense.

After an appeal has been fully heard, the appeals court renders an opinion on the procedures used in the case. If an error of law is found — such as an improper introduction of evidence or an improper statement by the prosecutor that was prejudicial to the defendant — the appeals court may reverse the decision of the trial court and order a new trial. If the lower-court decision is upheld, the case is finished, unless the defendant seeks a discretionary appeal to a higher state or federal court.

Over the last decade, criminal appeals have increased significantly in almost every state and the federal courts. Criminal case appeals make up close to 50

In order for a person to be convicted in criminal court, proof must be beyond a reasonable doubt. Even a suspected serial killer such as Rafael Ramirez, the accused "railway killer" considered responsible for at least eight murders in Texas, Kentucky, and Illinois, shown here at his trial, must be acquitted if there is not clear evidence of his guilt.

percent of the state appellate caseload and over 35 percent of the total federal caseload, which includes prisoner petitions and ordinary criminal appeals.[49] Today, a substantial number of these appeals involve drug-related cases and appeals of sentences where the offender was institutionalized. Most appeals usually occur after final trial court decisions on convictions and sentencing of the defendant.

proof beyond a reasonable doubt
The standard of proof needed to convict in a criminal case. The evidence offered in court does not have to amount to absolute certainty, but it should leave no reasonable doubt that the defendant committed the alleged crime.

EVIDENTIARY STANDARDS

Proof beyond a reasonable doubt is the standard required to convict a defendant charged with a crime at the adjudicatory stage of the criminal process. This requirement dates back to early American history and over the years has become the accepted measure of persuasion needed by the prosecutor to convince the judge or jury of the defendant's guilt. Many twentieth-century U.S. Supreme Court decisions have reinforced this standard by making "beyond a reasonable doubt a due process and constitutional requirement."[50] In *Brinegar v. United States* (1949), for instance, the Supreme Court stated:

> Guilt in a criminal case must be proven beyond a reasonable doubt and by evidence confined to that which long experience in the common-law tradition, to some extent embodied in the Constitution, has crystallized into rules of evidence consistent with that standard. These rules are historically grounded rights of our system, developed to safeguard men from dubious and unjust convictions with resulting forfeitures of life, liberty and property.[51]

The reasonable doubt standard is an essential ingredient of the criminal justice process. It is the prime instrument for reducing the risk of convictions based on factual errors.[52] The underlying premise of this standard is that it is better to release a guilty person than to convict someone who is innocent. Since the defendant is presumed innocent until proven guilty, this standard forces the prosecution to overcome this presumption with the highest standard of proof.

preponderance of the evidence The level of proof in civil cases; more than half the evidence supports the allegations of one side.

Unlike the civil law, where a mere **preponderance of the evidence** is the standard, the criminal process requires proof beyond a reasonable doubt for each element of the offense. As the Supreme Court pointed out in *In re Winship* (1970), where the reasonable doubt standard was applied to juvenile trials, "If the standard of proof for a criminal trial were a preponderance of the evidence rather than proof beyond a reasonable doubt, there would be a smaller risk of factual errors that result in freeing guilty persons, but a far greater risk of factual errors that result in convicting the innocent."[53] The various evidentiary standards of proof are analyzed and compared in Table 10.2

CRIMINAL TRIAL PRACTICES IN THE TWENTY-FIRST CENTURY

Criminal trial practices will likely undergo considerable change during the coming decades. What innovations can we expect in the twenty-first century? What are the trends in the trial process? Where is the criminal trial heading? Trials will likely continue to be adversarial in nature. Prosecutors, defense attorneys, and judges will reshape their roles, stressing community organization, sentencing reform, and mediation of criminal cases. The number of minority and female members of the judiciary should continue to grow.

Table 10.2
Evidentiary Standards of Proof—Degrees of Certainty

Standard	Definition	Ruling
Absolute certainty	No possibility of error; 100% certainty	Not used in civil or criminal law
Beyond reasonable doubt; moral certainty	Conclusive and complete proof, while leaving any reasonable doubt about the innocence or guilt of the defendant; allows the defendant the benefit of any possibility of innocence.	Criminal trial
Clear and convincing evidence	Prevailing and persuasive to the trier of fact	Civil commitments, insanity defense
Preponderance of evidence	Greater weight of evidence in terms of credibility; more convincing than an opposite point of view	Civil trial
Probable cause	U.S. constitutional standard for arrest and search warrants, requiring existence of facts sufficient to warrant that a crime has been committed	Arrest, preliminary hearing, motions
Sufficient evidence	Adequate evidence to reverse a trial court	Appellate review
Reasonable suspicion	Rational, reasonable belief that facts warrant investigations of a crime on less than probable cause	Police investigations
Less than probable cause	Mere suspicion; less than reasonable belief to conclude criminal activity exists	Prudent police investigation where safety of an officer or others is endangered

Another change that will continue to have an impact on the trial is the use of DNA evidence. DNA profiling involves scientifically matching the genetic material from hair, blood, and other bodily tissues and fluids found at a crime scene with samples taken from known suspects. (See Chapter 4.)

The use of DNA profiling in criminal trials received a boost in 1997 when the FBI announced that DNA testing has become so precise that experts no longer have to supply statistical estimates of accuracy while testifying at trial; they can now state in court that there exists "a reasonable degree of scientific certainty" that evidence came from a single suspect.

The FBI has implemented a combined DNA index system (CODIS). This computerized database allows DNA taken at a crime scene to be searched electronically, to find matches against samples taken from convicted offenders and other crime scenes. One database allows suspects to be identified; the second allows investigators to establish links between crimes. So far there have been more than one hundred instances in which offenders have been linked to unsolved cases. The use of DNA evidence should become commonplace in the twenty-first century.

Trial courts also are tapping into new communication technologies to improve the effectiveness of the criminal trial. Cellular phones, fax machines, computers, and teleconferencing systems that provide both audio and video linkages are routinely used by judges, prosecutors, and defense attorneys. In addition to the use of new equipment, trial experts believe that criminal cases can be handled efficiently (1) when trials are not interrupted by lengthy evidence and discovery arguments, (2) when lawyers and jurors act appropriately, and (3) when the judge rejects requests for delays and refuses to allow additional peremptory challenges.

Also, legal experts are still uncertain about the viability of completely televising criminal trials. Some believe it is not a bad thing because it exposes the judicial process to public scrutiny. Others feel the tabloid approach of a commercial enterprise like Court TV will continue to scare off the federal courts from ever allowing cameras into the courtroom.

According to some legal experts, our present criminal trial process is considered inadequate because it is very complicated, requires an inordinate amount of time, and the accuracy of jury verdicts is often questioned by the public. Serious questions exist regarding the use of unanimous verdicts and peremptory challenges. The key issue for the criminal trial is whether the current rules do justice to the system in modern times. Since the immediate source of the U.S. trial system is the English system of jurisprudence, a comparison of the American and English criminal trial processes (Table 10.3) can identify some of the changes that are beginning to take place.

SUMMARY

The number of cases disposed of by trials is relatively small in comparison with the total number that enter the criminal justice system. Nevertheless, the criminal trial provides the defendant with an important option. Unlike other steps in the system, the U.S. criminal trial allows the accused to assert the right to a day in court. The defendant may choose between a trial before a judge alone or a trial by jury. In either case, the purpose of the trial is to adjudicate the facts, ascertain the truth, and determine the guilt or innocence of the accused.

Criminal trials represent the adversary system at work. The state uses its authority to seek a conviction, and the defendant is protected by constitutional rights, particularly those under the Fifth and Sixth Amendments. When they involve serious crimes, criminal trials are complex legal affairs. Each jurisdiction relies on rules and procedures that have developed over many years to resolve legal issues. As the U.S. Supreme Court has extended the rights of the accused, the procedures have undoubtedly contributed to the complexities and delays within the system. Some solutions have included smaller juries, more efficient control of police misconduct, and reduced time delays between

Table 10.3
Comparing the American and English Criminal Trial Systems

Similarities	
Adversarial	
Trial by jury	
Presumption of innocence	
Proof beyond a reasonable doubt	
Independent judiciary	
Constitutional due process	
Major Differences	
American System	**English System**
Appointed or elected judges with political background	Appointed legal barristers
Prosecutors with political aspirations	Prosecutors are career civil servants
Freedom of the press	Limited media coverage
State permits television coverage	Prohibition on television coverage
Jury publicity in selection procedures	Limited attention given to jury process
Use of jury consultants in high-profile cases	No jury consultants
Governmental use of overcharging and plea bargaining	Limited use of overcharging
Little judicial influence over jury verdict	Judicial influence over jury
Jury unanimity required	Less than unanimous verdicts allowed
Extensive voir dire procedures	Voir dire handled outside of courtroom
Discussion of evidence during trial not permitted	Review of evidence allowed during trial
No questions permitted	Use of questions permitted
Judicial instructions on law only	Judicial summary on facts and law
Extensive use of peremptory challenges	No peremptory challenges

arrest, indictment, and trial. But the right to a fair trial, trial by jury, and the due process rights to counsel and confrontation need to be also guarded and protected in the twenty-first century.

An established order of steps is followed throughout a criminal trial, beginning with the selection of a jury, proceeding through opening statements and the introduction of evidence, and concluding with closing arguments and a verdict. The criminal trial serves both a symbolic and a pragmatic function for defendants who require a forum of last resort to adjudicate their differences with the state. The trial is the central test of the facts and law involved in a criminal case.

KEY TERMS

adjudication
confrontation clause
six-person jury
pro se
First Amendment
venire
voir dire
challenge for cause
peremptory challenge
bench trial
direct examination
cross-examination
real evidence
circumstantial (indirect) evidence
directed verdict
charge
verdict
writ of habeas corpus
in forma pauperis
proof beyond a reasonable doubt
preponderance of the evidence

INFOTRAC COLLEGE EDITION EXERCISES

G. K. Chesterton, the great English author, said on the issue of juries: "Our civilization has decided that determining the guilt or innocence of men is a thing too important to be trusted to trained men. When it wants a library catalogued, or the solar system discovered, or any trifle of that kind, it uses up wise specialists. But when it wishes anything done which is really serious, it collects twelve of the ordinary men standing around."

What is the meaning of Chesterton's statement? Is a fair and speedy trial by an impartial jury a due process right? Use *InfoTrac College Edition* to find articles about juries that would help you understand Chesterton's statement. Use key words such as "jury trial," "jury selection," and "peremptory challenge."

QUESTIONS

1. What are the steps involved in the criminal trial?
2. What are the pros and cons of a jury trial versus a bench trial?
3. What are the legal rights of the defendant in a trial process?
4. Trace the historical development of the right to counsel at the trial stage of the criminal justice system.
5. What is the significance of the Supreme Court decision in *Gideon v. Wainwright?*
6. "The burden of proof in a criminal trial to show that the defendant is guilty beyond a reasonable doubt is on the government in the adversary system of criminal justice." Explain the meaning of this statement.
7. What is evidence?
8. What will be the characteristics of the criminal trial in the twenty-first century?

NOTES

1. Patrick O'Driscoll, "Man Guilty of Murdering Gay Student," *USA Today,* 4 November 1999, 3A.
2. U.S. Constitution, Sixth Amendment.
3. *Pointer v. State of Texas,* 380 U.S. 400, 85 S.Ct. 1065, 13 L.Ed.2d 923 (1965).
4. *Coy v. Iowa,* 487 U.S. 1012, 108 S.Ct. 2798, 101 L.Ed.2d 857 (1988).
5. *Maryland v. Craig,* 497 U.S. 836, 110 S.Ct. 3157, 111 L.Ed.2d 666 (1990).
6. *Duncan v. Louisiana,* 391 U.S. 145, 88 S.Ct. 1444, 20 L.Ed.2d 491 (1968).
7. Ibid., at 157–58, 88 S.Ct. at 1451–52.
8. *Baldwin v. New York,* 399 U.S. 66, 90 S.Ct. 1886, 26 L.Ed.2d 437 (1970).
9. *Blanton v. North Las Vegas,* 489 U.S. 538, 109 S.Ct. 1289, 103 L.Ed.2d 550 (1989).
10. *Lewis v. United States,* 116 S.Ct. 2163 (1996).
11. *Williams v. Florida,* 399 U.S. 78, 90 S.Ct. 1893, 26 L.Ed.2d 446 (1970).
12. Ibid., at 101, 90 S.Ct. at 1906.
13. *Apodica v. Oregon,* 406 U.S. 404, 92 S.Ct. 1628, 32 L.Ed.2d 184 (1972).
14. *Powell v. Alabama,* 287 U.S. 45, 53 S.Ct. 55, 77 L.Ed.2d 158 (1932).
15. *Gideon v. Wainwright,* 372 U.S. 335, 83 S.Ct. 792, 9 L.Ed.2d 799 (1963); see also Yale Kamisar, "*Gideon v. Wainwright,* a Quarter Century Later," *Pace Law Review* 10 (1990): 343
16. *Argersinger v. Hamlin,* 407 U.S. 25, 92 S.Ct. 2006, 32 L.Ed.2d 530 (1972).
17. *Scott v. Illinois,* 440 U.S. 367, 99 S.Ct. 1158, 59 L.Ed.2d 383 (1979).
18. U.S. Constitution, Sixth Amendment.
19. *Faretta v. California,* 422 U.S. 806, 95 S.Ct. 2525, 45 L.Ed.2d 562 (1975).
20. *Martinez v. Court of Appeals of California,* 120 S.Ct. 684, 2000.
21. See American Bar Association, *Standards Relating to Speedy Trial* (Chicago: ABA, 1995).
22. *Klopfer v. North Carolina,* 386 U.S. 213, 87 S.Ct. 988, 18 L.Ed.2d 1 (1967).
23. Ibid., at 223, 87 S.Ct. at 993.
24. *Doggett v. United States,* 505 U.S. 162, 112 S.Ct. 2686, 120 L.Ed.2d 520 (1992).
25. *Estelle v. Williams,* 425 U.S. 501, 96 S.Ct. 1691, 48 L.Ed.2d 126 (1976); see also American Bar Association, "Fair Trial and Free Press," in *Standards for Criminal Justice* (Washington, D.C.: ABA, 1993).
26. *Nebraska Press Association v. Stuart,* 427 U.S. 539, 96 S.Ct. 2791, 49 L.Ed.2d 683 (1976).
27. Ibid., at 547, 96 S.Ct. at 2797.
28. *Gannett Co. v. DePasquale,* 443 U.S. 368, 99 S.Ct. 2898, 61 L.Ed.2d 608 (1979).
29. Ibid., at 370, 99 S.Ct at 2900.
30. *Press-Enterprise Co. v. Superior Court,* 478 U.S. 1, 106 S.Ct. 2735, 92 L.Ed.2d 1 (1986).
31. *El Vocero de Puerto Rico (Caribbean International News Corp. v. Puerto Rico),* 508 U.S. 147, 113 S.Ct. 2004, 124 L.Ed.2d 60 (1993).
32. *Richmond Newspapers, Inc. v. Virginia,* 448 U.S. 555, 100 S.Ct. 2814, 65 L.Ed.2d 973 (1980).
33. *Globe Newspaper Co. v. Superior Court for County of Norfolk,* 457 U.S. 596, 102 S.Ct. 2613, 73 L.Ed.2d 248 (1982).
34. Nicholas A. Pellegrini, "Extension of Criminal Defendant's Right to Public Trial," *St. John's University Law Review* 611 (1987): 277–89.
35. *In re Oliver,* 333 U.S. 257, 68 S.Ct. 499, 92 L.Ed. 682 (1948).
36. *Chandler v. Florida,* 449 U.S. 560 (1981); also American Bar Association, *Criminal Justice Standards, Fair Trial and Free Press* (Washington, D.C.: ABA, 1992).
37. Conference of State Court Administrators, *State Court Organization, 1987* (Williamsburg, Va.: National Center for State Courts, 1988), 10.
38. George Hayden, Joseph Senna, and Larry Siegel, "Prosecutorial Discretion in Peremptory Challenges: An Empirical Inves-

tigation of Information Use in the Massachusetts Jury Selection Process," *New England Law Review* 13 (1978): 768.

39. *Swain v. Alabama,* 380 U.S. 202, 85 S.Ct. 824, 13 L.Ed.2d 759 (1964).

40. *Batson v. Kentucky,* 476 U.S. 79, 106 S.Ct. 1712, 90 L.Ed.2d 69 (1986); see also Albert Alschuler and Randall Kennedy, "Equal Justice — Would Color-Conscious Jury Selection Help?" *American Bar Association Journal* 81 (1995): 36–37.

41. *Powers v. Ohio,* 479 U.S. 400, 111 S.Ct. 1364, 113 L.Ed.2d 411 (1991).

42. *Georgia v. McCollum,* 505 U.S. 42, 112 S.Ct. 2348, 120 L.Ed.2d 33 (1992).

43. *J.E.B. v. Alabama,* 511 U.S. 114 S.Ct. 1419, 128 L.Ed.2d 89 (1994).

44. See Charles McCormick, Frank Elliott, and John Sutton, Jr., *Evidence — Cases and Materials* (St. Paul: West, 1981), chap. 1.

45. See the fascinating case study of the *State's Case v. Dr. Webster* in Helen Thomson, *Murder at Harvard* (Boston: Houghton Mifflin, 1971).

46. *Chapman v. California,* 386 U.S. 18, 87 S.Ct. 824, 17 L.Ed.2d 705 (1967).

47. *Douglas v. California,* 372 U.S. 353, 83 S.Ct. 814, 9 L.Ed.2d 811 (1963).

48. *Ross v. Moffitt,* 417 U.S. 600, 94 S.Ct. 2437, 41 L.Ed.2d 341 (1974).

49. Brian J. Ostrom, *State Court Caseload Statistics, Annual Report, 1992* (Williamsburg, Va.: National Center for State Courts, 1994); National Center for State Courts, *Examining the Work of State Courts* (Williamsburg, Va.: National Center for State Courts, 1998); American Bar Association, *The State of Criminal Justice* (Chicago: ABA, 1997).

50. See *Brinegar v. United States,* 338 U.S. 160, 69 S.Ct. 1302, 93 L.Ed. 1879 (1949); *In re Winship,* 397 U.S. 358, 90 S.Ct. 1068, 25 L.Ed.2d 368 (1970).

51. *Brinegar v. United States,* 338 U.S. 160, 174, 69 S.Ct. 1302, 1310, 93 L.Ed. 1879 (1949).

52. See *In re Winship,* at 397.

53. Ibid., at 371, 90 S.Ct. at 1076.

chapter 11

Punishment and Sentencing

During his lifetime, Michael Riggs had been convicted eight times in California for such offenses as car theft and robbery. In 1996 he was once again in trouble, this time for shoplifting a $20 bottle of vitamins. After his trial, Riggs was sentenced to a term of 25 years–to–life under California's three-strikes law, which mandates a life sentence for anyone convicted of a third offense. The law enables a trial judge to treat a defendant's third offense, even a petty crime such as shoplifting, as if it were a felony for purposes of applying the law's mandatory sentencing provisions. Riggs must serve a minimum of 20.8 years before parole eligibility; without the three-strikes law, he would ordinarily have earned a maximum sentence of six months; if he had been convicted of *murder* he would have had to serve only 17 years. Riggs appealed his conviction to the Supreme Court in 1999, but the justices refused to rule on the case, leaving his sentence stand.[1]

The *Riggs* case illustrates the difficulty of finding proper and fair sentences for criminal offenders. Should we take into account a person's past record when we determine how he should be punished for his current crimes? Should public opinion be considered when we determine criminal punishments? When popular opinion, fueled by the media, demands revenge, politicians establish get-tough measures such as mandatory sentences for drug offenders and the death penalty for murder. Is Michael Riggs's life sentence for shoplifting the result of society's need for revenge? The facts of the case reveal that Riggs was homeless, hungry, a substance abuser, and extremely depressed after the death of his young son. Did this troubled person deserve a life sentence for shoplifting? ■

Historically, a full range of punishments were inflicted on criminal defendants, including physical torture, branding, whipping, and, for most felony offenses, death. During the Middle Ages, the philosophy of punishment was to "torment the body for the sins of the soul."[2] People who violated the law were considered morally corrupt and in need of strong discipline. If punishment was harsh enough, it was assumed, they would never repeat their mistakes. Punishment was also viewed as a spectacle that taught a moral lesson. The more gruesome and public the sentence, the greater the impact it would have on the local populace.[3] Harsh physical punishments would control any thoughts of rebellion and dissent against the central government and those who held political and economic control. Such barbaric use of state power is of course no longer tolerated in the United States. Exhibit 11.1 lists the most important forms of criminal punishment in modern U.S. society.

The controversy over punishment involves both its nature and extent: Are too many people being sent to prison?[4] Do people get widely different sentences for very similar crimes?[5] Is there discrimination in sentencing based on race, gender, or social class?[6] These are but a few of the most significant issues in the sentencing process.

This chapter first examines the history of punishment and then focuses on incarceration and capital punishment, the two most traditional and punitive forms of criminal sanctions used today. Chapter 12 reviews alternative sentences that have been developed to reduce the strain on the overburdened correctional

exhibit 11.1

Forms of Punishment

- Fine: a monetary payment made to the court, reflecting the costs to society of the criminal act
- Community sentence: a period of supervision in the community during which the criminal is required to obey predetermined rules of behavior and may be asked to perform tasks, such as making restitution to the victim
- Incarceration: a period of confinement in a state or federal prison, jail, or community-based treatment facility
- Capital punishment: death in the electric chair or gas chamber or by lethal injection

system; these sentences provide intermediate sanctions designed to control people whose behavior and personality make incarceration unnecessary. Such sanctions include probation and other forms of community correction.

THE HISTORY OF PUNISHMENT

The punishment and correction of criminals has changed considerably through the ages, reflecting custom, economic conditions, and religious and political ideals.[7]

From Exile to Fines, Torture to Forfeiture

In early Greece and Rome, the most common state-administered punishment was banishment, or exile. Only slaves were commonly subjected to harsh physical punishment for their misdeeds. Interpersonal violence, even attacks that resulted in death, were viewed as a private matter. These ancient peoples typically used economic punishments, such as fines, for such crimes as assault on a slave, arson, or housebreaking.

During the Middle Ages (fifth to eleventh centuries), there was little law or governmental control. Offenses were settled by blood feuds carried out by the families of the injured parties. When possible, the Roman custom of settling disputes by fine or an exchange of property was adopted as a means of resolving interpersonal conflicts with a minimum of bloodshed. After the eleventh century, during the feudal period, forfeiture of land and property was common punishment for persons who violated law and custom or who failed to fulfill their feudal obligations to their lord. The word **felony** actually comes from the twelfth century, when the term *felonia* referred to a breach of faith with one's feudal lord.

felony
A more serious offense that carries a penalty of incarceration in a state prison, usually for one year or more. Persons convicted of felony offenses lose such rights as the rights to vote, hold elective office, or maintain certain licenses.

wergild
Under medieval law, the money paid by the offender to compensate the victim and the state for a criminal offense.

During this period the main emphasis of criminal law and punishment was on maintaining public order. If in the heat of passion or while intoxicated a person severely injured or killed her neighbor, freemen in the area would gather to pronounce a judgment and make the culprit do penance or pay compensation called **wergild.** The purpose of the fine was to pacify the injured party and ensure that the conflict would not develop into a blood feud and anarchy. The inability of the peasantry to pay a fine led to the use of corporal punishment, such as whipping or branding, as a substitute penalty.

The development of the common law in the eleventh century brought some standardization to penal practices. However, corrections remained an amalgam of fines and brutal physical punishments. The criminal wealthy could buy their way out of punishment and into exile, but capital and corporal punishment

In earlier times, punishment was quite severe. Even kings, such as Charles I of England, were not immune from death by beheading.

were used to control the criminal poor, who were executed and mutilated at ever-increasing rates. Execution, banishment, mutilation, branding, and flogging were used on a whole range of offenders, from murderers and robbers to vagrants and Gypsies. Punishments became unmatched in their cruelty, featuring a gruesome variety of physical tortures often part of a public spectacle, presumably so that the sadistic sanctions would act as deterrents. But the variety and imagination of the tortures inflicted on even minor criminals before their death suggest that retribution, sadism, and spectacle were more important than any presumed deterrent effect.

Public Work and Transportation to the Colonies

By the end of the sixteenth century, the rise of the city and overseas colonization provided tremendous markets for manufactured goods and spurred the need for labor. Punishment of criminals changed to meet the demands created by these social conditions. Instead of being tortured or executed, many offenders were made to do hard labor for their crimes. **Poor laws,** developed at the end of the sixteenth century, required that the poor, vagrants, and vagabonds be put to work in public or private enterprises. Houses of correction were developed to make it convenient to assign petty law violators to work details. In London a workhouse was developed at Brideswell in 1557; its use became so popular that by 1576 Parliament ordered a Brideswell-type workhouse to be built in every county in England. Many convicted offenders were pressed into sea duty as galley slaves. Galley slavery was considered a fate so loathsome that many convicts mutilated themselves rather than submit to servitude on the high seas.

poor laws
Seventeenth-century laws in England that bound out vagrants and abandoned children as indentured servants to masters.

The constant shortage of labor in the European colonies also prompted authorities to transport convicts overseas. In England an Order in Council of 1617 granted a reprieve and stay of execution to people convicted of robbery and other felonies who were strong enough to be employed overseas. Similar measures were used in France and Italy to recruit galley slaves and workers.

Transporting convicts to the colonies became popular; it supplied labor, cost little, and was actually profitable for the government, since manufacturers and plantation owners paid for convicts' services. The Old Bailey Court in London supplied at least ten thousand convicts between 1717 and 1775. Convicts would serve a period as workers and then become free again.

The American Revolution ended the transportation of felons to North America, although it continued in Australia and New Zealand. Between 1787 and 1875, when the practice was finally abandoned, over 135,000 felons were transported to Australia.

Although transportation in lieu of a death sentence may at first glance seem advantageous, transported prisoners endured enormous hardships. Those who were sent to Australia suffered incredible physical abuse, including severe whippings and mutilation. Many of the British prison officials placed in charge of the Australian penal colonies could best be described as sociopaths or sadists.

The Rise of the Prison Between the American Revolution in 1776 and the first decades of the nineteenth century, the population of Europe and the United States increased rapidly. Transportation of convicts to North America was no longer an option. The increased use of machinery made industry capital intensive, not labor intensive. As a result, there was less need for unskilled laborers in England, and many workers could not find suitable employment.

The gulf between poor workers and wealthy landowners and merchants widened. The crime rate rose significantly, prompting a return to physical punishment and increased use of the death penalty. During the later part of the eighteenth century, 350 types of crime in England were punishable by death. Although many people sentenced to death for trivial offenses were spared the gallows, the use of capital punishment was extremely common in England during the mid-eighteenth century. Prompted by the excessive use of physical and capital punishment, legal philosophers argued that physical punishment should be replaced by periods of confinement and incapacitation. Jails and workhouses were commonly used to hold petty offenders, vagabonds, the homeless, and debtors. However, these institutions were not meant for hard-core criminals. One solution to imprisoning a growing criminal population was to keep prisoners in abandoned ships anchored in rivers and harbors throughout England. The degradation under which prisoners lived in these ships inspired John Howard, the sheriff of Bedfordshire, to write *The State of the Prisons* in 1777, which inspired Parliament to pass legislation mandating the construction of secure and sanitary structures to house prisoners.

penitentiary
A state or federal correctional institution for incarceration of felony offenders for terms of one year or more.

By 1820 long periods of incarceration in walled institutions called reformatories or **penitentiaries** began to replace physical punishment in England and the United States. These institutions were considered liberal reforms during a time when harsh physical punishment and incarceration in filthy holding facilities were the norm. The history of correctional institutions will be discussed further in Chapter 13. Incarceration has remained the primary mode of punishment for serious offenses in the United States since it was introduced in the early nineteenth century. Ironically, in our high-tech society, some of the institutions constructed soon after the Revolutionary War are still in use today. In recent times, prison as a method of punishment has been supplemented by a sentence to community supervision for less serious offenders, and the death penalty is reserved for those considered to be the most serious and dangerous.

THE GOALS OF MODERN SENTENCING

When we hear about a notorious criminal, such as serial killers Jeffrey Dahmer or Ted Bundy, receiving a long prison sentence or the death penalty for a particularly heinous crime, each of us has a distinct reaction. Some of us are gratified that a truly evil person "got just what he deserved"; many people feel safer because a dangerous person is now "where she can't harm any other innocent victims"; others hope the punishment serves as a warning to potential criminals that "everyone gets caught in the end"; some may actually feel sorry for the defendant — "He got a raw deal, he needs help, not punishment"; and still others hope that "when she gets out, she'll have learned her lesson." And when an offender is forced to pay a large fine, we say, "What goes around comes around."

Each of these sentiments may be at work when criminal sentences are formulated. After all, sentences are devised and implemented by judges, many of whom are elected officials and share the general public's sentiments and fears. The objectives of criminal sentencing today can usually be grouped into six distinct areas: general deterrence, incapacitation, specific deterrence, retribution/just desert, rehabilitation, and equity/restitution.

General Deterrence

What is the impact on the community when a criminal offender is punished? By punishing an offender severely, the state can demonstrate its determination to control crime and deter potential offenders. Too lenient a sentence might encourage criminal conduct; too severe a sentence might reduce the system's ability to dispense fair and impartial justice and may actually encourage criminality. For example, if the crime of rape were punished with death, rapists might be encouraged to kill their victims to dispose of the one person who could identify them; since they would already be facing the death penalty for rape, they would have nothing more to lose. Maintaining a balance between fear and justice is an ongoing quest in the justice system.

general deterrence
A crime control policy that depends on the fear of criminal penalties. General deterrence measures, such as long prison sentences for violent crimes, are aimed at convincing the potential law violator that the pains associated with crime outweigh its benefits.

Sentencing for the purposes of **general deterrence,** then, is designed to give a signal to the community at large: Crime does not pay! The message is impressive, but it may also be a case of wishful thinking. There is actually little clear-cut evidence that severe punishments influence criminal behavior trends. Nonetheless, criminal penalties have been toughened for many crimes; once arrested, people have a greater chance of being convicted today than in the past. As a result, prison sentences are lengthening, and the prison population is increasing. Despite these stern measures, there is still much crime.

Why does the threat of punishment have a less than expected influence on crime? Criminals may be too desperate or psychologically impaired by drugs and alcohol to be deterred by the threat of distant criminal punishment, or their economic circumstances may be too desperate for the threat of punishment to have an effect. Nonetheless, some experts believe that severe and draconian sentences can eventually bring down crime rates. They call for a get-tough policy featuring long, mandatory prison terms with little chance for early release.

Incapacitation

If an offender is a risk to society, he may be sentenced to a period of secure confinement. **Incapacitation** of criminals is a justifiable goal of sentencing because inmates will not be able to repeat their criminal acts while they are under state control. For some offenders, this means a period in a high-security state prison where behavior is closely monitored. Fixing sentence length involves determining how long a particular offender needs to be incarcerated to ensure that society is protected.

incapacitation
The policy of keeping dangerous criminals in confinement to eliminate the risk of their repeating their offense in society.

To some critics, incapacitation strategies seem of questionable utility because little association seems to exist between the number of criminals behind bars and the crime rate. Although the prison population jumped between 1980 and 1990, the crime rate also increased. In contrast, those who favor an incapacitation policy claim that the crime-reducing effect of putting people in prison has just taken a little longer than expected. The recent decline in the crime rate is a product of putting almost 2 million people behind bars. Opponents counter that crime rates have little to do with incarceration trends and that reductions in crime are related to other factors such as population makeup, police effectiveness, declining drug use, a strong economy, and other unrelated factors.

recidivism
Repetition of criminal behavior; habitual criminality. Recidivism is measured by (1) criminal acts that resulted in conviction by a court when committed by individuals who are under correctional supervision or who had been released from correctional supervision within the previous three years and (2) technical violations of probation or parole in which a sentencing or paroling authority took action that resulted in an adverse change in the offender's legal status.

specific deterrence
A crime control policy suggesting that punishment should be severe enough to convince convicted offenders never to repeat their criminal activity.

blameworthy
The culpability or guilt a person maintains for participating in a particular criminal offense.

just desert
The philosophy of justice asserting that those who violate the rights of others deserve to be punished. The severity of punishment should be commensurate with the seriousness of the crime.

Specific Deterrence

Experiencing harsh criminal punishments should convince convicted offenders that crime does not pay and **recidivism** is not in their best interests. The suffering caused by punishment should inhibit future law violations.

A few research efforts have found that punishment can have significant **specific deterrence** on future criminality, but they are balanced by research that has failed to find specific deterrence effects.[8] The specific deterrence goal of punishment is also weakened by the fact that about 70 percent of prison inmates have had prior convictions and more than 60 percent return to prison within three years of their release.[9]

Retribution/Just Desert

According to the retributive goal of sentencing, the essential purpose of the criminal process is to punish deserving offenders — fairly and justly — in a manner that is proportionate to the gravity of their crimes.[10]

Offenders are punished simply and solely because they deserve to be disciplined for what they have done; "the punishment should fit the crime."[11] It would be wrong to punish people to set an example for others or to deter would-be criminals, as the general deterrence goal demands. Punishment should be no more or less than the offender's actions deserve; it must be based on how **blameworthy** the person is; this is referred to as the concept of **just desert.**[12]

According to this view, punishments must be equally and fairly distributed to all people who commit similar illegal acts. Determining just punishments can be difficult because there is generally little consensus about the treatment of criminals, the seriousness of crimes, and the proper response to criminal acts.[13] Nonetheless, there has been an ongoing effort to calculate fair and just sentences by creating guidelines to control judicial decision making. This effort will be discussed in greater detail later in the chapter.

Rehabilitation

Can criminal offenders be effectively treated so that they can eventually readjust to society? It may be fairer to offer offenders an opportunity for rehabilitation rather than harsh criminal punishments. In a sense, society has failed criminal offenders, many of whom have grown up in disorganized neighborhoods and dysfunctional families. They may have been the target of biased police officers; and once arrested and labeled, the offender is placed at a disadvantage at home, at school, and in the job market.[14] Society is therefore obligated to help these unfortunate people who, through no fault of their own, experience social and emotional problems that are often the root of their criminal behavior.

The rehabilitation aspect of sentencing is based on a prediction of the future needs of the offender, not on the gravity of the current offense. For example, if a judge sentences a person convicted of a felony to a period of community supervision, the judge's actions reflect her belief that the offender can be successfully treated and presents no future threat to society. This faith is supported by studies showing that under the right circumstances rehabilitation efforts can be effective.[15]

The rehabilitation goal of sentencing has also been criticized by those who find little conclusive evidence exists that correctional treatment programs can prevent future criminality.[16] While the rehabilitative ideal has been undermined by such attacks, surveys indicate that the general public still supports the treatment goal of sentencing.[17] Many people express preferences for programs that are treatment oriented, such as early childhood intervention and services for at-risk children, rather than those that espouse strict punishment and incarceration policies.[18]

Equity/Restitution

Because criminals gain from their misdeeds, it seems both fair and just to demand that they reimburse society for its loss caused by their crimes. In the early common law, wergild and fines represented the concept of creating an equitable solution to crime by requiring the convicted offender to make restitution to both the victim and the state. Today, judges continue to require that offenders pay victims for their losses.

equity
The action or practice of awarding each his or her just due; sanctions based on equity seek to compensate individual victims and the general society for their losses due to crime.

The **equity** goal of punishment means that convicted criminals must pay back their victims for their loss, the justice system for the costs of processing their case, and society for any disruption they may have caused. In a so-called victimless crime, such as drug trafficking, the social costs might include the expense of drug enforcement efforts, drug treatment centers, and care for infants born to drug-addicted mothers. In predatory crimes, the costs might include the services of emergency room doctors, lost workdays and productivity, and treatment for long-term psychological problems. To help defray these costs, convicted offenders might be required to pay a fine, forfeit the property they acquired through illegal gain, do community service work, make financial restitution to their victim, and reimburse the state for the costs of the criminal process. Because the criminals' actions helped expand their personal gains, rights, and privileges at society's expense, justice demands that they lose rights and privileges to restore the social balance.[19]

Each factor that influences sentencing decisions is illustrated in Figure 11.1.

Imposing the Sentence

Regardless of the factors that influence the sentence, it is generally imposed by the judge, and sentencing is one of the most crucial functions of judgeship. Sentencing authority may also be exercised by the jury, or it may be mandated by statute (e.g., a mandatory prison sentence for a certain crime).

In most felony cases, except where the law provides for mandatory prison terms, sentencing is usually based on a variety of information available to the judge. Some jurisdictions allow victims to make impact statements that are considered at sentencing hearings. Most judges also consider a presentence investigation report by the probation department in making a sentencing decision. This report is a social and personal history, as well as an evaluation of the defendant's chances for rehabilitation within the community. Some judges give the presentence investigation report great weight; others may dismiss it completely or rely on only certain portions.

concurrent sentence
A prison sentence for two or more criminal acts that are served simultaneously, or run together.

When an accused is convicted of two or more charges, he must be sentenced on each charge. If the sentences are **concurrent,** they begin the same day and are

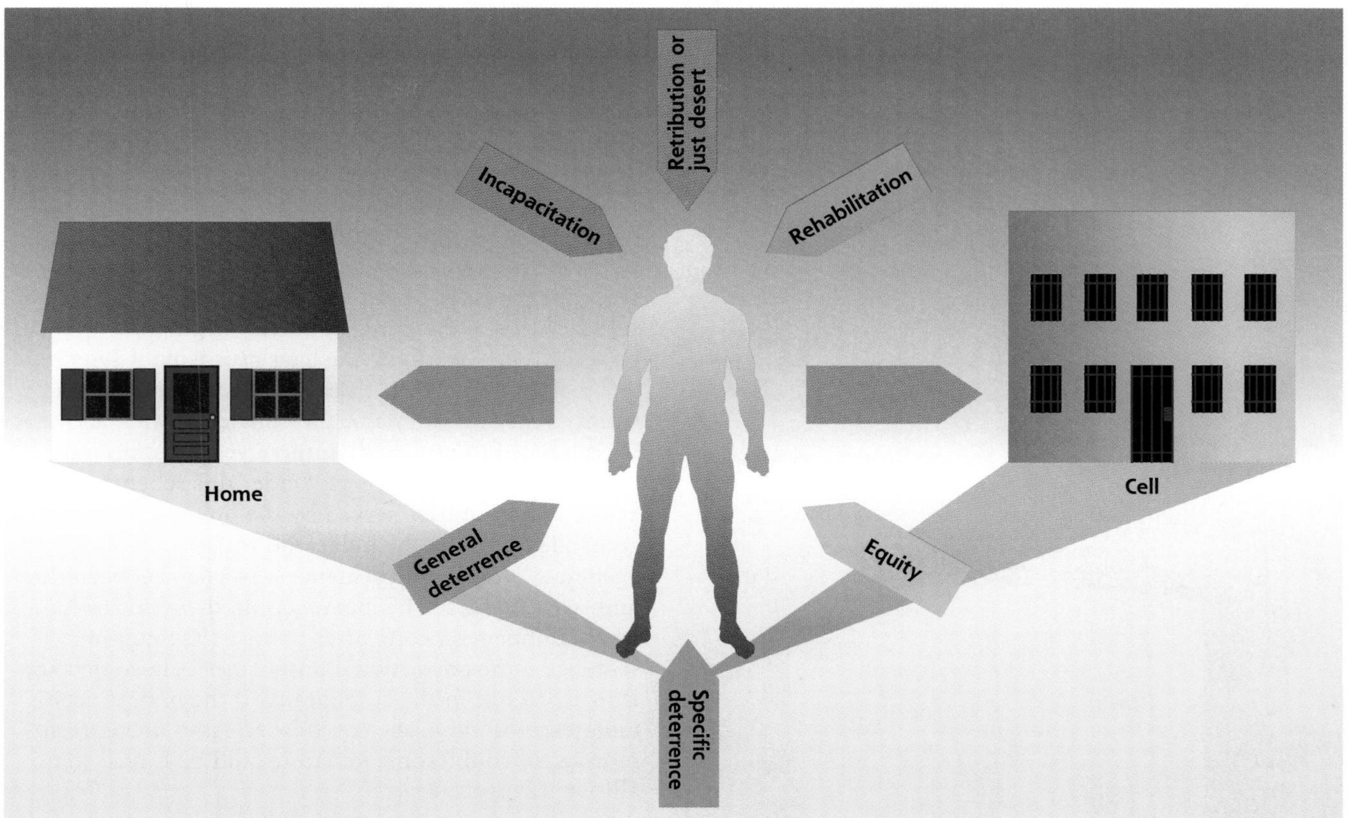

Figure 11.1
The factors influencing sentencing decisions

completed when the longest term has been served. For example, a defendant is convicted of burglarizing an apartment and assaulting its occupant; he is sentenced to three years on a charge of assault and ten years for burglary, with the sentences to be served concurrently. After ten years in prison, the sentences would be completed.

In contrast, receiving a **consecutive sentence** means that on completion of the sentence for one crime the offender begins serving time for the second of multiple crimes. If the defendant in the above example had been sentenced consecutively, he would serve three years on the assault charge and then ten years for the burglary. Therefore, the total term on the two charges would be thirteen years. Concurrent sentences are the norm; consecutive sentences are requested for the most serious criminals and for those who are unwilling to cooperate with authorities.

consecutive sentence
A prison sentence for two or more criminal acts that are served one after the other, or that follow one another.

indeterminate sentence
A term of incarceration with a stated minimum and maximum length, such as a sentence to prison for a period of from three to ten years. The prisoner would be eligible for parole after the minimum sentence had been served. Based on the belief that sentences should fit the criminal, indeterminate sentences allow individualized sentences and provide for sentencing flexibility. Judges can set a high minimum to override the purpose of the indeterminate sentence.

SENTENCING MODELS

When a convicted offender is sentenced to prison, the statutes of the jurisdiction in which the crime was committed determine the penalties that may be imposed by the court. Over the years, a variety of sentencing structures have been used in the United States. They include indeterminate sentences, determinate sentences, and mandatory sentences.

Indeterminate Sentences

In the 1870s, prison reformers, such as Enoch Wines and Zebulon Brockway, called for creation of **indeterminate sentences**, tailored to fit individual needs. Offenders, the argument went, should

Sentencing decisions are based on an amalgam of information available to the judge. Younger offenders may be given a more lenient sentence than hardened older criminals. The three teens shown on the monitor were charged with murdering an elderly man during a Florida hold-up. They were sentenced to life in prison. Should their age have been taken into consideration when punishment was considered?

only be placed in confinement until they were rehabilitated and then released on parole. Criminals were believed to be "sick" rather than bad; they could be successfully treated in prison. Rather than holding that "the punishment should fit the crime," reformers believed "the treatment should fit the offender."

The indeterminate sentence is still the most widely used type of sentence in the United States. Convicted offenders are typically given a "light" minimum sentence that must be served and a lengthy maximum sentence that is the outer boundary of the time that can be served. For example, the legislature might set a sentence of a minimum of three years and a maximum of twenty years for burglary; the convicted offender must be sentenced to no less than three years but no more than twenty years in prison. Under this scheme, the actual length of time served by the offender is controlled both by the judge and the correctional agency. A judge could sentence a burglar between three and twenty years. The inmate could then be paroled from confinement soon after serving the minimum sentence if the correctional authorities believe that she is ready to live in the community. If the inmate accumulates good time, she could be released in eighteen months; a troublesome inmate would be forced to do all twenty years.

The basic purpose of the indeterminate sentence is to individualize each sentence in the interests of rehabilitating the offender. This type of sentencing allows for flexibility not only in the type of sentence to be imposed but also in the length of time to be served.

Most jurisdictions that use indeterminate sentences employ statutes that specify minimum and maximum terms but allow judicial discretion to fix the actual sentence within those limits. The typical minimum sentence is at least one year; a few state jurisdictions require at least a two-year minimum sentence for felons.[20]

Determinate Sentences The indeterminate sentence has come under attack in recent years for a variety of reasons. It is alleged to produce great disparity in the way people are treated in the correctional system. For example, one offender may serve one year, and another may serve twenty years, for the same crime. Further, the indeterminate sentence is believed to take control of sentencing out of the hands of the judiciary and place it within the framework of corrections, especially when the minimum sentence is quite short. Every time an inmate who is granted early release via discretionary parole and commits a violent crime, the call goes up to get tough on prison inmates. In contrast, many inmates feel cheated by the system when they are denied parole, despite having a good prison record. The protections of due process maintained in the courtroom are absent in the correctional setting. Dissatisfaction with the disparity and uncertainty of indeterminate sentencing has prompted some states and the federal government to abandon it in favor of determinate sentencing models or structured sentencing models (discussed in the next section).

determinate sentence
A fixed term of incarceration, such as three years' imprisonment. Determinate sentences are felt by many to be too restrictive for rehabilitative purposes; the advantage is that offenders know how much time they have to serve — that is, when they will be released.

Determinate sentences, actually the first kind used in the United States, are today employed in about ten jurisdictions. As originally conceived, a determinate sentence was a fixed term of years, the maximum set in law by the legislature, to be served by the offender sentenced to prison for a particular crime. For example, if the law provided for a sentence of up to twenty years for robbery, the judge might sentence a repeat offender to a fifteen-year term; another, less experienced felon might receive a more lenient sentence of five years.

Although determinate sentences provide a single term of years to be served without benefit of parole, the actual time spent in prison is reduced by the implementation of "time off for good behavior." This concept was first used in 1817 in New York, and it was quickly adopted in most other jurisdictions. Good time is still in use today; inmates can accrue standard good time at a rate ranging from ten to fifteen days per month. In addition, some correctional authorities grant earned sentence reductions to inmates who participate in treatment programs, such as educational and vocational training, or who volunteer for experimental medical testing programs. More than half of a determinate sentence can be erased by accumulating both standard and earned good time.

Good-time laws allow inmates to calculate their release date at the time they enter prison by subtracting the expected good time from their sentence. However, good time can be lost if inmates break prison rules, get into fights, or disobey correctional officers. In some jurisdictions, former inmates can be returned to prison to serve the balance of their unexpired sentence when their good time is revoked for failing to conform to conditions set down for their release (e.g., not reporting to a postrelease supervisor or for abusing drugs).

Structured Sentences

Coinciding with the development of determinate sentencing has been the development of *sentencing guidelines* to control and structure the process and make it more rational. Guidelines are usually based on the seriousness of a crime and the background of an offender: The more serious the crime and the more extensive the offender's criminal background, the longer is the prison term recommended by the guidelines. For example, guidelines might require that all people convicted of robbery who had no prior offense record and who did not use excessive force or violence be given an average of a five-year sentence; those who used force and had a prior record will have three years added to their sentence. Guidelines eliminate discretionary parole but also allow inmates to reduce their sentence by acquiring time off for good behavior. By eliminating judicial discretion, they are designed to reduce racial and gender disparity.[21]

HOW ARE GUIDELINES USED?

Today, seventeen states use some form of structured sentencing. In seven states, *voluntary/advisory sentencing guidelines* (sometimes called *descriptive guidelines*) are used merely to suggest rather than mandate sentencing. In the other ten states, *presumptive sentencing guidelines* (sometimes called *prescriptive guidelines*) are used. In this instance, judges are required to use the guidelines to shape their sentencing decisions, and their sentencing decisions may be open to appellate review if they stray from the mandated sentences. Michigan, Washington, Oregon, Pennsylvania, Minnesota, North Carolina, and the federal government mandate that judges follow a set of comprehensive guidelines.[22]

Prescriptive guidelines are created by appointed sentencing commissions. The commission members determine what an "ideal" sentence would be for a particular crime and offender. There is, however, a great deal of variation within

Severity level of conviction offense (common offenses listed in italics)		Criminal History Score						
		0	1	2	3	4	5	6 or more
Murder, 2nd degree (intentional murder; drive-by-shootings)	X	306 *299—313*	326 *319—333*	346 *339—353*	366 *359—373*	386 *379—393*	406 *399—413*	426 *419—433*
Murder, 3rd degree Murder, 2nd degree (unintentional murder)	IX	150 *144—156*	165 *159—171*	180 *174—186*	195 *189—201*	210 *204—216*	225 *219—231*	240 *234—246*
Criminal sexual conduct, 1st degree Assault, 1st degree	VIII	86 *81—91*	98 *93—103*	110 *105—115*	122 *117—127*	134 *129—139*	146 *141—151*	158 *153—163*
Aggravated robbery, 1st degree	VII	48 *44—52*	58 *54—62*	68 *64—72*	78 *74—82*	88 *84—92*	98 *94—102*	108 *104—112*
Criminal sexual conduct, 2nd degree (a) & (b)	VI	21	26	30	34 *33—35*	44 *42—46*	54 *50—58*	65 *60—70*
Residential burglary Simple robbery	V	18	23	27	30 *29—31*	38 *36—40*	46 *43—49*	54 *50—58*
Nonresidential burglary	IV	12*	15	18	21	25 *24—26*	32 *30—34*	41 *37—45*
Theft crimes (over $2,500)	III	12*	13	15	17	19 *18—20*	22 *21—23*	25 *24—26*
Theft crimes ($2,500 or less) Check forgery ($200–$2,500)	II	12*	12*	13	15	17	19	21 *20—22*
Sale of simulated controlled substance	I	12*	12*	12*	13	15	17	19 *18—20*

Presumptive commitment to state imprisonment. First-degree murder is excluded from the guidelines by law and continues to have a mandatory life sentence.

Presumptive stayed sentence; at the discretion of the judge, up to a year in jail/or other nonjail sanctions can be imposed as conditions of probation. However, certain offenses in this section of the grid always carry a presumptive commitment to a state prison. These offenses include 3rd degree controlled substance crimes when the offender has a prior felony drug conviction, burglary of an occupied dwelling when the offender has a prior felony burglary conviction, second and subsequent criminal sexual conduct offenses, and offenses carrying a mandatory minimum prison term due to the use of a dangerous weapon (e.g., 2nd degree assault).

*One year and one day.

Figure 11.2
Sentencing guideline grid
Italicized numbers within the grid denote the range of months within which a judge may sentence without the sentence being deemed a departure. Offenders with nonimprisonment felony sentences are subject to jail time according to law.

SOURCE: Minnesota Sentencing Guidelines Commission, 1996.

prescriptive sentencing.[23] Some guidelines coexist with parole release, and some do not. Some deal with all crimes and others only with felonies. Some set narrow sentencing ranges, and some set broad ones.[24]

CONFIGURING GUIDELINES There are a number of ways to formulate guidelines. One method is to create a grid with prior record and current offense as the two coordinates and setting out specific punishment. Figure 11.2 shows Minnesota's guidelines. Note that as prior record and offense severity increase, so does recommended sentence length. After a certain point, probation is no longer an option, and the defendant must do prison time. A burglar with no prior convictions can expect to receive probation or an eighteen-month sentence for a house break-in; an experienced burglar with six or more prior convictions can get fifty-four months for the same crime, and probation is not an option.

The federal government uses a "cookbook" approach, but the guidelines are extensive and detailed. To determine the actual sentence, a magistrate must first determine the base penalty that a particular charge is given in the guidelines. For example, the federal guidelines give a base score (20) and mitigation factors for robbery. The base level can be adjusted upward if the crime was particularly serious or violent. For example, 7 points could be added to the robbery base if a firearm was discharged during the crime, or 5 points if the weapon was simply in the offender's possession. Similarly, points can be added to a robbery if a large amount of money was taken, a victim was injured, a person was abducted or restrained in order to facilitate an escape, or the object of the robbery was to steal weapons or drugs. Upward adjustments can also be made if the defendant was a ringleader in the crime, obstructed justice, or used a professional skill or position of trust (such as doctor, lawyer, or politician) to commit the crime. Offenders designated as career criminals by a court can likewise receive longer sentences.

Go to www.ussc.gov/general.htm **to find out information about the U.S. Sentencing Commission.**

Once the base score is computed, judges determine the sentence by consulting a sentencing table that converts scores into months to be served. Offense levels are set out in the vertical column, and the criminal history (ranging from one to six prior offenses) is displayed in a horizontal column, forming a grid that contains the various sentencing ranges (similar to the Minnesota guideline grid). By matching the applicable offense level and the criminal history, the judge can determine the sentence that applies to the particular offender.

HOW EFFECTIVE ARE GUIDELINES? Despite the widespread acceptance of guidelines, some nagging problems remain. A number of critics, including Michael Tonry, argue that they are rigid, harsh, and overcomplex; disliked by the judiciary; and should be substantially revised or totally eliminated.[25] Though they were designed to eliminate racial and social disparity, the effects of race, gender, and economic status continue to be debated.[26] Evaluations of the Minnesota guidelines show that African-American offenders are more likely to be charged with weapons violations and, consequently, more likely to receive prison terms than white offenders.[27] Similarly, possession of crack cocaine is punished far more severely by federal guidelines than possession of powdered cocaine. Critics charge that this amounts to racial bias because African Americans are much more likely to possess crack cocaine, whereas white offenders usually possess powdered cocaine.[28] Some jurisdictions give enhanced sentences if defendants have a prior juvenile conviction or if they were on juvenile probation or parole at the time of an arrest. African-American offenders are more likely than white offenders to have a prior record as a juvenile and therefore receive harsher sentences for their current crime.[29]

Some defense attorneys oppose the use of guidelines because they result in longer prison terms, prevent judges from considering mitigating circumstances, and reduce the use of probation. Even the widely heralded federal guidelines have had and will continue to have some dubious effects. The use of probation has diminished and the size of the federal prison population is increasing because guideline sentences are tougher and defendants have very little incentive to plea-bargain. They require incarceration sentences for minor offenders who in preguideline days would have been given community release; many of these petty offenders might be better served with cheaper alternative sanctions.[30] Because of these problems, sentencing expert Michael Tonry calls them "the most controversial and disliked sentencing reform initiative in United States history."[31]

In his important book *Sentencing Matters,* Tonry offers a prescription to improve structured sentencing guidelines that calls in part for the creation of ongoing sentencing commissions, creation of realistic guidelines, reliance on alternative sanctions, and a sentencing philosophy that stresses the "least punitive and intrusive appropriate sentence."[32]

mandatory sentence
A statutory requirement that a certain penalty shall be set and carried out in all cases on conviction for a specified offense or series of offenses.

Mandatory Sentences

Another effort to limit judicial discretion and at the same time get tough on crime has been the development of the **mandatory sentence.** Some states, for example, prohibit people convicted of certain offenses, such as violent crimes, and chronic offenders (recidivists) from being placed on probation; they must serve at least some time in prison. Other statutes bar certain offenders from being considered for parole. Mandatory sentencing legislation may impose minimum and maximum terms, but typically it requires a fixed prison sentence.

Mandatory sentencing generally limits the judge's discretionary power to impose any disposition but that authorized by the legislature; as a result, it limits individualized sentencing and restricts sentencing disparity. Mandatory sentencing provides equal treatment for all offenders who commit the same crime, regardless of age, sex, or other individual characteristics. The Policy, Programs, and Issues in Criminal Justice feature reviews two recent attempts to create get-tough mandatory sentences.

More than thirty-five states have already replaced discretionary sentencing with fixed-term mandatory sentences for such crimes as the sale of hard drugs, kidnapping, gun possession, and arson. The results have been mixed. Mandatory sentences have helped increase the size of the correctional population to record levels. They have also failed to eliminate racial disparity from the sentencing process.[33] Some state courts have ruled such practices unconstitutional. A survey conducted for the American Bar Association found that judges are unhappy with such laws because they are unfair to first-time offenders and limit judicial discretion.[34] As a result, many offenders who in the past might have received probation are now being incarcerated.

HOW PEOPLE ARE SENTENCED

What sentences do people actually receive for their criminal behavior? The federal government has sponsored a number of national surveys that chart sentencing practices. One survey of sentencing outcomes in the nation's seventy-five largest counties found that 69 percent of the defendants convicted of a felony were sentenced to incarceration and about 57 percent of those convicted of a misdemeanor were incarcerated.[35] All murder convictions resulted in a prison sentence, as did a majority of robbery (71%) and rape (56%) convictions. However, less than half of defendants convicted of drug trafficking (44%), burglary (43%), felony assault (40%), or a weapons offense (37%) were sentenced to prison. Overall, about one-third of convicted defendants received a sentence to probation (31%) without any incarceration. As Figure 11.3 shows, having a prior conviction significantly increased the likelihood of receiving prison incarceration as opposed to a more lenient jail or probation sentence.

Figure 11.3
Sentencing in large urban counties

SOURCE: Brian Reaves and Timothy Hart, *Felony Defendants In Large Urban Counties, 1996: State Court Processing Statistics* (Washington, D.C.: Bureau of Justice Statistics, 1999), 36.

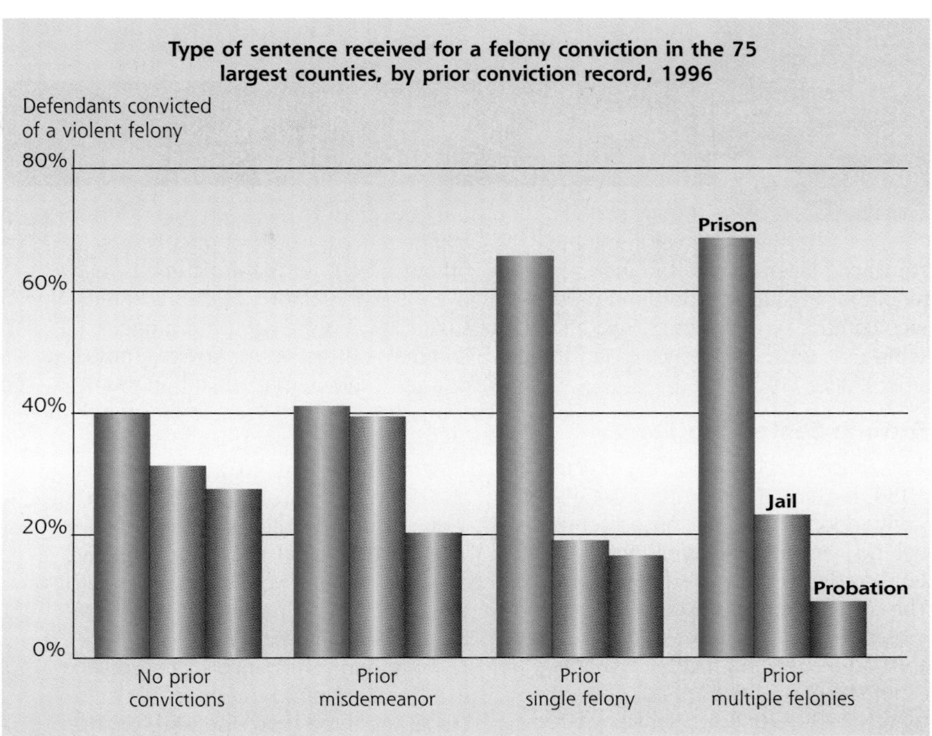

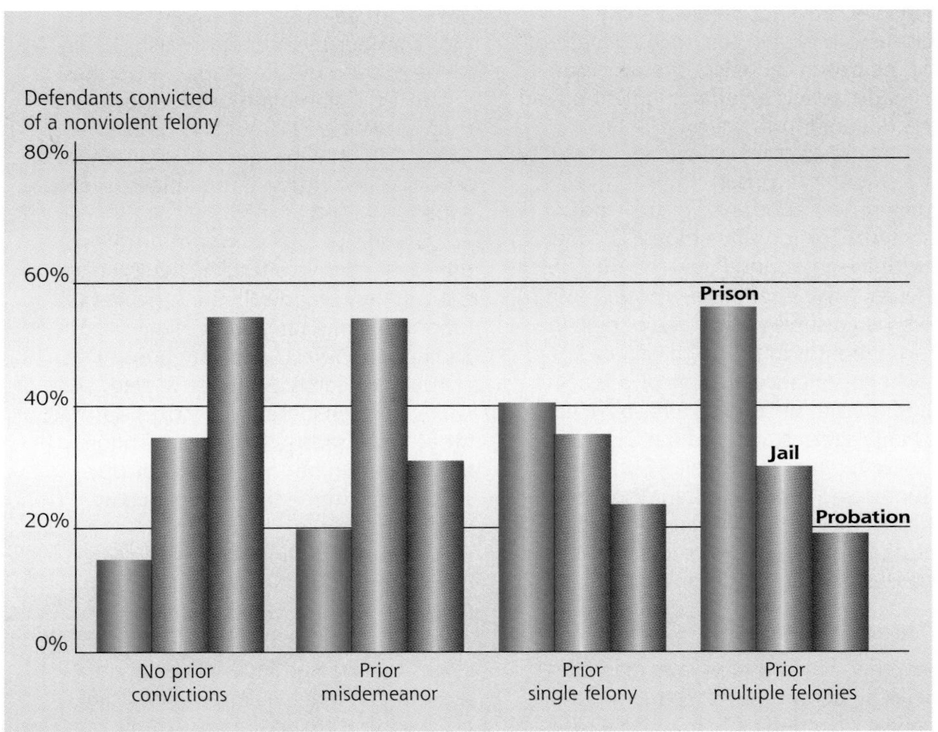

Policy, Programs, and Issues in Criminal Justice

LET'S GET TOUGH: TRUTH-IN-SENTENCING AND THREE-STRIKES LAWS

Public concern over crime has convinced lawmakers to toughen sentences for repeat offenders and those who commit serious crimes. Two efforts stand out: truth-in-sentencing and three-strikes laws.

Truth-in-Sentencing Laws

Truth-in-sentencing laws, first enacted in 1984, require offenders to serve a substantial portion of their prison sentence behind bars. Parole eligibility and good-time credits are restricted or eliminated. The movement was encouraged by the Violent Offender Incarceration and Truth-in-Sentencing Incentive Grants Program, part of the federal government's 1994 Crime Act, which offered funds to support the state costs involved with creating longer sentences. To qualify for federal funds, states must require persons convicted of a violent felony crime to serve not less than 85 percent of the prison sentence. The provision is already having an effect. Violent offenders released from prison in 1996 were sentenced to serve an average of eighty-five months in prison. Prior to release, they served about half of their prison sentence, or forty-five months. Under truth-in-sentencing laws requiring 85 percent of the sentence, violent offenders would serve an average of eighty-eight months in prison, based on the average sentence for violent offenders admitted to prison in 1996. By 1998 twenty-seven states and the District of Columbia met the federal Truth-in-Sentencing Incentive Grant Program eligibility criteria. Eleven states adopted truth-in-sentencing laws in 1995, one year after the 1994 Crime Act.

Three-Strikes Laws

Another new group of laws mandates lengthy periods of incarceration for repeat offenders, which in some cases can mean a life sentence for a minor felony. The new three-strikes-and-you're-out laws provide these lengthy terms for any person convicted of three felony offenses, even if the third crime is relatively trivial. California's statute three-strikes law is aimed at getting habitual criminals off the street. Anyone convicted of a third felony must do a minimum term of twenty-five years to life; the third felony does not have to be serious or violent. The federal Crime Act of 1994 also adopted a three-strikes provision, requiring a mandatory life sentence for any offender convicted of three felony offenses; twenty-two states have so far followed suit and passed some form of the three-strikes law.

Although welcomed by conservatives looking for a remedy for violent crime, the three-strikes policy is controversial because a person convicted of a minor felony can receive a life sentence. There are reports that some judges are defying three-strikes provisions because they consider them unduly harsh. Much to the chagrin of three-strikes advocates, two recent California court decisions, *People v. Romero* (1996) and *People v. Garcia* (1999), allows judges to disregard an earlier conviction if the judge believes a life term is unjustified.

Three-strikes laws may in fact help put some chronic offenders behind bars, but can they realistically be expected to lower the crime rate? Marc Mauer of The Sentencing Project, a private group that conducts research on justice-related issues, finds that the three-strikes approach may satisfy the public's hunger for retribution but makes little practical sense. First, "three-time losers" are at the brink of aging out of crime; locking them up for life should have little effect on the crime rate. Second, current sentences for chronic violent offenders are already severe, yet their punishment seems to have had little influence on reducing national violence rates. Mauer also suggests that a three-strikes policy will enlarge an already overburdened prison system, driving up costs, and, presumably, reducing resources available to house non-three-strikes inmates. Mauer also warns that African Americans face an increased risk of being sentenced under three-strikes statutes, expanding the racial disparity in sentencing. More ominous is the fact that police officers may be put at risk because two-time offenders would violently resist arrest, knowing that they face a life sentence.

The Costs Are High

Three-strikes laws have undeniable political appeal to legislators being pressured by their constituents to "do something about crime." Yet even if possibly effective against crime, any effort to deter criminal behavior through tough laws is not without costs. A study by the Rand Corporation, a California-based think tank, concluded that the state's three-strikes law may actually reduce serious felonies between 22 and 34 percent. However, the price of this reduction is an extra $4.5 to $6.5 billion per year in correctional costs in California alone. To put that in perspective, just the additional cost of the three-strikes policy would be sufficient to give more than 1 million students a full-tuition scholarship to the state university system!

Many states have passed three-strikes laws, but most have rarely invoked the penalty. California is one of the few to have used it with thousands of offenders; although many of these have committed serious crimes, as of 1996, 192 people had been sentenced to life for possession of marijuana. Because of its use with petty offenders, there are ongoing legal challenges to the use of three-strikes laws, and their future is still uncertain.

Can Three-Strikes Laws Work?

Although California officials attribute reduced crime rates to its three-strikes policy, others are skeptical about the approach. The Rand researchers argue that an alternative scheme would be to guarantee a full term in prison for seri-

Lawrence Olin, sentenced to 25 years to life for theft of blue jeans, on the "three strikes" California law.

ous felons without the possibility of probation, parole, or time off for good behavior. Their research shows that a guaranteed full-term policy would achieve the same benefits at a much lower cost.

As Mauer points out, "Three-strikes policies tend to incarcerate people at the tail end of their offending career, at a point when they may be on the verge of spontaneously 'aging out' of crime." A three-strikes policy also suffers because criminals typically underestimate their risk of apprehension while overestimating the rewards of crime. Given their inflated view of the benefits of crime, coupled with a seeming disregard of the risks of apprehension and punishment, it is unlikely a three-strikes policy can have a measurable deterrent effect on the crime rate. Even if such a policy could reduce the number of career offenders on the street, the drain in economic resources that might have gone for education and social welfare ensures that a new generation of young criminals will fill the offending shoes of their incarcerated brethren.

Critical Thinking

Is a policy that calls for spending billions on incarceration throwing money into the wind? Why or why not? After all, the number of people in prison already exceeds 1 million, and little conclusive evidence shows that incarceration alone can reduce crime rates. Might the funds earmarked for prison construction be used elsewhere with greater effect? Explain.

A large portion of the prison population consists of drug offenders. Although the number of people incarcerated for violent and property crimes has actually decreased in recent years, the number of incarcerated drug offenders has skyrocketed. Are the nation's interests best served by giving a life sentence to someone convicted of their third drug-trafficking charge, even if the crime involves selling a small amount of cocaine? Explain.

InfoTrac College Edition Research

To learn more about three-strikes laws, read

Kelly McMurry, "Three-Strikes Laws Proving More Show Than Go," *Trial* 33 (1997): 12.

Chi Chi Sileo, "Are Three-Strikes Laws Handcuffing The Courts?" *Insight on the News* 11 (1995): 14.

SOURCES: Paula M. Ditton and Doris James Wilson, *Truth in Sentencing in State Prisons* (Washington, D.C.: Bureau of Justice Statistics, 1999); Public Law No. 103-322, 108; "California Supreme Court Undercuts Three-Strikes Law," *Criminal Justice Newsletter,* 1 July 1996, 2; "Three-Strikes Laws Rarely Used, Except California's, Study Finds," *Criminal Justice Newsletter,* 17 September 1996, 4; "California Passes a Tough Three-Strikes-You're-Out Law," *Criminal Justice Newsletter,* 4 April 1993, 6; Rand Research Brief, *California's New Three-Strikes Law: Benefits, Costs and Alternatives* (Santa Monica, Calif.: Rand Corp., 1994); Marc Mauer, testimony before the U.S. Congress House Judiciary Committee on "Three Strikes and You're Out," 1 March 1994 (Washington, D.C.: The Sentencing Project, 1994); Lois Forer, *A Rage to Punish: The Unintended Consequences of Mandatory Sentencing* (New York: Norton, 1994).

exhibit 11.2

Findings from the National Survey of State and Federal Courts: How Are People Sentenced?

- 1996 was the first year state and federal courts convicted a combined total of over 1 million adults of felonies — state courts convicted 997,970 adults, and federal courts convicted 43,839 adults (accounting for 4% of the national total).
- In 1996, 69% of all convicted felons were sentenced to a period of confinement — 38% to state prisons and 31% to local jails. Jail sentences are for short-term confinement (usually for a year or less) in a county or city facility, and prison sentences are for long-term confinement (usually for over a year) in a state facility.
- State courts sentenced 38% of convicted felons to a state prison, 31% to a local jail, and 31% to straight probation with no jail or prison time to serve.
- Felons sentenced to a state prison in 1996 had an average sentence of five years but were likely to serve almost half (45%) of that sentence — or just over two years — before release, assuming that 1996 release policies continue in effect.
- The average sentence to local jail was six months. The average probation sentence was about three and one-half years.
- Besides being sentenced to incarceration or probation, 32% or more of convicted felons also were ordered to pay a fine, pay victim restitution, receive treatment, perform community service, or comply with some other additional penalty. A fine was imposed on at least 20% of convicted felons.

SOURCE: Jodi M. Brown and Patrick A. Langan, *Felony Sentences in the United States, 1996* (Washington, D.C.: Bureau of Justice Statistics, 1999).

Another national survey of sentencing practices that covered a wider sample of state and federal courts found similar results (Exhibit 11.2). As Table 11.1 shows, the average prison sentence is about three years, with violent crimes averaging a little more than six years and drug offenses a little more than two years. About one-third of all felons receive a probationary sentence.

The Sentencing Project has news publications and a search engine. Go to: www.sentencingproject.org/

What Factors Affect Sentencing?

What factors influence judges when they decide on criminal sentences? Crime seriousness and the offender's prior record are certainly considered. State sentencing codes usually include various factors that can legitimately influence the length of prison sentences, including the following:

- The severity of the offense
- The offender's prior criminal record
- Whether the offender used violence
- Whether the offender used weapons
- Whether the crime was committed for money

Research does in fact show a strong correlation between these legal variables and the type and length of sentence received. For example, judges seem less willing to use discretion in cases involving the most serious criminal charges such as terrorism, while employing greater control in low-severity cases.[36]

Table 11.1
Lengths of Felony Sentences Imposed by State Courts

Most Serious Conviction Offense	Average Maximum Sentence Length (in months) for Felons Sentenced To			
	Total	**Prison**	**Jail**	**Probation**
All offenses	38	62	6	41
Violent offenses	78	105	7	48
Property offenses	30	49	6	40
Drug offenses	28	51	6	42
Weapons offenses	29	45	5	35
Other offenses	24	42	6	40

NOTE: Means exclude sentences to death or to life in prison. Sentence-length data were available for 997,906 incarceration and probation sentences.

SOURCE: Jodi M. Brown and Patrick A. Langan, *Felony Sentences in the United States, 1996* (Washington, D.C.: Bureau of Justice Statistics, 1999).

Besides these legally appropriate factors, sentencing experts suspect that judges may also be influenced by the defendant's age, race, gender, and income. Considerations of such variables would be a direct violation of constitutional due process and equal protection, as well as of federal statutes, such as the Civil Rights Act. Limiting judicial bias is one of the reasons that states have adopted determinate and mandatory sentencing statutes. Do extralegal factors actually influence judges when they make sentencing decisions?

SOCIAL CLASS Evidence supports an association between social class and sentencing outcomes: Members of the lower class may expect to get longer prison sentences than more affluent defendants. One reason is that poor defendants may be unable to obtain quality legal representation or to make bail, factors that influence sentencing.[37] Racial status may also influence the association between incomes and sentence length. At least in some jurisdictions, minorities receive longer sentences than Caucasians if they are currently indigent or unemployed. Judges may possibly view their status as "social dynamite," considering them more dangerous and likely to recidivate than white offenders.[38]

Not all research efforts have found a consistent class–crime relationship, however, and the relationship may be more robust for some crime patterns than others.[39]

chivalry hypothesis
The view that the low female crime and delinquency rates are a reflection of the leniency with which police treat female offenders.

GENDER Does a defendant's gender influence how he or she is sentenced? Some theorists believe that women benefit from sentence disparity because the criminal justice system is dominated by men who have a paternalistic or protective attitude toward women; this is referred to as the **chivalry hypothesis.** Others argue that female criminals can be the victim of bias because their behavior violates what men believe is "proper" female behavior.[40]

Most research indicates that women receive more favorable outcomes the further they go in the criminal justice system: They are more likely to receive preferential treatment from a judge at sentencing than they are from the police officer making the arrest or the prosecutor seeking the indictment.[41] Favoritism crosses both racial and ethnic lines, benefiting African-American, white, and Hispanic women.[42] Gender bias may be present because judges perceive women as better risks than men. Women have been granted more lenient pretrial release conditions and lower bail amounts than men; women are also more likely to spend less time in pretrial detention.[43]

AGE Another extralegal factor that may play a role in sentencing is age. Judges may be more lenient with elderly defendants and more punitive toward younger ones.[44] Although sentencing leniency may be a result of judges' perception that the elderly pose little risk to society, such practices are a violation of the civil rights of younger defendants.[45] On the other hand, judges may also wish to protect the youngest defendants, sparing them the pains of a prison experience.[46]

victim impact statement
A postconviction statement by the victim of crime that may be used to guide sentencing decisions.

VICTIM CHARACTERISTICS Victim characteristics may also influence sentencing. They may be asked to make a **victim impact statement** before the sentencing judge. This gives the victim an opportunity to tell of their experiences and describe their ordeal; in the case of a murder trial, the surviving family can recount the effect the crime has had on their lives and well-being.[47] The effect of victim/witness statements on sentencing has been the topic of some debate. Some research finds that victim statements result in a higher rate of incarceration, but other efforts find that victim/witness statements are insignificant.[48]

A victim's personal characteristics may influence sentencing. Sentences may be reduced when victims have "negative" personal characteristics or qualities. For example, rapists whose victims are described as prostitutes or substance abusers or who have engaged in risky behaviors, such as hitchhiking or going to bars alone, receive much shorter sentences than those who assault women without these negative characteristics.[49]

RACE No issue concerning personal factors in sentencing is more important than the suspicion that race influences sentencing outcomes. Racial disparity in sentencing has been suspected because a disproportionate number of African-American inmates are in state prisons and on death row. The war on drugs has been centered in African-American communities, and politically motivated punitive sentencing policies aimed at crack cocaine have had a devastating effect on young African-American men. If, charges Michael Tonry, such punitive measures are allowed to continue or are even expanded, an entire cohort of young African Americans may be placed in jeopardy.[50] Because this issue is so important, it is the focus of the Race, Culture, and Gender feature on pages 346–347.

CAPITAL PUNISHMENT

The most severe sentence used in the United States is capital punishment, or execution. More than 14,500 confirmed executions have been carried out in America under civil authority, starting with the execution of Captain George Kendall in 1608. Most of these executions were for murder and rape. However, federal, state, and military laws have conferred the death penalty for other crimes, including robbery, kidnapping, treason (offenses against the federal government), espionage, and desertion from military service.

In recent years, the U.S. Supreme Court has limited the death penalty to first-degree murder and only then when aggravating circumstances, such as murder for profit or murder using extreme cruelty, are present.[51] The federal government still has provisions for granting the death penalty for espionage by a member of the armed forces, treason, and killing during a criminal conspiracy, such as drug trafficking. Some states still have laws assessing capital punishment for such crimes as aircraft piracy, ransom kidnapping, and the aggravated rape of a child, but it remains to be seen whether the courts will allow criminals to be executed today for any crime less than aggravated first-degree murder.

Today, the death penalty for murder is used in thirty-eight states and by the federal government with the approval of about 75 percent of the population. After many years of abolition, New York reinstated the use of the death penalty in 1995 and expanded its use to cover numerous acts, including serial murder, contract killing, and the use of torture.[52] There are currently more than thirty-three hun-

Timothy McVeigh is escorted to his cell after his trial in the Oklahoma City terrorist bombing. Does he deserve to die for his crime? If a calculating killer such as McVeigh, who killed more than one hundred innocent people, does not deserve to die, who does?

dred people on death row. Around seventy-five people are now executed each year, most having served ten years on death row before their execution.[53] As of 1999 lethal injection was the predominant method of death, though a number of states maintain the gas chamber and electric chair. In 1999 the U.S. Supreme Court refused to hear a case concerning Florida's use of the electric chair as the sole means of execution. Even though the chair has malfunctioned several times, sending up smoke and flames, the Court refused to consider whether this amounted to cruel and unusual punishment. Of the thirty-eight death penalty states, only Alabama, Georgia, Nebraska, and Florida still use the electric chair as the sole means of execution.[54] Although the death penalty is generally approved of in the United States, it fairs less well abroad. See the Race, Culture, and Gender feature on page 348.

No issue in the criminal justice system is more controversial or emotional than the implementation of the death penalty. Opponents and proponents have formulated a number of powerful arguments in support of their positions; these arguments are reviewed in the following sections.

Arguments for the Death Penalty

Let's look at some of the most common arguments for retaining the death penalty in the United States.

INCAPACITATION Supporters argue that death is the "ultimate incapacitation" and the only one that can ensure that convicted killers can never be pardoned, be paroled, or escape. Most states that do not have capital punishment provide the sentence of "life in prison without the chance of parole." However, forty-eight states grant their chief executive the right to grant clemency and commute a life sentence and may give "lifers" eligibility for various furlough and release programs.

Death penalty advocates believe that the potential for recidivism is a serious enough threat to require that murderers be denied further access to the public. Stephen Markman and Paul Cassell analyzed the records of 52,000 state prison inmates serving time for murder and found that 810 had previously been convicted of homicide and that these recidivists had killed 821 people following their

Race, Culture, and Gender

XYXYXYXY
XYXYXYXY
XYXYXYXY

RACE AND SENTENCING

Although critics of American race relations may think otherwise, research on sentencing has failed to show a definitive pattern of racial discrimination. Some works do indicate that a defendant's race has a direct impact on sentencing outcomes, but other efforts show that racial influence on sentencing is less clear-cut than anticipated. The disproportionate number of minority inmates may possibly be a result of crime-and-arrest patterns, not racial bias by judges when they hand out criminal sentences. Racial and ethnic minorities commit more crime, the argument goes, and therefore they are more likely to wind up in prison.

Despite this inconclusive evidence, racial disparity in sentencing has been suspected because a disproportionate number of minority inmates are in state prisons and on death row. Research shows that minority defendants suffer discrimination in a variety of court actions: They are more likely to be detained before trial than whites and, upon conviction, are more likely to receive jail sentences rather than fines. Prosecutors are less likely to divert minorities from the legal system than whites who commit the same crimes; minorities are less likely to win appeals than white appellants.

The relationship between race and sentencing is difficult to establish because their association may not be linear: Although minority defendants may be punished more severely for some crimes and under some circumstances, they are treated more leniently for others. For example, James Nelson studied misdemeanant sentencing in New York state and found that minorities were given more lenient sentences than whites if they had no prior arrest record; in contrast, African Americans with a prior arrest record received harsher sentences than whites with similar criminal backgrounds. Alexander Alvarez and Ronet Bachman's study of sentencing in Arizona found that Native Americans received harsher sentences for robbery and burglary and whites were punished more harshly for homicide.

Sociologist Darnell Hawkins explains this phenomenon as a matter of "appropriateness":

> Certain crime types are considered less "appropriate" for blacks than for whites. Blacks who are charged with committing these offenses will be treated more severely than blacks who commit crimes that are considered more "appropriate." Included in the former category are various white collar offenses and crimes against political and social structures of authority. The latter groups of offenses would include various forms of victimless crimes associated with lower social status (e.g., prostitution, minor drug use, or drunkenness). This may also include various crimes against the person, especially those involving black victims.

Race may have an impact on sentencing because some race-specific crimes are punished more harshly than others. African Americans receive longer sentences for drug crimes than do whites because (1) they are more likely to be arrested for crack cocaine possession and sales and (2) crack cocaine dealing is more severely punished by state and federal laws than other drug crimes. Because whites are more likely to use marijuana and methamphetamines, prosecutors are more willing to plea-bargain and offer shorter jail terms.

Racial bias has also been linked to the victim–offender status. Minority defendants are sanctioned more severely if their victim is white than if their target is a fellow minority group member. Judges may base sentencing decisions on the race of the victim, not the race of the defendant. For example, Charles Crawford and his associates found that African-American defendants are more likely to be prosecuted under habitual offender statutes if they commit crimes where there is a greater likelihood of a white victim (e.g., larceny and burglary) than if they commit violent crimes that are largely intraracial. Where there is a perceived "racial threat" due to interracial crime, punishments are enhanced.

System Effects

Sentencing disparity may also reflect race-based differences in criminal justice practices and policies associated with sentencing outcome. Probation presentence reports may favor white over minority defendants, causing judges to award whites probation more often than minorities. Defendants who can afford bail receive more lenient sentences than those who remain in pretrial detention; minority defendants are less likely to make bail because they earn less on average. Sentencing outcome is also affected by the defendant's ability to afford a private attorney and put on a vigorous legal defense that makes use of high-paid expert witnesses. These factors place the poor and minority group members at a disadvantage in the sen-

first convictions.[55] More than 250 inmates on death row today had prior homicide convictions; if they had been executed for their first offense, 250 innocent people would still be alive.[56]

DETERRENT Proponents of capital punishment argue that executions serve as a strong deterrent for serious crimes. Although capital punishment would probably not deter the few mentally unstable criminals, it could have an effect on the cold, calculating murderer, such as the hired killer or someone who kills

tencing process and result in sentencing disparity. Finally, although considerations of prior record may be legitimate in forming sentencing decisions, evidence shows that minorities are more likely to have prior records because of organizational and individual bias on the part of the police.

Jurisdictional Differences

Significant differences also exist in the racial influence on sentencing between different states. Some states exhibit little racial bias, and others demonstrate a great deal. Studies that use multiple-state data in their analyses may therefore miss the effects of race on sentencing within particular states.

In a thorough review of sentencing disparity, Samuel Walker and his associates identify what they call *contextual discrimination.* This term refers to the practices of judges in some jurisdictions to impose harsher sentences on African Americans who, for example, victimize whites or to give racial minorities prison sentences in "borderline" cases for which whites get probation. Sentencing disparity may also be influenced by regional sentencing practices: The greatest percentage of the African-American population lives in the South, where judges are more punitive to *all* defendants, regardless of race. According to their view, racism is very subtle and hard to detect but still exerts an influence in the court setting.

Are Sentencing Practices Changing?

If in fact racial discrepancies exist, new sentencing laws featuring determinate and mandatory sentences may be helping reduce disparity. For example, Jon'a Meyer and Tara Gray found that jurisdictions in California that use mandatory sentences for such crimes as drunk driving also show little racial disparity in sentences between whites and minority group members. Similarly, a national survey of sentencing practices conducted by the Bureau of Justice Statistics found that, although white defendants are somewhat more likely to receive probation and other nonincarceration sentences than black defendants (34% vs. 31%), there was little racial disparity in the length of prison sentences.

Critical Thinking

Do you think that sentences should be influenced by the fact that one ethnic or racial group is more likely to commit that crime? For example, critics have called for change in the way federal sentencing guidelines are designed, asking that the provisions that punish crack cocaine possession more heavily than powdered cocaine possession be repealed because African Americans are more likely to use crack and whites powdered cocaine. Do you approve of such a change? Explain.

InfoTrac College Edition Research

The issue of race and justice is of great concern to criminal justice policymakers. To review this issue, read

> Carolyn Wolpert, "Considering Race and Crime: Distilling Non-Partisan Policy from Opposing Theories," *American Criminal Law Review* 36 (1999): 265.

SOURCES: Travis Pratt, "Race and Sentencing: A Meta-Analysis of Conflicting Empirical Research Results," *Journal of Criminal Justice* 26 (1998): 513–25; Charles Crawford, Ted Chiricos, and Gary Kleck, "Race, Racial Threat, and Sentencing of Habitual Offenders," *Criminology* 36 (1998): 481–511; Jon'a Meyer and Tara Gray, "Drunk Drivers in the Courts: Legal and Extra-Legal Factors Affecting Pleas and Sentences," *Journal of Criminal Justice* 25 (1997): 155–63; Alexander Alvarez and Ronet Bachman, "American Indians and Sentencing Disparity: An Arizona Test," *Journal of Criminal Justice* 24 (1996): 549–61; Carole Wolff Barnes and Rodney Kingsnorth, "Race, Drug, and Criminal Sentencing: Hidden Effects of the Criminal Law," *Journal of Criminal Justice* 24 (1996): 39–55; Samuel Walker, Cassia Spohn, and Miriam DeLone, *The Color of Justice, Race, Ethnicity, and Crime in America* (Belmont, Calif.: Wadsworth, 1996), 145–46. Jo Dixon, "The Organizational Context of Sentencing," *American Journal of Sociology* 100 (1995):1157–98; Celesta Albonetti and John Hepburn, "Prosecutorial Discretion to Defer Criminalization: The Effects of Defendant's Ascribed and Achieved Status Characteristics," *Journal of Quantitative Criminology* 12 (1996): 63–81; Jimmy Williams, "Race of Appellant, Sentencing Guidelines, and Decision Making in Criminal Appeals: A Research Note," *Journal of Criminal Justice* 23 (1995); Joan Petersilia, *Racial Disparities in the Criminal Justice System* (Santa Monica, Calif.: Rand Corp., 1983); Darnell Hawkins, "Race, Crime Type and Imprisonment," *Justice Quarterly* 3 (1986): 251–69; James Nelson, "A Dollar or a Day: Sentencing Misdemeanants in New York State," *Journal of Research in Crime and Delinquency* 31 (1994): 183–201; Robert Crutchfield, George Bridges, and Susan Pitchford, "Analytical and Aggregation Biases in Analyses of Imprisonment: Reconciling Discrepancies in Studies of Racial Disparity," *Journal of Research in Crime and Delinquency* 31 (1994): 166–82.

Race, Culture, and Gender

XYXYXYXY
XYXYXYXY
XYXYXYXY

THE INTERNATIONAL USE OF THE DEATH PENALTY

The United States is not alone in using the death penalty. In Afghanistan in 1998, at least five men, convicted of sodomy by Islamic Shari'a courts, were placed next to walls and then buried under the rubble as the walls were broken over them. Two of the men did not die until the next day in a hospital. One man survived. In the same country, people can also be executed by being stoned, hanged from cranes, or having their throats slit. Nations that operate under Islamic law, such as Saudi Arabia, routinely employ the death penalty and publicly execute convicted criminals. In 1997 the Saudi government beheaded more than 100 criminals, including more than 50 drug smugglers; in 1996, 68 people were beheaded and 192 in 1995.

What is the state of capital punishment around the world? According to Amnesty International, the nonprofit human rights organization, by the end of 1998, sixty-seven countries had abolished the death penalty for all offenses and fourteen countries for all but exceptional offenses, such as wartime crimes. At least twenty-four countries that retained the death penalty in law were considered abolitionist in practice, in that they had not executed anyone for at least ten years or had made an international commitment not to carry out executions. Some countries reduced the scope of the death penalty. For example, in Tajikistan the number of crimes carrying a possible death sentence was reduced in 1998 from forty-four to fifteen.

Although the abolitionist movement is significant, over ninety countries still retain the death penalty; during 1998 at least 1,625 prisoners were executed in thirty-seven countries, and 3,899 people were sentenced to death in seventy-eight countries. These figures include only cases known to Amnesty International; the true figures are certainly higher.

Each year the vast majority of executions worldwide are carried out in a tiny handful of countries. In 1998 more than 80 percent of all known executions took place in China, the Democratic Republic of the Congo (DRC), the United States, and Iran. In China, 1,067 people were known to have been executed, although the true figure was believed to be much higher. More than 100 executions were carried out in the DRC. Sixty-eight people were executed in the United States. In Iran, 66 executions were reported, but the total was believed to have been higher. In addition, hundreds of executions were reported in Iraq, although there is no way to confirm reports.

Opposition to executions is growing in some areas, but in others, such as the Caribbean, the public is demanding increased use of the death penalty. In 1998 the governments of Jamaica, Guyana, and Barbados all expressed interest in speeding the use of the death penalty. More than 250 prisoners are currently on death row across the English-speaking Caribbean. Trinidad tops the list, with 107 prisoners convicted of capital crimes and awaiting execution; followed by Jamaica, with 47; and the Bahamas, with an estimated 40. In July 1998 the twin-island federation of St. Kitts and Nevis executed its first prisoner since becoming independent in 1983. Jamaica has ordered its first execution in a decade, that of a twenty-nine-year-old hitchhiker convicted of strangling a business executive who gave him a ride. Even Japan, a country that prides itself on low crime rates and nonpunitive forms of correction, executed 3 men in 1998; at the same time, Taiwan increased its executions, and at least 32 people were known to have been executed.

Executions of Juveniles

International human rights treaties prohibit anyone under eighteen years old at the time of the crime being sentenced to death. The International Covenant on Civil and Political Rights, the American Convention on Human Rights, and the U.N. Convention on the Rights of the Child all have provisions to this effect. More than one hundred countries have laws specifically excluding the execution of juvenile offenders or may be presumed to exclude such executions by being parties to one or another of the above treaties. A small number of countries, however, continue to execute juvenile offenders. Five countries since 1990 are known to have executed prisoners who were under eighteen years old at the time of the crime — Iran, Pakistan, Saudi Arabia, the United States, and Yemen. However, the United States leads the world in juvenile executions. Since 1976 there have been twelve executions of those who were under eighteen years old at the time of their crime, with nine of the twelve occurring in the 1990s. Seventy-two additional juveniles are on death row awaiting execution.

Critical Thinking

The movement toward abolition of the death penalty in the United States is encouraged by the fact that so many nations have abandoned it. Should we model our own system of punishments after other nations, or is our crime problem so unique that it requires the use of capital punishment? Explain.

InfoTrac College Edition Research

The death penalty remains a controversial issue around the world. To learn more, read

Stefanie Grant, "A Dialogue of the Deaf? New International Attitudes and the Death Penalty in America," *Criminal Justice Ethics* 17 (1998): 19.

Caroline Moorehead, "Tinkering with Death," *World Press Review* 42 (1995): 38.

SOURCES: Amnesty International USA, *Annual Report 1999: The Death Penalty: An Affront to Our Humanity* (Washington, D.C.: Amnesty International, 1999); Larry Rohter, "In Caribbean, Support Growing for Death Penalty," *New York Times*, 4 October 1998; Associated Press, "Chechen Pair Executed in Public," *Boston Globe*, 19 September 1997, 9; Reuters, "Saudi Beheadings Over 100 for 1997," *Boston Globe*, 28 September 1997, A29.

for profit; the fear of death may also convince felons not to risk using handguns during armed robberies.

Proponents argue that the deterrent effect of an execution can produce a substantial decline in the murder rate.[57] In one analysis of sixteen well-publicized executions, Steven Stack found that they may have saved 480 lives by immediately deterring potential murderers.[58] In a more recent survey, he concluded that well-publicized executions of criminals in California reduced the homicide rate 12 percent during the month of the execution.[59]

MORALLY CORRECT Advocates of capital punishment justify its use on the grounds that it is morally correct because it is mentioned in the Bible and other religious works. Although the U.S. Constitution forbids "cruel and unusual punishments," this prohibition would not include the death penalty since capital punishment was widely used at the time the Constitution was drafted. The "original intent" of the Founding Fathers was to allow the states to use the death penalty; capital punishment may be cruel, but it is not unusual.

The death penalty is morally correct because it provides the greatest justice for the victim and helps alleviate the psychic pain of the victim's family and friends. It has even been accepted by criminal justice experts who consider themselves *humanists,* people who are concerned with the value and dignity of human beings. As the noted humanist David Friedrichs argues, a civilized society has no choice but to hold responsible those who commit horrendous crimes. The death penalty makes a moral statement: There is behavior that is so unacceptable to a community of human beings that one who engages in such behavior forfeits his right to live.[60]

PROPORTIONAL Putting dangerous criminals to death also conforms to the requirement that the punishment must be proportional to the seriousness of the crime. Since we use a system of escalating punishments, it follows that the most serious punishment should be used to sanction the most serious crime. Before the brutality of the death penalty is considered, the cruelty with which the victim was treated should not be forgotten.

REFLECTS PUBLIC OPINION Those who favor capital punishment charge that a majority of the public believes that criminals who kill innocent victims should forfeit their own lives. Public opinion polls show that up to 80 percent of the public favors the death penalty, almost double the percentage of twenty years ago.[61] Public approval is based on the rational belief that the death penalty is an important instrument of social control, can deter crime, and is less costly than maintaining a murderer in prison for life.[62] Alexis Durham and his associates found that the 80 percent approval rating may actually be low, that almost everyone (95%) would give criminals the death penalty under some circumstances, and the most heinous crimes are those for which the public is most likely to approve capital punishment.[63]

UNLIKELY CHANCE OF ERROR The many legal controls and appeals currently in use make it almost impossible for an innocent person to be executed or for the death penalty to be used in a racist or capricious manner. Although some unfortunate mistakes may have been made in the past, the current system makes it virtually impossible to execute an innocent person. Federal courts closely scrutinize all death penalty cases and rule for the defendant in an estimated 60 percent to 70 percent of the appeals. Such judicial care should ensure that only those who are both truly guilty and deserving of death are executed.

In sum, those who favor the death penalty find it to be traditional punishment for serious crimes, one that can help prevent criminality; is in keeping with the traditional moral values of fairness and equity; and is highly favored by the public.

Arguments against the Death Penalty

Arguments for the death penalty are matched by those that support its abolition.

A general information center on the death penalty can be found at: www.essential.org/dpic/ **If you want information on the National Association of Sentencing Advocates, go to:** www.sproject.com/nasa.htm

POSSIBILITY OF ERROR Critics of the death penalty believe capital punishment has no place in a mature democratic society.[64] They point to the finality of the act and the real possibility that innocent persons can be executed. Examples of people wrongfully convicted of murder abound. Critics point to miscarriages of justice such as the case of Rolando Cruz and Alejandro Hernandez who, wrongfully convicted of murder, were released in 1995 after spending more than a decade on death row in the Illinois prison system; three former prosecutors and four deputy sheriffs who worked on the case were charged with fabricating evidence against the pair.[65] Cruz and Hernandez are certainly not alone. Jeffrey Blake went to prison for a double murder in 1991 and spent seven years behind bars before his conviction was overturned in 1998. It seems that the prosecution's star witness conceded that he lied on the stand, forcing Blake to spend a quarter of his life in prison for a crime he did not commit.[66] These wrongful convictions would have been even more tragic if they had been executed for their alleged crimes. A congressional report cited forty-eight cases in the past two decades in which people who served time on death row were released because of new evidence proving their innocence; one Maryland man served nine years on death row before DNA testing proved that he could not have committed the crime.[67] These findings show that even with the best intentions there is grave risk that an innocent person can be executed.[68]

According to research by Michael Radelet and Hugo Bedeau, there have been about 350 wrongful murder convictions this century, of which 23 led to executions. They estimate that about three death sentences are returned every two years in cases where the defendant has been falsely accused. More than half the errors stem from perjured testimony, false identifications, coerced confessions, and suppression of evidence. In addition to the 23 who were executed, 128 of the falsely convicted served more than six years in prison, 39 served more than sixteen years in confinement, and 8 died while serving their sentence.[69] It is their view that even though the system attempts to be especially cautious in capital cases, unacceptable mistakes can occur. Although there is careful review of death penalty sentences, relatively few stays of execution are actually granted (about two out of fifty); obviously, there is room for judicial error.[70]

UNFAIR USE OF DISCRETION Critics also frown on the tremendous discretion used in seeking the death penalty and the arbitrary manner in which it is imposed. Of the approximately 10,000 persons convicted each year on homicide charges, only 250 to 300 are sentenced to death, while an equal number receive a sentence of probation or community supervision only.[71] It is true that many convicted murderers do not commit first-degree murder and therefore are ineligible for execution, but it is also likely that many serious criminals who could have received the death penalty are not sentenced to death because of prosecutorial discretion. Some escape death by cooperating or giving testimony against their partners in the crime. A person who commits a particularly heinous crime and knows full well that she will receive the death penalty if convicted may be the one most likely to plea-bargain to avoid capital punishment. Is it fair to spare the life of a dangerous killer who cooperates with the prosecutor while executing another who does not?

VICIOUS CRIMINALS OFTEN GO FREE Some vicious criminals who grievously injure victims during murder attempts are spared the death penalty because a physician's skill saved the victim. Some notable cases come to mind. Lawrence Singleton used an axe to cut off the arms of a woman he raped, yet he served only eight years in prison because the victim's life was saved by prompt

Those who oppose the death penalty argue that the chance of error is too great to risk an innocent person's life. These five men were all death row inmates who were later released when new evidence exonerated them.

medical care (after being released from prison, Singleton killed a female companion in 1997). "David," a boy severely burned in a murder attempt, lives in fear because his assailant, his father, Charles Rothenberg, was paroled from prison after serving a short sentence.[72] Although these horrific crimes received national attention and the intent to kill the victim was present, the death penalty could not be applied because of the availability of effective medical treatment. Areas that have superior medical resources actually have lower murder rates than less well-equipped areas; for example, ambulance response time can reduce the death rate by expeditiously transporting victims to an appropriate treatment center.[73] It makes little sense to punish someone for an impulsive murder while sparing the life of those who intentionally maim and torture victims who happen by chance to live because of prompt medical care.

MISPLACED VENGEANCE Although critics acknowledge that the general public approves of the death penalty, they maintain that prevailing attitudes reflect a primitive desire for revenge and not "just desert." Public acceptance of capital punishment has been compared to the approval of human sacrifices practiced by the Aztecs in Mexico five hundred years ago.[74] It is ironic that many death penalty advocates also oppose abortion on the grounds that it is the taking of human life.[75] The desire to be vengeful and punitive outweighs their concern about taking life.

Even if the majority of the general public favors the death penalty, support has been associated with prejudice against racial minorities and the approval of revenge as a rationale for punishment.[76] Public support is not as strong as death penalty advocates believe: When surveys ask about a choice of punishments, such as life without parole, support for the death penalty declines from 80 percent to 50 percent.[77] Public opinion is influenced by such factors as the personal characteristics of the offender and the circumstances of the offense. Therefore, the public does not support death in many cases of first-degree murder.[78] It is possible that politicians favor the death penalty in the mistaken belief that the public favors such harsh punishment for criminal offenders.[79]

NO DETERRENT EFFECT Those opposed to the death penalty also find little merit in the argument that capital punishment deters crime. They charge that insufficient evidence exists that the threat of a death sentence can convince potential murderers to forgo their criminal activity. Most murders involve people who knew each other, very often friends and family members. Since murderers are often under the influence of alcohol or drugs or are suffering severe psychological turmoil, no penalty will likely be a deterrent. Most research concludes that the death penalty is not an effective deterrent.[80]

HOPE OF REHABILITATION The death sentence also rules out any hope of offender rehabilitation. There is evidence that convicted killers actually make good parole risks; convicted murderers are actually model inmates and, once released, commit fewer crimes than other parolees.

RACIAL BIAS One of the most compelling arguments against the use of the death penalty is that it is employed in a racially discriminatory fashion. Evidence indicates that prosecutors are more likely to recommend the death sentence for African Americans who kill white victims than they are in any other racial combination of victim and criminal — for example, whites who kill blacks.[81] It is not surprising then that, since the death penalty was first instituted in the United States, a disproportionate number of minorities have been executed. Charges of racial bias are supported by the disproportionate numbers of African Americans who have received the death sentence, are currently on death row, and who have been executed (53.5% of all executions). Racism was particularly blatant when the death penalty was invoked in rape cases: Of those receiving the death penalty for rape, 90 percent in the South and 63 percent in the North and West were black.[82] Today, about 40 percent of the inmates on death row are African Americans, a number disproportionate to the minority representation in the population.

White criminals arrested for homicide actually have a slightly greater chance of getting the death penalty than blacks do, and a majority of murderers executed since 1980 have also been white.[83] Does this statistical anomaly mean that discrimination in the use of the death penalty has either ended or that it never actually existed? The answer may be that simply calculating the relative proportion of each racial group sentenced to death may not tell the whole story. A number of researchers have found that the death penalty is associated with the race of the victim rather than the race of the offender. In most instances, prosecutors are more likely to ask for the death penalty if the victim was white. The fact that most murders involving a white victim also involve a white attacker (86%) accounts for the higher death sentence rate for white murderers.[84] With few exceptions, the relatively infrequent interracial murder cases involving a black criminal and a white victim (14%) are the most likely to result in the death penalty.[85] In contrast, since 1976 only two white criminals have been executed for murdering a black victim, the most recent being Kermit Smith, who was executed on January 24, 1995, in North Carolina for the kidnap, rape, and murder of a twenty-year-old college cheerleader.[86]

BRUTALITY Abolitionists believe that executions are unnecessarily cruel and inhuman and come at a high moral and social cost. Our society does not punish criminals by subjecting them to the same acts they themselves committed. Rapists are not sexually assaulted, and arsonists do not have their house burned down; why, then, should murderers be killed?

Robert Johnson has described the execution process as a form of torture in which the condemned are first tormented psychologically by being made to feel powerless and alone while on death row; suicide is a constant problem among those on death row.[87] The execution itself is a barbaric affair marked by the

brutalization effect
The belief that capital punishment creates an atmosphere of brutality that enhances, rather than deters, the level of violence in society. The death penalty reinforces the view that violence is an appropriate response to provocations.

smell of burning flesh and stiffened bodies. The executioners suffer from delayed stress reactions, including anxiety and a dehumanized personal identity.

The brutality of the death penalty may actually produce more violence than it prevents — the so-called **brutalization effect.**[88] Executions may increase murder rates because they raise the general violence level in society and because violence-prone people actually identify with the executioner, not with the target of the death penalty. When someone gets in a conflict with such individuals or challenges their authority, they execute them in the same manner the state executes people who violate its rules.[89] The brutalization effect was encountered by John Cochran and his associates when they studied the influence of a well-publicized execution in Oklahoma: After the execution, murders of strangers actually increased by one per month.[9] Follow-up research by William Bailey finds that (1) the brutalization effect extends to other types of murder (e.g., non-stranger murder) and (2) a vicarious brutalization effect may occur in which people in a state that does not practice capital punishment are influenced by news reports of executions in death penalty states.[91]

Because of its brutality, many enlightened nations have abandoned the death penalty with few ill effects. Abolitionists point out that such nations as Denmark and Sweden have long abandoned the death penalty and that 40 percent of the countries with a death penalty have active abolitionist movements.[92] It is ironic that citizens of countries that have eliminated the death penalty sometimes find themselves on death row in the United States. For example, a Paraguayan citizen, Angel Francisco Breard, age 32, was executed on April 14, 1998, in Virginia, for murder and attempted rape, despite a plea from the International Court of Justice that he be spared and intense efforts by the Paraguayan government to stay the execution.[93]

EXPENSE Some people complain that they do not want to support "some killer in prison for thirty years." Abolitionists counter that legal appeals drive the cost of executions far higher than the cost of years of incarceration. If the money spent on the judicial process were invested, the interest would more than pay for the lifetime upkeep of death row inmates. For example, in 1998 there were 508 men and 9 women on death row in California. Because of numerous appeals, the median time between conviction by a jury, sentencing by a judge, and execution averaged fourteen years. The cost of processing appeals is extremely costly, and the annual budget for the state's public defender staff of forty-five lawyers who represent inmates in death cases is $5 million.[94]

At least thirty states now have a sentence of life in prison without parole, and this can more than make up for an execution. Being locked up in a hellish prison without any chance of release (barring a rare executive reprieve) may be a worse punishment than a painless death by lethal injection. If vengeance is the goal, life without parole may eliminate the need for capital punishment.

Legal Issues The constitutionality of the death penalty has been a major concern to both the nation's courts and its concerned social scientists. In 1972 the U.S. Supreme Court in *Furman v. Georgia*[95] decided that the discretionary imposition of the death penalty was cruel and unusual punishment under the Eighth and Fourteenth Amendments of the U.S. Constitution. This case not only questioned whether capital punishment is a more effective deterrent than life imprisonment but also challenged the very existence of the death penalty on the grounds of its brutality and finality. The Supreme Court did not completely rule out the use of capital punishment as a penalty; rather, it objected to the arbitrary and capricious manner in which it was imposed. After *Furman,* many states changed statutes that had allowed jury discretion in imposing the death penalty.

In some states this was accomplished by enacting statutory guidelines for jury decisions; in others the death penalty was made mandatory for certain crimes only. Despite these changes in statutory law, no further executions were carried out while the Court pondered additional cases concerning the death penalty.

Then, in July 1976 the Supreme Court ruled on the constitutionality of five state death penalty statutes. In the first case, *Gregg v. Georgia,*[96] the Court found valid the Georgia statute holding that a finding by the jury of at least one "aggravating circumstance" out of ten is required in pronouncing the death penalty in murder cases. In the *Gregg* case, for example, the jury imposed the death penalty after finding beyond a reasonable doubt two aggravating circumstances: (1) The offender was engaged in the commission of two other capital felonies, and (2) the offender committed the offense of murder for the purpose of receiving money and other financial gains (e.g., an automobile).[97]

In probably one of the most important death penalty cases, *McLesky v. Kemp,* the Court upheld the conviction of a black defendant in Georgia, despite social science evidence that black criminals who kill white victims have a significantly greater chance of receiving the death penalty than white offenders who kill black victims. The Court ruled that the evidence of racial patterns in capital sentencing was not persuasive without a finding of racial bias in the immediate case.[98] Many observers believe that *McLesky* presented the last significant legal obstacle that death penalty advocates had to overcome and that, as a result, capital punishment will be a sentence in the United States for years to come (McLesky was executed in 1991).

Although the Court has generally supported the death penalty, it has also placed some limitations on its use. Rulings have promoted procedural fairness in the capital sentencing process. For example, the Court has limited the death penalty sentence to capital murder cases, ruling that it is not permissible to punish rapists with death.[99] It has prohibited prosecutors from presenting damaging evidence about the defendant's background unless it is directly relevant to the case.[100]

In 1998, attorneys for convicted murderer Karla Faye Tucker filed a last-minute writ of *habeas corpus* in an attempt to save their client from her scheduled execution. To view a copy of this writ, go to www.courttv.com/legaldocs/newsmakers/tucker

The Court has also reinforced the idea that mental and physical conditions such as age, though not excusing criminal behavior, can be considered as mitigating factors in capital sentencing decisions. In *Wilkins v. Missouri* and *Stanford v. Kentucky,* the Court set a limit of 16 years as the age of defendants who could be sentenced to death.[101] (Eight inmates currently on death row committed their crime at age 17 or younger.) These rulings effectively barred the use of capital punishment from minors under the age of 16 who have been waived or transferred from the juvenile to the adult court system.

The Court seems committed to maintaining the death penalty within boundaries of fairness and due process. It has reduced a defendant's ability to reappeal in a capital case by raising claims that were not included in the original legal motion.[102] It now allows victim impact statements to be made and gives prosecutors the right to include such statements in their closing argument, describing how the victims will be missed by their family and friends.[103] A judge now may, when the law allows, ignore a jury's recommendation for leniency and impose the death penalty.[104] These rulings, plus the failure to grant stays in numerous capital cases, underscore the Court's willingness to retain the death sentence.

death-qualified jury
The process during jury selection of removing any juror in a capital case who acknowledges that he or she will not convict knowing that there is a potential for the death penalty being applied. The U.S. Supreme Court has ruled that prosecutors have the right to discharge those jurors who would not consider the death penalty under any circumstances.

Death-Qualified Juries

Death-qualified juries are ones in which any person opposed in concept to capital punishment has been removed during voir dire. Defense attorneys are opposed to death qualification because it bars from serving on juries those citizens who oppose the death penalty and who may be more liberal and less likely to convict defendants. Death qualification creates juries that are nonrepresentative of the 20 percent of the public that opposes capital punishment.

In *Witherspoon v. Illinois* (1968), the Supreme Court upheld the practice of excusing jurors who are opposed to the death penalty.[105] The Court has made it easier to convict people in death penalty cases by ruling that any juror can be excused if his views on capital punishment are deemed by a trial judge to "prevent or substantially impair the performance of their duties."[106] The Court has also ruled that jurors can be removed because of their opposition to the death penalty at the guilt phase of a trial, even though they would not have to consider the issue of capital punishment until a separate sentencing hearing. In *Lockhart v. McCree* (1986), the Court also ruled that removing anti–capital punishment jurors does not violate the Sixth Amendment provision that juries represent a fair cross section of the community, nor does it unfairly tip the scale toward juries who are prone to convict people in capital cases.[107] So, it appears that for the present, prosecutors will be able to excuse jurors who feel that the death penalty is wrong or immoral.

Does the Death Penalty Deter Murder? The key issue in the capital punishment debate is whether it can actually lower the murder rate and save lives. Despite its inherent cruelty, capital punishment might be justified if it proved to be an effective crime deterrent that could save many innocent lives. Abolitionists claim it has no real deterrent value; advocates claim it does. Who is correct?

Considerable empirical research has been carried out on the effectiveness of capital punishment as a deterrent. In particular, studies have tried to discover whether the death sentence serves as a more effective deterrent than life imprisonment for capital crimes such as homicide. Three methods have been used:

- Immediate-impact studies, which calculate the effect a well-publicized execution has on the short-term murder rate
- Time-series analysis, which compares long-term trends in murder and capital punishment rates
- Contiguous-state analysis, which compares murder rates in states that have the death penalty with a similar state that has abolished capital punishment

Using these three methods over a sixty-year period, most researchers have failed to show any deterrent effect of capital punishment.[108] These studies show that murder rates do not seem to rise when a state abolishes capital punishment any more so than they decrease when the death penalty is adopted. The murder rate is also quite similar both in states that use the death penalty and neighboring states that have abolished capital punishment. Finally, little evidence shows that executions can lower the murder rate. For example, a test of the deterrent effect of the death penalty in Texas found no association between the frequency of execution during the years 1984–1997 and murder rates.[109]

Only a few studies have found that the long-term application of capital punishment may actually reduce the murder rate.[110] However, these have been disputed by researchers who have questioned the methodology used and indicate that the deterrent effects the studies uncover are an artifact of the statistical techniques used in the research.[111]

The general consensus among death penalty researchers today is that the threat of capital punishment has little effect on murder rates. It is still unknown why capital punishment fails as a deterrent, but the cause may lie in the nature of homicide. As noted earlier, murder is often a crime of passion involving people who know each other, and many murders are committed by people under the influence of drugs and alcohol — more than 50 percent of all people arrested for murder test positively for drug use. People involved in interpersonal conflict with friends, acquaintances, and family members and who may be under the influence of drugs and alcohol are not likely to be capable of considering the threat of the death penalty.

Murder rates have also been linked to the burdens of poverty and income inequality. Desperate adolescents who get caught up in the cycle of urban violence and become members of criminal groups and gangs may find that their life situation gives them little choice except to engage in violent and deadly behavior; they have few chances to ponder the deterrent impact of the death penalty.

The failure of the "ultimate deterrent" to deter the "ultimate crime" has been used by critics to question the value of capital punishment.

Despite the less than conclusive empirical evidence, many people still hold to the efficacy of the death penalty as a crime deterrent, and recent U.S. Supreme Court decisions seem to justify its use. Of course, even if the death penalty were no greater a deterrent than a life sentence, some people would still advocate its use on the grounds that it is the only way to permanently rid society of dangerous criminals who deserve to die.

SUMMARY

Punishment and sentencing have gone through various phases throughout the history of Western civilization. Initially, punishment was characterized by retribution and the need to fix sentences for convicted offenders. Throughout the middle years of the twentieth century, individualized sentencing was widely accepted, and the concept of rehabilitation was used in sentencing and penal codes. During the 1960s, however, experts began to become disenchanted with rehabilitation and concepts related to treating the individual offender. There was less emphasis on treatment and more on the legal rights of offenders. A number of states returned to the concept of punishment in terms of mandatory and fixed sentences.

Theorists suggest that the philosophy of sentencing has thus changed from a concentration on rehabilitation to a focus on incapacitation and deterrence, where the goal is to achieve equality of punishment and justice in the law and to lock up dangerous criminals for as long as possible.

Sentencing in today's criminal justice system is based on deterrence, incapacitation, and rehabilitation. Traditional dispositions include fines, probation, and incarceration, with probation being the most common choice.

A number of states have developed determinate sentences that eliminate parole and attempt to restrict judicial discretion. Methods for making dispositions more uniform include the institution of sentencing guidelines that create uniform sentences based on offender background and crime characteristics. Despite these changes, most states continue to use indeterminate sentences, which give convicted offenders a short minimum sentence after which they can be released on parole if they are considered "rehabilitated." Jurisdictions that use either determinate or indeterminate sentences allow inmates to be released early on good behavior.

The death penalty continues to be the most controversial sentence, with over half the states reinstituting capital punishment laws since the *Furman v. Georgia* decision of 1972. Although there is little evidence that the death penalty deters murder, supporters still view it as necessary in terms of incapacitation and retribution and cite the public's support for the death penalty and the low chance of error in its application. Opponents point out that mistakes can be made, that capital sentences are apportioned in a racially biased manner, and that the practice is cruel and barbaric. Nonetheless, the courts have generally supported the legality of capital punishment, and it has been used more frequently in recent years.

KEY TERMS

sanction
punishment
felony
wergild
poor laws
penitentiary
general deterrence
incapacitation
recidivism
specific deterrence
blameworthy
just desert
equity
concurrent sentence
consecutive sentence
indeterminate sentence
determinate sentence
mandatory sentence
chivalry hypothesis
victim impact statement
brutalization effect
death-qualified jury

INFOTRAC COLLEGE EDITION EXERCISES

Capital punishment provokes more debate than almost any other criminal justice issue. Some opponents oppose the death penalty on moral and religious grounds. They argue, for example, that humans are not infallible and that the sacredness of human life must be upheld, regardless of the circumstances. To learn more about the religious perspective on capital punishment, read

Kevin Doyle, "No Defense," *U.S. Catholic* 64 (1999): 18.
Patrick Glynn, "Conscience and the Public Square," *Brookings Review* 17 (1999): 24.

Some critics charge that the media are very inconsistent in their coverage of the death penalty. After a heinous crime is committed, mass media coverage of capital crimes goes through a pattern of antagonism against the perpetrator. Then, as the killer is about to be executed, they treat the condemned as a victim. To read more about this view, see Ed Bishop, "Here," *St. Louis Journalism Review* 29 (1999): 4.

How do people from abroad view the use of the death penalty in the United States? Read the following article to find out:
"The Death Penalty: An Outsider's View," *America* 178 (1998): 3.

QUESTIONS

1. Discuss the sentencing dispositions in your jurisdiction. What are the pros and cons of each?
2. Compare the various types of incarceration sentences. What are the similarities and differences? Why are many jurisdictions considering the passage of mandatory sentencing laws?
3. Discuss the issue of capital punishment. In your opinion, does it serve as a deterrent? What new rulings has the U.S. Supreme Court made on the legality of the death penalty?
4. Why does the problem of sentencing disparity exist? Do programs exist that can reduce disparate sentences? If so, what are they? Should all people who commit the same crime receive the same sentence? Explain.
5. Should convicted criminals be released from prison when correctional authorities are convinced they are rehabilitated? Why or why not?

NOTES

1. *Riggs v. California,* No. 98-5021 (1999).
2. Michel Foucault, *Discipline and Punishment* (New York: Vintage Books, 1978).
3. Graeme Newman, *The Punishment Response* (Philadelphia: Lippincott, 1978), 13.
4. Peter Greenwood with Allan Abrahamse, *Selective Incapacitation* (Santa Monica, Calif.: Rand Corp., 1982).
5. Kathleen Auerhahn, "Selective Incapacitation and the Problem of Prediction," *Criminology* 37 (1999): 703–34.
6. Kathleen Daly, "Neither Conflict nor Labeling nor Paternalism Will Suffice: Intersections of Race, Ethnicity, Gender, and Family in Criminal Court Decisions," *Crime and Delinquency* 35 (1989): 136–68.
7. Among the most helpful sources for this section are Benedict Alper, *Prisons Inside-Out* (Cambridge, Mass.: Ballinger, 1974); Gustave de Beaumont and Alexis de Tocqueville, *On the Penitentiary System in the United States and Its Applications in France* (Carbondale: Southern Illinois University Press, 1964); Orlando Lewis, *The Development of American Prisons and Prison Customs, 1776–1845* (Montclair, N.J.: Patterson-Smith, 1967); Leonard Orland, ed., *Justice, Punishment, and Treatment* (New York: Free Press, 1973); J. Goebel, *Felony and Misdemeanor* (Philadelphia: University of Pennsylvania Press, 1976); George Rusche and Otto Kircheimer, *Punishment and Social Structure* (New York: Russell & Russell, 1939); Samuel Walker, *Popular Justice* (New York: Oxford University Press, 1980); Newman, *The Punishment Response;* David Rothman, *Conscience and Convenience* (Boston: Little, Brown, 1980); George Ives, *A History of Penal Methods* (Montclair, N.J.: Patterson-Smith, 1970); Robert Hughes, *The Fatal Shore* (New York: Knopf, 1986); Leon Radzinowicz, *A History of English Criminal Law,* vol. 1 (London: Stevens, 1943), 5.
8. Gerald Wheeler and Rodney Hissong, "Effects of Sanctions on Drunk Drivers: Beyond Incarceration," *Crime and Delinquency* 34 (1988): 29–42; Jeffrey Fagan, "Cessation of Family Violence: Deterrence and Dissuasion," in *Crime and Justice,* vol. 11, ed. Lloyd Ohlin and Michael Tonry (Chicago: University of Chicago Press, 1989), 100–51.
9. Allen Beck and Bernard Shipley, *Recidivism of Prisoners Released in 1983* (Washington, D.C.: Bureau of Justice Statistics, 1989).
10. Charles Logan, *Criminal Justice Performance Measures for Prisons* (Washington, D.C.: Bureau of Justice Statistics, 1993), 3.
11. Alexis Durham, "The Justice Model in Historical Context: Early Law, the Emergence of Science, and the Rise of Incarceration," *Journal of Criminal Justice* 16 (1988): 331–46.
12. Andrew von Hirsh, *Doing Justice: The Choice of Punishments* (New York: Hill and Wang, 1976).
13. Alexis Durham, "Crime Seriousness and Punitive Severity: An Assessment of Social Attitudes," *Justice Quarterly* 5 (1988): 131–53.
14. Shawn Bushway, "The Impact of an Arrest on the Job Stability of Young White American Men," *Journal of Research in Crime and Delinquency* 35 (1998): 454–79.
15. For a review, see Arnulf Kolstad, "Imprisonment as Rehabilitation: Offenders' Assessment of Why It Does Not Work," *Journal of Criminal Justice* 24 (1996): 323–35.
16. Charles Logan and Gerald Gaes, "Meta-Analysis and the Rehabilitation of Punishment," *Justice Quarterly* 10 (1993): 245–64.
17. Richard McCorkle, "Research Note: Punish and Rehabilitate? Public Attitudes Toward Six Common Crimes," *Crime and Delinquency* 39 (1993): 240–52; D. A. Andrews, Ivan Zinger, Robert Hoge, James Bonta, Paul Gendreau, and Francis Cullen, "Does Correctional Treatment Work? A Clinically Relevant and Psychologically Informed Meta-Analysis," *Criminology* 28 (1990): 369–404; Francis Cullen, John Cullen, and John Wozniak, "Is Rehabilitation Dead?

The Myth of the Punitive Public," *Journal of Criminal Justice* 16 (1988): 303–16.

18. Francis Cullen, John Paul Wright, Shayna Brown, Melissa Moon, Michael Blankenship, and Brandon Applegate, "Public Support for Early Intervention Programs: Implications for a Progressive Policy Agenda," *Crime and Delinquency* 44 (1998): 187–204.

19. Jacob Adler, *The Urgings of Conscience: A Theory of Punishment* (Philadelphia: Temple University Press, 1991).

20. Paula Ditton and Doris James Wilson, *Truth in Sentencing in State Prisons* (Washington, D.C.: Bureau of Justice Statistics, 1999).

21. Jo Dixon, "The Organizational Context of Criminal Sentencing," *American Journal of Sociology* 100 (1995): 1157–98.

22. Michael Tonry, *Reconsidering Indeterminate and Structured Sentencing Series: Sentencing and Corrections: Issues for the 21st Century* (Washington, D.C.: National Institute of Justice, 1999).

23. Michael Tonry, *The Fragmentation of Sentencing and Corrections in America* (Washington, D.C.: National Institute of Justice, 1999).

24. Ibid., 11.

25. Michael Tonry, "The Failure of the U.S. Sentencing Commission's Guidelines," *Crime and Delinquency* 39 (1993): 131–49.

26. Terance Miethe and Charles Moore, "Socioeconomic Disparities under Determinate Sentencing Systems: A Comparison of Preguideline and Postguideline Practices in Minnesota," *Criminology* 23 (1985): 337–63.

27. Ibid.

28. Michael Tonry, "Racial Politics, Racial Disparities, and the War on Crime," *Crime and Delinquency* 40 (1994): 475–94.

29. Joan Petersilia and Susan Turner, *Guideline-Based Justice: The Implications for Racial Minorities* (Santa Monica, Calif.: Rand Corp., 1985).

30. Elaine Wolf and Marsha Weissman, "Revising Federal Sentencing Policy: Some Consequences of Expanding Eligibility for Alternative Sanctions," *Crime and Delinquency* 42 (1996): 192–205.

31. Tonry, "The Failure of the U.S. Sentencing Commission's Guidelines," 131.

32. Michael Tonry, *Sentencing Matters* (New York: Oxford University Press, 1996), 5.

33. Henry Scott Wallace, "Mandatory Minimums and the Betrayal of Sentencing Reform: A Legislative Dr. Jekyll and Mr. Hyde," *Federal Probation* 57 (1993): 9–16.

34. "Survey Finds Judges Unhappy with Mandatory Sentencing," *Criminal Justice Newsletter,* 1 October 1993, 3.

35. Brian Reaves and Timothy Hart, *Felony Defendants in Large Urban Counties, 1996: State Court Processing Statistics* (Washington, D.C.: Bureau of Justice Statistics, 1999).

36. Brent Smith and Kelly Damphouse, "Terrorism, Politics, and Punishment: A Test of Structural–Contextual Theory and the Liberation Hypothesis," *Criminology* 36 (1998): 67–92.

37. For a general look at the factors that affect sentencing, see Susan Welch, Cassia Spohn, and John Gruhl, "Convicting and Sentencing Differences among Black, Hispanic, and White Males in Six Localities," *Justice Quarterly* 2 (1985): 67–80.

38. Tracy Nobiling, Cassia Spohn, and Miriam DeLone, "A Tale of Two Counties: Unemployment and Sentence Severity," *Justice Quarterly* 15 (1998): 459–86.

39. Stewart D'Alessio and Lisa Stolzenberg, "Socioeconomic Status and the Sentencing of the Traditional Offender," *Journal of Criminal Justice* 21 (1993): 61–77.

40. Cecilia Saulters-Tubbs, "Prosecutorial and Judicial Treatment of Female Offenders," *Federal Probation* 57 (1993): 37–41.

41. See, generally, Janet Johnston, Thomas Kennedy, and I. Gayle Shuman, "Gender Differences in the Sentencing of Felony Offenders," *Federal Probation* 87 (1987): 49–56; Cassia Spohn and Susan Welch, "The Effect of Prior Record in Sentencing Research: An Examination of the Assumption That Any Measure Is Adequate," *Justice Quarterly* 4 (1987): 286–302; David Willison, "The Effects of Counsel on the Severity of Criminal Sentences: A Statistical Assessment," *Justice System Journal* 9 (1984): 87–101.

42. Cassia Spohn, Miriam DeLone, and Jeffrey Spears, "Race/Ethnicity, Gender and Sentence Severity in Dade County, Florida: An Examination of the Decision to Withhold Adjudication," *Journal of Crime and Justice* 21 (1998): 111–32.

43. Ellen Hochstedler Steury and Nancy Frank, "Gender Bias and Pretrial Release: More Pieces of the Puzzle," *Journal of Criminal Justice* 18 (1990): 417–32.

44. Dean Champion, "Elderly Felons and Sentencing Severity: Interregional Variations in Leniency and Sentencing Trends," *Criminal Justice Review* 12 (1987): 7–15.

45. Darrell Steffensmeier, John Kramer, and Jeffery Ulmer, "Age Differences in Sentencing," *Justice Quarterly* 12 (1995): 583–601.

46. Darrell Steffensmeier, Jeffery Ulmer, and John Kramer, "The Interaction of Race, Gender, and Age in Criminal Sentencing: The Punishment Cost of Being Young, Black, and Male," *Criminology* 36 (1998): 763–98.

47. *Payne v. Tennessee,* 111 S.Ct. 2597, 115 L.Ed.2d 720 (1991).

48. Robert Davis and Barbara Smith, "The Effects of Victim Impact Statements on Sentencing Decisions: A Test in an Urban Setting," *Justice Quarterly* 11 (1994): 453–69; Edna Erez and Pamela Tontodonato, "The Effect of Victim Participation in Sentencing on Sentence Outcome," *Criminology* 28 (1990): 451–74.

49. Rodney Kingsworth, Randall MacIntosh, and Jennifer Wentworth, "Sexual Assault: The Role of Prior Relationship and Victim Characteristics in Case Processing," *Justice Quarterly* 16 (1999): 276–302.

50. Michael Tonry, *Malign Neglect: Race, Crime and Punishment in America* (New York: Oxford University Press, 1995), 105–109.

51. *Coker v. Georgia,* 433 U.S. 584, 97 S.Ct. 2861, 53 L.Ed.2d 982 (1977).

52. "Many State Legislatures Focused on Crime in 1995, Study Finds," *Criminal Justice Newsletter,* 2 January 1996, 2.

53. Tracy Snell, *Capital Punishment, 1997* (Washington, D.C.: Bureau of Justice Statistics, 1998).

54. *Lopez v. Singletary,* No. 98-6065.

55. Stephen Markman and Paul Cassell, "Protecting the Innocent: A Response to the Bedeau–Radelet Study," *Stanford Law Review* 41 (1988): 121–70.

56. Snell, *Capital Punishment,* 2.

57. Stephen Layson, "United States Time-Series Homicide Regressions with Adaptive Expectations," *Bulletin of the New York Academy of Medicine* 62 (1986): 589–619.

58. Steven Stack, "Publicized Executions and Homicide, 1950–1980," *American Sociological Review* 52 (1987): 532–40; for a study challenging Stack's methods, see William Bailey and Ruth Peterson, "Murder and Capital Punishment: A Monthly Time-Series Analysis of Execution Publicity," *American Sociological Review* 54 (1989): 722–43.

59. Steven Stack, "The Effect of Well Publicized Executions on Homicide in California," *Journal of Crime and Justice* 21 (1998): 1–12.

60. David Friedrichs, "Comment — Humanism and the Death Penalty: An Alternative Perspective," *Justice Quarterly* 6 (1989): 197–209.

61. Kathleen Maguire and Ann Pastore, *Sourcebook of Criminal Justice Statistics, 1995* (Washington, D.C.: Government Printing Office, 1996), 183.

62. For an analysis of the formation of public opinion on the death penalty, see Kimberly Cook, "Public Support for the Death Penalty: A Cultural Analysis" (Paper presented at the annual meeting of the American Society of Criminology, San Francisco, November 1991).

63. Alexis Durham, H. Preston Elrod, and Patrick Kinkade, "Public Support to the Death Penalty: Beyond Gallup," *Justice Quarterly* 13 (1996): 705–36.

64. See, generally, Hugo Bedeau, *Death Is Different: Studies in the Morality, Law, and Politics of Capital Punishment* (Boston: Northeastern University Press, 1987); Keith Otterbein, *The Ultimate Coercive Sanction* (New Haven, Conn.: HRAF Press, 1986).

65. "Illinois Ex-Prosecutors Charged with Framing Murder Defendants," *Criminal Justice Newsletter* 28 (1997): 3.

66. Jim Yardley, "Convicted in Murder Case, Man Cleared 7 Years Later," *New York Times,* 29 October 1998.

67. House Subcommittee on Civil and Constitutional Rights, *Innocence and the Death Penalty: Assessing the Danger of*

Mistaken Executions (Washington, D.C.: Government Printing Office, 1993).

68. David Stewart, "Dealing with Death," *American Bar Association Journal* 80 (1994): 53.

69. Michael Radelet and Hugo Bedeau, "Miscarriages of Justice in Potentially Capital Cases," *Stanford Law Review* 40 (1987): 121–81.

70. Stewart, "Dealing with Death."

71. Patrick Langan and John Dawson, *Felony Sentences in State Courts, 1988* (Washington, D.C.: Bureau of Justice Statistics, 1990), 2.

72. "A Victim's Progress," *Newsweek,* 12 June 1989, 5.

73. William Doerner, "The Impact of Medical Resources on Criminally Induced Lethality: A Further Examination," *Criminology* 26 (1988): 171–77.

74. Elizabeth Purdom and J. Anthony Paredes, "Capital Punishment and Human Sacrifice," in *Facing the Death Penalty: Essays on Cruel and Unusual Punishment,* ed. Michael Radelet (Philadelphia: Temple University Press, 1989), 152–53.

75. Kimberly Cook, "A Passion to Punish: Abortion Opponents Who Favor the Death Penalty," *Justice Quarterly* 15 (1998): 329–46.

76. Steven Barkan and Steven Cohn, "Racial Prejudice and Support for the Death Penalty by Whites," *Journal of Research in Crime and Delinquency* 31 (1994): 202–09; Robert Bohm and Ronald Vogel, "A Comparison of Factors Associated with Uninformed and Informed Death Penalty Opinions," *Journal of Criminal Justice* 22 (1994): 125–43.

77. Kathleen Maguire and Ann Pastore, *Sourcebook of Criminal Justice Statistics, 1995* (Washington, D.C.: Government Printing Office, 1996), 183.

78. Gennaro Vito and Thomas Keil, "Elements of Support for Capital Punishment: An Examination of Changing Attitudes," *Journal of Crime and Justice* 21 (1998): 17–25.

79. John Whitehead, Michael Blankenship, and John Paul Wright, "Elite versus Citizen Attitudes on Capital Punishment: Incongruity between the Public and Policy Makers," *Journal of Criminal Justice* 27 (1999): 249–58.

80. William Bowers and Glenn Pierce, "Deterrence or Brutalization: What Is the Effect of Executions?" *Crime and Delinquency* 26 (1980): 453–84.

81. Jon Sorenson and Danold Wallace, "Prosecutorial Discretion in Seeking Death: An Analysis of Racial Disparity in the Pretrial Stages of Case Processing in a Midwestern County," *Justice Quarterly* 16 (1999): 559–78.

82. Lawrence Greenfield and David Hinners, *Capital Punishment, 1984* (Washington, D.C.: Bureau of Justice Statistics, 1985).

83. Gennaro Vito and Thomas Keil, "Capital Sentencing in Kentucky: An Analysis of the Factors Influencing Decision Making in the Post–*Gregg* Period," *Journal of Criminal Law and Criminology* 79 (1988): 493–503; David Baldus, C. Pulaski, and G. Woodworth, "Comparative Review of Death Sentences: An Empirical Study of the Georgia Experience," *Journal of Criminal Law and Criminology* 74 (1983): 661–85; Raymond Paternoster, "Race of the Victim and Location of Crime: The Decision to Seek the Death Penalty in South Carolina," *Journal of Criminal Law and Criminology* 74 (1983): 754–85.

84. Raymond Paternoster, "Prosecutorial Discretion and Capital Sentencing in North and South Carolina," in *The Death Penalty in America: Current Research,* ed. Robert Bohm (Cincinnati: Anderson, 1991), 39–52.

85. Vito and Keil, "Capital Sentencing in Kentucky," 502–503.

86. David Brown, "Man Is Executed in Carolina; Second of a White Who Killed a Black," *Boston Globe,* 25 January 1995, 3.

87. Robert Johnson, *Death Work: A Study of the Modern Execution Process* (Pacific Grove, Calif.: Brooks/Cole, 1990).

88. William Bailey, "Disaggregation in Deterrence and Death Penalty Research: The Case of Murder in Chicago," *Journal of Criminal Law and Criminology* 74 (1986): 827–59.

89. Gennaro Vito, Pat Koester, and Deborah Wilson, "Return of the Dead: An Update on the Status of *Furman*-Commuted Death Row Inmates," in *The Death Penalty in America: Current Research,* ed. Robert Bohm (Cincinnati: Anderson, 1991), 89–100; Gennaro Vito, Deborah Wilson, and Edward Latessa, "Comparison of the Dead: Attributes and Outcomes of *Furman*-Commuted Death Row Inmates in Kentucky and Ohio," in *The Death Penalty in America: Current Research,* ed. Robert Bohm (Cincinnati: Anderson, 1991), 101–12.

90. John Cochran, Mitchell Chamlin, and Mark Seth, "Deterrence or Brutalization? An Impact Assessment of Oklahoma's Return to Capital Punishment," *Criminology* 32 (1994): 107–34.

91. William Bailey, "Deterrence, Brutalization, and the Death Penalty: Another Examination of Oklahoma's Return to Capital Punishment," *Justice Quarterly* 36 (1998): 711–34.

92. Joseph Schumacher, "An International Look at the Death Penalty," *International Journal of Comparative and Applied Criminal Justice* 14 (1990): 307–15.

93. David Stout, "Clemency Denied, Paraguayan Is Executed," *New York Times,* 15 April 1998.

94. Don Terry, "California Prepares for Faster Execution Pace," *New York Times,* 17 October 1998, A7.

95. *Furman v. Georgia,* 408 U.S. 238, 92 S.Ct. 2726, 33 L.Ed.2d 346 (1972).

96. *Gregg v. Georgia,* 428 U.S. 153, 96 S.Ct. 2909, 49 L.Ed.2d 859 (1976).

97. Ibid., at 205–207, 96 S.Ct. at 2940–41.

98. *McLesky v. Kemp,* 428 U.S. 262, 96 S.Ct. 2950, 49 L.Ed.2d 929 (1976).

99. *Coker v. Georgia,* 430 U.S. 349, 97 S.Ct. 1197, 51 L.Ed.2d 393 (1977).

100. *Dawson v. Delaware,* 503 U.S. 159, 112 S.Ct. 1093, 117 L.Ed.2d 309 (1992).

101. *Wilkins v. Missouri* and *Stanford v. Kentucky,* 492 U.S. 361, 109 S.Ct. 2969, 106 L.Ed.2d 306 (1989).

102. *McKlesky v. Zant,* 49 CrL 2031 (1991).

103. *Payne v. Tennessee,* 501 U.S. 808, 111 S.Ct. 2597, 115 L.Ed.2d 720 (1991).

104. *Harris v. Alabama,* U.S. 115 S.Ct. 1031, 130 L.Ed.2d 1004 (1995).

105. *Witherspoon v. Illinois,* 391 U.S. 510, 88 S.Ct. 1770, 20 L.Ed.2d 776 (1968).

106. *Wainwright v. Witt,* 469 U.S. 412, 105 S.Ct. 844, 83 L.Ed.2d 841 (1985).

107. *Lockhart v. McCree,* 476 U.S. 162, 106 S.Ct. 1758, 90 L.Ed.2d 137 (1986).

108. Walter C. Reckless, "Use of the Death Penalty," *Crime and Delinquency* 15 (1969): 43; Thorsten Sellin, "Effect of Repeal and Reintroduction of the Death Penalty on Homicide Rates," in *The Death Penalty,* ed. Thorsten Sellin (Philadelphia: American Law Institute, 1959); Robert H. Dann, "The Deterrent Effect of Capital Punishment," *Friends Social Service Series* 29 (1935): 1; William Bailey and Ruth Peterson, "Murder and Capital Punishment: A Monthly Time-Series Analysis of Execution Publicity," *American Sociological Review* 54 (1989): 722–43; David Phillips, "The Deterrent Effect of Capital Punishment," *American Journal of Sociology* 86 (1980): 139–48; Sam McFarland, "Is Capital Punishment a Short-Term Deterrent to Homicide? A Study of the Effects of Four Recent American Executions," *Journal of Criminal Law and Criminology* 74 (1984): 1014–32; Richard Lempert, "The Effect of Executions on Homicides: A New Look in an Old Light," *Crime and Delinquency* 29 (1983): 88–115.

109. Jon Sorenson, Robert Wrinkle, Victoria Brewer, and James Marquart, "Capital Punishment and Deterrence: Examining the Effect of Executions on Murder in Texas," *Crime and Delinquency* 45 (1999): 481–93.

110. Isaac Ehrlich, "The Deterrent Effect of Capital Punishment: A Question of Life or Death," *American Economic Review* 65 (1975): 397.

111. For a review, see William Bailey, "The General Prevention Effect of Capital Punishment for Non-Capital Felonies," in *The Death Penalty in America: Current Research,* ed. Robert Bohm (Cincinnati: Anderson, 1991), 21–38.

chapter 12

Probation and Intermediate Sanctions

On November 23, 1999, Walter Turnbull, founder of the internationally known Boys Choir of Harlem, was spared a prison sentence for tax evasion when Federal District Court Judge Barbara Jones sentenced him to one year of probation. The fifty-four-year-old Turnbull had been convicted for failing to report $55,000 in income on his 1990 tax return. In rendering her decision, Judge Jones said, "Dr. Turnbull isn't just someone who does his job excellently. He goes way beyond that, contributing his own personal money at times to keep the choir going." The court had received thirty-five letters of support for Turnbull who, while overseeing the choir for the past thirty years, helped it grow into an institution that provides special musical training as well as educational and personal counseling for hundreds of inner-city children. Under federal sentencing guidelines, Turnbull could have received up to eight months in prison. ■

Turnbull's sentencing represents some of the core values of the probation sentence: Many of those convicted in criminal courts are deserving of a second chance; they present little threat to society; having learned their lesson, they are unlikely to recidivate. Considering these circumstances, it seems foolish to incarcerate them in an overcrowded and dangerous prison system, which inmates describe as "criminal universities" where deviant identities are reinforced.[1] It may be both more effective and less costly to have them remain in the community under the supervision of a trained court officer where they can receive treatment that will help them turn around their lives.

Considering the potential benefits and cost effectiveness of a probation sentence, it is not surprising that the number of probationers is at an all-time high. In addition, the need to create effective and efficient methods of controlling offenders in the community has also prompted correctional policymakers to develop new forms of community-based intermediate sanctions: fines, forfeiture, restitution, shock probation and split sentencing, intensive probation supervision, house arrest, electronic monitoring, and residential community corrections. These programs are designed to provide greater control over an offender and to increase the level of sanction without resorting to a prison sentence.

Both traditional probation and the newer intermediate sanctions have the potential to become reasonable alternatives to many of the economic and social problems faced by correctional administrators: They are less costly than jail or prison sentences; they help the offender maintain family and community ties; they can be structured to maximize security and maintain public safety; they can be scaled in severity to correspond to the seriousness of the crime. No area of the criminal justice system is undergoing more change and greater expansion than probation and intermediate sanctions.

This chapter reviews these criminal sanctions. It begins with a brief history of probation and covers probation as an organization, sentence, and correctional practice. Then we focus attention on such intermediate sanctions as intensive supervision, house arrest, and electronic monitoring.

probation
A sentence entailing the conditional release of a convicted offender into the community under the supervision of the court (in the form of a probation officer), subject to certain conditions for a specified time. The conditions are usually similar to those of parole. (*Note:* Probation is a sentence, an alternative to incarceration; parole is administrative release from incarceration.) Violation of the conditions of probation may result in revocation of probation.

PROBATION

Probation is a criminal sentence mandating that a convicted offender be placed and maintained in the community under the supervision of a duly authorized agent of the court. Once on probation, the offender is subject to certain rules and conditions that must be followed to remain in the community. The probation sentence is managed by a probation department that supervises offenders' behavior and treatment and carries out other tasks for the court. Although the term has many meanings, *probation* usually indicates a nonpunitive form of sentencing for convicted criminal offenders and delinquent youth, emphasizing maintenance in the community and treatment without institutionalization or other forms of punishment.[2]

The History of Probation The roots of probation can be traced back to the traditions of the English common law. During the Middle Ages, judges wishing to spare deserving offenders from the pains of the then commonly used punishments of torture, mutilation, and death used their power to grant clemency and stays of execution. The common-law practice of **judicial reprieve** allowed judges to suspend punishment so that convicted offenders could seek a pardon, gather new evidence, or demonstrate that they had reformed their behavior. Similarly, the practice of **recognizance** enabled convicted offenders to remain free if they agreed to enter into a debt obligation with the state. The debt would have to be paid only if the offender was caught engaging in further criminal behavior. Sometimes **sureties** were required — these were people who made themselves responsible for the behavior of an offender after he was released.

judicial reprieve
The common-law practice that allowed judges to suspend punishment so that convicted offenders could seek a pardon, gather new evidence, or demonstrate that they had reformed their behavior.

recognizance
During the Middle Ages, the practice of letting convicted offenders remain free if they agreed to enter a debt relation with the state to pay for their crimes.

sureties
During the Middle Ages, people who made themselves responsible for the behavior of offenders released in their care.

Early U.S. courts continued the practice of indefinitely suspending sentences of criminals who seemed deserving of a second chance, but it was John Augustus of Boston who is usually credited with originating the modern probation concept.[3] As a private citizen, Augustus began in 1841 to supervise offenders released to his custody by a Boston judge. Over an eighteen-year period, Augustus supervised close to two thousand probationers and helped them get jobs and establish themselves in the community. Augustus had an amazingly high success rate, and few of his charges became involved in crime again.

In 1878 Augustus's work inspired the Massachusetts Legislature to pass a law authorizing the appointment of a paid probation officer for the city of Boston. In 1880 probation was extended to other jurisdictions in Massachusetts, and by 1898 the probation movement had spread to the superior (felony) courts.[4] The Massachusetts experience was copied by Missouri (1887), by Vermont (1898), and soon after by most other states. In 1925 the federal government established a probation system for the U.S. district courts. The probation concept soon became the most widely used correctional mechanism in the United States.[5]

The Concept of Probation The philosophy of probation is that the average offender is not actually a dangerous criminal or a menace to society. Advocates of probation suggest that when offenders are institutionalized instead of being granted community release, the prison community becomes their new reference point, they are forced to interact with hardened criminals, and the "ex-con" label prohibits them from making successful adjustments to society. Probation provides offenders with the opportunity to prove themselves, gives them a second chance, and allows them to be closely supervised by trained personnel who can help them reestablish proper forms of behavior in the community.

Probation usually involves suspension of the offender's sentence in return for the promise of good behavior in the community under the supervision of the probation department. As practiced in all fifty states and by the federal government, probation implies a contract between the court and the offender in which the former promises to hold a prison term in abeyance while the latter promises to adhere to a set of rules or conditions mandated by the court. If the rules are violated, and especially if the probationer commits another criminal offense, probation may be revoked; **revocation** means that the contract is terminated and the original sentence is enforced. If an offender on probation commits a second offense that is more serious than the first, she may also be indicted, tried, and sentenced on the second offense. However, probation may be revoked simply because the rules and conditions of probation have not been met; it is not necessary for an offender to commit another crime.

revocation
An administrative act performed by a parole authority that removes a person from parole or a judicial order by a court removing a person from parole or probation, in response to a violation on the part of the parolee or probationer.

Each probationary sentence is for a fixed period of time, depending on the seriousness of the offense and the statutory law of the jurisdiction. Probation is considered served when offenders fulfill the conditions set by the court for that period of time; they can then live without state supervision.

Awarding Probation

Probationary sentences may be granted by state and federal district courts and state superior (felony) courts. In some states, juries may recommend probation if the case meets certain legally regulated criteria (e.g., if it falls within a certain class of offenses as determined by statute). Even in those jurisdictions that allow juries to recommend probation, judges have the final say in the matter and may grant probation at their discretion. In nonjury trials, probation is granted solely by judicial mandate.

In most jurisdictions, all juvenile offenders are eligible for probation, as are most adults. Some state statutes prohibit probation for certain types of adult offenders, usually those who have engaged in repeated and serious violent crimes, such as murder or rape, or those who have committed crimes for which mandatory prison sentences have been legislated.

suspended sentence
A prison term that is delayed while the defendant undergoes a period of community treatment. If the treatment is successful, the prison sentence is terminated.

The most common manner in which a probationary sentence is imposed is a direct sentence to probation (about 50%). It is also common (27%) for the judge to formulate a prison sentence and then suspend it if the offender agrees to obey the rules of probation while living in the community (a **suspended sentence**).[6] The term of a probationary sentence may extend to the limit of the suspended prison term, or the court may set a time limit that reflects the sentencing period. For misdemeanors, probation usually extends for the entire period of the jail sentence, and felonies are more likely to warrant probationary periods that are actually shorter than the suspended prison sentences. Some offenders (about 10%) receive some form of *split sentence* in which they must first serve a jail term before being released on probation. In about 10 percent of all cases, the imposition of the sentence to probation is suspended.[7] This step is usually taken to encourage the defendant to pursue a specific rehabilitation program, such as treatment for alcohol abuse. If the program is successfully completed, further legal action is not usually taken.

The Extent of Probation

There are approximately two thousand adult probation agencies in the United States. Slightly more than half are associated with a state-level agency, while the remainder are organized at the county or municipal level of government. About thirty states combine probation and parole supervision into a single agency.

At last count more than 3.4 million adults were under federal or state probation, equal to about two-thirds of all adults under some form of correctional supervision.[8] Little more than half of all offenders on probation have been convicted of a felony; 40 percent are on probation for a misdemeanor.

Each year slightly more than 1.7 million people are placed on probation, and about 1.6 million complete their probationary sentences; this imbalance has resulted in a steadily increasing probation population. In 1980, 1.1 million people were on probation, so the number of probationers has tripled in two decades (Figure 12.1). Some states, such as Texas and California, are now maintaining hundreds of thousands of probationers in their caseloads. Without probation, the correctional system would rapidly become overcrowded, overly expensive and unmanageable.

Figure 12.1
Probation populations in the United States, 1980–1999

SOURCE: Joan Petersilia, *Probation in the United States* (Washington, D.C.: National Institute of Justice, 1997). Updated 1999.

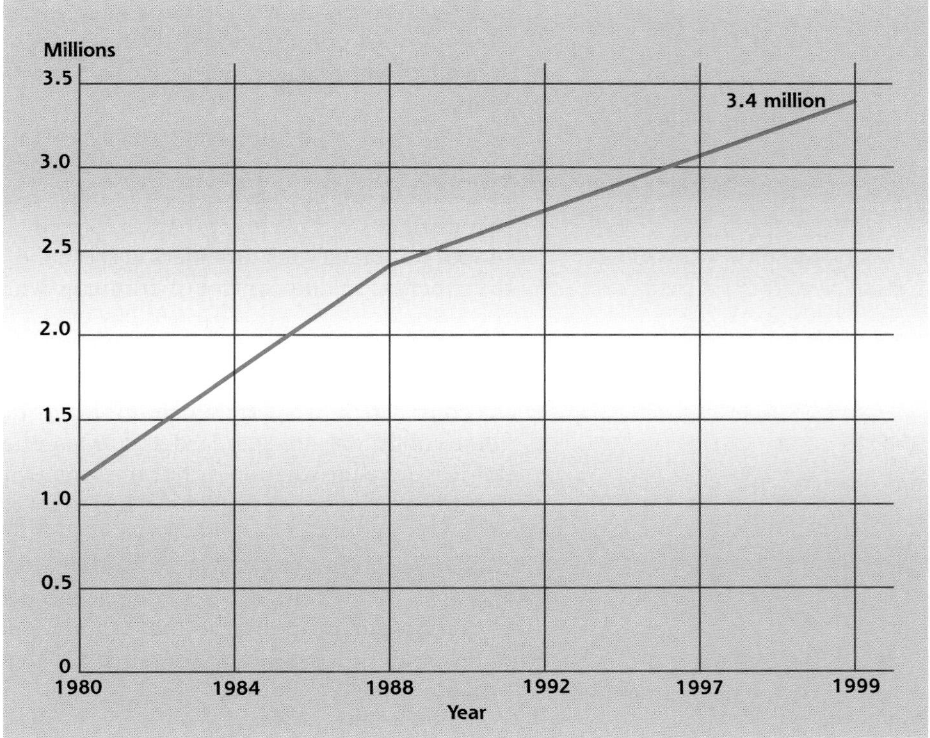

WHO IS ON PROBATION? Women make up about 21 percent of the nation's probationers, and men 79 percent. Approximately 64 percent of the adults on probation are white, and 35 percent are black; Hispanics represent 14 percent of probationers.

Most of those on probation (77%) are being actively supervised by a probation officer; about 9 percent are classified as inactive. In addition, probation officers are unaware of the whereabouts of 10 percent of their cases, who are classified as "absconded."

Eligibility for Probation

Several criteria are used in granting probation. On one level, the statutes of many states determine the factors that a judge should take into account when deciding whether to grant probation. Some states limit the use of probation in serious felony cases and for specific crimes whose penalties are controlled by mandatory sentencing laws. However, the granting of probation to serious felons is common; more than half of all probationers were convicted on felony offenses.

Some states have attempted to control judicial discretion by creating guidelines for granting probation. Judges often follow these guidelines, but probation decision making is varied: An individual offender granted probation in one jurisdiction might not be if tried in another. Probation is most often granted by a discretionary decision based on the beliefs and attitudes of the presiding judge and the probation staff.

A significant issue involving eligibility for probation is community supervision of convicted felons. Many people believe that probation is given to minor or first offenders who are deserving of a break. This is not actually the case. Many serious criminal offenders are given probation sentences, including people convicted on homicide (about 5%), rape (about 20%), and robbery (12%) charges.[9]

Although originally conceived as a way to provide a second chance for young offenders, probation today is also a means of reducing the population pressures on an overcrowded and underfunded correctional system. So there are two distinct sides to the probation, one involving the treatment and rehabilitation of nondangerous offenders deserving of a "second chance" and the other the supervision and control of criminals who might otherwise be incarcerated.

Conditions of Probation When probation is fixed as a sentence, the court sets down certain conditions for qualifying for community treatment. Some conditions are standard and are applied in every probation case (i.e., "Do not leave the jurisdiction"), but the sentencing judge usually has broad discretion to set specific conditions on a case-by-case basis. A presiding judge may not of course impose capricious or cruel conditions, such as requiring an offender to make restitution out of proportion to the seriousness of the criminal act.[10] For example, in one Illinois case, an appeals court ruled that requiring a probationer to make a public apology in the local newspaper for driving drunk was too punitive and a more drastic requirement than those authorized by the state's probation laws.[11]

Judges may, however, legally impose restrictions tailored both to fit the probationer's individual needs and/or to protect society from additional harm. For example, a child molester can be forbidden to associate with minor children.[12] In one case, a probationer was actually banished from the county in which he lived on the grounds that he was a popular figure among drug-using adolescents to whom he sold cocaine; barring him from his residence also gave him an opportunity for a fresh start.[13] Probationers' community supervision may be revoked if they fail to comply with these conditions and to obey the reasonable requests of the probation staff to meet their treatment obligations.[14]

The most common of these special conditions include residential placement, alcohol- or drug-abuse treatment and testing, mental health counseling, house arrest, and community service (the last two conditions are discussed later in this chapter); almost half of all probationers are given one or more special conditions.[15]

Administration of Probation Services Probation services are organized in a variety of ways, depending on the state and the jurisdiction in which they are located. Some states have a statewide probation service, but each court jurisdiction actually controls its local department. Other states maintain a strong statewide authority with centralized control and administration. Thirty states combine probation and parole services in a single unit; some combine juvenile and adult probation departments, whereas others maintain these departments separately.

The typical probation department is situated in a single court district, such as juvenile, superior, district, or municipal court. The relationship between the department and court personnel (especially the judge) is extremely close.

In the typical department, the chief probation officer (CPO) sets policy, supervises hiring, determines training needs, and may personally discuss with or recommend sentencing to the judge. In state-controlled departments, some of the CPO's duties are mandated by the central office; training guidelines, for example, may be determined at the state level. If, on the other hand, the depart-

A portable electronic device is used to check the whereabouts of a probationer who is wearing an electronic monitoring device.

ment is locally controlled, the CPO is invested with great discretion in the management of the department.

The line staff, or the probation officers (POs), may be in direct and personal contact with the entire supervisory staff, or they may be independent of the CPO and answer mainly to the assistant chiefs. Line staff perform the following major functions:

1. Supervise or monitor cases assigned to them to ensure that the rules of probation are followed.
2. Attempt to rehabilitate their cases through specialized treatment techniques.
3. Investigate the lives of convicted offenders to enable the court to make intelligent sentencing decisions.
4. Occasionally collect fines due the court or oversee the collection of delinquent payments, such as child support.
5. Interview complainants and defendants to determine whether criminal action should be taken, whether cases can be decided informally, whether diversion should be advocated, and so on. This last procedure, called *intake,* is common in juvenile probation.

Some POs view themselves as "social workers" and maintain a treatment orientation; their goal is to help offenders adjust in the community. Others are "law enforcers" who are more concerned with supervision, control, and public safety. An officer's style is influenced by both personal values and the department's general policies and orientation toward the goals of probation.[16]

DUTIES OF PROBATION OFFICERS Staff officers in probation departments are usually charged with four primary tasks: investigation, intake, diagnosis, and treatment supervision.

presentence investigation
An investigation performed by a probation officer attached to a trial court after the conviction of a defendant. The report contains information about the defendant's background, education, previous employment, and family; his or her own statement concerning the offense; prior criminal record; interviews with neighbors or acquaintances; and his or her mental and physical condition (i.e., information that would not be made record in the case of a guilty plea or that would be inadmissible as evidence at a trial but could be influential and important at the sentencing stage).

intake
The process in which a probation officer settles cases at the initial appearance before the onset of formal criminal proceedings; also, process in which a juvenile referral is received and a decision is made to file a petition in the juvenile court, release the juvenile, or refer the juvenile elsewhere.

In the investigative stage, the PO conducts an inquiry within the community to discover the factors related to the criminality of the offender. The **presentence investigation** is conducted primarily to gain information for judicial sentences, but in the event that the offender is placed on probation, the investigation becomes a useful testimony on which to base treatment and supervision.

Intake is a process by which POs interview cases that have been summoned to the court for initial appearances. Intake is most commonly used with juvenile offenders but may also be used with adult misdemeanant cases. During juvenile court intake, the petitioner (the juvenile) and the complainant (the private citizen or the police officer) may work with the PO to determine an equitable resolution of the case. The PO may settle the case without further court action, recommend restitution or other compensation, initiate actions that result in a court hearing, or recommend unofficial or informal probation.

Diagnosis is the analysis of the probationer's personality and the subsequent development of a personality profile that may be helpful in treating the offender. Diagnosis involves evaluating the probationer, based on information from an initial interview (intake) or the presentence investigation for the purpose of planning a proper treatment program. The diagnosis should not merely reflect the desire or purpose of labeling the offender neurotic or psychopathic, for example, but should "codify all that has been learned about the individual, organized in such a way as to provide a means for the establishment of future treatment goals."[17]

TREATMENT SUPERVISION Based on a knowledge of psychology, social work, or counseling and the diagnosis of the offender, the PO plans a treatment program that will, it is hoped, allow the probationer to fulfill the probation contract and make a reasonable adjustment to the community.

In years past, the probation staff had primary responsibility for supervision and treatment. Probation officers today rarely have hands-on treatment responsibility and instead employ the resources of the community to carry out this function. Attitudes toward treatment also seem to be changing. Probation officers seem less interested today in treating clients than in controlling their behavior.[18] Some experts have called for totally eliminating the personal involvement of POs in supervising treatment.[19] However, the increasing number of narcotics abusers in probation caseloads often overwhelms the availability of community-based substance abuse programs.[20]

The treatment function is a product of both the investigative and diagnostic aspects of probation. It is based on the PO's perceptions of the probationer, including family problems, peer relationships, and employment background. Treatment may also involve the use of community resources. For example, a PO who discovers that a client has a drinking problem may find a detoxification center willing to accept the client, a chronically underemployed offender may be given job counseling or training, and a person undergoing severe psychological stress may be placed in a therapeutic treatment program. In the case of juvenile delinquency, a PO may work with teachers and other school officials to help a young offender stay in school. Of course, most cases do not (or cannot) receive such individualized treatment.

Failure to adequately supervise probationers and determine whether they are obeying the rules of probation can result in the officer and the department being held legally liable for civil damages. For example, if a probationer with a history of child molestation attacks a child while working as a school custodian, the probationer's case supervisor could be held legally responsible for failing to check on the probationer's employment activities.[21]

The proper diagnostic, treatment, and investigative skills needed for effective probation work are difficult to find in a single individual. Probation officers often have social work backgrounds, and a master's degree in counseling or

A probationer involved in an anti-drug program helps paint a sign. Required treatment activity can be recommended by the presentence investigation and become part of the probation plan.

criminal justice may be a prerequisite for hiring or advancement in large departments. Today, most jurisdictions require officers to have a background in the social sciences and to hold at least a bachelor's degree.

PRESENTENCE INVESTIGATIONS An important task of POs is the investigation and evaluation of defendants coming before the court for sentencing. The court uses presentence investigation reports in deciding whether to grant probation, incarcerate, or use other forms of treatment.

The style and content of presentence investigations may vary among jurisdictions and also among individual POs within the same jurisdiction. Some departments require voluminous reports covering every aspect of the defendant's life; other departments, which may be rule oriented, require that officers stick to the basic facts, such as the defendant's age, race, sex, and previous offense record. Each department also has its own standards for presentence investigations.

At the conclusion of most presentence investigations, a recommendation is made to the presiding judge that reflects the department's sentencing posture on the case at hand. This is a crucial aspect of the report because the probation department's recommendation is followed in many but not all cases.

risk classification
Classifying probationers so that they may receive an appropriate level of treatment and control.

RISK CLASSIFICATION **Risk classification** involves classifying and assigning cases to a level and type of supervision on the basis of the clients' particular needs and the risks they present to the community. For example, some clients may receive frequent (intensive) supervision, whereas others are assigned to minimum monitoring by a PO.

A number of risk assessment approaches are used, but most employ such objective measures as the offender's age, employment status, drug abuse history, prior felony convictions, and number of address changes in the year prior to sentencing.[22] Efforts are under way to create more effective instruments using subjective information obtained through face-to-face interviews and encounters.[23]

Does classification make a dramatic difference in the success of probation? There is little clear-cut evidence that classification has a substantial impact on reducing recidivism. Even though probation administrators are often skeptical about their validity, they continue to use these scales and believe that may be a useful tool in case management and treatment delivery. The scales may validate the PO's self-perception of being a rational and scientific decision maker.[24] The classification of offenders aids the most important goal of supervision: reducing the risk the probationer presents to the community. In addition, classification schemes are in synch with desert-based sentencing models: The most serious cases get the most intensive supervision.[25]

How Successful Is Probation?

Probation is the most commonly used alternative sentence for a number of reasons: It is humane, it helps offenders maintain community and family ties, and it is cost effective. Incarcerating an inmate costs over $20,000 per year, while probation costs about $2,000 per year.[26]

Although unquestionably inexpensive, is probation successful? If most probation orders fail, the costs of repeated criminality would certainly outweigh the

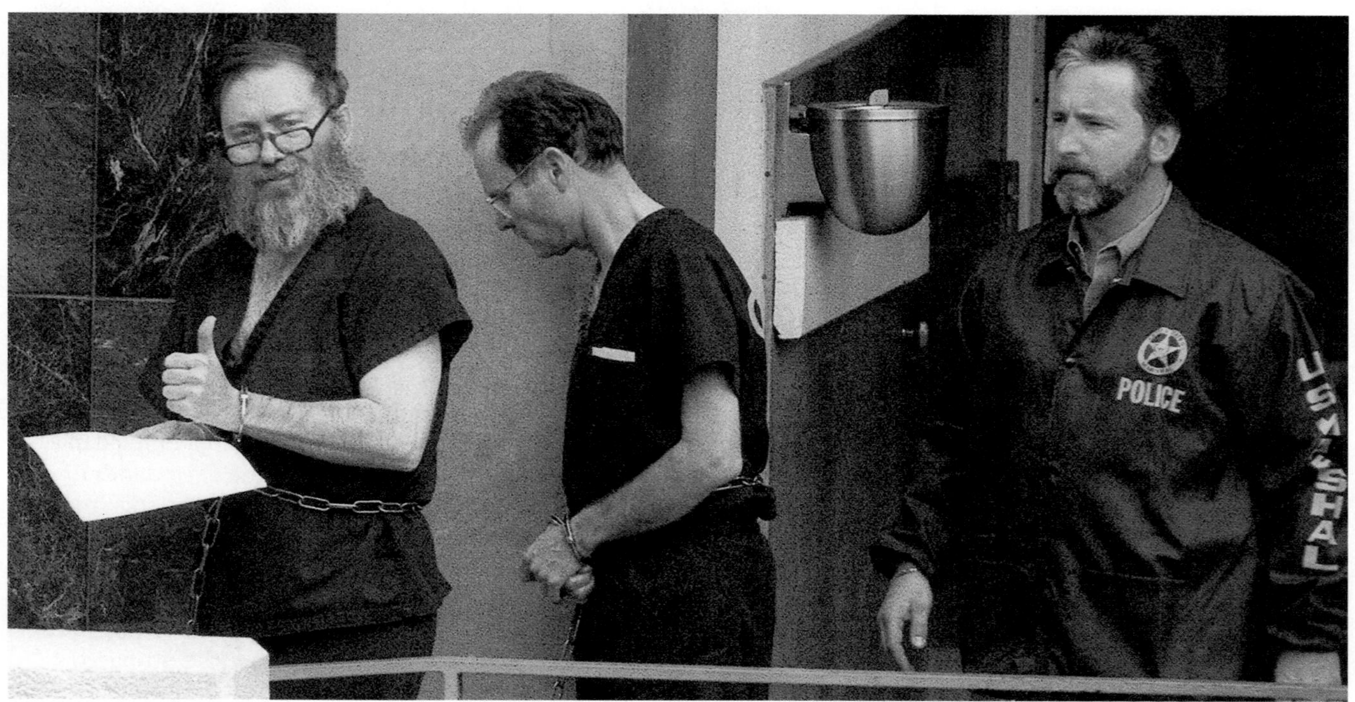

Larry Wayne Harris, in prison garb and chains, giving "thumbs up" after his arrest in 1998 on suspicion of possession of a deadly virus. After his arrest, it was found that Harris had been on probation for illegally obaining the bacteria which causes bubonic plague. Should people such as Harris be granted probation?

condition.[34] What type of acts caused their probation to be terminated? Most (87%) had been arrested for a new offense (but not charged or convicted). Others had tested positive for drug use, failed to report for drug testing/treatment, failed to report for counseling, left the jurisdiction without telling their probation officer, neglected to make restitution payment, made contact with known offenders, or failed to report a change in address.

The survey of probationers in prison inmates showed that based on the offense that brought them to prison, the 162,000 violators committed at least 6,400 murders, 7,400 rapes, 10,400 assaults, and 17,000 robberies while under supervision in the community an average of seventeen months.[35] Probation failures, then, were responsible for a significant number of highly serious crimes. These offenders are referred to as **avertable recidivists,** people whose crimes could have been avoided had they been harshly punished — in this case sent to prison — in the first place.

avertable recidivist
An offender who has been convicted of a prior offense but is free to violate the law because he or she has received a community sentence instead of incarceration. If he (she) has been imprisoned his (her) crimes would have been averted.

Legal Rights of Probationers

A number of important legal issues surround probation, one set involving the civil rights of probationers and another involving the rights of probationers during the revocation process.

CIVIL RIGHTS

The U.S. Supreme Court has ruled that probationers have a unique status and therefore are entitled to fewer constitutional protections than other citizens. One area of law involves the Fifth Amendment right of freedom from self-incrimination. The Supreme Court dealt with this issue in the case of *Minnesota v. Murphy* (1984).[36] In *Murphy,* the Supreme Court ruled that the probation officer–client relationship is not confidential, like physician–patient or attorney–client relationships. Furthermore, the *Murphy* decision held that a probation officer could even use trickery or psychological pressure to get information and turn it over to the police.

A second area of law involving probationers is search and seizure. In *Griffin v. Wisconsin* (1987), the Supreme Court held that a probationer's home may be searched without a warrant on the grounds that probation departments "have in mind the welfare of the probationer" and must "respond quickly to evidence of misconduct."[37]

REVOCATION RIGHTS

During the course of a probationary term, a violation of the rules or terms of probation or the commitment of a new crime can result in probation being revoked, at which time the offender may be placed in an institution. Revocation is not often an easy decision, since it conflicts with the treatment philosophy of many probation departments.

When revocation is chosen, the offender is notified, and a formal hearing is scheduled. If the charges against the probationer are upheld, the offender can then be placed in an institution to serve the remainder of the sentence. Most departments will not revoke probation unless the offender commits another crime or seriously violates the rules of probation.

Because placing a person on probation implies that probation will continue unless the probationer commits some major violation, the defendant has been given certain procedural due process rights at this stage of the criminal process. In three significant decisions, the U.S. Supreme Court provided procedural safeguards to apply at proceedings to revoke probation (and parole). In *Mempa v. Rhay* (1967), the Court unanimously held that a probationer was constitutionally entitled to counsel in a revocation-of-probation proceeding where the imposition of sentence had been suspended.[38] Then, in 1972, the Supreme Court in the case of *Morrissey v. Brewer* handed down an important decision detailing the

Mary Kay Le Tourneau, former fourth-grade teacher who had an affair with a 13-year-old boy and gave birth to his baby, has her handcuffs removed at the start of a hearing in February 1998 to determine if she should return to prison for violating conditions of her release. Le Tourneau's community release was revoked and she returned to serve a long prison sentence.

procedures required for parole revocation.[39] Because the revocations of probation and parole are similar, the standards in the *Morrissey* case affected the probation process as well. In *Morrissey* the Court required an informal inquiry to determine whether there was probable cause to believe the arrested parolee had violated the conditions of parole, as well as a formal revocation hearing with minimum due process requirements. However, in *Morrissey* the Court did not deal with the issue of right to counsel. Chief Justice Warren Burger stated, "We do not reach or decide the question whether the parolee is entitled to the assistance of retained counsel or to appointed counsel if he is indigent."

The question of the right to counsel in revocation proceedings came up again in the 1973 case of *Gagnon v. Scarpelli.*[40] In that decision, which involved a probationer, the Supreme Court held that both probationers and parolees have a constitutionally limited right to counsel in revocation proceedings. The *Gagnon* case can be viewed as a step forward in the application of constitutional safeguards to the correctional process. The provision of counsel helped give control over the unlimited discretion exercised in the past by probation and parole personnel in revocation proceedings.

With the development of innovative probation programs, courts have had to review the legality of changing probation rules and their effect on revocation. For example, courts have in general upheld the demand that restitution be made to the victim of crime.[41] Because restitution is designed to punish and reform the offender, rather than simply repay the victim, the probationer can be made legally responsible for paying restitution.

In *United States v. Granderson* (1994), the Supreme Court helped clarify what can happen to a probationer whose community sentence is revoked. Granderson was eligible for a six-month prison sentence but instead was given sixty months of probation. When he tested positively for drugs, his probation was revoked. The statute he was sentenced under required that he serve one-third his original sentence in prison. When the trial court sentenced him to twenty months, he appealed. Was his original sentence six months or sixty months? The Court found that it would be unfair to force a probationer to serve more time in prison than he would have if originally incarcerated and ruled that the proper term should have been one-third of the six months, or two months.[42]

The Future of Probation Probation will continue to be a sentence of choice in both felony and misdemeanor cases because it holds the promise of great cost savings at a time when many state budgets are being reduced.[43] In fact, defraying the cost of probation may be possible by asking clients to pay fees for probation services, a concept that would be impossible with prison inmates. At least twenty-five states now impose some form of fee on probationers to defray the cost of community corrections. Massachusetts has initiated day fees, which are based on the probationer's wages (the usual fee is between one and three days' wages each month).[44] An analysis of the probation fee system found that it may actually improve the quality of services afforded clients.[45] Texas requires judges to impose supervision fees unless the offender is truly unable to pay; fees make up more than half the probation department's annual budget.[46]

Probation is unquestionably undergoing dramatic changes. During the past decade, it has been supplemented and used as a restrictive correctional alternative. Expanding the scope of probation has created a new term, *intermediate sanctions,* to signify penalties that fall between traditional community supervision and confinement in jail or prison. These new correctional services are discussed in detail in the remainder of this chapter.

The Corrections Connections acts as a clearinghouse for information concerning the corrections industry. It offers links to about 20 community corrections sites at www.corrections.com/

INTERMEDIATE SANCTIONS

Community corrections has traditionally emphasized offender rehabilitation. The probation officer has been viewed as a caseworker or counselor whose primary job is to help the offender adjust to society. Offender surveillance and control has seemed more appropriate for law enforcement, jails, and prisons, than for community corrections.[47]

But since 1980 a more conservative justice system has reoriented toward social control. Although the rehabilitative ideals of probation have not been abandoned, new programs have been developed that add a control dimension to community corrections. These programs can be viewed as "probation plus," since they add restrictive penalties and conditions to community service orders. Being more punitive than probation, intermediate sanctions can be sold to conservatives, while they remain attractive to liberals as alternatives to incarceration.[48]

intermediate sanctions
The group of punishments falling between probation and prison; "probation plus." Community-based sanctions, including house arrest and intensive supervision, serve as alternatives to incarceration.

Intermediate sanctions include programs typically administered by probation departments: intensive probation supervision, house arrest, electronic monitoring, restitution orders, shock probation or split sentences, and residential community corrections.[49] Some experts also include high-impact shock incarceration, or boot camp experiences, within the definition of intermediate sanctions, but since these programs are typically operated by correctional departments, they are discussed separately in Chapter 13. Intermediate sanctions also involve sentences administered independently of probation staffs: fines and forfeiture, pretrial programs, and pretrial and posttrial residential programs. Intermediate sanctions therefore range from the barely intrusive, such as restitution orders, to the highly restrictive, such as house arrest accompanied by electronic monitoring and a stay in a community correctional center.

What are the advantages of creating a system of intermediate sanctions? Primary is the need to develop alternatives to prisons and jails, which have proved to be costly, ineffective, and injurious. Research indicates that more than 60 percent of all prison inmates are rearrested and returned to prison, many within a short period after their release.[50] Little evidence exists that incapacitation is either a general deterrent to crime or a specific deterrent against future criminality. Some correctional systems have become inundated with new inmates. Even states that have extensively used alternative sanctions have experienced rapid increases in their prison population; the pressure on the correctional system if alternative sanctions had not been an option is almost inconceivable.[51] Other nations have embraced alternative sanctions and despite rising crime rates have not experienced the explosion in the prison population that has occurred in the United States. This issue is explored further in the Race, Gender, and Culture feature.

Advantages of Intermediate Sanctions Intermediate sanctions also have the potential to save money. Although they are more expensive than traditional probation, they are far less costly than incarceration. If those offenders given alternative sanctions would have otherwise been incarcerated, the extra cost would be significant. In addition, offenders given intermediate sanctions generate income, pay taxes, reimburse victims, perform community service, and provide other cost savings that would be nonexistent had they been incarcerated. Intermediate sanctions are not likely to pay an immediate "corrections dividend" because many correctional costs are fixed, but they may reduce the need for future prison and jail construction.

Race, Gender, and Culture

XYXYXYXY
XYXYXYXY
XYXYXYXY

COMMUNITY SENTENCING ABROAD

While the crime rate has been declining in the United States for nearly a decade, get-tough measures such as "three strikes, you're out" has resulted in a steadily increasing prison population. Western European countries have crime rates similar to the United States, but their incarceration rates are much lower; criminal penalties there are not nearly as harsh as those in the United States. This disparity in punishment has not been lost on researchers such as legal scholar Michael Tonry, who has explored the differences between the United States and other Western democracies.

Tonry points out that crime trends seem to have an important impact on U.S. incarceration policies. As the crime rate goes up, so too does the media coverage of crime stories. Political figures, especially those running for office, feed off the media coverage and make crime an election focus. Because these events fuel public anxiety, there is an outcry for punitive measures to be taken against criminals. Politicians are happy to oblige their constituents and pass tough sanctions against criminals to show their sensitivity to the voters.

Tonry finds that crime has taken on increasing political importance since the 1964 presidential election. In the 1990s the overused phrase "get tough on crime" crossed party lines as lawmakers promised to implement harsh measures against criminals, regardless of whether the measures would actually reduce crime or are really needed. As crime rates fall, both the politicians and the public credit the get-tough stance for success, though little evidence shows that draconian measures actually reduce crime. For example, crime rates were already trending downward before harsh reform laws such as mandatory minimum sentencing and truth-in-sentencing laws were created; yet conservatives believe that these get-tough measures helped reduce crime rates.

Western European nations have taken a different approach to crime control. When rates of crime rose in European democracies, lawmakers focused on making punishment fair rather than harsh. Rather than mandatory sentencing, individual circumstances and the reasons for committing a crime are considered. Western European lawmakers also focus on punishments that are utilitarian and effective in reducing crime, rather than being punitive and retributive. They often rely on community sentences such as day fines, which are based on the offender's earnings and economic circumstances. The money collected from day fines not only punish the offender but also serve to benefit society. Western European judges have also been more likely to sentence offenders to community service. Community service, which was created in the United States, has quickly become the sentence of choice for minor crimes in European nations. Where community service hours can number in the thousands for an American criminal, European sentences often limit the number of hours to 240.

Critical Thinking

Incarceration sentences in Europe are substantially shorter than those in the United States. No European country has implemented mandatory sentences or truth in sentencing. Almost all efforts to control or reduce judicial discretion has been met with disapproval. Tonry points out this may be due to Western European judges and prosecutors being career civil servants, free from political concerns. Not having to worry about an upcoming election allows them to focus on what they believe is just, rather than when what is politically expedient. Would you encourage such practices in the United States? Why or why not?

InfoTrac College Edition Research

To learn more about community sentences abroad, read

Donald G. Evans, "Ontario's New Probation Supervision Model," *Corrections Today* 60 (1998): 126.

Donald G. Evans, "'What Works' in the United Kingdom," *Corrections Today* 60 (1998): 124.

SOURCES: Michael Tonry, "Why Are U.S. Incarceration Rates so High?" *Crime and Delinquency* 45 (1999): 419–38; "Parochialism in U.S. Sentencing Policy," *Crime and Delinquency* 45 (1999): 48–66.

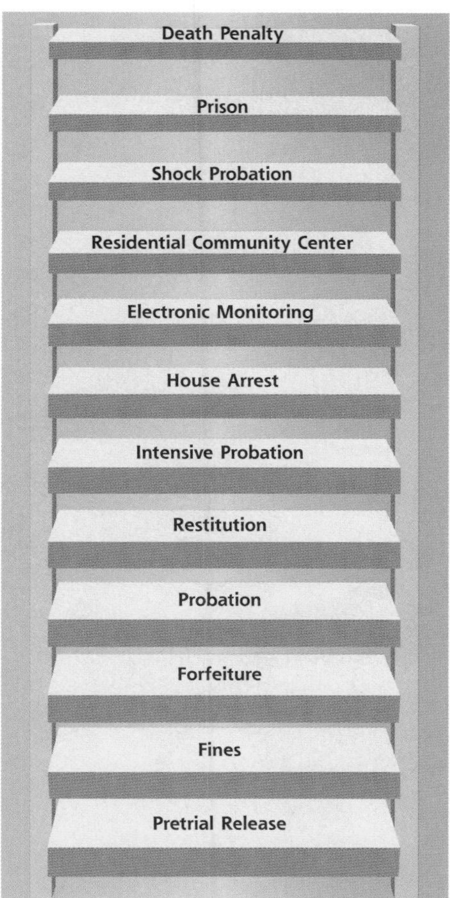

Figure 12.3
The punishment ladder

Intermediate sanctions also help meet the need for developing community sentences that are fair, equitable, and proportional.[52] It seems unfair to treat both a rapist and a shoplifter with the same type of probationary sentence, considering the differences in their crimes. As Figure 12.3 illustrates, intermediate sanctions can form the successive steps of a meaningful "ladder" of scaled punishments outside of prison, thereby restoring fairness and equity to nonincarceration sentences.[53] For example, forgers may be ordered to make restitution to their victims, and rapists can be placed in a community correctional facility while they receive counseling at a local psychiatric center. This feature of intermediate sanctions allows judges to fit the punishment to the crime without resorting to a prison sentence. Intermediate sentences can be designed to increase punishment for people whose serious or repeat crimes make a straight probation sentence inappropriate yet for whom a prison sentence would be unduly harsh and counterproductive.[54]

In the broadest sense, intermediate sanctions can serve the needs of a number of offender groups. The most likely candidates are convicted criminals who would normally be sent to prison but who pose either a low risk of recidivism or who are of little threat to society (such as nonviolent property offenders). Used in this sense, intermediate sanctions are a viable solution to the critical problem of prison overcrowding.

Intermediate sanctions can also reduce overcrowding in jails by providing alternatives to incarceration for misdemeanants and cut the number of pretrial detainees who currently make up about half the inmate population.[55] Some forms of bail already require conditions, such as supervision by court officers and periods of home confinement (conditional bail), that are a form of intermediate sanctions.

Intermediate sanctions can also potentially be used as halfway-back strategies for probation and parole violators. Probationers who violate the conditions of their community release could be placed under increasingly more intensive supervision before actual incarceration is required. Parolees who pose the greatest risk of recidivism might receive conditions that require close monitoring or home confinement. Parole violators could be returned to a community correctional center rather than a walled institution.

In the following sections, the forms of intermediate sanctions currently in use are more thoroughly discussed.

fine
Levying a money payment on offenders to compensate society for their misdeeds.

Fines

Fines are monetary payments imposed on offenders as an intermediate punishment for their criminal acts. They are a direct offshoot of the early common-law practice of requiring compensation be paid to the victim and the state (wergild) for criminal acts. Fines are still commonly used in Europe, where they are often the sole penalty, even in cases involving chronic offenders who commit fairly serious crimes.[56]

In the United States, fines are most commonly used in cases involving misdemeanors and lesser offenses. Fines are also frequently used in felony cases where the offender benefited financially. Investor Ivan Boesky paid over $100 million for violating insider stock-trading rules; the firm of Drexel Burnham Lambert paid a fine of $650 million in 1988 for securities violations.[57] A study sponsored by the federal government found that lower-court judges impose fines along or in tandem with other penalties in 86 percent of their cases; superior court judges imposed fines in 42 percent of their cases.[58]

Fines may be used as a sole sanction or combined with other punishments, such as probation or confinement. Judges commonly levy other monetary sanctions along

Financier Michael Milken after his release from federal prison. In addition to serving time behind bars, Milken was also required to do 5,400 hours of community service and pay a fine of $1.1 billion.

with fines, such as court costs, public defender fees, probation and treatment fees, and victim restitution, to increase the force of the financial punishment.[59] However, there is evidence that many offenders fail to pay fines and that courts are negligent in their efforts to collect unpaid fees; it has been estimated that defendants fail to pay upward of $2 billion in fines each year.[60]

In most jurisdictions, little guidance is given to the sentencing judge directing the imposition of the fine. Judges often have inadequate information on the offender's ability to pay, resulting in defaults and contempt charges. Because the standard sanction for nonpayment is incarceration, many offenders held in local jails are confined for nonpayment of criminal fines. Although the U.S. Supreme Court in *Tate v. Short* (1971) recognized that incarcerating a person who is financially unable to pay a fine discriminates against the poor, many judges continue to incarcerate offenders for noncompliance with financial orders.[61]

Research indicates that, given the facts of a case, judges do seem to use fines in a rational manner: Low-risk offenders are the ones most likely to receive fines instead of a jail sentence; the more serious the crime, the higher the amount of the fine. Offenders who are fined seem less likely to commit new crimes than those who receive a jail sentence.[62]

DAY FINES Because judges rely so heavily on offense seriousness to fix the level of fines, financial penalties may have a negative impact on success rates. The more serious the offense and the higher the fine, the greater are the chances that the offender will fail to pay the fine and risk probation revocation. To over-

day fine
A fine geared to the average daily income of the convicted offender in an effort to bring equity to the sentencing process.

come this sort of problem, some jurisdictions, such as New York City, are experimenting with **day fines.**[63]

A concept originated in Europe, day fines are geared to an offender's net daily income. In an effort to make them equitable and fairly distributed, fines are based on the severity of the crime, weighted by a daily-income value taken from a chart similar to an income tax table; the number of the offender's dependents are also taken into account. The day fine concept means that the severity of punishment is geared to the offender's ability to pay.

Several demonstration programs have been set up to determine the effectiveness of the day fine concept. An evaluation of the Staten Island, New York, project indicates that it is generally successful, enabling judges to increase the amount of fines collected while reducing the number of arrest warrants issued for failure to appear in postsentencing hearings; even if the fine could not be paid in full, more offenders paid something as opposed to nothing.[64] Day fines hold the promise of becoming an equitable solution to the problem of setting the amount of a fine according to the offender's ability to pay.

forfeiture
The seizure of personal property by the state as a civil or criminal penalty.

Forfeiture

Another intermediate sanction with a financial basis is criminal (in personam) and civil (in rem) **forfeiture.** Both involve the seizure of goods and instrumentalities related to the commission or outcome of a criminal act. For example, federal law provides that after arresting drug traffickers, the government may seize the boats they used to import the narcotics, the cars they used to carry the drugs overland, the warehouses in which the drugs were stored, and the homes paid for with the drug profits; on conviction, the drug dealers lose permanent ownership of these "instrumentalities" of crime.

Forfeiture is not a new sanction. During the Middle Ages, "forfeiture of estate" was a mandatory result of most felony convictions. The Crown could seize all of a felon's real and personal property. Forfeiture derived from the common-law concept of "corruption of blood" or "attaint," which prohibited a felon's family from inheriting or receiving his property or estate. The common law mandated that descendants could not inherit property from a relative who may have attained the property illegally: "[T]he Corruption of Blood stops the Course of Regular Descent, as to Estates, over which the Criminal could have no Power, because he never enjoyed them."[65]

Forfeiture was reintroduced to U.S. law with the passage of the Racketeer Influenced and Corrupt Organization (RICO) and the Continuing Criminal Enterprises Acts, both of which allow the seizure of any property derived from illegal enterprises or conspiracies. Although these acts were designed to apply to ongoing criminal conspiracies, such as drug or pornography rings, they are now being applied to a far-ranging series of criminal acts, including white-collar crimes. More than one hundred federal statutes use forfeiture of property as a punishment.

zero tolerance
The practice of seizing all instrumentalities of a crime, including homes, boats, and cars. It is an extreme example of the law of forfeiture.

Although law enforcement officials at first applauded the use of forfeiture as a hard-hitting way of seizing the illegal profits of drug law violators, the practice has been criticized because the government has often been overzealous in its application. For example, million-dollar yachts have been seized because someone aboard possessed a small amount of marijuana; this confiscatory practice is referred to as **zero tolerance.** This strict interpretation of the forfeiture statutes has come under fire because it is often used capriciously, the penalty is sometimes disproportionate to the crime involved, and it makes the government a "partner in crime."[66] It is also alleged that forfeiture unfairly targets a narrow ranges of offenders. For example, it is common for government employees involved in corruption to forfeit their pensions; employees of public companies are exempt from such punishment.[67]

Offenders doing community service work in New York. Community service orders, once considered an experimental innovation, have now become a standard sentencing alternative. Most reviews suggest that people actually complete their community service orders, but that they are just as likely to recidivate as people placed in traditional correctional programs.

restitution
A condition of probation in which the offender repays society or the victim of crime for the trouble the offender caused. Monetary restitution involves a direct payment to the victim as a form of compensation. Community service restitution may be used in victimless crimes and involved work in the community in lieu of more severe criminal penalties.

monetary restitution
A sanction that requires that convicted offenders compensate crime victims by reimbursing them for out-of-pocket losses caused by the crime. Losses can include property damage, lost wages, and medical costs.

community service restitution
An alternative sanction that requires an offender to work in the community at such tasks as cleaning public parks or working with disabled children in lieu of an incarceration sentence.

Restitution Another popular intermediate sanction is **restitution,** which can take the form of requiring offenders either to pay back the victims of crime (**monetary restitution**) or serve the community to compensate for their criminal acts (**community service restitution**).[68] Restitution programs offer offenders a chance to avoid a jail or prison sentence or a lengthier probation period. It may help them develop a sense of allegiance to society, better work habits, and some degree of gratitude for being given a second chance. Restitution serves many other purposes, including giving the community something of value without asking it to foot the bill for an incarceration stay and helping victims regain lost property and income.[69]

If monetary restitution is called for, the probation department typically makes a determination of victim loss and develops a plan for paying fair compensation. To avoid the situation in which a wealthy offender can fill a restitution order by merely writing a check, judges will sometimes order that compensation be paid out of income derived from a low-paid social service or public works job.

Community service orders usually require duty in a public nursing home, shelter, hospital, drug treatment unit, or works program; some young vandals may find that they must clean up the damage they caused to the school or the park. Judges sometimes have difficulty gauging the length of community service orders. One suggestion is that the maximum order should be no more than 240 hours and that this should be considered the equivalent of a six- to twelve-month jail term.[70] Whether these terms are truly equivalent remains a matter of personal opinion.

Judges and probation officers have embraced the concept of restitution because it appears to benefit the victim, the offender, the criminal justice system, and society.[71] Financial restitution is inexpensive to administer, helps avoid stigma, and provides compensation for victims of crime. Offenders ordered to do community service work have been placed in schools, hospitals, and nursing homes. Helping them avoid a jail sentence can mean saving the public thousands of dollars that would have gone to maintaining them in a secure institution, frees up needed resources, and gives the community the feeling that equity has been returned to the justice system.

Does restitution work? Most reviews rate it as a qualified success.[72] It is estimated that almost 90 percent of the clients successfully complete their restitution orders and that 86 percent have no subsequent contact with the justice system. Most restitution orders are met by a majority of program clients.[73]

shock probation
A sentence in which offenders serve a short prison term before they begin probation, to impress them with the pains of imprisonment.

split sentence
A practice that requires convicted criminals to spend a portion of their sentence behind bars and the remainder in the community.

Shock Probation and Split Sentencing

Shock probation and **split sentences** are alternative sanctions designed to allow judges to grant offenders community release only after they have sampled prison life. These sanctions are based on the premise that if offenders are given a taste of incarceration sufficient to shock them into law-abiding behavior, they will be reluctant to violate the rules of probation or commit another crime.

In a number of states and in the Federal Criminal Code, a jail term can actually be a condition of probation, known as split sentencing. About 10 percent of probationers are now given split sentences. The shock probation approach involves resentencing an offender to probation after a short prison stay. The shock comes because the offender originally received a long maximum sentence but is then eligible for release to community supervision at the discretion of the judge (usually within ninety days of incarceration). About one-third of all probationers in the fourteen states that use the program receive a period of confinement.[74] Evaluations of shock probation have shown it to be effective.[75]

Some states have linked the short prison stay with a boot camp experience, referred to as *shock incarceration,* in which young inmates undergo a brief but intense period of military-like training and hard labor designed to impress them with the rigors of prison life.[76] (Boot camp programs are discussed in greater detail in Chapter 13.) Shock probation and split sentencing have been praised as ways to limit prison time, reintegrate the client quickly into the community, maintain family ties, and reduce prison populations and the costs of corrections.[77] An initial jail sentence probably makes offenders more receptive to the conditions of probation, since it amply illustrates the problems they will face if probation is violated.

Split sentences and shock probation programs have been criticized by those who believe that even a brief period of incarceration can interfere with the purpose of probation, which is to provide the offender with nonstigmatizing, community-based treatment. Even a short-term commitment subjects probationers to the destructive effects of institutionalization, disrupts their life in the community, and stigmatizes them for having been in jail.

intensive probation supervision (IPS)
A type of intermediate sanction involving small probation caseloads and strict monitoring on a daily or weekly basis.

Intensive Probation Supervision

Intensive probation supervision (IPS) programs are another important form of intermediate sanctions (these programs are also referred to as intensive supervision programs). IPS programs, which have been implemented in some form in about forty states and today include about one hundred thousand clients, involve small caseloads of fifteen to forty clients who are kept under close watch by probation officers.[78]

The primary goal of IPS is decarceration: Without intensive supervision, clients would normally be sent to already overcrowded prisons or jails.[79] The second goal is control: High-risk offenders can be maintained in the community under much closer security than traditional probation efforts can provide. A third goal is reintegration: Offenders can maintain community ties and be reoriented toward a more productive life while avoiding the pains of imprisonment.

In general, IPS programs rely on a great degree of client contact to achieve the goals of decarceration, control, and reintegration.[80] Most programs have admissions criteria based on the nature of the offense and the offender's criminal background. Some programs, such as New Jersey's, exclude violent offenders; others will not take substance abusers. In contrast, some jurisdictions, such as Massachusetts, do not exclude offenders based on their prior criminal history. About 60 percent of existing programs exclude offenders who have already violated probation orders or who otherwise failed on probation.

IPS programs are used in several ways. In some states, IPS is a direct sentence imposed by a judge; in others, it is a postsentencing alternative used to divert offenders from the correctional system. A third practice is to use IPS as a case management tool to give the local probation staff flexibility in dealing with clients. Other jurisdictions use IPS in all three ways, in addition to applying it to probation violators to bring them halfway back into the community without resorting to a prison term.

THE EFFECTIVENESS OF IPS Evaluations indicate that IPS programs are generally successful, deliver more services than would normally be received by probationers, are cost effective, and produce recidivism rates equal to or better than those of offenders who have been confined.[81] However, evaluations have so far not been definitive, often ignoring such issues as whether the program met its stated goals, whether IPS is more attractive than other alternative sanctions, and which types of offenders are particularly suited for IPS. For example, IPS seems to work better for offenders with good employment records than it does for the underemployed or unemployed.[82] Younger offenders who commit petty crimes are the most likely to fail on IPS; ironically, people with these characteristics are the ones most likely to be included in IPS programs.[83]

Indications also exist that the failure rate in IPS caseloads is high, in some cases approaching 50 percent; IPS clients may even have a higher rearrest rate than other probationers.[84] It should come as no surprise that IPS clients fail more often because, after all, they are more serious criminals who might otherwise have been incarcerated and are now being watched and supervised more closely than probationers. Probation officers may also be more willing to revoke the probation of IPS clients because they believe the clients are a risk to the community and, under normal circumstances, would have been incarcerated. Why risk the program to save a few "bad apples"?

Although evidence that it can significantly reduce offending rates is still insufficient, IPS might be an attractive alternative to traditional correctional methods if it can be restricted to offenders who would most likely have been incarcerated without the availability of the IPS program. After thoroughly reviewing the impact of IPS, Betsy Fulton and her associates concluded that IPS programs are among the most popular alternatives to imprisonment in the United States and that, although IPS has not provided a solution to prison crowding, it is useful for those not meriting imprisonment but at high risk for probation.[85]

house arrest
A form of an intermediate sanction that requires that the convicted offender spend a designated amount of time per week in his or her own home — for example, from 5 P.M. Friday until 8 A.M. Monday.

House Arrest

The **house arrest** concept requires convicted offenders to spend extended periods of time in their own home as an alternative to an incarceration sentence. For example, persons convicted on a drunk-driving charge might be sentenced to spend between 6 P.M. Friday and 8 A.M. Monday and every weekday after 5:30 P.M. in their home for six months. Current estimates indicate that more than ten thousand people are under house arrest.

As with IPS programs, there is a great deal of variation in house arrest initiatives: Some are administered by probation departments, while others are simply judicial sentences monitored by surveillance officers. Some check clients twenty or more times a month (such as the Florida Community Control Program), while others do only a few curfew checks. Some use twenty-four-hour confinement, while others allow offenders to attend work or school. Regardless of the model used, house arrest programs are designed to be more punitive than IPS or any other community supervision alternative and are considered a "last chance" before prison.[86]

No definitive data exist indicating that house arrest is an effective crime deterrent, nor is there sufficient evidence to conclude that it has utility as a device to lower the recidivism rate. One evaluation of the Florida program found that nearly 10 percent of the house arrest sample had their probation revoked for technical violations within eighteen months of their sentencing.[87] Another evaluation of the same program found that recidivism rates were almost identical to a matched sample of inmates released from secure correctional facilities; four out of five offenders in both forms of correction recidivated within five years.[88]

Criticisms of house arrest also include charges that it has little deterrent value and seems more like being "grounded" than real punishment. They point to such cases as that of convicted Saudi arms dealer Adnan Khashoggi, whose "punishment" required him to be in his 30,000-square-foot luxury home — with its own swimming pool — between the hours of 1 A.M. and 8 A.M., with permission to take trips to Aspen and Fort Lauderdale.[89] Although these findings are troublesome, the advantages of house arrest in reducing costs and overcrowding in the correctional system probably make further experimentation inevitable.

Electronic Monitoring For house arrest to work, sentencing authorities must be assured that arrestees are actually at home during their assigned times. Random calls and visits are one way to check on compliance with house arrest orders. However, one of the more interesting developments in the criminal justice system has been the introduction of **electronic monitoring (EM)** devices to manage offender obedience to home confinement orders.[90] Electronic monitoring programs have been around since 1964, when Ralph Schwitzgabel of Harvard University experimented with linking offenders with a central monitoring station.[91] As Figure 12.4 shows, EM can be used with offenders at a variety of points in the criminal justice system, ranging from pretrial release to parole. Today, about fourteen thousand probationers are being monitored electronically.[92]

electronic monitoring (EM)
Requiring a convicted offender to wear a monitoring device as part of his or her community sentence. Electronic monitoring is typically part of a house arrest order and enables the probation department to ensure that the offender is complying with court-ordered limitations on his (her) freedom.

Electronically monitored offenders wear devices, which send signals to a control office, around their ankles, wrists, or necks. Two basic types of systems are used: active and passive. Active systems constantly monitor offenders by continuously sending a signal to the central office. If offenders leave their home at an unauthorized time, the signal is broken, and the "failure" is recorded. In some cases, the control officer is automatically notified electronically through a beeper. In contrast, passive systems usually involve random phone calls generated by computers to which the offenders have to respond within a particular time (such as thirty seconds). Some passive systems require offenders to place their monitoring device into a verifier box that then sends a signal to the control computer; another approach is to have the arrestee repeat words that are analyzed by a voice verifier and compared with tapes of the client's voice. Other systems use radio transmitters that receive a signal from a device worn by the offenders and relay it to the computer monitoring system via telephone lines.

Electronic monitoring supporters claim the EM has the benefits of relatively low cost and high security, while helping offenders avoid the pains of imprisonment in overcrowded, dangerous state facilities. Electronic monitoring is capital

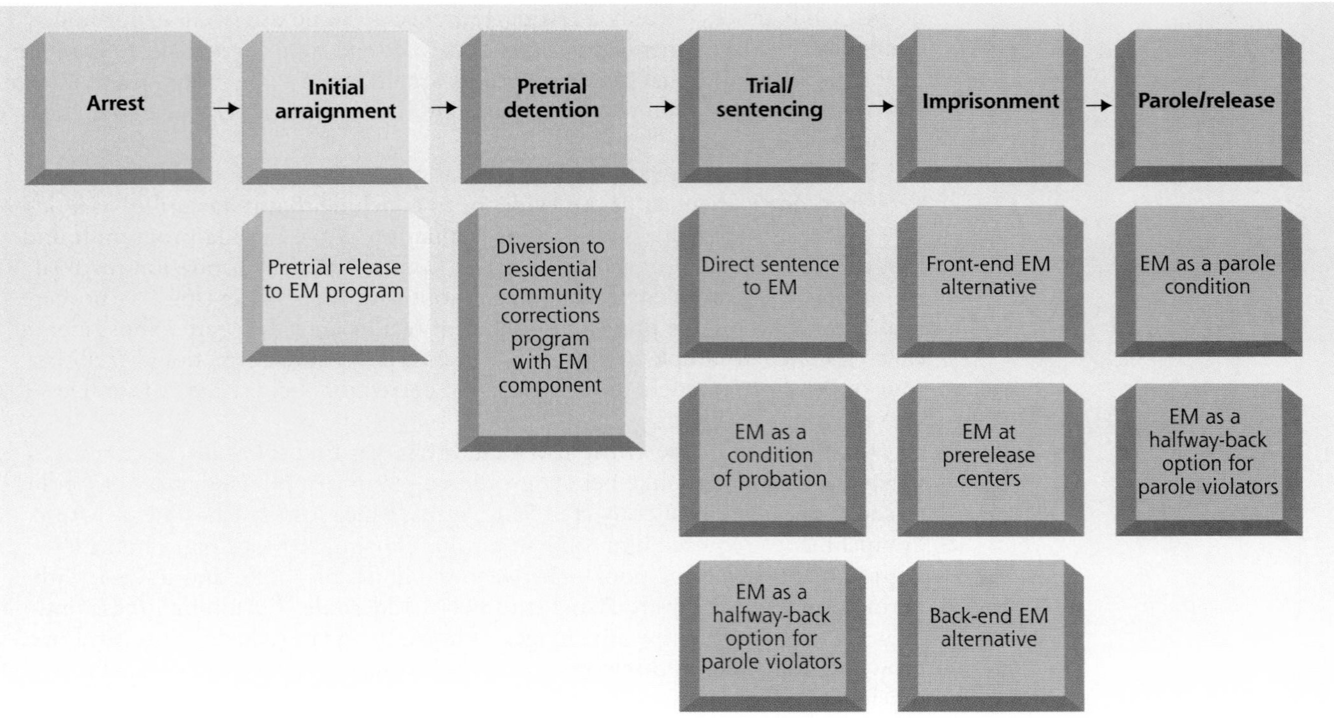

Figure 12.4
Key decision points where electronic monitoring programs are being used

SOURCE: James Byrne, Arthur Lurigio, and Christopher Baird, *The Effectiveness of the New Intensive Supervision Programs,* Research in Corrections Series, vol. 2, no. 2 (preliminary unpublished draft; Washington, D.C.: National Institute of Corrections, 1989).

intensive rather than labor intensive. Since offenders are monitored by computers, an initial investment in hardware rules out the need for hiring many more supervisory officers to handle large numbers of clients. It is not surprising then that the public supports EM as a cost-effective alternative to prison sentences that have proven ineffective.[93]

There are some indications that EM can be an effective addition to the galaxy of intermediate sanctions, providing the judiciary with an enhanced supervision tool.[94] Program evaluations with pretrial, probation, and parole groups indicate that recidivism rates are no higher than in traditional programs, costs are lower, and system overcrowding is reduced.[95] For example, when Kevin Courtright and his associates examined the cost-saving potential of using house arrest with EM as an alternative to incarceration for a drunk-driving population in a Pennsylvania county, they found that the program saved money and avoided new construction costs, without widening the net of social control.[96]

Some civil libertarians are troubled by the fact that EM can erode privacy and liberty. Do we really want U.S. citizens watched over by a computer? What are the limits of EM? Can it be used with mental patients? HIV carriers? Suicidal teenagers? Those considered high-risk future offenders? While promising to reduce the correctional population, EM actually has the potential to substantially increase it by turning homes into prisons.[97]

Although EM seems to hold great promise, both its effectiveness and its virtue have not been determined. It is not yet clear whether EM is a correctional savior or a temporary fad.[98]

Residents in a community correctional center help prepare and serve a meal.

residential community corrections (RCC)
A nonsecure facility, located in the community, that houses probationers who need a more secure environment. Typically, residents will be free during the day to go to work, school, or treatment and return in the evening for counseling sessions and meals.

Residential Community Corrections

The most secure intermediate sanction is a sentence to a **residential community corrections** (RCC) facility. Such a facility has been defined as "a freestanding nonsecure building that is not part of a prison or jail and houses pretrial and adjudicated adults. The residents regularly depart to work, to attend school, and/or participate in treatment activities and programs."[99]

Traditionally, the role of community corrections was supplied by the nonsecure halfway house, designed to reintegrate soon-to-be-paroled prison inmates back into the community. Inmates spend the last few months in the halfway house, acquiring suitable employment, building up cash reserves, obtaining an apartment, and developing a job-related wardrobe.

The traditional concept of community corrections has expanded. Today, the community correctional facility is a vehicle to provide intermediate sanctions as well as a prerelease center for those about to be paroled from the prison system. For example, RCC has been used as a direct sentencing option for judges who believe particular offenders need a correctional alternative halfway between traditional probation and a stay in prison. Placement in an RCC center can be used as a condition of probation for offenders who need a nonsecure community facility that provides a more structured treatment environment than traditional probation. It is commonly used in the juvenile justice system for youths who need a more secure environment than can be provided by traditional probation yet who are not deemed a threat to the community and do not require a secure placement.

Probation departments and other correctional authorities have been charged with running RCC centers that serve as a preprison sentencing alternative. In addition, some RCC centers are operated by private, nonprofit groups that receive referrals from the county or district courts and from probation or parole departments. For example, Portland House, a private residential center in Minneapolis, operates as an alternative to incarceration for young adult felony offenders. The twenty-five residents regularly receive group therapy and financial, vocational, educational, family, and personal counseling. Residents may work to earn a high school equivalency degree. With funds withheld from their earnings at work-release employment, residents pay room and board, family and self-support, and income taxes. Portland House appears to be successful. It is significantly cheaper to run than a state institution, and the recidivism rate of clients is much lower than that of those who have gone through traditional correctional programs.[100]

Besides being sole sentence and halfway houses, RCC facilities have also been residential pretrial release centers for offenders who are in immediate need of social services before their trial and as halfway-back alternatives for both parole and probation violators who might otherwise have to be imprisoned. In this capacity, RCC programs serve as a base from which offenders can be placed in outpatient psychiatric facilities, drug and alcohol treatment programs, job training, and so on. Some programs make use of both inpatient and outpatient programs to provide clients with specialized treatment, such as substance abuse management.[101]

day reporting center (DRC) A nonresidential community-based treatment program.

One recent development has been the use of RCC facilities as **day reporting centers (DRCs).**[102] Day reporting centers provide a single location to which a variety of clients can report for supervision and treatment. Used in Massachusetts, Connecticut, Minnesota, and other states, DRCs utilize existing RCC facilities to service nonresidential clients. They can be used as a step up for probationers who have failed in the community and a step down in security for jail or prison inmates.[103] An evaluation of the Metropolitan Day Reporting Center in Boston found that it was highly successful. Some of the features of the program are listed in Exhibit 12.1.

exhibit 12.1

Evaluation of the Metropolitan Day Reporting Center (MDRC)

- Inmates who participate in the MDRC are twice as likely to remain crime free after their release from the program when compared with inmates released directly from the county house of correction.
- Only 6 (1.3%) of 466 clients committed a new crime while in the program.
- Notably, 8 out of every 10 clients are either working or involved in a job search as part of their responsibilities as participants in the MDRC program.
- Nearly 17% (or 84 clients) were able to obtain their general education diploma while in the MDRC program.
- A small number of MDRC clients (12.3%) have had three or more previous incarcerations. This indicates that the MDRC provides service equally to what could be considered a traditional parole clientele as well as to many clients who resemble a traditional probation client.
- Over half (54.8%) of the clients have no prior offense. This indicates that criminal justice agencies are viewing the MDRC as a useful community correctional alternative for clients early in their criminal career.
- Most clients (59.7%) participate in some form of substance abuse treatment in addition to the two required Alcoholics Anonymous or Narcotics Anonymous meetings.
- As clients age, their likelihood of recidivating decreases. Clients living with a spouse or children produced very low recidivism rates (4.9% and 0.0%, respectively), while clients living with parents and siblings had significantly higher rates (25.4% and 16.7%, respectively).
- A majority (approximately 60.0%) of MDRC clients with three or more prior incarcerations do not recidivate.

SOURCE: Jack McDevitt, Marla Domino, Katrina Baum, and K. Suzanne Armfield, *MDRC: An Evaluation for the Center for Criminal Justice Policy Research,* (Boston: College of Criminal Justice, Northeastern University, 1997).

More than two thousand state-run community-based facilities are in use today. In addition, up to twenty-five hundred private, nonprofit RCC programs operate in the United States. About half also have inmates who have been released from prison (halfway houses) and use the RCC placement to ease back into returning to society. The remainder are true intermediate sanctions, including about four hundred federally sponsored programs.[104]

Despite the thousands of traditional and innovative RCC programs in operation around the United States, relatively few efforts have been made to evaluate their effectiveness. Those evaluations that do exist suggest that many residents do not complete their treatment regimen in RCC facilities, violating the rules or committing new offenses. Those that do complete the program have lower recidivism rates than the unsuccessful discharges.[105]

One reason that it is so difficult to assess RCC facilities is that programs differ considerably with respect to target population, treatment alternatives, and goals. While some are rehabilitation oriented and operate under loose security, others are control oriented and use such security measures as random drug and alcohol testing. Although critics question their overall effectiveness, RCC facilities appear to work for some types of offenders, and some treatment orientations seem to work better than others. It is possible that rather than being used as a "last resort" community alternative before sentence to a jail or prison, RCC placement might actually work better with first-time offenders who have relatively little experience with the criminal or juvenile justice systems.[106]

Can Intermediate Sanctions Work? Intermediate community-based sanctions hold the promise of providing cost-effective crime control strategies without widening the net of the criminal justice system.[107] They reduce overreliance on incarceration and exploding correctional construction costs.[108] Nonetheless, there are indications that, as currently situated, intermediate sanctions are no more effective in reducing recidivism than traditional forms of probation; because of the more intense monitoring involved, intermediate sanctions may result in more offenders being discovered to have committed technical violations.[109] Revocation for technical reasons helps increase rather than decrease the correctional population, an outcome in opposition to the stated goals of alternative sentencing.[110]

Some criminal justice professionals welcome the use of intermediate sanctions as a practical alternative to prison, whereas others are skeptical about the ability of community sentences to significantly reduce the correctional population. Skeptics John DiIulio and Charles Logan argue that it is a myth that prison crowding can be reduced, that new construction can be avoided, and that annual operating costs can be cut if greater advantage is taken of intermediate sanctions. The great majority of those under correctional supervision, they argue, have already been on probation and will eventually be supervised in the community. In other words, most convicted criminals are already experiencing an "intermediate sanction" for at least some part of their sentence. Of inmates currently in state prisons, 67 percent were given probation as an intermediate sanction one or more times on prior convictions, and over 80 percent have had prior convictions resulting in either probation or incarceration. On any day of the week, argue DiIulio and Logan, you will find three times as many convicts under alternative supervision as you will find under the watchful eye of a warden. And most of those in the warden's custody are probably there at least partly because they did not do well under some prior alternative.[111]

In contrast to this view, Michael Tonry and Mary Lynch suggest that intermediate sanctions can be a useful correctional tool. Not everyone who commits a crime is the same, and they should not receive identical punishments. Clients for intermediate sanction programs might be chosen from those already incarcerated, eliminating the threat of net widening. It might be possible, they suggest, to create "exchange rates" that create equivalent sentences for prison and community alternatives, such as three days in home confinement instead of one day in jail. Although intermediate sanctions are not a panacea for all offenders (as Tonry and Lynch put it, "There is no free lunch"), they conclude that for offenders who do not present unacceptable risks of violence, well-managed intermediate sanctions offer a cost-effective way to keep them in the community.[112]

RESTORATIVE JUSTICE As you may recall, restorative justice principles are a perfect fit for serving as the basis of intermediate sanctions. Maintaining "ownership" or jurisdiction over the conflict means that the resolution between criminals and victims should take place in the community in which it originated, not in some far-off prison. Victims should be given a chance to voice their stories and offenders can help compensate them financially or provide some service (e.g., fixing damaged property). Citizens and victims are asked to participate in conferences, sentencing circles, or mediations whenever possible.[113] The goal is to enable offenders to appreciate the damage they have caused, to make amends, and to be reintegrated back into society.

Today, alternative programs based on restorative principles are evolving. They hold great promise and may provide the key to developing effective programs. The Policy, Programs, and Issues in Criminal Justice feature describes in some detail a few prominent programs.

SUMMARY

Probation can be traced to the common-law practice of granting clemency to deserving offenders. The modern probation concept was developed by John Augustus of Boston, who personally sponsored two thousand convicted inmates over an eighteen-year period. Today, probation is the community supervision of convicted offenders by order of the court. It is a sentence reserved for defendants whom the magistrate views as having potential for rehabilitation without needing to serve prison or jail terms. Probation is practiced in every state and by the federal government and includes both adult and juvenile offenders.

In the decision to grant probation, most judges are influenced by their personal views and the presentence reports of the probation staff. Once on probation, the offender must follow a set of rules or conditions, the violation of which may lead to revocation of probation and reinstatement of a prison sentence. These rules vary from state to state but usually involve such demands as refraining from using alcohol or drugs, obeying curfews, and terminating past criminal associations.

Probation officers are usually organized into countywide departments, although some agencies are statewide and others are combined parole–probation departments. Probation departments have instituted a number of innovative programs designed to bring better services to their clients. These include restitution and diversionary programs, intensive probation, and residential probation.

In recent years, the U.S Supreme Court has granted probationers greater due process rights; today, when the state wishes to revoke probation, it must conduct a full hearing on the matter and provide the probationer with an attorney when that assistance is warranted.

To supplement probation, a whole new family of intermediate sanctions have been developed. These range from pretrial diversion to residential community corrections. Other widely used intermediate sanctions include fines and forfeiture, house arrest, and intensive probation supervision. Electronic monitoring (EM) involves a device worn by an offender under home confinement. While some critics complain that EM smacks of a "Big Brother Is Watching You" mentality, it would seem an attractive alternative to a stay in a dangerous, deteriorated, secure correctional facility. A stay in a community correctional center is one of the most intrusive alternative sentencing options. Residents may be eligible for work and educational release during the day while attending group sessions in the evening. Residential community correction is less costly than more secure institutions, while being equally effective.

It is too soon to determine whether these programs are successful, but they provide a hope of being lost-cost, high-security alternatives to traditional corrections. Alternatives to incarceration

Policy, Programs, and Issues in Criminal Justice

RESTORATIVE JUSTICE IN THE COMMUNITY

A number of new and innovative community programs based on restorative justice principles, four of which are discussed here, are being tested around the nation.

Minnesota

Minnesota has been a groundbreaker in restorative justice. Its Department of Corrections created the Restorative Justice Initiative in 1992, hiring Kay Pranis as a full-time restorative justice planner in 1994 — the first such position in the country. The initiative offers training in restorative justice principles and practices, provides technical assistance to communities in designing and implementing practices, and creates networks of professionals and activists to share knowledge and provide support.

Besides promoting victim–offender mediation, family group conferencing, and neighborhood conferencing, the department has introduced *sentencing circles.* Citizen volunteers and criminal justice officials from Minnesota have participated in training in the Yukon Territory, Canada, where peacemaking circles have been held since the late 1980s. In Minnesota the circle process is used by the Mille Lacs Indian Reservation and in other communities in several counties. The circle process usually has several phases. First, the Community Justice Committee conducts an intake interview with offenders who want to participate. Then, separate healing circles are held for the victim (and others who feel harmed) and the offender. The committee tries to cultivate a close personal relationship with victims and offenders and to create support networks for them. In the end, a sentencing circle, open to the community, meets to work out a sentencing plan.

Vermont

A pilot reparative probation program began in Vermont in 1994, and the first cases were heard by a reparative citizen board the following year. Three features distinguish this restorative justice initiative from most others in the United States: The Department of Corrections designed the program, it is implemented statewide, and it involves a sizable number of volunteer citizens. The process is straightforward. Following an adjudication of guilt, the judge sentences the offender to probation, with the sentence suspended and only two conditions imposed: The offender will commit no more crimes and will complete the reparative program. The volunteer board members meet with the offender and the victim and together discuss the offense, its effects on victim and community, and the life situations of victim and offender. All participants must agree on a contract, to be fulfilled by the offender. It is based on five goals: The victim is restored and healed, the community is restored, the offender understands the effects of the crime, the offender learns ways to avoid reoffending, and the community offers reintegration to the offender. Since reparative probation targets minor crimes, it is not meant as a prison diversion program. In 1998 the forty-four boards handled twelve hundred cases, accounting for more than one-third of the probation caseload. More than three hundred trained volunteers serve as board members. Ten coordinators handle case management and organization for the boards. The goal is to have the boards handle about 70 percent of the targeted probation cases. That only about 17 percent of offenders fail to complete their agreements or attend follow-up board meetings is a measure of the program's success. These offenders are referred back to the courts.

Travis County, Texas

Texas law now authorizes that each county develop a community justice council and community justice task force. The task force includes representatives of criminal justice agencies, social and health services, and community organizations. With task force assistance, the council, consisting of elected officials, handles planning and policymaking and prepares a community justice plan.

Many efforts are directed at juvenile offenses. In Austin, the Juvenile Probation Office offers victim–offender mediation for young people in trouble. For misdemeanors, juveniles may be diverted from court to neighborhood conference committees. These consist of panels of trained adult citizens who meet with juvenile offenders and their parents and together develop contracts tailored to the case.

Critical Thinking

Restorative justice may be the model that best serves alternative sanctions. How can this essentially humanistic approach be sold to the general public that now supports more punitive sanctions? For example, would it be feasible that using restorative justice with nonviolent offenders frees up resources for the relatively few dangerous people in the criminal population? Explain.

InfoTrac College Edition Research

To learn more about the restorative justice approach, see

Gordon Bazemore, "Restorative Justice and Earned Redemption: Communities, Victims, and Offender Reintegration," *American Behavioral Scientist* 41 (1998): 768.

Tag Evers, "A Healing Approach to Crime," *The Progressive* 62 (1998): 30.

Carol La Prairie, "The Impact of Aboriginal Justice Research on Policy: A Marginal Past and an Even More Uncertain Future," *Canadian Journal of Criminology* 41 (1999): 249.

SOURCE: Leena Kurki, *Incorporating Restorative and Community Justice into American Sentencing and Corrections* (Washington, D.C.: National Institute of Justice, 1999).

can help reduce overcrowding in the prison system and spare nonviolent offenders the pains of a prison experience. Although alternatives may not be much more effective than a prison sentence in reducing recidivism rates, they are far less costly and can free up needed space for more violent offenders. One promising approach is to use principles of restorative justice to shape intermediate sanctions.

KEY TERMS

probation
judicial reprieve
recognizance
sureties
revocation
suspended sentence
presentence investigation
intake
risk classification
avertable recidivist
intermediate sanctions
fine
day fine
forfeiture
zero tolerance
restitution
monetary restitution
community service restitution
shock probation
split sentence
intensive probation supervision (IPS)
house arrest
electronic monitoring (EM)
residential community corrections (RCC)
day reporting center (DRC)

INFOTRAC COLLEGE EDITION EXERCISES

In *Pennsylvania Board of Probation and Parole v. Scott,* the U.S. Supreme Court held that the exclusionary rule for illegally obtained evidence did not apply to parole revocation. Will it apply to probation? For one answer, see Duncan N. Stevens, "Off the Mapp: Parole Revocation Hearings and the Fourth Amendment," *Journal of Criminal Law and Criminology* 89 (1999): 1047.

Another legal issue is whether statements made in treatment programs can be used in probation revocation. Should probationers be given immunity from prosecution if they are required during the treatment to take responsibility for their actions and admit wrongdoing? See the following for one answer: Jonathan Kaden, "Therapy for Convicted Sex Offenders: Pursuing Rehabilitation without Incrimination," *Journal of Criminal Law and Criminology* 89 (1998): 347.

Cooperation between police agencies and probation officers may provide advantages that help suppress crime rates. The Boston Police Department was able to establish an effective gang program through a collaboration with local probation officers. To read about this unique combination, check out Brian McKay and Barry Paris, "Forging a Police–Probation Alliance," *FBI Law Enforcement Bulletin* 67 (1998): 27.

QUESTIONS

1. What is the purpose of probation? Identify some conditions of probation and discuss the responsibilities of the probation officer.
2. Discuss the procedures involved in probation revocation. What are the rights of the probationer?
3. Is probation a privilege or a right? Explain.
4. Should a convicted criminal make restitution to the victim? Why or why not? When is restitution inappropriate?
5. Should offenders be fined based on the severity of what they did or according to their ability to pay? Is it fair to gear day fines to wages? Why or why not? Should offenders be punished more severely because they are financially successful? Explain.
6. Does house arrest involve a violation of personal freedom? Does wearing an ankle bracelet smack of "Big Brother"? Would you want the government monitoring your daily activities? Could this be expanded, for example, to monitor the whereabouts of AIDS patients? Explain.
7. Would you want a community correctional center located in your neighborhood? Why or why not?

NOTES

1. Arnulf Kolstad, "Imprisonment as Rehabilitation: Offenders' Assessment of Why It Does Not Work," *Journal of Criminal Justice* 24 (1996): 323–35.

2. See, generally, Todd Clear and Vincent O'Leary, *Controlling the Offender in the Community* (Lexington, Mass.: Lexington Books, 1983).

3. For a history of probation, see Edward Sieh, "From Augustus to the Progressives: A Study of Probation's Formative Years," *Federal Probation* 57 (1993): 67–72.

4. Ibid.

5. David Rothman, *Conscience and Convenience* (Boston: Little, Brown, 1980), 82–117.

6. Lawrence Bonczar and Lauren Glaze, *Probation and Parole, 1998* (Washington, D.C.: Bureau of Justice Statistics, 1999).

7. Ibid.

8. Ibid.

9. Jodi Brown and Patrick Langan, *Felony Sentences in the United States, 1996* (Washington, D.C.: Bureau of Justice Statistics, 1999).

10. *Higdon v. United States,* 627 F.2d 893 (9th Cir., 1980).

11. *People v. Johnson,* 175 Ill.App.3d 908, 125 Ill. Dec. 469, 530 N.E.2d 627 (1988).

12. *Ramaker v. State,* 73 Wis.2d 563, 243 N.W.2d 534 (1976).

13. *United States v. Cothran,* 855 F.2d 749 (11th Cir., 1988).

14. *United States v. Gallo,* 20 F.3d 7 (1st Cir., 1994).

15. Patrick Langan and Mark Cuniff, *Recidivism of Felons on Probation, 1986–1989* (Washington, D.C.: Bureau of Justice Statistics, 1992).

16. Todd Clear and Edward Latessa, "Probation Officers' Roles in Intensive Supervision: Surveillance versus Treatment," *Justice Quarterly* 10 (1993): 441–62.

17. Ibid.

18. Patricia Harris, Todd Clear, and S. Christopher Baird, "Have Community Supervision Officers Changed Their Attitudes toward Their Work?" *Justice Quarterly* 6 (1989): 233–46.

19. John Rosencrance, "Probation Supervision: Mission Impossible," *Federal Probation* 50 (1986): 25–31.

20. David Duffee and Bonnie Carlson, "Competing Value Premises for the Provision of Drug Treatment to Probationers," *Crime and Delinquency* 42 (1996): 574–92.

21. Richard Sluder and Rolando Del Carmen, "Are Probation and Parole Officers Liable for Injuries Caused by Probationers and Parolees?" *Federal Probation* 54 (1990): 3–12.

22. Mark Cuniff, Dale Sechrest, and Robert Cushman, "Redefining Probation for the Coming Decade" (Paper presented at the annual meeting of the American Society of Criminology, San Francisco, November 1991).

23. Patricia Harris, "Client Management Classification and Prediction of Probation Outcome," *Crime and Delinquency* 40 (1994): 154–74.

24. Anne Schneider, Laurie Ervin, and Zoann Snyder-Joy, "Further Exploration of the Flight from Discretion: The Role of Risk/Need Instruments in Probation Supervision Decisions," *Journal of Criminal Justice* 24 (1996): 109–21.

25. Clear and O'Leary, *Controlling the Offender in the Community,* 11–29, 77–100.

26. Joan Petersilia, "An Evaluation of Intensive Probation in California," *Journal of Criminal Law and Criminology* 82 (1992): 610–58.

27. Joan Petersilia, Susan Turner, James Kahan, and Joyce Peterson, *Granting Felons Probation: Public Risks and Alternatives* (Santa Monica, Calif.: Rand Corp., 1985).

28. Langan and Cuniff, *Recidivism of Felons on Probation, 1986–1989.*

29. Cuniff, Sechrest, and Cushman, "Redefining Probation for the Coming Decade," 7–8.

30. Kathryn Morgan, "Factors Influencing Probation Outcome: A Review of the Literature," *Federal Probation* 57 (1993): 23–29.

31. Kathryn Morgan, "Factors Associated with Probation Outcome," *Journal of Criminal Justice* 22 (1994): 341–53.

32. Paula M. Ditton, *Mental Health and Treatment of Inmates and Probationers* (Washington, D.C.: Bureau of Justice Statistics, 1999).

33. Langan and Cuniff, *Recidivism of Felons on Probation, 1986–1989;* Allen Beck and Bernard Shipley, *Recidivism of Prisoners Released in 1983* (Washington, D.C.: Bureau of Justice Statistics, 1989).

34. Robyn L. Cohen, *Probation and Parole Violators in State Prison, 1991* (Washington, D.C.: Bureau of Justice Statistics, 1995).

35. Ibid.

36. *Minnesota v. Murphy,* 465 U.S. 420, 104 S.Ct. 1136, 79 L.Ed.2d 409 (1984).

37. *Griffin v. Wisconsin,* 483 U.S. 868, 107 S.Ct. 3164, 97 L.Ed.2d 709 (1987).

38. *Mempa v. Rhay,* 389 U.S. 128, 88 S.Ct. 254, 19 L.Ed.2d 336 (1967).

39. *Morrissey v. Brewer,* 408 U.S. 471, 92 S.Ct. 2593, 33 L.Ed.2d 484 (1972).

40. *Gagnon v. Scarpelli,* 411 U.S. 778, 93 S.Ct. 1756, 36 L.Ed.2d 656 (1973).

41. *United States v. Carson,* 669 F.2d 216 (5th Cir., 1982).

42. *United States v. Granderson,* 114 Ct. 1259, 127 L.Ed.2d 611 (1994).

43. Peter Finn, "Prison Crowding: The Response of Probation and Parole," *Crime and Delinquency* 30 (1984): 141–53.

44. "Law in Massachusetts Requires Probationers to Pay 'Day Fees,'" *Criminal Justice Newsletter,* 15 September 1988, 1.

45. Gerald Wheeler, Therese Macan, Rodney Hissong, and Morgan Slusher, "The Effects of Probation Service Fees on Case Management Strategy and Sanctions," *Journal of Criminal Justice* 17 (1989): 15–24.

46. Peter Finn and Dale Parent, *Making the Offender Foot the Bill, A Texas Program* (Washington, D.C.: National Institute of Justice, 1992).

47. Richard Lawrence, "Reexamining Community Corrections Models," *Crime and Delinquency* 37 (1991): 449–64.

48. Todd Clear and Patricia Hardyman, "The New Intensive Supervision Movement," *Crime and Delinquency* 36 (1990): 42–60.

49. For a thorough review of these programs, see James Byrne, Arthur Lurigio, and Joan Petersilia, eds., *Smart Sentencing: The Emergence of Intermediate Sanctions* (Newbury Park, Calif.: Sage, 1993). Hereinafter cited as *Smart Sentencing.*

50. Beck and Shipley, *Recidivism of Prisoners Released in 1983.*

51. S. Christopher Baird and Dennis Wagner, "Measuring Diversion: The Florida Community Control Program," *Crime and Delinquency* 36 (1990): 112–25.

52. Norval Morris and Michael Tonry, *Between Prison and Probation: Intermediate Punishments in a Rational Sentencing System* (New York: Oxford University Press, 1990).

53. Michael Tonry and Richard Will, *Intermediate Sanctions* (Washington, D.C.: National Institute of Justice, 1990).

54. Ibid., 8.

55. Michael Maxfield and Terry Baumer, "Home Detention with Electronic Monitoring: Comparing Pretrial and Postconviction Programs," *Crime and Delinquency* 36 (1990): 521–56.

56. Sally Hillsman and Judith Greene, "Tailoring Fines to the Financial Means of Offenders," *Judicature* 72 (1988): 38–45.

57. David Pauly and Carolyn Friday, "Drexel's Crumbling Defense," *Newsweek,* 19 December 1988, 44.

58. George Cole, Barry Mahoney, Marlene Thorton, and Roger Hanson, *The Practices and Attitudes of Trial Court Judges Regarding Fines as a Criminal Sanction* (Washington, D.C.: Government Printing Office, 1987).

59. Ibid.

60. George Cole, "Monetary Sanctions: The Problem of Compliance," in *Smart Sentencing.*

61. *Tate v. Short,* 401 U.S. 395, 91 S.Ct. 668, 28 L.Ed.2d 130 (1971).

62. Margaret Gordon and Daniel Glaser, "The Use and Effects of Financial Penalties in Municipal Courts," *Criminology* 29 (1991): 651–76.

63. "'Day Fines' Being Tested in New York City Court," *Criminal Justice Newsletter,* 1 September 1988, 4–5.

64. Laura Winterfield and Sally Hillsman, *The Staten Island Day-Fine Project* (Washington, D.C.: National Institute of Justice, 1993), 5–6.

65. C. Yorke, *Some Consideration on the Law of Forfeiture for High Treason,* 2d ed. (1746), 26; cited in David Freid, "Rationalizing Criminal Forfeiture,"*Journal of Criminal Law and Criminology* 79 (1988): 329.

66. Fried, "Rationalizing Criminal Forfeiture," 436.

67. James B. Jacobs, Coleen Friel, and Edward O'Callaghan, "Pension Forfeiture: A Problematic Sanction for Public Corruption," *American Criminal Law Review* 35 (1997): 57–92.

68. For a general review, see Burt Galaway and Joe Hudson, *Criminal Justice, Restitution, and Reconciliation* (New York: Criminal Justice Press, 1990); Robert Carter, Jay Cocks, and Daniel Glazer, "Community Service: A Review of the Basic Issues," *Federal Probation* 51 (1987): 4–11.

69. Douglas McDonald, "Punishing Labor: Unpaid Community Service as a Criminal Sentence," in *Smart Sentencing.*

70. Morris and Tonry, *Between Prison and Probation,* 171–75.

71. Frederick Allen and Harvey Treger, "Community Service Orders in Federal Probation: Perceptions of Probationers and Host Agencies," *Federal Probation* 54 (1990): 8–14.

72. Peter Schneider, Anne Schneider, and William Griffith, *Monthly Report of the National Juvenile Restitution Evaluation Project V* (Eugene, Ore.: Institute for Policy Analysis, 1981).

73. Sudipto Roy, "Two Types of Juvenile Restitution Programs in Two Midwestern Counties: A Comparative Study," *Federal Probation* 57 (1993): 48–53.

74. Louis Jankowski, *Probation and Parole, 1990* (Washington, D.C.: Bureau of Justice Statistics, 1991), 2.

75. Harry Allen, Chris Eskridge, Edward Latessa, and Gennaro Vito, *Probation and Parole in America* (New York: Free Press, 1985), 88.

76. Joan Petersilia, *The Influence of Criminal Justice Research* (Santa Monica, Calif.: Rand Corp., 1987).

77. Ibid.

78. Jodi Brown, *Correctional Populations in the United States, 1996* (Washington, D.C.: Bureau of Justice Statistics, 1999), 39.

79. Stephen Gettinger, "Intensive Supervision: Can It Rehabilitate Probation?" *Corrections Magazine* 9 (1983): 7–18.

80. James Byrne, Arthur Lurigio, and Christopher Baird, *The Effectiveness of the New Intensive Supervision Programs, Research in Corrections Series,* vol. 2, no. 2 (preliminary unpublished draft; Washington, D.C.: National Institute of Corrections, 1989).

81. Edward Latessa and Gennaro Vito, "The Effects of Intensive Supervision on Shock Probationers," *Journal of Criminal Justice* 16 (1988): 319–30.

82. James Byrne and Linda Kelly, "Restructuring Probation as an Intermediate Sanction: An Evaluation of the Massachusetts Intensive Probation Supervision Program" (Final report to the National Institute of Justice, Research Program on the Punishment and Control of Offenders, Washington, D.C., 1989).

83. James Ryan, "Who Gets Revoked? A Comparison of Intensive Supervision Successes and Failures in Vermont," *Crime and Delinquency* 43 (1997): 104–18.

84. Peter Jones, "Expanding the Use of Noncustodial Sentencing Options: An Evaluation of the Kansas Community Corrections Act," *Howard Journal* 29 (1990): 114–29; Michael Agopian, "The Impact of Intensive Supervision Probation on Gang-Drug Offenders," *Criminal Justice Policy Review* 4 (1990): 214–22.

85. Betsy Fulton, Edward Latessa, Amy Stichman, Lawrence Travis, "The State of ISP: Research and Policy Implications," *Federal Probation* 61 (1997): 65–75.

86. Joan Petersilia, *Expanding Options for Criminal Sentencing* (Santa Monica, Calif.: Rand Corp., 1987), 32.

87. S. Christopher Baird and Dennis Wagner, "Measuring Diversion: The Florida Community Control Program," *Crime and Delinquency* 36 (1990): 112–25.

88. Linda Smith and Ronald Akers, "A Comparison of Recidivism of Florida's Community Control and Prison: A Five-Year Survival Analysis," *Journal of Research in Crime and Delinquency* 30 (1993): 267–92.

89. Cited in Stephen Rackmill, "An Analysis of Home Confinement as a Sanction," *Federal Probation* 58 (1994): 45.

90. Robert N. Altman, Robert E. Murray, and Evey B. Wooten, "Home Confinement: A '90s Approach to Community Supervision," *Federal Probation* 61 (1997): 30–32.

91. Marc Renzema, "Home Confinement Programs: Development, Implementation, and Impact," in *Smart Sentencing.*

92. Brown, *Correctional Populations in the United States, 1996.*

93. Preston Elrod and Michael Brown, "Predicting Public Support for Electronic House Arrest: Results from a New York County Survey," *American Behavioral Scientist* 39 (1996): 461–74.

94. Joseph Papy and Richard Nimer, "Electronic Monitoring in Florida," *Federal Probation* 55 (1991): 31–33.

95. James Beck, Jody Klein-Saffran, and Harold Wooten, "Home Confinement and the Use of Electronic Monitoring with Federal Parolees," *Federal Probation* 54 (1990): 22–31.

96. Kevin E. Courtright, Bruce L. Berg, and Robert J. Mutchnick, "The Cost Effectiveness of Using House Arrest with Electronic Monitoring for Drunk Drivers," *Federal Probation* 61 (1997): 19–22.

97. Richard Rosenfeld, "The Scope and Purpose of Corrections: Exploring Alternative Responses to Crowding," *Crime and Delinquency* 37 (1991): 500.

98. For a more complete analysis of the EM controversy, see Ronald Corbett and Gary Marx, "Critique: No Soul in the New Machine: Technofallacies in the Electronic Monitoring Movement," *Justice Quarterly* 8 (1991): 399–414.

99. See, generally, Edward Latessa and Lawrence Travis III, "Residential Community Correctional Programs," in *Smart Sentencing.*

100. Updated with personal correspondence with Jan Cartalucca, administrative assistant, Tom Hayden, director, 8 January 1992.

101. Harvey Siegal, James Fisher, Richard Rapp, Casey Kelliher, Joseph Wagner, William O'Brien, and Phyllis Cole, "Enhancing Substance Abuse Treatment with Case Management," *Journal of Substance Abuse Treatment* 13 (1996): 93–98.

102. Dale Parent, *Day Reporting Centers for Criminal Offenders — A Descriptive Analysis of Existing Programs* (Washington, D.C.: National Institute of Justice, 1990); Jack McDevitt and Robyn Miliano, "Day Reporting Centers: An Innovative Concept in Intermediate Sanctions," in *Smart Sentencing.*

103. David Diggs and Stephen Pieper, "Using Day Reporting Centers as an Alternative to Jail," *Federal Probation* 58 (1994): 9–12.

104. For a description of these programs, see Edward Latessa and Lawrence Travis III, "Residential Community Correctional Pro-

grams," in *Smart Sentencing;* see also Byrne and Kelly, "Restructuring Probation as an Intermediate Sanction."

105. David Hartmann, Paul Friday, and Kevin Minor, "Residential Probation: A Seven-Year Follow-Up of Halfway House Discharges," *Journal of Criminal Justice* 22 (1994): 503–15.

106. Banhram Haghighi and Alma Lopez, "Success/Failure of Group Home Treatment Programs for Juveniles," *Federal Probation* 57 (1993): 53–57.

107. Peter R. Jones, "Community Corrections in Kansas: Extending Community-Based Corrections or Widening the Net?" *Journal of Research in Crime and Delinquency* 27 (1990): 79–101.

108. Richard Rosenfeld and Kimberly Kempf, "The Scope and Purposes of Corrections: Exploring Alternative Responses to Crowding," *Crime and Delinquency* 37 (1991): 481–505.

109. For a thorough review, see Michael Tonry and Mary Lynch, "Intermediate Sanctions," in *Crime and Justice, A Review of Research,* vol. 20, ed. Michael Tonry (Chicago: University of Chicago Press, 1996), 99–144.

110. Francis Cullen, "Control in the Community: The Limits of Reform?" (Paper presented at the International Association of Residential and Community Alternatives, Philadelphia, November 1993).

111. John DiIulio and Charles Logan, "The Ten Deadly Myths about Crime and Punishment in the U.S.," *Wisconsin Interest* 1 (1992): 21–35.

112. Michael Tonry and Mary Lynch, "Intermediate Sanctions."

113. Gordon Bazemore and Curt Taylor Griffiths, "Conferences, Circles, Boards, and Mediations: The 'New Wave' of Community Justice Decision Making," *Federal Probation* 61 (1997): 25–37.

chapter 13

Corrections: History, Institutions, and Populations

Luis Felipe is the founder of the New York chapter of the Almighty Latin Kings and Queens Nation, a branch of Chicago's notorious Latin Kings gang.[1] In 1997 federal Judge John S. Martin, Jr., sentenced Felipe, upon his conviction for murder, to life imprisonment plus forty-five years. The judge ruled that Felipe must serve the entire sentence in solitary confinement, prohibited from writing or being visited by anyone except his lawyer and close relatives. According to legal experts, these conditions are virtually unprecedented in their severity and the degree to which they will be monitored by a federal judge; they stand as an extreme example of a trend to make prison sentences more punitive.

Luis Felipe, gang leader, in Federal prison in Colorado

The story of prison inmate Luis Felipe is an all too familiar account of a life filled with displacement, poverty, and chronic predatory crime. The son of a Cuban prostitute, at the age of nine, he was sent to prison for robbery. On his nineteenth birthday in 1980, he immigrated to the United States and soon after became a street thug in Chicago where he joined the Latin Kings. After moving to the Bronx, in what has been described as a drunken accident, he shot and killed his girlfriend in 1981. He fled to Chicago and was not apprehended until 1984. Sentenced to nine years for second-degree manslaughter, Felipe ended up at Collins Correctional Facility in Helmuth, New York, where he started a fledgling New York prison chapter of the Latin Kings. As King Blood, Inka, First Supreme Crown, Felipe corresponded with Latin Kings in and out of prison. (At its peak, the gang was estimated to have about two thousand members.) But in 1993 and 1994, disciplinary troubles erupted throughout the Latin Kings; some members were stealing from the organization. Infuriated, King Blood wrote to his street lieutenants about disloyal Kings, ordering them to B.O.S. (beat on sight) and T.O.S. (terminate on sight). Even while he was in prison segregation, he was able to order the leader of the Latin Kings in the Rikers Island jail to commit murder; the victim ended up being badly slashed in the face. Another victim was choked and beheaded. A third victim was killed accidentally during an attempt on another man, and a fourth was gunned down. Federal authorities, who had been monitoring Felipe's mail, arrested thirty-five Latin Kings; thirty-four pled guilty and only Felipe insisted on a trial.

Since his sentencing in February 1997, Felipe has spent twenty-three hours a day in a 7 × 12-foot cell and allowed one hour to run in a hall outside his cell in a maximum-security facility in Colorado. Prison guards will not talk with him. Except for letters from his lawyer, Felipe receives no mail. "You cannot even imagine how I feel in here and how frustrating it is to be alone 24-7," he recently wrote to his attorney. "I feel real down and out . . . I am so terribly alone . . . I am afraid to think cause all that comes to my mind is agony . . . As day after day goes by I see that my whole life has been useless. I fought so hard to protect a dream that has become my most terrified nightmare. I have even tried to look for God but even that search has turned empty."[2]

The story of Luis Felipe's life is typical of a majority of prisoners in the vast American prison system. Many come from troubled backgrounds and have little hope or opportunity; all too many have emotional problems and grew up in abusive households. A majority are alcohol and drug dependent at the time of their arrest. Considered both dangerous and incorrigible, many find themselves, like Felipe, in super-maximum-security prisons where they spend most of their day confined to their cells. ■

prison
A state or federal correctional institution for incarceration of felony offenders for terms of one year or more.

jail
A place to detain people awaiting trial, to serve as a lockup for drunks and disorderly individuals, and to confine convicted misdemeanants serving sentences of less than one year.

Today, the correctional system has branches in the federal, state, and county levels of government. Felons may be placed in state or federal penitentiaries (**prisons**), which are usually isolated, high-security structures. Misdemeanants are housed in county **jails**, sometimes called reformatories or houses of correction. Juvenile offenders have their own institutions, sometimes euphemistically called schools, camps, ranches, or homes. Typically, the latter are nonsecure facilities, often located in rural areas, that provide both confinement and rehabilitative services for young offenders.

Other types of correctional institutions include ranches and farms for adult offenders and community correctional settings, such as halfway houses, for inmates who are about to return to society. Today's correctional facilities encompass a wide range, from maxi-maxi security institutions, such as the federal prison in Florence, Colorado, where the nation's most dangerous felons are confined, to low-security camps that house white-collar criminals convicted of such crimes as insider trading and mail fraud.

One of the great tragedies of our time is that correctional institutions, whatever form they may take, do not seem to correct. They are, in most instances, overcrowded, understaffed, outdated warehouses for social outcasts. The overcrowding crisis is the most significant problem faced by the prison today: Prisons now contain more than 1.2 million inmates. Prisons are more suited to control,

recidivism
Repetition of criminal behavior; habitual criminality. Recidivism is measured by (1) criminal acts that resulted in conviction by a court when committed by individuals who are under correctional supervision or who had been released from correctional supervision within the previous three years and (2) technical violations of probation or parole in which a sentencing or paroling authority took action that resulted in an adverse change in the offender's legal status.

punishment, and security than to rehabilitation and treatment. It is a sad but unfortunately accurate observation that today's correctional institution has become a revolving door and that all too many of its residents return time and again. Although no completely accurate statement of the **recidivism** rate is available, it is estimated that more than half of all inmates will be back in prison within six years of their release.[3]

Despite the apparent lack of success of penal institutions, great debate continues over the direction of their future operations. Some penal experts maintain that prisons and jails are not really places for rehabilitation and treatment but should be used to keep dangerous offenders apart from society and give them the "just deserts" for their crimes.[4] In this sense, prison success would be measured by such factors as physical security, length of incapacitation, relationship between the crime rate and the number of incarcerated felons, and inmates' perceptions that their treatment was fair and proportionate. The dominance of this correctional philosophy is illustrated by the facts that (1) presumptive and mandatory sentencing structures are now used in such traditionally progressive states as California, Massachusetts, and Illinois; (2) the number of people under lock and key has risen rapidly in the past few years despite the fact that the crime rate has declined; and (3) political candidates who are portrayed by their opponents as advocates of inmate rehabilitation soon find themselves on the defensive with voters.

Although the conservative tide in corrections is self-evident, many penal experts still maintain that prisons can be useful places for offender rehabilitation.[5] Many examples of the treatment philosophy still flourish in prisons: Educational programs allow inmates to get college credits; vocational training has become more sophisticated; counseling and substance abuse programs are almost universal; and every state maintains some type of early-release and community correctional programs.

In this chapter we explore the correctional system, beginning with the history and nature of correctional institutions. Then, in Chapter 14 we examine institutional life in some detail.

THE HISTORY OF CORRECTIONAL INSTITUTIONS

As you may recall, the original legal punishments were typically banishment or slavery, restitution (wergild), corporal punishment, and execution. The concept of incarcerating convicted offenders for long periods of time as a punishment for their misdeeds did not become the norm of corrections until the nineteenth century.[6]

Although the use of incarceration as a routine punishment began much later, some early European institutions were created specifically to detain and punish criminal offenders. Penal institutions were constructed in England during the tenth century, to hold pretrial detainees and those waiting for their sentence to be carried out.[7] During the twelfth century, King Henry II of England constructed a series of county jails to hold thieves and vagrants prior to the disposition of their sentence. In 1557 the workhouse in Brideswell, England, was built to hold people convicted of relatively minor offenses who would work to pay off their debt to society; those committing more serious offenses were held there prior to their execution.

Le Stinche, a prison in Florence, Italy, was used to punish offenders as early as 1301.[8] Prisoners were enclosed in separate cells, classified on the basis of gender, age, mental state, and crime seriousness. Furloughs and conditional release were permitted, and perhaps for the first time, a period of incarceration

"Prisoners Exercising" by Vincent Van Gogh. Painted in 1890, Van Gogh's work captures the despair of the nineteenth-century penal institution. The face of the prisoner in the center of the picture looking at the viewer is Van Gogh's.

replaced corporal punishment for some offenses. Although Le Stinche existed for five hundred years, relatively little is known about its administration or whether this early example of incarceration was unique to Florence.

The first penal institutions were foul places devoid of proper care, food, or medical treatment. The jailer, usually a shire reeve (sheriff), an official appointed by king or noble landholder as chief law enforcement official of a county, ran the jail under the "fee system." This required inmates to pay for their own food and services. Those who could not pay were fed scraps until they literally starved to death:

> In 1748 the admission to Southwark prison was eleven shillings and four pence. Having got in, the prisoner had to pay for having himself put in irons, for his bed, of whatever sort, for his room if he was able to afford a separate room. He had to pay for his food, and when he had paid his debts and was ready to go out, he had to pay for having his irons struck off, and a discharge fee . . . The gaolers [jailers] were usually "low bred, mercenary and oppressive, barbarous fellows, who think of nothing but enriching themselves by the most cruel extortion, and have less regard for the life of a poor prisoner than for the life of a brute."[9]

Jail conditions were deplorable because jailers ran them for personal gain; the fewer the services provided, the greater their profit. Early jails were catchall institutions that held not only criminal offenders awaiting trial but also vagabonds, debtors, the mentally ill, and assorted others.

hulk
A mothballed ship that was used to house prisoners in eighteenth-century England.

From 1776 to 1785 a growing inmate population that could no longer be transported to North America forced the English to house prisoners on **hulks,** abandoned ships anchored in harbors. The hulks became infamous for their degrading conditions and brutal punishments but were not totally abandoned until 1858. The writings of John Howard, the reform-oriented sheriff of Bedfordshire, drew attention to the squalid conditions in British penal institutions. His famous book, *The State of Prisons* (1777), condemned the lack of basic care given English inmates awaiting trial or serving sentences.[10] Howard's efforts to create humane standards in the British penal system resulted in the Penitentiary Act, by which Parliament established a more orderly penal system, with periodic inspections, elimination of the fee system, and greater consideration for inmates.

American Developments

Although Europe had jails and a variety of other penal facilities, it was in the United States that correctional reform was first instituted. The first American jail was built in James City in the Virginia colonies in the early seventeenth century. However, the "modern" American correctional system had its origin in Pennsylvania under the leadership of William Penn.

At the end of the seventeenth century, Penn revised Pennsylvania's criminal code to forbid torture and the capricious use of mutilation and physical punishment. These penalties were replaced with imprisonment at hard labor, moderate flogging, fines, and forfeiture of property. All lands and goods belonging to felons were to be used to make restitution to the victims of crimes, with restitution being limited to twice the value of the damages. Felons who owned no property were required by law to work in the prison workhouse until the victim was compensated.

Penn ordered that a new type of institution be built to replace the widely used public forms of punishment — stocks, pillories, gallows, and branding irons. Each county was instructed to build a house of corrections similar to today's jails. County trustees or commissioners were responsible for raising money to build the jails and providing for their maintenance, although they were operated by the local sheriff. Penn's reforms remained in effect until his death in 1718, when the criminal penal code was changed back to open public punishment and harsh brutality.

It is difficult to identify the first American prison. Alexis Durham has described the opening of the Newgate Prison of Connecticut in 1773 on the site of an abandoned copper mine. Newgate, which closed in the 1820s, is often ignored by correctional historians.[11] In 1785 Castle Island prison was opened in Massachusetts and operated for about fifteen years.

THE QUAKER INFLUENCE

The origin of the modern correctional system, however, is usually traced to eighteenth-century developments in Pennsylvania. In 1776 postrevolutionary Pennsylvania again adopted William Penn's code, and in 1787 a group of Quakers led by Benjamin Rush formed the Philadelphia Society for Alleviating the Miseries of Public Prisons. The aim of the society was to bring some degree of humane and orderly treatment to the growing penal system. The Quakers' influence on the legislature resulted in limiting the use of the death penalty to cases involving treason, murder, rape, and arson. Their next step was to reform the institutional system so that the prison could serve as a suitable alternative to physical punishment.

The only models of custodial institutions at that time were the local county jails that Penn had established. These facilities were designed to detain offenders, to securely incarcerate convicts awaiting other punishment, or to hold offenders who were working off their crimes. The Pennsylvania jails placed men, women, and children of all ages indiscriminately in one room. Liquor was often freely sold.

Under pressure from the Quakers to improve these conditions, the Pennsylvania State Legislature in 1790 called for the renovation of the prison system. The ultimate result was the creation of a separate wing of Philadelphia's **Walnut Street Jail** to house convicted felons (except those sentenced to death). Prisoners were placed in solitary cells, where they remained in isolation and did not have the right to work.[12] Quarters that contained the solitary or separate cells were called the **penitentiary house,** as was already the custom in England.

Walnut Street Jail
In 1790 a separate wing of Philadelphia's Walnut Street Jail was built to house convicted felons. This was the forerunner of the secure correctional system in the United States.

penitentiary house
A secure correctional facility, based on the Quaker concept that incarcerated criminals should do "penitence."

The new Pennsylvania prison system took credit for a rapid decrease in the crime rate — from 131 convictions in 1789 to 45 in 1793.[13] The prison became known as a school for reform and a place for public labor. The Walnut Street Jail's equitable conditions were credited with reducing escapes to none in the first four years of its existence (except for fourteen on opening day).

The Walnut Street Jail was not a total success. Overcrowding undermined the goal of solitary confinement of serious offenders, and soon more than one inmate was placed in each cell. The isolation had a terrible psychological effect on inmates, and eventually inmates were given in-cell piecework on which they worked up to eight hours a day. Despite these difficulties, similar institutions were erected in New York (Newgate in 1791) and New Jersey (Trenton in 1798).

THE AUBURN SYSTEM As the nineteenth century got underway, both the Pennsylvania and the New York prison systems were experiencing difficulties maintaining the ever-increasing numbers of convicted criminals. Initially, administrators dealt with the problem by increasing the use of pardons, relaxing prison discipline, and limiting supervision.

In 1816 New York built a new prison in Auburn, hoping to alleviate some of the overcrowding at Newgate. The Auburn Prison design became known as the **tier system** because cells were built vertically on five floors of the structure. It was also referred to as the **congregate system** since most prisoners ate and worked in groups. Later, in 1819, construction was started on a wing of solitary cells to house unruly prisoners. Three classes of prisoners were then created: One group remained continually in solitary confinement as a result of breaches of prison discipline; the second group was allowed labor as an occasional form of recreation; and the third and largest class worked and ate together during the day and were separated only at night.

tier system
The structure of early prisons having numerous floors or wings that stacked cells one over another.

congregate system
The Auburn Prison, one of the nation's first correctional facilities, was a congregate system since most prisoners ate and worked in groups.

Auburn system
The prison system developed in New York during the nineteenth century that stressed congregate working conditions.

The philosophy of the **Auburn system** was crime prevention through fear of punishment and silent confinement. The worst felons were to be cut off from all contact with other prisoners, and although they were treated and fed relatively well, they had no hope of pardon to relieve their solitude or isolation. For a time, some of the worst convicts were forced to remain totally alone and silent during the entire day; this practice caused many prisoners to have mental breakdowns, resulting in many suicides and self-mutilations. This practice was abolished in 1823.

The combination of silence and solitude as a method of punishment was not abandoned easily. Prison officials sought to overcome the side effects of total isolation while maintaining the penitentiary system. The solution adopted at Auburn was to keep convicts in separate cells at night but allow them to work together during the day under enforced silence. Hard work and silence became the foundation of the Auburn system wherever it was adopted. Silence was the key to prison discipline; it prohibited the formulation of escape plans, it prevented plots and riots, and it allowed prisoners to contemplate their infractions.

Inmates in a nineteenth-century prison return from a work detail in "lock step."

THE PENNSYLVANIA SYSTEM In 1818 Pennsylvania took the radical step of establishing a prison that placed each inmate in a single cell for the duration of his sentence. Classifications were abolished because each cell was intended as a miniature prison that would prevent the inmates from contaminating one another.

The new Pennsylvania state prison, called the Western Penitentiary, had an unusual architectural design. It was built in a semicircle, with the cells positioned along its circumference. Built back to back, some cells faced the boundary wall while others faced the internal area of the circle. Its inmates were kept in solitary confinement almost constantly, being allowed out for about an hour a day for exercise. In 1820 a second, similar penitentiary using the isolate system was built in Philadelphia and called the Eastern Penitentiary.

Pennsylvania system
The prison system developed during the nineteenth century that stressed total isolation and individual penitence as a means of reform.

Supporters of the **Pennsylvania system** believed that the penitentiary was truly a place to do penance. By advocating totally removing the sinner from society and allowing the prisoner a period of isolation in which to reflect alone on the evils of crime, the supporters of the Pennsylvania system reflected the influence of religion and religious philosophy on corrections. Solitary confinement (with in-cell labor) was believed to make work so attractive that upon release the inmate would be well suited to resume a productive existence in society.

The Pennsylvania system eliminated the need for large numbers of guards or disciplinary measures. Isolated from one another, inmates could not plan escapes or collectively break rules. When discipline was a problem, however, the whip and iron gag were used.

INCARCERATION PHILOSOPHIES Why did prisons develop at this time? One reason was that during this period of "enlightenment," a concerted effort was made to alleviate the harsh punishments and torture that had been the norm. The interest of religious groups, such as the Quakers, in prison reform was prompted in part by humanitarian ideals. Another factor was the economic potential of prison industry, viewed as a valuable economic asset in times of a short labor supply.[14]

The concept of using harsh discipline and control to "retrain" the heart and soul of offenders is the subject of an important book on penal philosophy: *Discipline and Punish* by French sociologist Michel Foucault.[15] Foucault's thesis is that as societies evolve and become more complex, they create increasingly more elaborate mechanisms to discipline their recalcitrant members and make them docile enough to obey social rules. In the seventeenth and eighteenth centuries, discipline was directed toward the human body itself, through torture. However, physical punishment and torture turned some condemned men into heroes and martyrs. Prisons presented the opportunity to rearrange, not diminish, punishment — to make it more effective and regulated. In the development of the nineteenth-century prison, the object was to discipline the offender psychologically; "the expiation that once rained down on the body must be replaced by a punishment that acts in the depths of the heart."[16]

Regimentation became the standard mode of prison life. Convicts did not simply walk from place to place; rather, they went in close order and single file, each looking over the shoulder of the preceding person, faces inclined to the right, feet moving in unison. The lock-step prison shuffle was developed at Auburn and is still used in some institutions today.[17]

When discipline was breached in the Auburn system, punishment was applied in the form of a rawhide whip on the inmate's back. Immediate and effective, Auburn discipline was so successful that when one hundred inmates were used to build the famous Sing Sing Prison in 1825, not one dared try to escape, although they were housed in an open field with only minimal supervision.[18]

Many fiery debates occurred between advocates of the Pennsylvania system and adherents of the Auburn system. Those supporting the latter boasted of its supposed advantages; it was the cheapest and most productive way to reform prisoners. They criticized the Pennsylvania system as cruel and inhumane, suggesting that solitary confinement was both physically and mentally damaging. The Pennsylvania system's devotees, on the other hand, argued that their system was quiet, efficient, humane, and well ordered and provided the ultimate correctional facility.[19] They chided the Auburn system for tempting inmates to talk by putting them together for meals and work and then punishing them when they did talk. Finally, the Auburn system was accused of becoming a breeding place for criminal associations by allowing inmates to get to know one another.

The Auburn system eventually prevailed and spread throughout the United States; many of its features are still used today. Its innovations included congregate working conditions, the use of solitary confinement to punish unruly inmates, military regimentation, and discipline. In Auburn-like institutions, prisoners were marched from place to place; their time was regulated by bells telling them to wake up, sleep, and work. The system was so like the military that many of its early administrators were recruited from the armed services.

Although the prison was viewed as an improvement over capital and corporal punishment, it quickly became the scene of depressed conditions; inmates were treated harshly and routinely whipped and tortured. Prison brutality flourished in these institutions, which had originally been devised as a more humane correctional alternative. In these early penal institutions, brutal corporal punishment took place indoors where, hidden from public view, it could become even more savage.[20]

PRISONS AT THE TURN OF THE CENTURY The prison of the late nineteenth century was remarkably similar to that of today. The congregate system was adopted in all states except Pennsylvania. Prisons were overcrowded, and the single-cell principle was often ignored. The prison, like the police department, became the scene of political intrigue and efforts by political administrators to control the hiring of personnel and dispensing of patronage.

contract system (convict)
The system used earlier in the twentieth century by which inmates were leased out to private industry to work.

convict-lease system
The system whereby the state leased its prisoners to a business for a fixed annual fee and gave up supervision and control.

Prison industry developed and became the predominant theme around which institutions were organized. Some prisons used the **contract system,** in which officials sold the labor of inmates to private businesses. Sometimes the contractor supervised the inmates inside the prison itself. Under the **convict-lease system,** the state leased its prisoners to a business for a fixed annual fee and gave up supervision and control. Finally, some institutions had prisoners produce goods for the prison's own use.[21]

The development of prison industry quickly led to the abuse of inmates, who were forced to work for almost no wages, and to profiteering by dishonest administrators and businessmen. During the Civil War era, prisons were major manufacturers of clothes, shoes, boots, furniture, and the like. Beginning in the 1870s, opposition by trade unions sparked restrictions on interstate commerce in prison goods.

REFORM MOVEMENTS Prison operations were also reformed. The National Congress of Penitentiary and Reformatory Discipline, held in Cincinnati in 1870, heralded a new era of prison reform. Organized by penologists Enoch Wines and Theodore Dwight, the congress provided a forum for corrections experts from around the nation to call for the treatment, education, and training of inmates.

One of the most famous people to attend the congress, Z. R. Brockway, warden at the Elmira Reformatory in New York, advocated individualized treatment, the indeterminate sentence, and parole. The reformatory program initiated by Brockway included elementary education for illiterates, designated library hours, lectures by faculty members of the local Elmira College, and a group of vocational training shops. From 1888 to 1920, Elmira administrators used military-like training to discipline the inmates and organize the institution. The military organization could be seen in every aspect of the institution: schooling, manual training, sports, supervision of inmates, and even parole decisions.[22] The cost to the state of the institution's operations was to be held to a minimum.

Although Brockway proclaimed Elmira to be an ideal reformatory, his actual achievements were limited. The greatest significance of his contribution was the injection of a degree of humanitarianism into the industrial prisons of that day (although there were accusations that excessive corporal punishment was used and that Brockway personally administered whippings).[23] Although many institutions were constructed across the nation and labeled reformatories based on the Elmira model, most of them continued to be industrially oriented.[24]

PRISONS IN THE TWENTIETH CENTURY The early twentieth century was a time of contrasts in the prison system of the United States.[25] At one extreme were those who advocated reform, such as the Mutual Welfare League led by Thomas Mott Osborne. Prison reform groups proposed better treatment for inmates, an end to harsh corporal punishment, the creation of meaningful prison industries, and educational programs. Reformers argued that prisoners should not be isolated from society and that the best elements of society — education, religion, meaningful work, self-governance — should be brought to the prison. Osborne went so far as to spend one week in New York's notorious Sing Sing Prison to learn firsthand about its conditions.

Opposed to the reformers were conservative prison administrators and state officials who believed that stern disciplinary measures were needed to control dangerous prison inmates. They continued the time-honored system of regimentation and discipline. Although the whip and the lash were eventually abolished, solitary confinement in dark, bare cells became a common penal practice.

Elmira Reformatory, training course in drafting, 1909. Inmates stand at drafting tables as guards watch and a supervisor sits at a fenced-off desk at the front of the hall. Elmira was one of the first institutions to employ education and training programs.

In time, some of the more rigid prison rules gave way to liberal reform. By the mid-1930s, few prisons required inmates to wear the red-and-white-striped convict suit and substituted nondescript gray uniforms. The code of silence ended, as did the lockstep shuffle. Prisoners were allowed "the freedom of the yard" to mingle and exercise an hour or two each day.[26] Movies and radio appeared in the 1930s. Visiting policies and mail privileges were liberalized.

PRISON INDUSTRY A more important trend was the development of specialized prisons designed to treat particular types of offenders. For example, in New York the prisons at Clinton and Auburn were viewed as industrial facilities for hard-core inmates, Great Meadow was an agricultural center to house nondangerous offenders, and Dannemora was a facility for the criminally insane. In California, San Quentin housed inmates considered salvageable by correctional authorities, while Folsom was reserved for hard-core offenders.[27]

Prison industry also evolved. Opposition by organized labor helped put an end to the convict-lease system and forced inmate labor. By 1900 a number of states had restricted the sale of prisoner-made goods on the open market. The worldwide Depression that began in 1929 prompted industry and union leaders to further pressure state legislators to reduce competition from prison industries. A series of evermore restrictive federal legislative initiatives led to the Sumners–Ashurst Act (1940), which made it a federal offense to transport interstate commerce goods made in prison for private use, regardless of the laws of the state receiving the goods.[28] The restrictions imposed by the federal government helped to severely curtail prison industry for forty years. Private entrepreneurs shunned prison investments because they were no longer profitable; the result was inmate idleness and make-work jobs.[29]

Despite some changes and reforms, the prison in the mid-twentieth century remained a destructive total institution. Although some aspects of inmate life improved, severe discipline, harsh rules, and solitary confinement were the way of life in prison.

hands-off doctrine
The legal practice of allowing prison administrators a free hand to run the institution even if correctional practices violate inmates' constitutional rights; ended with the onset of the prisoners' rights movement in the 1960s.

THE MODERN ERA The modern era has been a period of change and turmoil in the nation's correctional system. Three trends stand out. First, between 1960 and 1980, what is referred to as the prisoners' rights movement occurred. After many years of indifference (a policy referred to as the **hands off doctrine**), state and federal courts ruled in case after case that institutionalized inmates had rights to freedom of religion and speech, medical care, procedural due process, and proper living conditions. Inmates won rights unheard of in the nineteenth- and early twentieth-century prisons. Since 1980, however, an increasingly conservative judiciary has curtailed the growth of inmate rights.

Second, violence within the correctional system became a national concern. Well-publicized riots at New York's Attica Prison and the New Mexico State Penitentiary drew attention to the potential for death and destruction that lurks in every prison. Prison rapes and killings have become commonplace. The locus of control in many prisons shifted from the correctional staff to violent inmate gangs. In reaction, some administrators have tried to improve conditions and provide innovative programs that give inmates a voice in running the institution. Another reaction has been to tighten discipline and build new super-maximum-security prisons to control the most dangerous offenders. The problem of prison overcrowding has made attempts to improve conditions extremely difficult.

Third, the view that traditional correctional rehabilitation efforts have failed has prompted many penologists to reconsider the purpose of incapacitating criminals. Between 1960 and 1980, it was common for correctional administrators to cling to the **medical model,** which viewed inmates as "sick people" who were suffering from some social malady that prevented them from adjusting to society. Correctional treatment could help "cure" them and enable them to live productive lives once they returned to the community. In the 1970s, efforts were also made to help offenders become reintegrated into society by providing them with new career opportunities that relied on work-release programs. Inmates were allowed to work outside the institution during the day and return in the evening; some were given extended furloughs in the community. Work release became a political issue when Willie Horton, a furloughed inmate from Massachusetts, raped a young woman. Criticism of its "liberal" furlough program helped George Bush defeat Massachusetts Governor Michael Dukakis for the U.S. presidency in 1988; in the aftermath of the Horton case, a number of states, including Massachusetts, restricted their furlough policies.

medical model
A view of corrections holding that convicted offenders are victims of their environment who need care and treatment to transform them into valuable members of society.

Prisons have come to be viewed as places for control, incapacitation, and punishment, rather than as sites for rehabilitation and reform. Advocates of the *no frills,* or *penal harm, movement* believe that if prison is a punishing experience, would-be criminals will be deterred from crime and current inmates will be encouraged to go straight. Nonetheless, efforts to use correctional institutions as treatment facilities have not ended, and such innovations as the development of private industries on prison grounds have kept the rehabilitative ideal alive.

The alleged failure of correctional treatment, coupled with constantly increasing correctional costs, has prompted the development of alternatives to incarceration, such as intensive probation supervision, house arrest, and electronic monitoring (see Chapter 12). What has developed is a bifurcated correctional policy: Keep as many nonviolent offenders out of the correctional system as possible by means of community-based programs; incarcerate dangerous, violent offenders for long periods of time.[30] These efforts have been compromised by a growing get-tough stance in judicial and legislative sentencing policy, accented by mandatory minimum sentences for gun crimes and drug trafficking. Despite the development of alternatives to incarceration, the number of people under lock and key has skyrocketed.

In the following sections, we review the most prominent types of correctional facilities in use today.

JAILS

The nation's jails are institutional facilities with five primary purposes: (1) They detain accused offenders who cannot make or are not eligible for bail prior to trial; (2) they hold convicted offenders awaiting sentence; (3) they serve as the principal institution of secure confinement for offenders convicted of misdemeanors; (4) they hold probationers and parolees picked up for violations and waiting for a hearing; (5) they house felons when state prisons are overcrowded.

A number of formats are used to jail offenders. About fifteen thousand local jurisdictions maintain short-term police or municipal lockups that house offenders for no more than forty-eight hours before a bail hearing can be held; thereafter, detainees are kept in the county jail. In some jurisdictions, such as New Hampshire and Massachusetts, a house of corrections holds convicted misdemeanants, and a county jail holds pretrial detainees. Today, the jail is a multipurpose correctional institution whose other main functions are set out in Exhibit 13.1.

According to the most recent statistics, about half of jailed inmates are unconvicted, awaiting formal charges (arraignment), bail, or trial. The remaining half are convicted offenders who are serving time, awaiting parole or probation revocation hearings, or transferred from a state prison because of overcrowding.

Jails are typically a low-priority item in the criminal justice system. Because they are usually administered on a county level, jail services have not been sufficiently regulated, nor has a unified national policy been developed to mandate what constitutes adequate jail conditions. Many jails have consequently developed into squalid, crumbling holding pens.

Jails are considered to be holding facilities for the county's undesirables, rather than correctional institutions that provide meaningful treatment. They may house indigents who, looking for a respite from the winter's cold, commit a minor offense; the mentally ill who will eventually be hospitalized after a civil commitment hearing; and substance abusers who are suffering the first shocks of confinement. The jail rarely holds "professional" criminals, most of whom are able to make bail.[31] Instead, the jail holds the people considered detached from and disreputable in local society and who are frequently arrested because they are considered "offensive" by the local police. A recent survey in New York City found that on any given day more than twenty-eight hundred people with serious mental illness were being confined in jail, about 20 percent of the total inmate population.[32] The purpose of the jail is to "manage" these persons and keep them separate from the rest of society. By intruding in their lives, jailing them actually increased their involvement with the law.

exhibit 13.1

Jail Functions and Services

Receive individuals pending arraignment and hold them awaiting trial, conviction, or sentencing.

Readmit probation, parole, and jail-bond violators and absconders.

Temporarily detain juveniles pending transfer to juvenile authorities.

Hold mentally ill persons pending their movement to appropriate health facilities.

Hold individuals for the military, for protective custody, for contempt, and for the courts as witnesses.

Release convicted inmates to the communty on completion of sentence.

Transfer inmates to federal, state, or other authorities.

House inmates for federal, state, or other authorities because of crowding of their facilities.

Relinquish custody of temporary detainees to juvenile and medical authorities.

Sometimes operate community-based programs as alternatives to incarceration.

Hold inmates sentenced to short terms (generally under one year).

Source: Darrell K. Gilliard and Allen J. Beck, *Prison and Jail Inmates at Midyear 1996* (Washington, D.C.: Bureau of Justice Statistics, 1997).

Jail Populations A national effort has been made to remove as many people from local jails as possible through the adoption of both bail reform measures and pretrial diversion. Nonetheless, jail populations have been steadily increasing, due in part to the increased use of mandatory jail sentences for such common crimes as drunk driving and the use of local jails to house inmates for whom there is no room in state prisons.

Approximately 600,000 people are being held in the nation's local jails, and the jail population has been increasing about 5 percent each year.[33] There are also about 70,000 people who are assigned to jail but are being supervised in the community on work release, electronic monitoring, weekend programs, and so on. On an annual basis, about 10 million people are admitted to jail, and slightly less are released.

Whereas the number of jails has declined from a high of 4,037 in 1970 to about 3,500 today, the number of inmates has increased about 400 percent (from 160,683); there is thus a trend toward fewer but larger jails. In 1970 there were 79 inmates per 100,000 population; in 1990 that number had risen to 163 per 100,000; today there are 219 residents per 100,000. The increase in the jail population is a direct function of the nation's get-tough policy against drug offenders and offenses.

Jail Inmate Characteristics The removal of juveniles from adult jails has long been a national priority, but more than fifty thousand youths are admitted to adult jails each year. An estimated eighty-one hundred people under age 18 are housed in adult jails on a given day. Over two-thirds of these young inmates have been convicted or are being held for trial as adults in criminal court.

Male inmates make up about 90 percent of the local jail population. However, the female population, like the crime rate, has been growing at a faster pace. On average, the female jail population has grown 10.2 percent annually since 1985, whereas the male inmate population has grown by 6.1 percent annually.

A majority of local jail inmates are either black or Hispanic. White non-Hispanics make up about 41 percent of the jail population; black non-Hispanics, 41 percent; Hispanics, 16 percent; and other races (Asians, Pacific Islanders, Native Americans and Alaska Natives), 1.7 percent. Relative to the number of U.S. residents, black non-Hispanics are six times more likely than white non-Hispanics, over twice as likely as Hispanics, and over eight times more likely than persons of other races to have been held in a local jail. As Figure 13.1 shows, since 1984 the increase in the number of African-Americans doing jail time has increased dramatically. The increase helps fuel the suspicion in the African-American community of a dual standard in the justice system.

Most inmates were either doing time or awaiting trial on property crime charges, such as burglary, larceny, or motor vehicle theft. However, the number of drug offenders has increased markedly. In 1983 about 9 percent of the total population was in jail for drug-related crimes; that number has now increased to about 24 percent of all inmates. Many inmates were repeaters: more than 70 percent had a prior criminal record, and more than half had a criminal justice status (e.g., probationer, bailee, parolee) at the time of their arrest. About 40 percent were under the influence of alcohol at the time of their arrest, and an equal number had at one time or were currently being treated for substance abuse problems. There is also a strong association between prior physical and sexual abuse and jail inmate status: About 13 percent of males and 47 percent of female inmates report either physical or sexual abuse.[34] It is not surprising then that about 16 percent of those in local jails report either having a mental condition or an overnight stay in a mental hospital at least once in their lives.[35]

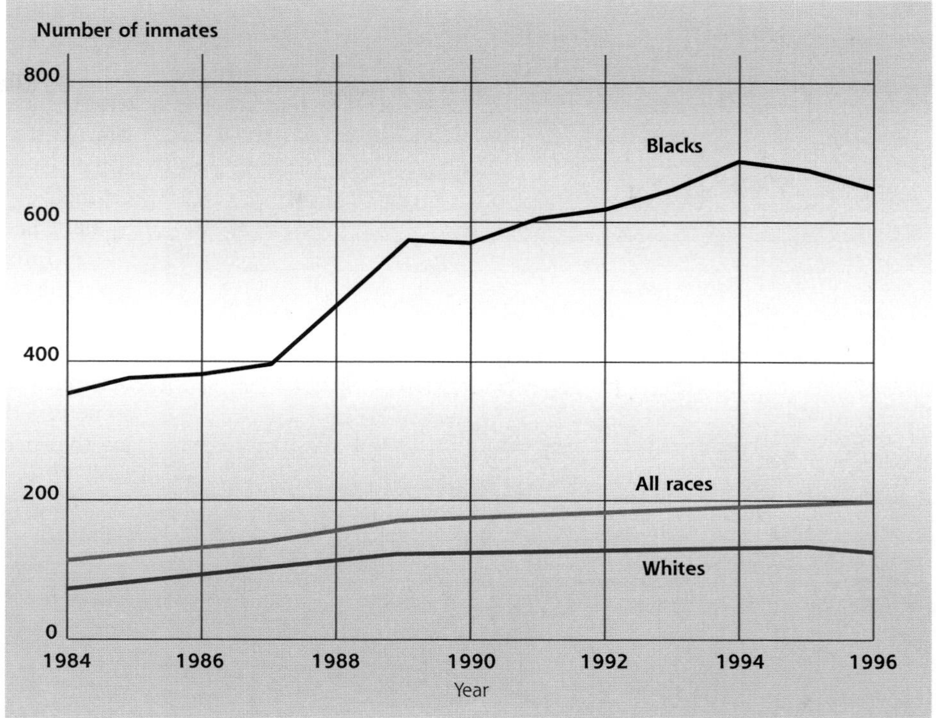

Figure 13.1
Number of jail inmates per 100,000 U.S. residents, by race, 1984–1996

SOURCE: Allen Beck et al., *Correctional Populations in the United States, 1996* (Washington, D.C.: Bureau of Justice Statistics, 1999), 22.

Jail Conditions Jails are the oldest and most deteriorated institutions in the criminal justice system. Because they are usually run by the county government (and controlled by a sheriff), it is difficult to encourage taxpayers to appropriate money for improved facilities. In fact, jails are usually administered under the concept of "custodial convenience," which involves giving inmates minimum standards of treatment and benefits while controlling the cost of jail operations. Jail employees are often underpaid, ill-trained, and lacking in professional experience.

Some jails are practically run by violent inmate cliques that terrorize other prisoners; one former IBM executive who served time in jail for writing bad checks relates this story:

> I've seen people raped, especially young kids. You can get a kid as young as 16. These young boys would come in and if they were fresh and young, the guys who run the tank and lived in the first cell, they would take the kid, forcibly hold him and someone would rape him. Some of them go to pieces just right there and then, kids who can't hack it and are torn apart.[36]

A report on incarceration in the United States by the Human Rights Watch found that because they are short-term facilities, jail often lack basic programs and services. Because of insufficient data and record keeping, violence-prone inmates are held in the same cells as first-time offenders. The report cited the case of an eighteen-year-old in California who committed suicide after being raped in a county jail and an AIDS-infected inmate who was denied a change of clothing, bedding, soap, towels, toothbrush, toilet paper, a Bible, or visitors; this inmate was left in a bare room and denied access to a telephone on the grounds that there was no disinfectant with which to clean the phone after he made a call.[37] About nine hundred people die in jail each year, and more than one-third of these are suicides.[38] Well aware of these problems, some judges are reluctant to sentence offenders to a jail term if they seem weak or vulnerable.[39]

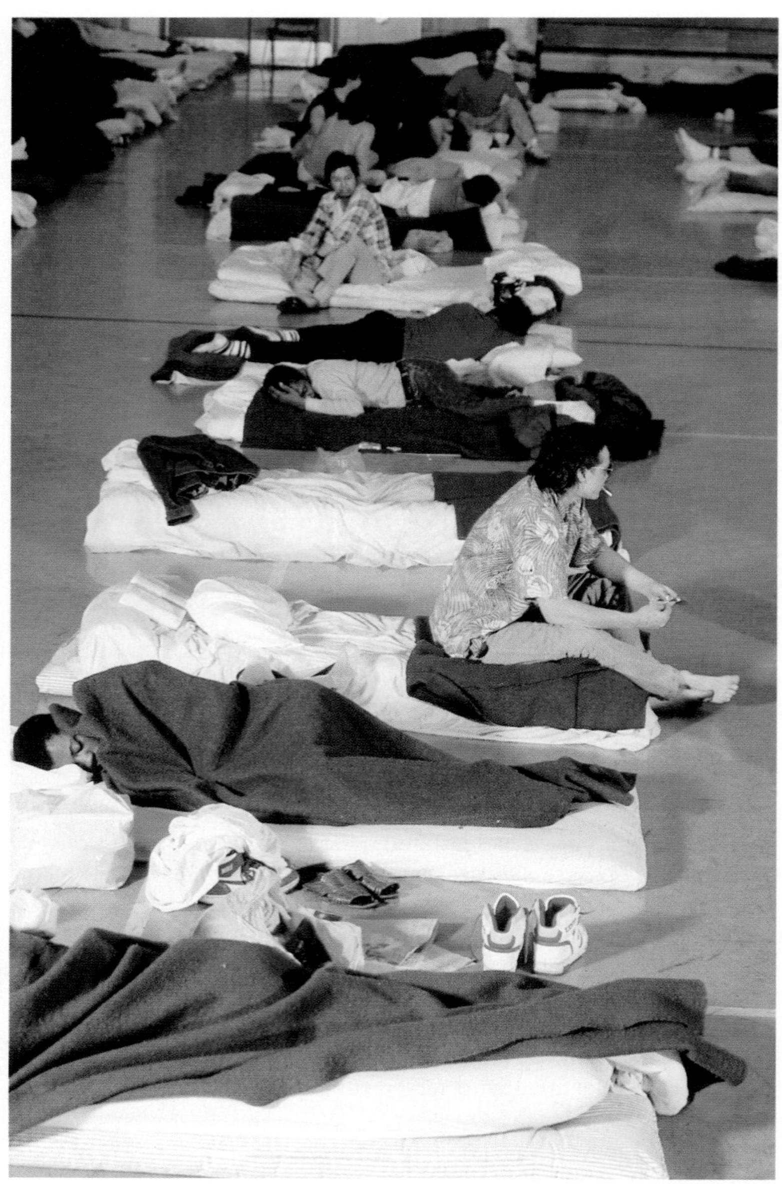

Inmates are sometimes forced to sleep outside of cells in overcrowded jails. Here a long line of inmates rest on floor mattresses in Illinois's Cook County Jail.

Although the number of jail inmates was slightly less than the stated capacity of jails as of 1998, some jails are so overcrowded that they simply have no room to put people. A moratorium has been placed on new admissions to some city jails, and many detainees are released on their own recognizance who might ordinarily have been forced to put up cash bail.[40]

A number of factors lead to jail overcrowding. One is the concerted effort being made to reduce or control particular crime problems, including substance abuse, spousal abuse, and driving while intoxicated (DWI). For example, some jurisdictions have passed legislation requiring that people arrested on suspicion of domestic violence be held in confinement for a number of hours to "cool off" before becoming eligible for bail. Other jurisdictions have attempted to deter drunk driving by passing mandatory jail sentences for people convicted of DWI; such legislation can quickly result in overcrowded jails.[41]

PRISONS

The Federal Bureau of Prisons and every state government maintain closed correctional facilities, also called prisons, penitentiaries, or reformatories. It is a vast and costly system. According to a 1999 report by the Bureau of Justice Statistics, the various states and the District of Columbia spend about $22 billion to build, staff, and maintain their prison facilities and to house the prisoners. The Federal Bureau of Prisons spends an additional $2.5 billion. This is an average annual cost of approximately $20,100 per inmate. What is most alarming is the rapid escalation of prison costs. State prison expenditures increased 83 percent from $12 billion in 1990 to $22 billion in 1996, an average of about 11 percent annually. Federal prison expenditures rose 160 percent, from $946 million in 1990 to $2.5 billion in 1996, an average of about 17 percent annually.[42]

Types of Prisons

Usually, prisons are organized or classified on three levels — maximum, medium, and minimum security — and each has distinct characteristics.

maximum-security prison
A correctional institution that houses dangerous felons and maintains strict security measures, high walls, and limited contact with the outside world.

MAXIMUM-SECURITY PRISONS Housing the most famous criminals and subject to films and stories, **maximum-security prisons** are probably the institutions most familiar to the public. Famous "max prisons" have included Sing Sing, Joliet, Attica, Walpole, and the most fearsome prison of all, the now-closed federal facility on Alcatraz Island known as The Rock.

A typical maximum-security facility is fortresslike, surrounded by stone walls with guard towers at strategic places. These walls may be twenty-five feet high, and sometimes inner and outer walls divide the prison into courtyards. Barbed wire or electrified fences are used to discourage escapes. High security, armed guards, and stone walls give the inmate the sense that the facility is impregnable and reassure the citizens outside that convicts will be completely incapacitated.

Inmates live in interior, metal-barred cells that contain their own plumbing and sanitary facilities and are locked securely either by key or electronic device. Cells are organized in sections called blocks, and in large prisons, a number of cell blocks make up a wing. During the evening, each cell block is sealed off from the others, as is each wing. Thus, an inmate may be officially located in, for example, Block 3 of E Wing.

Every inmate is assigned a number and a uniform on entering the prison system. Unlike the striped, easily identifiable uniforms of old, the maximum-security inmate today wears khaki attire not unlike military fatigues. Dress codes may be strictly enforced in some institutions, but closely cropped hair and other strict features are vestiges of the past.

During the day, the inmates engage in closely controlled activities: meals, workshops, education, and so on. Rule violators may be confined to their cells, and working and other shared recreational activities are viewed as privileges.

The byword of the maximum-security prison is security. Guards and other correctional workers are made aware that each inmate may be a dangerous criminal or violent and that, as a result, the utmost in security must be maintained. In keeping with this philosophy, prisons are designed to eliminate hidden corners where people can congregate, and passages are constructed so that they can be easily blocked off to quell disturbances. Some states have constructed **super-maximum-security prisons** (supermax prisons) to house the most predatory criminals. These high-security institutions can be independent correctional centers or locked wings of existing prisons.[43] Some supermax prisons lock inmates in their cells twenty-two to twenty-four hours a day, never allowing them out unless they are shackled.[44] The Criminal Justice and Technology feature discusses these supermax prisons.

super-maximum-security prison The newest form of a maximum-security prison that uses high-level security measures to incapacitate the nation's most dangerous criminals. Most inmates are in twenty-three hours per day lockdown.

A national survey of supermax prisons found that, though the costs of running these institutions is generally higher than in less secure facilities, they tend to be popular with correctional administrators who believe that isolating troublemakers helps them maintain order. The survey's major findings include the following:[45]

- Thirty-four prison systems are either operating or soon will open supermax facilities/units. Four others are considering the need for supermax facilities or are actively pursuing construction funds.
- Thirty-six prison systems cite the need to better manage violent and seriously disruptive inmates as a major factor in their jurisdictions' development of supermax housing; seventeen of these systems include gang members as appropriate candidates for supermax housing.
- Jurisdictions vary greatly in the length of time inmates are confined in supermax facilities and the criteria for admission and release. Approval authority for admission and release of inmates varies from the warden or superintendent to the director/commissioner of the prison system.
- Programs in supermax facilities range from "none available" to "cell-front only," television/video programming, or limited group programming.
- Jurisdictions differ in whether mentally ill and/or developmentally disabled inmates are placed in supermax housing.
- Transitional programming is available only in some jurisdictions.

Criminal Justice and Technology

SUPER-MAXIMUM-SECURITY PRISONS

More than thirty states and the federal government have constructed high tech, super-maximum-security, or supermax, prisons to house the most dangerous predatory criminals. These high-security institutions can be independent correctional centers or locked wings of existing prisons operating under such names as the *secure housing unit* or *maximum control unit.* However, there is no agreement on the precise definition of these units, so what is considered supermax in one jurisdiction may not be supermax in another. Their development represents a shift from previous correctional policy that favored dispersing the most troublesome inmates to different prisons in order to prevent them from joining forces or planning escapes. The supermax model finds that housing the most dangerous inmates in an ultra-secure facility eases their control while reducing violence levels in the general prison population.

The first federal maxi-maxi prison was located in Marion, Illinois, which was infamous for its tight security and isolated conditions. Marion has been supplanted by a new 575-bed facility in Florence, Colorado. This new prison has the most sophisticated security measures in the United States, including 168 videocameras and fourteen hundred electronically controlled gates. Inside the cells all furniture is unmovable; the desk, bed, and TV stand are made of cement. All potential weapons, including soap dishes, toilet seats, and toilet handles, have been removed. The cement walls are five thousand-pound quality, and steel bars are placed so they crisscross every eight inches inside the walls. Cells are angled so that inmates can see neither each other or the outside scenery (Figure A). This cuts down on communications and denies inmates a sense of location, in order to prevent escapes.

Getting out of prison seems impossible. There are six guard towers at different heights to prevent air attacks. To get out, the inmates would have to pass through seven three-inch-thick steel doors, each of which can be opened only after the previous one has closed. If a guard tower is ever seized, all controls are switched to the next station. If the whole prison is seized, it can be controlled from the outside. It appears that the only way out is via good works and behavior, through which an inmate can earn transfer to another prison within three years.

Threat of transfer to a supermax institution is used to deter inmate misbehavior in less restrictive institutions. Civil rights watchdog groups charge that these maxi-maxi prisons violate the United Nations standards for the treatment of inmates. They are typically located in rural areas, which makes staffing difficult in the professional areas of dentistry, medicine, and counseling. Senior officers would rather not work in these institutions, leaving the most difficult inmates in the hands of the most inexperienced correctional officers.

Critical Thinking

Super-maximum-security prisons are reminiscent of the old Pennsylvania system, which made use of solitary confinement and high security. Is this inhumane in our more enlightened age? Why or why not?

InfoTrac College Edition Research

To discover more about life in the supermax prison, read

"The Bomber Next Door: What Are the Most Dangerous Men in America Talking about at the Supermax Prison in Colorado?" *Time,* 22 March 1999, 55.

SOURCES: Richard H. Franklin, "Assessing Supermax Operations," *Corrections Today* 60 (1998): 126–28; Chase Riveland, *Supermax Prison: Overview and General Considerations* (Longmont, Colo.: National Institute of Corrections, 1998); Federal Bureau of Prisons, *State of the Bureau, 1995* (Washington, D.C.: Government Printing Office, 1996); Dennis Cauchon, "The Alcatraz of the Rockies," *USA Today,* 16 November 1994, 6a.

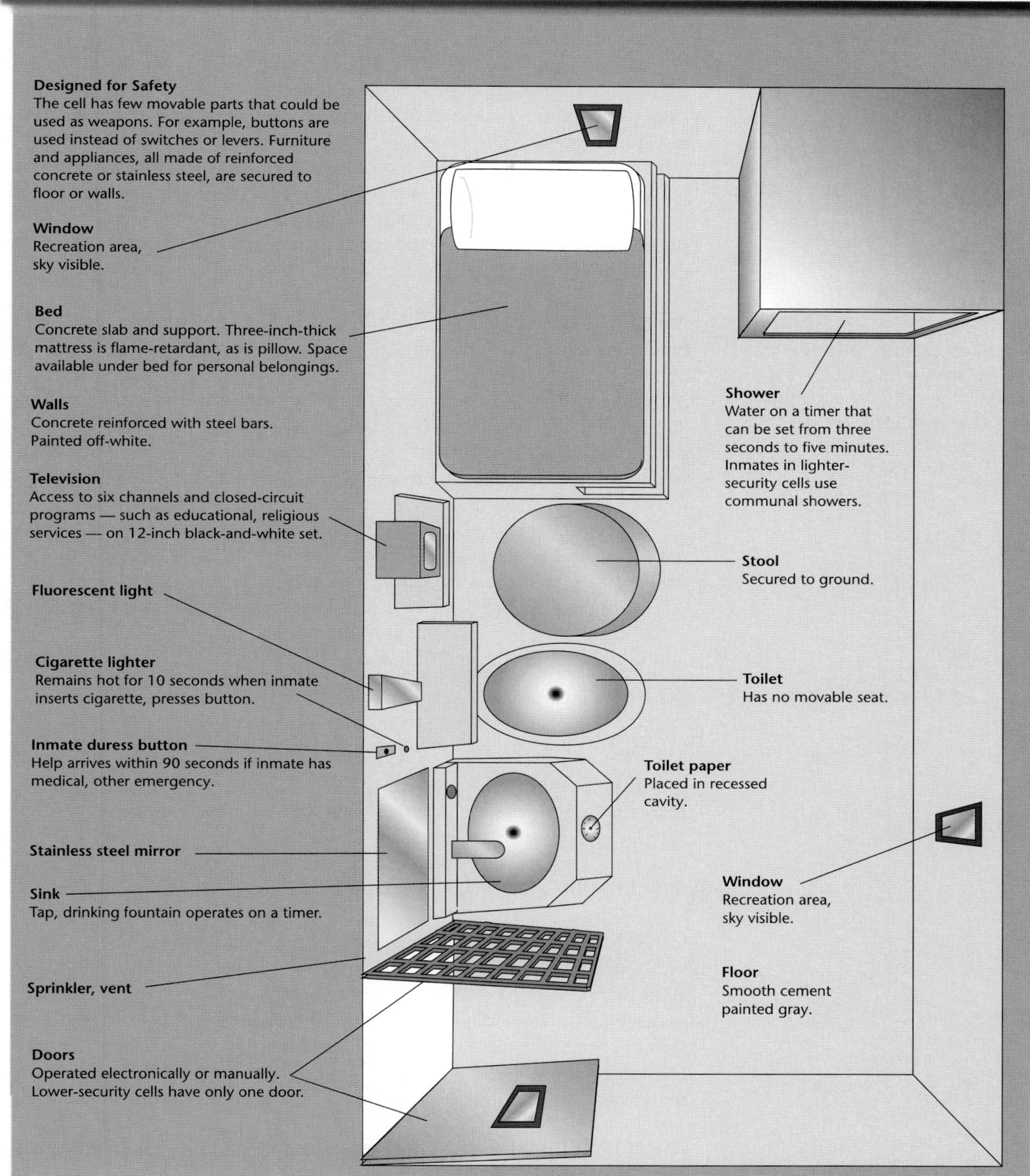

Figure A
Typical cell in a super-maximum-security prison
Some of the toughest felons in the federal prison system are held in a new penitentiary in Florence, Colorado. It is designed to be the most secure ever built by the government. Many inmates live in isolation, except for an hour a day of recreation. A high-security cell in the 575-bed facility has these features.

SOURCE: Louis Winn, United States Penitentiary, Administrative Maximum-Florence, Colorado.

medium-security prison
A less secure institution that houses nonviolent offenders and provides more opportunities for contact with the outside world.

MEDIUM-SECURITY PRISONS Similar in appearance to maximum-security prisons, in **medium-security prisons** the security and atmosphere are neither so tense nor so vigilant. Medium-security prisons are also surrounded by walls, but there may be fewer guard towers or other security precautions. For example, visitor privileges may be more extensive, and personal contact may be allowed, whereas in a maximum-security prison visitors may be separated from inmates by Plexiglas or other barriers (to prohibit the passing of contraband). While most prisoners are housed in cells, individual honor rooms in medium-security prisons are used to reward those who make exemplary rehabilitation efforts. Finally, medium-security prisons promote greater treatment efforts, and the relaxed atmosphere allows freedom of movement for rehabilitation workers and other therapeutic personnel.

minimum-security prison
The least secure institution that houses white-collar and nonviolent offenders, maintains few security measures, and has liberal furlough and visitation policies.

MINIMUM-SECURITY PRISONS Operating without armed guards or walls, **minimum-security prisons** usually house the most trustworthy and least violent offenders; white-collar criminals may be their most common occupants. Inmates are allowed a great deal of personal freedom. Instead of being marched to activities by guards, they are summoned by bells or loudspeaker announcements and assemble on their own. Work furloughs and educational releases are encouraged, and vocational training is of the highest level. Dress codes are lax, and inmates are allowed to grow beards or mustaches or demonstrate other individual characteristics.

Minimum-security facilities may have dormitories or small private rooms for inmates. Prisoners are allowed to own personal possessions that might be deemed dangerous in a maximum-security prison, such as radios.

Minimum-security prisons have been criticized for being like "country clubs"; some federal facilities for white-collar criminals even have tennis courts and pools (they are called derisively "Club Fed"). Yet they remain prisons, and the isolation and loneliness of prison life deeply affects the inmates.

Prison Inmate Characteristics

Surveys of prison inmates indicate that, as might be expected, the personal characteristics of prison inmates reflect common traits of arrestees: Inmates tend to be young, single, poorly educated, disproportionately male, and minority group members.[46] Many are either underemployed or unemployed prior to their arrest; many have incomes of less than $10,000 and suffer drug abuse and other personal problems.

GENDER Gender differences in the prison population are considerable. Women are actually underrepresented in prison, and not solely because they commit less serious crimes. The Uniform Crime Reports arrest statistics indicate that the overall male–female arrest ratio is today about 3.5 male offenders to 1 female offender; for violent crimes, the ratio is closer to 6 males to 1 female. Yet female inmates account for only about 10 percent of the prison population. Whereas the typical male inmate was a violent offender, most female inmates committed property offenses.

MINORITIES The prison system is populated disproportionately by minorities; black males in the United States are now incarcerated at a higher rate than in South Africa before the election of Nelson Mandela. As Figure 13.2 shows, about 6.6 percent of the population of African-American males are in prison or jail as opposed to less than 1 percent of the white male population. This condition severely decreases the life chances of African-American men, has a devastating effect on the black community, and is an ongoing national concern.[47]

TYPE OF OFFENSE What did the inmates do to earn their sentence? About half of all inmates are serving time for violent crimes. As Figure 13.3

Figure 13.2
Percent of U.S. adult population in state or federal prisons or in local jails, by race and sex, 1984–1996

SOURCE: Allen Beck et al., *Correctional Populations in the United States, 1996* (Washington, D.C.: Bureau of Justice Statistics, 1999), 4.

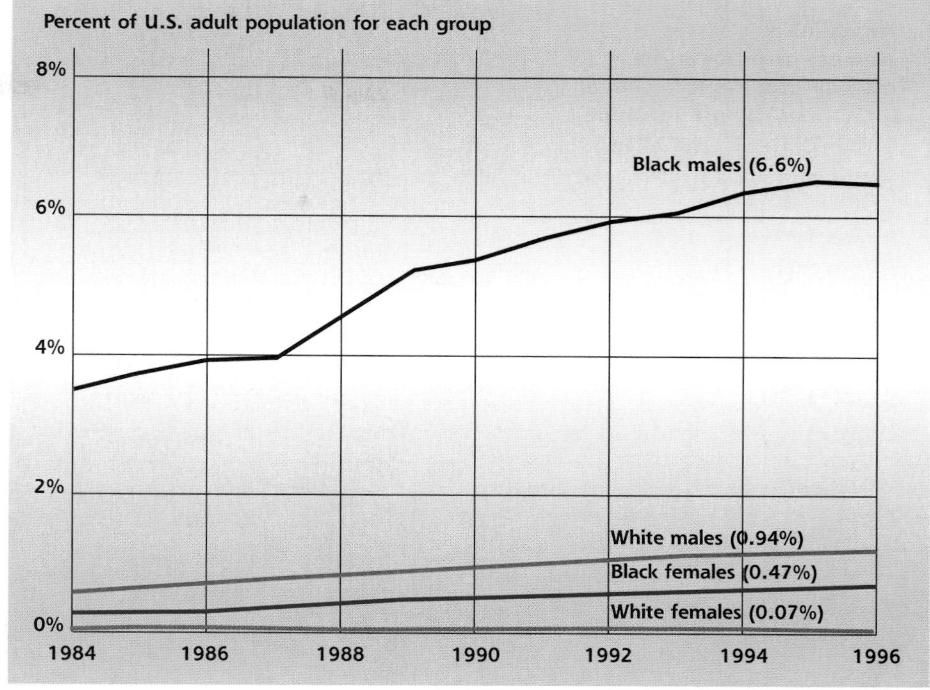

shows, the number of offenders doing time for drug and violent crimes has increased significantly during the past decade. This increase probably reflects the effect of mandatory minimum sentences for violent crime and drug offenders and the increased emphasis that law enforcement agencies are putting on the control of the drug trade.

SUBSTANCE ABUSE A strong association exists between substance abuse and inmate status. For example, one study of four hundred Texas inmates found that almost 75 percent suffered from lifetime substance abuse or dependence disorder, which is characterized by psychologists as (1) abuse of drugs for at least one continuous month (or repeated symptoms to occur over a longer period), (2) "failure to fulfill major role obligations," and (3) "substance-related legal problems."[48] About 80 percent of inmates report using drugs sometime during their life, and more than 60 percent are regular users. About half of the inmates report being either drunk, high, or both when they committed the crime that landed them in prison. Considering this background, it should come as no surprise that more inmates die from HIV-related disease than from prison violence.[49]

PHYSICAL ABUSE Like jail inmates, prison inmates also report a long history of physical abuse and mental health problems: About 19 percent report some form of physical abuse, including 57 percent of female offenders.[50] In addition, about 16 percent of state prison inmates report having some form of mental problems.[51] Mentally ill inmates are more likely to be arrested for violent offenses and to have suffered a variety of personal and emotional problems than the general inmate population. The picture that emerges is that prisons hold those people who face the toughest social obstacles in society. Only a few members of the educated middle-class wind up behind bars, and these people are usually held in low-security, "country club" institutions.

Figure 13.3
Number of prisoners in custody of state correctional authorities, by offense type, 1980–1996

SOURCE: Allen Beck et al., *Correctional Populations in the United States, 1996* (Washington, D.C.: Bureau of Justice Statistics, 1999), 6.

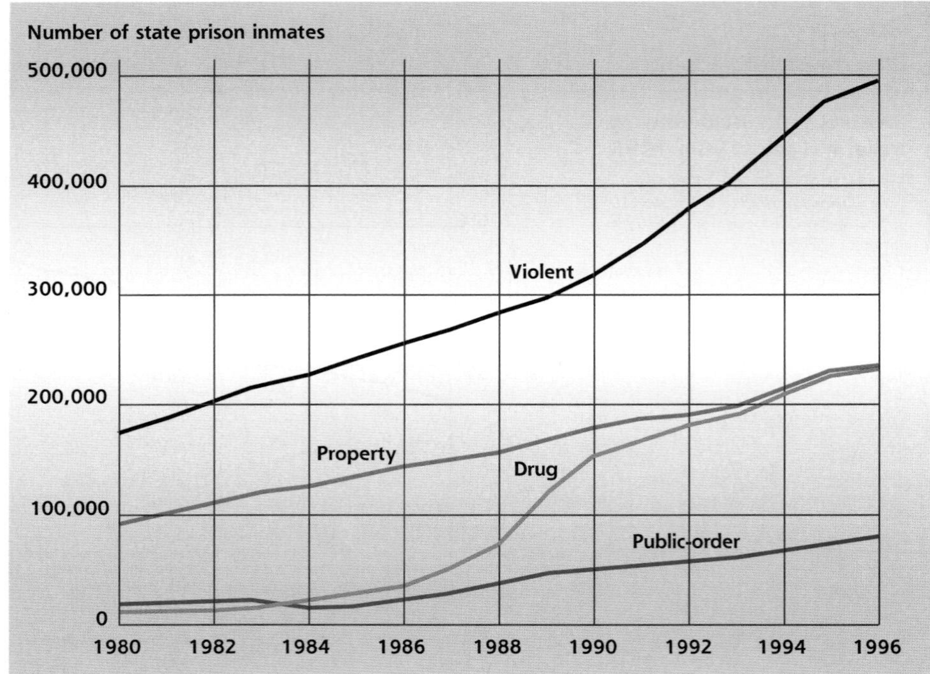

ALTERNATIVE CORRECTIONAL INSTITUTIONS

In addition to prison and jails, a number of other correctional institutions are operating around the United States. Some have been in use for quite some time, whereas others have been developed as part of an innovative or experimental program.

Prison Farms and Camps

Prison farms and camps are used to detain offenders. These types of facilities are found primarily in the South and the West and have been in operation since the nineteenth century. Today, about forty farms, forty forest camps, eighty road camps, and more than sixty similar facilities (vocational training centers, ranches, etc.) exist in the nation. Prisoners on farms produce dairy products, grain, and vegetable crops that are used in the state correctional system and other governmental facilities, such as hospitals and schools. Forestry camp inmates maintain state parks, fight forest fires, and do reforestation work. Ranches, primarily a western phenomenon, employ inmates in cattle raising and horse breeding, among other activities. Road gangs repair roads and state highways.

shock incarceration
A short prison sentence served in boot camp–type facilities.

boot camp
A short-term militaristic correctional facility in which inmates undergo intensive physical conditioning and discipline.

Shock Incarceration in Boot Camps

A recent approach to correctional care that is gaining popularity around the United States is **shock incarceration** in **boot camps.** Such programs typically include youthful, first-time offenders and feature military discipline and physical training (Figure 13.4). The concept is that short periods (ninety to one hundred eighty days) of high-intensity exercise and work will "shock" the inmate into going straight. Tough physical training is designed to promote responsibility and improve decision-making skills, build self-confidence, and teach socialization skills. Inmates are treated with rough intensity by drill masters who may call them names and punish the entire group for the fail-

Figure 13.4
Shock incarceration
Typical daily routines and schedule in a boot camp program

SOURCE: Cherie Clark, David Aziz, and Doris Mackenzie, *Shock Incarceration in New York: Focus on Treatment* (Washington, D.C.: National Institute of Justice, 1994), 5.

Rita finishes 50 sit-ups and springs to her feet. At 6 A.M. her platoon begins a 5-mile run, the last portion of this morning's physical training. After 5 months in New York's Lakeview Shock Incarceration Correctional Facility, the morning workout is easy. Rita even enjoys it, taking pride in her physical conditioning.

When Rita graduates and returns to New York City, she will face 6 months of intensive supervision before moving to regular parole. More than two-fifths of Rita's platoon did not make it this far; some withdrew voluntarily, and the rest were removed for misconduct or failure to participate satisfactorily. By completing shock incarceration, she will enter parole 11 months before her minimum release date.

The requirements for completing shock incarceration are the same for male and female inmates. The women in a separate housing area of Lakeview. Otherwise, men and women participate in the same education, physical training, drill and ceremony, drug education, and counseling programs. Men and women are assigned to separate work details and attend network group meetings held in inmates' living units.

Daily Schedule

A.M.	
5:30	Wake up and standing count
5:45-6:30	Calisthenics and drill
6:30-7:00	Run
7:00-8:00	Mandatory breakfast/cleanup
8:15	Standing count and company formation
8:30-11:55	Work/school schedules
P.M.	
12:00-12:30	Mandatory lunch and standing count
12:30-3:30	Afternoon work/school schedule
3:30-4:00	Shower
4:00-4:45	Network community meeting
4:45-5:45	Mandatory dinner, prepare for evening
6:00-9:00	School, group counselling, drug counseling, prerelease counseling, decision-making classes
9:00	Count while in programs
9:15-9:30	Squad bay, prepare for bed
9-30	Standing count, lights out

ure of one of its members. Discipline is so severe that some critics warn that it can amount to "cruel and unusual punishment" and generate costly inmate law suits.[52]

There is wide variation in the more than seventy-five programs now operating around the United States.[53] Some programs also include educational and training components, counseling sessions, and treatment for special-needs populations, whereas others devote little or no time to therapeutic activities. Some receive program participants directly from court sentencing, whereas others choose potential candidates from the general inmate population. Some allow voluntary participation and others voluntary termination.[54]

Shock incarceration programs can provide some important correctional benefits. New York houses inmates in these programs in separate institutions and provides most (but not all) "graduates" with extensive follow-up supervision. Although recidivism rates for these programs in New York are similar to those of traditional prisons, there are indications that both inmates and staff view shock incarceration as a positive experience.[55] It is estimated that the New York program has saved taxpayers hundreds of millions of dollars because boot camps are cheaper to build and maintain than traditional prisons. Other evaluations have found that a boot camp experience can improve inmates' attitudes and have the potential for enhancing their postcorrection lifestyle.[56]

Inmates at Swan Lake, Montana, Boot Camp stand at attention waiting for their class to begin. Boot camps stress strict discipline and rigorous physical training in order to promote responsibility, improve decision making, and build self-confidence.

Shock incarceration has the advantage of being a lower-cost alternative to overcrowded prisons because inmates are held in nonsecure facilities and sentences are short. Both staff and inmates seem excited by the programs, and even those who fail on parole report that they felt the shock incarceration was a valuable experience.[57] Of course, if shock incarceration is viewed as an exciting or helpful experience by its "graduates," they be encouraged to recidivate, since the threat of the prison experience has been weakened.

EVALUATING SHOCK INCARCERATION Is shock incarceration a correctional panacea or another fad doomed to failure? The results so far are mixed. The costs of boot camps are no lower than those of traditional prisons, but since sentences are shorter they do provide long-term savings. Some programs suffer high failure-to-complete rates, which makes program evaluations difficult (even if "graduates" are successful, it is possible that success is achieved because troublesome cases drop out and are placed back in the general inmate population). What evaluations exist indicate that the recidivism rates of inmates who attend shock programs are in some cases no lower than for those released from traditional prisons.[58]

Many of these evaluations have been conducted by Doris Layton Mackenzie and her associates. One study with James Shaw found that, although boot camp inmates may have lower recidivism rates than probationers and parolees, they have higher rates of technical violations and revocations.[59] Even though these results are disappointing, Mackenzie reports that both staff and inmates seem excited by the programs, and even those who fail on parole report that they felt boot camp was a valuable experience.[60] She also found, with Alex Piquero, that carefully managed boot camp programs can make a major dent in prison overcrowding.[61] Nonetheless, Mackenzie's extensive evaluations of the boot camp experience generate little evidence that they can significantly lower recidivism rates. Programs that seem to work best, such as those in New York, stress treatment and therapeutic activities, are voluntary, and are longer in duration.[62]

community treatment
The attempt by correctional agencies to maintain convicted offenders in the community instead of a secure facility; it includes probation, parole, and residential programs.

halfway house
A community-based correctional facility that houses inmates before their outright release so that they can become gradually acclimated to conventional society.

Community Correctional Facilities

One of the goals of correctional treatment is to help reintegrate the offender back into society. Placing offenders in a prison makes them more likely to adapt an inmate lifestyle than to reassimilate conventional social norms. As a result, the **community treatment** concept began to take off in the 1960s. State and federal correctional systems created community-based correctional models as an alternative to closed institutions. Many are **halfway houses** to which inmates are transferred just before their release into the community. These facilities are designed to bridge the gap between institutional living and the community. Specialized treatment may be offered, and the residents use the experience to cushion the shock of reentering society.

As you may recall, commitment to a community correctional center may also be used as an intermediate sanction and sole mode of treatment. An offender may be assigned to a community treatment center operated by the state department of corrections or to probation. Or the corrections department can contract with a private community center. This practice is common in the treatment of drug addicts and other nonviolent offenders whose special needs can be met in a self-contained community setting that specializes in specific types of treatment.

Halfway houses and community correctional centers can look like residential homes and in many instances were originally residences; in urban centers, older apartment buildings can be adapted for the purpose. Usually, these facilities have a central treatment theme — such as group therapy or reality therapy — that is used to rehabilitate and reintegrate clients.

Another popular approach in community-based corrections is the use of ex-offenders as staff members. These individuals have made the transition between the closed institution and society and can be invaluable in helping residents overcome the many hurdles they face in proper readjustment.

Despite the encouraging philosophical concept presented by the halfway house, evaluation of specific programs has not led to a definite endorsement of this type of treatment.[63] One significant problem has been a lack of support from community residents, who fear the establishment of an institution housing "dangerous offenders" in their neighborhood. Court actions and zoning restrictions have been brought in some areas to foil efforts to create halfway houses.[64] As a result, many halfway houses are located in decrepit neighborhoods in the worst areas of town — certainly a condition that must influence the attitudes and behavior of the inmates. Furthermore, the climate of control exercised in most halfway houses, where rule violation can be met with a quick return to the institution, may not be one that the average inmate can distinguish from his former high-security penal institution.

Despite these problems, the promise held by community correctional centers, coupled with their low cost of operations, has led to their continued use into the new millennium.

Private Prisons

Correctional facilities are now being run by private firms as business enterprises. In some instances, a private corporation will finance and build an institution and then contract with correctional authorities to provide services for convicted criminals. Sometimes the private concern will finance and build the institution and then lease it outright to the government.

This model has the advantage of allowing the government to circumvent the usually difficult process of getting voters to approve a bond issue and raising funds for prison construction. Another common method of private involvement is with specific service contracts; for example, a private concern might be hired to manage the prison health-care system, food services, or staff training.

The federal government has used private companies to run detention centers for illegal aliens who are being held for trial or deportation.[65] One private firm, the Corrections Corporation of America, runs a federal halfway house, two detention centers, and a 370-bed jail in Bay County, Florida. On January 6, 1986, the U.S. Corrections Corporation opened the first private state prison in Marion, Kentucky — a 300-bed minimum-security facility for inmates who are within three years of parole. Today, more than twenty companies are trying to enter the private prison market, five states are contracting with private companies to operate facilities, and more than ten others — including Oregon, New Mexico, and Florida — have recently passed laws authorizing or expanding the use of private prison contractors.[66]

Wackenhut Corrections Corporation, one of the largest private corrections companies in the world, keeps a home page at www.wackenhut.com **If you are interested in learning more about the arguments against private prisons, go to** www.amandla.org/osepp/prisoners/news_ppw.html

Although privately run institutions have been around for a few years, their increased use may present a number of problems. For example, will private providers be able to effectively evaluate programs, knowing that a negative evaluation might cause them to lose their contract? Will they skimp on services and programs in order to reduce costs? Might they not skim off the "easy" cases and leave the hard-core inmate to the state's care? And will the need to keep business booming require widening the net to fill empty cells? Must they maintain state-mandated liability insurance to cover inmate claims?[67] So far, private and state institutions cost about the same to operate.

Private corrections firms also run into opposition from existing state correctional staff and management who fear the loss of jobs and autonomy. Moreover, the public may be skeptical about an untested private concern's ability to provide security and protection.

Private corrections also face administrative problems. How will program quality be controlled? To compete on price, a private facility may have to cut corners to beat out the competition. Determining accountability for problems and mishaps will be difficult when dealing with a corporation that is a legal fiction and protects its officers from personal responsibility for their actions. And legal problems can emerge quickly: Can privately employed guards patrol the perimeter and use deadly force to stop escape attempts? The U.S. Supreme Court has ruled that private correctional officers have less immunity from lawsuits than state employees.

The very fact that individuals can profit from running a prison may also prove unpalatable to large segments of the population. Should profit be made from human tragedy and suffering? However, is a private correctional facility really much different from a private hospital or mental health clinic that provides services to the public in competition with state-run institutions? The issue that determines the future of private corrections may be one of efficiency and cost effectiveness, not fairness and morality.

In the abstract, a private correctional enterprise may be an attractive alternative to a costly correctional system, but these legal, administrative, and cost issues need to be resolved before private prisons can become widespread.[68] A balance must be reached between the need for a private business to make a profit and the integrity of a prison administration that must be concerned with such complex issues as security, rehabilitation, and dealing with highly dangerous people in a closed environment.[69] Research indicates that today private prisons are no more economical than public institutions and that other factors such as the size and security level of an institution are the key indicators of an institution's actual cost.[70]

CORRECTIONAL POPULATIONS

The nation's vast system of penal institutions now holds about 2 million people (counting jail and community corrections populations) and employs more than 250,000 to care for and guard them.

The nation's prison population has had a number of cycles of growth and decline.[71] Between 1925 and 1939, it increased at about 5 percent a year, reflecting the nation's concern for the lawlessness of that time. The incarceration rate reached a high of 137 per 100,000 U.S. population in 1939. Then, during World War II, the prison population declined by 50,000, as potential offenders were drafted into the armed services. By 1956 the incarceration rate had dropped to 99 per 100,000 U.S. population.

The postwar era saw a steady increase in the prison population until 1961, when 220,000 people were in custody, a rate of 119 per 100,000. During the Vietnam era (1961–1968), the prison population actually declined by 30,000. The incarceration rate remained rather stable until 1974, when the current dramatic rise began. The incarceration rate has been steadily rising, and there are now more than 400 people in prison per 100,000 population.

Why Is the Prison Population Rising?

How can this significant rise in the prison population be explained? Prison administrators have linked the growth of the correctional population to a change in public opinion, which has demanded a more punitive response to criminal offenders. Public concern about drugs and violent crime has not been lost on state lawmakers. Mandatory sentencing laws, which have been implemented by a majority of states and the federal government, increase eligibility for incarceration and limit the availability for early release via parole. Although probation and community sentences still predominate, structural changes in criminal codes and crime rates have helped produce an expanding correctional population. The growing punitiveness of sentencing has significantly increased the amount of time served in prison, and efforts are now under way to adopt truth-in-sentencing laws that require inmates to serve at least 85 percent of their sentence behind bars (Figure 13.5).[72]

As you may recall from Chapter 11, the conviction rate is increasing for crimes that are traditionally punished with a prison sentence, such as robbery and burglary. In addition, get-tough policies have helped curtail the use of parole and have reduced judicial discretion to impose nonincarceration sentences.[73] States fed up with juvenile crime have passed strict laws mandating that violent juveniles be waived or transferred to the adult court for treatment.[74] More than twenty thousand juveniles are being tried as adults each year and are therefore eligible for incarceration in adult facilities.

As Table 13.1 shows, the number of state inmates being sentenced to prison has undergone a slight decline between 1994 and 1996 (the last data available). It is possible that this trend may herald an eventual reduction in prison populations.

Prison Overcrowding

Inmates are routinely housed two and three to a cell or in large dormitory-like rooms that hold more than fifty people. Military bases and even tents have been used to house overflow inmates. In addition to detainees and misdemeanants, thousands of people convicted of felonies are being held in local jails because of prison crowding. State correctional authorities have attempted to deal with the overcrowding problem by building new facilities, using construction techniques that limit expenditures, such as modular and preassembled units. Precast concrete cells are fabricated as fully finished units and can be

Figure 13.5
Truth-in-sentencing laws require inmates to serve more of their sentences.

SOURCE: Paula Ditton and Doris James Wilson, *Truth in Sentencing in State Prisons* (Washington, D.C.: Bureau of Justice Statistics, 1999), 1.

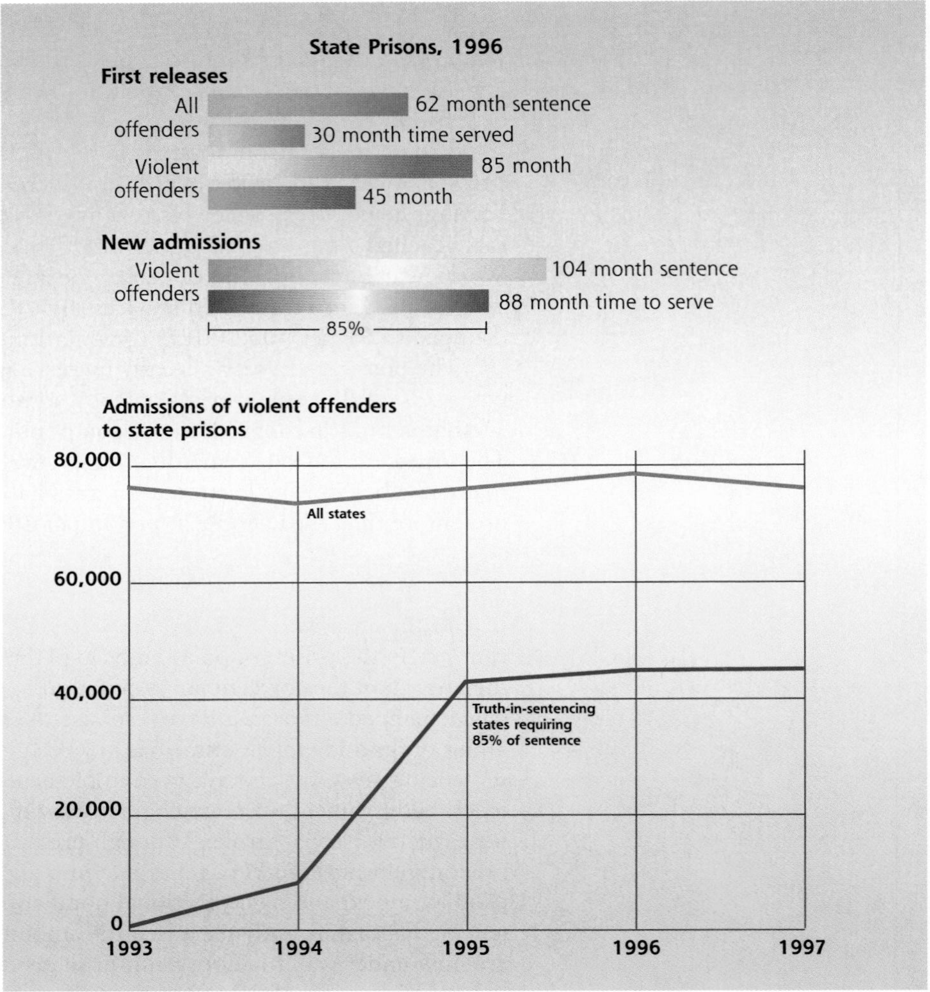

installed quickly. There is also an increasing need to maintain security in overcrowded facilities, and as the Criminal Justice and Technology feature on page 424 shows, correctional administrators may rely on high-tech advances to maintain order.

THE COST OF INCARCERATION The nation's prisons cost $24.5 billion in 1996, accounting for about 80 percent of all state correctional expenditures (the remaining 20 percent was for juvenile justice activities, probation and parole services, and community-based corrections). Average inmate cost was approximately $20,100 per state inmate and $23,500 per federal inmate.

So many people are now going to prison that the federal government estimates that a significant portion of the nation's population will at one time or another be behind prison gates. About 5 percent of the population, or more than 13 million people, will serve a prison sentence sometime during their life. As Table 13.1 shows, men are over eight times more likely than women to be incarcerated in prison at least once during their life. Among men, African Americans (28.5%) are about twice as likely as Hispanics (16.0%) and six times more likely than whites (4.4%) to be admitted to prison during their life. Among women, 3.6 percent of African Americans, 1.5 percent of Hispanics, and 0.5

Table 13.1
Who Goes to Prison: What Is the Likelihood of Getting an Incarceration Sentence?

Percent of Convicted Felons in State Courts Who Received a Prison Sentence

	1988	1990	1992	1994	1966	Probation Only Sentences
All offenses	44	46	44	45	38	29
Murder	91	91	93	95	92	5
Rape	69	67	68	71	63	21
Robbery	75	73	74	77	73	13
Aggravated assault	45	45	44	48	42	28
Burglary	54	54	52	53	45	29
Larceny	39	40	38	38	31	37
Drug trafficking	41	49	48	48	39	29

SOURCES: Patrick A. Langan and Jodi M. Brown, *Felony Sentences in State Courts, 1994* (Washington, D.C.: Bureau of Justice Statistics, 1997); Jodi M. Brown and Patrick A. Langan, *Felony Sentences in State Courts, 1996* (Washington, D.C.: Bureau of Justice Statistics, 1999).

percent of whites will enter prison at least once.[75] The extreme racial differences in the imprisonment rate are a key concern of the justice system. Do these differences reflect racial discrimination in the sentencing process? What can be done to reduce or eliminate this significant social problem?

Despite such ominous signs, the nation's prison population may be "maxing out." Budget cutbacks and belt tightening may halt the expansion of prison construction and the housing of ever more prisoners in already crowded prison facilities.[76] Although new modular construction techniques and double and triple bunking of inmates make existing prisons expandable, the secure population probably cannot expand endlessly. As costs skyrocket, some states are now spending more on prisons than on higher education. The public may begin to question the wisdom of a strict incarceration policy. There may also be fewer criminals to incarcerate. The waning of the crack cocaine epidemic in large cities may hasten this decline because street crimes will decline and fewer offenders will be eligible for the long penalties associated with the possession of crack.[77] As noted earlier, fewer people are now receiving a prison sentence than five years earlier, and if this trend holds the prison population will eventually decline.

In the final analysis, change in the correctional population may depend on the faith judges and legislators place in incarceration as a crime control policy. As long as policymakers believe that incarcerating predatory criminals can bring down crime rates, the likelihood of a significant decrease in the institutional population seems remote. If there is little evidence that this costly system does nothing to lower crime rates, less costly and equally effective alternatives may be sought.

Guard Deborah Gilmour, knocking on cell door in Mental Illness block at Joseph Harp Correctional Center, Lexington, Oklahoma. Up to 35 percent of all inmates may be suffering from some form of mental disorder. The cost of incarcerating special-needs inmates, such as the mentally ill, the elderly, and the HIV infected, has helped drive up the costs of corrections.

SUMMARY

Today's correctional institutions can trace their development from European origins. Punishment methods developed in Europe were modified and improved by American colonists, most notably William Penn. He replaced the whip and other methods of physical punishment with confinement in county institutions or penitentiaries.

Later, as needs grew, the newly formed states created their own large facilities. Discipline was harsh within them, and most enforced a code of total and absolute silence. The Auburn system of congregate working conditions during the day and isolation at night has been adopted in our present penal system.

The current correctional population has grown dramatically in the past few years. Although the number of inmates diminished in the late 1960s and early 1970s, it has since hit an all-time high. This development may reflect a toughening of sentencing procedures nationwide.

A number of institutions currently house convicted offenders. Jails are used for misdemeanants and minor felons. Because conditions are so poor in jails, they have become a major trouble spot for the criminal justice system.

Federal and state prisons — classified as minimum, medium, and maximum security — house most of the nation's incarcerated felons. However, their poor track record has spurred the development of new correctional models, specifically the boot camp, the halfway house, and the community correctional center. Nonetheless, the success of these institutions has been challenged by research efforts indicating that their recidivism rates are equal to those of state prisons. One newer development has been the privately run correctional institution. These are jails and prisons operated by private compa-

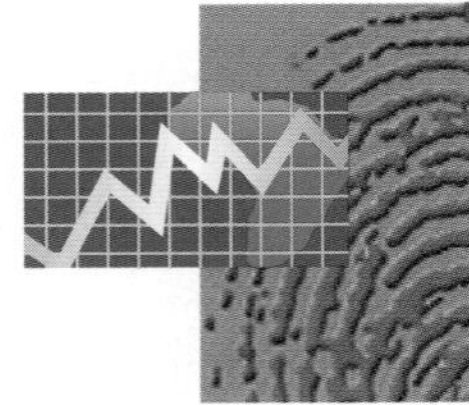

Criminal Justice and Technology

USING TECHNOLOGY TO INCREASE PRISON SECURITY

Advanced Technology

New and developing technologies are being used to increase prison safety, reduce escapes, and control contraband. A few of these advances are described here.

Deterring Prison Breaks

Special Technologies Laboratories (STL) has developed a new technology called ground-penetrating radar (GPR), which is able to locate tunnels that inmates used to escape. GPR works almost like an old-fashioned Geiger counter, held in the hand and swept across the ground by an operator. Instead of detecting metal, the GPR system detects changes in ground composition, including voids, such as those created by a tunnel.

Pulsed Radar

STL has also developed the GPR-X, a ground-penetrating radar that transmits energy into the ground. By measuring the time it takes for that energy to be reflected, it detects changes in ground material. GPR-X can detect contraband buried in the recreation yard, for instance, or a tunnel being built under the prison.

Heartbeat Monitoring

The weakest security link in any prison has always been the sally port, where trucks unload their supplies and where trash and laundry is taken out of the facility. Over the years, inmates have hidden in loads of trash, old produce, and laundry — any possible container that might be exiting the facility. Now it is possible to prevent escapes by monitoring inmates' heartbeats! The Advanced Vehicle Interrogation and Notification System (AVIAN) — being marketed by Geo Vox Security — works by identifying the shock wave generated by the beating heart, which couples to any surface the body touches. The system takes all frequencies of movement, such as the expansion and contraction of an engine and rain hitting the roof, and determines if there is a pattern similar to a human heartbeat.

Satellite Monitoring

Pro Tech Monitoring has developed a system to monitor offenders by satellite, using cellular technology combined with the federal government's global positioning system of satellites. While in the community, each offender wears an

nies, which receive a fee for their services. Used in a limited number of jurisdictions, they have been the center of some controversy. Can a private company provide better management of what has traditionally been a public problem?

The greatest problem facing the correctional system today is overcrowding, which has reached a crisis level. To help deal with the problems of overcrowding, corrections departments have begun to experiment with modular prison construction and the use of intermediate sanctions.

KEY TERMS

prison
jail
recidivism
hulk
Walnut Street Jail
penitentiary house
tier system
congregate system
Auburn system
Pennsylvania system
contract system
convict-lease system
hands-off doctrine
medical model
maximum-security prison
super-maximum-security prison
medium-security prison
minimum-security prison
shock incarceration
boot camp
community treatment
halfway house

ankle bracelet and carries a three-pound portable tracking device (smart box), programmed with information on her geographic restrictions. For instance, a sex offender may be forbidden to come within five miles of his victim's home or workplace, or a pedophile may be barred from getting close to a school. A satellite monitors the geographic movements of the offender, either in real time or by transmitting the information to the smart box, for later retrieval. The smart box and the ankle bracelet sound an alarm when boundaries are breached, alerting potential victims.

What the Future Holds

These new technologies are now available, but a number of others are under development, including the following:

- X-ray body scanners that test for concealed weapons and contraband hidden in body cavities
- Noninvasive drug testing, using eye scans and patches placed on the skin
- A smart gun that is computer coded so it cannot be fired by anyone other than the registered user
- A language translater, for use by law enforcement and correctional officers to communicate with nonnative inmates
- Walkthrough metal detectors that can pinpoint exactly where the metal is located on the body

Critical Thinking

Can these high-tech security devices present a challenge to the constitutionally protected rights of freedom and privacy? For example, is it fair to require convicted sex offenders to wear tracking devices after they have paid their "debt to society"? If so, should we monitor the spending of former thieves or the bank accounts of robbers?

InfoTrac College Edition Research

To read about some of the latest developments in prison security, check out

Stephen A. Donohue and Anthony J. Greloch, "Keeping It Simple," *Corrections Today* 59 (1997): 90.

Harry S. Sands, Jr., and Anthony H. Johnson, "Visitation in Absentia: New Technology Allows Inmates to Receive Visitors without Leaving Cells," *Corrections Today* 59 (1997): 96.

SOURCE: Gabrielle deGroot, "Hot New Technologies," *Corrections Today* 59 (1997): 60–63.

 INFOTRAC COLLEGE EDITION EXERCISES

Prison administrators are beginning to pay more attention to the communications and other technologies that have been developed for correctional facilities. In some cases, technology has been used for security purposes and in others to keep down costs. To find out more about the emerging technologies, read the following articles in *InfoTrac College Edition:*

Stewart Deck, "Illinois Prisons Upgrade Database to Tighten Reins on Cons," *Computerworld,* 15 February 1999.

Michelle Gaseau and Carissa Caramanis, "Technologies Bring New Era of Communication to Corrections," *Corrections Today* 61 (1999): 56.

InfoTrac College Edition has many interesting articles on the history of prisons and penal institutions. Read the two following pieces and then do a search on "prison history" to find other informative material.

Larry Goldsmith, "History from the Inside Out: Prison Life in Nineteenth-Century Massachusetts," *Journal of Social History* 31 (1997).

Jay Stuller, "There Never Was a Harder Place Than 'The Rock,'" *Smithsonian* 26 (1995): 84.

QUESTIONS

1. Would you allow a community correctional center to be built in your neighborhood? Why or why not?
2. Should pretrial detainees and convicted offenders be kept in the same institution? Explain.
3. What can be done to reduce correctional overcrowding?
4. Should private companies be allowed to run correctional institutions? Why or why not?
5. What are the drawbacks to shock incarceration?

NOTES

1. This section leans heavily on Jan Hoffman, "Judge's Sentence of Gang Leader Tests Limits of Punishment," *New York Times,* 26 October 1997, 31–33.

2. Ibid.

3. Allen Beck and Bernard Shipley, *Recidivism of Young Parolees* (Washington, D.C.: Bureau of Justice Statistics, 1987); see also John Wallerstedt, *Returning to Prison* (Washington, D.C.: Bureau of Justice Statistics, 1984).

4. See David Fogel, *We Are the Living Proof,* 2d ed. (Cincinnati: Anderson, 1978); Andrew von Hirsch, *Doing Justice: The Choice of Punishments* (New York: Hill and Wang, 1976); R. G. Singer, *Just Deserts — Sentencing Based on Equality and Desert* (Cambridge, Mass.: Ballinger, 1979).

5. Ted Palmer, *Correctional Intervention and Research* (Lexington, Mass.: Lexington Books, 1978); Michael Gottfredson, "The Social Scientist and Rehabilitative Crime Policy," *Criminology* 20 (1982): 29–42. The most widely cited source on the failure of rehabilitation is Robert Martinson; see Robert Martinson, Douglas Lipton, and Judith Wilks, *The Effectiveness of Correctional Treatment* (New York: Praeger, 1975).

6. Among the most helpful sources in developing this section were David Duffee, *Corrections: Practice and Policy* (New York: Random House, 1989); Harry Allen and Clifford Simonsen, *Correction in America,* 5th ed. (New York: Macmillan, 1989); Benedict Alper, *Prisons Inside-Out* (Cambridge, Mass.: Ballinger, 1974); Harry Elmer Barnes, *The Story of Punishment,* 2d ed. (Montclair, N.J.: Patterson-Smith, 1972); Gustave de Beaumont and Alexis de Tocqueville, *On the Penitentiary System in the United States and Its Applications in France* (Carbondale: Southern Illinois University Press, 1964); Orlando Lewis, *The Development of American Prisons and Prison Customs, 1776–1845* (Montclair, N.J.: Patterson-Smith, 1967); Leonard Orland, ed., *Justice, Punishment, and Treatment* (New York: Free Press, 1973); J. Goebel, *Felony and Misdemeanor* (Philadelphia: University of Pennsylvania Press, 1976); Georg Rusche and Otto Kircheimer, *Punishment and Social Structure* (New York: Russell & Russell, 1939); Samuel Walker, *Popular Justice* (New York: Oxford University Press, 1980); Graeme Newman, *The Punishment Response* (Philadelphia: Lippincott, 1978); David Rothman, *Conscience and Convenience* (Boston: Little, Brown, 1980).

7. F. Pollock and F. Maitland, *History of English Law* (London: Cambridge University Press, 1952).

8. Marvin Wolfgang, "Crime and Punishment in Renaissance Florence," *Journal of Criminal Law and Criminology* 81 (1990): 567–84.

9. Margaret Wilson, *The Crime of Punishment, Life and Letters Series,* no. 64 (London: Johnathon Cape, 1934), 186.

10. John Howard, *The State of Prisons,* 4th ed. (1792; reprint ed., Montclair, N.J.: Patterson-Smith, 1973).

11. Alexis Durham III, "Newgate of Connecticut: Origins and Early Days of an Early American Prison," *Justice Quarterly* 6 (1989): 89–116.

12. Lewis, *The Development of American Prisons and Prison Customs,* 17.

13. Ibid., 29.

14. Dario Melossi and Massimo Pavarini, *The Prison and the Factory: Origins of the Penitentiary System* (Totowa, N.J.: Barnes and Noble, 1981).

15. Michel Foucault, *Discipline and Punish* (New York: Vintage Books, 1978).

16. Ibid., 16.

17. David Rothman, *The Discovery of the Asylum* (Boston: Little, Brown, 1970).

18. Orland, *Justice, Punishment, and Treatment,* 143.

19. Ibid., 144.

20. Walker, *Popular Justice,* 70.

21. Ibid., 71.

22. Beverly Smith, "Military Training at New York's Elmira Reformatory, 1880–1920," *Federal Probation* 52 (1988): 33–41.

23. Ibid.

24. See Z. R. Brockway, "The Ideal of a True Prison System for a State," in *Transactions of the National Congress on Penitentiary and Reformatory Discipline,* reprint ed. (Washington, D.C.: American Correctional Association, 1970), 38–65.

25. This section leans heavily on Rothman, *Conscience and Convenience.*

26. Ibid., 23.

27. Ibid., 133.

28. 18 U.S.C., sec. 1761.

29. Barbara Auerbach, George Sexton, Franlin Farrow, and Robert Lawson, *Work in American Prisons: The Private Sector Gets Involved* (Washington, D.C.: National Institute of Justice, 1988), 72.

30. See, generally, Jameson Doig, *Criminal Corrections: Ideals and Realities* (Lexington, Mass.: Lexington Books, 1983).

31. John Irwin, *The Jail: Managing the Underclass in American Society* (Berkeley: University of California Press, 1985).

32. Correctional Association of New York: *Prison and Jails: Hospitals of Last Resort* (New York: Correctional Association of New York, 1998).

33. Darrell K. Gilliard, *Prison and Jail Inmates at Midyear 1998* (Washington, D.C.: Bureau of Justice Statistics, 1999).

34. Caroline Wolf Harlow, *Prior Abuse Reported by Inmates and Probationers* (Washington, D.C.: Bureau of Justice Statistics, 1999).

35. Paula M. Ditton, *Mental Health and Treatment of Inmates and Probationers* (Washington, D.C.: Bureau of Justice Statistics, 1999).

36. Cited in Ben Bagdikan and Leon Dash, *The Shame of the Prisons* (New York: Pocket Books, 1972), 32.

37. Human Rights Watch, *Prison Conditions in the United States* (New York: Human Rights Watch, 1991).

38. Victor Kappeler, Michael Vaughn, and Rolando Del Carmen, "Death in Detention: An Analysis of Police Liability for Negligent Failure to Prevent Suicide," *Journal of Criminal Justice* 19 (1991): 381–93.

39. "Judge Won't Subject Man to Jail 'Brutalities,'" *Omaha World Herald,* 10 April 1981, 21.

40. "Philadelphia Frees Defendants to Meet Goal on Jail Crowding," *Criminal Justice Newsletter,* 15 June 1988.

41. Fred Heinzlemann, W. Robert Burkhart, Bernard Gropper, Cheryl Martorana, Lois Felson Mock, Maureen O'Connor, and Walter Philip Travers, *Jailing Drunk Drivers: Impact on the Criminal Justice System* (Washington, D.C.: National Institute of Justice, 1984).

42. James J. Stephan, *State Prison Expenditures, 1996* (Washington, D.C.: Bureau of Justice Statistics, 1999).

43. Human Rights Watch, *Prison Conditions in the United States.*

44. "Suit Alleges Violations in California's 'Super-Max' Prison," *Criminal Justice Newsletter,* 1 September 1993, 2.

45. Chase Riveland, *Supermax Prison: Overview and General Considerations* (Longmont, Colo.: National Institute of Corrections, 1998).

46. Allen Beck, Darrell Gilliard, Lawrence Greenfeld, Caroline Harlow, Thomas Hester, Louis Jankowski, Tracy Snell, James Stephan, and Danielle Morton, *Survey of Prison Inmates, 1991* (Washington, D.C.: Bureau of Justice Statistics, 1993).

47. Marc Mauer, "Men in American Prisons: Trends, Causes, and Issues," *Men's Studies Review* 9 (1992): 10–12.

48. Roger Peters, Paul Greenbaum, John Edens, Chris Carter, and Madeline Ortiz, "Prevalence of DSM-IV Substance Abuse and Dependence Disorders among Prison Inmates," *American Journal of Drug and Alcohol Abuse* 24 (1998): 573–80.

49. Craig Hemmens and James Marquart, "Fear and Loathing in the Joint: The Impact of Race and Age on Inmate Support for Prison AIDS Policies," *Prison Journal* 78 (1998): 133–52.

50. Harlow, *Prior Abuse Reported by Inmates and Probationers,* 1.

51. Ditton, *Mental Health and Treatment of Inmates and Probationers,* 1.

52. James Anderson, Laronistine Dyson, and Jerald Burns, *Boot Camps: An Intermediate Sanction* (Lanham, Md.: University Press of America, 1999), 1–17.

53. Doris Layton Mackenzie, Robert Brame, David McDowall, and Claire Souryal, "Boot Camp Prison and Recidivism in Eight States," *Criminology* 33 (1995): 327–57.

54. Ibid., 328–29.

55. "New York Correctional Groups Praise Boot Camp Programs," *Criminal Justice Newsletter,* 1 April 1991, 4–5.

56. Velmer Burton, James Marquart, Steven Cuvelier, Leanne Fiftal Alarid, and Robert Hunter, "A Study of Attitudinal Change among Boot Camp Participants," *Federal Probation* 57 (1993): 46–52.

57. Doris Layton Mackenzie, "Book Camp Prisons: Components, Evaluations, and Empirical Issues," *Federal Probation* 54 (1990): 44–52; see also "Boot Camp Programs Grow in Number and Scope," *NIJ Reports* (November/December 1990): 6–8.

58. See, for example, Dale Sechrest, "Prison 'Boot Camps' Do Not Measure Up," *Federal Probation* 53 (1989): 15–20.

59. Doris Layton Mackenzie and James Shaw, "The Impact of Shock Incarceration on Technical Violations and New Criminal Activities," *Justice Quarterly* 10 (1993): 463–87.

60. Doris Layton Mackenzie, "Boot Camp Prisons: Components, Evaluations, and Empirical Issues," *Federal Probation* 54 (1990): 44–52.

61. Doris Layton Mackenzie and Alex Piquero, "The Impact of Shock Incarceration Programs on Prison Crowding," *Crime and Delinquency* 40 (1994): 222–49.

62. Mackenzie et al., "Boot Camp Prisons and Recidivism in Eight States," 352–53.

63. Correctional Research Associates, *Treating Youthful Offenders in the Community, an Evaluation Conducted by A. J. Reiss* (Washington, D.C.: Correctional Research Associates, 1966).

64. Kevin Krajick, "Not on My Block: Local Opposition Impedes the Search for Alternatives," *Corrections Magazine* 6 (1980): 15–27.

65. For a review, see John DiIulio, *Private Prisons* (Washington, D.C.: Government Printing Office, 1988); Joan Mullen, *Corrections and the Private Sector* (Washington, D.C.: National Institute of Justice, 1984).

66. "Many State Legislatures Focused on Crime in 1995, Study Finds," *Criminal Justice Newsletter,* 2 January 1996, 2.

67. Ira Robbins, *The Legal Dimensions of Private Incarceration* (Chicago: American Bar Association, 1988).

68. Lawrence Travis, Edward Latessa, and Gennaro Vito, "Private Enterprise and Institutional Corrections: A Call for Caution," *Federal Probation* 49 (1985): 11–17.

69. Patrick Anderson, Charles Davoli, and Laura Moriarty, "Private Corrections: Feast or Fiasco," *Prison Journal* 65 (1985): 32–41.

70. Travis Pratt and Jeff Maahs, "Are Private Prisons More Cost-Effective Than Public Prisons? A Meta-Analysis of Evaluation Research Studies," *Crime and Delinquency* 45 (1999): 358–71.

71. Data in this section come from Bureau of Justice Statistics, *Prisoners, 1925–1981* (Washington, D.C.: Government Printing Office, 1982).

72. Todd Clear, *Harm in American Penology: Offenders, Victims and Their Communities* (Albany: State University of New York Press, 1994).

73. Daniel Nagin, "Criminal Deterrence Research: A Review of the Evidence and a Research Agenda for the Outset of the 21st Century," in *Crime and Justice: An Annual Review* (Chicago: University of Chicago Press, 1997).

74. For more on this issue, see Marcy Rasmussen Podkopacz and Barry Feld, "The End of the Line: An Empirical Study of Judicial Waiver," *Journal of Criminal Law and Criminology* 86 (1996): 449–92.

75. Thomas P. Bonczar and Allen J. Beck, *Lifetime Likelihood of Going to State or Federal Prison* (Washington, D.C.: Bureau of Justice Statistics, 1997).

76. Timothy Noah, "Prison Population Boom Sputters to Halt as States Lack Funds to House Criminals," *Wall Street Journal,* 3 February 1992, A7.

77. Andrew Lang Golub, Farrukh Hakeem, and Bruce Johnson, *Monitoring the Decline in the Crack Epidemic with Data from the Drug Use Forecasting Program, Final Report* (Washington, D.C.: National Institute of Justice, 1996).

chapter 14

Prison Life

Precious Bedell spent more than nineteen years in a New York State prison after being convicted in 1980 for the death of Lashonda, her two-year-old daughter. She was granted a new trial in 1999 and allowed to plead guilty to second-degree manslaughter; given the time she had already served, Bedell was released immediately.

"I regret the tragedy that I caused in my life so deeply, I cannot tell you how deeply," Bedell, now in her mid-forties, said after her release. "No matter what I've done and what I've accomplished, it will never compensate for Lashonda's death." She said she would devote her life to developing programs to prevent child

Precious Bedell kisses her daughter Keisha as she leaves the Onondaga County courthouse a free woman after spending nineteen years in prison.

abuse and child neglect. "I strongly believe we should do this work on the outside before people come to prison," she said.

Bedell, who had her first child at age 16, was an unwed mother with a drug abuse problem when she was convicted of fatally beating her child. During her time at the state's Bedford Hills Correctional Facility, Bedell came to symbolize the potential for prison-based rehabilitation efforts; she became an inspiration to other inmates. She earned bachelor's and master's degrees, worked her way into a position of trust at the prison's Children's Center, started a Parents as Reading Partners program, and helped write handbooks about foster care, imprisoned parent's rights and responsibilities, and rage control. Her rehabilitation efforts caught the attention of a number of people who became her advocates, including actress Glenn Close, who met her while filming a documentary at the prison. Her two surviving children, both in their mid-twenties, also helped push for their mother's release over the years.[1]

The story of Precious Bedell is unfortunately so unique that it makes media headlines around the nation. Most inmates are not rehabilitated, and a majority return to prison soon after their release. The spotty record of correctional rehabilitation is not surprising considering the overcrowded correctional system. A significant percentage of facilities are old, decrepit, archaic structures: Twenty-five prisons were built before 1875, 79 between 1875 and 1924, and 141 between 1925 and 1949. In fact, some of the first prisons ever constructed, such as the Concord Reformatory in Massachusetts, are still in operation.

Although a majority of prisons are classified as medium security, more than half of all inmates are being held in large, maximum-security institutions. Despite the continuous outcry by penologists against the use of fortresslike prisons, institutions holding a thousand or more inmates still predominate. Prison overcrowding is a significant problem. As noted in Chapter 13, the prison system now holds over 1.2 million people (Figure 14.1). Many institutions are overcrowded and operating above stated capacity. Recreation and workshop facilities have been turned into dormitories housing thirty or more inmates in a single room. Most prison experts agree that a minimum of sixty square feet is needed for each inmate, but many prisons fail to reach this standard.

This giant, overcrowded system designed to reform and rehabilitate offenders is instead undergoing a crisis of massive proportions. Institutions are so overcrowded that meaningful treatment efforts are often a matter of wishful thinking; recidivism rates are shockingly high. Inmates are resentful of the deteriorated conditions, and correctional officers fear that the institution is ready to explode. In addition, correctional administrators have begun to adopt a "no-frills" policy in prison, removing privileges and making prisons truly places of punishment. The no-frills movement is a response to lawmakers' claims that crime rates are high because inmates no longer fear imprisonment. This chapter presents a brief review of some of the most important issues confronting the nation's troubled correctional system.

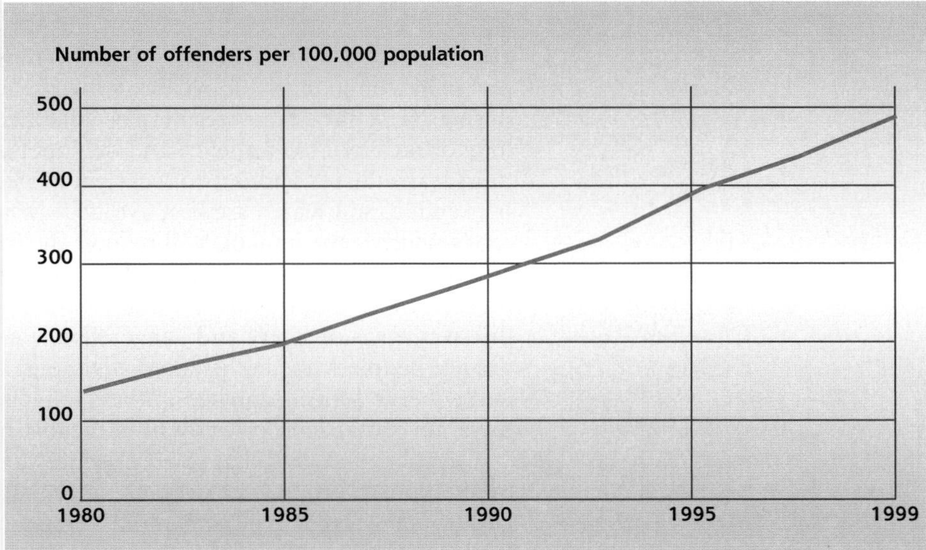

Figure 14.1
Federal and state incarceration rate, 1980–1999
The incarceration rate has more than tripled since 1980, and the number of inmates has skyrocketed to over 1.2 million.

SOURCE: U.S. Department of Justice, *Correctional Populations in the United States, 1996* (Washington, D.C.: Bureau of Justice Statistics, 1997). Updated 1999.

total institution
A regimented, dehumanizing institution such as a prison, in which like-situated people are kept in social isolation, cut off from the world at large.

MEN IMPRISONED

According to prevailing wisdom, prisons in the United States are **total institutions.** This means that inmates locked within their walls are segregated from the outside world, kept under constant scrutiny and surveillance, and forced to obey strict official rules to avoid facing formal sanctions. Their personal possessions are taken from them, and they must conform to institutional dress and personal appearance norms. Many human functions are strictly curtailed — heterosexual relationships and sex, friendships, family relationships, education, and participation in groups become privileges of the past.

Living in Prison

Inmates quickly learn what the term *total institution* really means. When they arrive at the prison, they are stripped, searched, shorn, and assigned living quarters. Before they get there, though, their first experience occurs in a classification or reception center, where they are given a series of psychological and other tests and are evaluated on the basis of their personality, background, offense history, and treatment needs. Based on the classification they are given, they will be assigned to a permanent facility. Hard-core, repeat, and violent offenders will go to the maximum-security unit; offenders with learning disabilities may be assigned to an institution that specializes in educational services; mentally disordered offenders will be held in a facility that can provide psychiatric care; and so on.

Once they arrive at the long-term facility, inmates may be granted a short orientation period and then given a permanent cell assignment in the general population. Due to overcrowding, they may be sharing a cell designed for a single inmate with one or more others. All previous concepts of personal privacy and dignity are soon forgotten. Personal losses include the deprivation of liberty, goods, and services, heterosexual relationships, autonomy and security.[2] Inmates may be subject to verbal and physical attack and threats, with little chance of legal redress. Although the criminal law applies to inmates as to any other citizen, it is rarely enforced within prison walls.[3] Therefore, part of living in prison involves learning to protect oneself and developing survival instincts.

Inmates in large, inaccessible prisons may find themselves physically cut off from families, friends, and associates. Visitors may find it difficult to travel great distances to see them; mail is censored and sometimes destroyed.

ADJUSTING TO PRISON Inmates may go through a variety of attitude and behavior changes, or cycles, as their sentence unfolds. During the early part of their prison stay, inmates may become easily depressed while considering the long duration of the sentence and the loneliness and dangers of prison life. They must learn the ins and outs of survival in the institution: Which persons can be befriended, and which are best avoided? Who will grant favors and for what repayment? Some inmates will request the regular payments be made to them in exchange for protection from rape and beatings. To avoid victimization, inmates must learn to adopt a lifestyle that shields them from victimization.[4] They must discover areas of safety and danger. Some learn how to fight back to prove they are not people who can be taken advantage of. While some kill their attackers and get even longer sentences, others join cliques that provide protection and the ability to acquire power within the institution.

Inmates may find that some prisoners have formed cliques, or groups, based on ethnic backgrounds or personal interests; they are likely to encounter Mafia-like or racial terror groups that must be dealt with. Inmates may be the victim of homosexual attacks. They may find that power in the prison is shared by terri-

Counselor Charlie Doty talks to an inmate in a Kentucky prison. Counseling and treatment are standard fare in most prisons. Whether prison-based rehabilitation can succeed in reducing recidivism rates is the subject of constant debate. The so-called "failure" of rehabilitation has encouraged harsh penal measures such as mandatory life sentences for "three time losers."

fied guards and inmate gangs; the only way to avoid being beaten and raped may be to learn how to beat and rape.[5] If they are weak and unable to defend themselves, new inmates may find that they are considered a "punk"; if they ask a guard for help, they are labeled a "snitch." After that, they may spend the rest of their sentence in protective custody, sacrificing the "freedom of the yard" and rehabilitation services for personal protection.[6]

COPING BEHAVIOR Despite all these hardships, many inmates learn to adapt to the prison routine. Each prisoner has his own method of coping, he may stay alone, become friends with another inmate, join a group, or seek the advice of treatment personnel. They may soon learn that their lifestyle and activities can contribute to their being victimized by more aggressive inmates: The more time they spend in closely guarded activities, the less likely they are to become the victims of violence; the more they isolate themselves from others who might protect them, the greater is their vulnerability to attack; the more visitors they receive, the more likely they are to be attacked by fellow inmates jealous of their relationship with the outside world.[7]

New inmates must learn to deal with the guards and other correctional personnel; these relationships will determine whether the inmates do "hard time" or "easy time." For example, when inmates housed in open institutions are sent out to work on roads or to do farm work, they may be forced to wear *stun belts* for security while they do their outdoor activities. Once confined in a stun belt, the inmate can receive a shock of fifty thousand volts and three to four milliamps for a period of eight seconds. Although not fatal, the shock is very painful, and victims are immediately incapacitated. Burns, which may take months to heal, may develop where the electrodes touch the skin above the left kidney. Critics charge that stun guns are brutal and can be used by correctional workers to terrorize or torture inmates whom they dislike or find offensive.[8]

Regardless of adaptation style, the first stage of the inmates' prison cycle is marked by a growing awareness that they can no longer depend on their traditional associates for help and support and that, for better or worse, the institution is a new home to which they must adjust. Unfortunately for the goal of rehabilitation, the predominant emotion that inmates must confront is boredom. The absence of anything constructive to do, the forced idleness, is what is often so frustrating and so damaging.[9]

CONFLICT AND HUSTLING Part of new inmates' early adjustment involves becoming familiar with and perhaps participating in the black market, the hidden economy of the prison — the hustle. Hustling provides inmates with a source of steady income and the satisfaction that they are beating the system.[10] Hustling involves sales of such illegal commodities as drugs (uppers, downers, pot), alcohol, weapons, or illegally obtained food and supplies. When prison officials crack down on hustled goods, it merely serves to drive up the price — giving hustlers greater incentive to promote their activities. Drugs and other contraband are smuggled into prison by visitors, carried in by inmates who are out on furlough or work-release programs, or bought from corrupt prison officials. Control of the prison drug trade is often the spark that creates violence and conflict.

Inmates must also learn to deal with the racial conflict that is a daily fact of life. Prisoners tend to segregate themselves, and if peace is to reign in the institution, they learn to stay out of each other's way. Often, racial groupings are quite exact; for example, Hispanics will separate themselves according to their national origin (Mexican, Puerto Rican, Colombian, etc.) Because racial disparity in sentencing is common in many U.S. courts, prisons are one place where minorities often hold power.

Inmates may find that the social support of inmate peers can make incarceration somewhat less painful. They may begin to take stock of their situation and enter into educational or vocational training programs, if they are available. Many turn to religion and take Bible classes. They heed the inmate grapevine to determine what the parole board considers important in deciding to grant community release. They may become more politically aware in response to the influence of other inmates, and the personal guilt they may have felt may be shifted to society at large. Why should they be in prison when those equally guilty go free? They learn the importance of money and politics. Eventually, they may be called on by new arrivals to aid them in adapting to the system.

Even in the harsh prison environment, inmates may learn to find a niche for themselves. They may be able to find a place, activity, or group in which they can feel comfortable and secure.[11] An inmate's niche is a kind of insulation from the pains of imprisonment, enabling him to cope and providing him with a sense of autonomy and freedom. Finding a niche may insulate inmates from attack, and research in fact indicates that prison victimization may be less prevalent than commonly believed. Not surprisingly, the relatively few victims of prison violence seem less psychologically healthy, more fearful than nonvictims, and less able to avoid the pains of imprisonment.[12]

Of course, not all inmates learn to cope. Some inmates repeatedly violate institutional rules; more than 10 percent of all inmates have six or more such infractions yearly.[13] Predicting who will become an institutional troublemaker is difficult, but rule-breaking behavior has been associated with being a younger inmate with a low IQ, possessing numerous juvenile convictions, being a repeat offender, and having victimized a stranger. Inmates who have limited intelligence and maintain low self-control may not be able to form adaptive coping mechanisms and manage the stress of being in prison.[14]

inmate subculture
The loosely defined culture that pervades prisons and has its own norms, rules, and language.

inmate social code
Unwritten guidelines that express the values, attitudes, and types of behavior that older inmates demand of young ones. Passed on from one generation of inmates to another, the inmate social code represents the values of interpersonal relations within the prison.

prisonization
Assimilation into the separate culture in the prison that has its own set of rewards and behaviors. This loosely defined culture that pervades prisons has its own norms, rules, and language. The traditional culture is now being replaced by a violent gang culture.

The Inmate Social Code

For many years, criminal justice experts maintained that inmates formed their own world with a unique set of norms and rules, known as the **inmate subculture.**[15] A significant aspect of the inmate subculture was a unique **inmate social code,** unwritten guidelines that expressed the values, attitudes, and type of behavior that older inmates demanded of young ones. Passed on from one generation of inmates to another, the inmate social code represented the values of interpersonal relations within the prison.

National attention was first drawn to the inmate social code and subculture by Donald Clemmer's classic book *The Prison Community,* in which he presented a detailed sociological study of life in a maximum-security prison.[16] Referring to thousands of conversations and interviews, as well as to inmate essays and biographies, Clemmer was able to identify a unique language, or *argot,* that prisoners use. In addition, Clemmer found that prisoners tend to group themselves into cliques on the basis of such personal criteria as sexual preference, political beliefs, and offense history. He found complex sexual relationships in prison and concluded that many heterosexual men will turn to homosexual relationships when faced with long sentences and the loneliness of prison life.

Clemmer's most important contribution may have been his identification of the **prisonization** process. This he defined as the inmate's assimilation into the existing prison culture through acceptance of its language, sexual code, and norms of behavior. Those who become the most "prisonized" will be the least likely to reform on the outside.

Using Clemmer's work as a jumping-off point, a number of prominent sociologists have set out to more fully explore the various roles in the prison community. The most important principles of the dominant inmate culture have been identified, including the following:

1. *Don't interfere with inmates' interests.* Within this area of the code are maxims concerning serving the least amount of time in the greatest possible comfort. For example, inmates are warned never to betray another inmate to authorities; in other words, grievances must be handled personally. Other aspects of the noninterference doctrine include "Don't be nosy," "Don't have a loose lip," "Keep off the other inmates' backs," and "Don't put another inmate on the spot."
2. *Don't lose your head.* Inmates are also cautioned to refrain from arguing, quarreling, or engaging in other emotional displays with fellow inmates. The novice may hear such warnings as "Play it cool" and "Do your own time."
3. *Don't exploit inmates.* Prisoners are warned not to take advantage of one another — "Don't steal from cons," "Don't welsh on a debt," and "Be right."
4. *Be tough and don't lose your dignity.* Although rule 2 forbids conflict, once it starts, an inmate must be prepared to deal with it effectively and thoroughly. Maxims include "Don't cop out," "Don't weaken," and "Be tough; be a man."
5. *Don't be a sucker.* Inmates are cautioned not to make fools of themselves and support the guards or prison administration over the interest of the inmates — "Be sharp."[17]

While some inmates violate the code and exploit their peers, the "right guy" is someone who uses the inmate social code as his personal behavior guide. He is always loyal to his fellow prisoners, keeps his promises, is dependable and trustworthy, and never interferes with inmates who are conniving against the officials.[18] The right guy does not go around looking for a fight, but he never runs away from one; he acts like a man.

Some prison experts believe that the prison experience transforms people and forces them to accept the inmate culture, but others argue that the culture is actually imported from the outside world.[19] In other words, inmate culture is affected as much by the values of newcomers and events on the outside as it is by traditional inmate values. Both socialization and importation may also possibly help define the way inmates adapt to the prison culture. For example, inmates who view violence as an acceptable alternative before entering prison are the ones most likely to adopt the inmate social code.[20]

The effects of prisonization may be long term and destructive. Many become hostile to the legal system, learning to use violence as a means of solving problems and to value criminal peers.[21] For some this change may be permanent; for others it is temporary, and they may revert to their "normal" life after release.

The New Inmate Culture

The importation of outside values into the inmate culture has had a dramatic effect on prison life. Although the "old" inmate subculture may have been harmful because its norms and values insulated the inmate from change efforts, it also helped create order within the institution and prevented violence among the inmates. People who violated the code and victimized others were sanctioned by their peers. An understanding developed between guards and inmate leaders: The guards would let the inmates have things their own way; the inmates would not let things get out of hand and draw the attention of the administration.

The old system may be dying or already dead in most institutions. The change seems to have been precipitated by the Black Power movement in the 1960s and 1970s. Black inmates were no longer content to fill a subservient role and challenged the power of established white inmates. As the Black Power movement gained prominence, racial tension in prisons created divisions that severely altered the inmate subculture. Older, respected inmates could no longer cross racial lines to mediate disputes. Predatory inmates could victimize others without fear of retaliation. Consequently, more inmates than ever are now assigned to protective custody for their own safety.

In the new culture, African-American and Latino inmates are much more cohesively organized than whites.[22] Their groups sometimes form out of religious or political affiliations, such as the Black Muslims; out of efforts to combat discrimination in prison, such as the Latino group La Familia; or from street gangs, such as the Vice Lords or Gangster Disciples in the Illinois prison system and the Crips in California. Where white inmates have successfully organized, it is in the form of a neo-Nazi group called the Aryan Brotherhood. Racially homogenous gangs are so cohesive and powerful that they are able to supplant the original inmate code with one of their own. Consider the oath taken by new members of Nuestra Familia (Our Family), a Latino gang operating in California prisons: "If I go forward, follow me. If I hesitate, push me. If they kill me, avenge me. If I am a traitor, kill me."[23]

WOMEN IMPRISONED

Before 1960 few women were in prison. Women's prisons were relatively rare and were usually an outgrowth of male institutions. Only four institutions for women were built between 1930 and 1950; in comparison, thirty-four women's prisons were constructed during the 1980s.

At the turn of the century, female inmates were viewed as morally depraved people who flaunted conventional rules of female behavior. The treatment of white and African-American women differed significantly. In some states, white women were placed in female-only reformatories designed to improve their deportment; black women were placed in male prisons, where they were subject to the chain gang and beatings.[24]

The place of women in the correctional system has changed rapidly. Today, more than eighty-five thousand women are in the state and federal systems, about 6.5 percent of the total inmate population. Although still small compared with the male inmate population, the female population has grown at a faster pace. Analyses of imprisonment rates from 1990 to 1997 reveal a 49 percent increase among men and a 71 percent increase among women in the number of sentenced prisoners per 100,000 residents.[25]

The female offender population has increased so rapidly for a number of reasons. Women have accelerated their crime rate at a faster pace than men. The get-tough policies that produced mandatory and determinate sentencing statutes also helped reduce the judicial discretion that has traditionally benefited women. As Meda Chesney-Lind points out, women are swept up in the get-tough movement and no longer receive the benefits of male chivalry. The use of sentencing guidelines means that such factors as family ties and employment record, two elements that usually benefit women during sentencing, can no longer be considered by judges.[26] Chesney-Lind notes that judges seem willing once again to view female offenders as "depraved" and outside the ranks of "true womanhood." Her work is discussed in greater detail in the Race, Culture, and Gender feature.

Female Institutions

State jurisdictions have been responding to the influx of female offenders into the correctional system by expanding the facilities for housing and treating them.[27] Women's prisons tend to be smaller than those housing male inmates.[28] Although some female institutions are strictly penal, with steel bars, concrete floors, and other security measures, the majority are nonsecure institutions similar to college dormitories and group homes in the community. Women's facilities, especially those in the community, commonly offer a great deal of autonomy to inmates and allow them to make decisions affecting their daily life.

Like men's prisons, women's prisons suffer from a lack of adequate training, health, treatment, and educational facilities. Psychological counseling often takes the form of group sessions conducted by laypeople, such as correctional officers. Most trained psychologists and psychiatrists restrict themselves to such activities as conducting intake classifications and court-ordered examinations and prescribing mood-controlling medication. Although many female inmates are parents and had custody of their children before their incarceration, little effort is made to help them develop better parenting skills. One program designed to help female inmates manage their children is described in Exhibit 14.1.

The lack of meaningful work opportunities is also a problem. Where vocational training exists, it is in areas with limited financial reward, hindering adjustment on release. Female inmates, many of whom were on the economic margin before their incarceration began, find little room for improvement during their prison experience.[29] Surveys also indicate that the prison experience does little to prepare women to reenter the workforce after their sentence has been completed. Gender stereotypes still shape vocational opportunities.[30] Female inmates are still being trained for "women's roles," such as child rearing, and not given the programming to make successful adjustments in the community.[31]

FEMALE INMATES Like their male counterparts, female inmates are young (most are under age 30), minority group members, unmarried, undereducated (more than half are high school dropouts), and either unemployed or underemployed.

Incarcerated women also have had a troubled family life. Significant numbers were at-risk children, products of broken homes and the welfare system; over half had received welfare at some time during their adult lives. They experienced a pattern of harsh discipline and physical abuse. Many claim to have been physically or sexually abused at some point in their life. This pattern continued in their adult life: Many female inmates were victims of domestic violence.

Race, Culture, and Gender

XYXYXYXY
XYXYXYXY
XYXYXYXY

WOMEN IN PRISON: VENGEFUL EQUITY

The number of women imprisoned in the United States has been expanding at a faster pace than the number of men. More than 100,000 women are locked up on any given day in the nation's prisons and jails. What can account for this increase, and are women suffering more than men due to the justice system's turn toward more punitive sanctions?

According to Meda Chesney-Lind, a highly respected feminist scholar, the soaring number of women under lock and key is not simply a product of the increasing reliance on imprisonment as a sanction, but because women's proportional "share" of the prison population has increased. This increase has occurred because of a significant change in society's response to women's crime. Where before the status of a female defendant, usually a nonviolent offender who was also a wife and mother might be taken into account, this is no longer possible under new mandatory sentences. Many female offenders are involved in drug offenses that are now heavily sanctioned. The "war on drugs" has placed an extremely harsh burden on poor and marginalized women. The war on drugs, Chesney-Lind claims, has become a "war on women." Though its intent was to get tough on drug kingpins and dealers, mandatory drug sentencing, especially in federal courts, has resulted in an explosion in the female inmate population; over one-third of incarcerated women are serving time solely for possession of illegal drugs. In addition, the new technologies being developed for drug testing has resulted in more parole and probation violations, further increasing the number of female inmates.

The result has been a dramatic change in the way the country responds to female offenders. The nation is becoming more punitive and treating men and women more equally. However, this has harmed women by increasing their share of the prison population; it is "equality with a vengeance."

The effort to treat men and women more equally has also triggered abuse of incarcerated women in male-dominated institutions. When male inmates in New York were videotaped while being strip searched, the state instituted a policy of also taping women's strip searches. The videotaping was done while male officers were in the vicinity, and the female inmates sued and won damages when they suspected that the videos were being watched by prison officials. Such sexually charged situations are particularly damaging to women who have a history of sexual and physical abuse. Because male correctional officers now are commonly assigned to women's prisons, there have also been major scandals involving the sexual exploitation and rape of female inmates. Few if any of these incidents are reported, and perpetrators rarely go to trial. Institutional workers cover for each other, and women who file complaints are offered little protection from vengeful guards.

While women are suffering because of this misguided effort at equity, they are also victimized because of perceived gender differences. Women are much more likely than men to suffer disciplinary complaints for trivial offenses and more likely to be punished with solitary confinement and other severe sanctions. There is clear evidence that women in prison are overpoliced and overcontrolled.

Critical Thinking

Chesney-Lind concludes that women in modern prisons suffer the "worst of both worlds": sometimes suffering because of gender differences; sometimes receiving "equity with a vengeance" that results in their sexual exploitation. Would an alternative approach, stressing community care and support, be a more effective method in reducing female crime rates and helping indigent women achieve their potential? Explain. Should prison be a last resort for female offenders? Why or why not?

InfoTrac College Edition Research

Are female inmates victimized because of their gender? How do sex-role stereotypes influence correctional programming and practices for female inmates? To find out, read
Pamela J. Schram, "Stereotypes about Vocational Programming for Female Inmates," *Prison Journal* 78 (1998): 244.

SOURCE: Meda Chesney-Lind, "Vengeful Equity: Sentencing Women to Prison," in *The Female Offender: Girls, Women and Crime* (Thousand Oaks, Calif.: Sage, 1997).

exhibit 14.1

Summer Program at the Bedford Hills Correctional Center

The Summer Program at the Bedford Hills Correctional Center in New York was started in 1978 by a Roman Catholic nun, Sister Elain Roulet, and a Franciscan brother, Tom Grady. The program allows mothers to spend from 9 A.M. to 3 P.M. with their child campers, playing basketball, putting on a talent show, and making crafts. The activities take place in the Children's Center, a separate room off the visiting areas usually available to inmates and their children during regular visiting hours. The children do not stay overnight at the facility but are shuttled to the homes of area residents who have agreed to house the children for the one-week summer camp, which runs from June through August. Children as young as three are accepted, and even youths in their late teens will attend.

Bedford Hills has other programs designed to strengthen family ties. A Family Reunion program allows inmates to spend two or three nights with family members in houses on the prison grounds, complete with kitchen and yard. Weekend programs, run year-round, allow children to stay overnight with host families and spend from 9 A.M. to 3 P.M. with their mothers. Children are matched with host families on the basis of likes and dislikes, favorite foods, and pets. Some hosts become attached to the children, requesting to be permanent sponsors.

SOURCES: Monte Williams, "When Mother Lives in Prison, A State Program Seeks to Sustain Maternal Bonds," *New York Times,* 18 August 1997, A17; John Wooldredge and Kimberly Masters, "Confronting Problems Faced by Pregnant Inmates in State Prisons," *Crime and Delinquency* 39 (1993):195–203.

A serious problem for women in prison is the disruption of their families. About three-fourths of all female inmates are mothers, and most were living with their children before their incarceration. Who takes care of the children while their mothers are incarcerated? Most children of incarcerated women are placed with their father, grandparent, other relative, or a family friend. About 10 percent wind up in foster homes or state facilities.

A significant number of female inmates report having substance abuse problems. About three-fourths have used drugs at some time in their lives, and almost half were involved with addictive drugs, such as cocaine, heroin, or PCP. There is actually little difference in major drug use between male and female offenders when measured over their life span or at the time of their current arrest. The incarceration of so many women who are low-criminal risks yet face a high risk of exposure to HIV (human immunodeficiency virus, which causes AIDS) and other health issues because of their prior history of drug abuse presents a significant problem.

The picture that emerges of the female inmate is troubling. After a lifetime of emotional turmoil, physical and sexual abuse, and drug use, it seems improbable that overcrowded, underfunded correctional institutions can forge a dramatic turnaround in the behavior of at-risk female inmates.

SEXUAL EXPLOITATION Daily life in women's prisons differs somewhat from that in male institutions. For one thing, unlike male inmates, women usually do not present an immediate physical danger to staff and fellow inmates. Relatively few engage in violent behavior, and incidents of inmate-initiated sexual aggression, so common in male institutions, are rare in women's prisons.[32] Nevertheless, there are numerous reports of female prisoners being sexually abused and exploited by male correctional workers who either use brute force or psychological coercion to gain sexual control over inmates.[33] Staff-on-inmate

Cynthia Hardin in the prison yard at Gatesville, Texas. Although there are far fewer women in prison than men, the rate of female incarceration is accelerating faster.

sexual misconduct covers a wide range of behaviors, from lewd remarks to voyeurism to assault and rape. A 1999 survey by the federal government's General Accounting Office (GAO) found that the federal government, forty-one states, and the District of Columbia had passed laws criminalizing some types of staff sexual misconduct in prisons. The GAO's in-depth analysis of the three correctional systems with the largest number of female inmates — the federal Bureau of Prisons, the California Department of Corrections, and the Texas Department of Criminal Justice — found that sexual misconduct persists despite efforts to correct problems and train staff. Between 1995 and 1998, female inmates made 506 allegations of staff sexual misconduct; 92 of them were sustained, generally resulting in staff firings or resignations. Each jurisdiction was involved in at least two civil lawsuits arising from staff sexual misconduct during this period.[34]

ADAPTING TO PRISON The rigid, anti-authority inmate social code found in many male institutions does not exist in female institutions.[35] Confinement for women, however, may produce severe anxiety and anger because of separation from families and loved ones and the inability to function in normal female roles. Unlike men, who direct their anger outward, female prisoners may turn to more self-destructive acts to cope with their problems. Female inmates are more likely than males to mutilate their own bodies and attempt suicide. For example, one common practice among female inmates is self-mutilation, or "carving." This ranges from simple scratches to carving the name of their boyfriend on their body or even complex statements or sentences ("To mother, with hate").[36]

make-believe families
Formed by women in prison to compensate for the loss of family and loved ones, a peer unit that contains mother and father figures.

Another form of adaptation to prison used by women is the **make-believe family.** This group contains masculine and feminine figures acting as fathers and mothers; some even act as children and take on the role of brother or sister. Formalized marriages and divorces may be conducted. Sometimes one inmate holds multiple roles, so that a "sister" in one family may "marry" and become the "wife" of another inmate. It is estimated that about half of all female inmates are members of make-believe families.[37]

Why do make-believe families exist? Experts suggest that they provide the warm, stable relationships otherwise unobtainable in the prison environment. People both in and out of prison have needs for security, companionship, affection, attention, status, prestige, and acceptance that can be filled only by having primary group relationships. Friends fill many of these needs, but the family better represents the ideal or desire for these things in a stable relationship.

CORRECTIONAL TREATMENT METHODS

Almost every prison facility uses some mode of treatment for inmates. This may come in the form of individual or group therapy programs or educational or vocational training.

Despite good intentions, rehabilitative treatment within prison walls is extremely difficult to achieve. Trained professional treatment personnel usually command high salaries, and most institutions do not have sufficient budgets to adequately staff therapeutic programs. Usually, a large facility may have a single staff psychiatrist or a few social workers. A second problem revolves around the philosophy of **less eligibility,** which has been interpreted to mean that prisoners should always be treated less well than the most underprivileged law-abiding citizen. Translated into today's terms, less eligibility usually involves the question "Why should inmates be treated to expensive programs denied to the average honest citizen?" Enterprising state legislators use this argument to block expenditures for prison budgets, and some prison administrators may actually agree with them.

less eligibility
The correctional practice demanding that prison inmates do not enjoy benefits that exceed those of the indigent poor who have never been convicted of a crime. For example, educational opportunities should not be provided that are not freely obtainable by anyone in the general public.

Finally, correctional treatment is hampered by the ignorance surrounding the practical effectiveness of one type of treatment program over another. What constitutes proper treatment has not yet been determined, and studies evaluating treatment effectiveness have suggested that few, if any, of the programs currently used in prisons actually produce significant numbers of rehabilitated offenders.

This section presents a selected number of therapeutic methods that have been used nationally in correctional settings and identifies some of their more salient features.

Group Counseling

Prison inmates typically suffer from a variety of cognitive and psychosocial deficits, such as poor emotional control, social skills, and interpersonal problem solving; these deficits are often linked to long-term substance abuse. Modern counseling programs help them to control emotions (e.g., understanding why they feel the way they do; how not to get too nervous or anxious; solving their problems creatively), to communicate with others (e.g., understanding what people tell them; communicating clearly when they write), to deal with legal concerns (e.g., keeping out of legal trouble; avoiding breaking laws), to manage general life issues (e.g., finding a job; dealing with difficult coworkers; being a good parent), and to develop and maintain social relationships (e.g., having good relations with others; making others happy; making others proud).[38] To achieve these goals, correctional systems use a variety of intensive individual and group techniques, including behavior modification, aversive therapy, milieu therapy, reality therapy, transactional analysis, and responsibility therapy.

special-needs inmate
Those correctional clients who require special care and treatment, such as the elderly, mentally ill, drug addicted, or AIDS infected.

Treating the Special-Needs Inmate

One of the challenges of correctional treatment is to care for **special-needs inmates.** These individuals can have a variety of social problems. Some are mentally ill but have been assigned to prison because the state has toughened its insanity laws. Others suffer mental problems developed during their imprisonment. An additional 1 to 6 percent of the inmate population is mentally retarded. Treating the mentally ill inmate has required the development and use of new therapies in the prison environment. Although some critics warn of the overuse of "chemical straitjackets" — psychotropic medications — to keep disturbed inmates docile, prison administrators have been found to have a genuine concern for these special-needs inmates.[39]

Restrictive crime control policies have also produced another special-needs group, elderly inmates who require health care, diets, and work and recreational opportunities that are different from those of the general population. Some correctional systems have responded to the growing number of elderly inmates by creating facilities tailored to their needs.[40] It is now estimated that more than twenty-two thousand inmates are over age 55, an increase of more than 40 percent since 1990.[41]

THE DRUG-DEPENDENT INMATE

Another special-needs group in prison are drug-dependent inmates. Although most institutions attempt to provide drug and alcohol treatment, these efforts are often inadequate. Government-sponsored surveys have found that an estimated half a million state inmates are in need of drug treatment; because of lack of funding and inadequate security measures, however, only one hundred thousand receive adequate treatment.[42]

Although the ideal drug treatment has yet to be identified, experimental efforts around the country use counseling sessions, instruction in coping strategies, employment counseling, and strict security measures featuring random urinalysis.

THE AIDS-INFECTED INMATE

The AIDS-infected prisoner is another acute special-needs inmate. Two groups of people at high risk of contracting HIV are intravenous drug users who share needles and males who engage in homosexual sex, two lifestyles common in prison. Although the numbers are constantly changing, the rate of HIV infection among state and federal prisoners has stabilized at around 2 percent. There were 23,548 HIV-infected inmates at the end of 1997, down from 23,881 in 1996. More encouraging, the number of deaths due to AIDS dropped from 907 in 1996 to 538 in 1997, a significant decline from 100 deaths per 100,000 state inmates in 1995 (the highest rate recorded) to 48 deaths per 100,000 inmates in 1997. Between 1991 (the first year of data collection) and 1996 about 1 in 3 state prisoner deaths were attributable to AIDS; during 1997 it was about 1 in 5.[43] At the end of 1997, the number of inmates with confirmed AIDS in state and federal prisons was five times higher than in the total U.S. population: about 55 per 10,000 prison inmates compared with 10 per 10,000 persons in the U.S. population.

Correctional administrators have found it difficult to arrive at effective policies to confront AIDS. Although all state and federal jurisdictions do some AIDS testing, only eighteen states and the Federal Bureau of Prisons conduct mass screenings of all inmates. Most states test inmates only if there are significant indications that they are HIV-positive. About 40 percent of all state prison inmates have never been tested for AIDS.

Most correctional systems are now training staff about AIDS. Educational programs for inmates are often inadequate because administrators are reluctant to give them information on the proper cleaning of drug paraphernalia and safe sex (since both drug use and homosexual sex are forbidden in prison).

Educational and Vocational Programs

Besides treatment programs stressing personal growth through individual analysis or group process, inmate rehabilitation is also pursued through vocational and educational training. Although these two kinds of training sometimes differ in style and content, they can also overlap when, for example, education involves practical, job-related study.

The first prison treatment programs were in fact educational. A prison school was opened at the Walnut Street Jail in 1784. Elementary courses were offered in New York's prison system in 1801 and in Pennsylvania's in 1844. An actual school system was established in Detroit's House of Corrections in 1870, and Elmira Reformatory opened a vocational trade school in 1876. Today, most institutions provide some type of educational program. At some prisons, inmates can obtain a high school diploma or a general educational development (GED) certificate through equivalency exams. Other institutions provide an actual classroom education, usually staffed by certified teachers employed full time at the prison or by part-time teachers who also teach full time at nearby public schools.

The number of hours devoted to educational programs and the quality and intensity of these efforts vary greatly. Some are full-time programs employing highly qualified and concerned educators, whereas others are part-time programs without any real goals or objectives. Although worthwhile attempts are being made, prison educational programs often suffer from inadequate funding and administration. The picture is not totally bleak, however. In some institutions, programs have been designed to circumvent the difficulties inherent in the prison structure. They encourage volunteers from the community and local schools to tutor willing and motivated inmates. Some prison administrators have arranged flexible schedules for inmate students and actively encourage their participation in these programs. In several states, statewide school districts serving prisons have been created. Forming such districts can make better-qualified staff available and provide the materials and resources necessary for meaningful educational programs.

Every state correctional system also has some job-related services for inmates. Some have elaborate training programs within the institution, whereas others have instituted prerelease and postrelease employment services. Inmates who hope to obtain parole need to participate in prison industry. Documenting a history of stable employment in prison is essential if parole agents are to convince prospective employers that the ex-offender is a good risk; postrelease employment is usually required for parole eligibility.[44]

A few of the more important work-related services are discussed in the following sections.

BASIC PRISON INDUSTRIES Prisoners are normally expected to work within the institution as part of their treatment program. Aside from saving money for the institution, prison work programs are supposed to help inmates develop good habits and skills. Most prominent among traditional prison industries are those designed to help maintain and run the institution and provide

Some prison rehabilitation programs are quite unique. Here inmates confer with a teacher in the horticulture class at Limestone Prison in Capshaw, Alabama.

services for other public or state facilities, such as mental hospitals. These include the following:

1. *Food services* Inmates are expected to prepare and supply food for prisoners and staff. These duties include baking bread, preparing meat and vegetables, and cleaning and maintaining kitchen facilities.
2. *Maintenance* The buildings and grounds of most prisons are cared for by inmates. Electrical work, masonry, plumbing, and painting are all inmate activities. Of a less skilled nature are such duties as garbage collection, gardening, and cleaning.
3. *Laundry* Most prisons have their own inmate-run laundries. Quite often, prison laundries will also furnish services to other state institutions.
4. *Agriculture* In western and southern states, many prisons farm their own land. Dairy herds, crops, and poultry are all managed by inmates. The products are used in the prison and in other state institutions.

VOCATIONAL TRAINING Most institutions also provide vocational training programs. In New York, for example, more than forty-two trade and technical courses are provided in organized training shops under qualified civilian instructors. Some of these courses not only benefit the inmate but also provide services for the institution. For example, New York has trained inmates to become dental laboratory technicians; this program provides dentures for inmates and saves the state money. Another New York program trains inmates to become optical technicians and has the added benefit of providing eyeglasses for inmates. Other New York correctional training programs include barber training, computer programming, auto mechanics, auto body work, and radio and television repair. The products of most of these programs save the taxpayers money, and the programs provide the inmates with practical experience. Many other states offer this type of vocational programming.

Despite the promising aspects of such programs, they have also been seriously criticized: Inmates often have trouble finding skill-related, high-paying jobs on their release; equipment in prisons is often secondhand, obsolete, and hard to come by; some programs are thinly disguised excuses for prison upkeep and maintenance; and unions and other groups resent the intrusion of prison labor into their markets.

work release
A prison treatment program that allows inmates to be released during the day to work in the community and returned to prison at night.

furlough
A correctional policy that allows inmates to leave the institution for vocational or educational training, for employment, or to maintain family ties.

WORK RELEASE To supplement programs stressing rehabilitation via in-house job training or education, more than forty-four states have attempted to implement **work release** or **furlough** programs. These allow deserving inmates to leave the institution and hold regular jobs in the community.

Inmates enrolled in work release may live at the institutions at night while working in the community during the day. However, security problems (e.g., contraband may be brought in) and the usual remoteness of prisons often make this arrangement difficult. More typical is the extended work release, where prisoners are allowed to remain in the community for significant periods of time. To help inmates adjust, some states operate community-based prerelease centers where inmates live while working. Some inmates may work at their previous jobs, while others seek new employment.

Like other programs, work release has its good and bad points. Inmates are sometimes reluctantly received in the community and find that certain areas of employment are closed to them. Citizens are often concerned about prisoners "stealing" jobs or working for lower than normal wages; consequently, such practices are prohibited by federal Public Law 89-176, which controls the federal work-release program.

To visit the home page of Better People, a Portland, Oregon, non-profit, volunteer employment and counseling program dedicated to finding employment for ex-inmates, go to betterpeople.org/

On the other hand, inmates gain many benefits from work release, including the ability to maintain work-related skills, to maintain community ties, and to make an easier transition from prison to the outside world. For those who have learned a skill in the institution, work release offers an excellent opportunity to test out a new occupation. For others, the job may be a training situation in which new skills are acquired. A number of states have reported that few work-release inmates abscond while in the community.

HELPING FEMALE OFFENDERS Critics have charged that educational and vocational programs are especially deficient in female institutions, which typically have offered only remedial-level education or occasional junior college classes. Female inmates were not being provided with the tools needed to succeed on the outside because the limited vocational training stressed what was considered traditional "women's work": cosmetology, secretarial work, and food services.

Today, forty-seven states have instituted some sort of vocational training programs for women; the other three states provide supplemental services for their few female inmates. Although the traditional vocation of sewing is the most common industrial program, correctional authorities are beginning to teach data processing, and female inmates are involved in such other industries as farming, printing, telemarketing, and furniture repair. Clearly, greater efforts are needed to improve the quality of work experiences for female inmates.

PRIVATE PRISON ENTERPRISE Opposition from organized labor ended the profitability of commercial prison industries, but a number of interesting efforts have been made to vary the type and productivity of prison labor.[45] The federal government helped put private industry into prisons when it approved the Free Venture Program in 1976. Seven states, including Connecticut, South Carolina, and Minnesota, were given grants to implement private industries within prison walls. This successful program led to the Percy Amendment (1979), federal legislation that allowed prison-made goods to be sold across state lines if the projects complied with strict rules, such as making sure unions were consulted and preventing manufacturers from undercutting the existing wage structure.[46] The new law authorized a number of Prison Industry Enhancement pilot projects. These were certified as meeting the Percy Amendment operating rules and were therefore free to ship goods out of state; by 1987 fifteen projects had been certified.

Today, private prison industries have used a number of models. One approach, the *state-use model,* makes the correctional system a supplier of goods and services that serves state-run institutions. For example, the California Prison Industry Authority (PIA) is an inmate work program that provides work assignments for approximately seven thousand inmates and operates seventy service, manufacturing, and agricultural industries in twenty-three prisons. These industries produce a variety of goods and services including flags, printing services, signs, binders, eye wear, gloves, office furniture, clothing, and cell equipment. PIA products and services are available to government entities, including federal, state, and local government agencies. Court-ordered restitutions/fines are deducted from the wages earned by PIA inmates and are transferred to the Crime Victims' Restitution Fund. PIA inmates receive wages between $.30 and $.95 per hour, before deductions.[47] In another approach, the *free-enterprise model,* private companies set up manufacturing units on prison grounds or purchase goods made by inmates in shops owned and operated by the corrections department. In the *corporate model,* a semi-independent business is created on prison grounds whose profits go to the state government and inmate laborers.[48] Despite widespread publicity, the partnership between private enterprise and the prison community has been limited to a few experimental programs. However, it is likely to grow in the future.

POSTRELEASE PROGRAMS A final element of job-related programming involves helping inmates obtain jobs before they are released and keep them once they are on the outside. A number of correctional departments have set up employment services designed to ease the transition between institution and community. Employment program staff assess inmates' backgrounds to determine their abilities, interests, goals, and capabilities. They also help them create job plans essential to receiving early release (parole) and successfully reintegrating into the community. Some programs maintain community correctional placements in sheltered environments that help inmates bridge the gap between institutions and the outside world. Services include job placement, skill development, family counseling, and legal and medical assistance.

Inmate Self-Help

Recognizing that the probability of failure on the outside is acute, inmates have attempted to organize self-help groups to provide the psychological tools needed to prevent recidivism.[49] Membership in these programs is designed to improve inmates' self-esteem and help them cope with common problems, such as alcoholism, narcotics abuse, or depression.

Some groups are chapters of common national organizations, such as Alcoholics Anonymous. Other groups are organized along racial and ethnic lines. For example, there are chapters of the Chicanos Organizados Pintos Aztlan, the Afro-American Coalition, and the Native American Brotherhood in prisons stretching from California to Massachusetts. These groups try to establish a sense of brotherhood so that members will work together for individual betterment. They hold literacy, language, and religion classes and offer counseling, legal advice, and pre-

Inmate self-help programs help residents identify the causes of their problems and develop strategies to overcome them.

release support. Ethnic groups seek ties with outside minority organizations, such as the National Association for the Advancement of Colored People (NAACP), the Black Muslims, the Urban League, La Raza, and the American Indian Movement, as well as the religious and university communities.

A third type of self-help group helps inmates find the strength to make it on the outside. The best known is the Fortune Society, which claims more than seven thousand members. Staffed by ex-offenders, the Fortune Society provides counseling, education, and vocational training to parolees. It even helps supervise offenders in the community in alternative to incarceration programs. They run a substance abuse treatment unit that provides individual and group counseling to clients sent by the New York City Department of Probation, provide HIV-prevention information, and work as an advocate group to improve prison conditions.[50]

Can Rehabilitation Work? Despite the variety and number of treatment programs in operation, questions remain about their effectiveness. In their oft-cited research, Robert Martinson and his associates (1975) found that a majority of treatment programs were failures.[51] Martinson found in a national study that, with few exceptions, rehabilitative efforts seemed to have no appreciable effect on recidivism; his research produced a "nothing works" view of correctional treatment.

Martinson's work was followed by efforts showing that some high-risk offenders were more likely to commit crimes after they had been placed in treatment programs than before the onset of rehabilitation efforts.[52] A slew of reviews have claimed that correctional treatment efforts aimed at youthful offenders provide little evidence that rehabilitation can occur within correctional settings. Evidence is scant that treatment efforts — even those that include vocational, educational, and mental health services — can consistently lower recidivism rates.[53]

The so-called failure of correctional treatment has helped promote a conservative view of corrections in which prisons are considered places of incapacitation and punishment, not treatment centers. Current policies stress eliminating the nonserious offender from the correctional system while increasing the probability that serious, violent offenders will be incarcerated and serve longer sentences. This view supports the utility of mandatory and determinate sentences for serious offenders and the simultaneous use of intermediate sanctions, such as house arrest, restitution, and diversion, to limit the nonserious offender's involvement in the system.

Although the concept of correctional rehabilitation is facing serious challenges, many experts still believe strongly in the rehabilitative ideal. Some believe that rehabilitation has just not been given a realistic chance because of inadequate budgets and programs.[54] Programs that teach interpersonal skills, utilize individual counseling, and make use of behavioral modification techniques have produced positive results both in the community and within correctional institutions.[55] Even where programs exist, there has been low-level participation of inmates (both men and women) in work, vocational, mental health, substance abuse, and parent counseling programs.[56] Other researchers have shown through careful analysis that, although not all programs are successful for all inmates, many treatment programs are effective and that participants, especially younger clients, have a better chance of success on the outside than those who forgo treatment. If administered properly, correctional treatment programs have success rates in the magnitude of 20 to 35 percent.[57] The characteristics associated with the most successful programs include the following:

- Services are intensive, lasting only a few months.
- Programs are cognitive, aimed at helping inmates learn new skills to better cope with personality problems such as impulsivity.
- Program goals are reinforced in a firm, fair manner, making use of rewards rather than punishments.
- Therapists related to clients in a sensitive and positive way. Therapists are trained and supervised in an appropriate manner.
- Clients are insulated from disruptive interpersonal networks and placed in environments where prosocial activities predominate.

Although institutional treatment is still the norm, a new movement within the prison system focuses less on treatment and more on security and punishment. This no-frills approach is discussed in the Policy, Programs, and Issues in Criminal Justice feature.

GUARDING THE INSTITUTION

Control of a prison is a complex task. On one hand, a tough, high-security environment may meet the goals of punishment and control but fail to reinforce positive behavior changes. On the other hand, too liberal an administrative stance can lower staff morale and place inmates in charge of the institution.

For many years, prison guards were viewed as ruthless people who enjoyed their positions of power over inmates, fought rehabilitation efforts, were racist, and had a "lock psychosis" developed from years of counting, numbering, and checking on inmates. This view has changed in recent years. Correctional officers are now viewed as public servants who are seeking the security and financial rewards of a civil service position.[58] Most are in favor of rehabilitation efforts and do not hold any particular animosity toward the inmates. The correctional officer has been characterized as a "people worker" who must be prepared to deal with the problems of inmates on a personal level and also as a member of a complex bureaucracy who must be able to cope with its demands.

Corrections officers play a number of roles within the institution. They supervise cell houses, dining areas, shops, and other facilities as well as perch up

Policy, Programs, and Issues in Criminal Justice

THE NO-FRILLS MOVEMENT

There is little question that some treatment does work and that the quest for offender rehabilitation should not be abandoned. Yet some correctional administrators and politicians believe that prisons should be places of punishment only and that all inmate privileges and treatment programs should be curtailed. Inmates in some states have suffered reduced visiting hours, removal of televisions and exercise gear, and substitution of cold sandwiches for hot meals. One county in Maryland plans to reintroduce chain gangs; instead of inmates being shackled to prevent their flight, they will be forced to wear stun belts. After detonation the belts give fleeing inmates an eight-second fifty thousand-volt jolt of electricity, which renders them helpless for up to ten minutes. Developed by Stun Tech Inc., more than one thousand belts have been sold to law enforcement and correctional agencies. Amnesty International has asked Congress to ban the belts in part because they can used for torture. Amnesty charges that the belts are "cruel, inhuman, and degrading."

Advocates of the no-frills, or penal harm, movement claim to be responding to the public's desire to get tough on crime. They are tired of hearing that some prison inmates get free education, watch cable TV, or get special educational programs. Some of the efforts to restrict inmates' rights include the following:

- The Alabama Department of Corrections (DOC) introduced no-frills chain gangs in each of the state's three prisons in 1994. Inmates in the gangs do not have telephones or visitation privileges, and recreation is limited to basketball on the weekends. Chain gang members include primarily parole violators and repeat offenders, especially offenders who are former gang members. After six months of good behavior, chain gang members return to the general population and are given standard inmate privileges.
- Throughout the 1990s, the Arizona DOC, supplementing the legislature's ban on weightlifting equipment, reduced the amount of property and clothing inmates may keep in their cells, the number of items for sale in the store, the number and types of movies and television programs they may watch, and the frequency of telephone calls.
- Effective January 1, 1996, the Kansas DOC introduced a formal incentive program in which incoming inmates have to earn a range of privileges, including television, handicrafts, use of outside funds, canteen expenditures, personal property, and visitation. Under a three-level system, new inmates who must spend their first 120 days (Incentive Level I) without disciplinary reports and participate in educational programs or work assignments earn increased privileges (Incentive Level II). After another 120 days of similar behavior, additional privileges are made available (Incentive Level III). Inmates are reduced one level for misbehavior. Furloughs were the only privilege the DOC banned permanently for all inmates.
- Complementing the action of his governor, the commissioner of corrections in Wisconsin reduced the amount of personal property inmates may own, established limits on the amount of personal clothing and electronic equipment they may keep, and introduced monitoring of telephone calls.
- A number of sheriffs have eliminated privileges in their jails: Seven sheriffs in Florida have eliminated television and weightlifting; seven jails in Los Angeles County have also eliminated weightlifting equipment; the Niagara County, New York sheriff eliminated free coffee; and the sheriff of Maricopa County (Phoenix) eliminated "girlie" magazines, hot lunches, most hot breakfasts, and coffee, and he reduced recreation time, television programming, visitation, and the number of items in the commissary.
- In 1995 the Federal Bureau of Prisons ordered — and federal legislation now requires — wardens to stop purchasing new or repairing old televisions in individual cells.

Many politicians embrace the no-frills prison idea to appeal to their vengeful, conservative constituents, but wardens and prison administrators are more wary of a policy that restricts inmate activities, increases boredom, and threatens their control over inmates. One approach is to limit privileges at first but return them as rewards for good behavior. Whether the no-frills approach is a political fad or a long-term correctional policy trend remains to be seen.

Critical Thinking

Do you believe that inmates should be "harmed" by their prison experience in order to shock them into conformity? Explain. The penal harm movement is the antithesis of the rehabilitation ideal. By "harming" inmates and taking away privileges, are correctional administrators giving up on the prison as a place of reform? Explain.

InfoTrac College Edition Research

Although the "no-frills" movement has its advocates, attempts to change behavior through treatment and rehabilitation efforts have not been abandoned. To read more about these efforts, look up Vicki Verdeyen, "Changing the criminal mind." *Corrections Today,* (61) Feb 1999, p. 52.

SOURCES: Peter Finn, "No-Frills Prisons and Jails: A Movement in Flux," *Federal Probation* 60 (1996): 35–49; W. Wesley Johnson, Katherine Bennett, and Timothy Flanagan, "Getting Tough on Prisoners: Results from the National Corrections Executive Survey, 1995," *Crime and Delinquency* 43 (1997): 24–41; Peter Kilborn, "Revival of Chain Gangs Takes a Twist," *New York Times,* 11 March 1997, A18.

on the walls, armed with rifles to oversee the yard and prevent escapes. Corrections officers also sit on disciplinary boards and escort inmates to hospitals and court appearances.

To visit the Correctional Officers Developmental Center, go to http://codc.nmu.edu/main/

The greatest problem faced by correctional officers is the duality of their role: maintainers of order and security and advocates of treatment and rehabilitation. Added to this basic dilemma is the changing inmate role. In earlier times, corrections officers could count on inmate leaders to help them maintain order, but now they are faced with a racially charged atmosphere in which violence is a way of life. Today, correctional work is filled with danger, tension, boredom, and little evidence that efforts to help inmates lead to success. And, unlike police officers, correctional officers apparently do not form a close-knit subculture with unique values and a sense of intergroup loyalty. Correctional officers experience alienation and isolation from inmates, the administration, and each other. Interestingly, this sense of alienation seems greatest in younger officers; evidence exists that later in their careers officers enjoy a revival of interest in their work and take great pride in providing human services to inmates.[59] It is not surprising that correctional officers perceive significant levels of stress related to such job factors as lack of safety, inadequate career opportunities, and work overload.[60]

Many state prison authorities have developed training programs to prepare guards for the difficulties of prison work. Guard unions have also commonly been formed to negotiate wages and working conditions with corrections departments.

Female Correctional Officers

The issue of female correctional officers in male institutions comes up repeatedly. Today, an estimated five thousand women are assigned to all-male institutions.[61] The employment of women as guards in close contact with male inmates has spurred many questions of privacy and safety and a number of legal cases. In one important case, *Dothard v. Rawlinson* (1977), the U.S. Supreme Court upheld Alabama's refusal to hire female correctional officers on the grounds that it would put them in significant danger from the male inmates.[62] Despite such setbacks, women now work side by side with male guards in almost every state, performing the same duties. Research indicates that discipline has not suffered because of the inclusion of women in the guard force. Sexual assaults have been rare, and more negative attitudes have been expressed by the female guards' male peers than by inmates. Most commentators believe that the presence of female guards can have an important beneficial effect on the self-image of inmates and improve the guard–inmate working relationship.

Interestingly, little research has been conducted on male correctional officers in female prisons, although almost every institution housing female offenders employs male officers. What research there is indicates that male officers are generally well received, and although there is evidence of sexual exploitation and privacy violations, female inmates generally believe that the presence of male correctional officers helps create a more natural environment and reduce tension. Both male and female inmates are concerned about opposite-sex correctional workers intruding on their privacy, such as being given assignments in which they may observe inmates dressing or bathing or in which they may come into physical contact, such as during searches or pat-downs.

PRISON VIOLENCE

Conflict, violence, and brutality are sad but ever-present facts of institutional life. Violence can involve individual conflict: inmate versus inmate, inmate versus staff, staff versus inmate. One common threat is sexual assault. Research has shown that prison rapes usually involve a victim who is viewed as weak and submissive and a group of aggressive rapists who can dominate the victim through their collective strength. Sexual harassment leads to fights, social isolation, fear, anxiety, and crisis. Nonsexual assaults may stem from an aggressor's desire to shake down the victim for money and personal favors, may be motivated by racial conflict, or may simply be used to establish power within the institution.

Violence can also involve large groups of inmates, such as the famous Attica riot in 1971, which claimed thirty-nine lives, or the New Mexico State Penitentiary riot of February 1980, in which the death toll was thirty-three. More than three hundred prison riots have occurred since the first one in 1774, 90 percent of them since 1952.[63]

A number of factors can spark such damaging incidents. They include poor staff–inmate communications, destructive environmental conditions, faulty classification, and promised but undelivered reforms. The 1980 New Mexico State Penitentiary riot drew national attention to the problem of prison riots. The prison was designed for 800 but actually held 1,135 prisoners; conditions of overcrowding, squalor, poor food, and lack of medical treatment abounded. The state government had been called on to improve guard training, physical plant quality, and relief from overcrowding but was reluctant to spend the necessary money.

Although revulsion over the violent riots in New Mexico and the earlier riot in New York's Attica prison led to calls for prison reform, prison violence has continued unabated. About 75–100 inmates are killed by their peers each year in U.S. prisons, 6 or 7 staff members are murdered, and some 120 suicides are recorded.

Individual Violence A number of explanations are offered for individual violence by prisoners.[64] One position holds that inmates are often violence-prone individuals who have always used force to get their own way. In the crowded, dehumanizing world of the prison, it is not surprising that some inmates resort to force to exert their dominance over others.

A second view is that prisons convert people to violence by their inhuman conditions, including overcrowding, depersonalization, and the threat of sexual assault. Even in the most humane prisons, life is a constant put-down, and prison conditions are a threat to the inmates' sense of self-worth; violence is an expected consequence of these conditions.

Violence may also result because prisons lack effective mechanisms to enable inmate grievances against either prison officials or other inmates to be handled fairly and equitably. Prisoners who complain about other inmates are viewed as "rats" or "snitches" and are marked for death by their enemies. Similarly, complaints or lawsuits filed against the prison administration may result in the inmate being placed in solitary confinement — "the hole." The frustration caused by living in a prison with a climate that promotes violence — that is, one that lacks physical security and adequate mechanisms for resolving complaints and where the "code of silence" protects violators — is believed to promote individual violence by inmates who might otherwise be controlled.

Collective Violence There are two distinct theories of the cause of collective violence. The first, called the *inmate-balance theory,* suggests that riots and other forms of collective action occur when prison officials make an abrupt effort to take control of the prison and limit freedoms. Crackdowns occur when officials perceive that inmate leaders have too much power and take measures to control their illicit privileges such as gambling or stealing food.[65]

According to the *administrative-control theory,* collective violence may also be caused by prison mismanagement, lack of strong security, and inadequate control by prison officials. Poor management may inhibit conflict management and set the stage for violence. Repressive administrations give inmates the feeling that nothing will ever change, that they have nothing to lose, and that violence is the only means for change.

Overcrowding caused by the rapid increases in the prison population has also been linked to prison violence. As the prison population continues to climb, unmatched by expanded capacity, prison violence may increase.

Controlling Violence

Can prison violence be controlled, despite the fact that inmate populations will not be declining significantly or become less aggressive and hostile? In his book *Governing Prisons,* John DiIulio suggests that prison management reform can help alter the violent institutional climate.[66] After studying prisons in three states, DiIulio found that management could be classified into three types. The *consensual model,* practiced in California, is based on the notion that prison government rests on the consent of the governed, the inmates. This model fails to provide a coherent basis for dealing with violence because it allows inmates a say in the management process. In Michigan, the *responsibility model* is used. Here, inmates' rehabilitation is keyed to their participation in prison operations, and staff members are required to be facilitators in the process. The responsibility model has also failed because it offers weak controls on inmate behavior and produces disillusionment and alienation among the staff. DiIulio found that the *control model* used in the Texas prison system has more promise for reducing violence. The Texas system stresses clearly defined rules of behavior, inmate conformity with rules and regulations, and strong, independent top-down leadership.

DiIulio believes that the bureaucratic organization that works in large private corporations and government agencies can save prisons. In this approach, prison administrators act in a caring yet efficient manner without prejudice and bias, and experienced correctional leaders create and enforce clear and fair rules. Although this system may seem logical, what is known about the operations of criminal justice agencies indicates that "informal" rules and behaviors often dominate at the expense of the formal system and that leaders may be more self-serving than selfless. The Texas prison system that DiIulio so admires was marked by overcrowding and brutality until subject to court-ordered reform. Even then, prison officials were reluctant to change and attempted to undermine reform efforts. The control model may seem appealing to some experts, but whether it can work in the "real world" remains to be seen.

PRISONERS' RIGHTS

Before the early 1960s it was accepted that on conviction an individual forfeited all rights not expressly granted by statutory law or correctional policy; inmates were *civilly dead.* The U.S. Supreme Court held that convicted offenders should expect to be penalized for their misdeeds and that part of their punishment was the loss of freedoms free citizens take for granted.

hands-off doctrine
The legal practice of allowing prison administrators a free hand to run the institution even if correctional practices violate inmates' constitutional rights; ended with the onset of prisoners' rights movement in the 1960s.

One reason that inmates lacked rights was that state and federal courts were reluctant to intervene in the administration of prisons unless the circumstances of a case clearly indicated a serious breach of the Eighth Amendment protection against cruel and unusual punishment. This judicial policy is referred to as the **hands-off doctrine.** The courts used three basic justifications for their neglect of prison conditions:

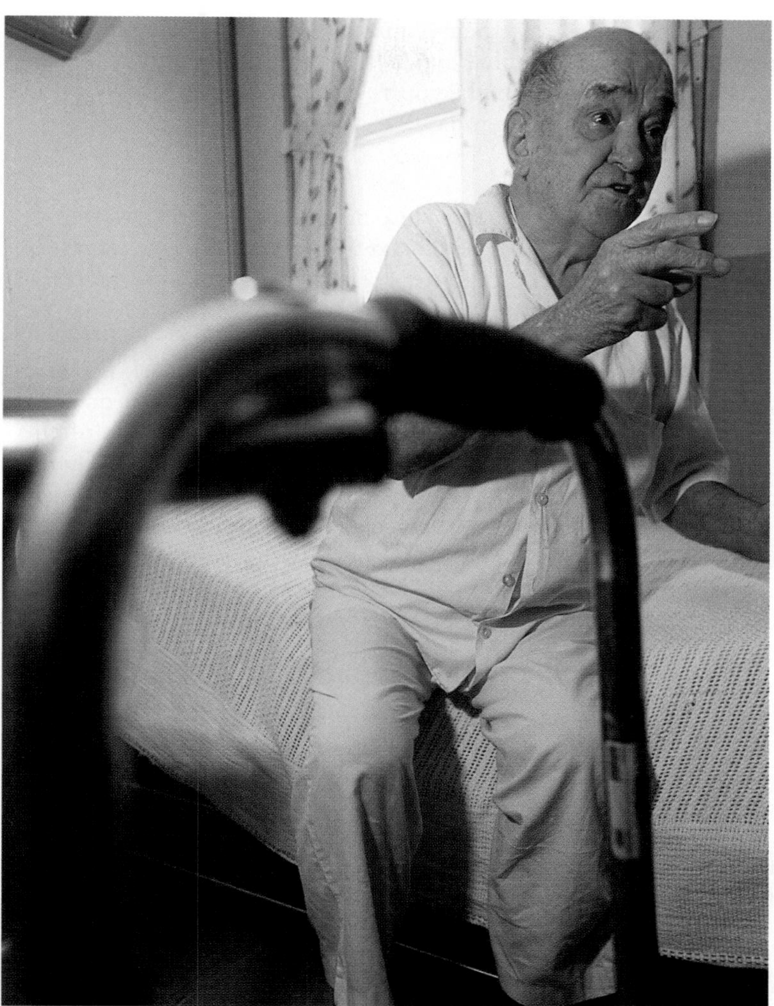

Because sentences are getting longer and health care is improving, the prison system must be prepared to deal with an increasing number of elderly inmates. John Bedarka is an 86-year-old man now in the thirtieth year of his life sentence for killing his wife's lover. He is in frail health and severely depressed. Should a prisoner such as Bedarka, who is little threat to society, be kept in confinement?

1. Correctional administration was a technical matter best left to experts rather than to courts ill equipped to make appropriate evaluations.
2. Society as a whole was apathetic to what went on in prisons, and most individuals preferred not to associate with or know about the offender.
3. Prisoners' complaints involved privileges rather than rights. Prisoners were considered to have fewer constitutional rights than other members of society.[67]

As the 1960s drew to a close, the hands-off doctrine was eroded. Federal district courts began seriously considering prisoners' claims concerning conditions in the various state and federal institutions and used their power to intervene on behalf of the inmates. In some ways, this concern reflected the spirit of the times, which saw the onset of the civil rights movement, and subsequently was paralleled in such areas as student rights, public welfare, mental institutions, juvenile court systems, and military justice.

Beginning the late 1960s, such activist groups as the NAACP Legal Defense Fund and the American Civil Liberties Union's National Prison Project began to search for appropriate legal vehicles to bring prisoners' complaints before state and federal courts. The most widely used device was the federal Civil Rights Act, 42 U.S.C. 1983:

> Every person who, under color of any statute, ordinance, regulation, custom, or usage of any State or Territory subjects, or causes to be subjected, any citizen of the United States or other person within the jurisdiction thereof to the deprivation of any rights, privileges, or immunities secured by the Constitution and laws shall be liable to the party injured in an action at law, suit in equity, or other proper proceeding for redress.

The legal argument went that, as U.S. citizens, prison inmates could sue state officials if their civil rights were violated — for example, if they were the victims of racial or religious discrimination.

The U.S. Supreme Court first recognized the right of prisoners to sue for civil rights violations in cases involving religious freedom brought by the Black Muslims. This well-organized group had been frustrated by prison administrators who feared its growing power and desired to place limits on its recruitment activities. In the 1964 case of *Cooper v. Pate,* however, the Supreme Court ruled that inmates who were being denied the right to practice their religion were entitled to legal redress under 42 U.S.C. 1983.[68] Although *Cooper* applied to the narrow issue of religious freedom, it opened the door to providing other rights for inmates.

The subsequent prisoners' rights crusade, stretching from 1960 to 1980, paralleled the civil rights and women's movements. Battle lines were drawn between prison officials hoping to maintain their power and resenting interference by the courts and inmate groups and their sympathizers, who used state and federal courts as a forum for demanding better living conditions and personal rights. Each decision handed down by the courts was viewed as a victory for one side or the other; this battle continues today.

substantive rights
Through a slow process of legal review, the courts have granted inmates a number of civil rights, including the rights to receive mail and medical benefits and to practice their religion.

jailhouse lawyer
An inmate trained in law or otherwise educated who helps other inmates prepare legal briefs and appeals.

Substantive Rights

Through a slow process of legal review, the courts have granted inmates a number of **substantive rights** that have significantly influenced the entire correctional system. The most important of these rights are discussed in the following sections.

ACCESS TO COURTS, LEGAL SERVICES, AND MATERIALS Without the ability to seek judicial review of conditions causing discomfort or violating constitutional rights, the inmate must depend solely on the slow and often insensitive administrative mechanism of relief within the prison system. Therefore, the right of easy access to the courts gives inmates hope that their rights will be protected during incarceration. Courts have held that inmates are entitled to have legal materials available and be provided with assistance in drawing up and filing complaints. Inmates who help others, so-called **jailhouse lawyers,** cannot be interfered with or harassed by prison administrators.

FREEDOM OF THE PRESS AND OF EXPRESSION Correctional administrators traditionally placed severe limitations on prisoners' speech and expression. For example, they have read and censored inmate mail and restricted their reading material. With the lifting of the hands-off doctrine, courts have consistently ruled that only when a compelling state interest exists can prisoners' First Amendment rights be modified; correctional authorities must justify the limiting of free speech by showing that granting it would threaten institutional security.

FREEDOM OF RELIGION Freedom of religion is a fundamental right guaranteed by the First Amendment. In general, the courts have ruled that inmates have the right to assemble and pray in the religion of their choice but that religious symbols and practices that interfere with institutional security can be restricted. Administrators can draw the line if religious needs become cumbersome or impossible to carry out for reason of cost or security. Granting special privileges can also be denied on the grounds that they will cause other groups to make similar demands.

MEDICAL RIGHTS In early prisons, inmates' right to medical treatment was restricted through the "exceptional circumstances doctrine." Using this policy, the courts would hear only those cases in which the circumstances totally disregarded human dignity, while denying hearings to less serious cases. The cases that were allowed access to the courts usually represented a situation of total denial of medical care.

To gain their medical rights, prisoners have resorted to class action suits (e.g., suits brought on behalf of all individuals affected by similar circumstances, in this case, poor medical attention). In the most significant case, *Newman v. Alabama* (1972), the entire Alabama prison system's medical facilities were declared inadequate.[69] The Supreme Court cited the following factors as contributing to inadequate care: insufficient physician and nurse resources, reliance on untrained inmates for paramedical work, intentional failure in treating the sick and injured, and failure to conform to proper medical standards. The *Newman* case forced corrections departments to upgrade prison medical facilities.

Inmates have the right to assemble and pray in the religion of their choice. Here, the Rev. Eugene Rivers preaches to inmates at Marion County Jail in Indiana.

It was not until 1976, in *Estelle v. Gamble,* that the Supreme Court clearly mandated an inmate's right to have medical care.[70] Gamble had hurt his back in a Texas prison and filed suit because he contested the type of treatment he had received and questioned the lack of interest that prison guards had shown in his case. The Supreme Court said, "Deliberate indifference to serious medical needs of prisoners constitutes the 'unnecessary and wanton infliction of pain,' proscribed by the Eighth Amendment."[71] Gamble was allowed to collect monetary damages for his injuries. The *Gamble* decision means that lower courts can decide, on a case-by-case basis, whether "deliberate indifference" to an inmate's medical needs occurred and to what damages the inmate is entitled.

cruel and unusual punishment Physical punishment or punishment that is far in excess of that given to people under similar circumstances and is therefore banned by the Eighth Amendment. The death penalty has so far not been considered cruel and unusual if it is administered in a fair and nondiscriminatory fashion.

CRUEL AND UNUSUAL PUNISHMENT The concept of **cruel and unusual punishment** is founded in the Eighth Amendment of the U.S. Constitution. The term itself has not been specifically defined by the Supreme Court, but the Court has held that treatment constitutes cruel and unusual punishment when it

- Degrades the dignity of human beings.[72]
- Is more severe (disproportional) than the offense for which it has been given.[73]
- Shocks the general conscience and is fundamentally unfair.[74]
- Is deliberately indifferent to a person's safety and well-being.[75]
- Punishes people because of their status, such as race, religion, and mental state.[76]
- Is in flagrant disregard of due process of law, such as punishment that is capriciously applied.[77]

State and federal courts have placed strict limits on disciplinary methods that may be considered inhumane. Corporal punishment all but ended after the practice was condemned in *Jackson v. Bishop* (1968).[78] Although the solitary confinement of disruptive inmates continues, its prolonged use under barbaric conditions has been held to be in violation of the Eighth Amendment. Courts have found that inmates placed in solitary have the right to adequate personal hygiene, exercise, mattresses, ventilation, and rules specifying how they earn their release.

OVERALL PRISON CONDITIONS Prisoners have long had the right to the minimal conditions necessary for human survival, such as the necessary food, clothing, shelter, and medical care to sustain human life. A number of attempts have been made to articulate reasonable standards of prison care and to make sure they are carried out. Courts have held that, although people are sent to prison for punishment, it does not mean that prison should be a punishing experience.[79] In the 1994 case of *Farmer v. Brennan,* the Court ruled that prison officials are legally liable if, knowing that an inmate faces a serious risk of harm, they disregard that risk by failing to take measures to avoid or reduce it. Furthermore, prison officials should be able to infer the risk from the evidence at hand; they need not be warned or told.[80]

Although inmates retain the right to reasonable care, if there is a legitimate purpose for the use of governmental restrictions, they may be considered constitutional. For example, it might be possible to restrict reading material, allow strip searches, and prohibit inmates from receiving packages from the outside if the restrictions are legitimate security measures. If overcrowded conditions require it, inmates may be double-bunked in cells designed for a single inmate.[81]

LEAVING PRISON

At the expiration of their prison term, most inmates return to society and try to resume their life there. For some inmates, their reintegration into society comes by way of **parole,** the planned community release and supervision of incarcerated offenders before the expiration of their full prison sentences. In states where determinate sentencing statutes have eliminated discretionary parole, offenders are released after having served their determinate sentence, less time off for good behavior and other credits designed to reduce the term of incarceration. Their release may involve supervision in the community, and rule violations can result in return to prison for the balance of their unexpired sentence.

parole
The early release of a prisoner from imprisonment subject to conditions set by a parole board. Depending on the jurisdiction, inmates must serve a certain portion of their sentences before becoming eligible for parole. The conditions of parole may require the individual to report regularly to a parole officer, to refrain from criminal conduct, to maintain and support his or her family, to avoid contact with other convicted criminals, to abstain from using alcohol and drugs, to remain within the jurisdiction, and so on. Violations of the conditions of parole may result in revocation of parole, in which case the individual will be returned to prison. The concept behind parole is to allow the release of the offender to community supervision, where rehabilitation and readjustment will be facilitated.

In a few instances, inmates are released after their sentence has been commuted by a board of pardons or directly by a governor or even the president of the United States. About 15 percent of prison inmates are released after serving their entire maximum sentence without any time excused or forgiven. And despite the efforts of correctional authorities, about seven thousand inmates escape every year from state and federal prisons (the number of escapes is actually declining, due in part to better officer training and more sophisticated security measures).[82]

Parole

Today, the parole population is over 700,000, increasing more than 150,000 in the past decade.[83] Regardless of the method of their release, former inmates face the formidable task of having to readjust to society. This means regaining legal rights they may have lost on their conviction, reestablishing community and family ties, and finding employment. After being in prison, these goals are often difficult to achieve.

Most correctional administrations allow inmates to become eligible for parole after completing their minimum sentence less good time. Parole is consid-

A former inmate works at Web Industries in Westborough, Massachusetts. Web has been committed to hiring former inmates and has employed over fifty during the past 25 years. Web's employees are given stock ownership in the company as part of their compensation, granting former inmates a chance to maintain a "stake in conformity."

ered a way of completing a prison sentence in the community under the supervision of the correctional authorities. It is not the same as a pardon; paroled offenders can be legally recalled to serve the remainder of their sentence in an institution if the parole authorities deem the offenders' adjustment inadequate because they fail to obey the conditions of their release or commit another crime while on parole.

The decision to parole is determined by statutory requirement. In about 40 percent of all prison-release decisions, parole is granted by a parole board, a duly constituted body of men and women who review inmate cases and determine whether offenders have reached a rehabilitative level sufficient to deal with the outside world. The board also dictates what specific parole rules parolees must obey.

Once released into the community, the offender is supervised by a trained staff of parole officers who help the offender search for employment and monitor the parolee's behavior and activities to ensure that the conditions of parole are met.

Parolees are subject to strict rules, standardized and personalized, that guide their behavior and set limits on their activities. If these rules are violated, they can be returned to the institution to serve the remainder of their sentence; this is known as a **technical parole violation.** Parole can also be revoked by the offender committing a second offense while in the community. The offender may even be tried and sentenced for this subsequent crime.

technical parole violation
Revocation of parole because conditions set by correctional authorities have been violated.

Parole is generally viewed as a privilege granted to deserving inmates on the basis of their good behavior while in prison. Parole has two conflicting sides, however. On one hand, the paroled offender is allowed to serve part of the sentence in the community, an obvious benefit for the deserving offender. On the other hand, since parole is a "privilege and not a right," the parolee is viewed as a dangerous criminal who must be carefully watched and supervised. The conflict between the treatment and enforcement aspects of parole has not been reconciled by the criminal justice system, and the parole process still contains elements of both.

In recent years the nation's parole system has come under increasing criticism from those who believe that it is inherently unfair to inmates and fails to protect the public. It is unfair to the inmate because the decision to release is based on the discretion of parole board members who are forced to make predictions about the inmate's future behavior, an uncertain activity at best. It fails to protect the public because predatory criminals released before the expiration of their sentence are free to once again attack innocent victims. The movement toward determinate and mandatory sentences has limited the availability of parole and restricted the discretion of parole boards.

MANDATORY PAROLE RELEASE In addition to inmates released at the discretion of correctional authorities, a significant number are released via mandatory parole — inmates whose discharge was a requirement of determinate sentencing statutes or good-time reductions but whose release was supervised by parole authorities. Mandatory release begins when the unserved portion of the maximum prison term equals the inmate's earned good time (less time served in jail awaiting trial). In some states, determinate sentences can be reduced by more than half with a combination of statutory and earned good time. If the conditions of their release are violated, mandatory releasees can have their good time revoked and be returned to the institution to serve the remainder of their unexpired term.

The remaining inmates are released for a variety of reasons, including expiration of their term, commutation of their sentence, and court orders to relieve overcrowded prisons.

The movement to create mandatory and determinate sentencing statutes has significantly affected parole. The number of people leaving prison via discretionary parole has declined substantially in the past few years. At one time more than 70 percent of releasees were granted discretionary parole, but that number has declined to 40 percent; in contrast, mandatory releases from prison as a result of a sentencing statute or good-time provision now compose 53 percent of those entering parole in 1998; in 1990 they were 41 percent.[84] Almost all mandatory parole releasees are in jurisdictions that rely heavily on determinate sentences, such as Washington and Minnesota. As the new truth-in-sentencing laws take effect, the number of parolees should decline. People will be spending more of their time in prison, and offenders who have served more time in prison may consequently have less time to spend on parole.

THE PAROLE BOARD In those states that have maintained discretionary parole, the authority to release inmates is usually vested in the parole board. State parole boards have four primary functions:

1. To select and place prisoners on parole
2. To aid, supervise, and provide continuing control of parolees in the community
3. To determine when the parole function is completed and to discharge from parole
4. To determine whether parole should be revoked, if violations of conditions occur

Most parole authorities are independent agencies with their own staff and administration, and a few parole boards are part of the state department of corrections. Arguments for keeping the board within a corrections department usually include the improved communication and availability of more intimate knowledge about offenders.

Most boards are relatively small, usually numbering fewer than ten members. Their size, coupled with their large caseloads and the varied activities they are expected to perform, can prevent board members from becoming as well acquainted with the individual inmates as might be desired.

PAROLE HEARINGS The actual (discretionary) parole decision is made at a parole-granting hearing. At this hearing the full board or a selected subcommittee reviews information, may meet with the offender, and then decides whether the parole applicant has a reasonable probability of succeeding outside of prison. Each parole board has it own way of reviewing cases. In some, the full board meets with the applicant; in others, only a few members do that. In a number of jurisdictions, a single board member can conduct a personal investigation and submit the findings to the full board for a decision.

At the hearing, parole board members consider such information as police reports of the crime, the presentence investigation, psychological testing and scores developed by prison mental health professionals, and institutional reports of disciplinary actions, treatment, and adjustment.[85] Letters may be solicited from the inmate's friends and family members. In some jurisdictions, victims may appear and make statements of the losses they suffered.

By speaking directly to the applicant, the board can also promote and emphasize the specific types of behavior and behavior changes it expects to see if the inmate is to eventually qualify for or effectively serve parole.

The inmate's specific rights at a parole-granting hearing also vary from jurisdiction to jurisdiction. In about half of the parole-granting jurisdictions, inmates are permitted counsel or are allowed to present witnesses on their behalf; other jurisdictions do not permit these privileges. Because the federal courts have declared that the parole applicant is not entitled to any form of legal representation, the inmate may have to pay for legal services where this privilege is allowed. In almost all discretionary parole-granting jurisdictions, the reasons for the parole decision must be given in writing, and in about half of the jurisdictions, a verbatim record of the hearing is made.

In the case of *Pennsylvania Board of Probation and Parole v. Scott,* the U.S. Supreme Court held that the exclusionary rule for illegally obtained evidence did not apply to parole revocation proceedings. The Court reasoned that the social costs of excluding incriminating evidence outweigh any benefits of protecting parolees from invasion of their privacy. *Scott* then allows evidence to be used in a parole revocation hearing that would be excluded from a criminal prosecution.[86]

PAROLE RULES Before release into the community, a parolee is given a standard set of rules and conditions that must be obeyed and conformed to. As with probation, the offender who violates these rules may have parole revoked and be sent back to the institution to serve the remainder of the sentence.

Parole rules may curtail or prohibit certain types of behavior while encouraging or demanding others. Some rules tend to be so moralistic or technical that they severely inhibit the parolee's ability to adjust to society. By making life unnecessarily unpleasant without contributing to rehabilitation, such parole rules reflect the punitive side of community supervision. Rules such as these can prohibit marriage, ban the use of motor vehicles, or forbid the borrowing of money. Parolees must often check in and ask permission when leaving their residences, and they may find that the rules bar them from associating with friends with criminal records, which, in some cases, severely limits their social life.

The way in which parole rules are stated, the kinds of things they forbid or encourage, and their flexibility vary between jurisdictions. Some states expressly forbid a certain type of behavior, and others will require permission to engage in it.

Each item in the parole conditions must be obeyed lest the offender's parole be revoked for a technical violation. In addition, the parole board can impose specific conditions for a particular offender, such as demanding that the parolee receive psychiatric treatment.

PAROLE SUPERVISION Once released into the community, the offender normally comes under the control of a parole agent who enforces parole rules, helps the parolee gain employment, and meets regularly with the parolee for reasons of treatment and rehabilitation.

Supervision in probation and parole is similar in some respects. In both, supervision attempts to help clients attain meaningful relationships in the community and uses similar enforcement, counseling, and treatment skills to gain that end. However, some major differences exist.

Parole officers deal with more difficult cases. The parolee has been institutionalized for an extended period of time; to be successful on parole, the former inmate must adjust to the community, which at first can seem a strange and often hostile environment. The parolee's family life has been disrupted, and the person may find it difficult to resume employment. The paroled offender may have already been classified by probation officers (in a presentence report) as dangerous or as a poor risk for community adjustment. Furthermore, a prison sentence probably does little to improve the offender's chances for rehabilitation.

To overcome these roadblocks to success, the parole officer may have to play a much greater role in directing and supervising clients' lives than the probation officer. Consequently, a significant number of parolees are sent back to prison for technical rule violations.

INTENSIVE SUPERVISION PAROLE To aid supervision, some jurisdictions are implementing systems that classify offenders on the basis of their supervision needs. Typically, a point or guideline system (sometimes called a **salient factor score**) based on prior record and prison adjustment divides parolees into three groups: (1) those who require intensive surveillance, (2) those who require social service rather than surveillance, and (3) those who require limited supervision.

salient factor score
A method developed by federal parole authorities to classify inmates for release.

intensive supervision parole (ISP)
A limited-caseload program for those parolees who need intensive surveillance. Parolees are required to meet more often with parole officers than routine parolees and may also have frequent drug testing, serve a term in a community correctional system, and be electronically monitored.

In some jurisdictions, parolees in need of closer surveillance are placed on **intensive supervision parole (ISP).** These programs use limited caseload sizes, treatment facilities, the matching of parolee and supervisor by personality, and shock parole (which involves immediate short-term incarceration for parole violators to impress them with the seriousness of a violation). ISP clients are required to attend more office and home visits than routine parolees. ISP may also require frequent drug testing, a term in a community correctional center, and electronic monitoring in the home. More than seventeen thousand parolees are under intensive supervision, fourteen hundred of whom are monitored electronically by computer.

Although ISP seems like an ideal way of limiting already overcrowded prison populations, little evidence shows that ISP programs are effective; in fact, they may produce a higher violation rate than traditional parole supervision. Limiting caseload size allows parole officers to supervise their clients more closely and spot infractions more easily.[87]

The Effectiveness of Parole

Parole recidivism rates are very high — approaching 50 percent or more. Of 423,700 parolees discharged from supervision in 1998, 45 percent had successfully met the conditions of their supervision, and 42 percent had been returned to incarceration either because of a rule violation or new offense. Absconders accounted for 9 percent of those discharged from parole in 1998, up from 1 percent of those discharged in 1990.

The cost of recidivism is acute. One federal survey of 156,000 parole violators serving time in the nation's prison system estimated that these offenders committed at least 6,800 murders, 5,500 rapes, 8,800 assaults, and 22,500 robberies while under supervision in the community an average of thirteen months. Of the parole violators in prison, 80 percent were in confinement following conviction for a new crime; the remaining 20 percent had been imprisoned for a technical violation. Over 40 percent of these technical violators, although not convicted of a new crime, had been arrested for a new crime while on parole supervision in the community. (An arrest for violating parole conditions was not counted as an arrest for a new crime.) Technical parole violators in prison who said they were not arrested for a new crime while on parole made up about 3 percent of the prison population. [88]

What did the technical parole violators do to warrant termination of their community release? The most common reasons for a technical violation were arrest for a new offense and failure to report to parole officers (presumably by absconding or leaving the jurisdiction).

WHY DO PEOPLE FAIL ON PAROLE? Why do so many released inmates end up back behind prison walls? The specter of recidivism is especially frustrating to the U.S. public: It is so difficult to apprehend and successfully prosecute chronic offenders that it seems foolish to grant them early release so that they can prey on more victims. There seems to be a strong association between prior and future offending: The parolees most likely to fail on release are the ones who have failed in the past; chronic offenders are the ones most likely to reoffend. Most research indicates that a long history of criminal behavior, maintenance of an antisocial personality, a record of substance abuse, and childhood experiences with family dysfunction are all correlated with postrelease recidivism.[89] Other factors that seem to predict parole violations include family criminality, criminal companions, and interpersonal conflict.[90] Many parolees were prior drug users and once released may revert to substance abuse. For example, a recent study of 237 parolees in Maryland found that 58 percent of those deemed successful on parole and 82 percent of the parole failures tested positively for drugs within a few months of their release.[91] This research suggests that parole successes may have earned their freedom by disguising their substance abuse from their parole supervisors.

Parolees fail because the psychological and economic reasons that led them to crime probably have not been eliminated by a stay in prison. Despite rehabilitation efforts, the typical ex-convict is still the same undereducated, unemployed, substance-abusing lower-class male he was when arrested. For example, one study of four hundred Texas inmates found that almost 75 percent suffered from lifetime substance abuse or dependence disorder.[92] It seems naïve to think that incarceration alone can help someone overcome these lifelong disabilities.

Being separated from friends and family, not sharing in conventional society, associating with dangerous people, and adapting to a volatile lifestyle probably has done little to improve offenders' personality or behavior. And when they return to society, it may be to the same destructive neighborhood and social groups that prompted their original law-violating behavior. Some ex-inmates may have to prove that the prison experience has not changed them: Taking drugs or being sexually aggressive may show friends that they have not lost their "heart."[93]

Ex-inmates may find their home life torn and disrupted when they are finally released. Wives of inmates report that they had to face the shame and stigmatization of having an incarcerated spouse while withstanding a barrage of calls from jealous husbands on the "inside" who tried to monitor their behavior and control their lives. Family visits to the inmate had become traumatic and strained interpersonal relationships because they often involved strip searches and other invasions of privacy.[94] Sensitive to these problems, some states have instituted support groups designed to help inmates' families adjust to their loneliness and despair.[95]

LOSING RIGHTS Ex-inmates may also find that going straight is an economic impossibility. Many employers are reluctant to hire people who have served time. Even if a criminal record does not automatically prohibit all chance of employment, why would an employer hire an "ex-con" when other applicants are available? If they lie about their prison experience and are later found out, ex-offenders will be dismissed for misrepresentation. Research shows that former inmates who gain and keep meaningful employment are more likely to succeed on parole than those who are unemployed or underemployed.[96] One reason that ex-inmates find it so difficult to make it on the outside is the legal restrictions they are forced to endure. These may include bars on certain kinds of employment, limits on obtaining licenses, and restrictions on their freedom of movement. One survey found that a significant number of states still restrict the activities of former felons.[97] Some of the more important findings are listed in Exhibit 14.2.

In general, states have placed greater restrictions on former felons, part of the get-tough movement. However, courts have considered individual requests by convicted felons to have their rights restored. It is common for courts to look at such issues as how recently the criminal offense took place and its relationship to the particular right before deciding whether to restore it.

A number of experts and national commissions have condemned the loss of rights of convicted offenders as a significant cause of recidivism. Consequently, courts have generally moved to eliminate the most restrictive elements of post-conviction restrictions.[98]

exhibit 14.2

Rights Lost upon Release from Prison

- Fourteen states permanently deny felons the right to vote; eighteen states suspend the right until after the correctional sentence has been completed.
- Nineteen states terminate parental rights.
- Twenty-nine states consider a felony conviction to be legal grounds for a divorce.
- Six states deny felons the opportunity for public employment.
- Thirty-one states disallow convicted felons the right to serve on juries.
- Twenty-five states prevent convicted felons from holding public office.
- Federal law prevents ex-convicts from owning guns. In addition, all states except Vermont employ additional legal measures to prevent felons from possessing firearms.
- Forty-six states require that felons register with law enforcement agencies. This requirement is up sharply in recent years; in 1986 only eight states required felons to register.
- Civil death, or the denial of all civil rights, is still practiced in four states.

Source: Kathleen Olivares, Velmer Burton, and Francis Cullen, "The Collateral Consequences of a Felony Conviction: A National Study of State Legal Codes 10 Years Later," *Federal Probation 60* (1996): 10–17

SUMMARY

On entering a prison, offenders must make tremendous adjustments to survive. Usual behavior patterns or lifestyles are radically changed. Opportunities for personal satisfaction are reduced. Passing through a number of adjustment stages or cycles, inmates learn to cope with the new environment.

Inmates also learn to obey the inmate social code, which dictates proper behavior and attitudes. If inmates break the code, they may be unfavorably labeled.

Inmates are eligible for a large number of treatment devices designed to help them readjust to the community once they are released. These include educational programs on the basic, high school, and even college levels, as well as vocational training programs. In addition, a number of treatment programs have offered inmates individualized and group psychological counseling. Work furloughs, conjugal visits, and coed prisons have also been employed.

Despite such measures, prisons remain forbidding structures that house desperate men and women. Violence is common in prisons. Women often turn their hatred inward and hurt themselves, and male inmates engage in collective and individual violence against others. The Attica and New Mexico riots are examples of the most serious collective prison violence.

In years past, society paid little attention to the incarcerated offender. The majority of inmates confined in jails and prisons were basically deprived of the rights guaranteed them under the Constitution. Today, however, the judicial system is actively involved in the administration of correctional institutions. Inmates can now take their grievances to courts and seek due process and equal protection under the law. The courts have recognized that persons confined in correctional institutions have rights — which include access to the courts and legal counsel, the exercise of religion, the rights to correspondence and visitation, and the right to adequate medical treatment.

Most inmates return to society before the completion of their prison sentence. The majority earn early release through time off for good behavior or other sentence-reducing mechanisms. In addition, about 40 percent of all inmates are paroled before the completion of their maximum term. Most state jurisdictions maintain an independent parole board whose members decide whether to grant parole. Their decision making is discretionary and is based on many factors, such as the perception of the needs of society, the correctional system, and the client. Once paroled, the client is subject to control by parole officers who ensure that the conditions set by the board (the parole rules) are maintained. Parole can be revoked if the offender violates the rules of parole or commits a new crime.

Ex-inmates have a tough time adjusting on the outside, and the recidivism rate is disturbingly high. One reason is that many states restrict their rights and take away privileges granted to other citizens.

KEY TERMS

total institution
inmate subculture
inmate social code
prisonization
make-believe family
less eligibility
special-needs inmate
work release
furlough
hands-off doctrine
substantive rights
jailhouse lawyer
cruel and unusual punishment
parole
technical parole violation
salient factor score
intensive supervision parole (ISP)

 INFOTRAC COLLEGE EDITION EXERCISES

What is the future of correctional institutions? Will the number of people in prison spiral even higher? Some experts believe that inmate populations will become almost exclusively made up of unskilled, poor, powerless, and angry populations coming from broken families and risky environments. To learn more about this chilling vision of the future, read the following article in using *InfoTrac College Edition:*
Ben M. Crouch, "Looking Back to See the Future of Corrections," *Prison Journal* 76 (1996): 468.

It is not surprising, considering the problems of the inmate population, that gangs flourish in prison. To see how administrators in one prison manage the gang problem, read
William Toller and Basil Tsagaris, "Managing Institutional Gangs: A Practical Approach Combining Security and Human Services," *Corrections Today* 58 (1996): 110.

Although the future may be troubling, efforts are now ongoing to make the prison experience one that prepares the inmate for successful rehabilitation in the outside world. In the twentieth century, various laws and government programs have been implemented to reintegrate inmates into society through meaningful and productive work. To read about them, check out
Gwen Smith Ingley, "Inmate Labor: Yesterday, Today and Tomorrow," *Corrections Today* 58 (1996): 28.

QUESTIONS

1. What are the benefits and drawbacks of coed prisons? Of conjugal visits?
2. Should women be allowed to work as guards in male prisons? What about male guards in female prisons? Why or why not?
3. Should prison inmates be allowed a free college education while noncriminals are forced to pay tuition? Why or why not? Do you believe in less eligibility for prisoners? Explain.
4. Define parole, including its purposes and objectives. How does it differ from probation?
5. What is the role of the parole board?
6. Should a former prisoner have all the civil rights afforded the average citizen? Explain. Should people be further penalized after they have paid their debt to society? Why or why not?

NOTES

1. Associated Press, "Glitch Wins Freedom for N.Y. Inmate," *New York Times,* 22 November 1999, 1.

2. Gresham Sykes, *The Society of Captives* (Princeton, N.J.: Princeton University Press, 1958).

3. David Eichenthal and James Jacobs, "Enforcing the Criminal Law in State Prisons," *Justice Quarterly* 8 (1991): 283–303.

4. John Wooldredge, "Inmate Lifestyles and Opportunities for Victimization," *Journal of Research in Crime and Delinquency* 35 (1998): 480–502.

5. David Anderson, *Crimes of Justice: Improving the Police, Courts, and Prison* (New York: Times Books, 1988).

6. Robert Johnson, *Hard Time: Understanding and Reforming the Prison* (Monterey, Calif.: Brooks/Cole, 1987), 115.

7. John Wooldredge, "Inmate Lifestyles and Opportunities for Victimization," *Journal of Research in Crime and Delinquency* 35 (1999): 480–502.

8. Lawrence Hinman, "Stunning Morality: The Moral Dimensions of Stun Belts," *Criminal Justice Ethics* 17 (1998): 3–6.

9. Kevin Wright, *The Great American Crime Myth* (Westport, Conn.: Greenwood Press, 1985), 167.

10. Sandra Gleason, "Hustling: The Inside Economy of a Prison," *Federal Probation* 42 (1978): 32–39.

11. Hans Toch, *Living in Prison* (New York: Free Press, 1977), 179–205.

12. Angela Maitland and Richard Sluder, "Victimization and Youthful Prison Inmates: An Empirical Analysis," *Prison Journal* 77 (1998): 55–74.

13. J. Stephan, *Prison Rule Violators* (Washington, D.C.: Bureau of Justice Statistics, 1989).

14. Leonore Simon, "Prison Behavior and Victim–Offender Relationships among Violent Offenders" (Paper presented at the annual meeting of the American Society of Criminology, San Francisco, November 1991).

15. John Irwin, "Adaptation to Being Corrected: Corrections from the Convict's Perspective," in *Handbook of Criminology,* ed. Daniel Glazer (Chicago: Rand McNally, 1974), 971–93.

16. Donald Clemmer, *The Prison Community* (New York: Holt, Rinehart & Winston, 1958).

17. Sykes, *The Society of Captives,* 1–36.

18. Gresham Sykes and Sheldon Messinger, "The Inmate Social Code," in *The Sociology of Punishment and Corrections,* ed. Norman Johnston et al. (New York: Wiley, 1970), 401–08.

19. John Irwin and Donald Cressey, "Thieves, Convicts, and the Inmate Culture," *Social Problems* 10 (1962): 142–55.

20. Brent Paterline and David Petersen, "Structural and Social Psychological Determinants of Prisonization," *Journal of Criminal Justice* 27 (1999): 427–41.

21. Ibid., 439.

22. James B. Jacobs, ed., *New Perspectives on Prisons and Imprisonment* (Ithaca, N.Y.: Cornell University Press, 1983); idem, "Street Gangs Behind Bars," *Social Problems* 21 (1974): 395–409; idem, "Race Relations and the Prison Subculture," in *Crime and Justice,* vol. 1, ed. Norval Morris and Michael Tonry (Chicago: University of Chicago Press, 1979), 1–28.

23. Stanley Penn, "Prison Gangs Formed by Racial Groups Pose Big Problem in West," *Wall Street Journal,* 11 May 1983, A1.

24. Nicole Hahn Rafter, *Partial Justice* (New Brunswick, N.J.: Transaction Books, 1990), 181–82.

25. Allen J. Beck and Christopher J. Mumola, *Prisoners in 1998* (Washington, D.C.: Bureau of Justice Statistics, 1999).

26. Meda Chesney-Lind, "Patriarchy, Prisons and Jails: A Critical Look at Trends in Women's Incarceration" (Paper presented at the International Feminist Conference on Women, Law and Social Control, Mont Gabriel, Quebec, July 1991).

27. Elaine DeCostanzo and Helen Scholes, "Women behind Bars, Their Numbers Increase," *Corrections Today* 50 (1988): 104–06.

28. This section synthesizes the findings of a number of surveys of female inmates, including DeCostanzo and Scholes, "Women behind Bars, Their Numbers Increase"; Ruth Glick and Virginia Neto, *National Study of Women's Correctional Programs* (Washington, D.C.: Government Printing Office, 1977); Ann Goetting and Roy Michael Howsen, "Women in Prison: A Profile," *Prison Journal* 63 (1983): 27–46; Meda Chesney-Lind and Noelie Rodrigues, "Women under Lock and Key: A View from Inside," *Prison Journal* 63 (1983): 47–65; Contact, Inc., "Women Offenders," *Corrections Compendium* 7 (1982): 6–11.

29. Merry Morash, Robin Harr, and Lila Rucker, "A Comparison of Programming for Women and Men in U.S. Prisons in the 1980s," *Crime and Delinquency* 40 (1994): 197–221.

30. Pamela Schram, "Stereotypes about Vocational Programming for Female Inmates," *Prison Journal* 78 (1998): 244–71.

31. Morash et al., "A Comparison of Programming for Women and Men in U.S. Prisons in the 1980s."

32. Candace Kruttschnitt and Sharon Krmpotich, "Aggressive Behavior among Female Inmates: An Exploratory Study," *Justice Quarterly* 7 (1990): 370–89.

33. "Sex Abuse of Female Inmates Is Common, Rights Group Says," *Criminal Justice Newsletter,* 16 December 1996, 2.

34. General Accounting Office, *Women in Prison: Sexual Misconduct by Correctional Staff* (Washington, D.C.: Government Printing Office, 1999).

35. Edna Erez, "The Myth of the New Female Offender: Some Evidence from Attitudes toward Law and Justice," *Journal of Criminal Justice* 16 (1988): 499–509.

36. Robert Ross and Hugh McKay, *Self-Mutilation* (Lexington, Mass.: Lexington Books, 1979).

37. Alice Propper, *Prison Homosexuality* (Lexington, Mass.: Lexington Books, 1981).

38. Dianna Newbern, Donald Dansereau, and Urvashi Pitre, "Positive Effects on Life Skills Motivation and Self-Efficacy: Node-Link Maps in a Modified Therapeutic Community," *American Journal of Drug and Alcohol Abuse* 25 (1999): 407–10.

39. Ira Sommers and Deborah Baskin, "The Prescription of Psychiatric Medication in Prison: Psychiatric versus Labeling Perspectives," *Justice Quarterly* 7 (1990): 739–55.

40. Judy Anderson and R. Daniel McGehee, "South Carolina Strives to Treat Elderly and Disabled Offenders," *Corrections Today* 53 (1991): 124–27.

41. American Bar Association, *The State of Criminal Justice* (Washington, D.C.: ABA, 1996).

42. "Few Inmates Get Drug Treatment, but Most Need It, GAO Finds," *Criminal Justice Newsletter,* 1 November 1991, 2.

43. Bureau of Justice Statistics, "Rates of HIV Infection and AIDS-Related Deaths Drop among the Nation's Prisoners," news release, 3 November 1999, 2.

44. Howard Skolnik and John Slansky, "A First Step in Helping Inmates Get Good Jobs after Release," *Corrections Today* 53 (1991): 92.

45. This section leans heavily on Barbara Auerbach, George Sexton, Franklin Farrow, and Robert Lawson, *Work in American Prisons, The Private Sector Gets Involved* (Washington, D.C.: National Institute of Justice, 1988).

46. Public Law 96-157, sec. 827, codified as 18 U.S.C., sec. 1761(c).

47. Courtesy of the Prison Industry Authority, 560 East Natoma Street, Folsom, CA 95630-2200.

48. Diane Dwyer and Roger McNally, "Public Policy, Prison Industries, and Business: An Equitable Balance for the 1990s," *Federal Probation* 57 (1993): 30–35.

49. This section leans heavily on Mark Hamm, "Current Perspectives on the Prisoner Self-Help Movement," *Federal Probation* 52 (1988): 49–56.

50. For more information, contact The Fortune Society, 39 West 19th Street, New York, NY 10011, (212) 206-7070. The e-mail address is info@fortunesociety.org.

51. Douglas Lipton, Robert Martinson, and Judith Wilks, *The Effectiveness of Correctional Treatment: A Survey of Treatment Evaluation Studies* (New York: Praeger, 1975).

52. Charles Murray and Louis Cox, *Beyond Probation: Juvenile Corrections and the Chronic Delinquent* (Beverly Hills, Calif.: Sage, 1979).

53. Steven Lab and John Whitehead, "An Analysis of Juvenile Correctional Treatment," *Crime and Delinquency* 34 (1988): 60–83.

54. Ted Palmer, "The Effectiveness of Intervention: Recent Trends and Current Issues," *Crime and Delinquency* 37 (1991): 330–46.

55. Mark Lipsey and David Wilson, "Effective Intervention for Serious Juvenile Offenders: A Synthesis of Research," in *Serious and Violent Juvenile Offenders: Risk Factors and Successful Interventions,* ed. Rolf Loeber and David Farrington (Thousand Oaks, Calif.: Sage, 1998).

56. Morash et al., "A Comparison of Programming for Women and Men in U.S. Prisons in the 1980s."

57. Paul Gendreau and Claire Goffin, "Principles of Effective Correctional Programming," *Forum on Correctional Research* 2 (1996): 38–41.

58. Lucien X. Lombardo, *Guards Imprisoned* (New York: Elsevier, 1981); James Jacobs and Norma Crotty, "The Guard's World," in *New Perspectives on Prisons and Imprisonment,* ed. James Jacobs (Ithaca, N.Y.: Cornell University Press, 1983), 133–41.

59. John Klofas and Hans Toch, "The Guard Subculture Myth," *Journal of Research in Crime and Delinquency* 19 (1982): 238–54.

60. Ruth Triplett and Janet Mullings, "Work-Related Stress and Coping among Correctional Officers: Implications from the Organizational Literature," *Journal of Criminal Justice* 24 (1996): 291–308.

61. Peter Horne, "Female Correction Officers," *Federal Probation* 49 (1985): 46–55.

62. *Dothard v. Rawlinson,* 433 U.S. 321 (1977).

63. David Duffee, *Corrections, Practice and Policy* (New York: Random House, 1989), 305.

64. Randy Martin and Sherwood Zimmerman, "A Typology of the Causes of Prison Riots and an Analytical Extension to the 1986 West Virginia Riot," *Justice Quarterly* 7 (1990): 711–37.

65. Bert Useem and Michael Resig, "Collective Action in Prisons: Protests, Disturbances, and Riots," *Criminology* 37 (1999): 735–60.

66. John DiIulio, *Governing Prisons: A Comparative Study of Correctional Management* (New York: Free Press, 1987).

67. National Advisory Commission on Criminal Justice Standards and Goals, *Corrections* (Washington, D.C.: Government Printing Office, 1973), 18.

68. *Cooper v. Pate,* 378 U.S. 546 (1964).

69. *Newman v. Alabama,* 92 S.Ct. 1079, 405 U.S. 319 (1972).

70. *Estelle v. Gamble,* 429 U.S. 97 (1976).

71. Ibid.

72. *Trop v. Dulles,* 356 U.S. 86, 78 S.Ct. 590 (1958); see also *Furman v. Georgia,* 408 U.S. 238, 92 S.Ct. 2726, 33 L.Ed.2d 346 (1972).

73. *Weems v. United States,* 217 U.S. 349, 30 S.Ct. 544, 54 L.Ed. 793 (1910).

74. *Lee v. Tahash,* 352 F.2d 970 (8th Cir., 1965).

75. *Estelle v. Gamble,* 429 U.S. 97 (1976).

76. *Robinson v. California,* 370 U.S. 660 (1962).

77. *Gregg v. Georgia,* 428 U.S. 153 (1976).

78. *Jackson v. Bishop,* 404 F.2d 571 (8th Cir. 1968).

79. *Bell v. Wolfish,* 99 S.Ct. 1873–1974 (1979); see "*Bell v. Wolfish:* The Rights of Pretrial Detainees," *New England Journal of Prison Law* 6 (1979): 134.

80. *Farmer v. Brennan,* 144 S.Ct. 1970 (1994).

81. *Rhodes v. Chapman,* 452 U.S. 337 (1981); for further analysis of *Rhodes,* see Randall Pooler, "Prison Overcrowding and the Eighth Amendment: The *Rhodes* Not Taken," *New England Journal on Criminal and Civil Confinement* 8 (1983): 1–28.

82. *Prison Escape Survey* (Lincoln, Neb.: Corrections Compendium, 1991).

83. Thomas Bonczar and Lauren Glaze, *Probation and Parole in the United States, 1998* (Washington, D.C.: Bureau of Justice Statistics, 1999).

84. Ibid.

85. Ronald Burns, Patrick Kinkade, Matthew Leone, and Scott Phillips, "Perspectives on Parole: The Board Members' Viewpoint," *Federal Probation* 63 (1999): 16–22.

86. Duncan N. Stevens, "Off the *Mapp:* Parole Revocation Hearings and the Fourth Amendment," *Journal of Criminal Law and Criminology* 89 (1999): 1047–60.

87. Thomas Hanlon, David N. Nurco, Richard W. Bateman, and Kevin E. O'Grady, "The Response of Drug Abuser Parolees to a Combination of Treatment and Intensive Supervision," *Prison Journal* 78 (1998): 31–44; Susan Turner and Joan Petersilia, "Focusing on High-Risk Parolees: An Experiment to Reduce Commitments to the Texas Department of Corrections," *Journal of Research in Crime and Delinquency* 29 (1992): 34–61.

88. Robyn L. Cohen, *Probation and Parole Violators in State Prison, 1991: Survey of State Prison Inmates, 1991* (Washington, D.C.: Bureau of Justice Statistics, 1995).

89. James Bonta, Moira Law, and Karl Hanson, "The Prediction of Criminal and Violent Recidivism among Mentally Disordered Offenders: A Meta-Analysis," *Psychological Bulletin* 123 (1998): 123–42.

90. Paul Gendreau, Tracy Little, and Claire Goggin, "A Meta-Analysis of the Predictors of Adult Offender Recidivism: What Works?" *Criminology* 34 (1996): 575–607.

91. Hanlon et al., "The Response of Drug Abuser Parolees to a Combination of Treatment and Intensive Supervision."

92. Roger Peters, Paul Greenbaum, John Edens, Chris Carter, and Madeline Ortiz, "Prevalence of DSM-IV Substance Abuse and Dependence Disorders among Prison Inmates," *American Journal of Drug and Alcohol Abuse* 24 (1998): 573–80.

93. J. E. Ryan, "Who Gets Revoked? A Comparison of Intensive Supervision Successes and Failures in Vermont," *Crime and Delinquency* 43 (1997): 104–18.

94. Laura Fishman, *Women at the Wall: A Study of Prisoners' Wives Doing Time on the Outside* (New York: State University of New York Press, 1990).

95. Leslee Goodman Hornick, "Volunteer Program Helps Make Inmates' Families Feel Welcome," *Corrections Today* 53 (1991): 184–86.

96. Hanlon et al., "The Response of Drug Abuser Parolees to a Combination of Treatment and Intensive Supervision."

97. Kathleen Olivares, Velmer Burton, and Francis Cullen, "The Collateral Consequences of a Felony Conviction: A National Study of State Legal Codes 10 Years Later," *Federal Probation* 60 (1996): 10–17.

98. See, for example, *Bush v. Reid,* 516 P.2d 1215 (Alaska, 1973); *Thompson v. Bond,* 421 F.Supp. 878 (W.D. Mo., 1976); *Delorne v. Pierce Freightlines Co.,* 353 F.Supp. 258 (D. Or., 1973); *Beyer v. Werner,* 299 F.Supp. 967 (E.D. N.Y., 1969).

chapter 15

Juvenile Justice

At thirteen years old, Nathaniel Abraham was the youngest person to be charged as an adult with murder in the state of Michigan.[1] Abraham was eleven years old when he fired a shot on October 29, 1997, from a .22-caliber rifle, fatally wounding eighteen-year-old Ronnie Lee Greene, Jr., who was standing 288 feet away from Abraham. As his trial began, Abraham's defense attorney told jurors in his opening statement that the shooting was a "very tragic, tragic accident" and that Abraham had the developmental abilities of a boy six to eight years old at the time of the killing. He argued that Abraham, one of the youngest people ever to face murder charges as an adult in the United States, was not capable of forming the intent to kill, as is

Nathaniel Abraham sits in a Michigan courtroom waiting to hear his fate.

required for a first-degree murder conviction. However, the prosecutor retorted that Abraham later bragged to friends about the killing. Prosecutors noted that Abraham had twenty-two scrapes with police and that his mother had also tried to have him ruled incorrigible in juvenile court.

After his conviction for murder, prosecutors sought a blended sentence of incarceration in a juvenile facility until age 21, followed by imprisonment in an adult facility. However, the sentencing judge ordered him to be held in juvenile detention until age 21, when he will be released. "While there is no guarantee Nathaniel will be rehabilitated at 21, it is clear 10 years is enough to accomplish this goal," said Judge Eugene Moore at the sentencing hearing. Moore went on to say that if society is committed to preventing future criminal behavior, rehabilitation through the juvenile system is the answer. "You clearly need to learn to think before you act. You have probably done the worst thing that can be done . . . you are going to have to come to terms with this," Moore told the boy.[2] ■

juvenile justice system
The system of agencies and organizations that deals with youths who commit acts of juvenile delinquency (crimes under a given age) and acts of noncriminal behavior (truancy and incorrigibility).

parens patriae
Power of the state to act on behalf of the child and provide care and protection equivalent to that of a parent.

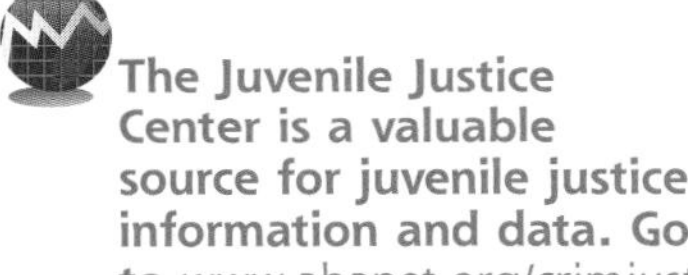
The Juvenile Justice Center is a valuable source for juvenile justice information and data. Go to www.abanet.org/crimjust/juvjus/home.html

balanced and restorative justice model
A new model of juvenile justice focusing on victim restoration, improving offender abilities, and protecting the public. Offenders, victims, and the community are all active participants.

The *Abraham* case, while certainly extreme, is representative of the very difficult choices that agents of the **juvenile justice system** are continually asked to make: How should troubled children be treated? What can be done to save dangerous young offenders? Should youthful law violators be given unique treatment because of their age, or should they be treated in a similar fashion to an adult committing the same crime?

Independent yet interrelated with the adult criminal justice system, the juvenile justice system is primarily responsible for dealing with juvenile and youth crime, as well as with incorrigible and truant children and runaways. First conceived at the turn of the century, the juvenile justice system was viewed as a quasi-social welfare agency that was to act as a surrogate parent in the interests of the child; this is referred to as the **parens patriae** philosophy. Today, some authorities still hold to the original social welfare principles of the juvenile justice system and argue that it is primarily a treatment agency that acts as a wise parent, dispensing personalized, individual justice to needy children who seek guidance and understanding. They recognize that many children who are arrested and processed to court come from the lowest economic classes. These at-risk children have grown up in troubled families, attend inadequate schools, and live in deteriorated neighborhoods. They are deserving of care and concern, not punishment and control. By sentencing Nathaniel Abraham to a juvenile facility, Judge Moore showed that he had not abandoned the hope of rehabilitation for even this violent youth.

In contrast to this view, those with a crime control orientation suggest that the juvenile justice system's parens patriae philosophy is outdated. They point to nationally publicized incidents of juvenile violence, such as the shootings at Columbine High School in Colorado, as indicators that serious juvenile offenders should be punished and disciplined, rather than treated and rehabilitated. They note that juveniles between the ages of 10 and 17 years commit about 12 percent of all murders in the United States.[3] It is not surprising then that they applaud when court rulings enhance the state's ability to identify and apprehend youthful law violators. For example, in 1995 the U.S. Supreme Court held in *Vernonia School District v. Acton* that public school athletes in middle and high schools can be required to submit to random drug testing even though the student did not engage in suspicious behavior.[4] Rulings such as *Vernonia* encourage those who want the state to be given a free hand to deal with juveniles who are disruptive at school and in the community.

It remains to be seen whether the juvenile justice system will continue on its path toward identification and control or return to its former role of a treatment-dispensing agency. There are also those who call for a totally new approach to the juvenile justice system, using the **balanced and restorative justice model,** which calls for offender–victim reconciliation, personal accountability, and community-based program developments.[5]

This chapter reviews the history of juvenile justice and discusses the justice system's processing of youthful offenders.

THE HISTORY OF JUVENILE JUSTICE

The modern practice of legally separating adult and juvenile offenders can be traced to two developments in English custom and law: the development of poor laws and the chancery court. Both were designed to allow the state to take control of the lives of needy but not necessarily criminal children.[6] They set the precedent for later American developments.

poor laws
Seventeenth-century laws in England that bound out vagrants and abandoned children as indentured servants to masters.

As early as 1535 the English passed statutes known as **poor laws**, which in part mandated the appointment of overseers who placed destitute or neglected children with families who then trained them in agricultural, trade, or domestic services; this practice was referred to as *indenture*. The Elizabethan poor laws of 1601 created a system of church wardens and overseers who, with the consent of the justices of the peace, identified vagrant, delinquent, and neglected children and took measures to put them to work. Often this meant placing them in poorhouses or workhouses or, more commonly, apprenticing them until their adulthood. The indenture, or *involuntary apprentice,* system set the precedent, which continues today, of allowing the government to take control of youths who had committed no illegal acts but who were deemed unable to care for themselves.

In contrast, *chancery courts* were concerned primarily with protecting property rights and welfare of more affluent minor children who could not care for themselves — children whose position and property were of direct concern to the monarch. They dealt with issues of guardianship and the use and control of property. Chancery courts operated under the parens patriae philosophy, which held that children were under the protective control of the state and its rulers were justified in intervening in their lives.[7] In the famous English case *Wellesley v. Wellesley,* a duke's children were taken from him in the name of parens patriae because of his scandalous behavior.[8]

The concept of parens patriae came to represent the primacy of the state and its power to act in "the best interests of the child." The idea that the state was legally obligated to protect the immature, the incompetent, the neglected, and the delinquent subsequently became a major influence on the development of the U.S. juvenile justice system in the twentieth century.

Care of Children in Early America

The forced apprenticeship system and the poor laws were brought from England to colonial America. Poor laws were passed in Virginia in 1646 and in Connecticut and Massachusetts in 1678 and continued in force until the early nineteenth century. They mandated care for wayward and destitute children. However, those youths who committed serious criminal offenses continued to be tried in the same courts as adults.

To accommodate dependent youths, local jurisdictions developed almshouses, poorhouses, and workhouses. Crowded and unhealthy, these accepted the poor, the insane, the diseased, and vagrant and destitute children. Middle-class civic leaders, who referred to themselves as **child savers**, began to develop organizations and groups to help alleviate the burdens of the poor and immigrants by sponsoring shelter care for youths, educational and social activities, and the development of settlement houses. In retrospect, their main focus seems to have been on extending governmental control over a whole range of youthful activities that previously had been left to private or family control, including idleness, drinking, vagrancy, and delinquency.[9]

child savers
Late nineteenth-century reformers in America who developed programs for troubled youths and influenced legislation creating the juvenile justice system.

The Child-Saving Movement

The child savers were responsible for creating a number of programs for indigent youths, including the New York House of Refuge, which began operations in 1825.[10] Its aim was to protect youths by taking them off the streets and reforming them in a family-like environment. Children were placed in the house by court order, sometimes over parental objections, for vagrancy or delinquency. Their stay depended on their needs, age, and work skills. While there they were required to do piecework provided by local manufacturers or to work part of the day in the community. The reality was far different from the intent. The institution was run more like a

Boys on the steps of an abandoned tenement building in New York City, about 1889. The child savers were concerned that children such as these if left alone would enter a life of crime. Critics accused them of class and race discrimination, and thought they sought to maintain control over the political system.

prison, however, with work and study schedules, strict discipline, and absolute separation of the sexes. So many children ran away because of this harsh program that the House of Refuge was eventually forced to adopt a more lenient approach.

Despite criticisms the concept enjoyed widespread popularity. In 1826 the Boston City Council founded the House of Reformation for juvenile offenders. Similar reform schools were opened in Massachusetts and New York in 1847.[11] Refuge managers believed that they were preventing poverty and crime, by training destitute and delinquent children and by separating them from their parents and adult criminals.[12]

The child savers also influenced state and local governments to create independent correctional institutions to house minors. The first of these *reform schools* opened in Westboro, Massachusetts, in 1848 and in Rochester, New York, in 1849. Other states soon followed suit — Ohio in 1850 and Maine, Rhode Island, and Michigan in 1860. Children lived in congregate conditions and spent their days working at institutional jobs, learning a trade where possible, and receiving some basic education. They were racially and sexually segregated, discipline was harsh and often involved whipping and isolation, and the physical care was of poor quality.

In 1853 New York philanthropist Charles Loring Brace helped develop the Children's Aid Society as an alternative for dealing with neglected and delinquent youths. Loring proposed rescuing wayward youths from the harsh environment of the city and providing them with temporary shelter and care. He then sought to place them in private homes in rural communities where they could engage in farming and agricultural work outside the harsh influence of the city. Although some placements proved successful, others resulted in the exploitation of children in a strange environment with few avenues of escape.

juvenile court
A court that has original jurisdiction over persons defined by statute as juveniles and alleged to be delinquents or status offenders.

ESTABLISHMENT OF THE ILLINOIS JUVENILE COURT: 1899 As the nation expanded, it became evident that private charities and public organizations were not caring adequately for the growing number of troubled youths. The child savers lobbied for an independent, state-supported **juvenile court,** and their efforts prompted the development of the first comprehensive juvenile court in Illinois in 1899. The Illinois Juvenile Court Act set up an independent court to handle criminal law violations by children under sixteen years of age, as well as to care for neglected, dependent, and wayward youths. The act also created a probation department to monitor youths in the community and to direct juvenile court judges to place serious offenders in secure schools for boys and industrial schools for girls. The ostensible purpose of the act was to separate juveniles from adult offenders and provide a legal framework in which juveniles could get adequate care and custody. By 1925 most states had developed juvenile courts.

The enactment of the Juvenile Court Act of 1899 was a major event in the history of the juvenile justice movement in the United States.

Although the efforts of the child savers to set up independent juvenile courts were originally seen as liberal reforms, modern scholars commonly view them as attempts to control and punish. Justice historians have suggested that the reform movement actually expressed the vested interests of the "ruling class."[13] Thus, according to this revisionist approach, the reformers applied the concept of parens patriae for their own purposes, including the continuance of middle- and upper-class values, the control of the political system, and the furtherance of a child labor system consisting of lower-class workers with marginal skills.

The Development of Juvenile Justice

The juvenile court movement quickly spread across the United States. In its early form it provided youths with quasi-legal, quasi-therapeutic, personalized justice. The main concern was the "best interests of the child," not strict adherence to legal doctrine, constitutional rights, or due process of law. The court was paternalistic, rather than adversarial. For example, attorneys were not required. Hearsay evidence, inadmissible in criminal trials, was commonly employed in the adjudication of juvenile offenders. Children were encouraged to admit their "guilt" in open court in violation of their Fifth Amendment rights. Verdicts were based on a "preponderance of the evidence," instead of being "beyond a reasonable doubt." Juvenile courts then functioned as quasi-social service agencies.

REFORM SCHOOLS Youngsters found delinquent in juvenile court could spend years in a state training school. Though priding themselves as nonpunitive, these early reform schools were generally punitive and based on the concept of reform through hard work and discipline. In the second half of the nineteenth century, the emphasis shifted from massive industrial schools to the cottage system. Juvenile offenders were housed in a series of small cabins, each one holding twenty to forty children, run by "cottage parents," who attempted to create a homelike atmosphere. The first cottage system was established in Massachusetts, the second in Ohio. The system was generally applauded for being a great improvement over the industrial training schools. The general movement was away from punishment and toward rehabilitation through attending to the needs of the individual and by implementing complex programs of diagnosis and treatment.[14] By the 1950s the influence of such therapists as Karen Horney and Carl Rogers promoted the introduction of psychological treatment in juvenile corrections. Group counseling techniques became standard procedure in most juvenile institutions.

LEGAL CHANGE In the 1960s and 1970s the U.S. Supreme Court radically altered the juvenile justice system when it issued a series of decisions that established the right of juveniles to receive **due process** of law:[15] The Court established that juveniles had the same rights as adults in important areas of trial process, including the right to confront witnesses, notice of charges, and the right to counsel. Exhibit 15.1 illustrates some of the most important legal cases bringing procedural due process to the juvenile justice process.

due process (juvenile)
The constitutional principle guaranteed by the Fifth, Sixth, and Fourteenth Amendments, which embodies the legal rights for children in judicial proceedings.

Besides the legal revolution brought about by the Supreme Court, Congress passed the Juvenile Justice and Delinquency Prevention Act of 1974 (JJDP Act) and established the federal Office of Juvenile Justice and Delinquency Prevention (OJJDP).[16] This legislation was enacted to identify the needs of youths and to fund programs in the juvenile justice system. Its main goal was to separate wayward, nondangerous youths from institutions housing delinquents and to remove adolescents from institutions housing adult offenders. In 1996 in a move reflecting the growing national frustration with serious delinquent offenders, the act was amended to make it easier to hold delinquents in adult penal institutions.

exhibit 15.1

Critical Cases in Juvenile Justice

Kent v. United States (1966) established that procedures concerning waiver (whether the juvenile court would hear a case or waive it to an adult court for trial) must measure up to the essentials of due process of law. A hearing, the right to counsel, and access to social records were required. (383 U.S. 541)

In re Gault (1967) held that juveniles at trial faced with incarceration were entitled to many of the rights granted adult offenders. These included counsel, notice of the charges, cross-examination of witnesses, and protection against self-incrimination. *Gault* mandated a more formalized juvenile court system. (387 U.S.1)

In re Winship (1970) ruled that the standard of proof in a delinquency proceeding that could result in a child's commitment must be "proof beyond a reasonable doubt" and not a "preponderance of the evidence." According to the Court, civil labels and good intentions do not obviate the need for criminal due process safeguards in juvenile courts. (397 U.S. 358)

McKeiver v. Pennsylvania (1971) held that juveniles were not afforded the constitutional right to a jury in a delinquency proceeding. The Court felt that this aspect of the adversarial process was not appropriate for the juvenile justice system. (403 U.S. 528)

Breed v. Jones (1975) established that the double jeopardy clause of the Fifth Amendment of the U.S. Constitution extends to juvenile offenders through the Fourteenth Amendment due process clause. Juveniles, henceforth, could not be tried in a juvenile court and then transferred to an adult court for a similar action. (421 U.S. 519)

Since 1975, the Court has decided a number of other important cases dealing with juvenile offenders.

Oklahoma Publishing Co. v. District Court (1977) ruled that a state court could not prohibit the publication of information obtained in an open juvenile proceeding. When photographs were taken and published of an eleven-year-old boy suspected of homicide and the local court prohibited further disclosure, the publishing company claimed that the court order was a restraint in violation of the First Amendment. The Supreme Court agreed. (430 U.S. 308)

Smith v. Daily Publishing Co. (1979) involved the discovery and subsequent publication of the identity of a juvenile suspect in violation of a state statute prohibiting publication. The Supreme Court declared the statute unconstitutional because it believed the state's interest in protecting the child was not of such magnitude as to justify the use of a criminal statute. (443 U.S. 97)

Fare v. Michael C. (1979) held that a child's request to see his probation officer at the time of interrogation did not operate to invoke his Fifth Amendment right to remain silent. According to the Court, the probation officer cannot be expected to offer the type of advice that an accused would expect from an attorney. (442 U.S. 707)

Eddings v. Oklahoma (1982) ruled that a defendant's age should be a mitigating factor deciding whether to apply the death penalty. (455 U.S. 104)

Schall v. Martin (1984) upheld a statute allowing for the placement of children in preventive detention before their trial. The Court concluded that it was not unreasonable to detain juveniles for their own protection. (467 U.S. 253)

(continued)

exhibit 15.1 (continued)

New Jersey v. T.L.O. (1985) determined that the Fourth Amendment applies to school searches. The Court adopted a "reasonable suspicion" standard, as opposed to "probable cause," to evaluate the legality of searches and seizures in a school setting. (469 U.S. 325)

Thompson v. Oklahoma (1988) ruled that imposing capital punishment on a juvenile murderer who was fifteen years old at the time of the offense violated the Eighth Amendment's constitutional prohibition against cruel and unusual punishment. (487 U.S. 815)

Stanford v. Kentucky and *Wilkins v. Missouri* (1989) concluded that the imposition of the death penalty on a juvenile who committed a crime between the ages of sixteen and eighteen was not unconstitutional and that the Eight Amendment's cruel and unusual punishment clause did not prohibit capital punishment. (492 U.S.109)

Vernonia School District v. Acton (1995) held that the Fourth Amendment's guarantee against unreasonable searches is not violated by the suspicionless drug testing of all students choosing to participate in interscholastic athletics. The Supreme Court expanded the power of public educators to ensure safe learning environments in schools. (515 U.S. 646)

United States v. Lopez (1995) ruled that Congress exceeded its authority under the Commerce Clause when it passed the Gun-Free School Zone Act, which made it a federal crime to possess a firearm within 1,000 feet of a school. (514 U.S. 549)

Figure 15.1
Status offenses

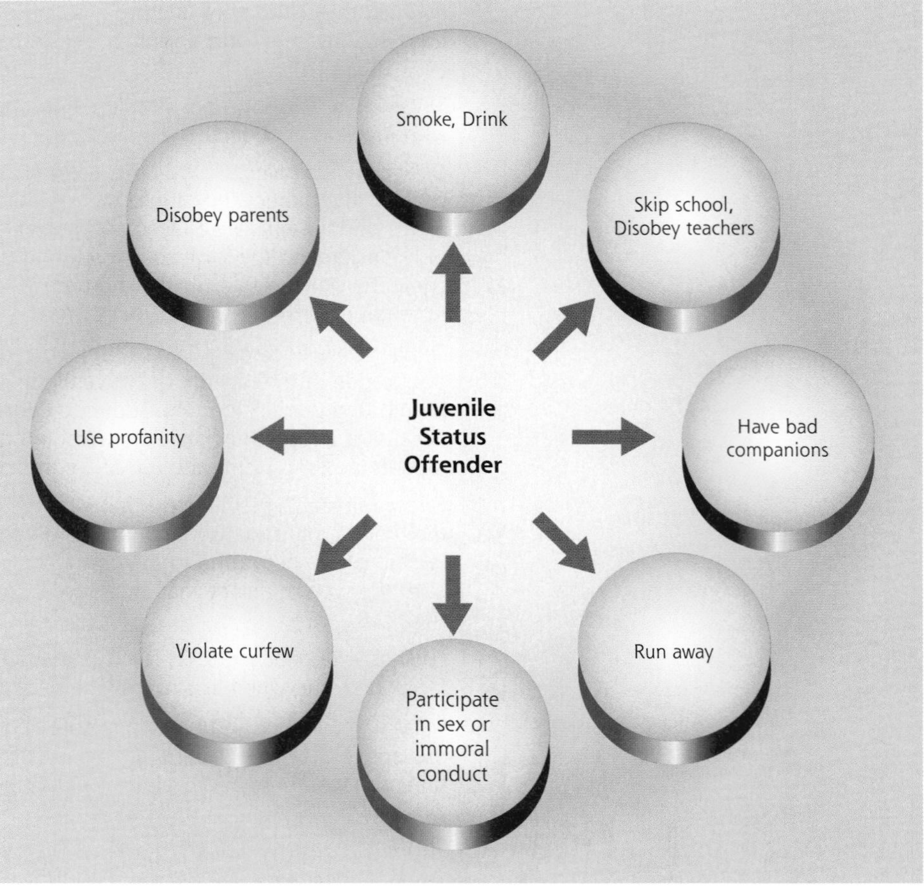

juvenile delinquency
Participation in illegal behavior by a minor who falls under a statutory age limit.

status offender
A juvenile who has been adjudicated by a judge of a juvenile court as having committed a status offense (running away, truancy, or incorrigibility).

JUVENILE JUSTICE TODAY

Today, the juvenile justice system has jurisdiction over two distinct categories of offenders — delinquents and status offenders.[17] **Juvenile delinquency** refers to children who fall under a jurisdictional age limit, which varies from state to state, and who commit an act in violation of the penal code. **Status offenders** include truants and habitually disobedient and ungovernable children. They are commonly characterized in state statutes as persons or children in need of supervision (PINS or CHINS). Most states distinguish such behavior from delinquent conduct to lessen the effect of any stigma on children as a result of their involvement with the juvenile court (see Figure 15.1). In addition, juvenile courts generally have jurisdiction over situations involving conduct directed at (rather than committed by) juveniles, such as parental neglect, deprivation, abandonment, and abuse.

The states have also set different maximum ages below which children fall under the jurisdiction of the juvenile court. Many states include all children under eighteen years of age, others set the limit at seventeen, and still others at sixteen (Exhibit 15.2). States may retain jurisdiction over children's sentence to juvenile institutions while they complete their sentence.

exhibit 15.2

Age Restrictions of Juvenile Courts

Youngest age for original juvenile court jurisdiction in delinquency matters:

Age	State
6	North Carolina
7	Maryland, Massachusetts, New York
8	Arizona
10	Arkansas, Colorado, Kansas, Louisiana, Minnesota, Mississippi, Pennsylvania, South Dakota, Texas, Vermont, Wisconsin

Oldest age for original juvenile court jurisdiction in delinquency matters:

Age	State
15	Connecticut, New York, North Carolina
16	Georgia, Illinois, Louisiana, Massachusetts, Michigan, Missouri, New Hampshire, South Carolina, Texas, Wisconsin
17	Alabama, Alaska, Arizona, Arkansas, California, Colorado, Delaware, District of Columbia, Florida, Hawaii, Idaho, Indiana, Iowa, Kansas, Kentucky, Maine, Maryland, Minnesota, Mississippi, Montana, Nebraska, Nevada, New Jersey, New Mexico, North Dakota, Ohio, Oklahoma, Oregon, Pennsylvania, Rhode Island, South Dakota, Tennessee, Utah, Vermont, Virginia, Washington, West Virginia, Wyoming

Oldest age over which the juvenile court may retain jurisdiction for disposition purposes in delinquency matters:

Age	State
17	Arizona, North Carolina
18	Alaska, Iowa, Kentucky, Nebraska, Oklahoma, Tennessee
19	Mississippi, North Dakota
20	Alabama, Arkansas, Connecticut, Delaware, District of Columbia, Florida, Georgia, Idaho, Illinois, Indiana, Louisiana, Maine, Maryland, Massachusetts, Michigan, Minnesota, Missouri, Nevada, New Hampshire, New Mexico, New York, Ohio, Pennsylvania, Rhode Island, South Carolina, South Dakota, Texas, Utah, Vermont, Virginia, Washington, West Virginia, Wyoming
22	Kansas
24	California, Montana, Oregon, Wisconsin, Colorado, Hawaii, New Jersey

SOURCE: Shay Bilchik, 1999 National Report Series, Juvenile Justice Bulletin: Juvenile Justice: A Century of Change. (Washington, D.C.: Office of Juvenile Justice and Delinquency Prevention, 1999.)

Teens behind bars in Florida. The juvenile justice system can maintain control over delinquent youths or transfer their jurisdiction to the adult court.

Some states exclude certain classes of offenders or offenses from the juvenile justice system. For example, youths who commit serious violent offenses such as rape or murder may be automatically excluded from the juvenile justice system and treated as adults on the premise that they stand little chance of rehabilitation within the confines of the juvenile system. Juvenile court judges may also transfer, or waive, repeat offenders whom they deem untreatable by the juvenile authorities.

The juvenile justice system has evolved into a parallel yet independent system of justice with its own terminology and rules of procedure. Exhibit 15.3 describes the basic similarities and differences between the juvenile and adult justice systems; Table 15.1 on page 478 points out how the language used in the juvenile court differs from that used in the adult system.

Today, the juvenile justice system is responsible for processing and treating almost 2 million cases of youthful misbehavior annually. Each state's system is unique, so it is difficult to give a precise accounting of the justice process. Moreover, depending on local practice and tradition, case processing often varies from community to community within a single state. Keeping this in mind, the following sections provide a general description of some of the key processes and decision points within juvenile justice. Figure 15.2 on page 479 illustrates a model of the juvenile justice process.

POLICE PROCESSING OF THE JUVENILE OFFENDER

According to the Uniform Crime Reports, police officers arrest more than 1.8 million juveniles under age 18 each year, including almost 600,000 under age 15.[18] Most larger police departments have separate juvenile detectives who handle delinquency cases and focus their attention on the problems of youth. In addition to conducting their own investigations, they typically take control of cases after an arrest is made by a uniformed officer.

exhibit 15.3

Similarities and Differences between Juvenile and Adult Justice Systems

Since its creation, the juvenile justice system has sought to maintain its independence from the adult system. Yet there are a number of similarities that characterize the institutions, processes, and law of the two systems.

Similarities

Police officers, judges, and correctional personnel use discretion in decision making in both the adult and the juvenile systems.

The right to receive *Miranda* warnings applies to juveniles as well as to adults.

Juveniles and adults are protected from prejudicial lineups or other identification procedures.

Similar procedural safeguards protect juveniles and adults when they make an admission of guilt.

Prosecutors and defense attorneys play equally critical roles in juvenile and adult advocacy.

Juveniles and adults have the right to counsel at most key stages of the court process.

Pretrial motions are available in juvenile and criminal court proceedings.

Negotiations and plea bargaining exist for juvenile and adult offenders.

Juveniles and adults have a right to a hearing and an appeal.

The standard of evidence in juvenile delinquency adjudications, as in adult criminal trials, is proof beyond a reasonable doubt.

Juveniles and adults can be placed on probation by the court.

Both juveniles and adults can be placed in pretrial detention facilities.

Juveniles and adults can be kept in detention without bail if they are considered dangerous.

After trial, both can be placed in community treatment programs.

Differences

The primary purpose of juvenile procedures is protection and treatment. With adults, the aim is to punish the guilty.

Age determines the jurisdiction of the juvenile court. The nature of the offense determines jurisdiction in the adult system.

Juveniles can be apprehended for acts that would not be criminal if they were committed by an adult (status offenses).

Juvenile proceedings are not considered criminal; adult proceedings are.

Juvenile court procedures are generally informal and private. Those of adult courts are more formal and are open to the public.

Courts cannot release identifying information about a juvenile to the press, but they must release information about an adult.

Parents are highly involved in the juvenile process but not in the adult process.

The standard of arrest is more stringent for adults than for juveniles.

Juveniles are released into parental custody. Adults are generally given the opportunity for bail.

Juveniles have no constitutional right to a jury trial. Adults have this right. Some state statutes provide juveniles with a jury trial.

Juveniles can be searched in school without probable cause or a warrant.

A juvenile's record is generally sealed when the age of majority is reached. The record of an adult is permanent.

A juvenile court cannot sentence juveniles to county jails or state prisons; these are reserved for adults.

The U.S. Supreme Court has declared that the Eighth Amendment does not prohibit the death penalty for crimes committed by juveniles ages 16 and 17 but it cannot be given to children under 16.

Most states do not have specific statutory provisions distinguishing the arrest process for children from that for adults. Some jurisdictions, however, give broad arrest powers to the police in juvenile cases by authorizing the officer to make an arrest whenever it is believed that the child's behavior falls within the jurisdiction of the juvenile court. Consequently, police may arrest youths for behavior considered legal for adults, including running away, curfew violations, and being in possession of alcohol.

When a juvenile is found to have engaged in delinquent or incorrigible behavior, police agencies are charged with the decision to release or to detain the child and refer her to juvenile court. Because of the state's interest in the child, the police generally have more discretion in the investigatory and arrest stages of the juvenile process than they do when dealing with adult offenders.

Table 15.1
Comparison of Terms Used in Adult and Juvenile Justice Systems

	Juvenile Terms	Adult Terms
The Person and the Act	Delinquent child	Criminal
	Delinquent act	Crime
Preadjudicatory Stage	Take into custody	Arrest
	Petition	Indictment
	Agree to a finding	Plead guilty
	Deny the petition	Plead not guilty
	Adjustment	Plea bargain
	Detention facility; child-care shelter	Jail
Adjudicatory Stage	Substitution	Reduction of charges
	Adjudicatory or fact-finding hearing	Trial
	Adjudication	Conviction
Postadjudicatory Stage	Dispositional hearing	Sentencing hearing
	Disposition	Sentence
	Commitment	Incarceration
	Youth development center; treatment center; training school	Prison
	Residential child-care facility	Halfway house
	Aftercare	Parole

This discretionary decision — to release or to detain — is based not only on the nature of the offense but also on police attitudes and the child's social and personal conditions at the time of the arrest. The following is a partial list of factors believed to be significant in police decision making regarding juvenile offenders:

- The type and seriousness of the child's offense
- The ability of the parents to be of assistance in disciplining the child
- The child's past contacts with police

Children in police custody can be detained prior to trial, interrogated, and placed in lineups. However, because of their youth and inexperience, children are generally afforded more protections than that given adults. Police must make sure they understand their constitutional rights before talking to them and, in most cases, will have a parent or guardian present to protect their interests.

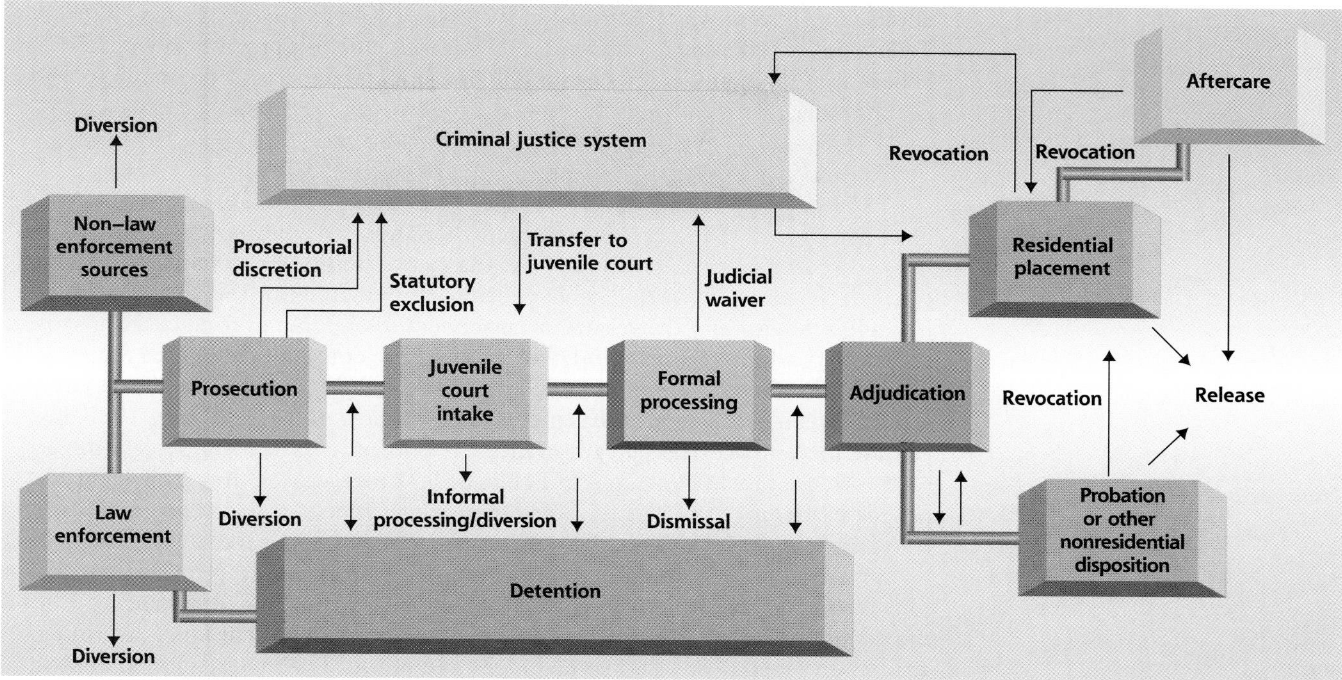

Figure 15.2
A model of the typical justice system and process

- The degree of cooperation obtained from the child and parents and their demeanor, attitude, and personal characteristics
- Whether the child denies the allegations in the petition and insists on a court hearing

Generally, cases involving violence and serious property offenses are most often referred to juvenile court. On the other hand, police often attempt to divert from court action minor disputes between juveniles, school and neighborhood complaints, petty shoplifting cases, runaways, and ungovernable children. The police may adjust a case by simply releasing the child at the point of contact on the street, giving an official warning and releasing the offender to the parents at the station house or the child's home, or referring the child to a social services program. In 1998, for example, 22 percent of arrests involving youths who were eligible in their state for processing in the juvenile justice system were handled exclusively within law enforcement agencies without further processing. Of the rest, 69 percent were referred to juvenile court, and 7 percent were referred directly to criminal court. The others were referred to a welfare agency or to another police agency.[19]

Legal Rights Once a juvenile has been taken into custody, the child has the same Fourth Amendment right to be free from unreasonable searches and seizures as an adult does. Children in police custody can be detained prior to trial, interrogated, and placed in lineups. However, because of their youth and inexperience, children are generally afforded more protections than adults. Police must be careful that the juvenile suspect understands his constitutional rights and, if there is some question, must provide access to a parent or guardian to protect the child's legal interests. For example, police often questioned juveniles in the absence of their parents or an attorney. Any incriminatory statements or confessions made by juveniles could be placed in evidence at their trials. That is no longer permissible, and children have the same (or more) *Miranda* rights as adults, a right that was confirmed in the case of *Fare v. Michael C.* (1979).[20] Today, police will interrogate a juvenile without an adult present only if they believe that the youth is unquestionably mature and experienced enough to understand her legal rights.

THE JUVENILE COURT PROCESS

After the police have determined that a case warrants further attention, they will bind it over to the prosecutor's office, which then has the responsibility for channeling the case through the juvenile court. The juvenile court plays a major role in controlling juvenile behavior and delivering social services to children in need. The most recent data available (1996) indicate that juvenile courts in the United States process an estimated 1.8 million delinquency cases per year.[21] The number of cases handled by juvenile courts increased by almost 50 percent since 1987, including increases of 144 percent in drug law violation cases, 100 percent in personal offense cases, 58 percent in public order offense cases, and 23 percent in property offense cases. This caseload increase has put a strain on juvenile court resources; the recent decline in crime rates may eventually reverse this trend.

Over the past century, the juvenile court has struggled to provide treatment for juvenile offenders while guaranteeing them constitutional due process. But the system has been so overwhelmed by the increase in violent juvenile crime and family breakdown that some judges and politicians have suggested abolishing the juvenile system. Even those experts who want to retain an independent juvenile court have called for its restructuring. Crime control advocates want to reduce the court's jurisdiction over juveniles charged with serious crimes and liberalize the prosecutor's ability to try them in adult courts. In contrast, child advocates suggest that the court scale back its judicial role and transfer its functions to community groups and social service agencies.[22] Despite these differing opinions, the juvenile court will likely remain a critical societal institution; there are few viable alternatives. The question is not whether there will be a juvenile court but what form it will take. Changes in court jurisdiction might include some of the following revisions listed in Exhibit 15.4.

exhibit 15.4

Possible Changes in the Juvenile Court

- Eliminating some of the court's delinquency function by transferring more jurisdiction to adult criminal court
- Removing status offenses from juvenile court
- Expanding the court's role over abuse and neglect cases
- Restructuring the juvenile court into a unified family court
- Utilizing alternative dispute resolution techniques
- Integrating the juvenile court with the private sector and volunteer resources
- Creating a comprehensive juvenile justice system where there is an appropriate response for each child who comes before the court

SOURCE: The Center for the Future of Children, *The Juvenile Court* (Los Altos, Calif.: David and Lucille Packard Foundation, 1996).

After arrest and before trial, the juvenile defendant is processed through a number of important stages within the juvenile court setting. These may include intake, detention, bail, plea bargaining, and waiver hearings. Each of these stages and processes is discussed in the following sections.

The Intake Process After police processing, the juvenile offender is typically remanded to the local juvenile court's *intake division.* At this juncture, court intake officers and/or probation personnel review and initially screen the child and the family to determine if the child needs to be handled formally or whether the case can be settled without the necessity of costly and intrusive official intervention. Their report helps the prosecutor decide whether to handle the case informally or bind it over for trial. The **intake** stage represents an opportunity to place a child in informal programs both within the court and in the community. The intake process also is critically important because more than half of the referrals to the juvenile courts never go beyond this stage.

intake
The process in which a probation officer settles cases at the initial appearance before the onset of formal criminal proceedings; also, process in which a juvenile referral is received and a decision is made to file a petition in the juvenile court, release the juvenile, or refer the juvenile elsewhere.

The Detention Process After a juvenile is formally taken into custody, either as a delinquent or as a status offender, the prosecutor usually makes a decision to release the child to the parent or guardian or to detain the child in a secure shelter pending trial.

Detention has always been a controversial area of juvenile justice. Far too many children have been routinely placed in detention while awaiting court appearances. Status offenders and delinquents have been held in the same facility, and in many parts of the country, adult county jails were used to detain juvenile offenders. The Juvenile Justice Act of 1974 placed emphasis on reducing the number of children placed in inappropriate detention facilities, and although successful, the practice continues.

detention
The temporary care of a child alleged to be a delinquent or status offender who requires secure custody, pending court disposition.

LEGAL ISSUES Most state statutes ordinarily require a hearing on the appropriateness of detention if the initial decision is to keep the child in custody. At this hearing, the child has a right to counsel and may be given other procedural due process safeguards, notably the privilege against self-incrimination and the right to confront and cross-examine witnesses. Most state juvenile court acts provide criteria to support a decision to detain the child. These include (1) the need to protect the child, (2) whether the child presents a serious danger to the public, and (3) the likelihood that the juvenile will return to court for adjudication. Whereas in adult cases the sole criterion for pretrial release may be the offender's availability for trial, juveniles may be detained for other reasons, including their own protection. Normally, the finding of the judge that the child should be detained must be supported by factual evidence. In the 1984 case of *Schall v. Martin,* the U.S. Supreme Court upheld the right of the states to detain a child before trial to protect his welfare and the public safety.[23]

REFORMING DETENTION There has been an ongoing effort to reform detention. The most important reform has been the successful effort to remove status offenders from lockups containing delinquents. After decades of effort,

Juvenile detainee confers with a detention officer. Detention centers tend to be overcrowded, and all too often youths are still detained in adult jails, where they may be subject to physical and sexual abuse.

almost all states have passed laws requiring that status offenders be placed in nonsecure shelters, rather than secure detention facilities, thereby reducing their contact with more dangerous delinquent youth (Figure 15.3).

Another serious problem is the detention of youths in adult jails. The practice is common in rural areas where there are relatively few separate facilities for young offenders.[24] The OJJDP has given millions of dollars in aid to encourage the removal of juveniles from adult lockups. These grants have helped jurisdictions develop intake screening procedures, specific release or detention criteria, and alternative residential and nonresidential programs for juveniles awaiting trial. By 1980 amendments to the act mandating the absolute removal of juveniles from jails had been adopted. Despite such efforts, many states are not complying with the removal provisions, and thousands of youths are annually detained in adult jails. Whatever the actual number jailed today, placing young offenders in adult jails continues to be a significant problem in the juvenile justice system. Juveniles detained in adult jails often live in squalid conditions and are subject to physical and sexual abuse. The practice is widely condemned, but eliminating the confinement of juveniles in adult institutions remains a difficult task.[25] Many youths who commit nonserious acts are still being held in adult jails — for example, runaways who are apprehended in rural areas; minority juveniles may be spending greater amounts of time in jail than white offenders for the same offense.[26]

A third problem is overcrowding caused by a tremendous increase in juveniles detained. Since 1985 the number of youths held in short-term detention facilities has increased by about 15 percent, or more than seventeen thousand children! In addition, the number of minority group children (African Americans and Hispanics) held in detention facilities has risen more than 30 percent, which has caused considerable concern to juvenile justice practitioners. Research shows that overcrowding of juvenile detention and disproportionate minority representation are pervasive and serious problems.[27]

Experts believe the steady increase in detention use may result from (1) a rise in serious crime by juveniles, (2) a growing link between juveniles and drug-related crimes, and (3) the involvement of younger children in juvenile offenses. A declining juvenile crime rate may help reduce these problems.

Bail If a child is not detained, the question of bail arises. Federal courts have not found it necessary to rule on the issue of a juvenile's constitutional right to bail because liberal statutory release provisions act as appropriate alternatives. Although only a few state statutes allow release on money bail, many others have juvenile code provisions that emphasize the release of the child to

Figure 15.3
Court data show a substantial decline in the use of detention in status offense cases.

SOURCE: Howard Snyder and Melissa Sickmund, *Juvenile Offenders and Victims: 1999 National Report* (Washington, D.C.: Office of Juvenile Justice and Delinquency Prevention, 1999), 207.

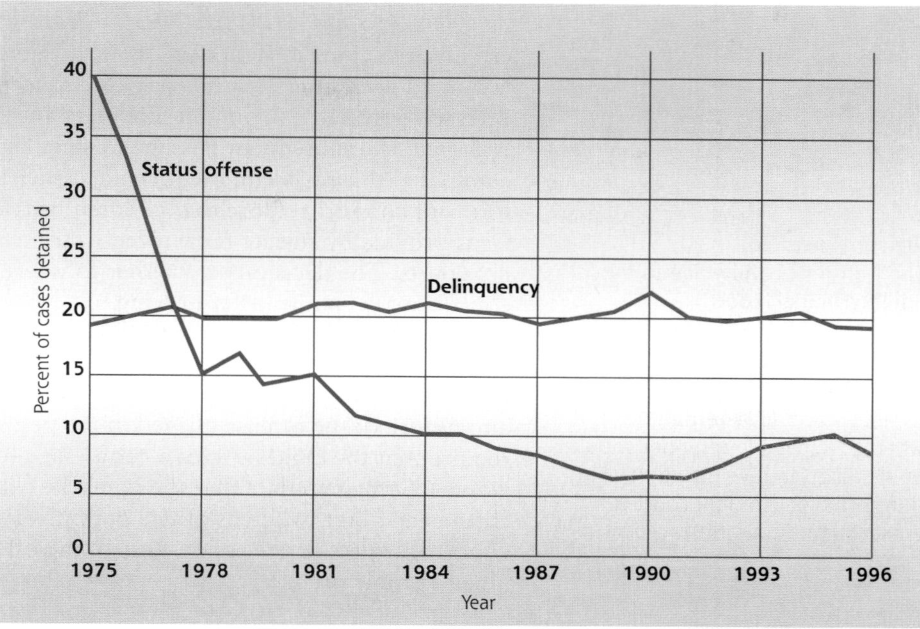

- In 1975 status offense cases were twice as likely as delinquency cases to involve secure detention between the time of referral to court and case disposition.
- By 1992 the likelihood that a status offense case would involve detention was less than half that for delinquency cases.
- In 1975 an estimated 143,000 status offense cases involved detention—in 1996, the figure was 39,100.

the parents as an acceptable substitute. A constitutional right to bail that on its face seems to benefit a child may have unforeseen results. For example, money bail might impose a serious economic strain on the child's family while conflicting with the protective and social concerns of the juvenile court. Considerations of economic liabilities and other procedural inequities have influenced the majority of courts confronting this question to hold that juveniles do not have a right to bail.

Plea Bargaining Before trial, juvenile prosecutors may attempt to negotiate a settlement to the case. For example, if the offender admits to the facts of the petition, she may be offered a placement in a special community-based treatment program in lieu of a term in a secure state facility. Or a status offense petition may be substituted for one of delinquency so that the adolescent can avoid being housed in a state training school and instead be placed in a more treatment-oriented facility.

If a bargain can be reached, the child will be asked to admit in open court that he did in fact commit the act of which he stands accused. State juvenile courts tend to minimize the stigma associated with the use of adult criminal standards by using other terminology, such as "agree to a finding" or "accept the petition" rather than "admit guilt." When the child makes an admission, juvenile courts require the following procedural safeguards: (1) The child knows of the right to a trial, (2) the plea or admission is made voluntarily, and (3) the child understands the charges and consequences of the plea.

waiver (juvenile)
The transfer of a juvenile to the adult (criminal) court.

transfer hearing
A preadjudication hearing in a juvenile court to determine whether a juvenile offender should be detained in juvenile court or transferred to criminal court for prosecution as an adult.

Waiver of Jurisdiction

Prior to the development of the first modern juvenile court in Illinois in 1899, juveniles were tried for violations of the law in adult criminal courts. The consequences were devastating; many children were treated as criminal offenders and often sentenced to adult prisons. Although the subsequent passage of state legislation creating juvenile courts eliminated this problem, the juvenile justice system did recognize that certain forms of conduct require that children be tried as adults. Today, most jurisdictions provide by statute for **waiver**, or transfer, of juvenile offenders to the criminal courts. The decision of whether to waive a juvenile to the adult, or criminal, court is made in a **transfer hearing.**

The transfer of a juvenile to the criminal court is often based on statutory criteria established by the state's juvenile court act, so waiver provisions vary considerably among jurisdictions. Most commonly considered are the child's age and nature of the offense alleged in the petition. For example, some jurisdictions require that the child be over a certain age (typically, 14) before they can be waived. Some mandate that the youth be charged with a felony before being tried as an adult, whereas others permit waiver of jurisdiction to the criminal court regardless of the seriousness of the offense (e.g., when a child is a petty albeit chronic offender).

LEGAL CONTROLS

Because of the nature of the waiver decision and its effect on the child in terms of status and disposition, the U.S. Supreme Court has imposed procedural protections for juveniles in the waiver process. In *Kent v. United States* (1966), the Supreme Court held that the waiver proceeding is a critically important stage in the juvenile justice process and that juveniles must be afforded minimum requirements of due process of law at such proceedings, including the right to legal counsel.[28] Then in *Breed v. Jones* (1975), the Court held that the prosecution of juveniles as adults in the California Superior Court violated the double jeopardy clause of the Fifth Amendment if they previously had been tried on the same charge in juvenile court.[29] The Court concluded that jeopardy attaches when the juvenile court begins to hear evidence at the adjudicatory hearing; this requires that the waiver hearing take place prior to any adjudication.

YOUTHS IN ADULT COURTS

Today, all states allow juveniles to be tried as adults in criminal courts in one of four ways:

1. *Concurrent jurisdiction* The prosecutor has the discretion of filing charges for certain offenses in either juvenile or criminal court.
2. *Excluded offenses* State laws exclude from juvenile court jurisdiction certain offenses that are either very minor, such as traffic or fishing violations, or very serious, such as murder or rape.
3. *Judicial waiver* After a formal hearing at which both prosecutor and defense attorney present evidence, a juvenile court judge may decide to waive jurisdiction and transfer the case to criminal court. This procedure is also known as *binding over* or *certifying* juvenile cases to criminal court.
4. *Reverse waiver* State laws mandate that certain offenses be tried in adult court; however, judges may decide that the case be tried in juvenile court.

Nearly every state has provisions for handling juveniles in adult criminal courts, and the trend is to make the waiver broader.[30] In thirty-one states, once a juvenile is tried in adult court, she is no longer eligible for juvenile justice on any subsequent offense. In order to get tough on juvenile crime, these efforts have limited the judge's ability to consider the individual circumstances that apply in each case.

THE EFFECT OF WAIVER The problem of youths processed in adult courts is a serious one. It is likely that more than fifteen thousand juvenile delinquency cases are now being transferred to the adult courts each year because more than eleven thousand judicial waivers alone occur each year. What is accomplished by treating juveniles like adults? Studies of the impact of the recent waiver statutes have yielded inconclusive results. Some juveniles whose cases are waived to criminal court are actually sentenced more leniently than they would have been in juvenile court. In many states, even when juveniles are tried in criminal court and convicted on the charges, they may still be sentenced to a juvenile or youthful offender institution, rather than to an adult prison. Some studies show that only a small percentage of juveniles tried as adults are incarcerated for periods longer than the terms served by offenders convicted on the same crime in the juvenile court; others have found that waived juveniles actually serve more time behind bars.[31] For example, they spend more time in juvenile detention awaiting trial (Figure 15.4). In the end, what began as a get-tough measure has had the opposite effect while costing taxpayers more money.[32]

Figure 15.4
Juveniles transferred to criminal court or awaiting transfer remained in detention longer than those awaiting juvenile court adjudication or disposition.

SOURCE: Howard Snyder and Melissa Sickmund, *Juvenile Offenders and Victims: 1999 National Report* (Washington, D.C.: Office of Juvenile Justice and Delinquency Prevention, 1999), 202.

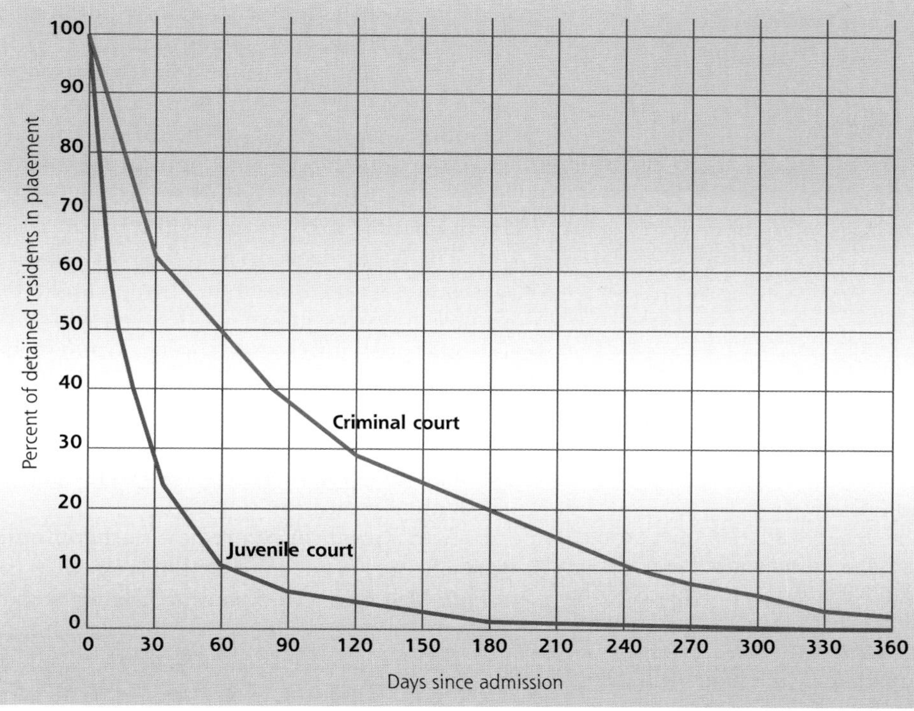

- Among juveniles detained while awaiting adjudication or disposition in juvenile court, 69% had been in the facility for at least seven days, 49% at least fourteen days, and 25% at least thirty days. By sixty days, only 11% remained in the facility; and by ninety days, 6% remained.
- Among detained juveniles awaiting a transfer hearing or awaiting criminal court processing, 89% had been in the facility for at least seven days, 80% at least fourteen days, and 64% at least thirty days. At sixty days, 50% remained in the facility, and by ninety days, 38% remained. After six months, nearly 20% remained, and after a full year, 4% remained.

Critics view these new methods of dealing with juvenile offenders as inefficient, ineffective, and philosophically out of step with the original concept of the juvenile court. Supporters view the waiver process as a sound method of getting the most serious juvenile offenders off the streets while ensuring that rehabilitation plays a less critical role in the juvenile justice system. No area of juvenile justice has received more attention recently than efforts to redefine the jurisdiction of the juvenile court.[33]

The Trial

There are typically two judicial hearings in the juvenile court process. The first, typically called an *initial appearance,* is similar to the arraignment. The child is informed of the charges against him, attorneys are appointed, bail is reviewed, and in many instances cases are settled with an admission of the facts, followed by a community sentence. If the case cannot be settled at this initial stage, it is bound over for trial.

During the adjudicatory or trial process, often called the *fact-finding hearing* in juvenile proceedings, the court hears evidence on the allegations stated in the delinquency petition. In its early development, the juvenile court did not emphasize judicial rule making similar to that of the criminal trial process. Absent were such basic requirements as the standard of proof, rules of evidence, and similar adjudicatory formalities. Proceedings were to be nonadversarial, informal, and noncriminal. Gradually, however, the juvenile trial process was the target of criticism because judges were handing out punishments to children without affording them legal rights. This changed in 1967 when the U.S. Supreme Court's landmark *In re Gault* decision radically altered the juvenile justice system.[34] In *Gault,* the Court ruled that the concept of fundamental fairness is applicable to juvenile delinquency proceedings. The Court granted critical rights to juvenile defendants, most importantly, (1) the notice of the charges, (2) the right to counsel, (3) the right to confront and cross-examine witnesses, (4) the privilege against self-incrimination, and (5) the right to a transcript of the trial record.

The *Gault* decision completely altered the juvenile trial process. Instead of dealing with children in a benign and paternalistic fashion, the courts were forced to process juvenile offenders within the framework of appropriate constitutional procedures. And though *Gault* was technically limited to the adjudicatory stage, it has spurred further legal reform throughout the juvenile system. Today, the right to counsel, the privilege against self-incrimination, the right to treatment in detention and correctional facilities, and other constitutional protections are applied at all stages of the juvenile process, from investigation through **adjudication** to parole.

adjudication
The determination of guilt or innocence; a judgment concerning criminal charges. The majority of offenders charged plead guilty; of the remainder, some cases are adjudicated by a judge and a jury, some are adjudicated by a judge without a jury, and others are dismissed.

After *Gault* the Supreme Court continued its trend toward legalizing and formalizing the juvenile trial process with the decision in *In re Winship* (1970), which held that a finding of delinquency in a juvenile case must be made with the same level of evidence used in an adult case: beyond a reasonable doubt.[35]

Although the informality of the traditional juvenile trial court was severely altered by *Gault* and *Winship,* the trend of increased rights for juveniles was somewhat curtailed when the Supreme Court held in *McKeiver v. Pennsylvania* (1971), that children do not have the same right to a jury trial as an adult.[36] The Court reasoned that juries were not an essential element of justice and if used in juvenile cases would end confidentiality.

Once an adjudicatory hearing has been completed, the court is normally required to enter a judgment against the child. This may take the form of declaring the child delinquent or a ward of the court or possibly even suspending judgment to avoid the stigma of a juvenile record. Following the entering of a judgment, the court can begin its determination of possible dispositions for the child.

disposition
For juvenile offenders, the equivalent of sentencing for adult offenders. The theory is that disposition is more rehabilitative than retributive. Possible dispositions may be to dismiss the case; release the youth to the custody of his or her parents; place the offender on probation; or send him or her to an institution or state correctional institution.

Disposition and Treatment

At the dispositional hearing, the juvenile court judge imposes a sentence on the juvenile offender based on her offense, prior record, and family background. Normally, the judge has broad discretionary power to issue a range of **dispositions** from dismissal to institutional commitment. In theory, the dispositional decision is an effort by the court to serve the best interests of the child, the family, and the community. In many respects, this postadjudicative process is the most important stage in the juvenile court system because it represents the last opportunity for the court to influence the child and control his behavior.

To ensure that only relevant and appropriate evidence is considered by the court during trial, most jurisdictions require a separate hearing to consider an appropriate disposition. The bifurcated hearing process ensures that the adjudicatory hearing is used solely to determine the merits of the allegations, whereas the dispositional hearing determines whether the child is in need of rehabilitation.

In theory, the juvenile court seeks to provide a disposition that represents an individualized treatment plan for the child. This decision is normally based on the presentence investigation of the probation department, reports from social agencies, and possibly a psychiatric evaluation. The judge generally has broad discretion in dispositional matters but is limited by the provisions of the state's juvenile court act. The following are typical juvenile court dispositions:

1. Suspended judgment
2. Probation
3. Placement in a community treatment program
4. Commitment to the state agency responsible for juvenile institutional care

In addition, the court may place the child with parents or relatives, make dispositional arrangements with private youth-serving agencies, or order the child committed to a mental institution.

JUVENILE SENTENCING REFORM

Over the past decade, juvenile justice experts and the general public have become aroused about the serious juvenile crime rate in general and about violent acts committed by children in particular. As a result, some law enforcement officials and conservative legislators have demanded that the juvenile justice system take a more serious stand with dangerous juvenile offenders. In the past two decades, many state legislatures have responded by toughening their juvenile codes (Exhibit 15.5). Some jurisdictions have passed mandatory or determinate incarceration sentences for juveniles convicted of serious felonies. The get-tough approach even allows the use of the death penalty for minors transferred to the adult system (Exhibit 15.6).[37] Many jurisdictions, however, have not abandoned rehabilitation as a primary dispositional goal and still hold to the philosophy that placements should be based on the least detrimental alternative. This view requires that judges employ the least intrusive measures possible to safeguard a child's growth and development.[38]

A second reform has been the concerted effort to remove status offenders from the juvenile justice system and restrict their entry into institutional programs. Because of the development of numerous diversion programs, many children who are involved in truancy and incorrigible behavior who ordinarily would have been sent to a closed institution are now being placed in community programs. There are far fewer status offenders in detention or institutions than ever before (see Figure 15.3).

exhibit 15.5

Some juvenile codes emphasize prevention and treatment goals, some stress punishment, and others seek a balanced approach. The following are philosophical goals stated in juvenile code purpose clauses, 1997.

Prevention/ Diversion/Treatment	Punishment	Both Prevention/Diversion/ Treatment and Punishment	
Arizona	Arkansas	Alabama	Nevada
District of Columbia	Georgia	Alaska	New Hampshire
Kentucky	Hawaii	California	New Jersey
Massachusetts	Illinois	Colorado	New Mexico
North Carolina	Iowa	Connecticut	North Dakota
Ohio	Louisiana	Delaware	Oklahoma
South Carolina	Michigan	Florida	Oregon
Vermont	Missouri	Idaho	Pennsylvania
West Virginia	Rhode Island	Indiana	Tennessee
		Kansas	Texas
		Maryland	Utah
		Maine	Virginia
		Minnesota	Washington
		Mississippi	Wisconsin
		Montana	Wyoming
		Nebraska	

- Most states seek to protect the interests of the child, the family, the community or some combination of the three.
- In seventeen states the purpose clause incorporates the language of the balanced and restorative justice philosophy, emphasing offender accountability, public safety, and competency development.
- Purpose clauses also address court issues such as fairness, speedy trials, and even coordination of services. In nearly all states, the code also includes protections of the child's constitutional and statutory rights.

*Arizona's statutes and court rules did not contain a purpose clause; however, the issue is addressed in case law.

SOURCE: Authors' adaptation of Torbet and Szymanski's *State legislative responses to violent juvenile crime: 1996–97 update* (unpublished background research), National Report Series–Juvenile Justice, 1999.

A third reform effort has been to standardize dispositions in juvenile court. As early as 1977, Washington passed one of the first determinate sentencing laws for juvenile offenders, resulting in other states adopting similar statutes.[39] All children found to be delinquent are evaluated on a point system based on their age, prior juvenile record, and type of crime committed. Minor offenders are handled in the community. Those committing more serious offenses are placed on probation. Children who commit the most serious offenses are subject to standardized institutional penalties. As a result, juvenile offenders who commit such crimes as rape or armed robbery are being sentenced to institutionalization for two, three, and four years. This approach is different from the indeterminate sentencing under which children who had committed a serious crime might be released from institutions in less than a year if correctional authorities believe that they have been rehabilitated.

exhibit 15.6

Most states that specify a minimum age for the death penalty set the minimum at age 16 or 18:

None specified	Age 16 (or less)	Age 17	Age 18
Arizona	Alabama	Georgia	California
Idaho	Arkansas (14)†	New Hampshire	Colorado
Louisiana	Delaware	North Carolina‖	Connecticut#
Montana	Florida	Texas	Federal system
Pennsylvania	Indiana		Illinois
South Carolina	Kentucky		Kansas
South Dakota*	Mississippi (13)‡		Maryland
Utah	Missouri		Nebraska
	Nevada		New Jersey
	Oklahoma		New Mexico
	Virginia (14)§		New York
	Wyoming		Ohio
			Oregon
			Tennessee
			Washington

SOURCE: Howard Snyder and Melissa Sickmund, *Juvenile Offenders and Victims: 1999 National Report.* (Washington, D.C.: Office of Juvenile Justice and Deliquency Prevention, 1999).

* Juveniles may be transferred to criminal court. Age can be a mitigating factor.

† See Arkansas Code Ann. 9–27–318(b)(2)(Repl.1991).

‡ The minimum age defined by statute is 13, but the effective age is 16 based on interpretation of U.S. Supreme Court decisions by the state attorney general's office.

§ The minimum age for transfer to criminal court is 14 by statute, but the effective age for a capital sentence is 16 based on interpretation of U.S. Supreme Court decisions by the state attorney general's office.

II The age required is 17 unless the murderer was incarcerated for murder when a subsequent murder occurred; then the age may be14.

See Conn. Gen. Stat. 53a–46a(g)(1).

NOTE: Minimum ages (at the time of the capital offense) reflect interpretation by state attorney general offices. States not listed do not have the death penalty.

probation
A sentence entailing the conditional release of a convicted offender into the community under the supervision of the court (in the form of a probation officer), subject to certain conditions for a specified time. The conditions are usually similar to those of parole. (*Note:* Probation is a sentence, an alternative to incarceration; parole is administrative release from incarceration.) Violation of the conditions of probation may result in revocation of probation.

THE JUVENILE CORRECTIONAL PROCESS

After disposition in juvenile court, delinquent offenders may be placed in some form of correctional treatment. Although many are placed in the community, more than one hundred thousand are now in secure facilities.

Probation

Probation is the most commonly used formal sentence for juvenile offenders, and many states require that a youth fail on probation before being sent to an institution (unless the criminal act is quite serious). Probation involves placing the child under the supervision of the juvenile probation department for the purpose of community treatment. Conditions of probation are normally

Boys in a juvenile institution sit down for their evening meal. Despite efforts to treat delinquents in the community, the institutional population is at an all-time high; more than 100,000 youths are in closed facilities.

imposed on the child by either statute or court order. There are general conditions, such as those that require the child to stay away from other delinquents or to obey the law. More specific conditions of probation include requiring the child to participate in a vocational training program, to attend school regularly, to obtain treatment at a child guidance clinic, or to make restitution. Restitution can be in the form of community service — for example, a youth found in possession of marijuana might be required to work fifty hours in a home for the elderly. Monetary restitution requires delinquents to pay back the victims of their crimes. Restitution programs have proven successful and have been adopted around the country.[40]

Juvenile probation is a major component of the juvenile justice system. Juvenile courts place more than 80 percent of adjudicated delinquents on some form of probation. It is the most widely used method of community treatment. The cost savings of community treatment, coupled with its nonpunitive intentions, are likely to keep probation programs growing.

commitment
Decision of judge ordering an adjudicated and sentenced juvenile offender to be placed in a correctional facility.

Institutionalization The most severe of the statutory dispositions available to the juvenile court involves **commitment** of the child to an institution. The committed child may be sent to a state training school or private residential treatment facility. These are usually minimum-security facilities with small populations and an emphasis on treatment and education. Some states, however, maintain facilities with populations over one thousand.

Most state statutes vary when determining the length of the child's commitment. Traditionally, many jurisdictions committed the child up to majority, which usually meant twenty-one years of age. This normally deprived the child of freedom for an extensive period of time — sometimes longer than an adult sentenced for the same offense would be confined. As a result, some states have passed legislation under which children are committed for periods ranging from one to three years.

To better handle violent juvenile offenders, some states have created separate or intermediate juvenile systems. Under such statutes, fourteen- to seventeen-year-olds charged with certain violent felonies are treated as adults, and if convicted, sentenced to new intermediate prisons, separated from both adult and regular juvenile offenders, for terms of two to five years.[41]

PROFILE OF INCARCERATED YOUTH The most recent available census of juvenile institutions (1997) indicates that about 125,805 young persons were being held in 1,121 public and 2,310 private residential facilities nationwide. Although the typical inmate was a white male, residential placement custody rates for black juveniles were substantially higher than rates for other groups. For every 100,000 non-Hispanic black juveniles in the population, 1,018 were in a residential placement facility; that rate is almost five times higher than the white incarceration rate of about 200 per 100,000 population. In nearly all states, a disproportionate number of minorities were in residential placement; the proportion of minorities in the juvenile population was 34 percent in 1997. The disproportionate number of minority youths incarcerated may mean that African Americans, Hispanics, and other minorities are more likely to be arrested and charged with serious crimes than are white youths.[42] However, researchers question whether the seriousness of the offense alone can explain differences in incarceration rates among racial groups. Minority youths are being incarcerated at a far greater rate than their representation in the general population. Some experts believe the overrepresentation of minorities in the nation's juvenile justice corrections system is even greater than previously thought and may be ten times that of whites in some states. The Juvenile Delinquency Act now requires states to assess disproportionate minority representations and racial issues at any level of the system. However, while minority representation remains disproportionately high, it is actually being reduced by federal initiatives that combat racism in the juvenile justice system (Figure 15.5).

Ninety-five percent of incarcerated juveniles are held for delinquent offenses — offenses that would be crimes if committed by adults. Thirty-five percent were held for person-oriented offenses; about 20 percent for alcohol, drug, and public order offenses; and more than 40 percent for property crimes.[43] Just over 5 percent were confined for a juvenile status offense, such as truancy, running away, or incorrigibility. The efforts made in recent years to keep status offenders out of institutions seem to have paid off.

DEINSTITUTIONALIZATION Some experts in delinquency and juvenile law question the policy of institutionalizing juvenile offenders. Many believe that large institutions are too costly to operate and only produce more sophisticated criminals. This dilemma has produced a number of efforts to remove youths from juvenile facilities and replace large institutions with smaller community-based facilities. For example, Massachusetts closed all its state training schools more than twenty years ago (subsequently, however, public pressure caused a few secure facilities to be reopened). Many other states have established small residential facilities operated by juvenile-care agencies to replace larger units.

Despite the daily rhetoric on crime control, public support for community-based programs for juveniles still exists. Although such programs are not panaceas,

Figure 15.5
Black juveniles are overrepresented at all stages of the juvenile justice system, compared with their proportion in the population.

SOURCE: Howard Snyder and Melissa Sickmund, *Juvenile Offenders and Victims: 1999 National Report* (Washington, D.C.: Office of Juvenile Justice and Delinquency Prevention, 1999), 192.

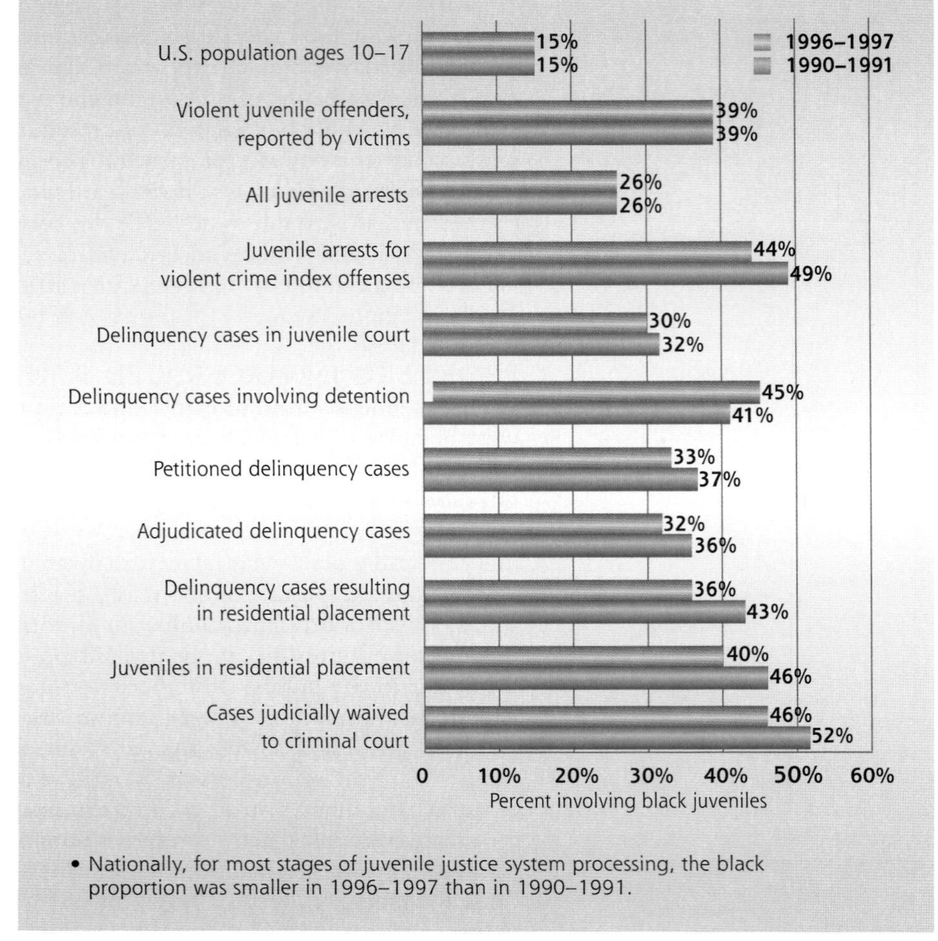

many experts still recommend more treatment and less incarceration for juvenile offenders. Utah, Maryland, Vermont, and Pennsylvania, for example, have dramatically reduced their reform school populations while setting up a wide range of intensive treatment programs for juveniles. Many large, impersonal, and expensive state institutions with unqualified staff and ineffective treatment programs have been eliminated.

STATUS OFFENDERS There has been an ongoing effort for almost thirty years to deinstitutionalize status offenders (DSO).[44] This means removing noncriminal youths from institutions housing delinquents in order to prevent them from interacting with violent and/or chronic offenders.

Since its inception, the DSO approach has been hotly debated. Some have argued that early intervention is society's best hope of forestalling future delinquent behavior and reducing victimization. Other experts maintain that legal control over status offenders is a violation of youths' rights. Still others have viewed status-offending behavior as a symptom of some larger trauma or problem that requires attention. These diverse opinions still exist today.

Since Congress passed the JJDP Act in 1974, all fifty states have complied with some aspect of the deinstitutionalization mandate. Millions of federal, state, and local dollars have been spent on the DSO movement. Vast numbers of programs have been created around the country to reduce the number of juveniles in secure confinement. What remains to be done, however, is to study the effect DSO has had on juveniles and the justice system.

treatment
The rehabilitative method used to effect a change of behavior in the juvenile offender, in the form of therapy, or educational or vocational programs.

THE RIGHT TO TREATMENT Courts have ruled that, unlike adults, juveniles who are committed to institutions have a right to **treatment.** This means that they must be given sufficient care and counseling to ensure their eventual rehabilitation. By so ruling, the courts have compared the system of dealing with juvenile offenders with the system of commitment for the mentally ill rather than that of adult criminals. Both the mental health and juvenile justice systems are based on the parens patriae philosophy, which mandates that people being held in state custody who have not committed a criminal act have a right to treatment. Their continued custody is illegal without a viable treatment program being made available.

Although the U.S. Supreme Court has not made a definitive ruling on this important issue, a series of lower federal court cases hold sway. For example, the case of *Martarella v. Kelly* (1972) established that status offenders held in custody must be furnished with adequate treatment; if not, their continued custody violates the Eighth and Fourteenth Amendments.[45] In *Inmates v. Affleck* (1972), a federal court required that minimum standards of treatment be implemented for juvenile offenders under institutional care.[46] In *Morales v. Turman* (1973), another federal court specifically found that juveniles at a training school in Texas have a legal right to treatment.[47] In accordance with these holdings, the Seventh U.S. Circuit Court of Appeals in *Nelson v. Heyne* (1974) upheld a constitutional right to treatment for institutionalized juveniles, under the Fourteenth Amendment.[48] The *Nelson* case is significant because it was the first federal appellate court decision to affirm a constitutional right to treatment. These decisions seem to indicate that juveniles do have a right, be it statutory or constitutional, to receive treatment and to be assured of a minimum standard of physical care if committed to an institution.

AFTERCARE *Aftercare* marks the final stage of the formal juvenile justice process. Its purpose is to help youths make the transition from residential or institutional settings back into the community. Effective aftercare programs provide adequate supervision and support services to help juvenile offenders avoid criminal activity. Examples of programs include electronic monitoring, counseling, treatment and community service referrals, education, work training, and intensive parole supervision.

Most juvenile aftercare involves parole. A juvenile parole officer provides the child with counseling, school referral, vocational training, and other services. Children who violate the conditions of parole may have their parole revoked and be returned to the institution. Unlike the adult postconviction process, where the U.S. Supreme Court has imposed procedural protections in probation and parole revocations, juveniles do not have such due process rights. State courts have also been reluctant to grant juveniles rights in this area, and those that have generally refuse to require that the whole array of rights be made available as they are to adult offenders. Since the *Gault* decision, however, many states have adopted administrative regulations requiring juvenile agencies to incorporate due process, such as proper notice of the hearing and the right to counsel in postconviction proceedings.

COMPREHENSIVE JUVENILE JUSTICE REFORM

What are the remedies for the current juvenile court system? Some suggest changing the jurisdiction of the juvenile courts. Others want to strengthen the legal rights of juveniles. The vast majority of experts believe there is an urgent need to develop successful dispositional programs. Over the last century, the juvenile court system has been transformed from a rehabilitative to a quasi-criminal court. Many states are toughening juvenile codes (Exhibit 15.7). With limited resources and procedural deficiencies, there is little likelihood of much change in the near future.[49]

A serious crisis exists in the U.S. juvenile justice system. How to formulate new policies and meet the needs of large numbers of children in trouble remains one of the most controversial issues facing our legal system. The National Juvenile Justice Action Plan of the federal government is a comprehensive response to this critical challenge.[50]

comprehensive juvenile justice The current reform model of balancing policies for juvenile offenders with preventive and community programs aimed at young people and successful control programs for aggressive offenders.

At a time when much attention is focused on the small group of serious juvenile offenders, a **comprehensive juvenile justice** strategy has been called for to deal with all aspects of juvenile crime. This strategy focuses on crime prevention and expanding options for handling juvenile offenders. The components of this strategy include (1) prevention in early childhood, (2) intervention methods for at-risk teenage youths, (3) graduated sanctions to hold serious juvenile offenders accountable for juvenile crimes, (4) proper utilization of juvenile detention and confinement, and (5) the placement of serious juvenile offenders into adult courts.[51]

Early Prevention

Research has identified certain risk factors that can possibly suggest future delinquency. For young children, these factors include abuse and neglect, domestic violence, family conflict, educational deficiencies, and health problems. Early childhood services may therefore prevent delinquency from occurring and make a child less vulnerable to future criminality. State legislatures are increasingly investing in state-funded early education programs, like Head Start, as a way to reduce juvenile crime, and Smart Start, designed to make sure children are healthy before starting school. Home visitation programs for new parents target families at risk because of child abuse and neglect. The Policy, Programs, and Issues in Criminal Justice feature explores this issue in greater depth.

For more information on gangs and crime, visit the National Youth Gang Centers home page at www.iir.com/nygc/
To learn about the issues surrounding school violence, go to the Center for the Prevention of School Violence's Web site at www.ncsu.edu/

Intervention Programs

Many jurisdictions are developing new intervention programs for at-risk teenage youths. An example of an effective national program is the Big Brother/Big Sister Program, a structured relationship that matches a volunteer adult with a youngster. More and more cities are finding that night curfews can also reduce gang violence and vandalism. Curfews may also contribute to a feeling of safety among residents of high-crime neighborhoods. Efforts also are being made to deter young people from becoming involved with gangs. Gang members ordinarily have higher rates of serious violent behavior.

Graduated Sanction Programs

Graduated sanction programs for juveniles are another solution that states are exploring across the country. Types of graduated sanctions include (1) immediate sanctions for nonviolent offenders, (2) intermediate sanctions that target repeat minor offenders and first-time serious offenders, and (3) secure care, which is reserved for repeat serious offenders and violent offenders. A survey conducted on more than 3,000 intervention programs found that about 425 of these programs showed success in

exhibit 15.7

From 1992 through 1997, legislatures in forty-seven states and the District of Columbia enacted laws that made their juvenile justice systems more punitive.

State	Changes in Law or Court Rule*			State	Changes in Law or Court Rule*		
Alabama	T		C	Montana	T	S	C
Alaska	T		C	Nebraska			
Arizona	T	S	C	Nevada	T		C
Arkansas	T	S	C	New Hampshire	T	S	C
California	T		C	New Jersey		S	C
Colorado	T	S	C	New Mexico	T	S	C
Connecticut	T	S	C	New York			
Delaware	T	S	C	North Carolina	T		C
D. of Columbia	T	S		North Dakota	T		C
Florida	T	S	C	Ohio	T	S	C
Georgia	T	S	C	Oklahoma	T	S	C
Hawaii	T		C	Oregon	T	S	C
Idaho	T	S	C	Pennsylvania	T		C
Illinois	T	S	C	Rhode Island	T	S	C
Indiana	T	S	C	South Carolina	T		C
Iowa	T	S	C	South Dakota	T		
Kansas	T	S	C	Tennessee	T	S	C
Kentucky	T	S	C	Texas	T	S	C
Louisiana	T	S	C	Utah	T		C
Maine			C	Vermont			
Maryland	T		C	Virginia	T	S	C
Massachusetts	T	S	C	Washington	T		C
Michigan		S	C	West Virginia	T		C
Minnesota	T	S	C	Wisconsin	T	S	C
Mississippi	T		C	Wyoming	T		C
Missouri	T	S	C				

- Transfer provisions—Laws made it easier to transfer juvenile offenders from the juvenile justice system (forty-five states).
- Sentencing authority—Laws gave criminal and juvenile courts expanded sentencing options (thirty-one states).
- Confidentiality—Laws modified or removed traditional juvenile court confidentiality provisions by making records and proceedings more open (forty-seven states).

*T = Transfer provisions; S = Sentencing authority; C = Confidentiality

SOURCE: Authors' adaptation of Torbet et al.'s *State responses to serious and violent juvenile crime* and Torbet and Szymanski's *State legislative responses to violent juvenile crime: 1996–97 update.*

juvenile treatment and control.[52] As a result, there is considerable information available for states to develop comprehensive graduated sanctions.

Reforming Institutionalization Another key to a comprehensive strategy is providing programs that deal with institutionalization. Many experts believe juvenile incarceration is overused, particularly for nonviolent offenders. That is exactly why the concept of deinstitutionalization was established by the Juvenile Justice and Delinquency Prevention Act of 1974. Considerable research

Policy, Programs, and Issues in Criminal Justice

PREVENTING DELINQUENCY WITH EARLY CHILDHOOD INTERVENTION

Prominent delinquency experts such as criminologist Terence Thornberry, a director at the Rochester Youth Development Study, are now attempting to link knowledge developed about the onset of a delinquent career with efforts to prevent delinquency. Two findings in particular support the idea that prevention programs should begin at an early age and should be comprehensive: (1) Although serious delinquency reaches its apex during adolescence, the onset of delinquent and antisocial behavior occurs much earlier for most offenders, and (2) there is no single pathway to delinquency. Using these findings, Thornberry and other experts have suggested that delinquency prevention should begin much before a child becomes a chronic offender and involved with the juvenile justice system.

Delinquency Prevention Begins before Birth

Delinquency prevention programs can begin as early as infancy — some programs even include prenatal care. Effective home visitation programs during pregnancy can improve a mother's prenatal health care and diet and can reduce her smoking and drug use. After the baby is born, home visitation programs can improve parenting behaviors. These factors reduce the chances of the early onset of antisocial behavior in children. In one program, which has been studied longitudinally over fifteen years, nurses provide prenatal and early childhood home visits. The program has produced positive interim results. Program participants posted a 75 percent reduction in state-verified cases of child abuse and neglect, a 32 percent reduction in emergency room visits, an 80 percent increase in employment by unmarried women, and a 43 percent reduction in subsequent children for unmarried women, as compared with a control group.

Child maltreatment — that is, physical or sexual abuse or neglect — has been identified as a risk factor for subsequent delinquency. Research shows that delinquency rates for children exposed to long-term, chronic parental neglect are particularly high. According to findings in the Rochester Youth Development Study, a long-term study of at-risk youths, child maltreatment places these children at risk for a variety of adolescent problem behaviors such as drug use, school failure, and teen pregnancy out of wedlock. Other studies have shown that maltreatment leads to a series of negative outcomes for children and youth, such as poor self-esteem, poor academic performance, teen pregnancy, and neurological disorders that affect learning and health. These findings underline the importance of including child maltreatment as a target of early prevention programs. Social support for parents and parent-training strategies can help prevent maltreatment. Providing social services to maltreated children may also decrease the risk of later delinquency.

Serving Youth with Multiple Needs

Children with multiple problem behaviors are overrepresented in the juvenile justice system. For example, a child may exhibit antisocial behavior, substance abuse, and academic failure. Therefore, both risk and protective factors need to be dealt with simultaneously through comprehensive services.

A number of approaches have been employed. Project Star and the Seattle Social Development Project provide skills development training for parents and children and family-centered and school-based initiatives. These programs target malleable risk factors such as parenting difficulties, family adversity, disturbed peer relations, and poor family social support and attempt to improve protective factors such as positive classroom atmosphere and rewarding school experiences. These and similar programs, such as the Starting Early–Starting Smart Program and the Kaleidoscope Program, emphasize the importance of matching services to individual needs. Individualized services should be provided for each adolescent within his or her natural environment rather than force-fitting the adolescent into the modular structure of programs.

Other areas to consider in recognizing and serving youth with multiple needs are fetal alcohol syndrome, attention deficit hyperactivity disorder, and victimization. Early identification and effective treatment of children with these and other needs would decrease the number of youths who come before the juvenile justice system. To accomplish this, better coordination is needed among governmental agencies at all levels.

Critical Thinking

Although early intervention strategies hold the promise of effective delinquency prevention, are there problems with labeling youths potential troublemakers before they actually violate the law? Explain.

Let's say an at-risk child needs special educational help in a boarding school that costs five times as much as a regular school. Should the government bear the cost of that educational experience to prevent delinquency? Why or why not? Should highly talented children be given the same type of aid to nurture their artistic or scientific abilities? Why or why not?

InfoTrac College Edition Research

Early childhood intervention programs may help improve a child's development and reduce the risk of future delinquency. To read more about these programs, check out Gerald W. Bracey, The impact of early intervention, *Phi Delta Kappan* (77) March 1996, p. 510.

SOURCE: Terence P. Thornberry, "Delinquency Prevention," *Juvenile Justice* 4 (1998): 12–15.

supports the fact that warehousing juveniles without proper treatment does little to deter future delinquent and criminal behavior. The most effective secure detention and corrections programs are those that provide individual services or a small number of participants. Large training schools have not reduced recidivism.

Part of the graduated sanction movement has been to create blended sanctions that combine correctional involvement in the juvenile and adult systems. Figure 15.6 illustrates this middle ground between the juvenile and adult justice systems.

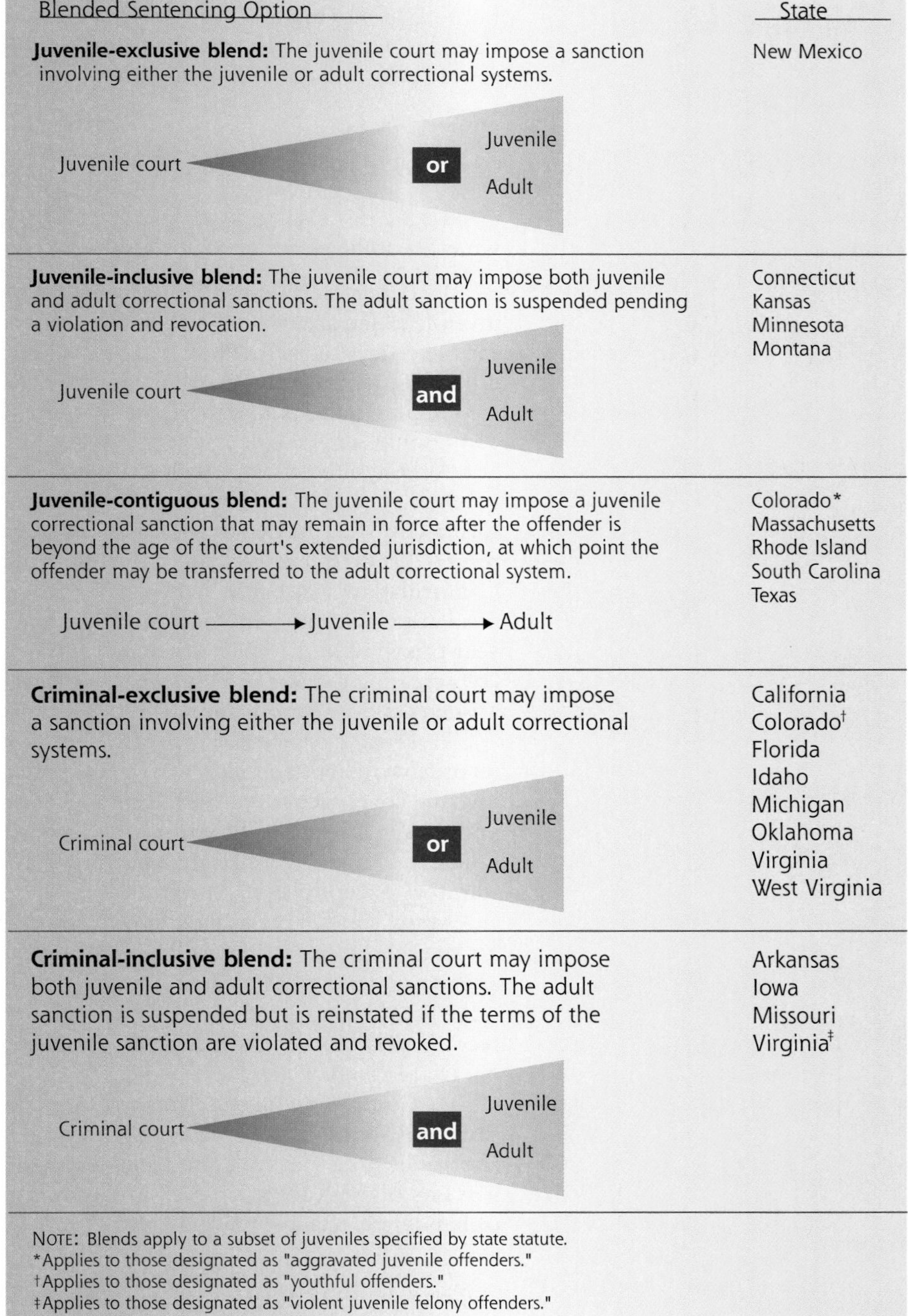

Figure 15.6
Blended sentencing options create a middle ground between traditional juvenile sanctions and adult sanctions.

SOURCE: Shay Bilchik, *1999 National Report Service: Juvenile Justice, A Century of Change* (Washington, D.C.: OJJDP, 1999), 19.

Increasing Waiver Treating juveniles like adults is the last component to an overall strategy for juvenile justice. This policy affects the numbers and types of juvenile cases going to adult courts. The number of delinquency cases waived to criminal court has grown from 7,200 in 1985 to upward of 15,000 today. As a result, more juvenile offenders are being sentenced as adults and incarcerated in adult prisons.

Getting tough on juvenile crime is the primary motivation for moving cases to the adult criminal justice system. Some commentators argue that transferring juveniles is a statement that juvenile crime is taken seriously by society; others believe the fear of being transferred serves as a deterrence. Whatever the stated purpose of moving cases to the adult court, more research is needed to substantiate the claim that the transfer process reduces crime and to designate the role it should play in a comprehensive crime control strategy.[53]

CURRENT AND FUTURE ISSUES IN JUVENILE JUSTICE

Beyond these issues, what are some of the major programs affecting juvenile justice today?

1. *Parental responsibility statutes* Related to a get-tough philosophy about juvenile crime are new laws to hold parents criminally and civilly responsible for the crimes of their children. The goal of these statutes is to prevent juvenile crime by requiring parents to be more accountable for their children. Some laws also require parents to participate with the juvenile in counseling programs or community service work.

Although the effectiveness of these laws has not been conclusively evaluated, parental responsibility laws have been adopted in a number of jurisdictions. California's law has misdemeanor sanctions against parents who fail ". . . to exercise reasonable care, supervision, protection and control over their children." The California law was expanded in 1988 so that violation of the provision brings a misdemeanor charge and may include a fine no greater than $2,500 and a one-year prison term. In 1995 Arizona, Louisiana, and Wyoming enacted comparable laws creating a crime of "improper" or "negligent" parental supervision, with misdemeanor sanctions similar to the law in California.[54]

2. *Privacy of juvenile records* For most of the twentieth century, juvenile records were kept confidential by case law or statute. The general rule was that juvenile court records — both legal and social — were considered confidential and thus inaccessible. Today, however, the record itself or the information contained in it can be opened by court order in many jurisdictions on the basis of statutory exception.

Many states have enacted laws authorizing a central repository for juvenile arrest records. Some states allow a juvenile adjudication for a criminal act, such as rape, to be used as evidence in a subsequent adult criminal proceeding for the same act, to show predisposition or criminal nature. In addition, a juvenile's records may be used during the disposition or sentencing stage of an adult criminal trial in some states.

3. *Controlling juvenile gun violence* Easy availability of guns is a significant contributor to teen violence. Research indicates a close tie among gun use, control of drug markets, and teen violence. Gang-related homicides almost always involve firearms. Unless significant efforts are made to control the spread of handguns, teenage murder rates should continue to rise.

At least thirty-five states have adopted legislation dealing with guns and children. In 1995 alone, nineteen states passed laws requiring schools to expel or suspend students for possessing weapons on school grounds.[55] At the federal level, laws have also been passed to restrict the possession, sale, and transfer of guns to juveniles. The Gun-Free Schools Act of 1994 requires local educational agencies receiving financial assistance to expel for one year any student who brings a firearm to school. The Youth Handgun Safety Act (part of the Omnibus Violent Crime Control and Law Enforcement Act of 1994) prohibits the possession or private transfer of a handgun to a juvenile. Although this legislation was enacted by the federal government, it is the state and local officials who can deal most effectively with juvenile gun violations.

SUMMARY

The juvenile justice system is concerned with delinquent children, as well as with those who are beyond the care and protection of their parents. Juveniles involved in antisocial behavior come under the jurisdiction of juvenile or family court systems. These courts belong to a system of juvenile justice agencies, including law enforcement, child care, and institutional services.

When a child is brought to the juvenile court, the proceedings are generally nonadversarial and informal. Representatives from different disciplines, such as lawyers, social workers, and psychiatrists, all play major roles in the judicial process.

In recent years the juvenile court system has become more legalistic by virtue of U.S. Supreme Court decisions that have granted children procedural safeguards. However, neither rehabilitation programs nor the application of due process rights has stemmed the growing tide of juvenile antisocial behavior. Perhaps the answer lies outside the courthouse in the form of job opportunities for juveniles, improved family relationships, and more effective school systems. How to cope with the needs of children in trouble remains one of the most controversial and frustrating issues in the justice system.

In the immediate future, the goals of the juvenile justice system are likely to be (1) reorganization of the juvenile system, (2) increased use of the juvenile waiver, (3) development of intermediate juvenile systems to handle violent offenders, and (4) tougher sentences. Perhaps the comprehensive juvenile justice strategy to reduce youth violence that was discussed is the most appropriate response to juvenile crime.

KEY TERMS

juvenile justice system
parens patriae
balanced and restorative justice model
poor laws
child savers
juvenile court
due process
juvenile delinquency
status offender
intake
detention
waiver
transfer hearing
adjudication
disposition
probation
commitment
treatment
comprehensive juvenile justice

 INFOTRAC COLLEGE EDITION EXERCISES

InfoTrac College Edition provides numerous articles on juvenile justice. You can use it to review many of the topics discussed in this chapter. For example, if you want to research the issues related to the abolition of the juvenile court, read

Barry C. Feld, "Abolish the Juvenile Court: Youthfulness, Criminal Responsibility, and Sentencing Policy," *Journal of Criminal Law and Criminology* 88 (1997): 68–136.

Stephen J. Morse, "Immaturity and Irresponsibility," *Journal of Criminal Law and Criminology* 88 (1997): 15–67.

For information on detention and incarceration issues, check out

Steven H. Rosenbaum, "Civil Rights Issues in Juvenile Detention and Correctional Systems," *Corrections Today* 61 (1999): 148.

QUESTIONS

1. Should status offenders be treated by the juvenile court? Explain. Should they be placed in confinement for running away or cutting school? Why or why not?
2. Should a juvenile ever be waived to adult court at the risk that the child will be incarcerated with adult felons? Why or why not?
3. Do you support the death penalty for children? Explain.
4. Should juveniles be given mandatory incarceration sentences for serious crimes, as adults are? Explain.
5. Is it fair to deny juveniles a jury trial? Why or why not?
6. Do you think the trend toward treating juveniles like adult offenders is desirable? Explain.

NOTES

1. Al Koski, "Trial Starts for Michigan Boy Charged with Murder," *Reuters Internet News,* 11 October 1999; L. L. Brasier and Desiree Cooper, "Abraham Jury Is Seated; Only 1 Member Is Black," *Detroit Free Press,* 29 October 1999, 1.

2. Keith Bradsher, "Boy Who Killed Gets 7 Years; Judge Says Law Is Too Harsh," *New York Times,* 14 January 2000, 1.

3. Howard Snyder and Melissa Sickmund, *Juvenile Offenders and Victims: 1999 National Report* (Washington, D.C.: Department of Justice, OJJDP, 1999). Herein cited as *Juvenile Offenders and Victims.*

4. *Vernonia School District v. Acton,* 515 U.S. 646, 115 S.Ct. 2386, 132 L.Ed.2d (1995).

5. Gordon Bazemore, "What's 'New' about the Balanced Approach," *Juvenile and Family Court Journal* 48 (1997): 1–21; see also Office of Justice Programs, "Balanced and Restorative Justice for Juveniles — a Framework for Juvenile Justice in the 21st Century" (Washington, D.C.: Department of Justice, OJJDP, 1997).

6. Material in this section depends heavily on Sanford J. Fox, "Juvenile Justice Reform: A Historical Perspective," *Stanford Law Review* 22 (1970): 1187–1205; Lawrence Stone, *The Family, Sex, and Marriage in England: 1500–1800* (New York: Harper & Row, 1977); Philippe Aries, *Century of Childhood: A Social History of Family Life* (New York: Vintage Press, 1962); Douglas R. Rendleman, "*Parens Patriae:* From Chancery to the Juvenile Court," *South Carolina Law Review* 23 (1971): 205–29; Wiley B. Sanders, "Some Early Beginnings of the Children's Court Movement in England," in *National Probation Association Yearbook* (New York: National Council on Crime and Delinquency, 1945); Anthony Platt, "The Rise of the Child-Saving Movement: A Study in Social Policy and Correctional Reform," *Annals of the American Academy of Political and Social Science* 381 (1979): 21–38; Anthony M. Platt, *The Child Savers: The Intervention of Delinquency* (Chicago: University of Chicago Press, 1969); Robert S. Pickett, *House of Refuge: Origins of Juvenile Reform in New York State, 1815–1857* (Syracuse, N.Y.: Syracuse University Press, 1969).

7. Douglas Besharov, *Juvenile Justice Advocacy: Practice in a Unique Court* (New York: Practicing Law Institute, 1974), 2; see also Jay Albanese, *Dealing with Delinquency — the Future of Juvenile Justice* (Chicago: Nelson-Hall, 1993).

8. 4 Eng.Rep. 1078 (1827).

9. Platt, *The Child Savers,* 11–38.

10. Fox, "Juvenile Justice Reform," 1188.

11. Pickett, *House of Refuge.*

12. Robert Mennel, *Thorns and Thistles* (Hanover, N.H.: University Press of New England, 1973); also Paul Cromwell, "Quaker Origins of Juvenile Justice Reform," *Juvenile and Family Court Journal* 38 (1987): 9–15.

13. Platt, *The Child Savers,* 116.

14. LaMar T. Empey, *American Delinquency: Its Meaning and Construction* (Homewood, Ill.: Dorsey Press, 1978), 515.

15. *Kent v. United States,* 383 U.S. 541, 86 S.Ct. 1045, 16 L.Ed.2d 84 (1966); *In re Gault,* 387 U.S. 1, 87 S.Ct. 1428, 18 L.Ed.2d 527 (1967): Juveniles have the right to notice, counsel, confrontation, and cross-examination and to the privileges against self-incrimination in juvenile court proceedings. *In re Winship,* 397 U.S. 358, 90 S.Ct. 1068, 25 L.Ed.2d 368 (1970): Proof beyond a reasonable doubt is necessary for conviction in juvenile proceedings. *Breed v. Jones,* 421 U.S. 519, 95 S.Ct. 1779, 44 L.Ed.2d 346 (1975): Jeopardy attaches in a juvenile court adjudicatory hearing, thus barring subsequent prosecution for the same offense as an adult.

16. Public Law 93-415 (1974).

17. For a comprehensive view of juvenile law, see, generally, Joseph J. Senna and Larry J. Siegel, *Juvenile Law: Cases and Comments,* 2d ed. (St. Paul: West, 1992).

18. FBI, *Crime in the United States, 1998* (Washington, D.C.: Government Printing Office, 1999), 220.

19. Howard N. Snyder, "Juvenile Arrests, 1998," *Juvenile Justice Bulletin* (December 1999): 12.

20. *Fare v. Michael C.,* 442 U.S. 707 (1979).

21. Anne L. Stahl, *Delinquency Cases in Juvenile Courts, 1996* (Washington, D.C.: Department of Justice, OJJDP, 1999), 1.

22. Fox Butterfield, "Justice Besieged," *New York Times,* 21 July 1997, A16.

23. *Schall v. Martin,* 467 U.S. 253, 104 S.Ct. 2403, 81 L.Ed.2d 207 (1984).

24. See *Juvenile Justice and Delinquency Prevention Act* of 1974, 42 U.S.C., sec. 5633.

25. Ira Schwartz, Linda Harris, and Laurie Levi, "The Jailing of Juveniles in Minnesota," *Crime and Delinquency* 34 (1988): 131; also Barry Krisberg and Robert DeComo, *Juveniles Taken into Custody — 1991* (San Francisco: National Council on Crime and Delinquency, 1993), 25.

26. Schwartz et al., "The Jailing of Juveniles in Minnesota," 134.

27. Eugene Rhoden, "Disproportionate Minority Representation — First Steps to a Solution," *Juvenile Justice* 2 (1994): 9.

28. 383 U.S. 541, 86 S.Ct. 1045, 16 L.Ed.2d 84 (1966).

29. 421 U.S. 519, 528, 95 S.Ct. 1779, 1785, 44 L.Ed.2d 346 (1975).

30. Alan Karpelowitz, *State Legislative Priorities — 1995* (Denver: National Conference of State Legislatures, 1995), 10.

31. Dale Parent et al., *Key Issues in Criminal Justice: Transferring Serious Juvenile Offenders to Adult Courts* (Washington, D.C.: National Institute of Justice, 1997).

32. Barry Feld, "The Juvenile Court Meets the Principle of the Offense: Legislative Changes in Juvenile Waiver Statutes," *Journal of Criminal Law and Criminology* 78 (1987): 471–533; see also John Kramer, Henry Sontheimer, and John Lemmon, "Pennsylvania Waiver to Adult Court" (Paper presented at the annual meeting of the American Society of Criminology, San Francisco, November 1991): Authors confirm that juveniles tried in adult courts are generally male, age 17 or older, and disproportionately minorities.

33. Parent et al., *Key Issues in Criminal Justice.*

34. 387 U.S. 1, 87 S.Ct. 1428, 18 L.Ed.2d 527 (1967).

35. 397 U.S. 358, 90 S.Ct. 1068, 25 L.Ed.2d 368 (1970).

36. 403 U.S. 528, 91 S.Ct. 1976, 29 L.Ed.2d 647 (1971).

37. Victor Streib, *Death Penalty for Juveniles* (Bloomington: Indiana University Press, 1987); also Paul Reidinger, "The Death Row Kids," *American Bar Association Journal* 70 (1989): 78; also, Note, "The Death Penalty and 8th Amendment, an Analysis of *Stanford v. Kentucky,*" *Yale Law Review* 35 (1990): 641.

38. See Joseph Goldstein, Anna Freud, and Albert Solnit, *Beyond the Best Interest of the Child* (New York: Free Press, 1973).

39. See Michael Serrill, "Police Write a New Law on Juvenile Crime," *Police Magazine* (September 1979): 47; see also A. Schneider and D. Schram, *Assessment of Juvenile Justice Reform in Washington State,* vols. 1–4 (Washington, D.C.: Department of Justice, Institute of Policy Analysis, 1983); T. Castellano, "Justice Model in the Juvenile Justice System — Washington State's Experience," *Law and Policy* 8 (1986): 479.

40. Anne Schneider, *Guide to Juvenile Restitution* (Washington, D.C.: Department of Justice, 1985).

41. "Colorado OKs New Way to Handle Violent Juvenile Offenders," *Criminal Justice Newsletter* 9 (1993): 4.

42. See John Wilson, "Disproportionate Minority Representation," *Juvenile Justice* 2 (1994): 21.

43. Melissa Sickmund, Howard Snyder, and Eileen Poe-Yamagata, *Juvenile Offenders and Victims: 1997 Update on Violence* (Washington, D.C.: Department of Justice, OJJDP, 1997), 18.

44. National Conference of State Legislatures, *A Legislator's Guide to Comprehensive Juvenile Justice, Juvenile Detention, and Corrections* (Denver: National Conference of State Legislators, 1996).

45. 349 F. Supp. 575 (S.D. N.Y., 1972).

46. 346 F. Supp. 1354 (D. R.I., 1972).

47. 364 F. Supp. 166 (E.D. Tex., 1973).

48. 491 F. 2d 352 (7th Cir., 1974).

49. Fox Butterfield, "Justice Besieged — Two Part Series on Juvenile Courts," *New York Times,* 21, 22 July 1997, 1.

50. Sarah Ingersoll, "The National Juvenile Justice Action Plan," *Juvenile Justice* 2 (1997): 11–21.

51. National Conference of State Legislators, *A Legislator's Guide to Comprehensive Juvenile Justice,* 1.

52. James Howell, ed., *Guide for Implementing the Comprehensive Strategy for Serious, Violent, and Chronic Juvenile Offenders* (Washington, D.C.: Department of Justice, OJJDP, 1995).

53. Carol J. DeFrances and Kevin Strom, *Juveniles Prosecuted in State Criminal Courts* (Washington, D.C.: Bureau of Justice Statistics, 1997).

54. OJJDP, *Juvenile Justice Reform Initiative in the States, 1994–1996* (Washington, D.C.: Government Printing Office, 1997).

55. Office of Justice Programs, *Reducing Youth Gun Violence* (Washington, D.C.: Department of Justice, OJJDP, 1996).

Glossary

accountability system Dealing with police corruption by making superiors responsible for the behavior of their subordinates.

actus reus An illegal act. The actus reus can be an affirmative act, such as taking money or shooting someone, or a failure to act, such as failing to take proper precautions while driving a car.

adjudication The determination of guilt or innocence; a judgment concerning criminal charges. The majority of offenders charged plead guilty; of the remainder, some cases are adjudicated by a judge and a jury, some are adjudicated by a judge without a jury, and others are dismissed.

adversarial procedure The procedure used to determine truth in the adjudication of guilt or innocence in which the defense (advocate for the accused) is pitted against the prosecution (advocate for the state), with the judge acting as arbiter of the legal rules. Under the adversary system, the burden is on the state to prove the charges beyond a reasonable doubt. This system of having the two parties publicly debate has proved to be the most effective method of achieving the truth regarding a set of circumstances. (Under the accusatory, or inquisitorial, system, which is used in continental Europe, the charge is evidence of guilt that the accused must disprove; the judge takes an active part in the proceedings.)

appellate court A court that reconsiders a case that has already been tried in order to determine whether the measures used complied with accepted rules of criminal procedure and were in line with constitutional doctrines.

Arizona v. Evans The 1995 U.S. Supreme Court case that added computer errors to the list of valid reasons that a search warrant might be issued in error but in good faith.

arraignment The step at which accused offenders are read the charges against them and are asked how they plead. In addition, the accused are advised of their rights. Possible pleas are guilty, not guilty, nolo contendere, and not guilty by reason of insanity.

arrest The taking of a person into the custody of the law, the legal purpose of which is to restrain the accused until he or she can be held accountable for the offense at court proceedings. The legal requirement for an arrest is probable cause. Arrests for investigation, suspicion, or harassment are improper and of doubtful legality. The police have the responsibility to use only the reasonable physical force necessary to make an arrest. The summons has been used as a substitute for arrest.

assigned counsel A lawyer appointed by the court to represent a defendant in a criminal case because the person is too poor to hire counsel.

Auburn system The prison system developed in New York during the nineteenth century that stressed congregate working conditions.

avertable recidivist An offender who has been convicted of a prior offense but is free to violate the law because he or she has received a community sentence instead of incarceration. If he (she) has been imprisoned his (her) crimes would have been averted.

bail The monetary amount for or condition of pretrial release, normally set by a judge at the initial appearance. The purpose of bail is to ensure the return of the accused at subsequent proceedings. If the accused is unable to make bail, he or she is detained in jail. The Eighth Amendment provides that excessive bail shall not be required.

bail bonding The business of providing bail to needy offenders, usually at an exorbitant rate of interest.

Bail Reform Act of 1984 Federal legislation that provides for both greater emphasis on release on recognizance for nondangerous offenders and preventive detention for those who present a menace to the community.

balanced and restorative justice model A new model of juvenile justice focusing on victim restoration, improving offender abilities, and protecting the public. Offenders, victims, and the community are all active participants.

beat A defined patrol area.

bench trial The trial of a criminal matter by a judge only. The accused waives any constitutional right to trial by jury.

Bill of Rights The first ten amendments to the U.S. Constitution.

biological theory The school of thought holding that certain biochemical, neurological, and genetic factors cause people to commit crime.

blameworthy The culpability or guilt a person maintains for participating in a particular criminal offense.

blue curtain The secretive, insulated police culture that isolated officers from the rest of society.

booking process The administrative record of an arrest, listing the offender's name, address, physical description, date of birth, and employer; the time of arrest; the offense; and the name of the arresting officer. Photographing and fingerprinting of the offender are also part of the booking process.

boot camp A short-term militaristic correctional facility in which inmates undergo intensive physical conditioning and discipline.

Boykin v. Alabama The 1969 U.S. Supreme Court decision upholding that a defendant's plea bargain can only be accepted if it is a voluntary affirmative statement in a judicial hearing.

broken windows model The term used to describe the role of the police as maintainers of community order and safety.

brutalization effect The belief that capital punishment creates an atmosphere of brutality that enhances, rather than deters, the level of violence in society. The death penalty reinforces the view that violence is an appropriate response to provocations.

Burger v. Kemp The 1987 U.S. Supreme Court decision upholding that no conflict of interest results when a defense attorney represents two defendants charged with the same crime as long as counsel acts competently and effectively.

bus sweep Police investigation technique where the police board a bus or train without suspicion of illegal activity and question passengers, asking for identification and seeking permission to search their baggage.

***Carriers* case** A fifteenth-century case that defined the law of theft and reformulated the concept of taking the possession of another.

challenge for cause Removing a juror because he or she is biased or has prior knowledge about a case, or for other reasons that demonstrate the individual's inability to render a fair and impartial judgment in a case.

charge In a criminal case, the specific crime the defendant is accused of committing.

charge In a criminal trial, the instructions the judge gives to the jury, regarding principles of law that should guide and control their decision.

child savers Late nineteenth-century reformers in America who developed programs for troubled youths and influenced legislation creating the juvenile justice system.

Chimel v. California The 1969 U.S. Supreme Court decision that limited the scope of a search made by a police officer to the immediate area under the defendant's control.

chivalry hypothesis The view that the low female crime and delinquency rates are a reflection of the leniency with which police treat female offenders.

choice theory The school of thought holding that people will engage in delinquent and criminal behavior after weighing the consequences and benefits of their actions. Delinquent behavior is a rational choice made by a motivated offender who perceives the chances of gain outweigh any perceived punishment or loss.

chronic offender A delinquent offender who is arrested five or more times before he or she is eighteen and who stands a good chance of becoming an adult criminal; these offenders are responsible for more than half of all serious crimes.

circumstantial (indirect) evidence Evidence not bearing on the fact in dispute but on various indirect circumstances from which the judge or jury might infer the existence of the fact (e.g., the defendant was seen in the house with wet clothing is circumstantial evidence that the person walked in the rain).

civil law All law that is not criminal, including torts (personal wrongs), contract, property, maritime, and commercial law.

commitment Decision of judge ordering an adjudicated and sentenced juvenile offender to be placed in a correctional facility.

common law Early English law, developed by judges, that incorporated Anglo-Saxon tribal custom, feudal rules and practices, and the everyday rules of behavior of local villages. Common law became the standardized law of the land in England and eventually formed the basis of the criminal law in the United States.

community service restitution An alternative sanction that requires an offender to work in the community at such tasks as cleaning public parks or working with disabled children in lieu of an incarceration sentence.

community treatment The attempt by correctional agencies to maintain convicted offenders in the community instead of a secure facility; it includes probation, parole, and residential programs.

complaint A sworn allegation made in writing to a court or judge that an individual is guilty of some designated (complained of) offense. This is often the first legal document filed regarding a criminal offense. The complaint can be "taken out" by the victim, the police officer, the district attorney, or another interested party. Although the complaint charges an offense, an indictment or information may be the formal charging document.

comprehensive juvenile justice The current reform model of balancing policies for juvenile offenders with preventive and community programs aimed at young people and successful control programs for aggressive offenders.

concurrent sentence A prison sentence for two or more criminal acts that are served simultaneously, and run together.

conflict theory The view that human behavior is shaped by interpersonal conflict and that those who maintain social power will use it to further their own needs.

confrontation clause The constitutional right of a criminal defendant to see and cross-examine all the witnesses against him or her.

congregate system The Auburn Prison, one of the nation's first correctional facilities, was a congregate system since most prisoners ate and worked in groups.

consecutive sentence A prison sentence for two or more criminal acts that are served one after the other, or that follow one another.

consensus view of crime The belief that the majority of citizens in a society share common ideals and work toward a common good and that crimes are acts that are outlawed because they conflict with the rules of the majority and are harmful to society.

consent search A voluntary agreement to allow a search with the knowledge that any evidence may be used at the defendant's trial.

constable In medieval England, an appointed official who administered and supervised the legal affairs of a small community.

contract system (attorney) Providing counsel to indigent offenders by having attorneys under contract to the county handle all (or some) such cases.

contract system (convict) The system used early in the twentieth century by which inmates were leased out to private industry to work.

convict-lease system The system whereby the state leased its prisoners to a business for a fixed annual fee and gave up supervision and control.

corpus dilecti The body of the crime, made up of the actus reus and mens rea.

court of last resort A court that handles the final appeal on a matter. The U.S. Supreme Court is the official court of last resort for criminal matters.

courtroom work group The phrase used to denote that all parties in the adversary process work together in a cooperative effort to settle cases with the least amount of effort and conflict.

crime A violation of societal rules of behavior as interpreted and expressed by a criminal legal code created by people holding social and political power. Individuals who violate these rules are subject to sanctions by state authority, social stigma, and loss of status.

crime control A model of criminal justice that emphasizes the control of dangerous offenders and the protection of society. Its advocates call for harsh punishments as a deterrent to crime, such as the death penalty.

crime fighter The police style that stresses dealing with hard crimes and arresting dangerous criminals.

criminal justice The decision-making points from the initial investigation or arrest by police to the eventual release of the offender and his or her reentry into society; the various sequential criminal justice stages through which the offender passes.

criminal law The body of rules that define crimes, set their punishments out, and mandate the procedures in carrying out the criminal justice process.

criminal procedure The rules and laws that define the operation of the criminal proceedings. Procedural law describes the methods that must be followed in obtaining warrants, investigating offenses, effecting lawful arrests, conducting trials, introducing evidence, sentencing convicted offenders, and reviewing cases by appellate courts.

critical view of crime The belief that the law is controlled by the rich and powerful who shape its content to ensure their continued economic domination of society. The criminal justice system is an instrument of social and economic repression.

cross-examination The process in which the defense and the prosecution interrogate witnesses during a trial.

cruel and unusual punishment Physical punishment or punishment that is far in excess of that given to people under similar circumstances and is therefore banned by the Eighth Amendment. The death penalty has so far not been considered cruel and unusual if it is administered in a fair and nondiscriminatory fashion.

curtilage The fields attached to a house.

cynicism The belief that most people's actions are motivated solely by personal needs and selfishness.

DARE Drug Abuse Resistance Education, a school-based antidrug program initiated by the Los Angeles Police Department and now adopted around the United States.

day fine A fine geared to the average daily income of the convicted offender in an effort to bring equity to the sentencing process.

day reporting center (DRC) A nonresidential community-based treatment program.

deadly force The ability of the police to kill suspects if they resist arrest or present a danger to the officer or the community. The police cannot use deadly force against an unarmed fleeing felon.

death-qualified jury The process during jury selection of removing any juror in a capital case who acknowledges that he or she will not convict knowing that there is a potential for the death penalty being applied. The U.S. Supreme Court has ruled that prosecutors have the right to discharge those jurors who would not consider the death penalty under any circumstances.

decriminalization Reducing the penalty for a criminal act but not actually legalizing it.

defeminization The process by which policewomen become enculturated into the police profession at the expense of their feminine identity.

deinstitutionalization The movement to remove as many offenders as possible from secure confinement and treat them in the community.

demeanor The way in which a person outwardly manifests his or her personality.

deposit bail The monetary amount set by a judge at a hearing as a condition of pretrial release, ordering a percentage of the total bond required to be paid by the defendant.

detention The temporary care of a child alleged to be a delinquent or status offender who requires secure custody, pending court disposition.

determinate sentence A fixed term of incarceration, such as three years' imprisonment. Determinate sentences are felt by many to be too restrictive for rehabilitative purposes; the advantage is that offenders know how much time they have to serve — that is, when they will be released.

deterrent effect Stopping or reducing crime by convincing would-be criminals that they stand a significant risk of being apprehended and punished for their crimes.

developmental theory The view that social interactions developed over the life course shape behavior. Some interactions, such as involvement with deviant peers, encourage law violations, whereas others, such as marriage and military service, may help people desist from crime.

direct examination The questioning of one's own (prosecution or defense) witness during a trial.

directed verdict The right of a judge to direct a jury to acquit a defendant because the state has not proven the elements of the crime or otherwise has not established guilt according to law.

discretion The use of personal decision making and choice in carrying out operations in the criminal justice system. For example, police discretion can involve the decision to make an arrest; prosecutorial discretion can involve the decision to accept a plea bargain.

displacement The process by which the presence of police officers in one area causes criminals to move to another, less well-guarded neighborhood.

disposition For juvenile offenders, the equivalent of sentencing for adult offenders. The theory is that disposition is more rehabilitative than retributive. Possible dispositions may be to dismiss the case; release the youth to the custody of his or her parents; place the offender on probation; or send him or her to an institution or state correctional institution.

diversion A noncriminal alternative to trial, usually featuring counseling, job training, and educational opportunities.

DNA profiling The identification of criminal suspects by matching DNA samples taken from their person with specimens found at the crime scene.

double marginality According to Alex, the social burden African-American police officers carry by being both minority group members and law enforcement officers.

Drug Enforcement Administration (DEA) The federal agency that enforces federal drug control laws.

due process The basic constitutional principle based on the concept of the privacy of the individual and the complementary concept of limitation on governmental power; a safeguard against arbitrary and unfair state procedures in judicial or administrative proceedings. Embodied in the due process concept are the basic rights of a defendant in criminal proceedings and the requisites for a fair trial. These rights and requirements have been expanded by appellate court decisions and include (1) timely notice of a hearing or trial that informs the accused of the charges against him or her; (2) the opportunity to confront accusers and to present evidence on one's own behalf before an impartial jury or judge; (3) the presumption of innocence under which guilt must be proven by legally obtained evidence and the verdict must be supported by the evidence presented; (4) the right of an accused to be warned of constitutional rights at the earliest stage of the criminal process; (5) protection against self-incrimination; (6) assistance of counsel at every critical stage of the criminal process; and (7) the guarantee that an individual will not be tried more than once for the same offense (double jeopardy).

due process (juvenile) The constitutional principle guaranteed by the Fifth, Sixth, and Fourteenth Amendments, which embodies the legal rights for children in judicial proceedings.

Durham rule A definition of insanity used in New Hampshire that required that the crime be excused if it was a product of a mental illness.

electronic monitoring (EM) Requiring a convicted offender to wear a monitoring device as part of his or her community sentence. Electronic monitoring is typically part of a house arrest order and enables the probation department to ensure that the offender is complying with court-ordered limitations on his (her) freedom.

entrapment A criminal defense that maintains the police originated the criminal idea or initiated the criminal action.

equity The action or practice of awarding each his or her just due; sanctions based on equity seek to compensate individual victims and the general society for their losses due to crime.

Escobedo v. Illinois The 1964 U.S. Supreme Court decision upholding that the Sixth Amendment, which guarantees the right to counsel, applies to preindictment interrogations when the accused asks to consult with an attorney.

exclusionary rule The principle that prohibits using evidence illegally obtained in a trial. Based on the Fourth Amendment "right of the people to be secure in their persons, houses, papers, and effects, against unreasonable searches and seizures," the rule is not a bar to prosecution because legally obtained evidence may be available that may be used in a trial.

Federal Bureau of Investigation (FBI) The arm of the U.S. Justice Department that investigates violations of federal law, gathers crime statistics, runs a comprehensive crime laboratory, and helps train local law enforcement officers.

felony A more serious offense that carries a penalty of incarceration in a state prison, usually for one year or more. Persons convicted of felony offenses lose such rights as the rights to vote, hold elective office, or maintain certain licenses.

felony court A state or federal court that has jurisdiction over felony offenses — serious crimes that carry a penalty of incarceration in a state or federal prison for one year or more.

field interrogation The questioning by police of a person suspected of a crime at the time of apprehension and arrest.

fine Levying a money payment on offenders to compensate society for their misdeeds.

First Amendment The U.S. constitutional amendment that guarantees freedom of speech, religion, press, and assembly and the right of the people to petition the government for a redress of grievances.

Florida v. Bostick The 1991 U.S. Supreme Court decision upholding the police investigation technique known as the *bus sweep,* where without probable cause the police can search a person's luggage.

foot patrol Police patrols that take officers out of cars and put them on a walking beat in order to strengthen ties with the community.

forfeiture The seizure of personal property by the state as a civil or criminal penalty.

Fourth Amendment The U.S. constitutional amendment that forbids unreasonable searches and seizures and requires probable cause for search warrants.

furlough A correctional policy that allows inmates to leave the institution for vocational or educational training, for employment, or to maintain family ties.

general deterrence A crime control policy that depends on the fear of criminal penalties. General deterrence measures, such as long prison sentences for violent crimes, are aimed at convincing the potential law violator that the pains associated with the crime outweigh the benefits.

Gideon v. Wainwright The 1963 U.S. Supreme Court case that granted counsel to indigent defendants in felony prosecutions.

good faith exception The principle of law holding that evidence may be used in a criminal trial even though the search warrant used to obtain it is technically faulty, if the police acted in good faith and to the best of their ability when they sought to obtain it from a judge.

grand jury A group (usually consisting of twenty-three citizens) chosen to hear testimony in secret and to issue formal criminal accusations (indictments). It also serves an investigatory function.

grass eaters A term to describe a police officer who accepts payoffs when everyday duties places him or her in a position to be solicited by the public.

halfway house A community-based correctional facility that houses inmates before their outright release so that they can become gradually acclimated to conventional society.

hands-off doctrine The legal practice of allowing prison administrators a free hand to run the institution even if correctional practices violate inmates' constitutional rights; ended with the onset of the prisoners' rights movement in the 1960s.

hearsay evidence Testimony that is not firsthand but related information told by a second party.

hot spots of crime Places from which a significant portion of all police calls originate. These hot spots include taverns and housing projects.

house arrest A form of an intermediate sanction that requires that the convicted offender spend a designated amount of time per week in his or her own home — for example, from 5 P.M. Friday until 8 A.M. Monday.

hue and cry A call for assistance in medieval England. The policy of self-help used in villages demanded that everyone respond if a citizen raised a hue and cry to get their aid.

hulk A mothballed ship that was used to house prisoners in eighteenth-century England.

hundred In medieval England, a group of one hundred families that had the responsibility to maintain the order and try minor offenses.

incapacitation The policy of keeping dangerous criminals in confinement to eliminate the risk of their repeating their offense in society.

index (Part I) crimes The eight crimes that, because of their seriousness and frequency, the FBI reports the incidence of in the annual Uniform Crime Reports. Index crimes include murder, rape, assault, robbery, burglary, arson, larceny, and motor vehicle theft.

indictment A written accusation returned by a grand jury charging an individual with a specified crime after determination of probable cause; the prosecutor presents enough evidence (a prima facie case) to establish probable cause.

indigent Person who is needy and poor or who lacks the means to hire an attorney.

in forma pauperis "In the manner of a pauper." A criminal defendant granted permission to proceed in forma pauperis is entitled to assistance of counsel at state expense.

indeterminate sentence A term of incarceration with a stated minimum and maximum length, such as a sentence to prison for a period of from three to ten years. The prisoner would be eligible for parole after the minimum sentence had been served. Based on the belief that sentences should fit the criminal, indeterminate sentences allow individualized sentences and provide for sentencing flexibility. Judges can set a high minimum to override the purpose of the indeterminate sentence.

information Like the indictment, a formal charging document. The prosecuting attorney makes out the information and files it in court. Probable cause is determined at the preliminary hearing, which, unlike grand jury proceedings, is public and attended by the accused and his or her attorney.

initial hearing The stage in the justice process during which the suspect is brought before a magistrate for consideration of bail. The suspect must be taken for an initial hearing within a "reasonable time" after arrest. For petty offenses, this step often serves as the final criminal proceedings, either by adjudication by a judge or the offering of a guilty plea.

inmate subculture The loosely defined culture that pervades prisons and has its own norms, rules, and language.

inmate social code Unwritten guidelines that express the values, attitudes, and types of behavior that older inmates demand of young ones. Passed on from one generation of inmates to another, the inmate social code represents the values of interpersonal relations within the prison.

insanity A legal defense that maintains a defendant was incapable of forming criminal intent because he or she suffers from a defect of reason or mental illness.

intake The process in which a probation officer settles cases at the initial appearance before the onset of formal criminal proceedings; also, process in which a juvenile referral is received and a decision is made to file a petition in the juvenile court, release the juvenile, or refer the juvenile elsewhere.

intensive probation supervision (IPS) A type of intermediate sanction involving small probation caseloads and strict monitoring on a daily or weekly basis.

intensive supervision parole (ISP) A limited-caseload program for those parolees who need intensive surveillance. Parolees are required to meet more often with parole officers than routine parolees and may also have frequent drug testing, serve a term in a community correctional system, and be electronically monitored.

intent An action that on its face indicates a criminal purpose — for example, breaking into a locked building or trespassing on someone's property; a guilty mind.

intermediate sanctions The group of punishments falling between probation and prison; "probation plus."

Community-based sanctions, including house arrest and intensive supervision, serve as alternatives to incarceration.

internal affairs The branch of the police department that investigates charges of corruption or misconduct made against police officers.

irresistible impulse test A test of criminal insanity where a person loses control and cannot stop from committing a crime because of mental illness.

jail A place to detain people awaiting trial, to serve as a lockup for drunks and disorderly individuals, and to confine convicted misdemeanants serving sentences of less than one year.

jailhouse lawyer An inmate trained in law or otherwise educated who helps other inmates prepare legal briefs and appeals.

judicial reprieve The common-law practice that allowed judges to suspend punishment so that convicted offenders could seek a pardon, gather new evidence, or demonstrate that they had reformed their behavior.

jury trial The process of deciding a case by a group of persons selected and sworn in to serve as jurors at a criminal trial, often as a six- or twelve-person jury.

just desert The philosophy of justice asserting that those who violate the rights of others deserve to be punished. The severity of punishment should be commensurate with the seriousness of the crime.

justice of the peace Established in 1326 England, the office was created to help the shire reeve in controlling the county and later took on judicial functions.

juvenile court A court that has original jurisdiction over persons defined by statute as juveniles and alleged to be delinquents or status offenders.

juvenile delinquency Participation in illegal behavior by a minor who falls under a statutory age limit.

juvenile justice system The system of agencies and organizations that deal with youths who commit acts of juvenile delinquency (crimes under a given age) and acts of noncriminal behavior (truancy and incorrigibility).

Knapp Commission A public body that led an investigation into police corruption in New York and uncovered a widespread network of payoffs and bribes.

landmark decision A decision handed down by the U.S. Supreme Court that becomes the law of the land and serves as a precedent for similar legal issues.

Law Enforcement Assistance Administration (LEAA) Funded by the federal government's Safe Streets Act, this agency provided technical assistance and hundreds of millions of dollars in aid to local and state justice agencies between 1969 and 1982.

law enforcer The police style that emphasizes the detection and apprehension aspects of police work. Law enforcers see the police role as one of enforcing all statutes and ordinances. According to this officer's view, duty is clearly set out in law, and the law enforcer stresses playing it "by the book."

law of precedent The legal principle by which the decision or holding in an earlier case becomes the standard with which subsequent similar cases are judged.

legalization The removal of all criminal penalties from a previously outlawed act.

less eligibility The correctional practice demanding that prison inmates do not enjoy benefits that exceed those of the indigent poor who have never been convicted of a crime. For example, educational opportunities should not be provided that are not freely obtainable by anyone in the general public.

life history A research method that uses the experiences of an individual as the unit of analysis, such as using the life experience of an individual gang member to understand the natural history of gang membership.

lower court A generic term referring to a court that has jurisdiction over misdemeanors and conducts preliminary investigations of felony charges.

M'Naghten rule A legal definition of insanity. According to M'Naghten, people are insane if they either do not know what they are doing or cannot distinguish between right and wrong.

make-believe families Formed by women in prison to compensate for the loss of family and loved ones, a peer unit that contains mother and father figures.

mandatory sentence A statutory requirement that a certain penalty shall be set and carried out in all cases on conviction for a specified offense or series of offenses.

Manhattan Bail Project The innovative experiment in bail reform that introduced and successfully tested the concept of release on recognizance.

Mapp v. Ohio The 1961 U.S. Supreme Court decision that applied the exclusionary rule to state criminal cases where evidence acquired through an unreasonable search and seizure must be excluded.

maximum-security prison A correctional institution that houses dangerous felons and maintains strict security measures, high walls, and limited contact with the outside world.

meat eaters A term used to describe a police officer who actively solicits bribes and vigorously engages in corrupt practices.

medical model A view of corrections holding that convicted offenders are victims of their environment who need care and treatment to transform them into valuable members of society.

medium-security prison A less secure institution that houses nonviolent offenders and provides more opportunities for contact with the outside world.

mens rea Guilty mind. The mental element of a crime or the intent to commit a criminal act.

methadone A synthetic narcotic used as a substitute for heroin in drug-control efforts.

minimum-security prison The least secure institution that houses white-collar and nonviolent offenders, maintains few security measures, and has liberal furlough and visitation policies.

***Miranda* warning** The result of two U.S. Supreme Court decisions (*Escobedo v. Illinois* and *Miranda v. Arizona*) that require police officers to inform individuals under arrest that they have a constitutional right to remain silent, that their statements can later be used against them in court, that they can have an attorney present to help them, and that the state will pay for an attorney if they cannot afford to hire one. Although aimed at protecting an individual during in-custody interrogation, the warning must also be given when the investigation shifts from the investigatory to the accusatory stage — that is, when suspicion begins to focus on an individual.

misdemeanor A minor crime usually punished by less than one year's imprisonment in a local institution, such as a county jail.

Missouri Plan A way of picking judges through nonpartisan elections as a means of ensuring judicial performance standards.

Mollen Commission An investigatory body formed in New York City in 1993 to scrutinize police misconduct.

monetary restitution A sanction that requires that convicted offenders compensate crime victims by reimbursing them for out-of-pocket losses caused by the crime. Losses can include property damage, lost wages, and medical costs.

National Crime Victimization Survey (NCVS) The ongoing victimization study conducted jointly by the Justice Department and the U.S. Census Bureau that surveys victims about their experiences with law violation.

neighborhood-oriented policing (NOP) Community policing efforts aimed at individual neighborhoods.

nolle prosequi The term used when a prosecutor decides to drop a case after a complaint has been formally made. Reasons for a nolle prosequi include evidence insufficiency, reluctance of witnesses to testify, police error, and office policy.

nonindex (Part II) crimes All other crimes except the eight index crimes recorded by the FBI. The FBI records all arrests made by police of Part II crimes.

nonintervention A justice philosophy that emphasizes the least intrusive treatment possible. Among its central policies are decarceration, diversion, and decriminalization. In other words, less is better.

official crime statistics Compiled by the FBI in its Uniform Crime Reports, these are a tally of serious crimes reported to police agencies each year.

order maintenance (peacekeeping) The order-maintenance aspect of the police role involves peacekeeping, maintaining order and authority without the need for formal arrest, "handling the situation," and keeping things under control by using threats, persuasion, and understanding.

parens patriae Power of the state to act on behalf of the child and provide care and protection equivalent to that of a parent.

parole The early release of a prisoner from imprisonment subject to conditions set by a parole board. Depending on the jurisdiction, inmates must serve a certain portion of their sentences before becoming eligible for parole. The conditions of parole may require the individual to report regularly to a parole officer, to refrain from criminal conduct, to maintain and support his or her family, to avoid contact with other convicted criminals, to abstain from using alcohol and drugs, to remain within the jurisdiction, and so on. Violations of the conditions of parole may result in revocation of parole, in which case the individual will be returned to prison. The concept behind parole is to allow the release of the offender to community supervision, where rehabilitation and readjustment will be facilitated.

particularity The requirement that a search warrant state precisely where the search is to take place and what items are to be seized.

penitentiary A state or federal correctional institution for incarceration of felony offenders for terms of one year or more.

penitentiary house A secure correctional facility, based on the Quaker concept that incarcerated criminals should do "penitence."

Pennsylvania system The prison system developed during the nineteenth century that stressed total isolation and individual penitence as a means of reform.

peremptory challenge The dismissal of a potential juror by either the prosecution or the defense for unexplained, discretionary reasons.

plain-view doctrine The doctrine that evidence in plain view to police officers may be seized without a search warrant.

plea bargaining The discussion between the defense counsel and the prosecution by which the accused agrees to plead guilty for certain considerations. The advantage to the defendant may be a reduction of the charges, a lenient sentence, or (in the case of multiple charges) dropped charges. The advantage to the prosecution is that a conviction is obtained without the time and expense of lengthy trial proceedings.

police brutality Usually involves such actions as the use of abusive language, unnecessary use of force or coercion, threats, prodding with nightsticks, stopping and searching people to harass them, and so on.

police chief The top administrator of the police department, who sets policy and has general control over all operating branches.

police–community relations Programs developed by police departments to improve relations with the community and develop cooperation with citizens. The forerunner of the community policing model.

police officer style The belief that the bulk of police officers can be classified into ideal personality types. Popular types include *supercops,* who desire to enforce only serious crimes, such as robbery and rape; *professionals,* who use a broad definition of police work; *service-oriented officers,* who see their job as a helping profession; and *avoiders,* who do as little as possible. The actual existence of ideal police officer types has been much debated.

police productivity The amount of order, crime control, and other law enforcement activities provided by an individual officer and consequently by the department as a whole.

poor laws Seventeenth-century laws in England that bound out vagrants and abandoned children as indentured servants to masters.

preliminary hearing (probable cause hearing) The step at which criminal charges initiated by an information are tested for probable cause; the prosecution presents enough evidence to establish probable cause — that is, a prima facie case. The hearing is public and may be attended by the accused and his or her attorney.

preponderance of the evidence The level of proof in civil cases; more than half the evidence supports the allegations of one side.

presentence investigation An investigation performed by a probation officer attached to a trial court after the conviction of a defendant. The report contains information about the defendant's background, education, previous employment, and family; his or her own statement concerning the offense; prior criminal record; interviews with neighbors or acquaintances; and his or her mental and physical condition (i.e., information that would not be made public record in the case of guilty plea or that would be inadmissible as evidence at a trial but could be influential and important at the sentencing stage).

pretrial detention Holding an offender in secure confinement before trial.

pretrial diversion A program that provides nonpunitive community-based alternatives to more intrusive forms of punishment such as jail or prison.

pretrial procedure A proceeding held before an official trial, such as a pretrial hearing, bail review, and pretrial diversion to a noncriminal program.

preventive detention The practice of holding dangerous suspects before trial without bail.

prison A state or federal correctional institution for incarceration of felony offenders for terms of one year or more.

prisonization Assimilation into the separate culture in the prison that has its own set of rewards and behaviors. This loosely defined culture that pervades prisons has its own norms, rules, and language. The traditional culture is now being replaced by a violent gang culture.

pro se The defense of self-representation.

proactive policing A police department policy emphasizing stopping crimes before they occur rather than reacting to crimes that have already occurred.

probable cause The evidentiary criterion necessary to sustain an arrest or the issuance of an arrest or search warrant; less than absolute certainty or "beyond a reasonable doubt" but greater than mere suspicion or "hunch." Probable cause consists of a set of facts, information, circumstances, or conditions that would lead a reasonable person to believe that an offense was committed and that the accused committed that offense. An arrest made without probable cause may be susceptible to prosecution as an illegal arrest under "false imprisonment" statutes.

probation A sentence entailing the conditional release of a convicted offender into the community under the supervision of the court (in the form of a probation officer), subject to certain conditions for a specified time. The conditions are usually similar to those of parole. (Note: Probation is a sentence, an alternative to incarceration; parole is administrative release from incarceration.) Violation of the conditions of probation may result in revocation of probation.

problem-oriented policing A style of police operations that stresses proactive problem solving, rather than reactive crime fighting.

proof beyond a reasonable doubt The standard of proof needed to convict in a criminal case. The evidence offered in court does not have to amount to absolute certainty, but it should leave no reasonable doubt that the defendant committed the alleged crime.

prosecutor Representative of the state (executive branch) in criminal proceedings; advocate for the state's case — the charge — in the adversary trial, for example, the attorney general of the United States, U.S. attorneys, attorneys general of the states, district attorneys, and police prosecutors. The prosecutor participates in investigations both before and after arrest, prepares legal documents, participates in obtaining arrest or search warrants, decides whether to charge a suspect and, if so, with which offense. The prosecutor argues the state's case at trial, advises the police, participates in plea negotiations, and makes sentencing recommendations.

psychoanalytic view of crime This position holds that criminals are driven by unconscious thought patterns, developed in early childhood, that control behaviors over the life course.

public defender An attorney generally employed by the government to represent poor persons accused of a crime at no cost to the accused.

Racketeer Influenced and Corrupt Organization Act (RICO) Federal legislation that enables prosecutors to bring additional criminal or civil charges against people whose multiple criminal acts constitute a conspiracy. RICO features monetary penalties that allow the government to confiscate all profits derived from criminal activities. Originally intended to be used against organized criminals, RICO also has been used against white-collar crime.

real evidence Any object produced for inspection at the trial (weapon, photograph).

reasonable competence standard The standard by which legal representation is judged: Did the defendant receive a reasonable level of legal aid?

recidivism Repetition of criminal behavior; habitual criminality. Recidivism is measured by (1) criminal acts that resulted in conviction by a court when committed by individuals who are under correctional supervision or who had been released from correctional supervision within the previous three years and (2) technical violations of probation or parole in which a sentencing or paroling authority took action that resulted in an adverse change in the offender's legal status.

recognizance During the Middle Ages, the practice of letting convicted offenders remain free if they agreed to enter a debt relation with the state to pay for their crimes.

rehabilitation perspective A model of criminal justice that views its primary purpose as helping to care for people who cannot manage themselves. Crime is an expression of frustration and anger created by social inequality that can be controlled by giving people the means to improve their lifestyle through conventional endeavors.

release on recognizance (ROR) A nonmonetary condition for the pretrial release of an accused individual; an alternative to monetary bail that is granted after the court determines that the accused has ties in the community, has no prior record of default, and is likely to appear at subsequent proceedings.

residential community corrections (RCC) A nonsecure facility, located in the community, that houses probationers who need a more secure environment. Typically, residents will be free during the day to go to work, school, or treatment and return in the evening for counseling sessions and meals.

restitution A condition of probation in which the offender repays society or the victim of crime for the trouble the offender caused. Monetary restitution involves a direct payment to the victim as a form of compensation. Community service restitution may be used in victimless crimes and involves work in the community in lieu of more severe criminal penalties.

restorative justice A view of criminal justice that advocates peaceful solutions and mediation rather than coercive punishments.

revocation An administrative act performed by a parole authority that removes a person from parole or a judicial order by a court removing a person from parole or probation, in response to a violation on the part of the parolee or probationer.

risk classification Classifying probationers so that they may receive an appropriate level of treatment and control.

salient factor score A method developed by federal parole authorities to classify inmates for release.

Santobello v. New York The 1971 U.S. Supreme Court decision upholding that promises of a prosecutor that are the foundation of a guilty plea must be honored by the government unless voided by a court.

search and seizure The legal term, contained in the Fourth Amendment to the U.S. Constitution, that refers to the searching for and carrying away of evidence by police during a criminal investigation.

search incident to a lawful arrest An exception to the search warrant rule; limited to the immediate surrounding area.

search warrant An order issued by a judge, directing officers to conduct a search of specified premises for specified objects or persons and bring them before the court.

self-defense A legal defense in which defendants claim that their behavior was legally justified by the necessity to protect their own life and property or that of another victim from potential harm.

self-incrimination Personal utterances or statements that can be used as evidence in a criminal matter. The Fifth Amendment prohibits law enforcement officials from using force or coercion to obtain incriminating statements from suspects in criminal cases.

self-report survey A research approach that requires subjects to reveal their own participation in delinquent or criminal acts.

sheriff The chief law enforcement officer in a county.

shire reeve In medieval England, the senior law enforcement figure in a county, the forerunner of today's sheriff.

shock incarceration A short prison sentence served in boot camp–type facilities.

shock probation A sentence in which offenders serve a short prison term before they begin probation, to impress them with the pains of imprisonment.

six-person jury The criminal trial of a defendant before a jury of six persons as opposed to a traditional jury of twelve persons.

Sixth Amendment The U.S. constitutional amendment containing various criminal trial rights, such as the right to public trial, right to trial by jury, and the right to confrontation of witnesses.

social agent The police style that believes that police should be involved in a wide range of activities without regard to their connection to law enforcement.

social control The ability of society and its institutions to control, manage, restrain, or direct human behavior.

social learning The view that behavior patterns are modeled and learned in interactions with others.

social process theory The view that an individual's interactions with key social institutions — family, school, peer group — shapes behavior.

social structure theory The view that a person's position in the social structure controls behavior. Those in the lowest socioeconomic tier are more likely to succumb to crime-promoting elements in their environment society, whereas those in the highest tier enjoy social and economic advantages that insulate them from crime-producing forces.

socialization The process in which a person learns to adapt to the cultural and social institutions in society.

source control Eradicating the drug problem through a policy of destroying crops and manufacturing plants located in source countries before they can be shipped to the United States.

special-needs inmate Those correctional clients who require special care and treatment, such as the elderly, mentally ill, drug addicted, or AIDS infected.

special-needs population A group of people whose personal problems need to be addressed by human services organizations — for example, the disabled, mentally ill, or substance abusers.

specific deterrence A crime control policy suggesting that punishment should be severe enough to convince convicted offenders never to repeat their criminal activity.

split sentence A practice that requires convicted criminals to spend a portion of their sentence behind bars and the remainder in the community.

stare decisis To stand by decided cases. The legal principle by which the decision or holding in an earlier case becomes the standard by which subsequent similar cases are judged.

status offender A juvenile who has been adjudicated by a judge of a juvenile court as having committed a status offense (running away, truancy, or incorrigibility).

sting operation An undercover police operation n which police pose as criminals to trap law violators.

stop and frisk The situation in which police officers who are suspicious of an individual run their hands lightly over the suspect's outer garments, to determine whether the person is carrying a concealed weapon. Also called a *patdown* or *threshold inquiry,* a stop and frisk is intended to stop short of any activity that could be considered a violation of Fourth Amendment rights.

Strickland v. Washington The 1984 U.S. Supreme Court decision upholding that defendants have the right to reasonably effective assistance of counsel (i.e., competent representation).

strict liability crime Illegal act whose elements do not contain the need for intent or mens rea; usually, acts that endanger the public welfare, such as illegal dumping of toxic wastes.

substantial capacity test A test of criminal insanity, where the lack of substantial capacity impairs the defendant's ability to conform his or her conduct to the dictates of law.

substantive criminal law A body of specific rules that declare what conduct is criminal and prescribe the punishment to be imposed for such conduct.

substantive rights Through a slow process of legal review, the courts have granted inmates a number of civil rights, including the rights to receive mail and medical benefits and to practice their religion.

super-maximum-security prison The newest form of a maximum-security prison that uses high-level security measures to incapacitate the nation's most dangerous criminals. Most inmates are in twenty-three hours per day lockdown.

sureties During the Middle Ages, people who made themselves responsible for the behavior of offenders released in their care.

suspended sentence A prison term that is delayed while the defendant undergoes a period of community treatment. If the treatment is successful, the prison sentence is terminated.

technical parole violation Revocation of parole because conditions set by correctional authorities have been violated.

teleconferencing Using audio and video linkups to allow people to communicate from distant locations.

Terry v. Ohio The 1968 U.S. Supreme Court decision upholding the right of the police to conduct a brief inquiry of a suspicious person when they believe such person may be dangerous.

threshold inquiry A term used to describe a stop and frisk.

tier system The structure of early prisons having numerous floors or wings that stacked cells one over another.

time-in-rank system For police officers to advance in rank they must spend an appropriate amount of time, usually years, in the preceding rank; that is, to become a captain an officer must first spend time as a lieutenant.

tithing In medieval England, a group of ten families who collectively dealt with minor disturbances and breaches of the peace.

tort The law of personal wrongs and damage. Tort-type actions include negligence, libel, slander, assault, and trespass.

Town of Newton v. Rumery The 1987 U.S. Supreme Court case that grants the prosecutor wide discretion in negotiating plea bargains as long as the defendant's legal rights are guaranteed.

total institution A regimented, dehumanizing institution such as a prison in which like-situated people are kept in social isolation, cut off from the world at large.

transfer hearing A preadjudication hearing in a juvenile court to determine whether a juvenile offender should be detained in juvenile court or transferred to criminal court for prosecution as an adult.

treatment The rehabilitative method used to effect a change of behavior in the juvenile offender, in the form of therapy, or educational or vocational programs.

Uniform Crime Reports (UCR) The FBI's yearly publication of where, when, and how much serious crime occurred in the prior year.

United States v. Mezzanatto The 1995 U.S. Supreme Court decision upholding that a defendant's statements in a plea bargain can be used against him or her if he or she goes to trial.

United States v. Ross The 1982 U.S. Supreme Court decision upholding that a warrantless search of an automobile is permissible if probable cause exists to believe that the vehicle contains criminal evidence.

United States v. Salerno The 1987 U.S. Supreme Court decision upholding that the practice of detaining dangerous suspects before trial without bail was constitutional.

unreasonableness A broad term often used in search-and-seizure law to make certain that a decision is based on reasonable facts and results in a fair and rational decision.

venire The group called for jury duty from which jury panels are selected.

verdict A finding of a jury or a judge on questions of fact at a trial.

vice squad Police officers assigned to enforce morality-based laws, such as those on prostitution, gambling, and pornography.

victim impact statement A postconviction statement by the victim of crime that may be used to guide sentencing decisions.

victimless crime An act that is in violation of society's moral code and therefore has been outlawed — for example, drug abuse, gambling, and prostitution. These acts are linked together because, although they have no external victim, they are considered harmful to the social fabric.

vigilantes A citizen group who tracked down wanted criminals in the Old West.

voir dire The process in which a potential jury panel is questioned by the prosecution and the defense in order to select jurors who are unbiased and objective.

waiver The act of voluntarily relinquishing a right or advantage; often used in the context of waiving one's right to counsel (e.g., *Miranda* warning) or waiving certain steps in the criminal justice process (e.g., the preliminary hearing). Essential to waiver is the voluntary consent of the individual.

waiver (juvenile) The transfer of a juvenile to the adult (criminal) court.

Walnut Street Jail In 1790 a separate wing of Philadelphia's Walnut Street Jail was built to house convicted felons. This was the forerunner of the secure correctional system in the United States.

watch system During the Middle Ages in England, men were organized in church parishes to guard at night against disturbances and breaches of the peace under the direction of the local constable.

watchman A police style that stresses reacting to calls for service rather than aggressively pursuing crime.

wergild Under medieval law, the money paid by the offender to compensate the victim and the state for a criminal offense.

widening the net The charge that programs designed to divert offenders from the justice system actually enmesh them further in the process by substituting more intrusive treatment programs for less intrusive punishment-oriented outcomes.

wiretapping The use of a concealed listening or recording device, done with judicial approval for the purpose of obtaining evidence of criminal activity.

work release A prison treatment program that allows inmates to be released during the day to work in the community and returned to prison at night.

writ of certiorari An order of superior court requesting that the record of an inferior court (or administrative body) be brought forward for review or inspection.

writ of habeas corpus A judicial order requesting that a person detaining another produce the body of the prisoner and give reasons for his or her capture and detention. Habeas corpus is a legal device used to request that a judicial body review the reasons for a person's confinement and the conditions of confinement. Habeas corpus is known as "the great writ."

zero tolerance The practice of seizing all instrumentalities of a crime, including homes, boats, and cars. It is an extreme example of the law of forfeiture.

Table of Cases

Name Index

Subject Index

E

T

Photo Credits

This page constitutes an extension of the copyright page. We have made every effort to trace the ownership of all copyrighted material and to secure permission from copyright holders. In the event of any question arising as to the use of any material, we will be pleased to make the necessary corrections in future printings. Thanks are due to the following authors, publishers, and agents for permission to use the material indicated.

Chapter 1
2: © Alan Tannebaum/CORBIS-Sygma; **5:** © Myung J. Chun—*Los Angeles Times Photo*; **7:** Brown Brothers; **12:** Frank Anderson/ The *Lexington Herald-Leader*; **21:** Shooting Star; **23:** © Allan Tannenbaum/CORBIS-Sygma; **29:** Reuters/Colin Braley/Archive Photos

Chapter 2
38: © David Butow/Saba; **46:** Ted Thai/ *Time* Magazine; **54:** AP/ Wide World Photos; **56:** © David Woo/*Dallas Morning News*/CORBIS-Sygma; **59:** © Andrew Lichtenstein/ Impact Visuals; **63:** AP/Wide World Photos; **66:** AP/Wide World Photos; **67:** Jim Lo Scalzo/*U. S. News & World Report*

Chapter 3
76: Attributed to George Cooke, ca. 1830, "Patrick Henry Arguing the Parson's Cause," Courtesy of the Virginia Historical Society, Richmond, VA; **79:** AP/Wide World Photos; **81:** A Wager of Battel. From *Le Coutume de Normandie*. 1450-1470; **85:** AP/Wide World Photos; **89:** © Ted Fitzgerald/ *Boston Herald*; **96:** © Robbie McClaren/Saba; **99:** © Alex Quesada/Matrix

Chapter 4
108: AP/Wide World Photos; **110:** © Shepard Sheerbell/Saba; **114:** Brown Brothers; **117:** AP/Wide World Photos; **120:** © Alex Quesada/Matrix; **129:** © John Zich; **130:** © Alex Quesada/Matrix

Chapter 5
134: © Brent Stirton/Liaison Agency; **140:** © Douglas Burrows/Gamma-Liaison Network; **143:** © David Butow/Saba; **147:** © George Rizer/*Boston Globe*. **149:** © 1999 Ken Horan; **151:** © 1998 Dan Lamont/ Matrix; **157:** © Mark Richards; **159:** AP/Wide World Photos

Chapter 6
164: © James Levine/Saba; **168:** Shooting Star; **169:** © Les Stone/CORBIS-Sygma; **174:** © Nola Tully/CORBIS-Sygma; **180:** Daniel LeClaire/Reuters/Archive Photos; **182:** © Alan Weiner/Gamma Liaison Network; **190:** Courtesy of AIS; **194:** Reuters/Lee Celano/Archive Photos

Chapter 7
202: © 1997 Alon Reininger/Contact Press Images; **207:** © Kim Kulish/Saba; **209:** © Rick Maiman/CORBIS-Sygma; **212:** © William Campbell/CORBIS-Sygma; **215:** © Jean Marc Giboux/ Gamma Liaison Network; **217:** © Joel Gordon; **219:** Photo Disc, Inc. **222:** Steve Liss/ *Time* Magazine

Chapter 8
226: © Ahmad Terry/*Rocky Mountain News*/CORBIS-Sygma; **231:** © Joel Gordon; **237:** © Ken Heinen; **242:** Photo by Therri Thuente, © 1997 *Los Angeles Daily News*; **248:** AP/Wide World Photos; **256:** © Kenneth Jarecke/Contact Press Images

Chapter 9
264: *Denver Rocky Mountain News*/Steven R. Nickerson/CORBIS-Sygma; **271:** © Peter Jordon/Matrix; **275:** © Alon Reininger/Contact Press Images; **277:** © Joel Gordon; **280:** Reuters/Gary Cameron/Archive Photos; **286:** AP/Wide World Photos; **290:** AP/Wide World Photos

Chapter 10
294: © Harry A. Barrios/*The Bakersfield Californian;* **296:** © Ahmad Terry/*Rocky Mountain News*/CORBIS-Sygma; **299:** © Kevin Moloney/Gamma Liaison Network; **301:** AP/Wide World Photos; **304:** © *Newsday,* photo by Dick Yarwood; **307:** © Todd Bigelow; **314:** © Steve Starr/Pool/CORBIS-Sygma; **317:** © Scott Goldsmith; **318:** © Ruben Ramirez/CORBIS-Sygma

Chapter 11
324: © David Turnley/CORBIS; **328:** The Granger Collection, New York; **334:** Phil Sheffield/*Tampa Tribune*/ Silver Image; **341:** *Los Angeles Times* photo/ Julie Markes; **345:** Bob Daemmrich/Agence France Presse /CORBIS-Bettmann; **351:** © 1999 Kevin Horan

Chapter 12
360: © Jacques Chenet/Woodfin Camp & Associates; **367:** © Joel Gordon; **369:** © A. Tannenbaum/CORBIS-Sgyma; **370:** © John Gurzinski/*Las Vegas Review Journal*; **374:** AP/Wide World Photos; **378:** © Louis Psihoyos/ Matrix; **380:** © Jacques Chenet/ Woodfin Camp & Associates; **385:** © Andrew Lichtenstein/Impact Visuals

Chapter 13
394: © Eastcott/Momatiuk/Woodfin Camp & Associates; **396:** © Lisa Terry/Gamma Liaison; **399:** van Gogh, Vincent: *Prisoner's Round,* (detail), 1890. Pushkin Museum of Fine Arts, Moscow. Scala/Art Resource, NY; **402:** Stock Montage, Inc.; **405:** American Correctional Association; **410:** © Michael Abramson/Woodfin Camp & Associates; **418:** © Eastcott/Momatiuk/Woodfin Camp & Associates; **423:** Erik Freeland/*U. S. News & World Report*

Chapter 14
428: © Joel Gordon; **430:** AP/Wide World Photos; **433:** Erik Freeland/ *U. S. News & World Report*; **440:** © David Butow; **444:** © A. Ramey/Woodfin Camp & Associates; **447:** AP/Wide World Photos; **453:** © Mark Peterson/Saba; **455:** © 1999 Kevin Horan; **457:** Jeffry Macmillan/ *U.S. News & World Report*

Chapter 15
466: © A. Ramey/Woodfin Camp & Associates; **468:** AP/Wide World Photos; **471:** The Granger Collection, New York; **476:** © Lui Xin/*Palm Beach Post*; **478:** © Sherman Zent/ *Palm Beach Post*; **482:** © A. Ramey/ Woodfin Camp & Associates; **490:** © A. Ramey/Woodfin Camp & Associates